AMERICAN CONSTITUTIONAL HISTORY

AMERICAN CONSTITUTIONAL HISTORY

AMERICAN CONSTITUTIONAL HISTORY

By ERIK McKINLEY ERIKSSON
Associate Professor of History, University of
Southern California, and DAVID NELSON
ROWE Research Staff, University of Chicago

W·W·NORTON & COMPANY INC
PUBLISHERS   *NEW YORK*

Copyright, 1933

W · W · NORTON & COMPANY, INC.

70 Fifth Avenue, New York

First Edition

PRINTED IN THE UNITED STATES OF AMERICA
FOR THE PUBLISHERS BY THE VAIL-BALLOU PRESS

CONTENTS

PREFACE ix

I. THE BEGINNING OF ENGLISH GOVERNMENTAL
EXPERIMENTS IN AMERICA 1

Evolution of the Constitution—The Constitutional Inherit-
ance from England—English Delay in Colonizing America—
Motives of English Colonization—First Attempts at Settle-
ment—The Charter of 1606—The Founding of Virginia
—The Charters of 1609 and 1612—Virginia as a Royal
Colony.

II. THE DEVELOPMENT OF THE NEW ENGLAND GOV-
ERNMENTS 16

The Plymouth Colony—The Massachusetts Bay Colony—
Rhode Island—Connecticut—New Hampshire.

III. THE COMPLETION OF THE COLONIAL GOVERN-
MENTS 34

Maryland—New York—New Jersey—Pennsylvania—Dela-
ware—North and South Carolina—Georgia—The Types of
Colonies—The Governor—The Council—The Assembly—
The Judiciary.

IV. TENDENCIES TOWARD UNION PRIOR TO 1763 62

The New England Confederation—Influence of the Wars
with France for Supremacy—Bases of English and French
Rivalry—Albany Conference of 1684—King William's War
—New York Conference of 1690—The Penn Plan of Union—
Queen Anne's War—Daniel Coxe's Plan of Union—King
George's War—The French and Indian War—The Albany
Congress of 1754—Richard Peters's Plan of Union—The
Franklin Plan of Union—English Successes—Influences
Toward Union in 1763.

V. CAUSES OF THE AMERICAN REVOLUTION 81

The Various Viewpoints—Development of an American Spirit
—England's Colonial Policy Prior to 1763—Attempted
Political Control—Attempted Economic Regulation—The

CONTENTS

Navigation and Trade Acts—The Manufacturing Acts—
Financial Legislation—The New Colonial Policy—The Gren-
ville Acts—The Stamp Act—The Townshend Acts—The
Boston Tea Party—The Intolerable Acts.

VI. THE CONTINENTAL CONGRESSES   109

Growth of Radicalism—Assembling of the First Continental
Congress—Work of the First Continental Congress—The
Continental Association—Lord North's Conciliatory Proposal
—Meeting of the Second Continental Congress—Accom-
plishments of the Second Continental Congress—Financial
Troubles—The Declaration of Independence—The French
Alliance—Adoption of the Articles of Confederation.

VII. FORMATION OF THE ORIGINAL STATE GOVERN-
MENTS   134

Recommendations by the Congress—New Hampshire's First
Constitution—South Carolina—Rhode Island and Connecticut
—Virginia—New Jersey—Delaware—Pennsylvania—Mary-
land—North Carolina—Georgia—New York—Massachusetts
—General Features of the State Constitutions.

VIII. THE CONFEDERATION GOVERNMENT   157

Character of the Articles of Confederation—Form of the
Confederation Government—Powers of Congress—Accomplishments of the Confederation Government—Financial Difficulties—Diplomatic and Commercial Troubles—Interstate
Controversies.

IX. THE FRAMING OF THE CONSTITUTION   183

The Calling and Organization of the Convention—The Personnel of the Constitutional Convention—Plans before the
Convention—Debate and Compromise—The Completed Constitution.

X. THE BATTLE OVER RATIFICATION   214

Attitude of the Framers Towards their Work—The Process
of Ratification—Federalists and Anti-Federalists—The Debate
over the Constitution in Contemporary Publications—Early
State Ratifications—The Battle in Massachusetts—Ratification
by Maryland, South Carolina, and New Hampshire—Ratification by Virginia—The New York Ratification Battle—The
Delayed Ratifications by North Carolina and Rhode Island.

XI. THE CREATION AND GROWTH OF GOVERNMENTAL
AGENCIES UNDER THE CONSTITUTION   239

Provisions for Establishing the New Government—The New
Government Organized—The Salaries of Federal Officials—

Congressional Expansion—Evolution of the Administrative
Departments—Growth of the Department of State—Develop-
ment of the Treasury Department—The Expansion of the
War Department—Creation and Development of the Navy
Department—The Department of Justice—Expansion of the
Post Office Department—The Establishment and Expansion
of the Department of the Interior—The Development of the
Newer Departments—The Independent Offices—Observations
on the Administrative Service—The Expansion of the Na-
tional Judiciary.

XII.   EXPANSION OF THE CONSTITUTION THROUGH
       AMENDMENT   279

       The Process of Amending the Constitution—Limitations on the
       Amending Power—The Bill of Rights—The Eleventh and
       Twelfth Amendments—The Civil War Amendments.

XIII. EXPANSION OF THE CONSTITUTION THROUGH
       AMENDMENT, (Continued)   302

       The Income Tax Amendment—Direct Election of Senators—
       The Prohibition Amendment—Woman Suffrage—The "Lame
       Duck" Amendment—Other Amendments Proposed by Con-
       gress—Additional Suggested Amendments.

XIV.   JUDICIAL INTERPRETATION OF THE CONSTITUTION   332

       The Doctrine of Judicial Review—The Case of Marbury vs.
       Madison—The Principle of Implied Powers—Interpretation
       of the Commerce Clause of the Constitution—The Supreme
       Court and State Powers.

XV.   LEGISLATIVE EXPANSION OF THE CONSTITUTION   355

       Liberal versus Strict Construction—Tariff Legislation—
       Financial Legislation as Recommended by Hamilton—Excise
       Legislation—Legislation Regarding Banks—The Budget Act
       of 1921—The Money System of the United States—Uses of
       the Congressional Power in Promoting Transportation Facili-
       ties—The Regulation of Interstate Commerce—Regulation
       of Business—Naturalization and Immigration—Miscellaneous
       Legislation—Congress and Slavery—Congress and the Ac-
       quisition of Territory—The Trend toward Social Legislation
       —The Electoral Power of Congress—Other Powers of Con-
       gress—Decline in the Prestige of Congress.

XVI.   THE RÔLE OF THE EXECUTIVE UNDER THE CON-
       STITUTION   388

       Colonial Experience with the Executive—The Articles of
       Confederation and the Executive Power—The Constitutional

Convention and the Executive—Arguments for the Executive in *The Federalist*—Evolution of the President's Powers—President Washington's Conception of his Office—Thomas Jefferson and the Presidency—President Jackson as Representative of the People—President Lincoln's War Leadership—Loss of Executive Prestige under President Johnson—President Hayes and the Veto Power—President Cleveland and Executive Independence—Executive Leadership by Presidents Theodore Roosevelt and Wilson—Proposals for Changing the Presidential System—Proposals to Make the President a Dictator.

XVII. CONSTITUTIONAL EFFECTS OF CUSTOM AND TRADITION   416

The Evolution of Political Parties—The Influence of Lobbies—The Election of a President—The No Third Term Tradition—The Presidential Succession—The President's Cabinet—Influence of Tradition on Foreign Relations—Other Traditions Affecting the President—Congressional Committees—The Party Caucus—Other Traditions Affecting Congress—The Courts and the Constitutionality of Laws.

XVIII. STATE AND FEDERAL RELATIONS   442

Dual Government in the United States—Constitutional Limitations on the States—Interstate Relations—Constitutional Guarantees to the States—Control of State Representation in Congress—Influence of Federal Subsidies on the States—Beginning of the "State Rights Fetish"—Nullification in South Carolina—Secession and Coercion—The State Rights Doctrine since the Civil War.

XIX. THE CONSTITUTION IN TIME OF WAR   462

The War Powers of Congress—War Powers of the President—Declarations of War—The Raising of Troops—War Finances—The President as Commander-in-chief—Interference with Constitutional Rights during the Civil War—President Lincoln and Slavery—Political Reconstruction of the South—Presidential Powers during the World War—Mobilization of War Resources during the World War—World War Reorganization of Governmental Agencies—Control of Public Opinion—Peace Time Preparations for War.

APPENDIX   491

Articles of Confederation 1781–1789.   491

Constitution of the United States 1789–   499

INDEX   515

PREFACE

SINCE the World War there has been manifested in this country a great zeal for the study of the Constitution of the United States. This has been due largely to the wave of patriotism which grew out of the war and also to a desire to combat the propaganda of radical agitators who have been urging the destruction of our form of government. Most of the states have placed laws on their statute books requiring the teaching of the Constitution in the schools. In some cases these laws do not affect college students except those who are candidates for teachers' credentials. Some of the states have much stricter laws requiring, as in California, that all students, before receiving a degree from a college or university in the state, must have taken an approved course dealing with the Constitution.

These laws which have been passed to insure the teaching of the Constitution are but one expression of the nation-wide enthusiasm for the study of this nation's basic law. The general observance of each seventeenth day of September as Constitution Day and the annual high school oratorical contest dealing with various phases of the Constitution are other outstanding evidences of popular interest.

Just what information the average college student or the general reader should be expected to acquire concerning the Constitution is a matter of opinion. The numerous published books dealing with the subject reveal the wide divergence of opinion. Some emphasize the genesis of the Constitution, others devote their whole attention to the Constitutional Convention and its work, others stress the development of constitutional law, while others deal almost entirely with the development of the government under the Constitution. A common method of imparting a knowledge of constitutional history is to include constitutional developments in a general treatment of American history. This has the advantage of supplying an adequate historical background but also the disadvantage of reducing the constitutional treatment to a minimum because of the necessity of including the social, economic, and cultural phases as well. Furthermore, many students do not have time available for such a complete course.

This volume is the result of the writers' experience in teaching American constitutional history to large numbers of students at the University of Southern California. This experience has demonstrated that most of those studying the subject are not well trained in American history and, therefore, are not adequately prepared for any highly technical expositions of constitutional development. It has been found that the best procedure is to present a general treatment of American constitutional history from the beginning to the present, emphasizing at all times the historical background. In this way the Constitution is seen as the product of a long process of historical evolution. Beginning with the English constitution, the genesis of the Constitution of the United States is traced through the colonial governments, the Continental Congresses, the original state constitutions, the Confederation period and the Constitutional Convention itself. Then an attempt is made to show in a general, non-technical way, how the Constitution was put into effect and how it has been expanded into the document which it is today.

It is hoped that this *American Constitutional History*, which follows the procedure outlined, will not only give to students and general readers a knowledge of the Constitution and how it has developed but will also tend to create in them a genuine respect for the American system of government and an appreciation of American constitutional ideals and principles.

The present writers have not undertaken to unearth new facts or to make new and unique interpretations in relation to American constitutional history. Every phase of the subject has been treated by eminent scholars and to them the writers of this volume acknowledge their great indebtedness.

To Professor G. G. Benjamin, Professor F. H. Garver, Dr. Bates Booth, and Mr. Trent Steele, of the Department of History, University of Southern California, who have read the manuscript in whole or in part, the authors are deeply grateful.

However, on the authors alone must be placed the blame for such errors as may be discovered in this volume.

Special thanks are due to Mrs. Minnie Louise Eriksson, Miss Mary Alice Reinhart, and Mr. August H. W. Reuber, who have given valuable assistance in the preparation and proof reading of the manuscript.

E. M. E.
D. N. R.

Pasadena, California
March 20, 1933

AMERICAN CONSTITUTIONAL HISTORY

Chapter One

THE BEGINNING OF ENGLISH GOVERN-
MENTAL EXPERIMENTS IN AMERICA

EVOLUTION OF THE CONSTITUTION

THE constitutional history of the United States did not begin with the Constitutional Convention of 1787 nor did it end with that event. The document drawn up at that time was not the result of a sudden inspiration as the English Prime Minister, William E. Gladstone, intimated when he said that the American Constitution was "the greatest work that was ever struck off at a given time by the brain and purpose of man." Rather, it was the result of a long evolutionary process extending back through the earlier national and colonial periods far into remote English history.

Since its adoption, the Constitution has continued to evolve into the document which is the basis of the United States government today. By formal amendment, by legislative expansion, by judicial interpretation, and through the influence of custom and tradition, the Constitution drawn up by an eighteenth century agricultural people has grown and has been adapted to the needs of a highly industrialized twentieth century society. To secure a perspective of this remarkable evolution it is necessary to survey the constitutional developments in England which were inherited by the Americans; to trace the constitutional experiments in the English colonies and during the periods of the Revolution and the Confederation; to study the Constitutional Convention and its work; and, finally, to observe the Constitution in operation during the period since 1789.

THE CONSTITUTIONAL INHERITANCE FROM ENGLAND

In considering the constitutional ideas and principles derived from England, a fundamental difference between the English and the American constitutions should be kept in mind. The

1

former is not a short written document but, on the contrary, is largely unwritten. Included in it are the numerous acts passed by Parliament together with such monumental documents as Magna Carta (1215), the Petition of Right (1628), and the Bill of Rights (1689). The American Constitution is a short written document containing only a few thousand words. Though it has been expanded in the various ways indicated, only the amendments formally adopted are regarded as a part of the Constitution.

Only a casual examination of English constitutional development is needed to reveal a number of extremely important ideas and principles which are included in the Constitution of the United States. Among these is the idea of a three branch government. The executive, of course, in England, was the king, who was at first extremely despotic. Gradually his powers were limited, and many of them were assumed by Parliament. This legislative organization was itself the result of a gradual development. The Anglo-Saxon kings had a group of advisers known as the Witenagemot. After the Norman conquest in 1066 this body became the Great Council or Magnum Concilium. In the course of time, there evolved from this body the Parliament which claimed and assumed the right to legislate. During the reign of Edward III (1327–1377) Parliament was recognized by law as having two houses, the House of Commons and the House of Lords. The former became a representative body with its members elected by those who held a certain amount of property. Incidentally, it should be noted that this undemocratic method of requiring the ownership of property as a basis for the suffrage was copied by the English colonies in America and prevailed well into the national period.

Among the powers assumed by Parliament similar to powers possessed by the American Congress were the initiation and control of taxation. By the early fifteenth century the House of Commons had acquired at least the theoretical right to originate financial bills, as is true of the American House of Representatives. Impeachment was another power assumed by Parliament and practised with some frequency before 1700. The Constitution of the United States definitely confers on Congress the power to impeach federal civil officers.

Privileges which came to be possessed by Parliament and which are recognized as belonging to Congress included freedom of speech in the legislative halls; freedom from arrest while attending legislative sessions or while going to or from them; the right to form their own organization and to choose their own officers; and the power to pass on the credentials of their members.

As early as the thirteenth century a judiciary branch of the English government had developed but it was not until after the Revolution of 1688 that the courts became entirely independent of the other two branches of the government. As in the United States so in England there had been developed lower courts and a court to hear appeals. Corresponding to the Supreme Court in this country was the Court of the King's Bench which heard appeals from the Court of Common Pleas and the Court of Exchequer.

The right to a jury trial was recognized, in fact, it was one of the guarantees contained in the famed charter of liberties, Magna Carta. In the American Constitution this right is safeguarded by the sixth and seventh amendments. One of the main points in the Petition of Right presented to King Charles I by Parliament in 1628 was a declaration that there should be no imprisonment without due process of law. This was very similar to provisions in the fifth and fourteenth amendments to the Constitution of the United States. Habeas Corpus writs were granted by the courts as early as the thirteenth century but were frequently evaded. In 1679 Parliament passed a definitive Habeas Corpus act which gave it the meaning recognized in the United States. It provided that any prisoner arrested for an alleged crime must, if he secured a writ of habeas corpus, be brought before a judge within a stated time for a decision whether he should be held for trial, discharged, or released on bail. The Bill of Rights, adopted in 1689, declared that excessive bail should not be required, nor excessive fines imposed, nor cruel and unusual punishments inflicted. One may read the same guarantees in the eighth amendment to the United States Constitution.

These illustrations will suffice to show the close relationship of the English and American constitutions. But it must not be supposed that the members of the Constitutional Convention of 1787 consciously borrowed these ideas and principles from England. For a hundred and eighty years prior to the convention, they and their predecessors had been carrying on constitutional experiments in America. What England had and what she developed in the way of constitutional ideas and principles during the colonial period, the colonists adapted to their own uses, developing and adding new ones as a result of their own experiences. Then when independence came they embodied their accumulated ideas of government in the state constitutions and finally in a national constitution.

In order to make this clear it is first necessary to review briefly the background of English colonization and then investigate with some care the formation and development of the colonial governments. Since the original United States was derived directly from thirteen English colonies it will contribute nothing to a knowledge of American constitutional history to study the colonizing efforts of Spain, France, the Netherlands or Sweden, except insofar as their activities affected the development of the thirteen colonies. Even though territories which were once controlled by these other countries have been incorporated into the United States, the effect has been felt along social, economic, and cultural lines rather than constitutional.

ENGLISH DELAY IN COLONIZING AMERICA

Compared with Spain, England was slow in attempting actual settlement in the New World. As early as 1497, John Cabot, an Italian in the employ of King Henry VII, sailed across the north Atlantic and reached the American coast, probably in the vicinity of Cape Breton Island. This voyage of discovery enabled England to claim a share in the western hemisphere. But for many years the English made no attempt to establish settlements in the region which they claimed. Apparently the only immediate result of Cabot's voyage was the opening up of the Newfoundland fisheries to the fishermen of England and other European countries.

Internal problems, particularly religious controversies, absorbed the interest of the English for many years. The action of

King Henry VIII in separating the Church in England from the jurisdiction of the pope in order to secure a divorce from his wife paved the way for bitter religious struggles which were destined to continue over a long period of time. While Henry himself had no thought or desire of making England Protestant, his action gave to the Protestants an opportunity to establish themselves. The reigns of Henry's two immediate successors were featured by bitter and at times bloody struggles between the Catholics and Protestants for control. When Elizabeth came to the throne of England late in 1558, she gave serious consideration to the securing of a religious settlement. The result was that, within a few months, Parliament had passed the Acts of Supremacy and Uniformity, establishing the Church of England as the state church.

MOTIVES OF ENGLISH COLONIZATION

While this settlement was unsatisfactory to many it at least had the effect of enabling the English to give some attention to affairs of the outside world. While the main interest of some Englishmen, such as John Hawkins and Francis Drake, was the plundering of Spanish commerce, others like Martin Frobisher, John Davis, and Sir Humphrey Gilbert were particularly concerned with seeking a northwest passage to the Far East. There were also existent in England many who were desirous of seeing English colonies planted on the American coast. The government was ready to sanction such colonies as a means of checking the growing power of Spain. Individuals were eager for an opportunity to acquire rich agricultural lands. Others saw opportunities for trade and commerce while still others hoped to gain wealth through finding gold. Some desired to go to the New World to convert the heathen Indians while quite a different religious motive animated those who wished to go to America to escape the control of the Church of England. As time went on an increasing number looked to American colonization as a means of escaping from the control of an arbitrary government. A factor of great importance in creating interest in colonization was the existence in England of many poor, unemployed persons who, together with an increasing criminal class, presented a serious social problem during Elizabeth's reign. Sending such persons across the Atlantic as colonists seemed a happy solution to a vexing problem.

FIRST ATTEMPTS AT SETTLEMENT

It remained for Sir Humphrey Gilbert to make the first effort to establish an English colony in America but he failed in two attempts in 1578 and 1583. The second venture came to an abrupt end when Gilbert, returning to England from Newfoundland, went down with his little ship in a storm off the Azores.

Undismayed by this failure, Gilbert's half-brother, Sir Walter Raleigh, applied for and received a patent granting him the privilege of discovery and settlement in America. He sent out an expedition which landed on Roanoke Island. The adjacent region was claimed for England and named Virginia in honor of Queen Elizabeth. The next year a settlement was made on the island but in 1586 the settlers deserted and returned to England. In the following year Raleigh sent out another group of settlers. They were left on the island while the vessels which had brought them returned to England. War with Spain caused the settlement to be neglected until 1591. When the relief expedition was finally sent it found that the settlers had all disappeared. What happened to them is still unknown, though it is supposed that they were carried away by either the Spanish or the Indians.

The failures of Raleigh demonstrated the futility of an individual attempting to carry the burden of American colonization. It remained for a stock company to plant the first permanent English settlement on the American coast. Stock companies had already proved successful in the development of trade. Among these was the Muscovy Company composed of a number of London merchants who received a charter authorizing them to carry on trade with Russia and other points. In 1581 the Levant Company was granted a charter to carry on trade with the region bordering on the eastern and southern shores of the Mediterranean Sea. What was destined to become the most important of the English trading companies, the East

India Company, was chartered in 1600. Similar successful trading companies were organized by the French, Dutch, and others.

THE CHARTER OF 1606

The success of the trading companies naturally led to the application of the stock company idea to the settlement of America. Stimulated by a favorable report submitted by George Weymouth, who visited the New England coast in 1604, a group of "knights, Gentlemen, Merchants, and other Adventurers" applied for and received from King James I a charter on April 10, 1606. This charter created two companies known as the London Company and the Plymouth Company. The companies were authorized to settle in the region of Virginia, a term then applied to the region from the present South Carolina to Nova Scotia. In authorizing settlements King James ignored the claims of both the Spanish and the French. The former especially offered strong objections to the projected English colonization but the English government ignored them.

By the terms of the charter the London Company was given authority to make settlements between the thirty-fourth and forty-first parallels while the other company was permitted to colonize between the thirty-eighth and the forty-fifth parallels. Neither company was to make settlements within a hundred miles of a settlement of the other. To supervise and regulate the affairs of the colonies there was to be set up in England a council of thirteen members called the Council of Virginia. This body was to be appointed by the king, who thus insured for himself control of the government of the projected colonies. In each of the colonies there was to be a resident council of thirteen members for the management of local affairs. While the charter granted to the colonists no specific political rights it did contain a statement that the colonists and their children should have and enjoy "all Liberties, Franchises, and Immunities, within any of our other Dominions, to all Intents and Purposes, as if they had been abiding and born, within this our Realm of *England*, or any of our other said Dominions." This provision, with similar statements in other charters, was to prove of considerable importance in the later colonial period and particularly during the pre-Revolutionary controversies when the colonists insisted on the observance of their rights as Englishmen.

THE FOUNDING OF VIRGINIA

In December, 1606, the London Company sent to America an expedition consisting of one hundred and twenty colonists on three ships. After a tedious voyage by way of the West Indies, consuming more than four months, the colonists arrived at the James River and established themselves on what was described as a half island and half peninsula. The village which they laid out was called Jamestown. The king had issued definite instructions regarding the settlement in Virginia: after establishing a fortified post the settlers were to till the soil, seek for gold, build up a trade with the Indians, and endeavor to find a passage through to the Pacific Ocean. Common storehouses were to be set up and in them were to be placed all the goods brought to the colony or produced there. From the storehouse each settler was to receive necessities while the surplus stored there was to be exported. In this way it was hoped to make the enterprise successful from an economic standpoint, but this proved to be a vain hope.

Not only did the economic organization prove faulty in practice but the type of government, the character of the early settlers, and the unfavorable environment were additional factors in bringing about the near failure of the enterprise. The names of the members of the local council were kept secret until Virginia was reached. The men selected hardly proved equal to the task of exercising absolute authority over their fellows. Jealousies and quarrels among the leaders prevented governmental efficiency. About the only bright spot in the early history of Jamestown was during the period in 1609 in which Captain John Smith was president of the council. He was the chief factor in keeping the colony alive, for he forced the lazy to work, obtained food from the Indians, and encouraged the sick and down-hearted.

Of the one hundred and four settlers who survived the voyage from England many were "gentlemen" while only a few were artisans and laborers. Such persons were hardly fit to endure the rigors of pioneer life in the New World. The unhealthy location of the village near a marsh inevitably led to many deaths from malaria. In spite of food supplies brought from England and corn secured from the Indians, famine conditions constantly prevailed. Indian attacks took an additional toll.

THE CHARTERS OF 1609 AND 1612

In an attempt to improve conditions some of the stronger men in the company, led by Sir Edwyn Sandys and Sir Thomas Smith, persuaded the king to issue a new charter in 1609. To replace the London Company, the new document created another corporation styled the "Treasurer and Company of Adventurers and Planters of the City of London for the first Colony in Virginia." Incorporators included fifty-six city companies of London and six hundred and fifty-nine individuals including many members of Parliament.

A liberal grant of land was given to the new company, extending two hundred miles north and two hundred miles south of Point Comfort, and inland "throughout from Sea to Sea, West, and Northwest." This gave Virginia a claim to an immense territory.

As was true of the first charter, the colonists were given no participation in their government though the company itself was given more authority by the king. While the king named the first treasurer and the governing council, the company was to have the right to choose their successors. The governing body was to be resident in London and was to have absolute authority in governing the colony. The council had the right to appoint a governor and such other officers as might be desired. No persons were to be allowed to go to the colony unless they first took the "Oath of Supremacy." This had the effect of establishing the Church of England as the official church of the colony.

The first governor sent out in 1609 was Sir Thomas Gates. Four hundred of the five hundred emigrants who sailed with him reached Jamestown in August but Gates did not arrive until the following spring, being delayed in the Bermudas. He found the colony in an almost hopeless condition for, of the nine hundred individuals who had come to Virginia, only about one-sixth were alive. Gates chose the easiest course and, taking the settlers on board the ship, he started to sail for England. Before leaving the James River he was intercepted by a vessel bearing a message informing him that a new governor, Lord Delaware, had arrived at Point Comfort with a hundred and fifty colonists and needed supplies.

Delaware remained in Jamestown less than a year. After his return to England in 1611 he continued to hold the office of governor until his death in 1618, but the actual work of governing was performed, meanwhile, by deputy governors. The first of these was Sir Thomas Dale who governed by military law, forcing the settlers to work like slaves and punishing with the greatest severity those who objected to his methods.

In 1612 a third charter for Virginia was granted. It placed under the control of the company the Bermudas, which however were sold two years later to a group known as the Somers Island Company. The charter also increased the powers of the company making it a real self-governing corporation. Quarterly meetings of the stockholders were authorized for the purpose of electing officers and making regulations for the colony. These quarterly meetings were known as the "General Court." But still no political privileges were granted to the actual settlers.

The very year in which this third charter was granted marked the beginning of the cultivation of tobacco which was to become the most important industry in colonial Virginia. Four years later a method of curing was developed which made it possible for the colonists to build up an important export trade. The abandonment of the communistic method of production and distribution was another influential factor in insuring the permanence of the colony. Grants of land to individuals and to groups pledged to bring over settlers soon resulted in spreading the original settlement and led to the creation of the plantation system. Not the least important factor in helping the colony to take root was the coming of women which stimulated the establishment of family life. The company, particularly in 1619, sent over several shiploads of unmarried women, who were quickly claimed by the lonely bachelors who, to secure wives, were glad to pay the cost of transportation amounting to one hundred and twenty pounds of first class tobacco for each person.

Mention should also be made of the introduction of the first negro slaves into Virginia in 1619. While this event was not very important at that time it marked the establishment in America of an institution which was destined to have a very important relation to the constitutional development of the United States.

But from the standpoint of constitutional development the most important event in the early history of Virginia was the holding of the first representative assembly in America. In 1618, the liberal members of the company, led by Sir Edwyn Sandys, gained control and proceeded to modify the arbitrary system of controlling the colony. A new governor, George Yeardley, was sent out with instructions to have the people of each hundred, ward, or plantation elect representatives to meet with the governor and the members of the council at Jamestown for the purpose of passing ordinances for the good of the colony. Accordingly, the new governor, after his arrival in April, 1619, had the settlements grouped into eleven "boroughs," from each of which two "burgesses" were to be elected. These burgesses met with the governor and the council in the Jamestown church on July 30, 1619. What they did after they assembled was not so important for they concerned themselves with such simple problems as the encouragement of diversified crops and the promotion of religion and morals. It was the fact of their meeting that was important for, in so doing, they definitely planted on American soil the representative system to which they had been accustomed in their native England.

While the inauguration of the House of Burgesses gave the settlers a voice in their local government it by no means conferred upon them complete self-government. The governor and the councilors were still to be chosen by the general court in England. Furthermore, the ordinances passed by the colonial assembly had to be approved by the general court, though it was equally true that the regulations passed by the general court had to be approved by the assembly.

In spite of the progress apparently made, the next few years were not particularly happy ones for Virginia. There were internal dissensions in the company which hindered efficiency. More serious was the fact that the Sandys faction, which controlled the company, had incurred the opposition of the king and his advisers because of its adherence to the group in Parliament which was attempting to limit the royal power. Since the king did not wish to violate the contract which he himself had made with the company he was forced to bide his time until some good reason presented itself for seeking a cancellation of the company's charter. An Indian uprising in 1622 in which more than three hundred settlers were killed, gave King James the opportunity which he had been seeking. His attorney-general accordingly brought suit in a court for the annulling of the charter on the ground of mismanagement by the company. The subservient court sustained the charges and the charter was cancelled.

By this action Virginia became the first of the royal colonies. The chief effect was to substitute control by the king for that of the company. In place of a governor chosen by the company there was sent out a royal governor to serve during the pleasure of the king who appointed him. The powers and duties of the governor were defined in his commission and instructions. The councilors of the company were replaced by appointees of the king. It was their duty to assist the governor and to restrain his actions in a limited manner. After a short delay recognition was given to the representative assembly by the new king, Charles I, who succeeded James in 1625. As was true before the cancellation of the charter, the governor, councilors, and burgesses convened as one house, but in 1676 the legislature was divided into two houses. This action was an important step in establishing the bicameral system which is such a prominent feature of American state and national governments.

The fact that the governor participated in legislation in addition to performing executive duties is evidence that the principle of checks and balances had not yet gained a foothold in Virginia. This was further shown by the fact that the assembly served as the final court of appeal, hearing appeals from the provincial courts. The English governing officials regarded the Virginia and other colonial legislatures as being wholly dependent upon the home government; a view which the American representative assemblies, however, refused to accept. They insisted particularly upon their right to control taxation. Even before the surrender of the charter the Virginia House of Burgesses had declared that the colony should not be taxed without its consent nor should any money be spent in the colony for governmental purposes without being authorized by the colonial legislature.

The attitude of the House of Burgesses in the matter of taxation was well illustrated during the governorship of Captain John Harvey who came to the colony in 1629. He apparently attempted to do in Virginia what the king was trying to do in England—to levy and collect taxes without legislative sanction. But the House of Burgesses strongly defended its asserted right to levy taxes and finally, in 1635, the governor was deposed and sent back to England. The king angrily denounced this action as an "assumption of royal power" and sent Harvey back to Virginia. But in 1641, when a new governor, Sir William Berkeley, was sent out his instructions recognized the legislative power of the Virginia assembly.

During the English Civil War, Virginia, under Governor Berkeley, remained loyal to the king. Not until 1652, when commissioners arrived from England on a war vessel, did the Virginians recognize the authority of Parliament. At that time the House of Burgesses drew up what they styled a "treaty" in which they declared that their submission was voluntary. They demanded that they be guaranteed freedom of speech and trade, and they also insisted on being exempted from all taxes not levied by themselves.

During the subsequent eight years, until the restoration of King Charles II, Virginia enjoyed a large degree of independence. The assembly even went so far as to assume the authority to elect governors during the period. In 1659, on the eve of the Restoration, the assembly chose Sir William Berkeley to be governor again. This proved to be a mistake for Berkeley proceeded to rule in a despotic and arbitrary manner. For fourteen years he prevented a new election of burgesses. Meanwhile he practically dictated the laws passed by the legislative body. Severe measures were taken against those who dissented from the Church of England, and heavy taxes were imposed while the government extravagantly spent money. These factors, together with economic hardships brought on by the British government's trade restrictions, known as Navigation Acts, and through the overproduction and the decline in the price of tobacco, aroused popular discontent. Still another grievance was added to the list in 1672 when the king granted Virginia, for a period of thirty-one years, to two of his favorites, Culpeper and Arlington, thus making it a proprietary colony. Poor crops, an epidemic among the cattle and the failure of the governor to protect the settlers against an Indian uprising finally provoked a rebellion under the leadership of Nathaniel Bacon, a member of the council. In the fall of the year Bacon died and his followers were scattered. Berkeley proceeded to execute fourteen who fell into his hands. Even King Charles was disgusted with this action for he is reported to have said, "That old fool has hanged more men in that naked country than I have done for the murder of my father." The governor was summoned back to England, his departure being marked by general rejoicing on the part of the colonists.

The chief importance of Bacon's Rebellion was that it forced the calling of a new assembly which passed laws, known as Bacon's laws, designed to limit the power of the governor and strengthen that of the House of Burgesses. By arousing in the smaller planters and farmers a group consciousness the rebellion had an effect in stimulating democratic ideas.

During the years following, the House of Burgesses continued to resist the efforts of Berkeley's successors to rule arbitrarily. When King James II was deposed by the bloodless revolution of 1688, the new monarchs, William and Mary, were required by Parliament to sign the Bill of Rights, and the attacks on the constitutional rights of the Virginians came to an end, at least temporarily.

SELECTED REFERENCES

Andrews, C. M., *Colonial Self-Government 1652–1689*, pp. 202–251.

Beard, C. A., and Beard, M. R., *The Rise of American Civilization*, Vol. I, pp. 1–32, 33–48.

Becker, Carl, *The Beginnings of the American People*, pp. 65–80.

Bolton, H. E., and Marshall, T. M., *The Colonization of North America 1492–1783*, pp. 104–125, 159–162, 183–188.

Channing, Edward, *History of the United States*, Vol. I, pp. 33–42, 115–140, 143–225, 225–236, 485–507; Vol. II, pp. 76–91.

Fisher, S. G., *The Colonial Era*, pp. 30–48.

Fiske, John, *Old Virginia and Her Neighbours*, Vol. I, pp. 41–222, 223–254; Vol. II, pp. 1–107.

Garner, J. W., and Lodge, H. C., *The History of the United States*, Vol. I, pp. 104–118.

Greene, E. B., *The Foundations of American Nationality*, pp. 1–18, 20–43, 45–65, 77–85.

Hart, A. B., *American History Told by Contemporaries*, Vol. I, pp. 145–167, 171–174, 200–233.

Jernegan, M. W., *The American Colonies 1492–1750*, pp. 1–25, 45–65.

Johnson, Allen, ed., *Readings in American Constitutional History 1776–1876*, pp. 14–17.

Johnston, Mary, *Pioneers of the Old South*, pp. 1–115, 132–140, 148–198.

MacDonald, William, ed., *Documentary Source Book of American History, 1606–1926* (Third edition), pp. 1–19, 20–22.

Osgood, H. L., *The American Colonies in the Seventeenth Century*, Vol. I, pp. 23–97; Vol. II, pp. 58–87; Vol. III, pp. 242–308.

Preston, H. W., ed., *Documents Illustrative of American History 1606–1863* (Sixth edition), pp. 1–28, 32–35.

Tyler, L. G., *England in America*, pp. 34–92, 105–117.

Chapter Two

THE DEVELOPMENT OF THE NEW ENGLAND GOVERNMENTS

THE PLYMOUTH COLONY

WHILE the London Company was actively engaged in settling Virginia, the Plymouth Company, which had been created by the same charter in 1606, was doing practically nothing. It did make an attempt to establish a settlement at the mouth of the Kennebec River but the venture ended in failure. Some members of the company, however, retained their faith in the possibilities of the New World, and in 1620, headed by Sir Fernando Gorges, they petitioned the king and received a charter which incorporated them as the Council for New England. To this Council was granted the land lying between the fortieth and forty-eighth parallels of latitude and extending westward to the Pacific Ocean. It was from this organization that the Pilgrims and Puritans who settled Massachusetts received their grants of land.

The Pilgrims, who were the first Englishmen to establish themselves in New England, came chiefly for religious reasons though they had other motives as well. They were members of a group of English Protestants who had refused to obey the laws requiring conformity to the Church of England. Disapproving of the idea of a national church and rejecting the episcopal system of church government in favor of a congregational organization, they withdrew from the Anglican Church and consequently were called "Separatists." Their non-conformity made them the subjects of prosecution under the laws of the country.

A small group of these Separatists lived at Scrooby Manor in Nottinghamshire in eastern England. Most of them were obscure individuals but among them were some men of marked ability such as William Brewster and John Robinson. In 1608, a group of these people, unwilling longer to endure interferences with their religious activities, fled secretly to the Netherlands where, after a short time, they settled in Leyden. They were soon joined by other Separatists until there were about two hundred persons in the congregation.

Though they were tolerated they did not feel comfortable among the Dutch. Their religious ideas differed from those of the people about them and they feared that, as the years passed, it would become increasingly difficult to preserve their religion intact. They also found the struggle for economic existence to be exceedingly difficult. At any time war might break out between Spain and the Netherlands due to the desire of the former to regain her lost province, and the Pilgrims feared that their able-bodied men would be involved. They also were fearful that they would eventually be assimilated by the Dutch through inter-marriage. Though they had suffered much in their original homes they still desired to be Englishmen.

Their dissatisfaction led them, after much debate, to determine to seek a new home in America. Accordingly, they sent John Carver as an agent to England to arrange for their passage to the New World. As the Virginia Company was then under the control of liberals headed by Sir Edwyn Sandys, no great difficulty was experienced in securing a grant of land from that company. Though no charter was secured from the king, the royal consent for settlement in America was secured with the understanding that the colonists were to conduct themselves peaceably. To finance the project a joint-stock company was organized with a group of London merchants supplying the necessary money. Each of the adult Pilgrims going to the New World was considered as owning one share of stock while each child between the ages of ten and sixteen years was credited with a half share.

Two vessels were secured to carry the colonists to their new home in America. They first went to England where the final preparations for the voyage were made. Finally, the two ships set out from Plymouth, but one, the *Speedwell*, proved unseaworthy and had to put back. As many as possible were then taken on board the other vessel, the *Mayflower*, which set sail on September 6, 1620, with one hundred and two passengers. Not more than about one-third of these were from the Leyden congregation. Some, including Captain Myles Standish, were not even Separatists, while a few were merely servants sent out by the merchants of the company to work for them.

The voyage across the Atlantic Ocean was a stormy one occupying more than two months. The *Mayflower* first sailed into the harbor of what is now Provincetown on Cape Cod, about two hundred miles north of the intended place of settlement. After a month spent in exploring the coast, a small boatload of Pilgrims made a landing on December 21, 1620 (new style) at Plymouth, so named after the port in England from which they had sailed. Five days later the *Mayflower* anchored in the harbor and all of the passengers were landed. With winter already setting in, it is not to be wondered at that the Pilgrims suffered so intensely before the arrival of spring that almost one-half of their number died.

Unlike the settlers of Jamestown, the Pilgrims had no charter so they had to make provision for their own government. While still on board ship, a number of the men had given evidence of discontent and had asserted that after they landed they would do as they pleased, "for none had power to command them" since the patent from the Virginia Company did not apply to New England. To forestall this mutinous element, forty-one men drew up, on November 21st (new style), a document since known as the "Mayflower Compact." This compact was the original expression in American history of the idea that men can establish a government for themselves by mutual consent. Yet the document was not, strictly speaking, a constitution, since it did not outline the form of a government or define its powers and limitations. The signers merely agreed to combine themselves "into a civill body politick" and promised "all due submission and obedience" to all laws that might be enacted thereafter.

Following this action, John Carver was elected governor and served until his death in April, 1621. He was succeeded by William Bradford, who was reëlected year after year, and his leadership contributed much to the success of the colony. As the business of the governor increased, assistants were chosen to aid him.

At first pure democracy prevailed in Plymouth for all the free male settlers met together to enact the laws. Later, as the colonists scattered throughout the surrounding country and new towns were established, representatives were chosen to meet at Plymouth to make the laws and conduct other necessary business.

As the Pilgrims had no legal right to settle in New England, it was necessary to secure a patent from the Council for New England. This patent was applied for and secured in the fall of 1621 by the English merchants backing the colony.

For a time the faulty economic system hindered the progress of the Plymouth colony. To insure the return of their money the financial backers of the Pilgrims had stipulated that a common storehouse should be erected and that all produce should be brought to it. Each was to receive only what he needed, regardless of his industry, a system similar to the one which had proved such a dismal failure in Jamestown. In the summer of 1623 the dissatisfaction with this system of common labor on the common land became so great that it was necessary to make small individual allotments of land. Four years later the colonists severed their partnership with the London merchants to whom they agreed to pay eighteen hundred pounds in nine equal annual installments, with an additional six hundred pounds to pay existing debts. After this arrangement a further distribution of land and other property was made among the colonists.

The colony of Plymouth never became very large and it was soon over-shadowed by the Massachusetts Bay colony which finally absorbed it in 1691.

THE MASSACHUSETTS BAY COLONY

The Massachusetts Bay colony was established by the Puritans, a numerous group in the Church of England who, like the Separatists, were dissatisfied with some of the forms and ceremonies of the church, but, unlike the Separatists, felt that the proper procedure was to remain in the church and attempt to "purify" it from within. However, both Kings James I and Charles I lacked sympathy with non-conformists in matters of religion and regarded them as a menace to the state.

Just after he became king, James I was petitioned by the Puritans to institute the reforms which they desired, but, instead of giving favorable attention to the request, the monarch threatened that he would either make them conform to the established church or he would "harry them out of the land, or else do worse." James was succeeded by Charles I who, acting through the notorious Bishop Laud, undertook to put a complete stop to the activity of non-conformists. This meant an increase in religious persecution making the situation extremely disagreeable to the Puritans.

But there were other factors which contributed to the discontent of the Puritans. They were opposed to the arbitrary methods used by the king in conducting the government and many of them felt that there was little hope for relief in that direction. Then, too, they were dissatisfied with the conditions of life about them, particularly the low standards of morality and the lack of strict Sunday observance. So, to escape from their unpleasant environment and at the same time better their economic condition, a large number of them planned to migrate to America. There they hoped to set up "a bulwark against the Kingdom of Anti-Christ."

As early as 1623 a fishing station had been established at Cape Ann, to the north of Plymouth, under the sponsorship of the "Dorchester Adventurers," a group of persons who leaned toward Puritanism. In 1628, a number of capitalists were added to the group which then took the name, "The Company of Adventurers for New England in America." A patent was secured from the Council for New England in March, 1628, granting a tract of land between points three miles south of the Charles River and three miles north of the Merrimac River and extending from the Atlantic to the Pacific. As the company lacked proper authority to govern its grant, an application was made to the king for a charter. This was granted in March, 1629, to the "Governor and Company of the Mattachusetts Bay in Newe-England," as the company was thereafter to be called.

This charter reaffirmed the land grant of the previous year and then outlined a form of government for the company. There were to be a governor, a deputy governor, and eighteen assistants chosen annually by the freemen from among their own number. Four times a year the freemen were to be assembled with the governor and the assistants in a general court for the purpose of making laws which, it was provided, were not to be contrary

THE NEW ENGLAND GOVERNMENTS

21

to those of England. Nothing was said about the location of
the chief office of the company, an omission which made it possible for the actual settlers to assume control instead of being
controlled from England as in the case of the Virginians. Permission was given to the company to transport settlers to
America and assurance was given that the colonists would enjoy
all the "liberties and Immunities" belonging to Englishmen in
the home country. No mention was made of religion.

Attracted by the liberal terms of this charter, twelve prominent Puritans signed, on August 29, 1629, what is called "The
Cambridge Agreement," in which they pledged themselves to
migrate to America by March, 1630, if they were given the
charter and if they and other freemen among the actual settlers
were given the power to control the company. The conditions
were complied with, following which new officers were chosen
including John Winthrop who was elected governor. Early in
1630 he sailed with eleven vessels for New England, thus in-
augurating the "Great Migration" which was to bring twenty
thousand colonists to the region within a decade. The first settlement was made at Salem, but within a year there were eight,
among them Boston.

Of the thousands who came to New England, a large portion
were seeking to escape religious persecution in the home land.
These were in hearty accord with the determination of their
leaders, such as Winthrop and John Cotton, to set up a Bible
commonwealth which would be securely protected against the
forces of "Anti-Christ." Those who came for reasons other than
religious were forced, however, to conform to the wishes of the
Puritan leaders. Religious toleration was entirely foreign to
those who were directing the destinies of the Massachusetts Bay
colony. What they set up in the New World was a theocracy
which was supported by the authority of the civil law. It is
an error, often made in the past, to regard Massachusetts as the
birthplace of religious freedom in this country.

It so happened that, of the hundreds who migrated to Massachusetts in 1630, only twelve were "freemen" of the company.
Since the charter had vested control of the colony's government
in the general court composed of the freemen, these twelve filled
the offices and held all the political power. Thus the first govern-

ment of the Massachusetts Bay colony was an oligarchy which, being in full accord with the clergy, gave the church leaders their whole-hearted support in carrying out their policies for both state and church.

But the desire for self-government was so strong in the English colonists that it was not long before they forced a change in the government. Trouble for the oligarchy began as early as October, 1630, when the first general court was held. At that time one hundred and nine settlers appeared and demanded to be made freemen. Action was postponed until the next spring when the petition was granted. It was required that all those admitted as freemen must be church members in the colony, meaning that they had to conform to the strict Puritan standards in religious matters for no others were allowed to become church members.

Though the number of freemen was increased they at first enjoyed no real power. Contrary to the charter, the members of the oligarchy decreed that the assistants, who were to hold office during good behavior, were to make the laws and elect the governor; the freemen were only allowed to elect new assistants when vacancies occurred. However, in May, 1632, the freemen voted that there must be an annual election of the governor and the assistants, and that each town should elect two delegates to act with those officers in levying taxes.

The next step towards representative government came in May, 1634. Delegates from each of the eight towns appeared at Boston and demanded that they be allowed to see the charter. Governor Winthrop did not dare to refuse and his attention was called to the fact that the law making power was vested in the general court of which the freemen were members. When the general court met a few days later three deputies were present from each town demanding the right to participate in the affairs of government. Though the charter did not provide for representation of the freemen it was recognized that it was impossible for all the freemen to attend and the representative system was put into effect in spite of the protests of the officials and leading clergymen.

While the new form of government had the appearance of being republican, it was neither liberal nor democratic. The freemen were only a small portion of the population and the rule that they must be church members was strictly enforced. The deputies were generally picked by the clergymen and the theocracy still continued in control. The governor and his assistants usually belonged to the most aristocratic class in the colony.

There were occasions on which the deputies disagreed with the assistants and since the former were more numerous they out-voted the latter. This led the assistants to claim that no measure could be passed unless it was approved by a majority of each group. The deputies resisted the claim which, if consented to, would give the assistants a veto power. Finally, the assistants, aided by John Cotton and other influential ministers, won their point and the general court became in effect a two house or bicameral legislature.

From the beginning the Massachusetts Bay colonists enjoyed a high degree of home rule, dealing with their political, eco-nomic, social, and religious problems as they saw fit, with little regard to the wishes of the government in England. King Charles I had hardly expected such a development and finally ordered the Massachusetts charter to be surrendered. The out-break of civil war in England enabled the colonists to disregard the order and, for almost another fifty years, the Puritan theocracy was able to continue in power with little effective opposition.

As the years passed and many more people came to Massa-chusetts who had little or no sympathy with the Puritans, the evidences of discontent with the government of the colony became more pronounced. This discontent was increased by the religious fanaticism displayed in the persecution of Quakers and alleged witches. After Charles II became king in 1660 he gave a ready ear to the complaints coming from Massachusetts for he had no sympathy with the Puritanic ideals of conduct and morality. Finally, in 1684, on the ground that the royal au-thority was being disregarded in the colony, the Massachusetts Bay charter was annulled by order of an English court.

Two years later, by order of King James II, Sir Edmund Andros was sent to America to serve as governor-general of the "Dominion of New England" which included New York and the Jerseys as well as all of the New England colonies. This action was part of a royal plan to secure direct control of all of the colonies in America by making them royal colonies. Andros did away with the representative assemblies and ruled the "Dominion" aided only by a council composed of men selected by the king. But when the governor-general attempted to levy and collect taxes he was met with strong protests similar to those which greeted the Stamp Act about three-quarters of a century later.

In 1688 the "glorious revolution" occurred in England which exiled King James and brought William and Mary to the throne as joint rulers. When the news reached Boston in the spring of 1689 the colonists rose against Andros and he was arrested and imprisoned. The other members of the "Dominion" also re-volted and all resumed their old forms of government.

In the case of Massachusetts Bay, however, the new English government refused to recognize the old charter but in its place issued a new one in 1691. This charter united Massachusetts Bay and Plymouth into one colony called merely Massachusetts. The theocratic government was definitely broken up by a pro-vision for religious freedom to all but Catholics and by the sub-stitution of a property test for the previous religious qualifica-tion for voters. Provision was made for a royal governor with veto power, but the two house legislature was continued under the name, "Great and General Court of Assembly." The council or upper house was to be composed of twenty-eight members elected annually by the general court. The lower branch of the general court was to be made up of two representatives elected from each town by those possessing a forty shilling freehold. It was provided that the king should have the power to pass on all laws passed by the colonial legislature. Courts could be created by the legislature but the power to appoint judges was vested in the governor and council. Appeal from the judgments of colonial courts to the Privy Council in England was to be permitted.

In short, the new charter, while allowing Massachusetts to retain a considerable amount of self-government, made provision for direct control by the home government in England. There-after, until the War for Independence, the constitutional history of Massachusetts is largely an account of the struggles of the representative assembly against what they regarded as encroachments on their power by the royal governors.

RHODE ISLAND

The settlement of Rhode Island was the direct result of the attempts of the Massachusetts Bay theocracy to preserve their colony from contamination by heretics. The exile of Roger Williams and Anne Hutchinson, chiefly for religious reasons, led to the forming of the new colony and with it there was definitely established for the first time in America the idea of religious liberty.

Roger Williams was the first to suffer banishment from the Puritan settlements. In 1631, he became pastor of the church at Salem and soon attracted attention by his liberal ideas. Among other things he denied the right of the civil authorities to legislate on matters of religion or in any way to exercise power over a person's religious beliefs. In other words, he stood for a complete separation of church and state. Finally, in the fall of 1635, he was ordered to appear before the general court to be tried for his opinions. He refused to retract his statements and was forthwith condemned to be banished. The authorities planned to send him to England but he escaped and fled through the forests southward to Narragansett Bay where, with five companions, he established early in 1636 a settlement known as Providence.

The exile of Williams temporarily checked the teaching of heretical ideas in Massachusetts Bay but the theocrats were soon to learn that force could not prevent people from formulating opinions which varied from those accepted as orthodox. If anything, Mrs. Anne Hutchinson constituted a greater menace to the established order than did Roger Williams because she had powerful supporters, including Sir Henry Vane who was elected governor of Massachusetts Bay in the spring of 1636. Mrs. Hutchinson of Boston first made herself obnoxious to the clergy by holding meetings at her house to discuss and criticize the sermon of the previous Sunday. This led to the formation of a doctrine of her own which held that salvation was through grace and not through works, as the clergy were preaching. Her teachings aroused considerable excitement and were bitterly opposed by most of the clergy and the magistrates. It was not until 1638 that they were able to secure an order from the general court for her banishment as a woman unfit to live in the colony. Not satisfied with this, the clergy had her excommunicated from the church so that, henceforth, she was to be regarded as "a Heathen and a Publican."

Mrs. Hutchinson and her husband fled to Narragansett Bay where they joined a group of settlers from Massachusetts who had, a short time before, founded Portsmouth. In the next year the town of Newport was established while, four years later, in 1643, Warwick was founded. Thus there were four towns, each independent of the others and each having its own government.

To safeguard the settlements from the encroachments of other colonies, Roger Williams went to England and, on March 14, 1643, he secured from the Long Parliament, which claimed to act in the name of the king, a patent which incorporated Providence, Portsmouth, and Newport under the name of Providence Plantations. It granted the people full power to rule themselves, provided that their acts were, as far as possible, in conformity with the laws of England. It was not until May, 1647, however, that a government was actually organized under this patent. Then a code was adopted which provided for a general court or legislature made up of six representatives from each town, including Warwick which then entered the corporation. The presiding officer, called the president, was to be aided in executive matters by one assistant from each town. All officers were to be elected annually. The president and the assistants acted as a court for the trial of important cases. An interesting provision of the code required that all acts of the general court must be submitted to a referendum of the freemen in each town; lack of a majority vote in any town would defeat the measure. Another noteworthy feature was the fact that membership in a particular church was not required of citizens.

After this government was set up the colony was not free from trouble. In 1651, the union was broken up by discord, but three years later was reorganized with Roger Williams as president. Even after that there was continuous anxiety due chiefly to the fact that neighboring colonies were claiming Rhode Island's territory. After the restoration of Charles II to the English throne in 1660 there was constant fear that the king would not recognize the patent of 1644 which had been granted by the Long Parliament which had rebelled against his father. Under these circumstances a skillful agent, John Clarke, was selected to present to the king a petition for a charter. Perhaps because Rhode Island had promptly recognized him after the restoration and because he wished to restrain Massachusetts which was claiming Rhode Island territory, the king granted the petition in July, 1663.

The charter designated the colony as "The Governor and Company of the English Collonie of Rhode-Island and Providence Plantations." The law making body, called the general assembly, was to consist of a governor, a deputy governor, ten assistants, and from two to six representatives from each town. The assistants and representatives were to be elected annually by the freemen while the governor and other officials were to be chosen by the assembly, which was to meet twice a year. In general the laws passed by this assembly were to conform to the laws of England but a notable exception was made in the matter of religious liberty. The provision, which, for the first time in American history, gave a constitutional sanction to religious liberty, declared that "noe person within the sayd colonye, at any tyme hereafter, shall bee any wise molested, punished, disquieted, or called in question, for any differences in opinione in matters of religion" so long as the civil peace of the colony was not disturbed.

Except for a short time between 1686 and 1689 when Rhode Island was included in the Dominion of New England, the colony continued under the charter of 1663. At times its independence, like that of the other chartered colonies, was endangered by threats of the home government to revoke the charter. Though several bills were introduced in Parliament for the purpose, none of them was passed. The Rhode Island charter was still in operation when the American War for Independence broke out. Even then the charter was not discarded but, after slight revision, was continued as the state constitution until 1842.

It has been said that Rhode Island was founded by those who had to leave Massachusetts Bay while Connecticut was established by those who wished to leave that colony. Those who were responsible for the first settlement of Connecticut were the members of the congregations of Newtown (now Cambridge), Dorchester, and Watertown located near Boston. These people looked with disapproval at the efforts of the Massachusetts oligarchy to Presbyterianize the churches of the colony. Therefore, under the influence of their liberal leaders they decided to migrate as a group to the Connecticut valley where they could develop their democratic Congregational system as they saw fit. There was also the feeling that they could better themselves economically on the rich farm lands of that valley.

The chief leader of the migrants was Thomas Hooker, the liberal minister of the Newtown church. Hooker was, like Roger Williams, a man "of creative ability, of inflexible purpose, of fine idealism"; but, unlike Williams, he was not a radical. He believed everything should be done in an orderly manner. Instead of publicly disputing with those with whom he could not agree in matters of politics and religion, he preferred to remove himself from their presence. Hooker's influence was constantly wielded to promote democracy in both the state and church. As Roger Williams finally succeeded in doing in Rhode Island, so in Connecticut, Hooker sought to give practical application to the ideas of the compact theory of the state, the doctrine of popular sovereignty, and the principle that the state exists for service to the public and should be held strictly responsible to the will of the majority.

At first the Massachusetts government refused to give its consent to the migration but finally gave its reluctant approval and granted a commission of government to those who were planning to go. The first settlers proceeded to the Connecticut in 1635 and by the end of 1636 there were about eight hundred people living in the towns of Hartford, Windsor, and Wethersfield. In 1637 the settlements were menaced by the Pequot Indians but, with the aid of Massachusetts troops, the Indians were practically exterminated, thus removing that danger.

These pioneers of Connecticut, it should be remembered, had no legal right to the land on which they had settled. At the time there was a Puritan settlement known as Saybrook, at the mouth of the Connecticut, which had been established under a grant made by the Council for New England. However, the settlers of Hartford and vicinity made an agreement with the Saybrook group whereby they were able to continue their colonization efforts without interference.

The next step was to provide a government for themselves. Accordingly, in January, 1639, representatives of the three towns met at Hartford and adopted a constitution which they called the Fundamental Orders of Connecticut. In the work of drawing up this document which has been described as "the first written constitution of modern democracy," and as "the first written constitution known to history that created a government," Thomas Hooker played a leading part.

This constitution provided for a general court or assembly which was to meet twice a year. It was to be composed of four deputies from each of the three towns. When new towns were established they should be entitled to representation on a basis to be determined by the general court. At the first meeting each year, the general court was to choose a governor and six assistants and such other officers as might be necessary. It was required that the governor be a member of one of the church congregations. No governor was to be elected more than once in two years. Only freemen were to have the right to vote or hold office. Though there was no requirement that the freemen should be church members, it is probable that, in practice, only those who were church members would be designated as freemen. Church and state were united by this constitution which declared that the purpose in banding together was not only to form a government but also "to mayntayne and preserve the liberty and purity of the gospell of our Lord Jesus which we now professe, as also the disciplyne of the Churches, which according to the truth of the said gospell is now practised amongst us."

For almost a quarter of a century the colony continued to prosper under the Fundamental Orders. The population grew and new towns were established, offering an increasingly strong bulwark against the Dutch to the westward.

Hardly had Hooker and his followers established themselves on the Connecticut River than another group of Puritans set up a colony west of them on Long Island Sound. In 1637, a number of Puritans under the lead of their minister, John Davenport, and Theophilus Eaton, a wealthy London merchant, had come to Massachusetts from England. Though urged to stay in Massachusetts they refused and, proceeding westward to the Sound, they founded New Haven in April, 1638. After acquiring title to the land from the Indians they proceeded, in June, 1639, to draw up a constitution known as the Fundamental Articles of New Haven.

Through this document, the settlers, who were strictly orthodox Puritans, undertook to set up a Bible Commonwealth that would be even more thorough-going than Massachusetts Bay. It provided that each year the freemen or "burgesses" should hold a general court for the purpose of electing a group of twelve men who should then have the power to make laws and conduct the affairs of the colony, subject only to the authority of the Scriptures. It was required that the freemen be members of the church.

Following this, other towns sprang up in the vicinity and each proceeded to set up a form of government similar to that of New Haven. In 1643, due to the danger from the Dutch and Indians, the various towns came together to form the New Haven confederation. A constitution was adopted which provided for a general court, composed of the magistrates and two deputies from each town, to meet at New Haven twice each year for the purpose of making laws. Only free burgesses, who must be church members, were to have the right to vote. There were to be a governor and a deputy governor elected annually by the free burgesses. These officers were to sit in and have votes in the general court. A rather elaborate judicial system was also provided but there was no provision for trial by jury. Under this form of government the New Haven colony continued until 1662 when it was united with Connecticut.

In the spring of 1661, the general court of Connecticut decided to petition for a charter. Governor John Winthrop, Jr., was placed in charge of the negotiations and, aided by influential Englishmen, succeeded in securing the charter in April, 1662. The definition of boundaries in the document included New Haven, much against its will. That colony, being strongly Puritan, was not favorably regarded by the king. Furthermore, it had been slow in recognizing him and had aroused his ire by sheltering some of the judges who had condemned his father to death. Because of these facts, its protests were unheeded and the union with Connecticut was consummated.

The government provided by this charter was very similar to that authorized by the Rhode Island charter of 1663. There was to be a general assembly composed of two representatives from each town, together with the governor, deputy governor, and twelve assistants. The representatives were to be elected annually by the freemen while the other officers were to be chosen each year by the general assembly. This body was to hold two meetings each year.

Under this charter Connecticut continued with slight modifications until long after independence was secured. When English authorities appeared to seize the charter in 1687, after Connecticut had been designated as a part of the Dominion of New England, the document was hidden, according to tradition, in a hollow oak which was thereafter known as the "Charter Oak." When Andros lost power after the deposition of James II, the charter was brought out and the government went on as before. Early in the eighteenth century there were attempts, as in the case of Rhode Island, to annul the charter by Parliamentary action, but nothing was done.

NEW HAMPSHIRE

Like Rhode Island and Connecticut, New Hampshire was largely an offshoot of the Massachusetts Bay colony. Originally, the area which came to be known as New Hampshire was included in the grant of land secured by the Council for New England in 1620.

During the next few years the Council made grants to various individuals and companies. Among the larger grants were those made to Captain John Mason and Fernando Gorges between 1622 and 1631. During the period various attempts at settlement were made in the region but none were attended by much success. The first such settlement in what came to be New Hampshire was made in 1623. Mason and Gorges were liberal in granting permission to settle on their land and, after 1631, the coast north of the Massachusetts Bay settlements became dotted with trading and fishing villages. The influx of population was considerably increased by fugitives from religious persecution in Massachusetts.

In 1635, Mason secured confirmation of a grant for the region between Salem and the Piscataqua River and gave it the name, New Hampshire. Thus he became the sole proprietor of this territory. Gorges, a little later, had his claim to the area between the Piscataqua and Kennebec rivers confirmed and named it Maine. Massachusetts Bay claimed that her charter gave her a right to most of New Hampshire. After Mason died in 1635, his heirs neglected New Hampshire and left the towns to look out for themselves. Taking advantage of this neglect, Massachusetts Bay absorbed these towns one after another, offering them protection in return for allegiance. When Gorges died, the towns in his territory were also left to shift for themselves, affording Massachusetts Bay an opportunity to absorb them also. The work of absorbing New Hampshire and most of Maine was finally accomplished in 1652 when Massachusetts Bay ran its northern boundary so as to include them.

The heirs of Mason and Gorges protested strongly against the action of Massachusetts but to little avail. Massachusetts finally purchased title to Maine from the Gorges heirs and retained possession of that region until 1820. As for New Hampshire, it was taken from Massachusetts and constituted a royal province in 1679. Its government consisted of a president and a council appointed by the king and an assembly elected by the people.

From 1686 to 1689, New Hampshire was included in the Dominion of New England. Thereafter, having no government, representatives of the four chief towns attempted unsuccessfully to establish one. Then, for a short time, the colony was again united with Massachusetts. In 1692 it was for a second time constituted as a royal colony with a governor appointed by the king. It remained a royal colony until the American War for Independence.

SELECTED REFERENCES

Andrews, C. M., *Colonial Self-Government*, pp. 41–73, 252–288.
Andrews, C. M., *Fathers of New England*, pp. 1–115.
Becker, Carl, *The Beginnings of the American People*, pp. 80–124.
Bolton, H. E., and Marshall, T. M., *The Colonization of North America 1492–1783*, pp. 135–151, 189–195.
Channing, Edward, *History of the United States*, Vol. I, pp. 271–351, 362–436; Vol. II, pp. 65–79, 155–203.
Cheney, E. P., *European Background of American History*, pp. 216–239.
Doyle, J. A., *The Puritan Colonies*, Vol. I, pp. 11–112, 220–319.
Fisher, S. G., *The Colonial Era*, pp. 82–149.
Fiske, John, *The Beginnings of New England*, pp. 60–198.
Garner, J. W., and Lodge, H. C., *The History of the United States*, Vol. I, pp. 148–176.
Greene, E. B., *The Foundations of American Nationality*, pp. 87–129, 186–195, 257–279.
Jernegan, M. W., *The American Colonies 1492–1750*, pp. 116–142, 147–160, 165–191.
MacDonald, William, ed., *Documentary Source Book of American History 1606–1926*, pp. 19, 22–26, 36–45, 50–53, 60–62, 66–72.
Osgood, H. L., *The American Colonies in the Seventeenth Century*, Vol. I, pp. 98–137, 141–199, 224–254, 301–370, 392–467; Vol. III, pp. 309–335, 378–443.
Pease, T. C., and Roberts, A. S., eds., *Selected Readings in American History*, pp. 10–16, 28–33, 47–54.
Preston, H. W., ed., *Documents Illustrative of American History 1606–1863* (Sixth edition), pp. 29–31, 36–61, 78–84, 96–129.
Tyler, L. G., *England in America*, pp. 148–281, 297–317.
Weeden, W. B., *Economic and Social History of New England*, Vol. I, pp. 8–164.
Wertenbaker, T. J., *The First Americans 1607–1690*, pp. 87–114.

Chapter Three

THE COMPLETION OF THE COLONIAL GOVERNMENTS

MARYLAND

SHORTLY after the Puritans commenced their colonizing activity in New England, a project to the southward was launched to serve as an asylum for Catholics who were, by the laws of England, deprived of religious and political privileges. The originator of the colonization scheme in what came to be known as Maryland was George Calvert. He had been quite prominent in English political affairs, having been one of King James's supporters in Parliament and having also served as one of the secretaries of state. His conversion to Catholicism barred him from further office holding but King Charles II offered him some compensation for this by raising him to the Irish peerage with the title of Lord Baltimore. Calvert had also shown an interest in trade and colonial development as a member of the East India Company, the Virginia Company, and the Council for New England.

In 1620 he had purchased some land in Newfoundland. Three years later he secured from King James I a patent recognizing him as proprietor of this area which he called Avalon. In 1627 he went to the island with the intention of remaining but found it unsuitable for colonization. He then went to Virginia but was not allowed to remain there because he would not take the oath of supremacy. Returning to England, he sought and finally secured from King Charles a grant of that portion of Virginia which lay north of the Potomac River. The Virginians protested in vain against this action.

Before a royal charter could be issued, George Calvert died, and the document was given to his son, Cecilius Calvert, the second Lord Baltimore. This younger Calvert had the same desire as his father to develop the resources of the grant and he had an even stronger desire to make it a haven for Catholics. This charter, which was issued in June, 1632, was much more specific in its description of boundaries than some charters, those of Virginia for example, had been. Roughly speaking, Maryland, as the area was called in the charter, was to be bounded on the south by the southern bank of the Potomac River, on the east by the Atlantic Ocean, on the north by the fortieth parallel, and on the west by the meridian which marked the source of the Potomac River.

This land was granted to Lord Baltimore as proprietor on such terms that he became virtually a feudal lord, owning not only the land but exercising important political powers in it. There was a remarkable freedom from control by the king. It was merely required that the king's over-lordship should be recognized by delivering to him each year two Indian arrows and also one-fifth of such gold and silver as might be mined in the colony.

The proprietor and his heirs were given the power to make laws with "the advice, assent, and approbation of the Free-Men" or their representatives who should be assembled for the purpose. It was required that the laws be reasonable and "not repugnant or contrary" to the laws of England.

Instead of settlers in the colony receiving their land from the king as in a royal colony, they were to receive it from the proprietor on the payment of quitrent or on such other terms as he saw fit. He also had the power to set up manors of the mediaeval feudal type and to establish manorial courts. This was the first instance in the English colonies of what could be called a constitutional provision for a separate court system. In passing, it might be observed that only a few manors were established in Maryland. The institution was not suited to conditions in America and so failed to take root. The proprietor could also impose fines, imprisonment, or other punishment, and could even inflict the death penalty. In brief, he was the sole source of executive, judicial, and military authority.

After receiving this charter, Lord Baltimore undertook to send out a colonizing expedition. In November, 1633, two small vessels set sail from England carrying about two hundred emigrants, perhaps half of whom were Catholics. Early in the next year a settlement was made at St. Marys, near the mouth of the Potomac. This site was a healthy one and so much of the trouble that had afflicted the early Virginian settlers was avoided. Most of those who first went to Maryland were accustomed to work and had little difficulty fitting into the new life.

Cecilius Calvert himself did not come to America but exercised his authority through a governor named by himself. The first governor, his brother, Leonard Calvert, was also the chief justice of the colony. He was assisted by members of a council appointed by the proprietor. The requirement that the freemen should be assembled was observed and the first assembly was held in 1634. While the people were settled in or close to St. Marys all the freemen met together, but as the settled area expanded a system of proxies developed. This proved unsatisfactory as it enabled the governor and a few others holding the proxies to outvote the freemen who were present.

Gradually, small political sub-divisions known as hundreds were set up and, in 1639, these began sending representatives to the assembly. By 1650 the representative system was fully established. In that same year the legislative body was divided into two houses; the upper was composed of the councilors and other members appointed by the proprietor and was regarded as representing his interests; the lower house was made up of the representatives elected from the hundreds by the freemen. No laws could be enacted without the consent of both houses, nor were they valid without the approval of the governor and the proprietor. In this way the proprietor retained a large measure of control over legislation, even though, in 1638, he had been forced to concede to the freemen the right to initiate laws.

In addition to its legislative function this two house assembly occasionally acted as a court of law. Most of the cases, however, were tried before the local courts or before the governor and his council sitting as a court.

Affairs in the colony did not proceed with entire smoothness. At first there was trouble with Virginia over territorial rights, but this dispute was settled by the king in favor of Maryland. When the civil war broke out in England the population of the colony was divided, one group supporting Parliament and the other the king. The existence of a Parliamentary group was due to a large influx of Puritans. As the controversy continued, questions relating to religion also arose. To prevent trouble the proprietor appointed William Stone, a Protestant, to be governor in 1647. This governor was required to take an oath that he would not molest anyone on account of his religion. Shortly afterwards, the assembly passed the famous toleration act of 1649 which declared that no person or persons "professing to believe in Jesus Christ, shall from henceforth bee anywaies troubled, Molested or discountenanced for or in respect of his or her religion nor in the free exercise thereof within this Province . . . nor in any way compelled to the beliefe or exercise of any other Religion against his or her consent." The denial of the doctrine of the Trinity was made an offense. Punishment was also provided for those guilty of blasphemy and Sabbath-breaking. It will be seen that this act did not grant complete toleration to all but only to those who were Christians.

After Charles I had been beheaded and the Commonwealth had been set up in England, commissioners were sent to America in 1652 to secure the allegiance of Virginia and Maryland. The latter agreed to recognize the authority of the Commonwealth. However, the commissioners were not satisfied with Governor Stone's attitude so they deposed him, turning the government over to a committee which called a new assembly controlled by Protestants. This assembly then passed an act disfranchising the Catholics, and undertook to destroy charter rights of the proprietor. Calvert, assuming that the authority of the commissioners was at an end when Oliver Cromwell became the Lord Protector of England, ordered Stone and his other officials to resume their offices. This led to a civil war between the Puritans and the followers of the proprietor, who were called "Papists." The Puritans won and it seemed that Lord Baltimore would be deposed as proprietor. In fact, Virginians were planning to unite Maryland and Virginia into one colony. But in 1657, the proprietor succeeded in having his rights restored and the government which he had set up was resumed. The Toleration Act which had been changed to disfranchise the Catholics was also restored, but this did not end the difficulties between the Catholics and Protestants.

After 1660 there was increased friction between the proprietor and the colonists. Finally, at the time of the English revolution of 1688, a revolution also broke out in Maryland. The government at St. Marys was overthrown and a convention called which petitioned King William and Queen Mary to abolish the proprietor's rights and make Maryland a royal colony. The monarchs complied with the second request by depriving the proprietor, who was then Charles Calvert, of his political powers. A royal governor was sent over and for about a quarter of a century Maryland was a royal province. However, much to the disgust of the "Association in Arms for the Defence of the Protestant religion, and for asserting the right of King William and Queen Mary to the Province of Maryland" which had staged the revolution in the colony, the proprietor was allowed to retain his rights to ungranted lands and to the revenues from the quitrents. In 1715 full proprietary rights were restored to the fourth Lord Baltimore and from then until the War for Independence Maryland remained under the political and economic control of the Calvert family.

NEW YORK

At about the same time that the English began seriously the task of colonizing in North America, the Dutch began planning to establish colonies of their own in the New World as well as in the Far East. Accordingly, as early as 1597, companies were formed to trade with the West Indies and, in 1602, the Dutch East India Company was chartered. To it was granted, by the government of the Netherlands, authority to make conquests, to plant colonies and to set up governments.

It was as an employee of the Dutch East India Company that Henry Hudson sailed up the river which now bears his name. He was seeking a passage to India. While he failed in this, his explorations gave the Dutch a claim to a share of the continent. In 1614, a company of merchants were given a charter by the States General of the Netherlands, granting them a trade monopoly in the region, called New Netherland, which lay between the fortieth and forty-fifth degrees of latitude. This company built a fort and trading post at "Fort Nassau" near the present Albany, and thus the beginning of the permanent settlement of the locality was made.

In 1621, this first company was replaced by the Dutch West India Company which received a charter granting it monopolistic trade privileges and the power to plant colonies in America and elsewhere. Two years later a ship was dispatched to New Netherland bearing thirty families. Two forts were built, one, called Fort Orange, on the site of the present Albany, and the other, a second "Fort Nassau," on what was later called the Delaware River, near the site of the present Camden, New Jersey. In 1626, Peter Minuit arrived bearing a commission as director-general. He proceeded to buy the island of Manhattan from the Indians, paying for it with goods valued at twenty-four dollars. A fort was built at what now is called The Battery and the name, New Amsterdam, was given to the island. Peace was made with the Indians and with the English at Plymouth. However, the latter warned the Dutch that they were trespassing on English soil.

As a means of stimulating settlement in New Netherland, the Dutch West India Company, in 1629, issued a "charter of privileges" setting up a patroon system which was a modified form of feudalism. Under this system, any person could receive a grant of land extending sixteen miles along one bank of the Hudson River or eight miles on each bank and stretching indefinitely to the east or west, provided that he agreed to settle fifty persons over the age of fifteen on the land within four years. The patroons, as the owners of such tracts were called, were granted extensive governmental, judicial, and economic privileges.

At first the only central government was that exercised by the governor or director-general who was appointed by and represented the Dutch West India Company. In 1642, the director-general reluctantly granted a demand of the settlers that he have an advisory council of five members. In December, 1653, delegates from the various towns that had been established by that time met at New Amsterdam to protest against the arbitrary government of the colony, which issued orders and made laws, "odious to every free born man," without the consent of the people. Peter Stuyvesant, who was then director-general, furiously denied the right of the delegates to meet and protest against his actions. Said he, "We derive our authority from God and the Company, not from a few ignorant subjects." However, a few years later, in 1664, with a war in progress between the Dutch and the English, Stuyvesant found it desirable to court the support of the people. Accordingly, the election of a provisional assembly was authorized, to be composed of twenty-four delegates or two from each town. Little was accomplished by this organization, however, as the English seized the colony shortly after the assembly met.

By 1664, the Dutch colony had expanded considerably. Settlements were to be found about Fort Orange, on the banks of the Hudson, on the west end of Long Island, on Staten Island, on the Jersey Coast, and on the Delaware River, in addition to the main settlement, New Amsterdam. The expanding English colonies were crowding these settlements on both the east and the south. Finally, in March, 1664, King Charles II granted to his brother, the Duke of York, all that territory which lay between Connecticut and the Delaware River. The Duke shortly dispatched a fleet to America which, on August 26, 1664, forced Stuyvesant to surrender New Amsterdam and with it, all of New Netherland. The town was renamed New York and the same name was given to the whole colony. This seizure of New Netherland was carried out in accordance with the plans which had been made by the English to weaken the Dutch who had developed into powerful commercial rivals.

The grant which the Duke of York had received from the king made him proprietor of the region which he had seized. He was given the power to establish "such Laws, Orders, Ordinances, Directions and Instruments" as he saw fit, provided they were not contrary to the laws of England. In addition, he was empowered to appoint such officers as he might wish to carry on governmental activities within the colony. No mention was made of a legislative body to represent the people.

In the exercise of his authority, the Duke appointed Richard Nicolls to be governor with an advisory council also appointed by the Duke. The inhabitants were allowed to retain their property. A code was drawn up, known as the Duke's Laws, which was a mixture of ideas derived from the laws of Massachusetts and New Haven and from the customs of the Dutch, with a few new ideas added. This code provided for trial by jury, equal taxation, religious toleration, and suffrage on a basis of land holding, but no provision was made for a representative assembly.

During the subsequent years this omission caused trouble but the Duke refused to grant the pleas for such an assembly. In 1681, difficulties arose over taxation. This led the Duke, in the next year, to send over Thomas Dongan as governor, with instructions to call together representatives of the people to advise the governor and council in the making of laws and in matters pertaining to taxation. The assembly thus called met in October, 1683, and passed several laws. It also passed what was called the "Charter of Franchises and Liberties."

When the Duke of York became King James II of England in 1685, he abolished this assembly and made New York a royal colony under the control of a governor and council. Shortly afterwards, the colony was included in the Dominion of New England in accordance with the king's plans to unify the control of the colonies. In May, 1689, a rebellion took place against the authority which James had set up. This rebellion was led by Jacob Leisler, who seized power and proclaimed King William and Queen Mary. For a time Leisler was virtually a dictator. Early in 1691, the English monarchs sent out a new governor to whom Leisler surrendered. The governor then summoned a representative assembly which first met on April 9, 1691.

From that time until the War for Independence began, New York remained a royal province. From the constitutional viewpoint, the chief feature of the intervening period was the persistent encroachment of the representative assembly on the prerogatives of the king and the royal governor. Since the suffrage was limited to those having a freehold worth forty pounds or more, it could not be said that the assembly was fighting for the mass of the people. Rather it was seeking favors for the privileged few. But in the course of time, rival leaders, seeking the support of the masses, began to stress the rights of the people generally.

The king and his governors insisted that permanent grants

should be made for governmental purposes and that expenditures should be determined by the governor and council. Gradually, however, the assembly changed the procedure and finally they assumed the power to vote the governor his salary for one year at a time. They also succeeded in having the money raised through taxation placed in charge of a provincial treasurer chosen by themselves, thus making certain that expenditures would be in accordance with their wishes. They overrode the objections of the council by citing actions of the English House of Commons. Further, they denied to the council the right even to amend money bills.

To prevent the governor from defeating their measures by keeping in existence an assembly, the members of whom he might have won over to his support, the assembly passed a bill providing for elections every three years. This measure was disallowed by the English government as an "infringement upon the prerogative of the Crown."

This and other actions on the part of the agents of the Crown and, particularly, the conduct of the royal governor were naturally subjects of discussion and criticism in the press. Some of this criticism appeared in the *New York Weekly Journal* which was published by John Peter Zenger. This aroused the wrath of the governor who, in 1734, had Zenger thrown into prison to await trial for criminal libel. As no New York lawyer dared defend him, his friends secured the services of Andrew Hamilton, a noted lawyer of Philadelphia. The chief justice, who owed his position to the governor, presided at the trial. He instructed the jury to decide merely whether or not Zenger had published the articles as charged, leaving it to the judge to decide whether the material was libelous. But Hamilton, in a brilliant appeal to the jury, persuaded them to disregard the judge's instructions, and pass judgment on the question of libel. The result was that the jury, convinced that the liberty of the people was at stake, voted to acquit Zenger. This episode and its outcome constituted a landmark in the development of freedom of the press in the English colonies. Freedom of the press was destined to become an American constitutional idea for it is guaranteed by the first amendment to the Constitution.

NEW JERSEY

Shortly after the Duke of York had received from King Charles II in 1664, the grant of the territory held by the Dutch, he in turn granted the portion known as the Jerseys to two of his favorites, Sir George Carteret and Sir John Berkeley. These men, as proprietors, assumed the power to provide a government for their possession. In 1665, they sent over Philip Carteret as governor. He brought with him a plan of government which bore the official title of "The Concession and Agreement of the Lords Proprietors." This document provided that the governor should appoint six men to serve in a council to advise him in the conduct of the government. It was further provided that the freemen should elect, from among their own number, twelve deputies to act with the governor and the council as a legislative body to be known as the general assembly. After local sub-divisions had been established, these twelve deputies were to be replaced by another group made up of one representative elected annually from each of these local areas.

The general assembly was to have the power to pass such laws as might be necessary for the government of the colony, provided such laws were not contrary to the laws of England or to the wishes of the proprietors. Religious liberty was supported in the Jerseys by the provision that no laws were to be enacted which interfered with liberty of the conscience.

Furthermore, the assembly was empowered to lay equal taxes, to erect governmental sub-divisions, to establish cities and forts, to allot lands, to naturalize foreigners, to provide armed forces, to provide for the support of the governor and the government in general, and to take steps for the collection of the quitrents due the proprietors.

After existing for a few years as a joint proprietary colony, New Jersey was divided. In 1674, Sir Berkeley sold his interest in the colony to Edward Byllynge and John Fenwick for one thousand pounds. These men were Quakers and apparently they purchased Berkeley's share in the region in the expectation of establishing an independent colony for members of their sect. These men soon transferred their rights to a new group of

Quakers, including William Penn. In 1676 these Quaker proprietors made an agreement with Sir George Carteret whereby they received West New Jersey while Carteret retained East New Jersey.

Soon Quakers in considerable numbers began arriving in West New Jersey. Settlers coming in 1677 brought with them a document, drawn up chiefly by Penn, styled "Concessions and Agreements," giving the people a very liberal government. The law making power was to be vested in a board of commissioners appointed by the proprietors acting with an assembly elected by the people. No laws were to be passed contrary to the "Concessions" or to the laws of England. The settlers were guaranteed various liberties including the right to trial by jury, the right to petition, and religious freedom. These guarantees constituted the first bill of rights to be put into operation in America.

In 1680, Byllynge secured title to West New Jersey. The chief change he made in the government was to substitute a single executive for the commissioners provided by the "Concessions." Seven years later, on the death of Byllynge, Daniel Coxe, a London merchant, secured possession of the colony and undertook to develop its commercial possibilities. During the next year, however, the territory was included in the Dominion of New England. After King James II had been dethroned, Coxe was restored to his proprietary rights but he soon sold the colony to the West New Jersey Society.

Meanwhile, in 1682, following the death of Carteret, East New Jersey had been sold to William Penn and eleven Quaker associates. A plan of government, called the "Fundamental Constitutions," was formulated but was never put into effect. Like West New Jersey, East New Jersey was included in the Dominion of New England. After the English Revolution of 1688 the colony was returned to its proprietors.

For a number of years following the accession of William and Mary to the English throne, the two Jerseys were allowed to remain in the possession of their proprietors. Considerable difficulty was experienced because of internal dissension and disputes over the authority of the proprietors. But, in 1702, an agreement was reached whereby East and West New Jersey were consolidated into one colony under a royal governor.

Though in many of the subsequent years, the royal governor of New York also served as the governor of New Jersey, the latter otherwise remained as a separate royal colony until the American Revolution.

PENNSYLVANIA

While the Quakers were interested in the settlement of New Jersey, their main effort to found a colony in America took place across the Delaware River in what came to be called Pennsylvania, under the promotion of William Penn. By birth and family connections, Penn belonged to the English aristocracy. His father was Sir William Penn who had been an admiral in the navy under Cromwell and then had managed to retain his place under Charles II. The younger Penn was sent to Oxford to acquire cultural polish so as to be fitted to assume his proper place in society, but while there he became, in 1667, an adherent of the Society of Friends, much to the disgust of his father.

All dissenters in England were subject to penalties under the law, but the Quakers, being regarded as dangerous radicals, were treated even more harshly than others who refused to acknowledge the supremacy of the Church of England. Even young Penn, in spite of his social position, did not escape being imprisoned for taking part in the illegal religious meetings held by the Quakers.

When Admiral Penn died he left to his son a fine inheritance, which included a claim of about sixteen thousand pounds against the king. The younger Penn had been much interested in the Quaker project of establishing a colony in America. The older colonies there, such as Massachusetts, had proved anything but hospitable to the members of the Society of Friends. In view of this it seemed desirable to develop a separate colonization project, which explains the Quaker interest in West New Jersey. In 1681, Penn, pressing his claim against Charles II, received from the king a large grant of land in America which was named Pennsylvania. This grant made it possible for the Quaker leader to apply, under favorable conditions and on a rather large scale, his ideas of government and religion.

The charter which Penn received from the king described the boundaries of Pennsylvania in a fairly definite way, yet con-

troversies arose with New York on the north and with Maryland
on the south. It was not until 1760 that these disputes were
settled. Then Pennsylvania accepted the forty-second degree as
the northern boundary and thirty-nine degrees and forty-four
minutes as the southern boundary. Seven years later the Mason
and Dixon line was surveyed to fix the boundary between Maryland and Pennsylvania. This line later became famous in
American history as marking the division between the North
and the South. The Delaware River formed the boundary on
the east while the western boundary was fixed by the charter as
a line five degrees west of that river.

Penn was given by the charter powers and privileges quite
similar to those granted earlier proprietors. He was to have
the right to make laws not contrary to the laws of England with
the consent of the freemen and he was to have the power to
appoint officials. Compared with those of Lord Baltimore in
Maryland, however, Penn's powers were considerably limited.
Any person in the colony was to have the right to appeal
to the Privy Council in England from any judgment of a Pennsylvania court. All laws had to be submitted to the Privy Council
for approval or disapproval. The charter further required that
the navigation laws be observed. The proprietor was to be
allowed to levy customs duties except in cases where Parliament
had acted to impose such duties. Penn was to maintain an agent
in England who could be held accountable for violations of the
navigation acts. No taxes were to be levied in the colony "unless
the same be with the consent of the pprietary [sic], or chiefe
Governor and assembly, or by Act of parliament in England."
This seemed to imply the right of Parliament to tax within
the colony, a matter of more than passing interest because of
the conflict which arose in the colonies about eighty-four years
later. Perhaps to lessen objections to granting the charter to a
Quaker, it was stated in the document that, if twenty or more
persons in the colony so desired, the Bishop of London was to
have the right to send a "preacher or preachers" of the Church
of England to serve them.

To promote the settlement of Pennsylvania, Penn prepared
and widely circulated a prospectus setting forth the advantages
of going there. To the settlers already in his territory he sent

a message in which he promised to set up an assembly for the purpose of making laws. In the fall of 1682 he himself arrived with a hundred colonists and proceeded to lay out Philadelphia.

Before he left England, Penn had drawn up a "Frame of Government" and a code of laws for his colony. After coming to Pennsylvania he proceeded to apply the Frame of Government with some modifications. It was his intent to serve as governor himself with an agent or deputy to act in his absence. A large council was to be elected by the land holding or tax paying freemen. In addition there was to be an assembly, also elected by the freemen, which should approve or disapprove of laws prepared by the council. In practice this plan did not work, and by 1701 the Frame of Government had been so modified as to provide for a governor and council appointed by the proprietor. The council was considered the upper house of the legislature while the assembly was the lower. The latter was recognized as the stronger of the two.

Probably the outstanding feature of Penn's colony was its emphasis on real religious liberty. Penn had undertaken to conduct a "Quaker experiment in government" yet he had no desire to bar those of other religious faiths. With his advice and consent, the Pennsylvania assembly passed a law which granted freedom of religion not only to Protestant Christians but to Catholics and Jews as well. Consequently the colony became a place of refuge for people of many different beliefs who had fled from Europe to avoid persecution.

But it should not be assumed that the proprietor had no trouble with his colony. One of his first difficulties was with the home government after the Revolution of 1688. The fact that he had been friendly with the Stuart kings, Charles II and James II, directed suspicion against him. He was also accused of failing to preserve order in his colony and of having permitted the violation of the navigation acts. The result was that, in 1692, Pennsylvania was taken from him and made a royal colony under the governor of New York. In two years, however, Penn was restored to the control of his colony.

There was also considerable trouble between the assembly and the proprietor's representatives in the colony. Penn, who spent little time in Pennsylvania, was much grieved and disappointed at this turn of events. In 1701, he had ordained that the members of the assembly should be elected annually. Subsequently, the assembly assumed powers he had not intended it to have: it curtailed the governor's power to make appointments, it controlled his actions by making his salary dependent on their annual or semi-annual vote, and it elected a treasurer to keep the funds of the colony. One of the more serious assembly-proprietor disputes, which developed after William Penn had died and the colony was in the hands of his descendants, was over the taxation of the estates belonging to the proprietor. In ·1764, the quarrel became so bitter that a strong group, which included Benjamin Franklin, sought to have the proprietary government replaced by a royal government. Nothing came of this, however.

Another matter which caused friction between the colony and the English government was the question of oaths. The Quakers did not believe in oaths but deemed a solemn affirmation sufficient. When attempts were made in Pennsylvania to substitute affirmations for oaths, the laws were disallowed by the government in England. Finally, the latter yielded to the extent of relieving the Quakers from taking oaths. This concession had some significance in connection with later constitutional development in this country for the Constitution of the United States allows the president to take either an oath or an affirmation when entering upon the duties of his office. Furthermore, by Article VI, all senators and representatives, all members of state legislations, and all executive and judicial officers of either the United States or the separate states are required to pledge support to the Constitution either "by Oath or Affirmation."

The Quaker opposition to war also caused trouble for the colony during the wars between the English and French in the period from 1689 to 1763. The Quaker believed that he should not bear arms himself and he often went so far as to hold that a Quaker member of the legislature should not even vote appropriations for military purposes. As a result such appropriations were often refused by a Quaker controlled assembly. When pressure became too great they preferred to give up their seats in the assembly to non-Quakers rather than violate their beliefs.

In spite of all its woes and troubles the proprietary control of Pennsylvania was maintained until the American War for

Independence gave its inhabitants an opportunity to set up their own state government.

DELAWARE

By the end of the first quarter of the seventeenth century, four nations had undertaken colonization on the eastern coast of North America. These were Spain, France, England, and the Netherlands. The fifth to seek a place for itself in America was Sweden. The establishment of New Sweden in the present Delaware was largely the result of the enterprise of William Usselinx who had been a founder of the Dutch West India Company. He sought and received from King Gustavus Adolphus of Sweden in 1626 a charter for a commercial company similar to the Dutch company. Because of the Thirty Years' War in Europe and the death of Gustavus Adolphus, the project of establishing a colony in America was delayed until 1638. In that year about fifty colonists set out under the leadership of Peter Minuit who, it will be recalled, had earlier been director-general of New Netherland. They settled on the Delaware River in territory claimed by the Dutch and erected Fort Christina near the present location of Wilmington.

The colony of New Sweden never enjoyed a prosperous development, and fifteen years after its founding it had only about two hundred inhabitants. The Dutch resented the presence of the Swedes whom they regarded as trespassers, but as long as the Thirty Years' War continued no action was taken since Sweden and the Netherlands had a common interest in the conflict. Following the Peace of Westphalia in 1648, however, the Dutch soon proceeded against their neighbors in America with the result that New Sweden was placed under the jurisdiction of New Netherland.

When the Duke of York seized the Dutch colony he also secured New Sweden which came to be known as Delaware. In 1682, the Duke granted Delaware to William Penn and in that same year the Pennsylvania assembly passed an Act of Union which united the two under the same government. From then until the American Revolution they had the same governors, but from 1702 Delaware was allowed its own assembly. Thus, while both belonged to the same proprietor, they were virtually separate colonies. With the outbreak of the Revolution each became an independent state.

NORTH AND SOUTH CAROLINA

For some time before any organized attempt was made to colonize the region south of Virginia, attention had been drawn to it by reports of the fertility of its soil. Some settlers from Virginia had even moved into the area, establishing themselves in the Albemarle River valley. The territory had been included in the London Company's grant of 1606 but after the Virginia charter was revoked in 1624, it reverted to the Crown. In 1629, Sir Robert Heath had received a grant to the territory which was called Carolina lying between the thirty-first and the thirty-sixth degrees of north latitude. No attempt had been made to settle the region so the grant was considered invalid.

As a reward to those who had helped restore him to the throne, King Charles II made a grant of the region to eight men who were to act as joint proprietors. They were the Earl of Clarendon, General George Monk, Lord John Berkeley, Sir William Berkeley, Lord William Craven, Sir John Colleton, Sir George Carteret and Lord Anthony Ashley. By a charter issued in 1663 and amended two years later to enlarge the boundaries, these eight were given complete sovereignty over the land between 29° and 36° 30' and extending from "sea to sea." For this they were to pay the king twenty marks a year and one-fourth of all the gold or silver found in the region.

The proprietors were to have the chief power to make laws, but these were not to be contrary to the laws of England nor were they to "extend to the binding, charging, or taking away of the right or interest of any person or persons, in their freehold, goods or chattels whatsoever." The people were to have a right to participate in the making of the laws. The proprietors were given authority to allow dissenters to settle in their territory, thus making possible religious toleration. Nevertheless, the Church of England was to be the official church of the colony.

Apparently the proprietors expected to develop a prosperous business producing and exporting to England and other British colonies such things as "silks, wines . . . raisins . . . almonds, oyl, and olives." The charter granted them the privilege of bringing these goods into English ports free of duties for a period of seven years. Needless to say, this privilege proved of little value and the proprietors were destined to disappointment in their hopes for economic gain from their colony.

The first step toward establishing a government in Carolina was taken in 1664 when a governor was sent out by the proprietors to take charge of the settlements which had been established on the Albemarle River by Virginians. This governor, William Drummond, proceeded to appoint a council and also called together representatives of the freeholders to form, with the council, a general assembly. This legislative body first met in 1665. Eventually, a more definite plan was developed in northern Carolina whereby the proprietors appointed the governor and other prominent officials including the members of the council. Twelve representatives were chosen by the freemen to sit with the governor and the council with the authority to make laws, subject to the veto of the governor and the proprietors. The courts were created by this assembly but the judges were appointed by the governor.

While this type of government was being developed in the colony, the proprietors were attempting to put into operation a plan called "The Grand Model" or "The Fundamental Constitutions of Carolina." This fantastic document was drafted by the famous English philosopher, John Locke, in 1669. At that time he was secretary to Lord Ashley and was also serving as clerk of the Carolina proprietors. The Fundamental Constitutions provided for a feudal government in which an aristocracy based upon land ownership would exercise the political power. High sounding titles were provided for officials. There were to be territorial subdivisions bearing such names as counties, seignories, baronies, and precincts. A system of courts was also provided for and there was to be a grand council and a parliament. This "Grand Model" was the first constitutional document in American history to provide for a two house or bicameral legislature. Locke's work proved of little practical value and the document is of interest chiefly as a curiosity in American constitutional development. The Fundamental Constitutions were not suited to conditions in the New World and were not viewed with favor by the colonists who strenuously resisted attempts to put them into operation.

Meanwhile plans were being formulated for settlement in the southern part of the Carolinas. In April, 1670, almost a hundred colonists landed on the Ashley River and laid out the original Charles Town. Others soon migrated to this locality and within fifteen years there were about twenty-five hundred people living in the vicinity. About 1680, the Charles Town settlement was moved between the Cooper and Ashley rivers and eventually its name was changed to Charleston.

The government of this colony was conducted by a governor representing the proprietors, by a "parliament" elected by the freeholders and by a council chosen by the parliament. The quarrel over this and such matters as quitrents led to a rebellion and the expulsion of the governor, John Colleton.

At the same time trouble was occurring in the Albemarle colony in northern Carolina which resulted in the expulsion of the governor from that colony also. To settle the difficulties, the proprietors, in 1691, sent out Philip Ludwell to act as governor of both colonies, though he actually lived at Charleston, while a deputy governor represented him in the north. Each colony, however, retained its own legislative organization. In the southern colony the legislative machinery was revamped to include the governor, a council of seven appointed by the proprietors acting as the upper house, and a lower house, called the "Common House of Assembly," elected by the people. At first the judicial power was vested in the governor and council.

The discontent in the Carolinas was only temporarily mollified, however, and soon new troubles developed. The people in the southern colony complained because the proprietors afforded them little help against hostile Indians. They also objected to legislation which required all dissenters to pay taxes for the support of the Anglican Church. The culmination of the difficulties came when the proprietors disallowed a measure designed to secure the election of members of the assembly from separate districts. This precipitated a rebellion in 1719 which overthrew the proprietary government. The home government, long dissatisfied with affairs in the Carolinas, took advantage of this action and sent a provisional royal governor to take charge of affairs in South Carolina.

North Carolina had been given its own governor in 1713 so that it was virtually a separate colony from that time. After the overthrow of the proprietors in South Carolina the division of the Carolinas was emphasized still more. Finally deciding that it was useless to continue their control any longer, the proprietors agreed to turn North Carolina over to the English government, also. The agreement was ratified by Parliament in 1729 and, from that date until the Revolution, North and South Carolina were separate royal colonies.

GEORGIA

Of the thirteen colonies which formed the original United States, the last to be settled was Georgia. The chief motive for its first colonization was philanthropic rather than religious or economic. In this respect it differed from every other colony.

The moving spirit in planning this colony was General George Oglethorpe. He was a member of Parliament and had become interested in the unfortunates of the country through visits to various prisons as chairman of a committee appointed to make such visits and recommend reforms. Oglethorpe was convinced that many persons who were imprisoned for debt did not deserve such treatment. He was convinced that they would be able to better their lot if they were colonized in the New World. He therefore sought a grant of land and a charter to permit the carrying out of his conviction.

A number of factors combined to secure favorable action on the petition. At the time a number of German Protestants, who had been subjected to persecution in the principality of Salzburg, were seeking refuge under the English flag. There was much sympathy for them in England and it was felt that they could well be taken care of in a new colony in America. Furthermore, the English government was anxious to establish a settlement south of South Carolina to furnish a buffer against the encroachments of the Spanish in Florida, and a protection against the Indians. Yet another favoring factor was the desire of the English to establish a post strategically located for participation in the southwestern fur trade.

The charter, which was granted in June, 1732, designated a group of twenty men, including Oglethorpe, as "one body politic and corporate, in deed and in name, by the name of the Trustees for establishing the colony of Georgia." The land granted lay between the Savannah and Altamaha rivers and extended from the Atlantic Ocean to the "south seas." The trustees, who were to all intents and purposes, proprietors, were given the authority to establish governmental agencies in the colony for a period of twenty-one years, after which Georgia was to become a royal colony. They could appoint a governor, judges and other officials, as they saw fit, with the exception of officers who should be appointed by the king to collect and receive revenues which should be due to the English government. The governor was to be required to give security as a guarantee that he would enforce the trade and navigation laws. Courts could be created but nothing was said concerning a representative assembly.

The trustees could also enact laws for the colony but these were subject to the Privy Council's approval or disapproval. All laws were required to be in conformity with the laws of England. The charter stated that all persons, "except papists, shall have a free exercise of religion, so they be contented with the quiet and peaceable enjoyment of the same, not giving offence or scandal to the government." Quakers were specifically granted the right to make affirmations instead of taking oaths.

It was stated that the trustees could grant lands, but no grant was to be larger than five hundred acres. An annual report was to be made each year to the English government of all money received or spent. Slavery in the colony was prohibited by a provision stating that all inhabitants of the colony should be free.

Shortly after the charter was granted, preparations began for the actual colonization of Georgia. Financial aid to the extent of ten thousand pounds was authorized by act of Parliament in 1732. Georgia was the only one of the thirteen colonies which received direct financial help from the home government. Early in 1733, about a hundred persons, men, women, and chil-

dren, led by Oglethorpe, reached America and founded Savannah at the mouth of the river bearing that name. While the first
settlers were largely of the debtor class, many others came to
the colony in subsequent years; among these were German
Protestants and Scotch Highlanders, together with some Swiss,
Jews, and Portuguese. About twenty years after the colony was
established a considerable tide of immigration set in from the
Carolinas and Virginia.

During the period in which the trustees controlled Georgia
its progress was disappointingly slow. As the population grew,
an increasing dissatisfaction developed with the policy of the
trustees. The prohibition of the slave trade and the importation
of rum met with the greatest disapproval, but finally, in 1749,
the ban on both was lifted.

The absence of a real colonial government was another source
of grievance. For years the only existing government was that
of the municipality of Savannah, and as the settlements spread,
all outside of Savannah were without participation in the government. An insistent demand for a representative assembly
arose, but it was not until 1751 that the demand was granted.
Two years later the trustees' period of control came to an end
and Georgia became a royal colony with a government similar
to that of the other royal colonies. Under royal control it enjoyed considerable prosperity, so much so that it can be said
that it joined the Revolution in 1775, not so much because of
any grievance of its own but because of its sympathy with the
other colonies.

THE TYPES OF COLONIES

Having traced the specific constitutional developments in each
of the thirteen colonies it is in order to make a few observations
concerning the general characteristics of the whole group. Considered from the standpoint of types, the colonies underwent
considerable changes from the time of their founding until they
broke away from England. At the time of their establishment
three were of the corporate type, that is, they were founded by
regularly chartered corporations organized by persons interested
in trade and economic exploitation. These were Virginia, New
York, and Delaware.

Another four were independent, that is, they were founded by people acting without the authority of a charter. Massachusetts (considering Plymouth as the beginning of that colony), Rhode Island, Connecticut, and North Carolina (referring to the Albemarle settlements) were, in this sense, originally independent colonies.

The remaining six, New Hampshire, Maryland, New Jersey, South Carolina, Pennsylvania, and Georgia, were, at their founding, proprietary colonies. That is, they were established by an individual or a group of individuals, acting under a charter or a patent obtained directly or indirectly (as in the case of New Hampshire) from the Crown.

It would hardly be proper to classify any of the colonies as charter colonies at the time of their founding or later as the use of the term would only cause confusion. Both the corporate and proprietary colonies were established under written charters or patents.

By the time the colonies revolted from their mother country their types had been changed very much. Only three of the proprietary colonies survived to 1775: Maryland, Pennsylvania, and Delaware. Two colonies, which originated through independent action, soon became corporate colonies through charters granted by the Crown to a group of the settlers organized in the form of a corporation. These charters permitted almost complete self-governing powers under a republican form of government. For this reason these colonies are sometimes described as republican colonies. The two, Connecticut and Rhode Island, were still corporate in form when the separation from England took place.

Originally none of the thirteen was a royal colony but, beginning with Virginia in 1624, seven had become royal colonies before 1775. That is, they were governed without charters and were controlled by the English government, to a considerable degree, through royal governors and councils appointed by the Crown. The seven were: New Hampshire, New York, New Jersey, Virginia, North Carolina, South Carolina, and Georgia. xMassachusetts might well be classified as a royal colony but it would be better to call it semi-royal or semi-corporate, for, from 1691 to 1774, it was governed under a charter permitting an elective council and a lower house elected by the people but with royal control through a governor appointed by the Crown.

THE GOVERNOR

Considering the structure of the colonial governments as they existed as the colonial period neared its close, one observes that all had an executive head called the governor. However, in the various types of colonies his powers and importance varied considerably. In the royal colonies the governor was appointed by the Crown and served only during the pleasure of his royal master. He was the representative of the Crown in the colony, and his first duty was to the Crown rather than to the people of his colony, and this fact he had constantly to keep in mind during conflicts with the popular assemblies. The governors were expected to keep the home government supplied with full information on colonial conditions; to recommend legislation to the colonial legislatures; to transmit laws passed by the legislatures with their consent to the home government for approval or disapproval; and, in general, to execute the royal will in the colonies over which they ruled.

Often royal governors were chosen, not because of competence, but through influence or favoritism. Naturally, many of them had little understanding of or sympathy with their subjects, and consequently aroused bitter opposition against all royal control. Their frequent use of the veto did not tend to lessen their unpopularity. Occasionally, competent royal governors were sent to America but even they were regarded by large numbers of the people as the symbols of an obnoxious outside authority.

In the proprietary colonies the governor's position was much the same as in the royal colonies, except that the proprietors did the appointing, subject to the approval of the Crown, and that the governor represented the proprietors instead of the English government. In the corporate colonies, Connecticut and Rhode Island, the governors were elected by the assemblies by which they were therefore controlled, and consequently played a relatively unimportant part.

THE COUNCIL

In each of the colonies there was a group of men generally designated as the council, though in Rhode Island and Connecticut they were called the assistants. In those two colonies they shared the executive functions with the governor; in the other colonies the council merely assisted the governor, whose duties were to be performed with their advice and consent. In the two corporate colonies and in Massachusetts the council was elected by the qualified voters; in the royal colonies the members were appointed by the Crown, generally from a list nominated by the royal governor; while in the proprietary colonies the council was selected by the proprietor.

Not only did the council or assistants, as the case might be, assist the governor in his executive duties, but with him constituted the upper house of each colonial legislature, whose approval of all laws was required. The council usually was made up of the most aristocratic individuals in each colony.

THE ASSEMBLY

Though the term "assembly" was frequently applied to the whole legislature it was generally understood to refer to the lower house which, in each colony, was elected by the qualified voters. Theoretically each assembly represented all the people in the particular colony, but because of the general restrictions on the suffrage, many people had no voice in the selection of the members. Nor was there equality of representation. Instead of creating districts of about the same population to give equal representation to all, the prevailing method was to assign to each county, town or other subdivision an arbitrary number of representatives. Often, after the population of a colony had increased, with a large portion in the so-called "back country," the preponderance of representation was left in the hands of the older settlements near the coast, in the "tidewater" area. This produced much dissatisfaction and not a little trouble at times. The Constitution of the United States reflects the general dissatisfaction with the colonial type of representation in the first article which provides for representation in the lower house of

Congress from the states in proportion to their population and also provides for a census to be taken every ten years so that the proper proportion of representatives might be maintained.

These colonial assemblies developed an organization similar in some respects to the English House of Commons. They set up committees for the consideration of various measures, thus establishing precedents for the later state and national governments. The presiding officer, elected by the assembly itself, was known as the speaker, who in some cases was quite influential in the politics of the colony.

The actual influence of the assemblies was much greater than that of the councils. The power to initiate legislation and to control financial measures was gradually assumed by the assemblies which found precedents in the history of the House of Commons. By controlling the finances, the assemblies were able to effectively restrict the governors, who, at least in the case of the royal colonies, theoretically possessed almost unlimited powers. Much of the constitutional history of the colonial period could be devoted to accounts of how the assemblies resisted the measures of the governors and in turn successfully encroached on what were supposed to be the rights of those officials. Long before the colonial period ended, the assemblies had become the most important cogs in the governmental machinery of their respective colonies.

THE JUDICIARY

The colonial courts were based on English legal experience almost entirely. In all of them the English common law was administered, but there was no uniformity in the type of courts as each colony had its own system. To deal with petty cases justices of the peace were appointed in the various colonies. Generally there were to be found county courts in which the more important criminal and civil cases were tried. These were the *nisi prius* or jury courts. Appeals were made to a higher court which, in most of the colonies, was made up of the governor and the council or assistants. Two of the colonies, however, had separate supreme courts with judges appointed by the governors. Appeals from the colonial courts could be made to the Privy Council in England, representing the Crown.

The fact that the governors and councils so generally acted as courts makes it obvious that there was not yet a full acceptance of the idea of a three branch government with each branch having separate powers. This is shown further by the executives' participation in legislation and by the aid the councils or assistants afforded the governors in carrying on the executive functions. Nevertheless, the colonial period saw great progress made toward the acceptance of the three branch government principle featured by the separation of powers. This principle was later more fully applied in the state and national constitutions.

SELECTED REFERENCES

Andrews, C. M., *Colonial Self-Government*, pp. 22–40, 74–201, 232–251.

Beard, C. A., *Readings in American Government and Politics*, pp. 1–16.

Becker, Carl, *Beginnings of the American People*, pp. 125–134.

Bolton, H. E., and Marshall, T. M., *The Colonization of North America 1492–1783*, pp. 125–129, 162, 164–178, 188, 189, 196–211, 221–231.

Channing, Edward, *History of the United States*, Vol. I, pp. 241–268, 438–483, 499–507; Vol. II, pp. 13–25, 31–59, 94–126, 203–209.

Doyle, J. A., *English Colonies in America*, Vol. I, pp. 275–296.

Fisher, S. G., *The Colonial Era*, pp. 62–81, 177–206, 303–312.

Fisher, S. G., *Evolution of the Constitution of the United States*, pp. 26–69.

Fiske, John, *Old Virginia and Her Neighbours*, Vol. I, pp. 255–318; Vol. II, pp. 270–307.

Fiske, John, *The Dutch and Quaker Colonies*, Vol. I, pp. 58–294; Vol. II, pp. 1–167.

Garner, J. W., and Lodge, H. C., *The History of the United States*, Vol. I, pp. 125–147, 180–218.

Greene, E. B., *The Foundations of American Nationality*, pp. 67–77, 130–153, 155–177, 281–309, 311–326.

Jernegan, M. W., *The American Colonies 1492–1750*, pp. 65–76, 194–213, 267–293.

Johnson, Allen, ed., *Readings in American Constitutional History 1776–1876*, pp. 6–9, 18–25.

Johnston, Mary, *Pioneers of the Old South*, pp. 116–131, 140–147, 199–211.

MacDonald, William, ed., *Documentary Source Book of American History 1606–1926* (Third edition), pp. 31–35, 53–55, 63–66, 74–78, 80–84, 95–103.

Orth, S. P., and Cushman, R. E., *American National Government*, pp. 9–32.

Osgood, H. L., *The English Colonies in the Seventeenth Century*, Vol. II, pp. 119–197, 200–225.

Pease, T. C., and Roberts, A. S., eds., *Selected Readings in American History*, pp. 36–38.

Preston, H. W., ed., *Documents Illustrative of American History 1606–1863* (Sixth edition), pp. 62–77, 130–145, 148–169.

Tyler, L. G., *England in America*, pp. 118–148.

Chapter Four

TENDENCIES TOWARD UNION
PRIOR TO *1763*

THE formation of the American Union was not a sudden accomplishment. Though finally brought about by the common grievances of the colonists against the home government, union was not a new idea in 1775. Prior to the close of the French and Indian War in 1763 there had been manifested numerous tendencies toward uniting the colonies; no less than twenty plans or proposals for union are known to have been made.

THE NEW ENGLAND CONFEDERATION

One of the most notable plans for colonial union, and the first to be put into effect, was the so-called New England Confederation. Beginning in 1637, several proposals were made for a confederation of the New England colonies but no action was taken until 1643. In May of that year, commissioners representing Massachusetts Bay, Plymouth, Connecticut, and New Haven met at Boston and drew up a document consisting of a preamble and eleven articles. Rhode Island was not invited to the meeting nor was it allowed to enter the confederation later, chiefly because of the unwillingness of Massachusetts Bay to deal with its heretical neighbor.

In the preamble the reasons for banding together were stated. Since the population of the several colonies was widely scattered, since the "sad distractions" (civil war) in England made it difficult to secure advice and protection from the home land, since they were hemmed in by people of different nationalities (obviously referring to the Dutch in New Netherland and the French in Canada), and since there was constant danger from the Indians, the colonists felt that it was their "bounden duty" to enter into an association for mutual help.

The official name of the confederation was "The United Colonies of New-England." In the second article it was stated that, "The said United colonies, for themselves and their posterities doe joyntly and severally, hereby enter into a firme and perpetuall league of friendship and amytie, for offence and defence, mutuall advise and succour, upon all just occations, both for preserveing and propagateing the truth and liberties of the Gospel, and for their owne mutuall safety, and wellfare."

Each member colony had complete jurisdiction over its internal affairs and was independent except in a few matters, such as military operations, which were in charge of the confederation. Two commissioners, who were required to be church members, represented each colony. They met once a year and oftener if necessary, alternating between Boston, Plymouth, Hartford, and New Haven. The consent of at least six of the commissioners was required before war could be declared. However, if one of the colonies was invaded, the others were to come to its aid without waiting for action by the commissioners. In case of war, men and money were to be furnished in proportion to the number of male population between the ages of sixteen and sixty. It is interesting to note that the articles contained provisions for the return of fugitive slaves and for the extradition of fugitives from justice. The commissioners were authorized to draw up other agreements for the common good and for the prevention of misunderstandings between the member colonies.

Though the confederation did not end until 1684 its usefulness was practically over a score of years earlier. During its short life it must be admitted that it served some useful purposes. The commissioners frequently discussed Indian affairs and, in 1675, the confederation was instrumental in ending the dangerous Indian uprising known as King Philip's War. There were occasions when the members would not coöperate as, in 1653, when Massachusetts Bay refused to join in a war on the Dutch. In 1662 the confederation received a serious blow when the provision in the articles guaranteeing the independence of each colony was violated by amalgamation of Connecticut and New Haven. Two years later the menace of the Dutch was eliminated when New Netherland was taken over by the English, and one of the chief reasons for forming the confederation was removed. After another twenty years, featured chiefly by inactivity and neglect, the New England Confederation disappeared, bringing to an end the first American experiment in union.

INFLUENCE OF THE WARS WITH FRANCE FOR SUPREMACY

Meanwhile a rivalry was developing between the British and French which was to have important consequences in the New World. Between 1689 and 1763 they waged four wars for world as well as American supremacy. These wars did much to promote the idea of union among the English colonists, as is evidenced by a number of noteworthy plans formulated during the period. Furthermore, the fighting gave to these colonists valuable experience in inter-colonial coöperation and in military operations which was to prove useful in the revolution against England.

BASES OF ENGLISH AND FRENCH RIVALRY

It was perhaps inevitable that the English and French should clash in America. The latter had earnestly begun their colonization of New France in 1608 when Quebec was laid out by Samuel de Champlain. From that place the French pushed westward up the St. Lawrence valley, establishing military and fur trading posts and missions. This expansion was interrupted for a time by a war with England in 1629 when Quebec was captured. However, three years later the French were restored to their colony and were able to proceed with their westward penetration, eventually reaching the western shore of Lake Michigan.

Under Louis XIV, who became king of France in 1643, a great zeal for national expansion was manifested. The king himself was interested in his colony in North America, but it was his minister of finance, Jean Baptiste Colbert, who had the most influence on the colonial policy of France. Colbert was a firm believer in the mercantilist theory and under his direction it was strictly applied. He organized industry and commerce on a national basis and protected them to the best of his ability against the competition of foreigners. He undertook the further development of the French colonies to make them more useful and profitable to the Crown.

Accordingly, the government of New France was reorganized to provide a more direct control by the home government. Emigration to the colony was encouraged and the economic development of the region was promoted. Particular attention was given to the expansion of the fur trade and to exploration. In 1671, the French took formal possession of the whole area surrounding the Great Lakes. Two years later Marquette and Joliet discovered the upper Mississippi River and so afforded the French a claim to additional territory. Then, in 1682, La Salle made his epochal voyage down the Mississippi to the Gulf of Mexico, climaxing his effort by a ceremony in which he formally claimed the whole Mississippi valley for his king, naming the area Louisiana in honor of Louis XIV. Thus the French claimed and possessed the entire region to the north and west of the English settlements. To safeguard their possessions they erected an increasing number of forts at strategic points, from which the missionaries and fur traders carried on their activities among the Indians.

Until near the close of the seventeenth century, the French and English settlements were so far apart that there was little friction between them. But as both were rapidly expanding it was only a matter of time until they clashed. Yet, at first, it was not so much territorial rivalry as it was rivalry in the fur trade that brought the two nationalities into conflict. In the south, English fur traders, chiefly from Virginia and the Carolinas, found themselves in competition with the French as well as the Spanish, while, in the far north, the English Hudson's Bay Company afforded rivalry to the French fur traders.

But it was in the central region, occupied by the powerful Iroquois Indians, that the most intense competition was developed. This was especially true after Thomas Dongan became governor of New York in 1681. The French were making desperate efforts to win over the Iroquois through their missionaries and through the use of military force but Dongan outmaneuvered them. He sent out agents who easily convinced the Indians that English goods were cheaper than the French. The

Indians naturally preferred to trade with the English when they found they could receive more rum and other articles for their furs than they could receive from the French.

ALBANY CONFERENCE OF 1684

In further promoting his plans, which contemplated the ruin of the French in Canada, Governor Dongan took a step which should be noted as an influence towards union. He sent an invitation to the officials of the other English colonies to meet at Albany for a conference with the chiefs of the Five Nations, as the Iroquois were frequently called. The meeting was held in July, 1684, with representatives present from Massachusetts Bay, New York, Maryland and Virginia, and a treaty was drawn up between the English and the Five Nations. The Indians had come to the conference seeking help in an expected war with the French and they interpreted the treaty as a pledge of such aid by the English. The English regarded the act as an acknowledgment of their sovereignty. At any rate, the Iroquois became the allies of the English and remained so during the subsequent wars for supremacy fought between the English and the French.

KING WILLIAM'S WAR

Open hostilities between the British and the French were delayed, however, until James II was deposed from the English throne by the bloodless Revolution of 1688. Both James and his predecessor, Charles II, received pensions from the French government with the result that the English and French remained on friendly terms, at least nominally. But when William and Mary became the joint monarchs of England in 1689, following the exile of James, the situation was radically changed. As stadtholder of the Dutch Republic, William had saved the Dutch territory from conquest by Louis XIV. In accomplishing this he had formed a number of alliances, culminating in the powerful League of Augsburg, organized in 1686.

In the fall of 1688, Louis aroused the League by sending troops into Germany. To more effectively oppose him, William took steps to bring England into the war. This was accomplished in May, 1689, when the League was transformed into the "Grand Alliance," composed of Great Britain, Austria, Spain, Holland, Sweden, Savoy, the elector of Brandenburg and others. The war waged between this group and France, 1689 to 1697, was called the War of the Grand Alliance.

With England and France at war, it was not long before hostilities also broke out in America in King William's War. Compared to the fighting in Europe what took place in America was relatively unimportant, but to the colonists the situation was serious enough. Trouble started when the Iroquois massacred the inhabitants of the French settlement of La Chine, near Montreal, in the summer of 1689. The French and their Indian allies retaliated by raids on the outlying settlements of Maine and New Hampshire. In 1690, they were responsible for a fearful massacre of the English and Dutch settlers at Schenectady, New York.

NEW YORK CONFERENCE OF 1690

This event had the effect of thoroughly arousing the English. Had the Dominion of New England still been in existence the northern colonies would have had the unity necessary to deal with the situation. But the colonists had demonstrated that they did not relish a union forced on them by the king, particularly when such a union involved the loss of their right to participate in the government. But the situation called for coöperation and it was decided to hold a conference to determine a course of action. The call for the conference was issued by the Massachusetts General Court on March 19, 1690. Five colonies responded by sending commissioners to New York which had been designated as the meeting place. Massachusetts, Maryland, Connecticut, and New York were each represented by two commissioners while Plymouth was represented by one. An agreement was drawn up, on May 1, 1690, which provided for raising eight hundred and fifty-five troops for the defence of Albany. Of these, New York was to furnish four hundred; Massachusetts, one hundred and sixty; Plymouth, sixty; Connecticut, one hundred and thirty-five; and Maryland, one hundred. The Lieutenant Governor of New York was to be commander of these troops. No attempt was made to form a permanent organization, but the conference was important as a demonstration of the possibility of inter-colonial coöperation.

Following this New York conference, the English colonists took the aggressive. Port Royal in Acadia was captured and an expedition was organized for the capture of Quebec, but this proved unsuccessful. The next year the French recaptured Port Royal and their province of Acadia. In the following years, nothing decisive took place in America, and when the war was ended by the Treaty of Ryswick in 1697 the situation stood much as it had eight years earlier.

THE PENN PLAN OF UNION

About the time the war closed in 1697, a notable plan for colonial union was drawn up by William Penn. During the previous year, the English Board of Trade had been petitioned to consolidate the colonies. The Board of Trade, however, reporting that such consolidation was impractical, inspired Penn to make his proposals. His plan was labelled, "A Briefe and Plaine Scheam how the English Colonies in the North parts of America, viz.: Boston, Connecticut, Road Island, New York, New Jerseys, Pensilvania, Maryland, Virginia, and Carolina may be made more usefull to the Crowne, and one another's peace and safty with an universall concurrence."

This plan included a congress composed of two deputies appointed by each colony to meet at least once a year in time of war and not less than once in two years in time of peace. The meeting place was to be as central as possible, New York being suggested as a good place. A high commissioner, appointed by the Crown, was to preside over the congress and act as commander-in-chief of the colonial military forces in case of war. It was suggested that the governor of New York might well be appointed to act also as the king's commissioner.

The congress was to consider and adjust differences between the colonies, to prevent injury to commerce, and to devise means of protection against enemies. In case of war it was to fix the quotas of men and money to be supplied by each colony.

Though Penn's plan was not adopted it stands, historically,

as the first plan for a general union of the colonies to be proposed by an American.

QUEEN ANNE'S WAR

For a few years following the Treaty of Ryswick, there was peace in Europe and America. However, it was not long before events so shaped themselves in Europe as to bring on another war. It had been the constant aim of William III to maintain a balance of power in Europe by means of the Grand Alliance. This balance was threatened by the efforts of Louis XIV of France to gain virtual control of Spain by placing a relative on the throne of that country. The Spanish king had no direct heirs and a quarrel developed between the French Bourbons and the Austrian Hapsburgs over succession to the throne. William of England intervened and made an agreement with Louis whereby the Spanish possessions were to be divided. But when the Spanish king died it was found that he had ignored this agreement and had made Philip of Anjou, grandson of Louis XIV, his sole heir. The powerful French king then broke his agreement with William and gave his approval to the procedure whereby his grandson was crowned as King Philip V of Spain.

This action had the practical effect of uniting the extensive Spanish empire to the already strong French empire. To William this was sufficient cause for war but neither his Dutch nor English subjects were anxious to enter a conflict for the purpose of helping a Hapsburg secure some of the Spanish possessions or even to preserve the balance of power. But in 1701, James II died and Louis proceeded to arouse the English people by immediately recognizing the son of James as king of England. Then the English merchants were irritated by new commercial restrictions imposed by the Spanish, influenced, as was believed, by the French. The Dutch, on their part, were fired with a war spirit by the appearance of French troops in the border provinces of Spanish Netherlands. Thus the stage was set for another war but William did not live to see its beginning. This war, which started in 1702, is known as the War of the Spanish Succession. In American history it is called Queen Anne's War from the name of the English ruler at the time.

While the war was fought chiefly in Europe there were some events of importance in America. Probably the outstanding achievement of the colonists was the capture of Acadia by New England militia. In 1713 a compromise peace was effected through the Treaty of Utrecht. By its terms, the English not only retained Acadia which they renamed Nova Scotia but they were also given possession of Newfoundland, a matter of great importance to the New England fishermen. In the treaty, the French also recognized the English protectorate over the Iroquois Indians.

DANIEL COXE'S PLAN OF UNION

Just before the war started there had been some discussion of colonial union but nothing had been done. The war itself revealed a deplorable lack of coöperation between the colonies, notably between New York and the New England colonies. But it was not until several years after the Treaty of Utrecht that anyone again broached the subject of union. The most noteworthy plan then brought forward was that of Daniel Coxe of New Jersey. In a volume published in London in 1722 he proposed that the colonies should be united in a "legal, regular, and firm establishment." There was to be a "great council" composed of two deputies elected annually by the legislative body of each colony. This council was to consult for the general good and it was to fix the quotas of men and money to be provided by each colony for the common defence. Each colony was to be allowed to raise its quotas in its own way. There was also to be a "supreme governor" or governor-general who was to preside over the council and who was to have a veto power over its actions. The individual colonial governors were to be subordinate to him.

Though Coxe argued that such "a coalition or union would lay a sure and lasting foundation of dominion, strength, and trade," his plan apparently received little consideration. The colonies were not yet ready for union.

KING GEORGE'S WAR

For a quarter of a century following the peace of Utrecht the English and the French refrained from warfare. Nevertheless, during the period, they were developing intense rivalry for world supremacy. Not only in Europe, but in Africa, Asia, and America their interests clashed. Each was seeking commercial supremacy and each was ready to use every governmental resource, military or otherwise, to bring it about.

In North America both were rapidly expanding. The French concluded that possession of the Ohio valley was essential to their welfare, regarding it as an indispensable link between their Mississippi and St. Lawrence colonies. The English, whose settlements were rapidly filling up the "Old West," the region lying east of the Appalachians, also viewed the region of the Ohio as necessary for their own expansion. With both nationalities claiming the region and seeking to possess it, conflict was bound to occur sooner or later.

Allied to France was Spain, whose king had, in 1733, formed with France what was called the Family Compact, aimed chiefly at England. In 1739, trouble arose between the Spanish and the English which led to war. Five years later the French entered the conflict which soon involved the other leading European powers. From that time on the war was called the War of the Austrian Succession, and in America it was known as King George's War.

Ostensibly the war was fought to preserve the territorial integrity of Austria but it developed into another test of strength between the English and the French. About the time that England and Spain started fighting, the ambitious Frederick the Great of Prussia seized the province of Silesia belonging to Austria, taking advantage of the supposed weakness of the young queen, Maria Theresa. Frederick's action was taken in spite of the agreement previously made by Prussia, England, and France to guarantee the integrity of the Austrian empire. Instead of punishing Prussia for its aggression, France, seeking to gain the Austrian Netherlands, allied herself with Prussia. To prevent France from securing possession of the coast provinces of Austria and so promoting her maritime strength, England entered the war on the side of Austria. Thus the war, which was fought in Europe and America, developed into what was primarily a struggle for sea power.

From the point of view of the English, the war was largely a failure. Her armies met with defeat while Prussia retained Silesia and the French invaded the Netherlands. On the sea the English demonstrated their superiority over the French but made little use of their advantage in this respect.

In America the chief event of the war was the capture of the strongly fortified Louisburg located on Cape Breton Island. This fortress served as a defence of the entrance to the St. Lawrence; it afforded shelter to the French fishermen who constituted a menace to the New England fishing interests; it served as a convenient port from which French privateers darted out to play havoc with British commerce; and it also served as a base of operations for expeditions against the English colonies. Therefore, it was with great pride and joy that the English colonists hailed the capture of this Gibraltar of America, in 1745, by an expedition of their own militia aided by a few English naval vessels. After that little of importance was accomplished in America.

By 1748, all parties concerned were tired of war and the Treaty of Aix-la-Chapelle was drawn up to bring the hostilities to a close. Having failed to get the French out of the Netherlands by force, the English found it necessary to restore Louisburg to its former possessors as the price for the evacuation of that territory. This was viewed by the English colonists with great disgust and was regarded by them as a betrayal of their interests. So far as America was concerned, and for that matter, Europe, the war might as well not have been fought. Certainly it settled nothing of importance. The peace established proved to be nothing more than a temporary truce for, in a few years, England and France were again at war.

THE FRENCH AND INDIAN WAR

The trade and territorial rivalries of the two nationalities in America became increasingly keen in the period between 1748 and 1754 when war again broke out. One point of dispute was Acadia which had been granted to the English by the Treaty of Utrecht. The French claimed that it included only the small peninsular area of the present Nova Scotia while the English insisted that it included much additional territory. Both undertook to make good their claims by force, if necessary. There was also a rivalry over the control of the waterway between the Hudson and the St. Lawrence rivers. The English definitely controlled the Hudson for some distance above Albany while the French just as definitely controlled the Richelieu River which formed the northern portion of the waterway. The dispute raged over the control of Lakes Champlain and George and the strip of land constituting the portage between the latter lake and the Hudson. The French had gained a clear advantage by erecting a fort at Crown Point on Lake Champlain. Their presence there was regarded as a serious menace to the English, particularly to those who had settled in the upper Connecticut valley.

The Great Lakes basin was yet another region in which the Anglo-French rivalry was growing more bitter. The French had established forts and trading posts at strategic points, including Forts Niagara, Frontenac, and Detroit, while the English had moved up the Mohawk valley and had strongly established themselves at Oswego on Lake Ontario. There, taking advantage of their acknowledged sovereignty over the Iroquois, they developed a fur trading business surpassing that of their rivals at nearby Fort Niagara. Naturally, the French were anxious for an opportunity to force the English out of Oswego and, at the same time, win over the Iroquois.

A fourth, and what proved to be the precipitating cause of the war, was the increasingly bitter rivalry for the possession of the Ohio valley. Without it, the only safe communication for the French between Canada and Louisiana was the hazardous and lengthy northern route by way of the upper Mississippi and the Great Lakes. As the first important step in securing possession of the region, the French governor-general of Canada, in 1749, dispatched Celeron de Bienville on an expedition which took him from Lake Erie to the Allegheny River, down that river to the Ohio, thence down to the Miami River, up that stream and down the Maumee River back to Lake Erie. At various points Bienville formally claimed possession of the territory for his king. His procedure was to issue a proclamation of French sovereignty, then to nail to a tree a sheet of tin bearing the French coat-of-arms, and finally to bury a leaden plate stating that the Ohio basin belonged to France.

The Bienville expedition actually accomplished little of its purpose to insure French possession of the region, but the reports brought back concerning the activities of the English in the area served to stimulate the French to take further action. In 1752, the French, with the aid of some Indians, destroyed the English post on the Miami River, Fort Pickawillany. In the following year, Marquis Duquesne, who had become governor-general of Canada, sent a force of fifteen hundred men to occupy the Ohio country. This expedition erected a fort at Presque Isle (the present Erie, Pennsylvania), and, before winter set in, they also built Fort Le Boeuf on French Creek, a branch of the Allegheny.

Reports of these French activities had the effect of arousing the English to take measures to safeguard their own interests. Virginia, in particular, was deeply concerned by what was transpiring as it claimed the Ohio country by the provisions of the charter of 1609. Furthermore, in 1749, a group of powerful Virginians chartered as the Ohio Company had obtained from the king of England a grant of half a million acres of land on the Ohio River, which they had agreed to settle. The next year the company had sent Christopher Gist to explore the region. His favorable report stimulated Virginian trading and colonization activity, Fort Pickawillany being one of their projects.

But with the French taking the aggressive, the English position in the Ohio country was seriously threatened and it was necessary for them to act before their cause was lost. Late in the summer of 1753, the English secretary of state for the colonies issued instructions to the colonial governors to use force to repel the French if they invaded English territory. Acting under this authority, Governor Robert Dinwiddie of Virginia sent George Washington to warn the French to vacate the Ohio country.

Washington, though at the time only twenty-one years of age, was experienced in the ways of the frontier and knew how to deal with the Indians. Late in the fall of 1753 he set out. He was joined by Christopher Gist who acted as his guide. He finally reached Fort Le Boeuf and delivered his message to the French commander there. The latter stated that he would forward Dinwiddie's letter of warning to Duquesne but meanwhile would remain where he was.

The report of this French defiance was carried back to Governor Dinwiddie who immediately began preparations for war. A small detachment of colonial troops was sent in February, 1754, to build a fort at the forks of the Ohio, but they were captured by a force of French and Indians and their fortification destroyed. In its place the French erected a stronger one which they named Fort Duquesne. Meanwhile, Washington, who had become leader of the English forces because of the death of the appointed commander, was approaching with a larger force. As he neared Fort Duquesne it became evident that the French, in superior numbers, would soon attack him. A rude fortification, styled Fort Necessity, was hastily constructed. It proved insufficient, however, for Washington's troops to ward off the enemy and, after a bloody fight, he was forced to surrender. For the time being the French were masters of the situation and the English were effectively eliminated from the Ohio country.

THE ALBANY CONGRESS OF 1754

In spite of Washington's defeat, it was difficult to arouse the colonies to action. The French encroachments did, however, have the effect of bringing the majority of them together in the largest inter-colonial conference held up to that time. This gathering, known as the Albany Congress of 1754, was held at the call of the English Board of Trade which instructed the colonial governors to recommend to their legislatures that commissioners be appointed to meet in a convention for the purpose of making a treaty with the Iroquois and also to form a union or confederation of the colonies for mutual defence. The meetings started in June and lasted for several weeks.

In addition to many Indians there were present twenty-five delegates from New Hampshire, Rhode Island, Massachusetts, Connecticut, New York, Pennsylvania, and Maryland. Strange though it may seem, Virginia was not represented nor were any of the other southern colonies. The congress was only partly successful in carrying out its objectives. The Indians who had become very much dissatisfied by the evidences of English weakness in the face of French aggressions were at least somewhat soothed by the conference and kept from going over to the enemy. The matter of forming a union of the colonies was regarded by the delegates as extremely important, so they set up a committee to propose a plan.

RICHARD PETERS'S PLAN OF UNION

Among the proposals apparently considered was one by Richard Peters, a delegate from Pennsylvania. His plan was purely military in character. He suggested that the colonies be divided into four groups, with the evident idea that the members of each group would have common interests and would be able most effectively to work together in case of war. Under this plan, which was not adopted, the three southern colonies, Georgia, South and North Carolina, would have constituted one group; Virginia, Maryland, Delaware and Pennsylvania, a second; New Jersey and New York, a third; and the four New England colonies, a fourth.

THE FRANKLIN PLAN OF UNION

The Albany Congress finally adopted the Franklin Plan of Union, so called because of the important part played in its formulation by Benjamin Franklin of Pennsylvania. The plan proposed that Parliament should be requested to pass an act to permit the formation "of one general government" in America. This government was to be administered by a president-general, "appointed and supported by" the Crown, and a grand council representing the colonies. It was to be composed of forty-eight members to be elected by the colonial assemblies for a term of three years. Each colony was to be accorded representation according to the amount of taxes it paid, but each colony was to have at least two representatives while none was to have more than seven. Massachusetts and Virginia were to have seven representatives each, Pennsylvania six and the other colonies were to have the remaining twenty-eight to begin with. This council was to meet at least once a year.

The president-general, with the advice of the grand council, was to have the power to declare war on, and to make treaties with, the Indians, to regulate trade with the Indians, to authorize new settlements, to "lay and levy such general duties, imposts, or taxes" as deemed just on each colony according to its ability to pay, to raise and pay troops, to build forts, to approve the appointment of military officers, to appoint civil officers of the union, and to appoint a special treasurer for each colony as well as a general treasurer.

The president-general was to nominate military officers and commission them after their appointment had been approved by the grand council. He was to have a veto power over the acts of the grand council and was to execute such acts as might be approved.

Though it was stated that each colony was to be left to manage its own affairs and though it was made clear that no acts should be passed contrary to the laws of Parliament, the Franklin plan met with neither the approval of the colonies nor the English government. The colonies felt that it left too much control in the hands of the Crown, while the English government thought it was too democratic. There were certainly some good features in the plan, some of which served as precedents for the later Constitution of the United States, among which were the idea of the colonial central government to control military affairs; and the power to levy taxes. Just what influence the proposed union would have had is, of course, a matter of speculation. But had it been put into effect it is probable that many of the irritating events which brought on the War for Independence would have been avoided. That war might have been postponed or even avoided altogether.

Because of the failure of the Franklin plan the French and Indian War had to be fought with the old machinery. It is true that some degree of uniformity was secured in the conduct of Indian affairs by the appointment of two superintendents, one in the south and the other in the north. So far as military affairs were concerned, there was only blundering inefficiency and failure for several years. In 1755, General Edward Braddock met with a disastrous defeat while attempting to capture Fort Duquesne and in the next year the English lost Oswego.

However, in 1756, the war assumed a different aspect. The previous fighting in America had been carried on without a declaration of war, while the home governments pretended to be at peace with each other. Meanwhile changes were taking place in the diplomatic alignment of the European nations. Austria had succeeded in allying herself with Russia and France against Prussia. England, to protect Hanover, the possession of George II, promptly allied herself with Prussia. Since there was no longer any need for a pretense of peace, England and France mutually declared war late in the spring of the year. From that time on the conflict, known in Europe as the Seven Years' War, was a real world war, with heavy fighting in Europe, America, and Asia.

ENGLISH SUCCESSES

Gradually, the English came to the conclusion that they must have a stronger and more efficient leadership if their cause were to prevail. The result was a cabinet reorganization in 1757 which placed William Pitt in office as the Principal Secretary of State in charge of foreign affairs and also in charge of the war. He proceeded to build up the army and navy to a high standard of efficiency, replacing incompetent commanders with younger and more active officers. The results of the new policy were soon apparent. In America, the British, aided by thousands of colonial troops, captured one French stronghold after another. Louisburg and Forts Frontenac, Duquesne, and Niagara were wrested from the French in 1758 and, in the next year, Quebec was captured. The year 1760 saw the French lose Montreal and her remaining forts in the region of the Great Lakes. During the same year the French power in India was broken. The war might have ended then had not Spain entered it, in 1761, as an ally of France. This postponed peace for two years but, in 1763, the Treaty of Paris was signed by England, France, and Spain.

By the terms of the treaty, France was entirely eliminated from North America. England received Canada, and all of Louisiana east of the Mississippi except the Island of Orleans. This settlement removed the most serious menace to the welfare of the English colonists.

Though the war had not produced a union of the colonies

it did more than anything previous to promote the idea of union. It demonstrated what could be done by coöperation under competent leadership; it increased the feeling of self-reliance on the part of the colonists, a feeling that was promoted by the removal of the French menace. The war, furthermore, had given military experience to about twenty-five thousand colonials. Incidentally, the contemptuous manner in which these colonial troops were often treated by the British officers did not help put the Americans in a mood to accept the actions of the British government in the period following the close of the war.

INFLUENCES TOWARD UNION IN 1763

It is obvious that, by 1763, there were definite forces operating to bring about a union of the colonies. The most important conditions essential in the development of a nation were present. In the first place the inhabitants of the thirteen colonies were predominantly English. While no accurate statistics are available it has been estimated that as high as eighty-two percent were of English blood. Many others, such as the Scotch, Irish, Scotch-Irish, and Welsh, came from the British Isles. Probably not more than ten percent of the people were from continental Europe. The common language was English and the political institutions were of English derivation. While it is true that, politically, there were three types of colonies, the corporate, the royal, and the proprietary, yet a casual examination will reveal more similarities than differences among them. Legal procedure in all of the colonies was based on the English common law; the prevailing ideas of representation and governmental organization were all based on English precedents; the history common to all of them was English.

Geographical contiguity was also an influence in promoting union. The colonies extended in an unbroken chain from Maine to Georgia, bounded on the east by the Atlantic Ocean and on the west by the Appalachian highland. At first, of course, the colonies had been isolated from each other but, as population filled in, this isolation tended to become less and less noticeable.

In 1763, it was possible, as it was earlier, to note differences in the economic and social life of the northern, central, and southern groups of the colonies, but these differences were not sufficient to prevent union.

Religion might be mentioned as another force operating towards union. Throughout the colonies the people were for the most part Protestants. It is true that various sects differed very much from each other and that there was much intolerance, yet, on the whole, the colonists had more that was similar than that was different in their religion.

Up to 1763 these factors had not been influential enough to bring about a union. But the stage was set. It remained only for the home government to inaugurate and attempt to enforce a policy which threatened what the colonists regarded as their rights to make union a reality. So it came about that the union, long discussed, was finally accomplished between 1763 and 1776.

SELECTED REFERENCES

Bolton, Herbert Eugene, and Marshall, Thomas Maitland, *The Colonization of North America 1492–1783*, pp. 257–274, 359–383.

Fisher, S. G., *Evolution of the Constitution of the United States*, pp. 215–266.

Fiske, John, *New France and New England*, Vol. I, pp. 1–132, 233–359.

Frothingham, Richard, *Rise of the Republic of the United States*, pp. 86–149.

Garner, J. W., and Lodge, H. C., *The History of the United States*, Vol. I, pp. 270–341.

Greene, Evarts Boutell, *The Foundations of American Nationality*, pp. 207–224, 357–386.

Jernegan, Marcus Wilson, *The American Colonies 1492–1750*, pp. 322–352.

MacDonald, William, ed., *Documentary Source Book of American History 1606–1926* (Third edition), pp. 45–50.

Palfrey, John Gorham, *History of New England*, Vol. II, pp. 3–68.

Preston, Howard W., ed., *Documents Illustrative of American History 1606–1863* (Sixth edition), pp. 85–95, 146–147, 170–187.

Chapter Five

CAUSES OF THE AMERICAN REVOLUTION

THE VARIOUS VIEWPOINTS

MORE has been written about the American Revolution and its causes than any other phase of this country's history. Various reasons have been assigned for the conflict which brought about the United States, the reasons in some cases depending upon the partisan viewpoints of the particular writers. Thus, out of the bitterness of the strife with England, there developed what was long destined to be the traditional American notion of the Revolution, namely, that the unjust, arbitrary, cruel, and unconstitutional acts of King George III finally drove his loyal but liberty loving subjects to revolt in order to free themselves from his tyranny.

Another viewpoint, that of the Tories who upheld the conduct of the British government, was that the Revolution was brought on by the scheming of demagogues and by the desire of law evaders and smugglers in America to escape a just control imposed on them by the home government which was acting entirely within its constitutional rights.

The Whigs in England were, in general, opposed to the king and, in some cases, openly sympathized with the American colonists in their resistance to the English governmental policies. Consequently, in later years, leading Whig historians of England promoted the idea that the struggle in America was but one phase of a struggle long waged in England by the middle class, capitalistic group against the domination of a landed aristocracy headed by the king himself.

At the time of the World War, when the United States was associated with England in a common cause, a great deal of propaganda was issued to promote friendliness between the people of the two countries. With this in view much was said to the effect that the Revolution had really been unnecessary and that it had been due merely to an unfortunate misunderstanding between the home government and the colonists.

Fortunately, there has developed among the writers of history what may best be described as a scientific attitude. Discarding traditional and partisan explanations, and turning to contemporary sources for their information, twentieth century historians of acknowledged competence have devoted their best efforts to the task of discovering a rational explanation as to why the thirteen colonies broke away from the mother country and established themselves as a new nation. The result of these modern researches has been to supply an explanation that is logical and sound and which is based on facts rather than on emotions or partisan considerations. Instead of undermining patriotism the modern viewpoint should strengthen it by giving a true understanding of what took place when the foundations of the United States were being laid.

In brief, the now generally accepted point of view is that an expanding English imperialism came into conflict with the idea of home rule which had long been developing in the colonies. Instead of attempting to reconcile their ideas of imperial control to colonial home rule, the English governmental leaders, obviously failing to understand clearly the nature of their problem, pursued a highly legalistic course. During the years following the French and Indian War, they sought to force the American colonies to accept the whole program of imperialistic control but at every point they met with stubborn resistance. Finally their persistence produced an explosion and as a result the thirteen colonies were lost to England forever.

It is a simple matter to say that the Revolution resulted from the conflict of imperialistic control and colonial home rule but the explanation is well-nigh meaningless unless one has an understanding of the nature of English imperialistic control both before and after 1763, and unless one has a clear conception of home rule as it existed in the thirteen colonies.

Probably no one was more competent to speak of the Revolution and its causes than John Adams. Nor was he loath to express himself. In the years following his retirement from the presidency of the United States, he freely expressed his opinions, and in 1815 wrote in a letter, "The revolution was in the minds of the people, and in the union of the colonies, both of which were accomplished before hostilities commenced." A few years later he wrote that the factors which had led to armed revolt should be "sought in the country from the first plantation in America." This was Adams's way of saying that, during a period of over a hundred and fifty years, the colonists had been de· veloping in their economic life, as well as religious, racial, social, cultural, and political, to the point where they had comparatively little in common with the English in the home country. England had sought, during that whole period, to direct the colonial development but had failed. Following the close of the war with France, the British government undertook to do what it had previously failed to accomplish, that is, to make the thirteen colonies an integral part of the imperial system. But it was too late. The American spirit of independence had been developed to such a degree that the attempts at control produced only the permanent loss of the colonies.

DEVELOPMENT OF AN AMERICAN SPIRIT

Long before the break occurred, the colonists had become distinctively American rather than English. While, as has been pointed out, a variety of motives led to the establishment of the English colonies, there had been, from the first, an underlying reason which was held by the home government in sanctioning colonization: that the colonies should serve as sources of supply for such articles as England herself could not produce and, further, that the colonies should serve to create a market for goods manufactured in the home land. Incidentally, the exchange of goods was expected to promote the growth of English shipping.

The result was a disappointment to England. Separated from the home country by three thousand miles of ocean and faced by the necessity of wresting a living from a strange wilderness, the colonists developed an economic life far different from what was intended. For example, in Virginia it had been expected that the settlers would produce pitch, tar, turpentine, and potash. Instead tobacco growing became the chief concern of the people. In New England, it had been intended that the settlers would secure and send to England materials for shipbuilding. The shipbuilding materials were secured but, for the most part, they were used by the New Englanders for building their own ships. Besides engaging in shipbuilding and commerce, contrary to the original intent, the New Englanders engaged in farming and fishing.

And so it was in the other colonies. The settlers turned their efforts to such economic enterprises as would benefit them most and which the geographic and climatic conditions of the New World made possible. Thus a distinct American economic life had been developed.

Various other factors contributed to convert the colonists into Americans. Many of them were dissenters in religion who had come from England to escape the domination of the Anglican church. In the New World, there was gradually established the idea of religious freedom in contrast to the condition which existed in the home land. This difference in religion had an influence in changing the colonists from Englishmen to Americans. Incidentally, the fear that a system of Anglican bishops would be set up in America, a fear that grew stronger as the eighteenth century progressed, was of some influence in bringing about the Revolution. It was very noticeable in the period between 1763 and 1775 that the Anglican ministers generally supported the position of the home government while the Congregational and Presbyterian ministers were just as zealous in stirring up discontent.

Racially, the colonists were mostly English. Yet, by the end of the colonial period, many settlers of non-English stocks had migrated to America. Among these were the Scotch-Irish, the Irish, and the Germans. These people, in large part, settled in the back country where they had little contact with the English authority. Such relations as they did have with the official class did not tend to create in them a respect for the authority of England. When difficulties developed with the home government, these non-English settlers generally supported the patriot cause.

In their social life also the colonists were vastly different from the people of England. In the New World tradition counted for little. While it should not be supposed that no attention was paid to class distinctions in America, the evident fact is that those distinctions did not mean much in practice. America had become the land of opportunity where even the person who had been in the humblest circumstances in the Old World could hope to rise in the social scale. The ownership of property was the key which unlocked the door to social preferment and securing property in the land of plenty was possible to all. Most of those who acquired property became only moderately wealthy. Some, however, came into possession, through special grants, of large tracts of land and became comparatively wealthy. These large landowners, with some of the wealthier merchants, and the higher officials of the colonial governments, constituted the only American aristocracy. Those outside of this select group, and particularly those who had no voice in affairs of government because of their lack of property, were easily influenced to support the patriot cause in the period of the Revolution for, by driving out the aristocrats, they could hope to participate in the privileges which the few had monopolized for themselves. The American aristocracy, while a perhaps feeble counterpart of the English aristocracy, was to the mass of the colonists a symbol of oppression and therefore something to be done away with when the opportunity offered.

Culturally, the colonists had made some progress. They had, in fact, developed a culture suited to the simple life which they lived, but their achievements along this line were viewed, for the most part, by the English with contempt. In securing the elements of an education better opportunities were afforded in the colonies than in England but in higher education there was little comparison. It is true that there existed several colleges, Harvard, Yale, William and Mary, King's (now Columbia), and a few other smaller institutions, but even they afforded little opportunity for the development of real scholarship. Some individuals in the colonies had large libraries but they were exceptions. Even in language, the colonists tended to differ from the people in England. New words like *papoose* and *pow-wow* were borrowed from the Indians while other words were acquired from the Dutch, French, Spanish, and Germans. Other words were invented as *egg-plant* and *bottom-lands*. These new words, together with the development of vulgarisms and a carelessness in the use of the rules of grammar, contributed to the development of a distinctive American language.

In their political life also, the colonists had developed along lines that were distinctly American. To be sure the town and county forms of local government in the colonies were modelled after the local governments in England, but there was a vast difference in the degree to which the people participated in these local governments on the two sides of the Atlantic. In England, political participation was limited to a small proportion of the population through the requirement of a forty shilling freehold. In America, a similar suffrage requirement generally existed and, in addition, there were qualifications for voting such as religion, nationality, race, character, and residence. At all times the proportion of the people eligible to vote in the colonies was small and an even smaller proportion actually voted. Yet, in the colonies, there was always the possibility of overcoming the restrictions and becoming a participant in the affairs of government, a possibility which did not exist in England. The local governments were, in many cases, training schools for those who became members of the colonial assemblies. There the representatives of the people were wont to act, not in the interests of England, but in their own. As has been shown, they not only resisted the efforts of governors to rule arbitrarily but they constantly encroached on the prerogatives of those officials and their councils.

Thus, by 1763, the colonists had lost the characteristics which had stamped them as Englishmen and had become a distinctive type who could properly be called American. They had developed a spirit which was truly American rather than English. Colonial interests came first with them; English interests were secondary. While commercial relations had some influence, the chief tie that held the colonies to England in 1763 was a loyalty based mostly on sentiment. In the period between 1763 and 1775 that tie was broken by the actions of a blundering, short-sighted English officialdom and separation was the inevitable result.

ENGLAND'S COLONIAL POLICY PRIOR TO 1763

It has been suggested that the English government tried unsuccessfully to control the course of colonial political and economic development. How this control was attempted and why it failed needs to be understood if one is to grasp the significance of what happened in the decade before 1775. In other words, it is necessary to study England's "old colonial policy" prior to the close of the French and Indian War in order to comprehend the "new colonial policy" put into effect after that war.

ATTEMPTED POLITICAL CONTROL

An important phase of the old colonial policy was the attempted political control of the colonies. In the consideration of the development of the individual colonies it has been noted that laws passed by the colonial legislatures were required to be in conformity with the laws of England and that they were subject to veto by the Crown. Judicial decisions, as has been pointed out, could be appealed from the colonial courts to the Privy Council in England. There has also been observed the tendency to convert the colonies into royal colonies with governors and councils appointed by the Crown. Seven had thus been brought under the more direct control of the home government while another had a royal governor but elected its own council. At various times, proposals had been made in Parliament to revoke the charters of the two corporate colonies but no action had been taken. Even the proprietary colonies which survived to the period of the Revolution had not been free from the danger of conversion into royal colonies. However, as has been shown, the control of the royal officials in the colonies was largely a fiction because of the power which the colonial assemblies had assumed in matters of finance.

In England itself elaborate machinery was set up to deal with colonial problems. Theoretically, the king exercised jurisdiction over the colonies but, in practice, it was the Privy Council, composed of the king and his close councilors, and a number of special boards and committees that actually dealt with colonial matters. The Privy Council, of course, was an historical body tracing its origin back to *curia regis* or king's council set up by the Norman kings after the conquest of England in the eleventh century. It handled colonial affairs as only one of its numerous functions. In particular, as has been mentioned, it acted as a court of appeals from the decisions of colonial courts. Statistics reveal, however, that only slightly more than sixty such appeals were made during the colonial period. It was also the Privy Council rather than the king that exercised the veto over colonial legislation. It appears that, out of considerably more than eight thousand laws submitted, about five percent were disallowed. But the veto of many of these laws had little effect since frequently they were repassed by the colonial legislatures in a modified form. Since it usually took several months to send a law to England and receive back a report of the action taken on it, it was possible for the legislatures in the colonies virtually to nullify the veto imposed by authority of the Crown.

Among the special agencies set up in England for colonial control was a sub-committee of the Privy Council called the Lords of Trade, organized in 1675. In 1696 this group was replaced by an agency styled the Board of Commissioners for Trade and Plantations or, as it was generally called, the Board of Trade. It was made up of eight officials as ex-officio members and eight others who were not connected with the king's ministry. Little actual authority was delegated to the Board of Trade but it was very active in collecting information, advising and instructing royal officials in the colonies, and in making recommendations to the Privy Council concerning such matters as the veto of colonial laws.

Mention should also be made of a number of regular English governmental agencies which exercised some measure of control over the colonies. The secretary of state for the southern department had charge of the colonies and was responsible for the initiation of administrative and military policies in connection with them. The secretary of war was in direct charge of military affairs in the colonies. The bishop of London was the administrator of the affairs of the Anglican church in America. In addition, there was the Treasury Board in charge of finances, and, subordinate to it, the Customs Board which was responsible for the enforcement of the navigation and trade laws which constituted the basis of the attempted economic control of the colonies.

It is apparent from the foregoing account that England had

an elaborate system for the political control and regulation of the colonies. Yet the control was more apparent than real. In practice the colonies enjoyed an extremely large measure of home rule.

ATTEMPTED ECONOMIC REGULATION

Even more obnoxious to the colonists than the system of political control was the English program designed to regulate their economic life. In developing this program, the English government had acted in accordance with the mercantilist theory which, generally speaking, controlled European thought on economic subjects, particularly during the seventeenth and eighteenth centuries. All the European nations subscribed to the theory. In fairness to the English, it should be said that their application of the theory was mild compared to the system of economic control imposed by such countries as Spain, yet it proved extremely distasteful to many of the liberty loving inhabitants of the thirteen colonies.

The mercantilist theory held that a national state should strive to make itself as strong and wealthy as possible and at the same time make itself independent of the outside world. In order to accomplish these aims, the development of a national merchant marine was to be encouraged and a strong navy was to be built up for its protection. Home agriculture was to be stimulated by government aid and protection so as to make the nation self-sufficient in the matter of food products. The production of raw materials needed by the country's manufactures was also to be encouraged. Likewise the country's industries were to be developed to provide the manufactured goods needed by the nation and, incidentally, to provide the people with employment. A favorable balance of trade was to be maintained by an excess of exports over imports, thus keeping gold and silver flowing into rather than out of the country. In this scheme of things, colonies were to exist solely for the benefit of the home country, supplying such raw materials as the home land could not produce and serving as a market for the manufactures of the mother country. In no case were the colonies to be allowed to develop economic enterprises competing with those in the home country.

THE NAVIGATION AND TRADE ACTS

In applying the mercantilist theory, the English Parliament passed several series of laws which may be classified as navigation and trade acts, manufacturing acts, and financial acts. The first English navigation law had been passed as early as 1381 and in subsequent years additional acts had been placed on the statute books. But it was not until 1651, when Oliver Cromwell was head of the English government, that the first navigation law seriously affecting the American colonies was passed. This law was designed to cripple the Dutch who had become powerful commercial rivals. By the provisions of this act no goods produced in America, Africa, or Asia could be brought to England or any of its possessions except in ships which had English owners and captains and which had crews which included a majority of English subjects. No goods produced in European countries were to be imported into England or its dependencies except in English ships or ships of the country producing the goods being shipped. All goods brought into England from foreign countries had to be shipped directly from a port of the producing country.

After the Restoration in 1660, a new navigation and trade law was enacted. In addition to continuing the main features of the 1651 act, it added the requirement that ships carrying goods to or from England must be built either in England or in one of her colonies. It was further specified that "noe Sugars Tobaccho Cotton Wool Indigoes Ginger Fustick or other dyeing wood of the Growth Production or Manufacture of any English Plantations in America Asia or Africa" should be carried to any place except to England or to one of the English dependencies.

In 1663, another act was placed on the statute books designed to control colonial imports for the benefit of the English merchants. It provided that, with a few enumerated exceptions including salt, Madeira wine, and horses and provisions produced in Ireland or Scotland, all European goods intended for the colonies in America, Africa, and Asia must be shipped in English ships and by way of England. It also provided that colonial goods must be sent to England and be unloaded there before permission would be granted for shipping them to foreign countries.

By these requirements England could place taxes on both the European and colonial goods when they came into the English ports for reshipment to their ultimate destination. This law obviously was designed to benefit the merchants of England.

Nine years later, in 1672, another act was passed which was intended to "put teeth" in the previous acts. The colonists had been taking advantage of the privilege under the law of 1660 of shipping sugar, tobacco, and other enumerated goods to other English colonies to send these goods to European countries instead. To prevent this, it was stated that henceforth vessels taking on board such articles in the colonies must either give bond to insure shipment to England or else pay certain specified duties, including five shillings for each hundred weight of white sugar, one penny for each pound of tobacco, and so on.

One of the most important of all the acts regulating trade was the so-called Molasses Act of 1733. It struck at a trade that had been developed between the New England colonies in particular and the islands of the West Indies, especially those owned by the French. In exchange for their agricultural products, lumber, and fish, the New Englanders secured molasses from the French plantations. The molasses was manufactured by the New Englanders into rum which was partly consumed in the colonies while the surplus was carried to Africa and exchanged for negro slaves. These slaves were then sold to the West Indian planters. Thus was developed the famous "triangular trade" which was very profitable to the colonists in America.

Not only was the prosperity of the French colonies promoted by this sale of molasses but it was also stimulated by the sale of their sugar in the European markets, largely displacing English sugar. The English planters in the West Indies were naturally displeased at the prosperity of their French rivals so Parliament was urged to pass a law prohibiting the importation of any foreign sugar, molasses, or rum into England or any of its possessions. Since a considerable number of these English plantation owners were members of the House of Commons they were able to secure the passage of the Molasses Act. By its provisions duties of nine pence a gallon on rum, six pence a gallon on molasses, and five shillings a hundred weight on sugar were to be paid when those goods were imported into the American colonies or any other possession from any colony or plantation in America not belonging to England.

Other navigation and trade acts passed in 1696, 1706, and 1722 acted further to increase the restrictions on trade. It should be mentioned that some of the acts tended to benefit the colonies by granting bounties on goods which England wished to have produced. For instance, in 1706, bounties were authorized to the amount of one pound a ton on masts, four pounds a ton on tar and pitch, six pounds a ton on hemp, and three pounds a ton on resin and turpentine.

THE MANUFACTURING ACTS

A second series of acts passed by Parliament had to do with manufacturing in the colonies. In 1699, on the demand of the English woolen manufacturers, the Woolen Act was passed. It prohibited the exportation of woolen goods from the colonies or from one colony to another. The next year it was enacted that woolen goods manufactured in England might be imported into the colonies free of duty. The result of this legislation was to stop rather effectively the colonial manufacture of woolen cloth for sale, though it did not stop people from making cloth for their own use.

Another colonial enterprise which was the subject of unfavorable legislation was the beaver hat industry. In 1731, it was disclosed that, in New England and New York, there were being manufactured each year about ten thousand beaver hats, which were the dress hats of the period. Immediately, on the demand of the hat manufacturers of England, Parliament decreed that the colonies could export no hats to England nor send them from one colony to another. No one was to make hats unless he had served an apprenticeship of seven years. No manufacturer was to be allowed more than two apprentices.

It had been the purpose of England to encourage the production of iron in the colonies but not the manufacture of iron products. As early as 1643, John Winthrop had set up a smelting furnace in Massachusetts and from this beginning a considerable iron industry had developed in the colonies, which included manufacturing as well as the production of the raw material.

Finally, in response to the demands of the English manufacturers, Parliament passed acts in 1750 and 1757 which encouraged the production of bar and pig iron by permitting them to be imported into England from the colonies free of duties. To stop the manufacture of iron products in the colonies, it was provided that no machinery or equipment was to be set up in any of them for the purpose of rolling or slitting iron or for making steel.

FINANCIAL LEGISLATION

The third type of English economic legislation had to do with colonial finances. From the beginning, there had been a scarcity of money in the colonies. In spite of the hopes of the early settlers, no gold or silver mines were found so little specie was in circulation except such as came in from the foreign colonies. Most of this specie soon found its way to England in payment of goods purchased from the merchants of that country. For years much of the trade in the colonies had to be carried on by the bartering of commodities. Beginning with Massachusetts in 1690, the colonies adopted the expedient of issuing paper money which, being fiat in character, soon depreciated in value. Ostensibly to maintain a sound money system but incidentally to protect English creditors, Parliament, in 1751, prohibited the issuing of paper money in New England. Thirteen years later the prohibition was extended to all the colonies. This did much to arouse colonial discontent, the more so because no other form of money was provided to aid the colonists in carrying on their business.

Another financial law passed in 1752 provided that English creditors could collect from their American debtors, of whom there were many, by levying on the lands, tenements, and slaves of the latter. In making such a levy the affidavit of the creditor living in England was to be accepted in colonial courts as testimony on an equal basis with that given by the colonial debtor in person.

Had this elaborate body of laws passed by Parliament to regulate the economic life of the colonies been enforced it would have ruined the colonists. But it is evident that the laws were not strictly applied prior to 1763. The manufacturing acts were frequently evaded and England found difficulty in enforcing its financial legislation. In regard to the navigation and trade acts, it is obvious that they were honored in the breach rather than the observance. After 1700, England established vice-admiralty courts in America to deal with smuggling cases. In these courts the cases were tried without juries by judges appointed by the English government. The colonists claimed that such courts violated their rights as Englishmen. In spite of such courts, much smuggling went on. Customs officials were also freely bribed to allow cargoes to come into colonial ports in violation of the laws. Everywhere there was laxity and inefficiency on the part of the English officials. The triangular trade went on as though the Molasses Act had never been passed. Even during the wars with France the English colonists persisted in carrying on trade with the colonies of the enemy.

THE NEW COLONIAL POLICY

In 1760, William Pitt, who was then the prime minister, issued orders that the Molasses Act should be enforced in order to stop the trade with the enemy. However, before much had been done to carry out the order, Pitt was dismissed from office by King George III who succeeded to the throne in that year. The new king and his ministers felt strongly that a more rigid control of the American colonies was necessary but it took some time to formulate a policy. The end of the war with France and her allies in 1763, as has been noted, left England in possession of Canada and Florida. The acquisition of these territories made necessary new arrangements for their government. At the same time the unrest of the Indians in the West, culminating in Pontiac's War in the spring of 1763, called for a new Indian policy to be put into effect. On the recommendation of the Board of Trade, the king, in October, 1763, issued the Proclamation of 1763, creating three new provinces, East Florida, West Florida, and Quebec, and providing royal governments for them. By the proclamation the English government also took over the complete regulation of the Indian trade. All land beyond "the Heads or Sources of any of the Rivers which fall into the Atlantic Ocean from the West and North West" were reserved to the Indians. No white settlers were, for the time being, allowed to go into the region and any who had gone into it were to move out. It was planned, though not so stated, that eventually cessions would be secured from the Indians and opened to settlement.

It apparently did not occur to those who drew up the proclamation that it deprived several of the old colonies of territory which they claimed under their charters. Nor did the British officials understand the psychological effect of the restrictions on the hearty American pioneers who felt that they had a right to go where they wished. There can be no doubt that the Proclamation of 1763 was one of the grievances that eventually drove the colonists to revolt.

But this was only the beginning of a program to bring all the English colonies under a closer control by the home government. The close of the French and Indian War had left England with a debt of over one hundred twenty-nine and a half million pounds. The acquisition of new territories had increased the annual cost of maintaining the army and navy from seventy thousand pounds to an amount five times as great. It seemed to the English ministry, headed by Lord Bute, that it would be a good idea to station part of the army in America, avowedly to keep the Canadians and Indians in submission, and force the colonists to pay part of the expense. At the same time, it was decided that the existing laws should be enforced so as to yield the maximum revenue. It was discovered that duties collected in the American colonies each year amounted to only about two thousand pounds while the cost of collection was about four times as great. New forms of revenue, such as a stamp tax, were also to be put into effect. In short, the new policy placed the emphasis on money raising rather than on the regulation of trade.

What seemed necessary and proper to the English officials certainly was not expedient. The surrender of Canada by the French removed what had long been regarded as the chief menace to the safety of the English colonies. The colonists felt that, with this danger removed, there was no need of maintaining a large body of troops among them. As for the cost of the war, they were convinced that they had done their share and should not be asked to do more. By the action of their own colonial legislatures, the colonists had been heavily taxed to support their own troops who had aided the English forces in subduing the French and Indians. Altogether the colonies had supplied over two and a half million pounds for war expenses. In 1765, they still owed about three-quarters of a million pounds which had to be raised by taxation.

Nor did the colonists feel that it was fair to say that they were paying only two thousand pounds a year into the royal treasury. This may have been the amount of the duties collected in America but, as a matter of fact, the Americans were indirectly contributing several hundred thousand pounds annually to the English government. For example, it was estimated that one-third of the cost to the colonists of English manufactured goods represented taxes paid on the goods in England before they were shipped to America. What the Americans paid was offset only to a slight degree by bounties paid on certain colonial products by the English government.

Another factor which made it inexpedient to inaugurate the new policy was the economic depression which was beginning to be felt in the colonies even before the war with France had ended. During the years between 1763 and 1775 the depression became more serious. The measures put into effect during the period by the English government and the steps taken by the colonists to resist these measures naturally accentuated the depression, causing increasing discontent.

THE GRENVILLE ACTS

Before the new policy could be put into effect, Bute resigned and was succeeded by George Grenville, a man who believed that the laws should be enforced to the letter. The first thing he did was to order all customs officials who had been living in England while their work was performed by deputies in the colonies to return immediately to America and diligently perform their duties. He also ordered naval vessels to seize ships engaged in illegal trade.

He then submitted to Parliament a list of proposed laws which were soon enacted. One of the new laws was the Sugar

Act, passed on April 5, 1764. It placed heavy duties on certain enumerated articles imported into the colonies, including ten shillings a ton on Portuguese, Spanish, or other wine, except French wine which could not be brought in; seven pounds on each ton of Madeira wine; and two shillings on each pound of foreign silk; and one pound and two shillings on each hundred weight of foreign sugar. In addition this law made perpetual the Molasses Act though it reduced the duty on foreign molasses from six pence to three pence a gallon. The importation of foreign rum into the colonies was forbidden but British rum could be imported free of duty. Stricter regulations were also included in the act to prevent trade in violation of the law.

The act further stated that all money received in payment of the duties on colonial imports should be kept as a separate fund "to be, from time to time, disposed of by parliament, towards defraying the necessary expences of defending, protecting, and securing, the *British* colonies and plantations in *America.*"

To supplement the revenues to be secured from the operation of the Sugar Act and other laws on the statute books, Grenville recommended to Parliament that a stamp tax be imposed on the colonists. Before doing so he asked the colonists to suggest other means of raising revenue but he was answered with petitions protesting against being taxed at all except by their own assemblies. These petitions the House of Commons refused to consider under a rule prohibiting the reception of petitions dealing with financial measures. On March 22, 1765, the Stamp Act was passed by Parliament with only slight opposition in the House of Commons. There the vote was two hundred and five to forty-nine while there was no opposition in the House of Lords. The act was a very lengthy one, consisting of a preamble and one hundred and seventeen paragraphs. It required that, after November 1, 1765, stamps should be purchased and placed on all kinds of legal documents, licenses, bonds, playing cards, dice, newspapers, pamphlets, and other articles "throughout the colonies and plantations in *America.*"

It was expected that the revenues derived from the operation of the Sugar Act, the Stamp Act, and other acts, would pay the expense, at least in large part, of maintaining in America ten thousand soldiers. The remaining cost of caring for these soldiers was to rest squarely on the individual colonies under the provisions of the Quartering Act passed in April, 1765. The act provided that the colonies should supply barracks for the soldiers. If the barracks were not sufficient the troops should be quartered in inns and other public houses. If these were not sufficient, the soldiers, it was stated, should be provided with quarters in "uninhabited houses" or other buildings. The soldiers were to be fed at a fixed price and, in addition, were to be supplied without charge "with Fire, Candles, Vinegar, and Salt, Bedding, Utensils for dressing their Victuals, and Small Beer or Cyder, not exceeding Five Pints, or Half a Pint of Rum mixed with a Quart of Water, to each Man." Furthermore, the colonies were to furnish transportation for the troops at a fixed rate, any charge above this rate to be paid by the colonies.

THE STAMP ACT

All of these acts were extremely distasteful to the colonists but it was the Stamp Act which aroused the greatest opposition for it was an internal tax. All over the colonies mob uprisings took place. Those who had accepted positions as stamp commissioners were forced to resign. Among these were men like Richard Henry Lee of Virginia, later a prominent patriot leader, who had sought appointments to sell the stamps, not realizing what a storm the act would create. The sale of stamps was effectively prevented while steps were being taken to secure the repeal of the act. Among the more important protests against the act were the "Virginia Resolves," formulated by Patrick Henry and passed by the Virginia House of Burgesses on May 29, 1765. This document asserted that the settlers in America had brought with them the rights of Englishmen and that these rights had been passed on to their posterity. One of the most important of these rights of Englishmen was that of being taxed by themselves or by persons chosen by themselves. In the case of Virginia that right had been recognized by the British government. Any attempt of others to tax them, the resolves declared, tended to destroy British as well as American liberty.

These resolves are important as an early formulation of American constitutional views on taxation.

A more elaborate statement of American constitutional ideas was soon forthcoming. On June 8, 1765, the Massachusetts House of Representatives sent a circular letter to the other colonies proposing a meeting at New York to consult together concerning their troubles and to petition for relief. Accordingly, on October 7th, twenty-seven delegates from nine colonies met at New York and remained in session until October 23rd, in what came to be called the Stamp Act Congress. The nine colonies were Massachusetts, Rhode Island, Connecticut, New York, New Jersey, Pennsylvania, Delaware, Maryland, and South Carolina. The members were generally quite conservative as was shown by their choice of Timothy Ruggles of Massachusetts as chairman. Ruggles later sided with the English when the break between the colonies and the home government occurred.

Several documents were drawn up by the congress, including petitions to the king, the House of Lords, and the House of Commons. But the most important document was a "declaration of the rights and grievances of the colonists in America," drafted by John Dickinson of Pennsylvania and adopted on October 19th. After professing allegiance to the Crown and "all due subordination" to Parliament, it was stated that the colonists were entitled "to all the inherent rights and liberties" of natural born Englishmen in Great Britain. Then followed an exposition of the American constitutional views on taxation. The document declared, "That it is inseparably essential to the freedom of a people, and the undoubted right of Englishmen, that no Taxes be imposed on them but with their own consent, given personally, or by their representatives." This was the statement which was later paraphrased into "No taxation without representation." Continuing, it was stated that the people of the colonies were not and could not be because of "their local circumstances" represented in the House of Commons. The only representatives of the colonists were those chosen by themselves, and therefore "no taxes ever had been, or can be constitutionally imposed on them, but by their respective legislatures."

The document then went on to protest specifically against the Stamp Act and other acts as having "a manifest tendency to subvert the rights and liberties of the colonists," and as constituting hindrances to trade and business.

It is apparent that the colonial view concerning representation was quite different from the view which prevailed in England. The English view was that of "virtual representation," that is, a member of the House of Commons, no matter by whom elected, represented all Englishmen wherever located. The American view, which still prevails in this country, was that a person elected to a legislative body represented the people of the district from which he was chosen.

Certainly, Parliament did not repeal the Stamp Act because it accepted the American constitutional views. A much greater influence was the evident fact that stamps could not be sold because of mob violence. Another factor was the decline in trade between England and the colonies. A colonial boycott of British goods caused exports to America to decline to one-fourth of what they had been. The result was that British merchants joined in the demands for the repeal of the act. Yet another factor favorable to repeal was a change in the British ministry which saw Grenville replaced by Rockingham who was friendly to the colonies. Finally, after a hard fight in the House of Lords, the Stamp Act was repealed on March 18, 1766.

The news of this action occasioned much rejoicing in America, but there would have been less joy had the colonists taken time to ponder on other acts Parliament had passed about the same time. In fact, on the very day of the Stamp Act repeal there was placed on the statute books what was called the Declaratory Act, stating that Parliament "had, hath, and of right ought to have, full power and authority to make laws and statutes of sufficient force and validity to bind the colonies and people of *America*, subjects of the crown of *Great Britain*, in all cases whatsoever." It also declared all colonial actions denying that Parliament possessed such powers to be "utterly null and void to all intents and purposes whatsoever."

Parliament also renewed the Quartering Act, changing it slightly to make it more effective. Some changes were also made in the Sugar Act of 1764; the most important was to lower the duty on molasses to one penny a gallon instead of three. It was to be collected on all molasses imported into the colonies whether it came from British or foreign possessions. In other words, the purpose was no longer to regulate trade but simply to collect a tax.

THE TOWNSHEND ACTS

It was not long before another change took place in the English ministry, bringing William Pitt again into power as prime minister with Charles Townshend as chancellor of the exchequer. Pitt soon became ill and so was unable to direct the affairs of government; therefore, each minister was left to formulate his own program and to urge Parliament to adopt it. Accordingly, Townshend submitted recommendations for new revenues to be raised in America, thus making a practical application of the claim set forth in the Declaratory Act.

Townshend's plans were approved by Parliament which, in 1767, passed several acts commonly referred to as the Townshend acts. One of these acts placed duties on certain enumerated articles imported into the colonies from Great Britain. The articles were glass, red and white lead, painters' colors, paper, and tea. The revenues secured were to be used to pay the governors, judges, and other officials in the colonies, thus making them independent of the colonial assemblies. Naturally, the colonists were alarmed at this for it deprived them of the weapon which had proved most effective in the fight for home rule. Also very distasteful to the colonists was the specific authorization given for the use of writs of assistance in seeking out violators of the revenue acts. For years the colonists had been objecting to the use of such writs which were virtually blank search warrants authorizing customs officers to secure the help of a constable or other public official in searching any building in the day time and seizing goods found which had been imported contrary to the laws of England. There had been some doubt as to what courts had authority to issue the writs so the Townshend Act clarified the matter by stating that they could be issued by any colonial superior or supreme court.

Other Townshend measures approved by Parliament provided for a reorganization of the customs service in America.

An American Board of Commissioners of the Customs was to be located at Boston for the purpose of supervising the collection of duties. Vice-admiralty courts were to be established at Boston, Philadelphia, and Charleston to deal with cases of smuggling.

Another act passed in 1767 and often associated with the Townshend acts was that which suspended the New York assembly for failing to comply with the Quartering Act. It was not until 1769 that the compliance was secured and the suspension was lifted.

The taxes imposed by the Townshend acts were described as external, that is, they were levied on goods brought into the colonies from the outside. While objecting strenuously to internal taxes as provided by the Stamp Act and expressing opposition to all other forms of taxation imposed by Parliament, the colonists had not, prior to 1767, denied the right of Parliament to impose external taxes. But after the Townshend acts were passed the argument was advanced that Parliament had no constitutional right to levy even external taxes. The chief exponent of this viewpoint was John Dickinson who had received his legal training in England. In his widely read "Letters of a Pennsylvania Farmer," published between December 2, 1767 and February 15, 1768, he asserted that the new tax program was a usurpation of power. In unfolding his argument he sought to make a distinction between a tax and an imposition. An imposition, he stated, was a fiscal arrangement for the regulation of trade while a tax was a "gift of the people to the crown, to be employed for public uses." Since taxes had to be given by people of their own free will they had to be internal. The colonies had been given the right in their charters to impose internal taxes, so Parliament had no right to impose them. The Townshend acts, he further argued, were really internal taxes since they aimed to take property from the colonists "by laying duties on the manufactures of Great-Britain which they MUST take." These duties were not impositions for the regulation of trade and since they took money from the colonists without their consent they were unconstitutional. The weakness, of course, in Dickinson's argument was that the acts of Parliament were a part of the English constitution and therefore could not be unconstitutional.

Other important statements in opposition to the Townshend acts were contained in the circular letter, adopted by the Massachusetts House of Representatives on February 11, 1768, and sent to the other colonial assemblies. This letter was largely an elaboration of the colonial argument that taxation without representation was wrong, violating, as was claimed, "the natural and constitutional rights" of the colonists. This emphasis on natural rights is of special interest for it reveals the influence on the colonists of the liberal political philosophers of England, particularly John Locke. That Locke's two *Treatises on Government* had been widely read in the colonies is clear from the frequent allusions to natural rights which are to be found in the colonial documents of the period.

Another interesting document expressing opposition to the Townshend acts was the "Virginia Resolves of 1769." These resolutions were drawn up by George Mason and introduced in the Virginia House of Burgesses by none other than George Washington. After adoption by the burgesses these resolves were sent to the assemblies of the other colonies.

Opposition to the Townshend acts was not confined to resolutions and verbal argument. A widespread boycott of British goods was put into effect which resulted in a decline of colonial imports from England amounting to about a half million pounds in 1769.

The loss of business, together with the all too apparent fact that manufacturing was being stimulated in America by the Townshend acts, led Lord North, who became prime minister in 1770, to recommend to Parliament the repeal of the taxes with the exception of the tax of three pence a pound on tea. This tax was retained to maintain the principle that Parliament had the right to tax.

At about the same time that Lord North was making his recommendation for the repeal of the revenue features of the Townshend acts, there occurred an event in America which had considerable influence in inflaming the colonists. This was the "Boston Massacre" of March 5, 1770. A mob attack on British soldiers stationed in Boston resulted in several citizens being killed and others wounded. For this shooting the soldiers were tried in a colonial court where they were defended by John

Adams. All were found not guilty except two who were convicted of manslaughter and sentenced to be "burned in the hand" and to be dismissed from the military service. In the trial it was brought out that the citizens had provoked the shooting by first attacking the troops. Nevertheless, it was generally accepted throughout the colonies that innocent colonists had been ruthlessly massacred by the soldiers of a tyrannous government.

After the excitement of the Boston Massacre had died down, the colonies assumed for a time an appearance of calmness. The merchants, who had gladly enlisted the support of the laboring classes and others of the disenfranchised classes to supply the mob actions against those unwilling to abide by agreements not to import British goods, feared that they would lose control. So following the partial repeal of the Townshend acts they cancelled their non-importation agreements, gave up politics and devoted themselves to business. As a result the imports from England, which had declined to about one million six hundred thousand pounds in 1769, rose to over four million two hundred thousand pounds in 1771.

THE BOSTON TEA PARTY

But this period of calm was not destined to last long, for in April, 1773, the British government again stirred the Americans to opposition by a new tea act. The refusal of the American colonists to import British tea in any large quantities because of the tea tax worked a hardship on the East India Company which, in 1773, had about seventeen million pounds of tea in England. To relieve the company, Parliament voted to allow the company to send tea to America free of all duties in England but with the requirement that the three pence a pound tax should be collected in America. A number of ships were loaded with tea and sent to America consigned to special agents. Instead of appointing regular tea merchants the company made the mistake of choosing as its agents men who had opposed the non-importation agreements and who were therefore unpopular. The offended merchants raised the cry of monopoly and again joined hands with the radical elements to defeat the new policy.

At only one port was the tea allowed to land. That was at

Charleston where it was stored in a warehouse until it was sold three years later by the American revolutionists and the proceeds used to buy war materials. The ships carrying tea to New York and Philadelphia were forced to return to England without landing their cargoes. Three ships came into the Boston harbor laden with tea. The royal governor, Thomas Hutchinson, was determined that the tea should be landed and sold. But he was frustrated by a mob which, dressed as Indians, went on board the vessels during the night of December 16, 1773, and threw overboard the tea, valued at about fifteen thousand pounds.

THE INTOLERABLE ACTS

This so-called "Boston Tea Party" aroused the wrath of the English officials who determined to punish the colonists for what had been done. Accordingly, Lord North recommended to Parliament the enactment of measures to put down the disorders in America and to secure "dependence of the colonies upon the crown and Parliament of Great Britain." The subservient Parliament responded by passing the coercive or, as the Americans called them, the intolerable acts.

The first of these new laws was the Boston Port Act, dated March 31, 1774, which closed the port of Boston until the destroyed tea should be paid for by the people of the city. This action had the effect of creating a sympathy for Boston which was expressed from one end of the colonies to the other. From all points money and food were sent for the relief of the people of the city.

Following the Boston Port Act, the Massachusetts Government Act was placed on the statute books by Parliament on May 20, 1774. This law did away with the elected council and substituted a council of from twelve to thirty-six members to be appointed by the Crown as in the other royal colonies. All judges, court officials, and sheriffs were made subject to appointment by the royal governor. Local town meetings, except for the regular meetings held to elect local officials, were prohibited unless the written consent of the governor was first secured. Another provision stated that jurymen were to "be summoned and returned by the sheriffs" of the counties instead of being "elected, nominated, or appointed, by the freeholders and inhabitants of the several towns within the said respective counties."

At the same time Parliament passed what was known as the Administration of Justice Act. It provided that any official accused of murder while engaged in enforcing the laws in Massachusetts should, if the governor thought a fair trial could not be had in that colony, have his case tried in some other colony or in Great Britain. In view of the fair trial which the soldiers who participated in the Boston massacre had received it seemed that this act was entirely uncalled for and unwarranted.

A fourth act to punish Boston was the Quartering Act. It seems that the Boston authorities had so interpreted the old Quartering Act as to permit them to provide barracks for the troops on an island in the harbor. The new act of 1774 provided that, if barracks were not supplied where they were needed, suitable quarters must be found for them by the local authorities. If they failed to do so, the governor was authorized to order the use of inns, alehouses, or any building that was not inhabited to house the troops.

Another act, not directly related to the other four, and yet associated with them in the minds of the colonists, was the Quebec Act. By this law the French colonists in the province of Quebec were granted freedom of religion which meant that Catholicism in that part of America was given official sanction by the British government. This aroused much opposition, particularly among the New England Puritans. The Quebec Act also made some changes in the government of the province and also extended its boundaries south to the Ohio and west to the Mississippi. This enraged the inhabitants of some of the older colonies because it not only took permanently from them territory which they claimed under their colonial charters but placed the area under the jurisdiction of a Catholic province.

Apparently the British officials were surprised at the opposition aroused in America to the five "intolerable" acts. But it was these acts which enabled the American radicals to organize an opposition to the British policy far more effective than any up to that time. Economic issues had been displaced by political issues and henceforth the radical element, rather than the merchants who favored moderation, was to control the situation. The assembling of the First Continental Congress made it clear that the radicals had the upper hand. Finally, the blunders and misjudgments of the British king, ministry, and members of Parliament—for all were to blame—had driven the colonists to the verge of revolt. The First and Second Continental Congresses served to crystallize and consolidate the opposition to England, and out of their activities a new nation, the United States of America, came into existence.

SELECTED REFERENCES

Beard, C. A., and Beard, M. R., *The Rise of American Civilization*, Vol. I, pp. 189–227.

Becker, Carl, *Beginnings of the American People*, pp. 161–200, 202–245.

Beer, G. L., *British Colonial Policy, 1754—1765*, pp. 72–315.

Bolton, H. E., and Marshall, T. M., *The Colonization of North America 1492–1783*, pp. 343–357, 403–424, 425–451.

Channing, Edward, *History of the United States*, Vol. III, pp. 1–154.

Faulkner, H. U., *American Economic History*, pp. 140–158.

Fisher, S. G., *The Struggle for American Independence*, Vol. I, pp. 6–136, 145–205.

Fiske, John, *The American Revolution*, Vol. I, pp. 14–62, 77–111.

Frothingham, Richard, *Rise of the Republic of the United States*, pp. 158–455.

Garner, J. W., and Lodge, H. C., *The History of the United States*, Vol. I, pp. 342–381.

Greene, E. B., *The Foundations of American Nationality*, pp. 178–186, 226–254, 338–355, 388–412, 414–431.

Howard, G. E., *The Preliminaries of the Revolution*, pp. 102–205, 242–295.

Jernegan, M. W., *The American Colonies 1492–1750*, pp. 270–297.

Lecky, W. E. H., *The American Revolution, 1763–1783* (arranged by J. A. Woodburn), pp. 38–135, 152–194.

MacDonald, William, ed., *Documentary Source Book of American History 1606–1926* (Third edition), pp. 55–59, 72–74, 78–79, 90–92, 103–109, 113–162.

Martin, C. E., *An Introduction to the Study of the American Constitution*, pp. 14–18.

Parrington, V. L., *The Colonial Mind 1620–1800*, pp. 179–247.

Pease, T. C., and Roberts, A. S., eds., *Selected Readings in American History*, pp. 73–115.

Schlesinger, A. M., *New Viewpoints in American History*, pp. 160–181.

Smith, T. C., *The Wars between England and America*, pp. 28–62.

Trevelyan, G. O., *The American Revolution*, Part I, pp. 1–253.

Van Tyne, C. H., *The American Revolution 1776–1783*, pp. 3–24.
Van Tyne, C. H., *The Causes of the War of Independence*, pp. 55–86, 198–238, 311–368.
Wilson, Woodrow, *History of the American People*, Vol. II, pp. 98–221.

Chapter Six

THE CONTINENTAL CONGRESSES

GROWTH OF RADICALISM

FOR a decade the radical leaders, such as Samuel Adams, had been busy creating sentiment against the British government and developing an organization that would enable them to control the situation in the colonies. At the time when high excitement prevailed in the colonies over the Stamp Act the opponents of the measure had organized groups which took the name of Sons of Liberty. Later the Massachusetts radicals had formed committees of correspondence in various towns to exchange views with each other and with those in other colonies who were opposed to the British policies. Virginia, in 1773, took up the idea and developed it further by forming a colonial committee of correspondence. Other colonies then formed committees of their own, modelled after those of either Virginia or Massachusetts or a combination of the two. Furthermore, liberal use had been made of newspapers and pamphlets to spread the arguments against the measures of the home government and to crystallize public opinion in favor of the radical points of view. Still another device for consolidating the forces of opposition was the Stamp Act Congress. This had proved something of a disappointment to the radicals because they had not been able to control it. It is a significant fact that nine years were to elapse before another congress was called. By that time the radicals were confident that they could control an inter-colonial gathering. The advocates of moderation were just as certain that they could dominate a new congress as they had the Stamp Act Congress of 1765. With both the radicals and the moderates in favor of the move it was not difficult to bring about the gathering which came to be known as the First Continental Congress of 1774.

ASSEMBLING OF THE FIRST CONTINENTAL CONGRESS

While the holding of a congress composed of delegates from all the colonies had been proposed by various town gatherings as well as by many individuals, it was Virginia which actually issued the call for such a congress. When the news of the passage of the Boston Port Act arrived in Virginia, the House of Burgesses was in session. They resolved to set aside June 1, the day the act was to go into effect, as a day of prayer and fasting. Because of this action the royal governor ordered their dissolution. Undaunted by this, the burgesses met in a tavern on May 27th and, after choosing Peyton Randolph as their chairman, resolved to call a provincial congress to choose delegates to a continental congress. At the same time they instructed their committee of correspondence to invite the other colonies to attend the proposed congress.

The suggestion was taken up by the Massachusetts House of Representatives which, on June 17th, locked its doors to bar a message of dissolution from the governor and resolved that a committee should be appointed to meet with similar committees from the other colonies at Philadelphia on September 1, 1774. Colony after colony took up the idea and eventually all but Georgia chose delegates to go to Philadelphia. In Georgia the influence of the royal officials was very great. Furthermore, the colony had suffered little from British control so that there were only a few radicals to be found there. Consequently it proved impossible to get delegates appointed to attend the First Continental Congress.

Altogether fifty-six delegates from the other twelve colonies finally arrived at Philadelphia, most of them in time to begin the sessions of the congress on September 5th in the Carpenters' Hall. The delegates from New York, Pennsylvania, Virginia, North Carolina, and South Carolina had been chosen by provincial conventions. These conventions themselves had been called in various ways. In Virginia it was the burgesses in an irregular meeting who had called the convention. In New York, Pennsylvania, and South Carolina, the conventions had been called by committees, while in North Carolina the provincial convention had been an outgrowth of county meetings held in spite of a proclamation by the royal governor forbidding such meetings as illegal. In three of the colonies, Massachusetts, Rhode Island, and Connecticut, the delegates had been elected by the assemblies. In three other colonies the delegates had been chosen by committees of correspondence while in the remaining colony various methods had been employed in selecting the men to go to Philadelphia. The number of delegates from each colony varied from two to nine.

In no sense was the First Continental Congress a legislative body. The instructions of the delegates indicated that they were to assemble together in an advisory and consultative capacity only. Three of the delegations were instructed to call attention to the violation of American rights and to seek means of preserving American liberty. Two were to seek action looking towards the repeal of the obnoxious laws passed by Parliament. Four were instructed to devise means for securing the union and harmony of the empire. The three others were to consult for the good of the colonies.

Only eleven of the members of the congress were merchants while most of the remainder were lawyers or representatives of agricultural interests. Among the prominent men present was Peyton Randolph of Virginia, who was elected president of the congress. Charles Thomson, who was not a delegate, it should be mentioned, was elected secretary. Besides Randolph, there were present from Virginia George Washington, Patrick Henry, Richard Henry Lee, and three others. Other prominent men who attended as delegates were John Sullivan of New Hampshire; John and Samuel Adams of Massachusetts; Stephen Hopkins of Rhode Island; Roger Sherman and Silas Deane of Connecticut; John Jay, James Duane, and Philip Livingston of New York; Joseph Galloway, John Dickinson, and Thomas Mifflin of Pennsylvania; Caesar Rodney, Thomas McKean, and George Read of Delaware; William Livingston of New Jersey; Matthew Tilghman and Samuel Chase of Maryland; Richard Caswell of North Carolina; and John and Edward Rutledge of South Carolina.

WORK OF THE FIRST CONTINENTAL CONGRESS

In the early stages of the congress harmony prevailed among the delegates. Serious consideration was given to a plan of union proposed by Joseph Galloway, the leader of the moderates, but finally the sentiment of the radicals prevailed and the plan was rejected. Galloway's plan, based largely on the Franklin plan of 1754, proposed a super-government for the colonies to be composed of a president-general appointed by the Crown and a federative colonial council made up of deputies elected every three years by the individual colonial legislatures. Parliament was to have the right to veto the acts of this council while the council, in turn, was to have the power to veto acts of Parliament which had to do with the colonies.

On September 17th, the radicals further demonstrated their superiority over the moderates who favored compromise by securing the approval of the Suffolk resolves which had been adopted a short time before by a convention in Suffolk County in Massachusetts. These resolutions declared that no obedience was due to the acts of Parliament passed earlier in the year and that the tax gatherers should pay no money into the treasury of the province until the constitutional government of the colony should be restored.

Another measure adopted by the congress which demonstrated the radical control was a "declaration of Rights." On September 7th, a committee composed of two delegates from each colony had been set up "to state the rights of the colonies in general, the several instances in which those rights are violated or infringed, and the means most proper to be pursued for obtaining a restoration of them." The report of this committee was finally adopted on October 14th. This document, which dealt only with developments since 1763, contained ten resolutions enumerating the rights which, it was declared, belonged to the colonists "by the immutable laws of nature, the principles of the English constitution, and the several charters or compacts."

The right "to life, liberty and property" was asserted and "all the rights, liberties, and immunities" belonging to persons born in England were claimed. It was declared that the provincial legislatures alone had the right to deal with matters of taxation, internal or external, and with all matters of "internal polity," subject only to the veto of the Crown. The right was conceded to Parliament to pass acts "as are bona fide," confined to the regulation of external trade "for the purpose of securing the commercial advantages of the whole empire to the mother country, and the commercial benefits of its respective members." The rights to peaceably assemble, to consider grievances, and to petition the king were also asserted. It was further declared that it was "unconstitutional, dangerous and destructive to the freedom of American legislation" to have legislative councils appointed by the Crown. As examples of the violations of these rights, the whole list of British acts from 1763 to the Intolerable Acts of 1774 were enumerated. "To these grievous acts and measures, Americans cannot submit," it was declared.

THE CONTINENTAL ASSOCIATION

The most important accomplishment of the First Continental Congress was the formation of the Continental Association. On September 30th, a committee was appointed to formulate "a plan for carrying into effect the non-importation, non-consumption and non-exportation" resolutions previously adopted. On October 20th the final report of the committee was signed by fifty-three members of the congress. To carry out their purposes, the agreement stated that "we do, for ourselves, and the inhabitants of the several colonies, whom we represent, firmly agree and associate, under the sacred ties of virtue, honour and love of our country."

After December 1, 1774, no goods were to be imported from Great Britain, Ireland, or from the British possessions outside of America. Even the slave trade was to be stopped. After March 1, 1775, no goods, the importation of which was prohibited, were to be purchased or consumed. The non-consumption of East India tea was especially stressed. After September 10, 1775, no goods were to be exported to Great Britain, Ireland, or the British West Indies. In order to make it possible to get along without British goods, "frugality, economy, and industry" were to be encouraged and "agriculture, arts and the manufactures of this country, especially that of wool," were to be promoted. Extravagance and dissipation were to be discouraged, "especially all horse-racing, and all kinds of gaming, cock fighting, exhibitions of shews, plays, and other expensive diversions and entertainments." Even the expenses connected with mourning a deceased relative or friend were to be reduced. No merchant was to be allowed to take advantage of the scarcity of goods to raise prices.

Since the congress had no authority to legislate it could not make the agreement legally binding. However, a method was devised for making the Association effective and that was through the force of public opinion. In each town, city, and county the qualified voters were to elect committees "whose business it shall be attentively to observe the conduct of all persons touching this association." The names of violators of the Association were to be published in the newspapers "to the end, that all such foes to the rights of British-America may be publicly known, and universally contemned as the enemies of American liberty; and thenceforth we respectively will break off all dealings with him or her." Any North American colonies or provinces which refused to accede to the Association or which violated its terms were to be barred from all "trade, commerce, dealings or intercourse whatsoever" with the others and were to be held "as unworthy of the rights of freemen, and as inimical to the liberties of their country." The Association was to remain in effect until the obnoxious acts previously complained of were repealed by Parliament.

Before adjourning on October 26th, the First Continental Congress prepared addresses to the people of the British American colonies, to the people of Canada, and to the people of Great Britain. A petition to the king was also drawn up. May 10, 1775, was set as the date for a second congress to assemble.

It was not long before the effects of the first congress were apparent. Throughout the colonies its measures were endorsed and steps were taken to make the Association operative. Soon the papers were filled with accounts of rioting, burning, and tarring and feathering resorted to as means of enforcing the Association. No longer were merchants permitted to decide for themselves whether or not they would join the movement to boycott British goods. Failure to adhere to the Association invited mob action in many instances.

Adherence became throughout the colonies the test of a patriot while opposition to the Association became a distinguishing mark of a Tory or loyalist. During the fall of 1774 and the early part of 1775, the colonists quickly divided into groups according to their views on the Association and on the general relations of the colonies with the home government. The loyalists, of course, included most of the high governmental officials in America. Forced to make a choice, many of the clergy of the Anglican church together with a large portion of the landowners, business, and professional men joined the loyalists. The fact that the aristocrats generally chose to side with the loyalists was in part accounted for by the fact that they were unwilling to yield equal participation in the provincial governments to the masses who were to be found in the radical or patriot ranks. While some of the aristocrats adhered to the patriot cause, the main force of the patriots was made up of laborers and small farmers—those who had been generally disfranchised.

Just how many of the colonists became loyalists and how many patriots it is impossible to say with accuracy. However, a statement made by John Adams may be accepted as a fair estimate. His conclusion was that about one-third of the people were loyalists, one-third patriots, and the other one-third indifferent. Though in the minority, the patriots soon demonstrated that they were much stronger than the loyalists. They were much better organized and, it might be said, were more enthusiastic and zealous in giving practical application to their convictions than were the loyalists.

LORD NORTH'S CONCILIATORY PROPOSAL

While the patriots and loyalists were consolidating their forces in America, certain developments were taking place in England which had considerable influence in shaping future events. In January, 1775, Parliament began a consideration of the American petition to the king and other matters related to the colonies. A motion was introduced by the Earl of Chatham, the great Whig leader, to withdraw the troops from Boston but the motion was defeated. He then proposed a plan of conciliation based upon concessions by both Parliament and the colonies but this plan was also rejected. Then Lord North rather unexpectedly took the initiative and introduced in Parliament a conciliatory resolution. This resolution was passed by Parliament on February 27, 1775. It stated that if any colony would undertake, by the authority of its legislature, to provide its share for the common defence and to make provision for the support of its civil government and its courts, Parliament would refrain from levying any taxes on such colony except for the regulation of trade.

This conciliatory proposal fell far short of satisfying the colonies. It made no mention of the grievances which had brought the First Continental Congress into existence. Even though it might have had some merit this was soon offset by an act passed by Parliament on March 30, 1775, known as the New England Restraining Act. It was designed to prevent all trade by the New England colonies with any place except Great Britain, Ireland, or the British West Indies and also to prohibit these colonies from carrying on fishing activities on the Newfoundland banks. In April the Restraining Act was extended to all the remaining colonies except New York, North Carolina, and Georgia. These actions could hardly have any other effect than to further antagonize the colonies and bring them to the verge of war.

The crisis was first reached in Massachusetts. There a military officer, General Thomas Gage, had been made the governor late in the spring of 1774. Early in the fall of that year he refused to allow a meeting of the lower house of the legislature but the representatives met nevertheless and declared themselves to be a provincial congress. They soon appointed a committee of safety and the task of organizing troops and gathering military supplies was commenced. General Gage was kept informed by his agents concerning these proceedings. On the night of April 18, 1775, he sent a body of troops to seize the military stores at Concord. The patriots, warned by William Dawes and Paul Revere, gathered to offer resistance. A skirmish took place at Lexington on the morning of the 19th and later in the day heavier fighting took place at Concord. The British were forced to retreat back to Boston under the constant fire of the patriot "minute men." The patriots followed and when April 20th dawned Boston was in a state of siege. Soon the news was spread to the other colonies and great excitement prevailed everywhere. Preparations were made from one end of the colonies to the other to put troops in the field to aid Massachusetts.

MEETING OF THE SECOND CONTINENTAL CONGRESS

Such was the situation in the colonies when the Second Continental Congress assembled at Philadelphia on May 10, 1775. The royal governors had attempted to prevent delegates from being chosen to this congress but the patriots out-maneuvered them. Delegates were chosen in all thirteen of the colonies, in some cases by conventions, in other cases by the assemblies. The personnel of this congress when it started the first of its seven sessions was much the same as that of the First Continental Congress. Notable additions were Benjamin Franklin of Pennsylvania and John Hancock of Massachusetts, who was elected president. After a short time Thomas Jefferson became a member of the congress, replacing George Washington.

Though the Second Continental Congress was called without legal authorization and though it lacked a constitutional basis, it became a *de facto* government through necessity. The members apparently were reluctant to assume governmental functions, preferring at first to regard themselves as advisers rather than as directors of the colonies. As the months and years passed the congress was forced to exercise more and more the functions of a central government. After the colonial governments were replaced by state governments the congress assumed a more definite character, for then its members were backed by the authority of the state legislatures which chose them. Nevertheless, the actions of the congress were at all times dependent upon the states. Without their acquiescence the congress could accomplish nothing. In particular, congress lacked the power to tax. All it could do was to determine how much money was needed and then request each state to pay its quota which was determined by the proportion of the state's population to that of all of the states. These facts must be kept in mind if one is to understand the history of the Second Continental Congress. In view of its dependence on the states and in view of the fact that it had no constitutional basis, it is hardly fair to criticize the congress for its inefficiency which certainly was very apparent.

ACCOMPLISHMENTS OF THE SECOND CONTINENTAL CONGRESS

During the period from 1775 to 1781, the Continental Congress exercised both legislative and executive functions for there was no attempt to establish a separate executive branch of government. Likewise, there was no effort made to set up a national judiciary except prize courts to deal with captured English vessels during the course of the Revolution. In voting on measures, each state was allowed but one vote.

The term of service of the delegates was not fixed but each state determined that matter for itself. One year terms became customary, however. Likewise each state chose as many delegates as it pleased, the number varying from one to twelve. Each delegate received such compensation for his services as his home state saw fit to pay. To carry out its measures, the congress set up a number of committees. These included the important committees on finance, army, and foreign affairs. By 1781, these committees had given way to what were called offices, including the office of foreign secretary, superintendent of finance, secretary of war, and secretary of marine.

The first important act of the Second Continental Congress in May, 1775, was to declare war on the English government. A little later, on June 12th, it issued a proclamation recommending "a day of public humiliation, fasting and prayer." Then the congress turned its attention to the practical problems confronting it because of the commencement of hostilities in Massachusetts. On June 14th, it voted that "an American continental army" should be raised and it also agreed to take over the troops then besieging Boston as the nucleus of the army. On the next day the congress chose one of its own members, George Washington, to be the commander-in-chief. Washington was chosen not merely because he had gained military experience in the French and Indian War but because of his prominence in

Virginia. His selection was expected to insure the support of the southern colonies in the war.

It must be said that the Continental Army did not prove very satisfactory from the military point of view, yet it was superior to the state militia. The volunteer system was adhered to, though late in the war the congress recommended to the states that compulsory service be inaugurated. Little was done to carry out this recommendation, however. In attempts to encourage enlistments the states resorted to the pernicious bounty system. There were instances where a thousand dollars were paid for enlistment for a few months of service.

Another defect in the Continental Army was that its personnel was enlisted for only short periods of time instead of for the duration of the war. The congress lacked both courage and understanding in this matter. Yet, had it recommended to the states that troops be enlisted for the duration of the war, the recommendation probably would have been rejected or, at least, disregarded. As it was, the term of service was from four to six months though there were numerous instances of shorter terms. General Washington repeatedly called to the attention of the congress the defects in the army but nothing was done about it. Perhaps nothing could be done to remedy the situation in view of the nature of the congress. During the war a total of four hundred thousand men was raised but at no one time did Washington have over twenty-six thousand men at his command and these were usually poorly equipped, ragged, and hungry. At no time did the British have more than forty-two thousand troops in America yet it took seven years to defeat them. The wonder is that the Americans won as many victories as they did. Had it not been for the genius of Washington and the patriotism of a comparatively few men, together with the French alliance, it may well be doubted whether independence would have been achieved.

Another matter to which the congress gave its attention in October, 1775, was the creation of a navy. A marine committee was set up with authority to grant naval commissions and to fit out vessels of war. It was from this committee that John Paul Jones received the commission under which he commanded various ships and rendered the conspicuous service which is familiar to most Americans. The congress also authorized the fitting out of privateers to prey on British commerce. It should be pointed out that in the appointment of naval officers the members of congress could not avoid being influenced by local political considerations. Efficiency was sacrificed to the necessity of satisfying each state in the matter of granting commissions.

The congress also took over the direction of Indian affairs and assumed charge of the postal system, both of which had been in charge of the British government. Benjamin Franklin, who had held a similar position under the British until his dismissal in 1774, was made postmaster-general in charge of the Continental post office.

FINANCIAL TROUBLES

One of the important matters to which the congress was early forced to turn its attention was the financing of the war. Taxing power, as has been indicated, was not granted to the congress. Nor was there any possibility of securing a grant of such power for the Americans were in no mood to be taxed to support a war waged in opposition to taxes. Naturally, the congress turned to the easiest method they could think of which was the issuing of fiat money. The British government had stopped the issuance of paper money but there was nothing to restrain the Second Continental Congress. Accordingly, the printing presses were started in June, 1775, and, by November, 1779, two hundred and forty-one million dollars in paper money had been issued. In addition the states issued paper to the amount of more than two hundred and nine million dollars. The result inevitably was a great depreciation in the value of the currency. Prices rose and finances generally were disarranged. Washington found it difficult to secure supplies for his troops because no one wished to accept the paper money. The British, on the other hand, had little difficulty in getting what they wanted since they paid gold for their supplies.

In 1779 the congress sought to bolster its currency by inducing the states to make it legal tender. Though the states complied the situation was not improved. In 1780 the congress passed an act providing for the redemption of the currency at one-fortieth of its face value. This only had the effect of causing further depreciation until, by the spring of 1781, the Continental bills were practically worthless. It was no longer possible to use them as a medium of exchange. Only speculators were willing to accept them—at the rate of five hundred to a thousand dollars for one dollar in gold.

Making requisitions on the states helped the revolutionary finances hardly at all. It was easy for the congress to fix quotas of money for the states to furnish but it was quite a different matter to secure the money. The states either ignored the requisitions or, if they paid, they paid with their own paper money which made the situation as bad as it had been before or worse. Late in 1780, the congress, despairing of securing any help from the states through its requests for money, asked the states to pay their quotas in food products. Even this failed to meet the needs of the army so Washington, to prevent his soldiers from starving, was forced to collect supplies from the surrounding country, giving what were called commissary certificates in payment whether the farmers wished to accept them or not.

Since the efforts made to finance the war through paper money and requisitions on the states proved so futile it was fortunate that representatives of the congress sent to Europe were able to negotiate some loans. Altogether about $7,830,000 were borrowed from the French and Spanish governments and from private bankers in Holland. Efforts were also made to borrow money from private Americans but with disappointing results. Nevertheless about one million six hundred thousand dollars was obtained in this way. It is of interest to note that the congress even promoted lotteries in efforts to raise money.

THE DECLARATION OF INDEPENDENCE

Without doubt, the most important accomplishment of the Second Continental Congress was the adoption of the Declaration of Independence. When the war broke out the idea of independence was entertained by relatively few people. To all except the most radical the object of fighting was to prevent the British government from coercing the colonies and from substituting imperial control for home rule. This was shown in the declaration of the causes and necessity of taking up arms, adopted by the congress on July 6, 1775. It stated, in part, "We have not raised armies with ambitious designs of separating from Great-Britain, and establishing independent states. We fight not for glory or for conquest. . . . In our own native land, in defence of the freedom that is our birth-right, and which we ever enjoyed till the late violation of it—for the protection of our property, acquired solely by the honest industry of our fore-fathers and ourselves, against violence actually offered, we have taken up arms."

Though the congress, on July 31, 1775, rejected Lord North's conciliatory resolution as "unreasonable and insidious," it nevertheless was seeking for a reconciliation with the English government on other terms than those offered. On July 8th the members of the congress signed a petition to the king which was carried to England by a special messenger. This "olive branch" petition was the last offer of reconciliation made by the congress. On August 23, the very day on which the petition was to have been presented to the king's minister, the king issued a proclamation of rebellion which declared that the American colonies had "at length proceeded to open and avowed rebellion, by arraying themselves in a hostile manner, to withstand the execution of the law, and traitorously preparing, ordering and levying war against us." All English subjects and officers were called upon to exert themselves "to suppress such rebellion, and to bring the traitors to justice." A few days later the "olive branch" petition was definitely rejected.

But even the rejection of the petition and the proclamation of rebellion were not sufficient to create a strong sentiment for independence. This was shown by the action on the subject taken by several of the colonies. In the period from September to December, 1775, North Carolina, Maryland, Pennsylvania, New Jersey, and New York declared, through their provisional governments, their opposition to independence. A similar declaration was made by the town of Portsmouth, New Hampshire, while in January, 1776, the New Hampshire provincial congress declared that they had never sought independence.

A few more grievances apparently were needed to bring the colonies to the verge of separation. They were not long in making their appearance. In November, 1775, the king, in opening a new session of Parliament, called attention to the rebellion in America. Parliament proceeded to pass an act prohibiting all trade or intercourse with the colonies during the course of the rebellion. This act converted many Americans to the idea of independence. The Continental Congress showed its defiance of the act in the spring of 1776 by declaring the American ports open to all countries except those subject to the British king.

Another influence in favor of separation was the action of the British government in hiring foreign soldiers to fight the Americans. The war was not popular in England and it proved difficult to secure enlistments. This forced the government to seek mercenaries with the result that Germans, many of them Hessians, were hired to go to America for the purpose of putting down the rebellion. During the course of the war more than thirty thousand German mercenaries were sent to America. The American resentment towards the English government because of this was certainly an influence of importance in bringing about independence.

One of the greatest factors in promoting the idea of independence was Thomas Paine's *Common Sense,* a pamphlet published at Philadelphia in January, 1776. This work, many thousands of copies of which were sold, convinced many who had been hesitating that independence was necessary. Paine ridiculed the idea of a king. He wrote, "Of more worth is one honest man to society . . . than all the crowned ruffians that ever lived." The happiness and security of the English people, he further argued, were due to their character rather than to the English constitution. The Americans had no reason to hope for anything from that constitution; their course must be to rid themselves of it and set up a new government of their own. Reconciliation would only result in ruin to the Americans because England was governed by self-interest and that self-interest would continue to determine colonial policies regardless of any temporary arrangement that might be made. The argument of the imperialists that the strength of Great Britain and her colonies must be united so that the world might be defied, Paine answered by declaring, "Our plan is commerce . . . and friendship with the world." He also stressed the great distance between England

and America as "a strong and natural proof that the authority of the one over the other was never the design of Heaven." From every point of view, Paine declared, independence was a necessity. "The blood of the slain, the weeping voice of Nature cries, ' 'Tis time to part,' " he concluded.

The effect of these various influences began to be noticeable during the first quarter of 1776. On February 2, a group of revolutionists meeting in Savannah, Georgia, instructed that colony's delegates to the Continental Congress to vote for all measures that they should "think calculated for the common good." In the latter part of March the South Carolina delegates were granted similar ambiguous authority while, early in May, Rhode Island voted to concur in any actions taken by the congress for annoying the enemy and for holding the colonies together. North Carolina, aroused by a loyalist uprising, was more definite in its instructions for, on April 12th, its delegates were empowered "to concur with the delegates of the other Colonies in declaring Independency, and forming foreign alliances."

But it remained for Virginia to initiate the action which led to the adoption of the Declaration of Independence. In that colony the leading men had for some time desired a separation from England. As early as April, 1775, Richard Henry Lee, the head of one of Virginia's most important families, had written to Patrick Henry expressing himself in favor of immediate independence. The burning of Norfolk on January 1, 1776, by order of the royal governor, Lord Dunmore, together with the publication of Paine's *Common Sense*, had served to inflame the Virginians further. On May 15th, a convention which was then exercising governmental authority in Virginia instructed its delegates in the congress to introduce a motion declaring the united colonies to be "free and independent states." The delegates were authorized to vote not only for independence but also for the formation of foreign alliances and for the development of a confederation of the colonies.

In obedience to these instructions, resolutions were introduced in the congress on June 7th, by Richard Henry Lee, the chairman of the delegation from Virginia, declaring "That these united colonies are, and of a right ought to be, free and independent states," and proposing foreign alliances and the formation of a confederation.

At the time these resolutions were introduced no positive action could be taken since not enough of the colonies had taken a stand in favor of independence. After a short delay, it was decided, on June 10th, to appoint a committee to draw up a formal declaration and, meanwhile, to postpone definite action until the various colonies should have the opportunity to instruct their delegates. These instructions were soon forthcoming from all but New York. Connecticut and New Hampshire quickly fell in line while in Massachusetts independence was endorsed by the town meetings. New Jersey, which had a strong loyalist element and which had previously instructed against independence, gave its approval to the idea of independence on June 22. In Pennsylvania, a convention of patriots voted on June 24 in favor of independence, thus reversing the previous action of the colony. A convention was assembled in Maryland in the latter part of June and through it the colony's delegates in the congress were instructed to vote for independence. Delaware failed to instruct its delegates definitely but when the final vote came it was found arrayed with the advocates of independence. In New York, the presence of a strong loyalist group was sufficient to prevent definite instructions for independence from being given.

Finally, on July 1, Lee's resolution declaring the independence of the colonies was taken up and debated. Those who favored the resolution contended that its adoption would merely be a recognition of an existing situation. Furthermore, they argued, a declaration of independence would aid in the negotiation of foreign alliances. The advocates of delay, headed by John Dickinson, insisted that the time was not ripe for independence; that some of the colonies had not definitely instructed in favor of it; that military success rather than a declaration of independence would result in foreign alliances; and, that it was desirable to form a confederation before declaring independence.

After the debate was closed, a preliminary vote was taken which showed only nine colonies on the affirmative side. It was decided to postpone the final vote until the next day. During the intervening period the advocates of independence worked hard. The two Delaware delegates present on the first were divided but the third delegate, Caesar Rodney, was hastily summoned and arrived in time to put the Delaware vote in the affirmative column on the second. Three of the Pennsylvania delegation, John Dickinson, Robert Morris, and James Wilson, were opposed while only Benjamin Franklin and John Morton were in favor of independence. Dickinson and Morris were persuaded to absent themselves on the second while Wilson was induced to vote in favor of the resolution. The South Carolina delegates were persuaded to vote in favor of the declaration on the ground that it would promote the best interests of their state as well as the interests of all Americans. While the delegates did not know it at the time, an event had taken place in their home state which insured approval of their action. That was an unsuccessful attack on Charleston by the British on June 28th. Thus, when the vote was taken on Lee's resolution on July 2, twelve of the delegations were in favor while New York refrained from voting.

However, the congress had demonstrated, by appointing a committee to draft a formal declaration of independence, that it did not intend to make the mere adoption of Lee's resolution stand as its official and final action. The committee, which had been named on June 11th, consisted of Thomas Jefferson, John Adams, Benjamin Franklin, Roger Sherman, and R. R. Livingston. Most of the actual work of drafting the formal declaration was performed by Jefferson though, from time to time, he received suggestions from the other members of the committee. On June 28th, a preliminary report was made to the congress and additional suggestions were received. Finally, on July 4th, the completed report was brought before the congress and adopted by the vote of the same twelve states which had previously adopted Lee's resolution. On the following day copies, signed only by John Hancock and Charles Thomson, the president and secretary of the congress, were sent to the various state governments. This placed the idea of independence squarely before the New York provincial congress which approved of it on July 9th.

The document was not ordered by the Continental Congress

to be engrossed until July 19, and it was not until August 2 that it was signed by fifty members while it was signed by other members even later.

It was not until July 6 that the Declaration of Independence was first made public. On that date it was published in the Pennsylvania *Evening Post*. It was much later before the people in the distant states learned of the Declaration. But as the news spread, the patriots everywhere indulged in joyful celebrations featured by the destruction of all remaining symbols of royal authority. The people took special delight in burning portraits of the king, while in New York City a leaden statue of the king, erected only a few years earlier, was torn down and melted into bullets. Everywhere people were forced to make a final choice of which side they would support. The war henceforth was to be waged not only against England but against those in America who were loyal to the British cause.

The Declaration of Independence has rightly been given first rank among American historical documents. Its formal adoption on July 4, 1776 brought into existence a new nation, and it is this fact that gives significance to the annual celebration of the day. It is true that England did not officially recognize American independence until 1783 but, nevertheless, Americans have regarded and always will regard the day when independence was formally declared as the nation's birthday.

An analysis of the Declaration of Independence reveals that it is divided into five parts. The opening paragraph explains the reason for drawing up and adopting the formal declaration, stating that "a decent respect to the opinions of mankind" required a statement of reasons for separating from England. Next comes a list of "self-evident" truths. Among these were the declarations "that all men are created equal; that they are endowed by their Creator with certain inalienable rights; that among these are life, liberty and the pursuit of happiness; that, to secure these rights, governments are instituted among men, deriving their just powers from the consent of the governed; that, whenever any form of government becomes destructive of these ends, it is the right of the people to alter or abolish it, and to institute a new government, laying its foundation on such principles, and organizing its powers in such form, as to them shall seem most likely to effect their safety and happiness."

Then follows a list of twenty-eight charges against King George III to show that his reign had been "a history of repeated injuries and usurpations, all having in direct object the establishment of an absolute tyranny" over the American colonies. Thus, on the king was placed the blame, not only for what he had done, but also for what his ministers and Parliament had done. It was this section of the Declaration which was largely responsible for creating the popular notion, so long held in the United States, that George III had brought on the War for Independence by his tyrannous actions.

The next section of the Declaration contains a complaint against the British people. They had frequently been appealed to by the colonists but had been "deaf to the voice of justice and of consanguinity." In the fifth part of the document, its closing paragraph, Lee's independence resolution is to be found in its entirety. Not only was it declared that the "united colonies are, and of right ought to be, free and independent states," but it was also asserted "that, as free and independent states, they have full power to levy war, conclude peace, contract alliances, establish commerce, and do all other acts and things which independent states may of right do."

The Declaration of Independence has been subjected to some criticism since its adoption. It has been asserted that it is full of "glittering generalities," and that the principles set forth in it were not new. It is true that the ideas expressed in the document had been generally accepted by the patriots before July 4, 1776, for some of them had been set forth in other earlier American documents such as the Declaration of Rights drawn up by the First Continental Congress. Very obviously some of the ideas were borrowed from the writings of John Locke. Nevertheless it was Jefferson who put the ideas together in a form acceptable to the American people. As Edward Channing, the historian, wrote, "Never in the whole range of the writings of political theorists has the basis of government been stated so succinctly. . . . Jefferson possessed the faculty of combining words in phrases that remain in one's memory throughout life. He stated ideas that were well known, that were common, that were hackneyed; but they are ideas which the American people have not yet grown tired of reading and hearing."

THE FRENCH ALLIANCE

The matter of forming foreign alliances as was also proposed in Lee's resolutions of June 7, 1776, was not so quickly accomplished. As early as November 29, 1775, the Second Continental Congress had created a secret "Committee of Correspondence with our friends abroad," an action which, it might be said, was the beginning of American foreign relations. In the spring of 1776, this committee sent Silas Deane as a secret agent to secure aid from the French. The latter were unwilling at the time to risk a war with England but did give secret aid to the Americans through a pseudo commercial company organized by Pierre Augustin Caron de Beaumarchais.

After the Declaration of Independence, the Continental Congress appointed a committee to draft a form of a treaty to be proposed to European nations. John Adams apparently performed most of the work of drafting the treaty which was approved by the congress on September 17, 1776. Benjamin Franklin was then appointed to go to France to act with Deane and Arthur Lee (who had previously joined Deane there) as a commission to negotiate with France. The three, on December 23, 1776, presented to Vergennes, the French foreign minister, what has been described as "the first formal diplomatic note" in American history. However, Vergennes would not promise anything more than a continuance of the secret aid, refusing openly to recognize American independence.

France doubtless was anxious for revenge on England for the crushing defeat inflicted on her by the latter a few years earlier. She also wished to regain her old leadership and prestige in Europe. She was entirely willing to see England lose her colonies because it would weaken her traditional enemy and would benefit French commerce. But the French had learned to be cautious. They did not wish to recognize the United States openly until they were quite certain that the Declaration of Independence would be made valid by force of arms. Furthermore, France wished to have Spain as her ally if she became involved in another war with England.

Certainly the military events of the latter part of 1776 and early 1777 did not give the French any reason to anticipate ultimate success for the Americans. But when the news of the decisive American victory at Saratoga and Burgoyne's surrender on October 14, 1777, reached France, the French government changed its attitude and, on December 12, notified Franklin and his fellow commissioners that American independence would be recognized and that a treaty would be negotiated.

On February 6, 1778, two treaties were signed by the American commissioners and by Conrad Alexander Gérard, then secretary of Vergennes and later destined to be the first French minister to the United States. One of these was a treaty of amity and commerce; the other was a treaty of alliance. It was declared in the latter that the object of the alliance was to effectively maintain "the liberty, sovereignty, and independence absolute and unlimited" of the United States. Neither party was to make peace until this purpose had been accomplished.

This alliance, the first and last entered into by the United States, was a notable achievement for the American commissioners, for the Second Continental Congress, and for its committee of foreign affairs which had replaced the original committee of correspondence. Through this treaty the Americans received the help of the French navy and army, as well as increased loans of money. The coöperation of a French fleet and the help of a French army were important factors in forcing the surrender of Cornwallis at Yorktown on October 19, 1781, an event which practically brought the War for Independence to a close so far as the fighting was concerned.

ADOPTION OF THE ARTICLES OF CONFEDERATION

The third proposal, made to the Second Continental Congress by Richard Henry Lee on June 7, 1776, was for the formation of a confederation of the states. Long before that date, however, the subject of a confederation had been discussed. As early as July 21, 1775, Benjamin Franklin presented to the congress a constitution for a confederation of the colonies but no action was taken at the time. Franklin proposed that the North American colonies should form a league of friendship for the purpose of promoting their general welfare and their common defence. While each colony was to retain jurisdiction over matters within its own limits there was to be a general congress, the members of which were to be chosen annually, to manage the affairs of the proposed confederacy. Each colony was to share the expenses of the confederacy and was also to have a number of delegates in the congress in proportion to the number of male inhabitants from sixteen to sixty years of age. Each delegate was to be allowed one vote. There was to be an executive council of twelve chosen by the congress from among its own members. When the congress was in recess this council was to manage the affairs of the confederacy. Amendments proposed by the congress would become effective after ratification by the assemblies in a majority of the colonies. It is evident that there were some points of superiority in Franklin's plan over the plan later adopted and put into effect.

Following Franklin's proposal nothing was done to bring about the formation of a confederation until after the introduction of the Lee resolution in June, 1776. On June 12, 1776, a committee consisting of one delegate from each state was appointed to draft articles of confederation. Among the more important members of this committee were Roger Sherman, Samuel Adams, Edward Rutledge, and John Dickinson. It was the latter who was chiefly responsible for the original draft of the articles.

On July 12, 1776, the committee presented a report to the congress which then secretly considered the proposed articles in committee of the whole during a period of several weeks. The consideration was interrupted when the congress was forced by the British advance to flee from Philadelphia to Baltimore. It was not until April, 1777, that the matter was again taken up. Then the congress resolved to give two days a week to the articles until they should be "wholly discussed." But after three months the press of other business made it necessary again to lay the articles aside. In the fall of 1777 the congress for a third time resumed the discussion of the proposed articles of confederation. The advocates of a confederation feared that such an organization could not be formed at all if it were not formed while the war was still going on. Finally, after another month of debate, the first constitution of the United States was completed by the congress on November 17, 1777, and submitted to the state legislatures with a request that they consider the document "and if approved by them, they are advised to authorize their delegates to ratify the same in the Congress of the United States; which being done, the same shall become conclusive."

The majority of the states soon gave their approval to the Articles of Confederation and instructed their delegates in the congress to sign the document. Thus on July 9, 1778, the signatures of most of the delegates from New Hampshire, Massachusetts, Rhode Island, Connecticut, New York, Pennsylvania, Virginia, and South Carolina were affixed to the articles. Then followed in order, North Carolina on July 21; Georgia on July 24; New Jersey on November 26, 1778; Delaware on May 5, 1779; and Maryland on March 1, 1781. The long delay on the part of Maryland was due to her refusal to ratify until the states having western lands should agree to cede such lands to the congress of the proposed confederation.

While the ratification of the articles by Maryland on March 1, 1781 was celebrated at Philadelphia by the discharge of cannon and by fireworks, the action did not result in the immediate demise of the Second Continental Congress. Not until November 5, 1781 was it definitely replaced by the congress provided for in the Articles of Confederation.

SELECTED REFERENCES

Bancroft George, *History of the United States*, Vol. IV, pp. 423–452.
Beard, C. A., and Beard, M. R., *The Rise of American Civilization*, Vol. I, pp. 228–287.
Becker, Carl, *Beginnings of the American People*, pp. 251–274.
Bolton, H. E., and Marshall, T. M., *The Colonization of North America 1492–1783*, pp. 451–545.
Channing, Edward, *History of the United States*, Vol. III, pp. 145–206, 279–303, 315–342, 445–458.
Fisher, S. G., *The Struggle for American Independence*, Vol. I, pp. 240–274, 309–435.

Fiske, John, *The American Revolution*, Vol. I, pp. 127–197; Vol. II, pp. 1–24.

Foster, J. W., *A Century of American Diplomacy*, pp. 8–40.

Frothingham, Richard, *The Rise of the Republic of the United States*, pp. 263–286, 311, 312.

Garner, J. W., and Lodge, H. C., *The History of the United States*, Vol. I, pp. 382–421; Vol. II, pp. 423–543.

Garver, F. H., "Attendance at the First Continental Congress," Pacific Coast Branch of the American Historical Association, *Proceedings*, 1929, pp. 21–40.

Garver, F. H., "The Transition from the Continental Congress to the Congress of the Confederation," *Pacific Historical Review*, Vol. I (June, 1932), pp. 221–234.

Greene, E. B., *The Foundations of American Nationality*, pp. 431–510.

Hart, A. B. *Formation of the Union*, pp. 70–95.

Johnson, Allen, ed., *Readings in American Constitutional History 1776–1876*, pp. 34–47.

Latané, J. H., *A History of American Foreign Policy*, pp. 1–22.

MacDonald, William, ed., *Documentary Source Book of American History 1606–1926* (Third edition), pp. 162–194.

Parrington, V. L., *The Colonial Mind 1620–1800*, pp. 248–263.

Pease, T. C., and Roberts, A. S., eds., *Selected Readings in American History*, pp. 110–130, 137–141, 149–154.

Preston, H. W., ed., *Documents Illustrative of American History 1606–1863* (Sixth edition), pp. 192–205, 210–217.

Schlesinger, A. M., *The Colonial Merchants and the American Revolution, 1763–1776*, pp. 308–393.

Tyler, M. C., *The Literary History of the American Revolution*, Vol. I, pp. 296–315, 452–474; Vol. II, pp. 35–49, 51–61, 72–77.

VanTyne, C. H., *The American Revolution 1776–1783*, pp. 23–101, 175–226, 248–268.

VanTyne, C. H., *The Causes of the War of Independence*, pp. 411–455.

Wilson, Woodrow, *History of the American People*, Vol. II, pp. 223–329.

Chapter Seven

FORMATION OF THE ORIGINAL STATE
GOVERNMENTS

THE outbreak of hostilities between Great Britain and the colonies early in 1775 was soon followed, in the royal colonies, by the overthrow of the royal officials and the assumption of the governing power by irregular revolutionary bodies which were called committees, provincial congresses, or conventions. In the proprietary colonies a similar procedure was followed, though more gradually than in the royal colonies, until the powers of the governmental agencies set up by the proprietors were virtually nullified. Only in the two self-governing corporate colonies, Connecticut and Rhode Island, was the machinery of government left undisturbed.

RECOMMENDATIONS BY THE CONGRESS

As the months passed it became obvious that some more definite forms of government would have to be set up in place of the old ones. Yet the colonies hesitated to form state governments as long as there appeared to be a possibility of reconciliation with the home government. In their dilemma, a number of colonies sought advice from the Continental Congress as to what they should do. Thus an inquiry from New Hampshire was answered in November, 1775, by a recommendation that a temporary government based on the authority of the people should be formed. A little later similar advice was given to South Carolina.

A few months later, on May 10, 1776, the congress, influenced doubtless by the rising tide of independence sentiment, passed a resolution recommending that all the colonies which had not yet acted should "adopt such government as shall, in the opinion of the representatives of the people, best conduce to the happiness and safety of their constituents in particular,

and America in general." Five days later an explanatory preamble was added to the resolution. It stated that the colonies
had been deprived of the protection of the Crown, that the
petitions of the colonists for the redress of grievances had not
been answered, and that the British government had resorted
to force including the use of foreign mercenaries. It appeared,
continued the preamble, "absolutely irreconcileable to reason
and good Conscience . . . to take the oaths and affirmations"
necessary to support any government representing Great Britain.
It was necessary, therefore, to suppress all British authority and
to set up governments as recommended in the previously
adopted resolution.

NEW HAMPSHIRE'S FIRST CONSTITUTION

Meanwhile, New Hampshire had followed the recommendation made earlier and had adopted, on January 5, 1776, through
a congress "the first constitution framed by an American Commonwealth." This constitution was intended to be temporary
as the members of the congress which framed it expected an
early reconciliation with Great Britain. This expected reconciliation failed to materialize so the constitution remained in
effect until replaced by a more detailed document on June 2,
1784.

The constitution of 1776 provided for a two house legislature,
the lower house being called the house of representatives or assembly and the upper, the council. The latter was to be composed of twelve members chosen from the counties by the
people. The council was to elect its own president and secretary.
Members of both houses were to be elected annually. New
Hampshire's constitution of 1784 provided for a legislature or
general court consisting of a senate with twelve members and
a house of representatives. Both senators and representatives
were to be elected annually by the voters. No provision was
made for a separate executive department in the 1776 constitution but the executive functions were, in practice, exercised by
the council and its president. In its 1784 constitution, New
Hampshire provided for an executive to be elected annually
by the voters. This executive was to be called the president and

was to be assisted by a council. Apparently the colonial court system was to be continued though no direct mention was made of the matter in the 1776 constitution. The 1784 constitution provided that judges should be appointed for terms of five years by the president and council.

The legislature was to appoint all civil officers for the colony and all county officials with a few exceptions, according to the 1776 constitution. Generals and field officers of the militia and "all officers of the Army" were likewise to be appointed by the legislature. All bills "for raising, levying and collecting money," it was further provided, should originate in the lower house. The 1784 constitution gave the power of impeachment to the house of representatives and the power to conduct impeachment trials to the senate.

SOUTH CAROLINA

South Carolina's first constitution, drawn up and adopted by a provincial congress on March 26, 1776, was a more comprehensive document than was New Hampshire's original constitution. It remained in effect for only two years for, in 1778, it was replaced by a new constitution. In the former, provision was made for a legislature consisting of a legislative council and a general assembly. The assembly was to be made up of two hundred and two members elected every two years from twenty-eight districts. From its own membership the general assembly was to elect biennially the thirteen members of the legislative council. The legislature was to have the power to appoint executive officers as well as officers of the army and navy. While all general power to make laws was vested in the legislature, subject to the approval or disapproval of the president, the right to originate money bills was reserved to the lower house. The legislative council was not allowed even to amend such bills though it could reject them. The constitution of 1778 changed the names of the two houses of the legislature to senate and house of representatives.

There was no provision for a governor but instead there was to be a "president and commander-in-chief" and a vice president elected for two years by the legislature. Assisting and advising the president there was to be a privy council composed of the vice president and three members of each house of the legislature. It is interesting to note that the president was given the power to veto bills passed by the legislature, but he could not adjourn, prorogue, or dissolve that body. By the 1778 constitution the title of South Carolina's executive was changed to governor and mention of the veto power was omitted.

A rather definite judiciary was also provided for by the South Carolina constitution. Justices of the peace were to be nominated by the legislature and commissioned by the president. The privy council also acted as a court of chancery which automatically fixed the term of the judges of that court at two years, the period for which the privy council was to be elected. All judges, other than those mentioned, were to be appointed by the legislature and were to hold office during good behavior. Little change was made in the 1778 constitution concerning the judiciary.

RHODE ISLAND AND CONNECTICUT

The next two colonies to act were Rhode Island and Connecticut. Rhode Island acted in May, 1776, while Connecticut, after taking provisional action on June 14, made its action permanent on October 10, 1776. Since these colonies were, as has been pointed out, virtually self-governing, it was not necessary for them to draw up new constitutions providing for new machinery of government. All that was required was that their legislatures or general courts should adopt the colonial charters as state constitutions based on the authority of the people rather than the Crown. While taking this action the Connecticut general court also adopted a bill of rights consisting of four articles. From 1776 to 1818 in the case of Connecticut, and from 1776 to 1842 in the case of Rhode Island, the two states had governments practically identical with those of the colonial period. Each, it will be recalled, had a two house legislature composed of representatives of the freemen in a lower house and the assistants in an upper house. These two houses were continued as were the governors and deputy governors elected annually by the freemen of the corporation gathered in general assemblies. Judges also continued to be chosen annually by general assemblies.

VIRGINIA

Virginia was the fifth state to adopt a state constitution prior to the adoption of the Declaration of Independence. This constitution was drawn up by a convention on June 29, 1776, and remained in effect until 1830. The document as adopted was composed of three parts, a bill of rights, a declaration of independence, and a frame of government.

The Virginia declaration of independence, written by Thomas Jefferson as was the national Declaration, contained a justification of the colony's action in separating from Great Britain and setting up a new government. This declaration was made a preamble to the frame of government.

Beginning with the statement that "all men are by nature equally free and independent" with the inherent right to enjoy life and liberty, the bill of rights went on to assert that all power is vested in the people and is derived from them. Since government is instituted for the people it can be changed at any time by a majority of the voters. Magistrates should be regarded as trustees and servants of the people and there should be no exclusive or hereditary privileges. The three branches of the government ought to be separate and distinct. Suffrage ought to be conferred on all men who presented "sufficient evidence of permanent common interest with, and attachment to, the community." The people could not be forced to obey laws or to pay taxes unless passed or levied with their consent given directly or through their representatives. Then followed an enumeration of rights which had come to be regarded as absolutely essential and which still are among the most highly prized American rights, as they should be. These were the right to a speedy and impartial jury trial, no excessive bail, no cruel or unusual punishments, no general warrants, freedom of the press, and freedom of religion.

The frame of government consisted of twenty-one sections. It provided for a legislature called the general assembly to be composed of two houses called the house of delegates and the senate. The delegates were to be elected annually. Each county was to elect two, while certain other districts, cities, and counties were to elect one each. The senators were to be elected for terms of four years from districts. One-fourth were to be replaced each year, a precedent for the later Constitution of the United States which provides that one-third of the United States senators shall be replaced every two years. All bills were to originate in the house of delegates but they could be amended or rejected by the senate with the exception of money bills which could only be accepted or rejected in the form submitted by the lower house. To the house of delegates was given the power to impeach civil officers including judges. Impeachment trials, instead of being conducted by the senate, were to be conducted by the whole legislature with the state attorney-general acting as prosecutor.

There was to be a governor elected for a term of one year by the legislature with each house voting separately. No governor was to serve more than three successive terms and, after leaving the office, he was not to be again eligible for the office until four years had elapsed. He was to be assisted and advised by a privy council or council of state composed of eight members chosen by the legislature through a joint ballot. Every three years two members of this privy council were to be replaced by the legislature.

A definite judiciary was also provided for by the Virginia constitution of 1776. There were to be county courts, a general court, an admiralty court, courts of chancery and, in addition, a supreme court of appeal to hear appeals from other courts and to pass on the constitutionality of laws passed by the legislature. All judges were to be elected by the legislature through a joint ballot of the two houses, with the exception of the justices of the peace in the counties who were to be appointed by the governor. Judges were to hold office during good behavior.

NEW JERSEY

Yet another state constitution to be adopted before the formal adoption of the Declaration of Independence by the Continental Congress was that of New Jersey. This constitution was adopted by a convention on July 2, 1776, and was published on the next day. It remained in effect until 1884. It provided for a two house legislature consisting of a legislative council and a general assembly. One member of the council or upper house and three members of the general assembly were to be elected annually from each county.

There was to be a governor elected annually by the legislature and a vice president chosen by the legislative council. The governor was to preside over the council and to have a vote in it. He was to exercise the executive power in the state, to command the state's military forces, and to commission all officers appointed by the legislature. The vice president was to act for the governor in the latter's absence.

A court system was also provided for including justice of peace courts, inferior courts of common pleas in the counties, a supreme court, and a court of appeals consisting of the governor and the council. Except for this court of appeals the judges were to be appointed by the legislature for terms of from five to seven years.

DELAWARE

Delaware was the first state to adopt a constitution after the Declaration of Independence. Its constitution was drawn up by a convention and was proclaimed on September 21, 1776. It remained in effect until 1792 when it was replaced by a new document.

The legislature provided for by the constitution of 1776 was to consist of a lower house called the house of assembly and an upper house called the council. The former was to be composed of seven members elected annually from each of the three counties; the latter was to be made up of three members elected from each of the three counties for terms of three years. However, one-third of the members of the upper house from each county were to retire each year unless reëlected. All money bills were to originate in the house of assembly but could be amended or rejected by the council. All army officers were to be appointed by a joint ballot of the two houses of the legislature. To the house of assembly was given the power to impeach civil officers but impeachment trials were to be conducted by the council—a direct precedent for the impeachment procedure later included in the Constitution of the United States.

Instead of a governor there was to be a president chosen for a three year term by a joint ballot of the legislature. After serving a term the president was to be ineligible for another term until three years had passed by. He was to be assisted and advised by a privy council composed of two members chosen by each house of the legislature. With the advice of this privy council he could grant pardons and reprieves, embody and command the militia, and appoint all civil officers not otherwise provided for by the constitution.

There were to be various courts in Delaware ranging from justice of peace courts to a supreme court. Judges of the latter were to be appointed by a joint ballot of the president and the legislature. Justices of the peace were to be nominated by the legislature and appointed by the president. Other judicial officials were to be chosen by the president and the privy council.

While Delaware did not make a bill of rights a part of its constitution, its constitutional convention did adopt twenty-three resolutions which set forth the rights of the people.

PENNSYLVANIA

Just one week after the Delaware constitution had been proclaimed, Pennsylvania, which had been joined with Delaware under the proprietorship of the Penn family, adopted a constitution which remained in effect until 1790. The Pennsylvania constitution was adopted by a convention presided over by Benjamin Franklin. Unlike the constitutions previously considered the Pennsylvania constitution made provision for a legislature of only one house to be called the house of representatives. The members were to be chosen annually from the counties and, in a few cases, from cities. While the number of representatives was temporarily fixed it was arranged that after three years representation should be from districts in proportion to the number of persons who were taxable. No representative was to serve more than four years out of each seven. Besides the usual powers to choose its own officers and to judge the elections and qualifications of its own members, the house of representatives was to have the right to expel members, to grant charters of incorporation, to appoint delegates to the Continental Congress, to reform the penal laws, and to establish schools and universities. The house of representatives was also to have the power to impeach state officials but in impeachment trials the members of the executive council were to act as judges.

The executive power was vested in a president and council. One member of this council was to be chosen by the freemen in each of the eleven counties while a twelfth member was to be elected from Philadelphia, all for three year terms. From the membership of the council a president and vice president were to be chosen annually by a joint vote of the legislature and the council. The president and council were to have unusually broad powers. They were to appoint judicial, military, and naval officers; to conduct business with other states; to recommend measures to the legislature; to grant pardons and reprieves; to see that all laws were executed; and to grant licenses; as well as act as judges in impeachment trials, as has been mentioned. The president was also to be the commander-in-chief of the state's military forces but he was not to lead them in person.

Beginning with justice of peace courts there was to be a system of courts including courts of sessions, courts of common pleas, and orphan's courts with a supreme court crowning the system. The justices of peace were to be elected by the freeholders of the counties and cities while the higher judges, as has been pointed out, were to be appointed by the president and council.

A curious device provided for by the original Pennsylvania constitution was the council of censors to be elected by the voters every seven years. The censors were to inquire whether the legislature had observed the constitution and to inform the public of their findings. They could, by a two-thirds vote, call a convention to amend the constitution. It should be mentioned that this council of censors proved of no importance in practice.

An important part of the constitution was a bill of rights consisting of sixteen articles. It stated that all men are born equally free and independent, with natural rights. The bill of rights went on to stress freedom of religion. It declared that sovereignty rested in the people and that officials were servants of the people. Government was established for the common good and, if it failed in this purpose, the people had the right to overthrow it. Rotation in office was stated to be a means of securing freedom from oppression. All elections were to be free. While all men were to contribute to the public defence no contributions were to be exacted except by legal processes.

In criminal trials the accused was to have the right to witnesses in his own defence; he was to have a jury trial; he was not to be compelled to testify against himself; nor was he to be deprived of his liberty except by the laws of the land or the judgment of his peers. Freedom of speech and of the press were guaranteed. There were to be no searches or seizures without warrants. The people were guaranteed the right to bear arms but a standing army was declared to be dangerous. The military power was to be subordinate to the civil power. All men were to have the right to migrate from one state to another and were to have the right to settle vacant land in order to form a new state. This remarkable bill of rights concluded with a guarantee of the right of the people to assemble together and to petition for the redress of grievances.

MARYLAND

On November 11, 1776, a convention in Maryland adopted a constitution for that state which was destined to remain in effect until 1851. It provided for a two house legislature called the general assembly, the upper house of which was designated as the senate and the lower house as the house of delegates. The latter was to be made up of four members from each county and two each from Baltimore and Annapolis, all elected annually; the former was to be composed of fifteen members elected for a term of five years. For the election of these senators the voters were to select two "electors" from each county and one each from Baltimore and Annapolis. These electors or any twenty-four of them were to meet and elect either from their own number or from the people fifteen "men of the most wisdom, experience, and virtue." This was a precedent for the electoral college later established by the Constitution of the United States for the election of the national president and vice president.

The house of delegates was to have the power to judge the elections and qualifications of its members, to expel members, to originate all money bills, to inquire into "all complaints . . . as the grand inquest" of the state, and to commit any person to the public jail to remain until discharged by law. The senate was to have the power to judge the elections and qualifications of its members, to fill vacancies in its own membership, to originate any bills other than money bills, and to amend any house bills other than money bills.

There was to be a governor elected annually by a joint ballot of the legislature. No governor was to serve more than three years and after leaving office was not to be eligible again until four years had elapsed. He was to be advised and assisted by a council elected by the legislature. The governor was to command the land and sea forces of the state, to grant reprieves and pardons according to law, and to lay embargoes during recesses of the legislature if he saw fit. It was specifically stated that he was not to exercise any power by virtue of the laws or customs of Great Britain.

A judiciary system was provided consisting of justices of peace, county courts, and a general court. All judges were to be appointed by the governor and were to serve during good behavior. Any judge could be removed on conviction for misbehavior in a court of law.

Maryland's constitution was one of the few which provided a method of amendment. It was required that a proposed amendment should be passed by the legislature, then published three months before a new election of members of the house of delegates, and then repassed by the new legislature before it could become a part of the constitution.

An important part of the constitution was a bill of rights consisting of forty-two articles. It asserted the validity of the compact theory of government and declared that sovereignty was vested in the people. The powers of government, it was stated, should be separated so that each of the three branches would exercise its own functions. There was to be free petition to the legislature for the redress of grievances.

Open and free trial of cases should be held where they arose, with full safeguards for the accused. No man was to be compelled to give evidence against himself. No cruel or unusual punishments were to be inflicted nor was excessive bail to be required. No person was to be imprisoned unless by the judgment of his peers or in accordance with the provisions of law. Blank search warrants were not to be allowed. The legislature was to pass no ex-post-facto laws or bills of attainder and there was to be no forfeiture of estates except on conviction for murder or treason.

There was to be a well regulated militia but no standing army. Troops were not to be quartered with citizens except in time of war. Except for soldiers, no person was to be subject to martial law.

Other articles in this elaborate bill of rights provided that there should be no long terms of office holding but, on the contrary, there should be rotation in office. There was to be freedom of religion but the legislature was to be allowed to levy taxes for the support of the Christian religion. Freedom of the press was also guaranteed. No commercial monopolies were to be allowed nor were titles of nobility to be permitted.

NORTH CAROLINA

The last of the state constitutions to be drawn up in 1776 was that of North Carolina. This constitution, which was adopted by a convention on December 18, 1776, remained in effect until 1868. By its provisions there was to be a general assembly composed of a senate and a house of commons. There were to be one senator and two members of the house of commons from each county. In addition, each of the six towns was to elect one member of the lower house. Members of both houses were to have terms of one year. Each house was to have the right to choose its own officers and to pass on the elections and qualifications of its own members. Generally speaking, civil and military officers were to be appointed by joint ballots of the legislature. The power of impeachment was also vested in the legislature.

A governor elected annually by a joint ballot of the legislature was to exercise the executive powers. No governor was to serve more than three terms in any six years. He was to be the commander of the militia with the power to mobilize them during recesses of the legislature. He was also empowered to draw and apply money appropriated by the legislature, to lay embargoes during recesses of the legislature, to grant pardons and reprieves, to fill vacancies among officers appointed by the legislature during recesses of that body, and to commission officers appointed by the legislature. A council of state consisting of seven members was to be elected annually by the legislature for the purpose of advising the governor.

Various courts were provided for including those of justices of the peace, admiralty courts, and supreme courts of law and equity. Judges were to be elected by joint ballots of the legislature and were to hold office during good behavior.

A bill of rights consisting of twenty-five articles was included in this North Carolina constitution. Among the most important articles was that which declared that sovereignty was vested in the people. It was declared that there should be no exclusive privileges or immunities for anyone. The powers of government were to be separated. No agency except the legislature was to have the power to suspend laws. Elections were to be held frequently.

In criminal prosecutions the accused was to have the right to be informed of the charge against him and to have witnesses for the defence. He was not to be compelled to testify against himself and was to be allowed a jury trial with a unanimous vote required for conviction. There was to be no excessive bail required nor were the imposition of excessive fines or cruel or unusual punishments to be permitted. No blank search warrants were to be allowed. Freemen were not to be imprisoned nor was their property to be confiscated except by the law of the land. If any freeman was "restrained of his liberty" he was to have the right to a legal inquiry into the reasons for it.

Freedom of the press, freedom of worship, and the right to assemble were other guarantees contained in this bill of rights. There was to be no taxation except by the legislature. The people were guaranteed the right to bear arms. Standing armies were declared to be dangerous and it was stated that the military power should be subordinate to the civil power. It was also specifically declared that there should be no hereditary privileges, no monopolies, and no ex-post-facto laws.

GEORGIA

Georgia's constitution was adopted on February 5, 1777 by a convention meeting at Savannah. This document remained operative only until 1785 when it was replaced by a new constitution. Like that of Pennsylvania, the Georgia constitution of 1777 provided for a unicameral legislature called the house of assembly. It was to be composed of about seventy-two members elected annually by the counties and some of the towns. No extraordinary powers were granted to this legislature.

The executive power was to be exercised by a governor and council elected annually by the house of assembly. They were not to serve more than one year in every three years. The executive council was to elect its own president who was to act in place of the governor in case of the latter's absence. It was required that the council attend the meetings of the legislature. Acting together, the governor and council could reprieve criminals and call special sessions of the legislature. The governor was to command the military and naval forces of the state.

It was provided that there should be courts in each county and a supreme court for the state. While the constitution was not clear on the subject, the judges were apparently to be appointed by the legislature.

There was no bill of rights in this first Georgia constitution but there were a few provisions in it safeguarding civil rights.

NEW YORK

The occupation of New York by the British forces caused some delay there in the task of organizing a state government. It was not until April 20, 1777 that a convention adopted a constitution which John Jay had been chiefly instrumental in drafting. This constitution was not replaced by a new document until 1821.

By the provisions of the first New York constitution there was to be a two house legislature consisting of the senate and the assembly. The senate was to have twenty-four members elected from four senatorial districts for terms of four years. One-fourth of them were to be replaced each year. The assembly was to be composed of at least seventy members elected annually from the counties of the state. The legislature was to have the power to adjust the representation but at no time was the number of senators to exceed one hundred or the assemblymen three hundred. Besides possessing ordinary legislative powers, the New York legislature was to have the power to naturalize foreigners. The assembly was to have the power to impeach civil officers but impeachment trials were to be conducted by a court composed of the president of the senate, the senators, and the supreme court justices.

Every three years a governor and a lieutenant governor were to be elected by a majority of the qualified voters of the state. The powers and functions assigned to these officials obviously served as a direct precedent for the framers of the national constitution when they were drawing up the provisions relating to the national executive department. The New York governor was to command the military and naval forces of the state. He was also empowered to call special sessions of the legislature, to grant reprieves and pardons except in the case of treason and murder (for which only the legislature could grant reprieves and pardons), to send messages and recommendations to the legislature, to correspond with the Continental Congress and other states, and to execute the laws of the state. The lieutenant governor was to serve as president of the senate and was to have a vote in case of a tie. In case the governorship should be vacated by death, removal, or otherwise, the lieutenant governor was to succeed to the office.

The governor was not given the power of veto but, instead, provision was made for a council of revision consisting of the governor, the chancellor, and two or more judges of the supreme court. This council was to pass on all acts of the legislature and to veto such as they saw fit. Acts might be passed over the veto by a two-thirds vote of the legislature.

Neither the governor nor the legislature was to have the power to make appointments. Instead there was provided a council of appointment composed of the governor and one senator from each senatorial district elected by the assembly.

There were to be justices of peace courts, county courts, and a supreme court. The supreme court justices and the "first" judge of each county court were to hold office during good behavior. The other county judges and justices of the peace were to have three year terms. All judges were to be selected by the council of appointment. It should also be mentioned that there was to be a court of final appeals to hear appeals from the supreme court. This appeals court, which had the same personnel as the impeachment court, was to be composed of the president of the senate, the senators, and the judges of the supreme court.

The New York constitution makers did not draw up a special bill of rights but they did adopt the national Declaration of Independence as a part of the state constitution. In addition, several provisions designed to safeguard civil rights were included in the body of the constitution. Among these was the guarantee of freedom of conscience and religion. No minister of the gospel, it was stated, was to hold any state office. A strong militia was to be the safeguard of the people. Those whose religious beliefs would not permit military service were to be allowed to buy their exemption. The right to a jury trial was to remain inviolate. Finally, it was provided that no bills of attainder should be passed.

MASSACHUSETTS

Massachusetts was the last of the thirteen colonies to adopt a state constitution. It had been the first to break away from the British authority for it had established a provisional government in 1774, following the passage of the coercive acts by Parliament. On July 19, 1775, the council had been recognized as the legal successor of the royal governor. Later, on May 1, 1776, the words "government and people" were substituted for "the king" in all commissions and legal processes. With these changes the colony continued under its charter for several years. In 1777 the legislature constituted itself a convention by holding a joint session of the council and house of representatives and proceeded to draw up a state constitution. This document was then submitted to the voters who rejected it by a five to one majority. Apparently the people objected to the legislature assuming the right to act as a constitutional convention though a similar thing had been done in other colonies.

Finally, on September 1, 1779, a convention elected for the purpose of framing a state constitution met at Cambridge. The constitution which it adopted, largely the work of John Adams, was submitted to the voters and was ratified by the small majority of three hundred and ninety-three out of a total vote of eleven thousand seven hundred and one. Thereafter the constitutional convention again assembled and declared the constitution to be in effect. This constitution was so well drawn that it has remained in effect to the present time though, in 1917, it was rather thoroughly amended.

It should be emphasized that the Massachusetts constitution was the only one of the original thirteen to be ratified by the voters though later, in 1784, the second New Hampshire constitution received a popular ratification. It is not difficult to see why the earlier constitutions were not so ratified. In the first place there was no precedent for submitting the documents to the voters for their approval or disapproval. Then, too, it was generally felt that haste was necessary. A requirement of popular ratification would cause undesirable delay. Further, there would have been danger in holding ratification elections. With many of the patriots absent in the military service the loyalists would perhaps have been in the majority and so would have been able to defeat the ratification. At any rate a ratification election would have given the loyalists an opportunity to organize. But, by 1780, Massachusetts had been sufficiently purged of loyalists to make it perfectly safe to hold an election for the purpose of ratifying the state constitution.

The Massachusetts constitution provided for a bicameral legislature composed of the senate and the house of representatives. There were to be forty senators elected annually from districts by the qualified voters. Every town of one hundred and fifty inhabitants was to elect annually one representative. For each two hundred and twenty-five additional inhabitants a town was to be allowed to elect another representative. The legislature was to meet at least once a year. It was to have the power to create courts and to appoint all executive officers except those whose selection was provided for by the constitution. Further, the legislature was to have authority to levy taxes with the proviso that it was to evaluate the property in the state at least every ten years. The house of representatives was empowered to impeach civil officers but the senate was to act as the impeachment court. The penalty on conviction in an impeachment trial was to include eviction from office and future ineligibility. The convicted person was also to be liable to further punishment under the laws of the state. These provisions regarding impeachment were very similar to those later inserted in the Constitution of the United States.

All money bills were to originate in the house of representatives but the senate was to have the right to propose or agree to amendments to such bills. This, too, was very much like the provision finally included in the national Constitution. Another item that served as a precedent for a national constitutional provision was that which stated that a member of the house could not be arrested while going to, attending, or returning from the legislature.

An executive department was provided for consisting of a governor, lieutenant governor, and a council. The governor and lieutenant governor were to be elected annually by the qualified voters in town meetings. The votes were to be counted by the legislature. If there were no majority, the house of representatives was to select two of the highest four and from these two the senate was to select one. This procedure was to be followed in the case of either the governor or lieutenant governor. These provisions suggest where the framers of the national Constitution got their idea for electing a president and vice president in case the electoral college failed to elect. Of course, the provisions in the national Constitution are somewhat different. Assisting and advising the governor was to be a council of nine members elected annually from the senators by a joint ballot of the legislature. If the governor's office was vacated it was to be filled by the lieutenant governor.

The governor was to have the power to call the legislature in special session, and he could also dissolve the legislature. He was to command the army and navy of the state. The governor was to have a qualified power of veto. With the advice of the council he could grant pardons except in the case of impeached persons. He was to choose judges and commission military officers after they had been elected by the officers of lower rank in the army. All expenditures of public funds had to be approved by the governor. In order to guarantee his independence from the legislature he was to receive a fixed salary—an interesting and important provision.

As has been mentioned, the legislature was given the power

to create courts while the governor, with the advice of the council, was empowered to appoint judges. At the bottom of the court system were to be the justices of the peace holding office for seven years. At the top was to be a supreme court. All judges other than justices of the peace were to hold office during good behavior. They could be removed by the governor with the consent of the council and at the request of the legislature. It is interesting to note that the judges of the supreme court were required to give opinions to the governor or to the legislature on request. Another provision required that all cases dealing with marriage, divorce, and alimony were to be tried before the governor and council until the legislature made some other arrangement.

Included in the Massachusetts constitution were a preamble and a bill of rights consisting of thirty articles. In this portion of the document was set forth the prevailing natural rights philosophy. As in the national Declaration of Independence, all men were declared to be "born free and equal." Popular sovereignty was proclaimed and it was declared that officials of the government were the servants and agents of the people. No hereditary titles or ranks in the government were to be permitted. Government, it was stated, was constituted for the common good; when it failed to promote this common good the people were to have the right to overthrow it. Rotation in office was asserted to be a means of preventing oppression. No taxes were to be levied except by legislative action and there were to be no "unjust requisitions."

There was to be free and quick remedy under the laws for all injuries to person, property, or character. No person was to be held for a crime unless he were informed of the charge against him. He was to be allowed an opportunity for defence and was not to be required to testify against himself. No punishments were to be inflicted without just judgment under the law of the land, nor were punishments to be cruel or unusual. The right to trial by jury was specifically safeguarded.

Freedom of religion was guaranteed, as were freedom of the press, freedom of speech, and freedom to assemble. No ex-post-facto laws were to be passed. The right of persons to bear arms was also guaranteed. In time of peace troops were not to be quartered in the homes of civilians without their consent. Except for the military, no person was to be subject to martial law unless by action of the legislature. Finally, the bill of rights declared that there should be absolute separation of the legislative, executive, and judicial powers in order that there might "be a government of laws and not of men."

During the period of the Revolution, in July, 1777, to be specific, Vermont also drew up a constitution and declared itself to be a state. However, this action was not recognized by the thirteen states and Vermont had no part in forming the original United States. Not until 1791 was it admitted to the union. In view of these facts it seems unnecessary to give attention here to the Vermont constitution.

GENERAL FEATURES OF THE STATE CONSTITUTIONS

From the foregoing analysis of the thirteen original state constitutions it is possible to draw certain obvious conclusions. For instance, it is clearly apparent that in these constitutions the early Americans embodied the ideas of government that they had derived from English and colonial practice, and from the writings of such men as John Locke and Montesquieu. The influence of these and other eighteenth century political philosophers is reflected in the frequent allusions in the constitutions to popular sovereignty, to the compact theory of government, to natural rights, and to the separation of powers. Certainly the idea of the separation of powers was clearly embodied in these first constitutions for they all set up, more or less definitely, legislative, executive, and judicial branches of government, each with its functions and powers at least partly defined. But there was little application of the idea of checks and balances, with three coördinate branches of government acting as a check on each other as in the case of the government of the United States under the Constitution. The tendency was to give a preponderance of power to the legislature, especially to the lower house.

The fear and dislike of the royal governors doubtless explains why the office of governor was so circumscribed by these first constitutions. It is significant that in only one state, South Carolina, was the governor, or president as he was called, given an unqualified veto while the last two states to adopt constitutions, New York and Massachusetts, would go no further than to give him a qualified veto. The distrust of the governor was further shown by the requirement in most of the states that he should act with the advice of a council created by the legislature. The tendency to place the power to appoint officials in the hands of the legislature also reveals the popular fear of the governor. The fact that in most of the states the governor (or corresponding officer) was to be chosen by the legislature is yet another evidence of the desire to control him. The provision for a one year term for the governor in all but three of the states is still another indication that the people feared him.

Another conclusion regarding these first state constitutions was that they were all written documents. Furthermore they were all short and concise, outlining a form of government and stating its powers, which are the chief things a constitution should do. There was a careful avoidance of material that was purely legislative in character such as is found in some of the present day constitutions. Only the Massachusetts constitution contained a preamble which is now considered an essential part of a constitution. A bill of rights is also considered a part of a complete constitution. Six of the original state constitutions, those of Virginia, Pennsylvania, Maryland, North Carolina, New York, and Massachusetts, contained elaborate bills of rights while a lengthy bill of rights was also included in the second New Hampshire constitution of 1784. In addition, all the remaining states, except Rhode Island, had clauses in their constitutions safeguarding the rights of the people. While a provision for amendment is now regarded as an essential feature of a constitution, the majority of the original constitutions made no mention of the matter.

Though all of the constitutions provided for republican forms of government, they fell far short of establishing democracy. Everywhere strict qualifications were imposed on candidates for office so that only a few men could possibly be eligible. Seven of the states required some sort of a religious test as a qualification for office. These were Massachusetts, Delaware, Pennsylvania, Maryland, North Carolina, South Carolina, and Georgia. Possession of considerable property was also a common qualification necessary for office holders. For example, in New Jersey, members of the legislative council were required to be residents for a year of the county from which elected and were further required to own property in the county worth one thousand pounds. Members of the general assembly had to meet the same residence requirement and own property worth five hundred pounds. In Maryland the governor was required to be more than twenty-five years of age, to be a resident of the state for five years preceding his election, and to own property in the state worth five thousand pounds, of which at least one-fifth must be "of freehold estate." As another example, Massachusetts required that a senator must have a freehold worth three hundred pounds or other property to the value of six hundred pounds. In addition, he must have been a resident of the state for five years and must also be a resident of the district from which he was chosen. The property requirement for a representative was one-third that of a senator. The governor was required to be a resident of the state for seven years preceding his election, to own a freehold of one thousand pounds and to be of the Christian religion.

Nor was there much liberality in the matter of the suffrage. The age of twenty-one or over was universally required of voters. Residence was also a general requirement though there were some exceptions. White men alone could vote in Virginia, South Carolina, and Georgia. The color question was not raised in the other ten states. Property requirements were imposed on voters and in some cases religious tests had to be passed. For instance, in South Carolina, voters were required "to acknowledge the being of a God, and to believe in a future state of rewards and punishments." In New Jersey voters were required to reside twelve months in the county where they wished to vote and, in addition, they must own property worth fifty pounds. In New Hampshire, Pennsylvania, and North Carolina, resident taxpayers were allowed to vote while Georgia extended the ballot to white inhabitants "of any mechanic trade." With these exceptions all the states required that a person, in order to be eligible to vote, should possess a freehold or its equivalent.

In spite of their shortcomings the original state constitutions were extremely important in the development of American constitutional practice. In them was embodied the best thinking of the period regarding government. They served as a direct link between the colonial charters and the later national Constitution. As has been pointed out in a few instances, the framers of the national document borrowed a number of important ideas from these state constitutions.

SELECTED REFERENCES

Bancroft, George, *History of the United States*, Vol. V, pp. 111–125.

Channing, Edward, *History of the United States*, Vol. III, pp. 431–444.

Fisher, S. G., *Evolution of the Constitution of the United States*, pp. 70–89, 190–214.

Greene, E. B., *The Foundations of American Nationality*, pp. 547–555.

Haines, B. M., and Haines, C. G., *The Constitution of the United States*, pp. 57–63.

Holcombe, A. N., *State Government in the United States*, pp. 40–72.

Johnson, Allen, ed., *Readings in American Constitutional History 1776–1876*, pp. 63–73.

Landon, J. S., *Constitutional History and Government of the United States*, pp. 57–64.

Long, Breckinridge, *Genesis of the Constitution of the United States of America*, pp. 167–196.

Nevins, Allan, *The American States During and After the Revolution*, pp. 117–170.

Pease, T. C., and Roberts, A. S., eds., *Selected Readings in American History*, pp. 131–136.

Schouler, James, *Constitutional Studies*, pp. 29–69.

Thorpe, F. N., *A Short Constitutional History of the United States*, pp. 69–81.

VanTyne, C. H., *The American Revolution 1776–1783*, pp. 136–156.

Chapter Eight

THE CONFEDERATION GOVERNMENT

CHARACTER OF THE ARTICLES OF CONFEDERATION

A CURSORY examination of the constitutional history of the period from 1781 to 1789 reveals that the state governments were, on the whole, much better organized and more efficient than the national government under the Articles of Confederation. This was not the result of an accident or of blundering; rather, it was the result of deliberate purpose. The simple truth of the matter is that the men who drew up the Articles of Confederation did not wish to establish a strong national government. All they sought to accomplish was to create a constitutional government to act as the agent of the states in carrying out certain common purposes. The states, deriving their authority directly from the people according to the prevailing political theory, were to remain supreme.

It is easy to criticize the Confederation government for its weaknesses and inefficiency for it was certainly both weak and inefficient. It is just as simple a matter to condemn those who drew up the Articles of Confederation for their short-sightedness. But, before passing too harsh a judgment on the framers of the Articles, it is well to recall that they were fighting for independence because Great Britain had attempted to impose stricter imperialistic control over them. Naturally, since they were striving to throw off one form of outside control, the states were not willing to submit to another form of external control even though the controlling agency were their own creation. It was to take a period of near chaos—what John Fiske called "The Critical Period"—to force the country to accept the idea of a strong central government.

The document described by its framers as *"Articles of Confederation and perpetual Union between the States"* consists of a preamble and thirteen articles. The first article stated that the confederation should be called "The United States of America." The next two articles indicate to some extent why the Confederation government was so helpless, for each state, it was declared, was to retain "its sovereignty, freedom and independence" as well as "every power, jurisdiction and right" not "expressly delegated" to the congress of the United States. While the preamble used the expression "perpetual union" the third article qualified this by stating that the purpose of the states was to "enter into a firm league of friendship with each other for their common defence, the security of their liberties, and their mutual and general welfare."

Then followed several provisions similar to ones later incorporated in the Constitution of the United States. The free inhabitants of each state were to "be entitled to all privileges and immunities of free citizens" in the other states. The people of each state were also to be free to enter or leave any other state and to carry on trade and commerce in other states on the same basis as the citizens of those states. Fugitives from justice were to be extradited from any state on the formal demand of the executive of the state from which they had fled. "Full faith and credit" were to be given in each state "to the records, acts and judicial proceedings of the courts and magistrates of every other State."

FORM OF THE CONFEDERATION GOVERNMENT

The form of the government provided for by the Articles of Confederation was extremely simple. It was to be a one branch government consisting of a congress made up of from two to seven delegates from each state. These delegates were to be elected annually "in such manner as the legislature of each State shall direct." No person was to act as a delegate for more than three out of each six years. A delegate was not to be eligible for any office "under the United States" which paid a salary or fee. Each state was to "maintain" its delegates as it saw fit. Obviously, because he was thus made dependent on his state for salary and expenses, a delegate would tend to be state minded rather than nationally minded. There was to be freedom of speech and debate in congress and no delegate was to be called to account out of congress for what he had said while in congress. Delegates were also to be free from arrest or imprisonment while going to or from or while attending congress, "except for treason, felony, or breach of the peace." These last two provisions were almost identical with clauses later inserted in the Constitution. Congress was to meet annually on the first Monday in November. The votes on all questions were to be taken by states with each state allowed but one vote.

Congress was to choose its own presiding officer who was to be called the president of the congress of the United States. No president was to serve more than one year in any period of three years. At various times, it has been asserted that John Hanson of Maryland, and not George Washington, was the first president of the United States because the former was elected president of the Confederation congress at its first session on November 5, 1781. A mere glance will reveal the difference in the titles of the two. Furthermore, there was a vast difference in the functions of the two. The president of the congress of the United States under the Articles was the presiding officer of a legislative body; the president of the United States is an executive officer charged by the Constitution with the performance of certain definite duties. It would be just as logical to say that John Hancock was the first president of the United States because he was president of the Continental Congress at the time of the Declaration of Independence as to give the honor to John Hanson.

In fact, what executive functions the Confederation government performed were either exercised by the whole congress or assigned to committees. The most important committee, which was authorized by the Articles, was the "Committee of the States" consisting of one delegate from each state. It was to conduct the government during the recesses of congress but was to exercise no powers for which the consent "of nine states in the Congress of the United States assembled" was required. Congress was also authorized to appoint "such other committees and civil officers" as it deemed necessary "for managing the general affairs of the United States" subject to the direction of congress itself. Under this authority congress continued, with modifications from time to time, the special offices or departments which had been set up by the Second Continental Congress for the purpose of administering such matters as finance and foreign affairs.

No national judiciary was provided for by the Articles except that congress was authorized to establish courts "for the trial of piracies and felonies committed on the high seas" and also prize courts "for receiving and determining finally appeals in all cases of captures." Congress was also to be the "last resort on appeal" in disputes between two or more states regarding "boundaries, jurisdiction or any other cause whatever." On petition of either party involved in a controversy "concerning the private right of soil claimed under different grants of two or more States" congress was also to effect a settlement. In settling boundary disputes or the other controversies mentioned congress was to set up commissions by a complicated process described in the Articles. It should be mentioned that, in practice, congress accomplished little in the way of settling disputes and controversies between the states.

POWERS OF CONGRESS

Only a few powers were delegated to the Confederation congress by the Articles and the most important of these could be exercised only by the votes of nine states. These included the power to declare war, to grant letters of marque and reprisal in time of peace, to make treaties or alliances, to coin money, to regulate the value of its own coin and that issued by the states, to determine the amounts "necessary for the defence and welfare of the United States, or any of them," to emit bills of credit, to borrow money, to appropriate money, to decide the number of naval vessels to be built or purchased, to fix the number of the land or naval forces, or to appoint a commander-in-chief for the army or navy.

By a vote of the majority of the states, congress was also empowered to fix the standard of weights and measures throughout the United States, to regulate trade with and manage all affairs with the Indians who were "not members of any of the States," to establish and regulate post offices throughout the United States and to establish postage rates, to appoint officers of the land forces except regimental officers who were to be appointed by the states, to appoint all naval officers, to commission all officers in the service of the United States, to make rules and regulations for the land and naval forces of the United States, and, finally, to direct the operations of the military and naval forces of the United States.

After congress had fixed the number of the land forces, it was "to make requisitions from each State for its quota, in proportion to the number of white inhabitants in such State." This requisition was to be binding on the state and its legislature was to immediately appoint regimental officers, raise and equip the quota of troops "at the expense of the United States," and march them, at the time set by congress, to the place appointed by that body. In practice this meant nothing for the states did as they pleased in the matter. If they failed to furnish their quotas, which was often the case, congress absolutely lacked power to coerce them.

All national expenses were to be paid out of a common treasury on the order of congress but that body had no taxing power. It was to secure the required money by making requisitions on the states "in proportion to the value of all land within each State, granted to or surveyed for any person" together with the buildings and improvements on such land. The value of the land and improvements was to be fixed by a method to be determined by congress. Each state was to raise its proportion of the national expenses through taxes levied by its own legislature. Here again, congress proved helpless because it could not force the states to pay their quotas. In practice it found that it could not satisfactorily determine the value of the lands within the states and the result was confusion. The states paid only what they pleased which, at times, was nothing at all.

And so it was in all matters. Though the thirteenth article specifically declared that "Every State shall abide by the determinations of the United States in Congress assembled, on all questions which by this confederation are submitted to them," and, further, that "the articles of this confederation shall be inviolably observed by every State," the history of the Confederation makes it apparent that the states paid little or no attention to congress or to what the Articles said. Helplessness characterized congress at every turn. It could neither secure obedience at home nor command proper respect in foreign countries.

ACCOMPLISHMENTS OF THE CONFEDERATION GOVERNMENT

Before considering in detail the weaknesses and failures of the Confederation government something should be said of its accomplishments. The most notable of these were the conclusion of the War for Independence through the Treaty of Paris negotiated in 1783, the drafting of the Land Ordinance of 1785, and the formulation of the Northwest Ordinance of 1787.

On June 14, 1781, the Continental Congress had appointed a peace commission composed of Benjamin Franklin, John Adams, John Jay, Henry Laurens, and Thomas Jefferson. However, since negotiations with Great Britain were not begun until early in 1782, it is apparent that the accomplishments of the peace commission must be credited to the Confederation congress. After preliminary negotiations carried on between Franklin and Richard Oswald and others on behalf of the British, a provisional treaty was signed on November 30, 1782 by the first four named American commissioners. (Jefferson had refused to serve.) This treaty, it should be noted, had been made without the knowledge of the French and in violation of the instructions of congress which had stated that any arrangement made with Great Britain was to leave the treaties of 1778 with the French in full force. The treaty of alliance with France had declared that neither the United States nor France was to make peace without the consent of the other. However, Franklin was able to soothe the feelings of Vergennes, the French foreign minister, to such an extent that he not only overlooked what seemed to be an act of bad faith on the part of the Americans but shortly afterwards consented to another French loan to the United States amounting to six million livres or something over a million dollars.

Shortly afterwards both the French and Spanish made peace with England and, on September 3, 1783, a final treaty between the United States and Great Britain was signed at Paris. It included exactly the same terms which had been embodied in the preliminary treaty of the year before which, meanwhile, had been approved by the Confederation congress. The definitive treaty of 1783 was ratified by congress on January 14, 1784 and by Great Britain on the ninth of April in the same year.

First and foremost, the treaty recognized the thirteen United States as "free, sovereign, and independent states." In the second article the boundaries were defined in such a way as to give the United States all the territory extending east and west between the Atlantic Ocean and the Mississippi River and north and south between Canada and East and West Florida. American fishermen were given the right to fish off Newfoundland and also the privilege of drying and curing their fish in certain uninhabited places. No impediment was to be placed in the way of creditors on either side in their efforts to collect bona fide debts previously contracted.

Congress was to "earnestly recommend" to the state legislatures that provision be made for the restitution of the confiscated property of loyalists. These loyalists were to be free to come and go anywhere in the states during a period of one year while seeking such restitution. No future confiscations or prosecutions were to be commenced against any person because of the part he had taken in the war. There was to be a mutual restoration of prisoners and the British government was, "with all convenient speed, and without causing any destruction, or carrying away any negroes or other property of the American inhabitants," to evacuate all forts and other places in the United States. As the event proved, "convenient speed" in this case was to mean thirteen years. As it was then thought that the Mississippi River had its source in Canada, it was provided that both subjects of Great Britain and citizens of the United States were to enjoy free navigation of that river.

The negotiation of the treaty of peace was a notable accomplishment for it gave formal recognition by Great Britain to the Declaration of Independence adopted seven years earlier. But the treaty was by no means an unalloyed blessing. Out of it, as will be seen, grew problems which the Confederation government was to find itself helpless to solve.

A second important accomplishment of the Confederation congress was the enactment of the Land Ordinance of 1785. It will be recalled that Maryland had refused to ratify the Articles of Confederation until assured that states having claims to western lands would give up such claims in favor of the Confederation government. However, it was some time before the actual cessions of land were made. The Confederation congress bent its efforts to complete the cessions and, by 1786, had secured the surrender of the various states' claims to all of the territory north of the Ohio River. The land south of that river was not finally ceded until after the Constitution had gone into effect, Georgia being the last state to cede its western lands.

While seeking the cession of these western lands, congress promised the states that the ceded lands would be disposed of for the common benefit and it also promised that as soon as these lands were settled they would be formed into republican states which would be made a part of the union on an equal basis with the original states. It was in fulfillment of the first promise that the Land Ordinance of 1785 was passed. To make it convenient to dispose of the public land a system of land surveys, known as the "rectangular" system, was established by the act. This system has been followed ever since by the United States government in surveying public lands.

Under this system a line was first laid out running east and west. This was called the base line. Perpendicular to it other lines known as meridian lines were run at intervals of six miles. The area between every two of these meridian lines was described as a range. Then other lines were run six miles apart and parallel to the base line. This resulted in dividing the ranges into six mile squares known as townships. Each township was then subdivided into thirty-six areas, each one mile square, called sections. These sections were capable of as much subdivision as might be desired. The law of 1785 provided for the surveying of seven ranges based on a line running due west from the point where the boundary of Pennsylvania is intersected by the Ohio River.

In addition to providing this efficient survey system, the Land Ordinance prescribed the terms on which the lands were to be sold. One section in each township was to be reserved for the support of schools, following a precedent which had been established by the New England colonies. The rest of the surveyed land was to be sold to the highest bidders in plots of a section or more but the bidders were required to pay at least one dollar for each acre. Auctions were to be held in each state with each being assigned a proportion of the land to be sold.

Land did not sell as rapidly as congress had expected. This was chiefly because the minimum price of six hundred and forty dollars for a section was more than poor men, who would naturally have been attracted to the land, could afford to pay. Settlement was also discouraged by disordered conditions in the west. The British, who had refused to evacuate the forts in that part of the American territory, advised the Indians not to cede their lands north of the Ohio to the agents of congress. The result was that congress, in spite of its best efforts, could guarantee neither safety of life nor security of title to those who might purchase land and move into the west.

However, congress did succeed in disposing of some of the land to large land companies. One of these, the Ohio Company of Associates which was composed of revolutionary veterans of New England who held paper promises of pay from congress, in 1787, purchased one and a half million acres on the Muskingum River for one million dollars. In payment the company tendered the certificates of indebtedness held by its members. Another large land company interested in settling the Ohio country was the Scioto Company. A third company, which secured a large grant between the Big and Little Miami rivers, was the Symnes Company composed largely of New Jersey and Pennsylvania veterans. In 1788 the Ohio Company actually started a settlement at Marietta while, at almost the same time, a settlement was begun by the Symnes Company.

Not only did congress provide a system of surveying and disposing of the public land in the west but it also took steps to carry out its promise to organize the territory and provide it with governmental machinery as a preliminary to incorporation in the union. Congress had implied authority to do this under the eleventh of the Articles of Confederation. This stated that Canada might accede to the Confederation and be admitted into the union, "but no other colony shall be admitted into the same unless such admission be agreed to by nine states." In 1784 an ordinance drafted by a committee headed by Thomas Jefferson was adopted by congress. This called for the division of the western lands "ceded or to be ceded" into fourteen terri-

tories or colonies. These were to establish temporary governments and, after any of them had twenty thousand inhabitants,
it could establish a permanent government. When it acquired
a population as great as the least populous of the original states
it was to be admitted to the Confederation as a state. Jefferson
had proposed that slavery should be prohibited in these states
but this proposal was rejected by congress. He had also proposed
fantastic names for the new states such as Sylvania, Michigania,
Illinoia, Metropotamia, Polypotamia, and Pelisipia, but these
names were also omitted from the ordinance as adopted.

Because of dissensions in congress the Ordinance of 1784 was
never put into effect. The delay in developing and putting into
operation a plan for the political organization of the region
caused considerable unrest in the west, particularly in the settled
area in the southwest. In 1785 the inhabitants of the region, now
a part of Tennessee but then claimed by North Carolina, took
matters into their own hands and organized what they called
the State of Franklin. North Carolina voiced strong objections
to this procedure so congress took no action to recognize the self-
constituted state. In 1788 the State of Franklin finally passed
out of existence.

Congressional delay in putting into operation a plan for the
west continued until 1787. Then the appearance of Manasseh
Cutler with an offer on behalf of the Ohio Company to buy a
large tract in the Ohio country seems to have stimulated congress to act. At any rate, it proceeded to enact, on July 13, 1787,
what is known as the Northwest Ordinance of 1787. This document, which is rightly considered as one of the most important
in American history, was the basis for the American territorial
system through which the original thirteen states have been
expanded to forty-eight.

The ordinance applied only to the region lying north of the
Ohio and extending westward to the Mississippi. For this territory congress was to create a temporary government consisting
of a governor, a secretary, and three judges, all appointed by
congress. The governor and the judges were to make laws for
the territory, which laws were to be reported to congress which
might disapprove of them. The governor was to act as commander-in-chief of the militia and was to appoint and com-

mission all officers below the rank of general officers. He was also to appoint necessary civil officers in each county or township.

As soon as there were five thousand free adult male inhabitants in the territory representatives to the number of at least twenty-five were to be elected from the counties or townships to serve in a general assembly. This assembly was to be made up of a house of representatives, the governor, and a legislative council. The five members of this council were to be nominated by the representatives but were to be appointed by congress for five year terms. Representatives were required to be residents of the territory and to own two hundred acres of land while members of the council were required to be residents of the district and to own five hundred acres of land. To qualify as a voter a man was required to be a resident of the territory and to own fifty acres of land. The general assembly was to have power to pass laws for the territory subject to the veto of the governor. A delegate to congress was to be elected by a joint ballot of the council and the house of representatives. He was to have the right to participate in debates but not to vote on questions before congress.

The ordinance set up tentative boundaries for three states to be formed out of the territory and it also provided for the possible formation of two additional states. When any of these divisions had acquired sixty thousand inhabitants it was to be permitted to adopt a permanent constitution providing for a republican form of government and was to be admitted to the union "on an equal footing with the original states in all respects whatsoever." It was this promise and provision for future statehood that made the ordinance such an extraordinary document.

But there were other provisions in the ordinance which were of interest and importance. For instance, there was the statement that "Religion, morality and knowledge, being necessary to good government and the happiness of mankind, schools and the means of education shall for ever be encouraged." Of great historical importance was the article which prohibited slavery or involuntary servitude in the territory except as a punishment for crime. Though a similar statement had been rejected by congress when it formulated the ordinance of 1784, there was practically no objection to the inclusion of the anti-slavery article in the Ordinance of 1787.

A bill of rights safeguarding the liberties of the inhabitants of the territory was also incorporated in the ordinance. This bill is interesting in that it reveals prevailing ideas concerning the rights of the people at the time when the Constitution was being framed. Among the rights guaranteed were freedom of religion, the benefit of the writ of habeas corpus, and trial by jury. The people were always to have "a proportionate representation" in the legislature. All judicial proceedings were to be in accordance with the common law. Bail was to be permitted for accused persons except "for capital offences, where the proof shall be evident or the presumption great." Fines were to be moderate and no cruel or unusual punishments were to be inflicted. No person was to be deprived of his liberty or property except "by the judgment of his peers, or the law of the land." No laws were to be made which interfered with or affected private contracts.

During the period of the Confederation no progress was made in giving practical application to the Northwest Ordinance beyond setting up a temporary government for the whole territory with General Arthur St. Clair as the first governor. After a national government was established under the Constitution the ordinance was reënacted by congress and, in 1790, a similar ordinance was enacted for the region south of the Ohio River. The Northwest Ordinance remained in operation for fifty years and even after that time its principles were retained in other legislation passed by congress. An examination of the present territorial governments of Alaska, Hawaii, and Porto Rico, will reveal a striking similarity to the second form of temporary government provided for by the Northwest Ordinance of 1787.

FINANCIAL DIFFICULTIES

It is obvious that the Confederation government was defective both because of its form and because of its lack of powers. The lack of a separate national executive and judiciary and the consequent absence of separation of powers were serious defects as was the provision for equality of voting power for all of the states whether large or small. In practice, the lack of authority to coerce either the states or individuals was a great handicap to the Confederation government. Congress could make requests or recommendations but had no way of forcing obedience to its wishes. Altogether too much power was retained by the states. Congress could not raise troops except through the state governments. Nor could it enforce contracts since it lacked both the power and the machinery for coercion. But even more serious than these deficiencies was the lack of power to levy and collect taxes and to control finances generally, and the inability to enforce treaties, and to control foreign and interstate commerce. Finally, the requirement that no amendments should be added to the Articles of Confederation, "unless such alteration be agreed to in a Congress of the United States, and be afterwards confirmed by the Legislatures of every State," effectively prevented any of the defects from being remedied.

From the very beginning of its existence, the Confederation government was embarrassed financially. Congress, it will be recalled, was authorized to determine the amount of money required for the common defence and for the promotion of the general welfare and it was also empowered to appropriate money for these purposes out of a common treasury. This treasury was to be supplied through requisitions on the states. In other words, congress had the power and even the obligation to contract debts but it had no power to raise money for the payment of those debts. All it could do was literally to beg the state legislatures to furnish their proportion of the required money. But all too often the states ignored the requisitions entirely or paid only a portion of the requested amount. Thus, during the years 1782 and 1783, congress requested ten million dollars but received only fifteen percent of that amount. During the year 1785 the income from requisitions averaged only about thirty-two thousand dollars a month, a sum far less than that required for the expenses of the government.

For congress to seek relief through the issue of paper money was out of the question as the Second Continental Congress had exhausted the possibilities in that direction. The only recourse left was to borrow money. As an aid in organizing credit facilities, congress incorporated the Bank of North America, following a recommendation made in 1781 by Robert Morris, the superintendent of finance. While this bank did not prove as useful as expected it did render some service to the government during the years 1782 and 1783.

Whenever possible the government issued certificates of indebtedness in payment of its obligations. Thus, in 1783, to avert what threatened to be serious trouble with the officers of the Continental army, congress awarded them certificates which, taken at face value, were equivalent to full pay for five years. But, by that time, the credit of congress had sunk so low that these certificates were worth only fifteen cents on the dollar. Had it not been for loans secured abroad the situation would have been hopeless indeed. Following the war the Dutch were the only ones who would lend money to the United States and they did so with increasing reluctance. At the beginning of 1784, the foreign debt of the United States, owed to France, Spain, and Holland, amounted to $7,830,517. During the period from the beginning of 1784 to 1789, the principal of the foreign debt was augmented by loans of $2,296,000, all secured in Holland. Meanwhile, congress failed to pay the interest on its foreign debts so that this item increased from $67,037 in 1784 to $1,640,071 by the end of 1789.

Likewise, the interest on domestic obligations remained unpaid. At the end of 1783, congress, on domestic certificates of indebtedness totalling $27,293,000, owed interest amounting to $3,109,000. Six years later the interest had increased to $11,493,858.

Attempts were made to amend the Articles of Confederation so as to provide some more satisfactory source of income for congress but all the attempts proved fruitless. On February 3, 1781, before the Articles had gone into effect, a proposal was submitted to the states for an amendment which would have granted congress the power to levy a five percent duty on all imports with a few enumerated exceptions. Twelve states approved but Rhode Island defeated the proposition by refusing to ratify in spite of strong pressure brought to bear on her.

In 1783 the idea of a national tariff was revived when congress submitted to the states an amendment to the Articles proposing specific duties on liquors, sugar, tea, coffee, molasses, and pepper, and ad valorem duties on all other goods. This tariff was to remain in effect for twenty-five years and the proceeds from it were to be used only for the payment of the interest on the public debts. To lessen objections to the amendment, it was provided that the duties should be collected by state officers. By 1786 nine states had ratified the amendment. In that year three more gave their approval but New York absolutely refused to ratify. Following the final defeat of this amendment the financial condition of the Confederation government became steadily worse, causing increased alarm to the moneyed and business interests of the country who were convinced that the only remedy lay in the establishment of a stronger central government.

If the financial condition of the central government was bad, the situation in the individual states was even worse. Undeterred by the fact that the currency issued both by the Continental Congress and by the states during the Revolution had depreciated to almost the vanishing point, a number of the states again resorted to the issuing of fiat money. Everywhere "paper money" parties appeared and contested for the political control of the individual states. In seven of them, Georgia, South Carolina, North Carolina, Pennsylvania, New Jersey, New York, and Rhode Island, the advocates of paper money won out. Not only were large amounts of depreciated paper currency issued but, to the dismay of the creditor class, laws were frequently passed requiring the acceptance of the paper in payment of debts. "Stay" laws, designed to suspend debt payments, were also passed in a number of cases. In Massachusetts where the paper money advocates failed to gain control, a critical situation developed when an uprising of the debtor class took place in 1786 under the leadership of Daniel Shays, a revolutionary veteran. The insurrectionists, who were subdued with great difficulty, sought to force the issuance of paper money and also the suspension of debt collections. This uprising, known as Shays's Rebellion, did much to convince hesitating conservatives that conditions in the country needed to be changed, and that quickly.

DIPLOMATIC AND COMMERCIAL TROUBLES

In its foreign relations and especially in its attempts to secure favorable commercial treaties, congress also displayed conspicuous weaknesses. During the period from May 7, 1784 until the Confederation government ended its existence, John Jay served as secretary for foreign affairs. In 1784, Thomas Jefferson was sent to France as minister plenipotentiary while, from 1785 to 1788, John Adams was minister to Great Britain.

With France relations were on a much more satisfactory basis than was true in the case of other countries. The treaty of commerce negotiated with France in 1778 remained in effect but the privileges which it granted to the United States were not very important. By the treaty Americans were granted most favored nation privileges, that is, they were not to pay any higher duties in French ports than were paid by the most favored nations. The French were to enjoy a similar privilege in American ports. As for the French West Indies, it was provided that only American ships of limited tonnage could trade with them. Further only certain enumerated goods were to be carried to specified ports of these islands and nothing but rum and molasses could be carried from them. In spite of these restrictions a considerable number of American vessels engaged in trade with the French during the Confederation period. But all efforts to secure more favorable commercial privileges from the government of France during the period were unsuccessful.

Other commercial treaties were negotiated by the Confederation government with the Netherlands in 1782, with Sweden in 1783, and with Prussia in 1785. All of these treaties granted to the United States most favored nation privileges. In practice, however, these treaties proved of little benefit for only a small amount of trade was carried on with the countries mentioned.

All attempts to negotiate a commercial treaty with Great Britain proved futile. The colonies had enjoyed important trade privileges with Great Britain and the British West Indies in spite of the navigation and trade acts. But after the colonies became independent states they found themselves deprived of all privileges of trade. Certain American goods such as naval stores and unmanufactured goods were permitted to enter British ports but they had to be carried, for the most part, in British ships. Similarly, British goods, such as rum, molasses, sugar, as well as manufactured goods, were carried to the United States in British vessels. At the end of the Confederation period three-fourths of the total American commerce was with Great Britain and most of this commerce was carried in British ships. Nine-tenths of all American imports, chiefly in the form of manufactured goods, came from Great Britain or its possessions. This condition was viewed with great displeasure by Americans, particularly by the manufacturers who found themselves unable to compete with the British, and by the shippers who viewed with jealous eyes the large number of British ships crowding the ports of the United States.

Availing themselves of a right conferred by the Articles of Confederation to impose "such imposts and duties on foreigners, as their own people are subjected to," various states passed laws imposing tariffs on British goods and tonnage duties on British ships. In some states British ships were prohibited from taking on board American goods. But these restrictions proved ineffectual for there was no uniformity in the action taken by the states. What one state did would be nullified by a jealous neighboring state.

John Adams persistently sought to negotiate a commercial treaty with Great Britain but without success. The British ministry, with irrefutable logic, pointed out that it would be useless to make a commercial treaty with the United States as long as the thirteen states had the power to impose trade restrictions as they saw fit.

The states could neither agree among themselves on a uniform policy of trade restriction nor were they willing to grant congress the power to pass navigation laws as a means of forcing from the British a favorable commercial treaty. On April 30, 1784, congress asked the states for authority for fifteen years to pass a navigation act prohibiting the importation or exportation of goods in ships owned or operated by subjects of countries with which the United States had no commercial treaty. The states received the request coldly and, after two and a half years, the proposed amendment remained unratified. In the fall of 1786 congress again appealed to the states for authority in the matter but to no avail. The northern commercial states were anxious for some action to be taken while the middle states were also favorable. But in the southern states the proposition to give congress the power to pass a navigation act was viewed with disfavor because of the fear that it would result in benefit only to northern commerce while southern interests would be injured.

Serious as were the commercial troubles, they constituted only one phase of the difficulties with Great Britain during the Confederation period. The treaty of 1783 had not specified the time for the withdrawal of British troops from American territory but had merely stated that it should take place "with all convenient speed." Years passed and still the British continued to occupy posts in the northwest, including Oswego, Niagara, and Detroit. While the motives of the British were obviously to maintain themselves in strategic positions for profitable participation in the fur trade and to establish an Indian buffer state between Canada and the United States, they presented other excuses for their failure to withdraw. They pointed out that the provision in the treaty which stated that no obstacles would be placed in the way of British merchants seeking to collect debts in the United States had not been lived up to. Furthermore they claimed rightly that the states had failed to make restitution to loyalists whose property had been confiscated though the treaty had stated that congress would recommend to the states that they make such restitution. In vain it was pointed out to the British that congress had agreed to do nothing more than "recommend," and that, therefore, the Confederation government should not be held responsible in the matter.

It was not until 1794, after the new Constitution had been put into effect, that John Jay succeeded in negotiating a treaty, settling, though in an unsatisfactory manner, the questions with Great Britain which the Confederation government had found itself utterly helpless to settle.

With Spain also serious diplomatic and commercial difficulties were experienced by the United States during the "critical period." That country persistently refused to negotiate a commercial treaty with the Confederation government nor would

it agree to a satisfactory settlement of other important questions. One of these had to do with the boundary between the
United States and West Florida. By the treaty of 1783 the
United States and Great Britain had agreed to fix the boundary
between the Mississippi and Apalachicola rivers at the thirty-
first parallel. However, in the secret preliminary treaty of 1782
there had been a provision to the effect that, if Great Britain
retained the Floridas, the boundary should be "a line drawn
from the mouth of the river Yassous, where it unites with the
Mississippi, due east, to the river Apalachicola," a line which
corresponded to 32° 28'. This had been the boundary fixed by
the British in 1767. But, when Spain made peace with Great
Britain in 1783, she received back the Floridas and immediately
set up a claim that West Florida should extend to 32° 28'. In
subsequent years the Indians from acknowledged Spanish territory raided American settlements in the disputed area and
even further north. The Spanish authorities made no attempt
to restrain or punish these Indians but, on the contrary, seem
to have encouraged their activities. The inability of congress to
settle the boundary question or to protect Americans in the
southwest stirred up considerable resentment and dissatisfaction.

Even more serious than the boundary question was the question of navigating the lower Mississippi. The treaty of 1783
between the United States and Great Britain had guaranteed
subjects of both countries the right to freely navigate that river.
But the Spanish claimed that, since they controlled both banks
of the lower part of the river, the British had no right to grant
anyone the privilege of navigating the lower part of that stream.
The treaty of 1763 ending the French and Indian War had
granted British subjects the right to navigate the Mississippi
but the Spanish declared that this right could not be transferred
by Great Britain.

In accordance with their views, the Spanish denied to Americans the right to navigate that part of the river which flowed
through their territory. This was a serious matter to the settlers
in the west who were forced to rely chiefly on water transportation to carry on trade. It was essential to their economic welfare
to be able to float their goods down the many streams of the

west to the Mississippi and then down that stream to New Orleans for reloading on ocean going vessels for shipment to the markets of eastern United States and elsewhere.

After Don Diego de Gardoqui arrived in Philadelphia in 1785 to serve as the Spanish *chargé d'affaires*, John Jay, the secretary for foreign affairs, entered into negotiations with him. His instructions from congress were to secure a settlement of the boundary and navigation questions in accordance with the American views. Gardoqui refused to recognize the validity of the American claims so Jay sought permission from congress to yield for twenty-five years the right to navigate the Mississippi and to leave the boundary question for future settlement in return for a favorable commercial treaty. The New England and the middle states favored Jay's proposal because they were more interested in commercial advantages than they were in the welfare of the southwest but the five southern states were opposed. Since the vote of nine states was required for the approval of a treaty the Jay proposals came to nothing. It was not until a decade later, after the government under the Constitution was well established, that the Treaty of San Lorenzo was negotiated with Spain. Though it granted commercial privileges and recognized the American claims regarding the West Florida boundary, it provided for only a temporary settlement of the question of navigating the Mississippi and of the "right of deposit," as the privilege of landing goods at New Orleans for reloading on ocean going vessels was called. Continued trouble over this last mentioned question eventually resulted, in 1803, in the purchase of the vast Louisiana territory which gave to this country the control of the entire Mississippi River.

Another obstacle to the free expansion of American commerce was the activity of Barbary pirates. For many years the countries of northern Africa, including Morocco, Algiers, Tunis, and Tripoli, had been preying on the ships of all nations in the Mediterranean Sea. Instead of taking united action to suppress these obnoxious pirates by force, the European countries, even those which were most powerful, had been content to pay tribute to the rulers of these corsairs in order that their merchant ships might be free from attack.

Before the Revolution, the ships of the American colonies

shared in the protection afforded by the payments made to these Barbary powers by Great Britain. As many as a hundred colonial vessels had engaged in the Mediterranean trade, carrying wheat, flour, rice, and dried fish to the ports there where good prices had been secured. But following the Revolution the colonies, having become independent states, found themselves deprived of the protection they had enjoyed as British dependencies.

John Adams and Thomas Jefferson attempted to negotiate a treaty with the Barbary powers but were told that it would cost about a million dollars to secure treaties with all four of them. As congress had no such sum available the negotiations made no progress. Finally, in 1787, on the payment of about ten thousand dollars, the United States succeeded in negotiating a treaty with Morocco. This failed to improve matters much since the other three powers continued to seize American vessels and to sell their crews into slavery. Since congress could neither buy them off nor suppress them by force, American commerce in the Mediterranean dwindled to practically nothing. After the Constitution had gone into effect and the national government had acquired means of raising money, treaties were negotiated, from 1795 to 1797, with Algiers, Tripoli, and Tunis. Still later, losing patience with the pirates, the United States resorted to force to compel the Barbary corsairs to respect the American flag. This was in sharp contrast with the helplessness displayed by the government under the Articles of Confederation.

In spite of all the obstacles and even though few commercial treaties were negotiated, it must not be supposed that American shipping interests were inactive. Yankee initiative soon discovered markets where trade could be carried on without the sanction of treaties. As early as 1784, for example, trade was begun with the Orient when a vessel, appropriately named the *Empress of China*, sailed from New York. Soon a profitable trade was developed with the Far East.

Even with European countries Americans found it possible to carry on some trade notwithstanding the absence of commercial treaties. Thus, in 1785, almost as many American vessels entered the port of Lisbon, Spain as entered from all the European countries.

INTERSTATE CONTROVERSIES

Another factor which caused dissatisfaction with the Confederation government was its inability to settle controversies between the states though the ninth of the Articles of Confederation stated that "The United States in Congress assembled shall also be the last resort on appeal in all disputes and differences now subsisting or that hereafter may arise between two or more States concerning boundary, jurisdiction or any other cause whatever."

The states, instead of coöperating with each other, were inclined to treat their neighbors like foreign countries. It was a common occurrence for states to impose tariffs and tonnage duties on the commerce of other states. A good example was the state of New York. The city of New York, then having a population of about thirty thousand, depended on Connecticut for its firewood and on the New Jersey farmers for its vegetables, poultry, butter, and cheese. Seeing in this trade an opportunity for revenue, New York, early in 1787, imposed tariff duties on the products of its neighbors just as though they were foreigners. New Jersey immediately retaliated by imposing a tax of eighteen hundred dollars annually on a lighthouse that New York had recently built on Sandy Hook. In Connecticut, a mass meeting of merchants was held and it was unanimously agreed to suspend all trade with New York.

It is true that, in 1782, the Confederation government, in accordance with the procedure described in the Articles of Confederation, did settle a dispute between Connecticut and Pennsylvania over the valley of Wyoming in favor of the latter. But a few years later attempts of Pennsylvanians to expel Connecticut citizens from the valley might have resulted in war between the two states had not the Pennsylvania legislature disavowed the action and ordered the payment of reparations to those who had been mistreated.

During the period of the Confederation, a four-cornered quarrel was carried on between Vermont, which wished to be a state but which was not recognized as such, and New York, New Hampshire, and Massachusetts, all of whom asserted their right to territory over which Vermont claimed jurisdiction. For a time it appeared that there would be a war involving at least Vermont, New York, and New Hampshire. The crisis was averted when George Washington, not congress, in 1784, persuaded the governor of Vermont to give up claims to territories which New Hampshire and New York asserted belonged to them. The difficulties in relation to Vermont were not finally settled until it was admitted to the union as a state shortly after the Constitution had gone into effect.

Another controversy that was ended satisfactorily through the efforts of the states concerned rather than through any action of congress was that between Maryland and Virginia. The former, claiming that its colonial charter had made the southern bank of the Potomac River instead of the middle of the river its southern boundary, proceeded to impose trade restrictions on Virginians using the river. Virginia, which controlled the entrance to Chesapeake Bay, retaliated by imposing duties on goods entering the bay destined for Maryland.

Before a crisis was reached in the relations of the two states it was decided, on the suggestion of James Madison, to hold a conference. Accordingly, on March 20, 1785, five commissioners, two chosen by the Virginia legislature and three by the Maryland legislature, met at Alexandria, Virginia. However, most of their eight day session was held at Mt. Vernon whence they were invited by George Washington who, as a planter forced to use the Potomac, was very anxious for a satisfactory settlement of the controversy. With good feeling promoted no doubt by Washington's hospitality, the commissioners had no difficulty in reaching an agreement for the joint use of the river by the two states.

The success of this Alexandria or Mt. Vernon convention soon led to the calling of another convention which, in turn, led directly to the calling of what became the Constitutional Convention. When the report of the commissioners was presented to the Maryland legislature that body not only approved the report but also recommended that Pennsylvania and Delaware be invited to a new convention to consider commercial questions. The Virginia legislature went even further. After approving the settlement which had been effected with Maryland, it voted to invite all of the states to send commissioners to Annapolis, Maryland, for a general meeting to consider commercial problems.

Though the meeting was called for the first Monday in September, 1786, it was not until the eleventh that the Annapolis convention began its session. Only twelve commissioners were present from five states, New York, New Jersey, Delaware, Pennsylvania, and Virginia. Four other states, New Hampshire, Massachusetts, Rhode Island, and North Carolina, appointed commissioners but they did not attend the convention. Among the prominent men present were James Madison and Edmund Randolph of Virginia, Alexander Hamilton of New York, and John Dickinson of Delaware who was chosen president of the convention. Because of the small number of states represented the convention made no attempt to discuss commercial difficulties. The main business accomplished was to adopt, on September 14, a report formulated by Hamilton and addressed to the legislatures of the five states represented.

This report called attention to the defects in the Confederation government "of a nature so serious, as, in the view of your commissioners, to render the situation of the United States delicate and critical, calling for an exertion of the united virtue and wisdom of all the members of the confederacy." Because of this condition the commissioners requested their legislatures to "use their endeavors" to secure the agreement of all of the states to send commissioners to Philadelphia on the second Monday of May, 1787, "to take into consideration the situation of the United States, to devise such further provisions as shall appear to them necessary to render the constitution of the federal government adequate to the exigencies of the Union," and to report their action to congress for ratification by that body after which it was to be sent to all of the state legislatures for confirmation. The report concluded with a statement that copies were to be sent "from motives of respect" to congress and to the executives of the states not represented at Annapolis.

It has been charged that certain men who were responsible for the Annapolis Trade Convention had no desire for their gathering to succeed in the purpose for which it was ostensibly called but, rather, that they were merely seeking an opportunity to secure the calling of a general convention to change the existing central government without the people generally becoming aware of their real intent. Such a charge was made by the French *chargé d'affaires* in a letter written to the French minister of foreign affairs shortly after the adjournment of the Annapolis convention. Whether or not the charge was true, there can be no doubt but that the propertied classes of the country were anxious for a stronger central government. This is revealed by the correspondence of such representative men as James Madison, Alexander Hamilton, George Washington, and others. After years of anxiety and misgivings these men were destined to see the realization of their hopes for, exactly one year after the Annapolis convention adjourned, a new Constitution was signed at Philadelphia.

SELECTED REFERENCES

Bancroft, George, *History of the United States,* Vol. VI, pp. 1–206.

Beard, C. A., *An Economic Interpretation of the Constitution of the United States,* pp. 52–63.

Beard, C. A., and Beard, M. R., *The Rise of American Civilization,* Vol. I, pp. 287–310.

Channing, Edward, *History of the United States,* Vol. III, pp. 463–491, 528–550.

Farrand, Max, *The Fathers of the Constitution,* pp. 1–107.

Faulkner, H. U., *American Economic History,* pp. 175–186.

Fiske, John, *The Critical Period of American History, 1783–1789,* pp. 101–222.

Frothingham, Richard, *Rise of the Republic of the United States,* pp. 569–584.

Gay, S. H., *James Madison,* pp. 76–87.

Greene, E. B., *The Foundations of American Nationality,* pp. 565–583.

Haines, B. M., and Haines, C. G., *The Constitution of the United States,* pp. 63–86.

Johnson, Allen, ed., *Readings in American Constitutional History 1776–1876,* pp. 74–99.

Landon, J. S., *The Constitutional History and Government of the United States,* pp. 65–81.

Latané, J. H., *A History of American Foreign Policy,* pp. 36–71.

Lodge, H. C., *George Washington,* Vol. II, pp. 1–29.

Long, Breckinridge, *Genesis of the Constitution of the United States of America,* pp. 197–212.

MacDonald, William, ed., *Documentary Source Book of American History 1606–1926,* pp. 195–216.

McLaughlin, A. C., *The Confederation and the Constitution 1783–1789,* pp. 3–183.

Morse, J. T., Jr., *John Adams*, pp. 226–240.

Morse, J. T., Jr., *Thomas Jefferson*, pp. 77–95.

Orth, S. P., and Cushman, R. E., *American National Government*, pp. 39–52.

Pease, T. C., and Roberts, A. S., eds., *Selected Readings in American History*, pp. 141–148, 163–179.

Preston, H. W., ed., *Documents Illustrative of American History 1606–1863*, pp. 218–250.

Schlesinger, A. M., *New Viewpoints in American History*, pp. 184–193.

Schuyler, R. L., *The Constitution of the United States*, pp. 36–84.

The Federalist (Everyman's Library edition of 1911), Nos. 15–22, pp. 66–110.

Warren, Charles, *The Making of the Constitution*, pp. 3–54.

Chapter Nine

THE FRAMING OF THE CONSTITUTION

THE CALLING AND ORGANIZATION OF THE CONVENTION

AT first the Confederation Congress demonstrated no willingness to call a convention as suggested by the Annapolis report. But a number of the states showed that they favored the proposition by proceeding to appoint delegates to attend such a convention. On December 4, 1786, Virginia chose seven delegates to go to Philadelphia while, by the middle of February, 1787, several other states had followed her example. Some states, including New York, instructed their delegates in congress to use their efforts to induce that body to call a convention.

Apparently convinced that a gathering to revise the Articles of Confederation would be held whether called by congress or not, that body finally yielded and, on February 21, 1787, adopted a resolution stating "That, in the opinion of Congress, it is expedient that, on the second Monday in May next, a convention of delegates, who shall have been appointed by the several states, be held at Philadelphia, for the sole and express purpose of revising the Articles of Confederation."

Following this action all the states which had not acted, with the exception of Rhode Island, proceeded to appoint delegates. Rhode Island, which was, at the time, under the control of the "paper money" party, had no desire for a stronger central government and so refused to coöperate with the other states in revising the Articles. In all of the other states the delegates were appointed by joint ballots of the legislatures with the exception, of course, of Georgia and Pennsylvania which had unicameral legislatures by which the delegates were chosen.

Charles A. Beard, in his very interesting *Economic Interpretation of the Constitution of the United States*, has pointed out that the business and propertied interests who wished to strengthen the central government insured their control of the convention by having the delegates chosen by the state legislatures. Because of the general prevalence of property qualifications for legislators, delegates chosen by them would be almost certain to have economic interests which would make them desire to strengthen the central government. Mr. Beard, after investigating each delegate who attended the convention, arrived at the following conclusions: Most of the delegates were lawyers and the majority came from towns near or on the coast. No delegate "in his immediate personal economic interests" was a representative of the mechanic or small farming class. On the contrary, at least five-sixths of those chosen to attend the convention "were immediately, directly, and personally interested in the outcome of their labors at Philadelphia, and were to a greater or less extent economic beneficiaries from the adoption of the Constitution." Seventy-four delegates were chosen but of these only fifty-five, at one time or another, attended the convention. Of these fifty-five, a total of forty were holders of public securities. Fourteen had invested in lands for speculative purposes; twenty-four possessed money loaned at interest; at least eleven were interested in the mercantile business, in manufacturing, and in shipping; while fifteen owned property in the form of slaves.

Because of the difficulties of travel and because of the delay in some cases in appointing delegates, a majority of the states were not represented at Philadelphia on May 14, the date set for beginning the convention. Therefore the members present adjourned from day to day until May 25 when twenty-nine delegates were assembled representing seven states. An organization was then perfected. On the motion of Robert Morris, George Washington was unanimously chosen president of the convention. William Jackson was elected secretary though he was not a delegate. It was decided that each state should be allowed one vote on all matters decided by the convention. It was also voted to maintain strict secrecy in regard to the convention and its work.

Before considering the work of the Constitutional Convention some attention should first be given to the personnel of that body. In such a small group—the average attendance was only thirty—the personality, character, and experience of the individual delegates were bound to be factors of unusual importance.

First and foremost among those present was George Washington of Virginia. He was one of the richest men in the country, but it was his great public services which had earned for him the universal respect and admiration of his countrymen. He had been a member of the First Continental Congress and had also served in the Second Continental Congress until he had been appointed commander-in-chief of the Continental army. It was largely the result of his genius that independence had been secured. One of his last acts as commander of the army had been, by personal intervention, to persuade his subordinate officers not to take any drastic action in relation to the Confederation Congress when it failed to make provision for their pay. After the Revolution, he had retired to his plantation home at Mt. Vernon. He continued, however, to be interested in public affairs and, as his correspondence reveals, was somewhat active in creating sentiment for a stronger government. As the presiding officer of the Constitutional Convention he could not, with propriety, take much part in the discussions. The debates show that he spoke only once and that was on the closing day.

Far more influential in the actual formulation of the new Constitution than Washington was James Madison, also from Virginia. He had a philosophical mind and was well read in political history. Many of the ideas which were finally incorporated in the Constitution were suggested by him. He was active in debate and when he spoke it was with clearness and logic. To the historian, Madison contributed a great service by keeping a private journal of the proceedings of the Convention. His record, which is much more complete and informative than the official journal kept by the secretary, was purchased, with other papers, by the national government after Madison's death and was first published in 1840. Since that time *Madison's Debates* have been made available in various editions. Prior to their publication only the meagre official proceedings, which had been published by order of Congress in 1819, were available. Because of the prominent part which Madison played in the Constitutional Convention some of his enthusiastic admirers have referred to him as "The Father of the Constitution." To bestow such a title on him is hardly fair for it detracts credit from other men who were also "Fathers of the Constitution."

Another member of the Virginia delegation, and its nominal head, was Governor Edmund Randolph. In private life he was a lawyer who enjoyed a lucrative practice. Since everything that he wished for was not incorporated in the Constitution he refused to sign it though later he actively worked for its ratification.

George Mason was another eminent Virginian present at the Philadelphia convention. He had been prominent in the drafting of the Virginia state constitution. In the Constitutional Convention he sought to have incorporated in the new Constitution a provision requiring property holding as a qualification for membership in the national legislature. Failing to gain this end, he refused to sign the completed Constitution and later opposed its ratification by Virginia.

Among the Pennsylvania delegates was the venerable Benjamin Franklin, then eighty-one years of age. He had been one of the signers of the Declaration of Independence; in fact, he had helped draft that document. With a great reputation in both America and Europe as a scientist, philosopher, and diplomat, he was naturally treated with great respect by the other delegates. He had little to do with the actual formulation of the Constitution, however. His chief part in the convention seems to have been as a peacemaker when it appeared that the delegates would not be able to agree on what should go into the document. Though he signed the Constitution he was known to be doubtful of its success.

Much more active in the convention was Franklin's colleague, James Wilson. He deserves to be ranked with Madison on the basis of actual influence on the completed Constitution. A brilliant lawyer, he had served in the Second Continental Congress and had been a signer of the Declaration of Independence. He had also served in the Confederation Congress.

Robert Morris, "the financier of the Revolution," the super-intendent of finance during the early part of the Confederation period, and a signer of the Declaration of Independence, was also present. He had little to do, however, with the drafting of the Constitution.

His relative, Gouverneur Morris, also from Pennsylvania, was on the contrary, one of the most active delegates in the Constitutional Convention. He had an extraordinary command of language and, in addition, was very clever and witty. Though he talked much, what he said did not carry the weight it might have had he been trusted more by his fellow delegates. The final wording of the Constitution was chiefly the work of Gouverneur Morris.

Thomas Mifflin, who had served in both the First and Second Continental Congresses and who, in 1783, had been president of the Confederation Congress, was also one of the Pennsylvania delegates to the Constitutional Convention. He played only a minor part, however, in the drafting of the Constitution.

From Massachusetts came "the handsome and charming Rufus King." He was a strong exponent of the doctrine of sep-aration of powers and he also believed in the principle of judicial control. Both King and his associate, Nathaniel Gorham, were members of the Confederation Congress. The latter had been president of the congress from June, 1786 to February, 1787. Incidentally, both King and Gorham had extensive mercantile interests.

Elbridge Gerry, who was also a merchant and who had served in the Confederation Congress in 1783–85, was another delegate from Massachusetts. He participated frequently in the debates of the convention. He took a strong stand against democracy, declaring that "The evils we experience flow from the excess of democracy." The Constitution as finally drafted failed to satisfy him so he refused to sign it.

Three outstanding delegates from Connecticut were William Samuel Johnson, Roger Sherman, and Oliver Ellsworth. Sher-man had served in the First and Second Continental Congresses and had signed the Declaration of Independence. All three had served in the Confederation Congress, Johnson being a member of that body at the time of the Constitutional Convention. These Connecticut delegates were fearful that a government would be established that would be too strong to work well so they employed their efforts to restrain those who were inclined to ignore the rights of individual states. Ellsworth and Johnson were lawyers while Sherman was engaged in business. The last named had, by his own efforts, risen from poverty to a comfortable state in life. He was one of the few self-made men who served in the Constitutional Convention.

New Hampshire was represented by John Langdon and Nicholas Gilman who were, at the time, members of the Confederation Congress. They did not attend the convention until it was more than half over.

The outstanding delegate from New York was Alexander Hamilton who had played such a prominent part in having the convention called. Though one of the ablest men in the convention he had but slight influence in the drafting of the Constitution. This was because of his aristocratic and even monarchial tendencies. The majority of the delegates were unwilling to support the extreme propositions which he presented to the convention. At first he was outvoted by his colleagues from New York, John Lansing and Robert Yates. When the convention was about half over they withdrew, thus depriving him of a vote since the instructions of the New York delegates required that a majority of them should decide the state's vote. Subsequently he also returned to New York but occasionally went back to Philadelphia. He was present on the last day and signed the Constitution, the only delegate from New York to do so.

Prominent in the New Jersey delegation was William Livingston, the first and only governor of the state from 1778 until his death in 1790. However, his fellow delegate, William Paterson, played a much more important part in framing the Constitution. He was a leading exponent of the small state views in the convention.

Important members of the Delaware delegation were George Read and John Dickinson. The former had served in both the First and Second Continental Congresses. The latter had been a member of all the important American congresses from the Stamp Act Congress to the Annapolis convention. He had written the *Farmer's Letters* in opposition to the Townshend acts. The Constitutional Convention represented his second experience in making a constitution for the United States, for he had been chairman of the committee which had framed the Articles of Confederation. In the convention of 1787 he demonstrated that he was not fully converted to the idea of a strong central government. He was not present on the last day of the convention but, nevertheless, signed the Constitution by proxy.

The most prominent delegate from Maryland was Luther Martin. He was a lawyer of high ability and, at the time of the convention, was the attorney general of his state. It was suspected that he had been sent to Philadelphia by certain interests to oppose the establishment of a strong government. This suspicion, coupled with the fact that he was a tiresome speaker, prevented him from having as much influence in the drafting of the Constitution as he might otherwise have had. He left the convention before it had completed its work.

From South Carolina came John Rutledge, a lawyer, who had served in the Stamp Act Congress, the two Continental Congresses, and the Confederation Congress, and who had been the first governor of his state. Another delegate from South Carolina was General Charles Cotesworth Pinckney of revolutionary fame. His cousin, Charles Pinckney, also represented South Carolina. The last named played a conspicuous part in the convention but did not influence the final draft of the Constitution as much as was once supposed.

Other delegates to the Constitutional Convention who might be mentioned were Hugh Williamson and William Blount of North Carolina; William Few, William Pierce, and Abraham Baldwin of Georgia; and Pierce Butler of South Carolina. All of these men except Williamson and Baldwin were members of the Confederation Congress at the time of the Constitutional Convention.

Taken altogether, the delegates to the Constitutional Convention were a notable group. They were in no sense "demigods" as Thomas Jefferson, with a touch of sarcasm, called them. But they were well equipped for the task of making a

Constitution for nearly all of them were well educated and well read, and, in addition, had enjoyed valuable experience in state and national affairs. Not all the outstanding men of the country were included in the convention, however. Among those missing were Jefferson and John Adams who were, at the time, ministers to France and Great Britain, respectively. Nor were such radicals as Samuel Adams or Patrick Henry present. The former was not elected as a delegate while the latter, though elected, declined to serve. Both were opponents of the proposition to establish a stronger central government. In the same category were Richard Henry Lee and James Monroe of Virginia, neither of whom was elected as a delegate. Nor was John Hancock elected a delegate. He was governor of Massachusetts at the time. Another man not elected to serve in the convention was John Jay of New York. From 1784 to 1789, he was secretary of foreign affairs under the Confederation Congress. John Marshall, later to become famous as Chief Justice of the United States, was another who was not elected as a delegate though he favored a stronger government. Others might be mentioned but the above list will suffice to show that there were other men in the country who had as much ability as those who were delegates. Nevertheless, the delegates to the Constitutional Convention were a fairly representative group.

Though most of the delegates, as has been pointed out, had certain economic interests to promote, it should not be supposed that they therefore acted with unanimity on all matters that came before the convention. Such was far from being the case. At almost every step conflicts of interest were apparent. An analysis of the debates of the convention reveals the existence of a variety of groups among the delegates. There were those who believed that the convention should confine itself to a revision of the Articles of Confederation. Opposed to them were the majority who felt that an entirely new Constitution should be adopted. Then there was the small state group opposed by the large state group. The nationalists, who wished to subordinate the states to the national government, were opposed by the federalists, meaning at that time those who wished to preserve the relation of the states and the central government much as it was under the Articles of Confederation. Other alignments which were apparent at different times were the north against the south, the free states versus the slave states, the old states against the new ones, the advocates of democracy against the aristocrats, and those who favored commercial interests in opposition to agricultural interests.

PLANS BEFORE THE CONVENTION

Though the sessions of the convention did not begin until some days after the scheduled date, the delegates who arrived early did not waste their time entirely. Even before the date set for assembling, Madison had been working on a plan of government. Early in April he had written to his fellow delegates from Virginia suggesting that they would be expected to make "some leading proposition" to the convention. He had then proceeded to outline views very similar to those contained in the Virginia plan later presented to the convention. It was Madison's idea that the best of the Articles of Confederation should be incorporated in a new Constitution which should provide for a three branch national government. He thought neither state independence nor consolidation of the states "into one simple republic" to be desirable but advocated taking a middle position "which will at once support a due supremacy of the national authority, and leave in force the local authorities so far as they can be subordinately useful."

After the Virginia delegates arrived in Philadelphia they held meetings daily. They also mingled with other delegates after their arrival in order to ascertain their views. In this way they were able to determine a course of procedure. It is therefore evident that the plan presented to the convention on May 29, 1787 by Governor Randolph was the work of the whole Virginia delegation based, however, largely on the proposals made by Madison. The plan is worthy of careful study because it was used as a basis for the convention's work and because it contained important ideas which were incorporated in the Constitution.

This plan, known variously as the Virginia, Randolph, or large state plan, was presented in the form of fifteen resolutions. Though the first resolution declared "that the articles of Confederation ought to be so corrected & enlarged as to accomplish the objects proposed by their institution," the form of government proposed in the remaining resolutions was entirely different from the Confederation government. In other words, the Virginia plan, while professing to revise the Articles of Confederation, proposed an entirely new Constitution.

Provision was made in this plan for a national legislature composed of two branches. The members of the "first branch" or lower house were to be elected by the people of the several states. The members of the "second branch" or upper house were to be elected by the lower house from a list of persons nominated by the individual state legislatures. Representation of each state in the national legislature, it was stated, "ought to be proportioned to the Quotas of contribution, or to the number of free inhabitants, as the one or the other rule may seem best in different cases." Members of both houses were to have definite terms and fixed salaries. Minimum age limits for members were also to be set.

Each branch of the legislature was to have the right to initiate legislation. All the powers vested in the Confederation Congress were to be transferred to the proposed national legislature which, in addition, was to have the right to legislate in all cases where "the separate States are incompetent, or in which the harmony of the United States may be interrupted by the exercise of individual Legislation." Furthermore, the national legislature was to have the power to veto state laws contrary to the national Constitution and it was also to be empowered to coerce any state which failed to "fulfill its duty" under the national Constitution.

There was to be a national executive but it was not stated whether it should be a single or a plural executive. The executive was to be chosen by the national legislature for a definite term of years and was to receive a fixed compensation. It was further proposed that the executive should not be eligible for more than one term. In the executive were to be vested all the executive "rights" exercised by the Confederation Congress and, in addition, "a general authority to execute the National laws."

The executive "and a convenient number" of the national

judiciary were to constitute "a council of revision" with power to examine every act of the national legislature before it became effective and to veto such acts if they saw fit. This council of revision was also to examine acts of state legislatures which had been negated by the national legislature and was empowered to reject the legislative veto. However, the national legislature could overcome the veto of the council of revision in each case by repassing the act or by again negating the state act.

A third distinct department of government was also outlined in the Virginia plan. There was to be a national judiciary consisting of "one or more supreme tribunals" and inferior courts. The judges of these courts were to be chosen by the national legislature. They were to hold office during good behavior and were to receive fixed salaries. The national courts were to have jurisdiction in cases involving piracies or felonies on the high seas, captures from an enemy, "cases in which foreigners or citizens of other states applying to such jurisdictions may be interested," cases arising out of the collection of the national revenue, impeachments of national officers, and all cases involving "the national peace and harmony."

Other provisions in the Virginia plan called for the admission of new states, for a guarantee by the United States of a republican form of government for each state, for the amendment of the new "Articles of Union" without the consent of the national legislature being required, and for state officials to be bound by oath to support "the articles of Union."

After making these drastic proposals, the plan closed by ingenuously stating that "the amendments which shall be offered to the Confederation" by the convention should, after approval by congress be sent to the states for ratification by conventions chosen by the people after the respective state legislatures had recommended that such conventions should be called.

Another plan, apparently quite similar to the Virginia plan, was submitted to the convention by Charles Pinckney of South Carolina, also on May 29. However, it was not considered by the convention but was used by the committee of detail, as will be mentioned later. Nothing was heard of the Pinckney plan outside of the convention until its *Journal* was published in

1819. At that time, Secretary of State John Q. Adams wrote to Pinckney asking for a copy of his plan to be included in the publication. Pinckney sent a copy of what he thought was his plan. He stated that he had among his papers several drafts of the plan which he had submitted to the convention and he was not certain of the exact form of his original proposals.

After the publication of the *Journal,* including what purported to be the Pinckney plan, Madison, in private correspondence, declared that the plan published was not in harmony with his records. But his views were not made public and the plan as published was accepted as authentic. Curiously enough, when Madison's papers were first published after his death, the editor, failing to note the criticisms which his subject had made of the alleged Pinckney plan, borrowed the plan as published in the *Journal* and included it in Madison's notes on the debates of the Constitutional Convention. This, of course, gave added validity to the plan and caused many persons to acclaim Pinckney as the real father of the Constitution. In recent years, scholars, including John Franklin Jameson, Andrew Cunningham McLaughlin, and Max Farrand, have demonstrated that what was published as the Pinckney plan was in reality a copy of an advance draft of the Constitution prepared by the committee of detail. This accounts for its similarity to the completed Constitution.

A third plan, drawn up by a committee representing the small states, was presented to the convention by William Paterson of New Jersey on June 15. It is variously referred to as the Paterson, New Jersey, or small state plan. The plan was presented in the form of nine resolutions. Instead of discarding entirely the existing machinery of government as proposed by the Virginia plan, the Paterson resolutions merely suggested "that the articles of Confederation ought to be so revised, corrected & enlarged, as to render the federal Constitution adequate to the exigencies of Government, & the preservation of the Union." Specifically, it was proposed that the powers of congress should be enlarged so as to permit that body to pass acts for raising revenue through duties on imports, through certain stamp taxes, and through charges for postage on letters and packages. Congress was also to have the power to pass acts for the regulation of interstate and foreign commerce. However, punishment for violation of commercial regulations was to be imposed by the state courts in the state where the violation took place though appeal could be made from the state courts to the judiciary of the United States. Congress was to be authorized to make requisitions on the states in proportion to their population, counting only three-fifths of the slaves. If a state failed to pay its requisitions within a specified time, congress was to have power to pass an act authorizing and directing the collection of the requested amount in the non-complying state.

There was included a proposal for a plural executive to be elected by congress. The persons making up this executive department were to serve for definite terms and were to receive fixed salaries. They were to be ineligible for reëlection and were to be removable by congress on application by a majority of the state executives. The proposed federal executives were to execute acts passed by congress, to appoint federal officers not otherwise provided for, and to direct all military operations though none of them were to be in active command of troops.

In the New Jersey plan it was further proposed that there should be a federal judiciary consisting of "a supreme Tribunal." The judges were to be appointed by the executive. They were to serve during good behavior and were to receive fixed salaries. This federal tribunal was to conduct all impeachment trials of federal officers. It was also to be the last court of appeal in all cases having to do with the rights of ambassadors, captures from an enemy, piracies and felonies on the high seas, all cases involving foreigners, all cases involving the construction of treaties, and, finally, all cases arising out of acts passed by congress for the purpose of regulating trade or collecting revenue.

All acts passed by congress in accordance with its old or revised powers and all treaties of the United States were to "be the supreme law of the respective States so far forth as those Acts or Treaties shall relate to the said States or their Citizens." The state courts were to be bound by these acts and treaties anything in the state laws to the contrary notwithstanding. In case either states or individuals opposed the execution of federal laws or treaties the federal executive was to be authorized "to call forth ye power of the Confederate States" to compel obedience to the acts or observance of the treaties.

The New Jersey plan concluded with resolutions calling for the admission of new states, for a uniform rule of naturalization in all of the states, and for holding citizens of a state committing an offense in another state responsible on the same basis as if they were citizens of that state.

Obviously, the adoption of the New Jersey plan would have made a vast improvement in the Articles of Confederation. A comparison of the plan with the completed Constitution reveals that some of its provisions found a place, though in modified form, in the completed document. But in spite of all of the improvements and additional powers which it proposed the New Jersey plan differed in one fundamental respect from the Virginia plan and that was in regard to the legislative branch of the government. Under the former plan the small states would retain their equality with the large states while under the Virginia plan the large states would control the national legislature. The adjustment of this difference in point of view between the large and small states has generally been regarded as the outstanding accomplishment of the Constitutional Convention.

A fourth plan was presented to the convention by Alexander Hamilton on June 18. On that date he made a long speech, occupying five or six hours, in the course of which he outlined a plan which contained eleven articles. He proposed that there should be a bicameral legislature with the lower house called the assembly and the upper house called the senate. The members of the assembly were to be chosen for three years while the members of the senate were to be chosen for life terms by electors who had, in turn, been chosen by the people. The senate was to have power to declare war. It was also to approve or reject all appointments of officers except the heads of the departments of foreign affairs, war, and finance.

There was to be a supreme executive called the governor. He likewise was to be chosen for a life term by electors. This executive was to have not only the power to negate laws about to be passed but also the right to negate the execution of all laws already passed.

A national judiciary was to be established with judges who were to hold office for life. The national legislature was to have power to establish courts in each of the states to deal with "all matters of general concern." State laws contrary to the Constitution or laws of the United States were to be void. To more effectively prevent such laws from being passed, the state executives were to be appointed by the general government and each state executive was to "have a negative upon the laws about to be passed in the State."

Hamilton's plan was so extreme in its proposals that it received little consideration in the convention. Even those who wished for a strong central government were not willing to go as far as Hamilton. The government which he advocated was far too aristocratic and even monarchistic in its form and powers to be received with favor by the delegates. In only a few particulars is it possible to trace similarity between Hamilton's plan and the completed Constitution.

DEBATE AND COMPROMISE

Early in the convention's session, Edmund Randolph presented three resolutions embodying the basic ideas of the Virginia plan. The third and most important of these stated "that a *national* Government ought to be established consisting of a supreme Legislative, Executive and Judiciary." After some debate the resolution was adopted. This showed that the delegates from most of the states were desirous, not of revising the Articles of Confederation in accordance with the call for the convention and with the instructions from their home legislatures, but of adopting a new frame of government. Only Connecticut opposed the resolution while New York lost its vote on the question because its delegation was divided.

Though the decision to establish a "national" government was reached rather easily it proved anything but easy to work out the details regarding its form and powers. During the early days of the convention, before Paterson introduced his resolutions, the Virginia plan served as the chief basis for the debates. It was considered in committee of the whole and by June 5 a considerable portion of it had been accepted by the committee. It was agreed, in general terms, that there should be national legislative, executive, and judiciary departments. It was further agreed that the legislature should consist of two houses. Then the real troubles of the convention began. At first it was decided that the lower house should be popularly elected as provided by the Virginia plan. The "second branch," it was decided, in accordance with the wishes of John Dickinson, should be chosen by the state legislatures.

The small states were far from being satisfied with the first tentative settlement of the question of representation. They objected to what was called "proportional" representation as they wished to retain their equal voting power in the national legislature. Representatives of these states secured a reconsideration of the question and soon the delegates were engaged in earnest debate. After the debate was over votes were taken on June 11 which revealed seven states in favor and three opposed to proportional representation in the lower house and six in favor and five opposed to proportional representation in the upper house. Though temporarily defeated, small state leaders were determined not to yield the principle of equal representation, at least in the upper house.

There the matter stood when the committee of the whole ended its deliberations. On June 13, this committee presented to the convention a report consisting of nineteen resolutions based on the Virginia plan. In fact practically everything that had been proposed in that plan had been accepted by the committee except the idea of coercion of the states by the national government.

Before consideration of the report began, William Paterson asked for time to prepare a new plan for presentation to the convention. Shortly afterwards, on June 15, he laid before the delegates the New Jersey plan, previously described. This plan and the Virginia plan were then referred to the committee of the whole and were there debated for several days. Paterson was the chief spokesman on behalf of the plan which he had presented. He stressed the fact that the delegates had no authority to do more than revise the Articles of Confederation. He dwelt much on the idea of equal sovereignty as established by the Articles and expressed the opinion that, if the states gave up their sovereignty, it would mean their extinction. Randolph, defending his plan, took the view that the delegates did not have to adhere to the letter of their instructions. "When the Salvation of the Republic was at stake, it would be treason to our trust," he declared, "not to propose what we found necessary."

It was during this debate that Hamilton introduced his plan for a new government. He rejected the New Jersey plan as entirely unsatisfactory and also took the view that it would be difficult to establish a satisfactory government on the Virginia plan. He presented his own plan, previously outlined, as superior to both. However, he failed to turn the course of the debate away from the Paterson and Virginia plans. Finally, on June 19, a vote was taken which resulted seven to three in favor of adhering to the plan which had been presented to the convention by Randolph. Only New Jersey, Delaware, and New York favored the Paterson or New Jersey plan while the vote of Maryland was divided. The New Hampshire delegates had not yet arrived at the convention—in fact, they did not arrive until about the end of July.

Following this vote in the committee of the whole, the convention began its delayed consideration of the report on the Virginia plan. Item by item it was taken up and debated anew. On June 20, it was voted unanimously to omit the word "national" from the plan. Since the advocates of a "national" government had demonstrated that they were in control of the convention the vote cannot be interpreted to mean that the idea of a government supreme over the states was given up. When the resolution providing for a two branch legislature was brought to a vote it carried by a seven to three vote with Maryland again divided.

Close to the end of June the convention began a consideration of the resolution providing for proportional representation in the legislature. In opposition to it the small state dele-

gates took a determined stand. The debates became so heated
that Franklin proposed that the daily sessions of the convention should be opened with prayer "imploring the assistance
of Heaven." The proposal was not adopted because some
of the delegates feared that such action would arouse suspicion among outsiders that there was dissension in the convention.

On June 29 a vote was taken on the question of proportional representation in the first branch of the legislature and
it was carried, six states to four. Delaware, New Jersey, New
York, and Connecticut were opposed while again the vote of
Maryland was divided. Then the debate continued over the
question of representation in the second branch. Ellsworth, on
behalf of the Connecticut delegation, demanded that the states
should be equally represented in this house. In vain Madison
and others argued that the small states had nothing to fear from
the large states. When the vote was taken on July 2, five states
favored proportional representation while five favored equal
representation in the senate. Georgia's vote was divided.

The delegates were unwilling to see the convention broken
up by a deadlock on this question so, on motion of General
C. C. Pinckney, a grand committee was elected consisting of
one delegate from each state. The committee included at least
six advocates of equal representation in the upper house. They
were Oliver Ellsworth of Connecticut, Robert Yates of New
York, William Paterson of New Jersey, Gunning Bedford of
Delaware, Luther Martin of Maryland, and Abraham Baldwin
of Georgia. The remaining five were by no means the strongest
advocates of the large state view that could have been chosen.
Massachusetts was represented by Elbridge Gerry, Pennsylvania by Benjamin Franklin, Virginia by George Mason, North
Carolina by William R. Davie, and South Carolina by John
Rutledge.

After assembling and choosing Gerry as their chairman, the
committee went over the arguments that had been presented
in the convention on the question of representation. Finally, on
the motion of Franklin, a report was adopted which recommended that, in the first branch of the legislature, each state
should have one member for every forty thousand inhabitants

with each state allowed at least one member. All bills for raising or appropriating money were to originate in this branch and were not to be amended by the second branch. In the second branch each state was to have an equal vote.

On July 5, this report was presented to the convention. It was immediately attacked by the more ardent of the advocates of the large state view but their opposition to the compromise as proposed proved futile. On July 16, by a vote of five to four, the convention accepted what has since been called "The Great Compromise." North Carolina deserted the large state ranks and voted for it while Maryland, Delaware, New Jersey, and Connecticut also supported it. Georgia, South Carolina, Virginia, and Pennsylvania were the states opposed. The Massachusetts vote was divided; the New York delegates had left the convention; and the New Hampshire delegates had not yet arrived. Though disappointed at the result, the large state men made no move to reverse the decision or to break up the convention.

As the convention proceeded with its work it gradually added to the list of resolutions originally presented. The Virginia plan, beginning with fifteen resolutions, had grown to nineteen when it emerged from the committee of the whole on June 13. By July 26, the number of resolutions had increased to twenty-three.

Feeling that the propositions before them needed to be clarified and systematized, the delegates decided to elect a committee of detail consisting of five members to redraft the resolutions. The convention then adjourned from July 26 to August 6 to give the committee time to perform its task. The five committeemen were among the most capable men in the convention. Four of them were lawyers. John Rutledge was chosen chairman of the committee, the other members of which were Edmund Randolph, Nathaniel Gorham, Oliver Ellsworth, and James Wilson.

By diligent effort the committee was able to accomplish the task assigned in the ten day period allowed. Not only did they take into consideration the twenty-three resolutions based on the Virginia plan and the great compromise but they also drew ideas and phraseology from the New Jersey and Pinckney plans, from the Articles of Confederation, and from the state constitutions.

On August 6, the committee of detail presented its report to the convention in the form of twenty-three compact articles. Then for five weeks, working six hours a day in spite of the intense heat of what was described as a very hot summer even for Philadelphia, the delegates examined and discussed the document very fully. Every word was scrutinized and numerous changes were made.

Having decided on the form of the national legislature, the convention was confronted with the necessity of definitely defining its powers. The Virginia plan had proposed that the legislature should be given the legislative rights enjoyed by the Confederation Congress and, in addition, the power "to legislate in all cases to which the separate States are incompetent." This, the delegates decided, was too general so it was finally agreed to delegate to the Congress of the United States, as the legislature was to be called, certain distinct powers.

It was also necessary to decide on a basis for representation in the lower house. Representation was to be based on the population of the individual states according to the great compromise but the question of whether or not slaves should be counted remained to be settled. The southern states wished to count the slaves but the northern states opposed this. The same question of counting the slaves again came up in connection with a proposal to give Congress the power to levy direct taxes on the states in proportion to their population. In this connection the southern states naturally were opposed to counting the slaves. An agreement was finally reached whereby only three-fifths of the slaves were to be counted in computing the population for the purposes of representation and direct taxation. Earlier writers on the subject stressed this agreement as one of the important compromises devised by the convention but more recent investigators have pointed out that the settlement was effected by applying a principle that had been included in a proposed amendment to the Articles of Confederation that had been discussed in congress in 1783.

The convention was agreed that the new Congress should be given the power to regulate commerce. The experiences of the "critical period" had demonstrated clearly the necessity of such regulation. However, some of the delegates insisted that some limitations should be placed on the power to regulate. While a number of delegates, including some from the south, were outspoken in their denunciations of slavery others declared that Congress should not be given the power to prohibit the importation of slaves. A number of southerners also expressed the fear that their export trade would be ruined unless Congress was forbidden to impose export taxes. An agreement was finally reached whereby Congress was given the power to regulate foreign and interstate commerce and trade with the Indian tribes with the provisos that it could not prohibit the importation of slaves prior to 1808 and that no export duties should be levied. No tax exceeding ten dollars a head was to be levied on imported slaves. In the completed Constitution the power to regulate commerce was further qualified by provisions that "No preference shall be given by any regulation of commerce or revenue to the ports of one State over those of another: nor shall vessels bound to, or from, one State, be obliged to enter, clear, or pay duties in another."

To reach an agreement regarding the national executive proved to be a very difficult matter. The subject, as Max Farrand has pointed out, was discussed on twenty-one different days and thirty separate votes were taken on the method of electing the executive. Among the proposals considered were popular election, election by congress, and election by electors chosen by the state legislatures. A compromise was reached early in September whereby the president, as it had been decided to call the executive, and also a vice president, were to be chosen by electors appointed in each state in such manner as the legislature of the state should decide. The number of electors was to be equal to the number of the state's senators and representatives in Congress.

The question of the length of the term of the executive also proved perplexing. Proposals ranged all the way up to a life term. At one time the convention favored a seven year term with the proviso that the executive should be ineligible for reëlection. The compromise on this matter was that the term should be four years with no limit placed on the number of

terms a president could serve. Custom, however, has entered
in to fix two terms as the maximum length of service. Extraordinary powers, far greater than those which had been given
the state executives, were given the president. However, as
will be made clear, he was to be held in check in various ways.

Concerning a national judiciary, the convention was far less
definite than it was in the case of the legislative and executive
departments. Provision was made for a Supreme Court to be
established by Congress. Inferior courts could also be established
by Congress if that body saw fit. The judicial power was defined
in broad terms but nowhere was it stated that the United States
courts should have the power to pass on the constitutionality
of laws. But the debates of the convention indicate that leading delegates, such as King, Gerry, Wilson, Gouverneur Morris,
Madison, Mason, and Martin, expected this power to be exercised by the courts nevertheless.

So far stress has been laid on the disagreements of the delegates and the consequent necessity of numerous compromises.
But, as a recent writer on the subject, R. L. Schuyler, has
pointed out, the agreements of the convention were more significant than the disputes. For instance, there was little controversy over the proposition to set up a three branch
government, featured by the separation of powers, and endowed
with power to raise revenues and to regulate commerce. The
disputations arose over ways and means to give effect to the
wishes of the majority. There were delegates who earnestly
sought to change words, phrases, or clauses yet these same
delegates were, for the most part, in complete harmony with
the chief purposes of the convention.

Towards the last, the delegates showed signs of weariness
from their long and intensive labors and consequently there
was a tendency to abruptly reject proposals for minor changes.
Shortly after the questions in relation to the presidency had
been settled the majority decided that the Constitution was
ready to be given its final form. Accordingly, on September 8,
a committee on style, consisting of five members, was appointed.
The five were William Samuel Johnson, Rufus King, James
Madison, Alexander Hamilton (who had returned to the con-

vention), and Gouverneur Morris. The credit for the final wording of the Constitution must be chiefly given to the last named.

On the twelfth of September, the committee on style made its report. After a delay of one day for the printing of the document, three days were spent in carefully going over it and making final minor changes. Then the Constitution was ordered to be engrossed and, on Monday, September 17, was presented to the convention for the signatures of the delegates. Because some members had declared that they would not sign the document, Gouverneur Morris devised a form that would give at least the appearance of unanimity, as follows, "Done in Convention by the Unanimous Consent of the States present. . . . In Witness whereof We have hereunto subscribed our Names." Morris then induced Benjamin Franklin to move the adoption of this form and to support it with a speech.

In this notable address, which was read by his colleague, James Wilson, the venerable statesman said, "I confess that there are several parts of this Constitution which I do not at present approve, but I am not sure I shall never approve them. For having lived long, I have experienced many instances of being obliged by better information or fuller consideration, to change opinions even on important subjects, which I once thought right, but found to be otherwise. It is therefore that, the older I grow, the more apt I am to doubt my own judgment, and to pay more respect to the judgment of others. . . . In these sentiments, Sir, I agree to this Constitution, with all its faults, if they are such; because I think a general government necessary for us. . . . I doubt too whether any other convention we can obtain may be able to make a better Constitution."

Franklin went on to say that he was astonished to find the Constitution "approaching so near to perfection as it does; and I think it will astonish our enemies, who are waiting with confidence to hear that our councils are confounded, like those of the Builders of Babel; and that our States are on the point of separation, only to meet hereafter for the purpose of cutting one another's throats. Thus I consent, sir, to this Constitution because I expect no better, and because I am not sure that it is not the best. The opinions I have had of its errors I sacrifice to the public good."

In closing, Dr. Franklin said, "On the whole, Sir, I cannot help expressing a wish that every member of the convention who may still have objections to it, would with me, on this occasion, doubt a little of his own infallibility—and to make manifest our unanimity, put his name to this instrument."

Then, at the last moment, Nathaniel Gorham of Massachusetts suggested that the Constitution would be more acceptable to the people if the number of members in the lower house of Congress were increased. Washington, in the only speech which he made in the convention, supported the proposal and a change was quickly adopted and approved by the delegates whereby one representative would be allowed for each thirty thousand of the population instead of for every forty thousand.

A vote was then taken on the Constitution as finally engrossed and it was unanimously approved by the states represented. Thirty-eight delegates personally signed the document while John Dickinson, who was absent, signed it by proxy. Three delegates, Edmund Randolph, George Mason, and Elbridge Gerry, refused to sign.

While the signing was going on, there took place an incident which was recorded by Madison and which, though often repeated, may well be recounted once more. "Whilst the last members were signing it Doctor Franklin looking towards the President's chair, at the back of which a rising sun happened to be painted, observed to a few members near him, that painters had found it difficult to distinguish in their art a rising from a setting sun. 'I have,' said he, 'often and often in the course of the session, and the vicissitudes of my hopes and fears as to its issue, looked at that behind the President without being able to tell whether it was rising or setting. But now at length I have the happiness to know that it is a rising and not a setting sun.' "

THE COMPLETED CONSTITUTION

The Constitution, as finally adopted, consisted of a preamble and seven articles. Though the whole document contains only about four thousand words and can be read aloud in twenty-three minutes, yet, to quote James B. Bryce, the English statesman who published in 1888 *The American Commonwealth*, "History knows few instruments which in so few words lay down equally momentous rules on a vast range of matters of the highest importance and complexity."

In the preamble the purposes of the Constitution were stated. It read as follows, "WE THE PEOPLE of the United States, in Order to form a more perfect Union, establish Justice, insure domestic Tranquillity, provide for the common defence, promote the general Welfare, and secure the Blessings of Liberty to ourselves and our Posterity, do ordain and establish this CONSTITUTION for the United States of America."

The expression "WE THE PEOPLE of the United States" was destined in later years to be the cause of considerable controversy, especially in the years before the Civil War when the states rights controversy was being hotly waged. The southerners took the view that the Constitution was a compact of the states; northerners, including the great champion of the union, Daniel Webster, insisted that the expression in the preamble proved that it was a compact of the people of the whole country and that it therefore could not be broken by the action of a state. As a matter of fact, in the earlier drafts of the Constitution each state was mentioned in a statement beginning "We the people of the states of . . . " In view of the fact that Rhode Island was not represented in the convention and because it was feared some of the states would not ratify the document, the final draft was changed by omitting mention of the individual states.

Almost one-half of the Constitution is included in the first article which deals with the legislative branch of the government. This article definitely provided for a "Congress of the United States" to consist of a lower house called the House of Representatives and an upper house called the Senate. A representative was required to be at least twenty-five years of age, seven years a citizen of the United States, and an inhabitant, when elected, of the state from which he was chosen. Representatives were to be elected every two years by the qualified voters of the states and were to be apportioned among the states in accordance with the spirit of the "great compromise." Each decade a census was to be taken for the purpose of determining the population of each state and thus afford a basis for a new apportionment. Pending the taking of the first census each state was assigned a definite number of representatives, making a total of sixty-five for the first Congress. However, a lesser number participated in the organization of the first House of Representatives in 1789 since Rhode Island and North Carolina had not yet ratified the Constitution.

Because of the rapid increase in population the size of the House grew until, after the reapportionment based on the 1910 census, the number of representatives reached four hundred and thirty-five. This large and unwieldy number was attained in spite of congressional acts which drastically increased the number of people required for each representative. After the 1920 census no reapportionment was made in spite of the constitutional requirement. After the 1930 census a reapportionment was made which, by considerably increasing the number of people required for each representative, kept the total number at four hundred and thirty-five. The number of persons required for each representative is now 282,974 compared with 30,000 when the Constitution became effective.

The Constitution, as has been made clear, provided for two senators from each state. The original Senate of twenty-two members has been expanded to ninety-six by the admission of new states to the union. The senators were to be elected by the state legislatures, a provision recently changed by the seventeenth amendment which provides for election by the people of the states. After the first election the senators were to be divided into three classes so that the terms of one-third of them would expire every two years. A senator was to be at least thirty years of age, nine years a citizen of the United States, and a resident of the state from which he was elected.

Each house was made the sole judge of the elections and qualifications of its members and each, by a two-thirds vote, could expel members. Each house could determine its own procedure and no restriction was placed on either house in the matter of organization other than the requirement that the House should elect a speaker and that the vice president of the

United States should preside over the Senate. Members of
Congress were to receive salaries fixed by law and paid out of
the United States treasury, an important change from the
Confederation procedure. Freedom of speech and freedom from
arrest while going to or from, or while attending Congress, were
guaranteed representatives and senators with stated exceptions.

Besides being granted all the legislative powers which had
been enjoyed by the Confederation Congress, Congress was
also granted extremely important new powers. Altogether,
eighteen powers, new and old, were enumerated. First among
the new ones was the "Power to lay and collect Taxes, Duties,
Imposts and Excises, to pay the Debts and provide for the
common Defence and general Welfare of the United States."
This is the famous "elastic clause" which has permitted the
passage of numerous acts by which the Constitution has been
greatly expanded. Hardly less important was the power to
regulate foreign and interstate commerce. Other new powers
included the right to pass patent and copyright laws, to punish
counterfeiting of United States coins or securities, to pass
naturalization acts, to enact uniform bankruptcy laws, to create
inferior courts, and to exercise exclusive jurisdiction over
property belonging to the national government. Furthermore,
Congress was to provide "for organizing, arming, and disciplining the Militia" and was to have the power to call out the
militia "to execute the Laws of the Union, suppress Insurrections and repel invasions." In addition to the old power to
raise troops, Congress was empowered to "support Armies"
though no appropriation for the purpose was to be made for
a longer period than two years. Finally came the "implied
powers" clause which has also been of great importance in
promoting expansion of the Constitution through acts of
Congress. Following the enumeration of the powers of Congress
the Constitution sets forth certain limitations on both Congress
and the states.

The second article, dealing with the executive department,
prescribes the term of the president and vice president and
their method of election as finally decided by the convention.
It should be mentioned that some change was later made in
the method of election by the twelfth amendment. Both the

president and vice president must be at least thirty-five years of age, natural born citizens of the United States, and fourteen years resident within the United States.

Important powers were granted to the president by the Constitution. He was to have the power to make appointments and treaties with the "Advice and Consent" of the Senate. He was to be commander-in-chief of the army and the navy. He could grant reprieves and pardons for all offences against the United States except in impeachment cases. He could influence legislature through messages to Congress and through the exercise of a veto. Above all he was to execute the laws of the United States. To prevent him from misconducting himself or usurping power, it was provided that he, as well as all civil officers of the United States, might be removed from office by "Impeachment for, and Conviction of, Treason, Bribery, or other high Crimes and Misdemeanors." Impeachment proceedings were to be instituted by the House of Representatives and the trials were to be conducted by the Senate.

In creating the office of president, the framers of the Constitution made an outstanding contribution to the science of government. No such office had ever been created before for it was modelled after neither the governorships nor the kingships of the past. A distinct "presidential system" of government was inaugurated by the Constitution. It and the cabinet system of Great Britain have been the chief models for popular governments of modern times.

Provision was made in the third article for the judiciary. As has been mentioned, the framers of the Constitution went no further than to state that there should be a Supreme Court and such inferior courts as Congress "may from time to time ordain and establish." The judicial power of the United States courts was to "extend to all Cases, in Law and Equity, arising under this Constitution, the Laws of the United States, and Treaties made, or which shall be made, under their Authority." The jurisdiction of the courts was also to extend to cases affecting ambassadors, public ministers, or consuls; to admiralty cases; to controversies "to which the United States shall be a Party"; to controversies between two or more states (thus affording a means of settling disputes such as had been so troublesome during the Confederation period); to cases involving a state and citizens of another state or citizens of different states; to cases where citizens of the same state claimed land under grants from different states; and, finally, to cases involving a state or its citizens and foreign states or their subjects. The eleventh amendment later removed from the United States courts jurisdiction over cases involving a state and citizens of another state or of a foreign country.

In only two types of cases was the Supreme Court to have original jurisdiction—in cases affecting ambassadors, public ministers, or consuls, and in cases in which a state shall be a party. To prevent any abuse in the matter this article also defined treason.

The fourth article contained a number of important miscellaneous provisions such as that for the admission of new states and that guaranteeing to every state a republican form of government. In the fifth article were set forth the methods by which the Constitution might be amended. This will be considered in detail later.

Three unrelated provisions were included in the sixth article. The first of these, inserted for the benefit of the holders of government securities, stated that all debts of the Confederation government should be valid against the United States under the Constitution. Another provision required both state and national officers to be bound by oath or affirmation to support the Constitution of the United States. The other provision, which embodies the compromise of the convention on the proposal to give the national government power to coerce the states, is so important that it deserves to be quoted in full, as follows, "This Constitution, and the Laws of the United States which shall be made in Pursuance thereof; and all Treaties made, or which shall be made, under the Authority of the United States, shall be the supreme Law of the Land; and the Judges in every State shall be bound thereby, any Thing in the Constitution or Laws of any State to the Contrary notwithstanding."

The seventh and last article of the Constitution contained

the "schedule," that is, the provision for putting the document into effect. Ratification by conventions in nine states was to make the Constitution effective for those states.

Before bringing to a close this consideration of the completed Constitution mention, at least, should be made of the important principles embodied in it. Some of these principles have been made apparent by the above analysis of the document. Among these principles is that known as "federal dualism," whereby a strong central government exists which is supreme in its own field while, at the same time, there exist states supreme in their own affairs. Under this dual system there are certain powers delegated to the central government and other powers reserved to the states. In some respects the central and state governments exercise concurrent powers while other powers are prohibited to either or both.

There are those who contend that the Constitution recognizes the sovereignty of the people. One of the chief arguments in support of this is the language of the preamble which, however, is misleading, as has been pointed out. Accepting the general principle of popular sovereignty, one does not have to admit that the Constitution is based upon it. As history has demonstrated, there is plenty of room for disagreement on the question. The states rights advocates can build a very plausible case for their viewpoint by showing that it is the states that rest on popular sovereignty and that the Constitution was the creation of the states. The proponents of the national viewpoint can present just as plausible arguments on their side. The tendency, historically, has been for the central government to rest more and more on the will of the people expressed directly rather than through state governments. Direct election of United States senators is an illustration of this.

While there was little of democracy in the original Constitution, there was in the document a definite recognition of the principle of representative government or what the members of the Constitutional Convention called republican government.

The principle of the supremacy of the national Constitution, laws, and treaties has been made clear by the analysis of the sixth article of the Constitution. Mention has also been made of the principles of separation of powers and the principle of checks and balances. Another principle that is obvious is that the government is limited in its powers. The limitations placed on the government by the Constitution and its first ten amendments were chiefly intended to safeguard the liberties of the people. Finally, the principle of an independent judiciary with the implied if not expressed power of judicial review was included in the original Constitution.

SELECTED REFERENCES

Beard, C. A., *An Economic Interpretation of the Constitution of the United States*, pp. 64–216.
Beard, C. A., *Readings in American Government and Politics*, pp. 38–53.
Beck, J. M., *The Constitution of the United States*, pp. 52–172, 198–244.
Chandler, J. A. C., *Genesis and Birth of the Federal Constitution*, pp. 267–300.
Channing, Edward, *History of the United States*, Vol. III, pp. 494–516.
Farrand, Max, *The Fathers of the Constitution*, pp. 108–142.
Farrand, Max, *The Framing of the Constitution of the United States*, pp. 1–210.
Fiske, John, *The Critical Period of American History 1783–1789*, pp. 230–305.
Gay, S. H., *James Madison*, pp. 88–114.
Greene, E. B., *The Foundations of American Nationality*, pp. 584–601.
Johnson, Allen, ed., *Readings in American Constitutional History 1776–1876*, pp. 98–125.
Johnson, Allen, *Union and Democracy*, pp. 25–45.
Landon, J. S., *The Constitutional History and Government of the United States*, pp. 82–110.
Lodge, H. C., *Alexander Hamilton*, pp. 50–65.
Lodge, H. C., *George Washington*, Vol. II, pp. 29–35.
Martin, C. E., *An Introduction to the Study of the American Constitution*, pp. 30–78.
McLaughlin, A. C., *The Confederation and the Constitution 1783–1789*, pp. 184–276.
McMaster, J. B., *History of the People of the United States*, Vol. I, pp. 417–524.
Munro, W. B., *The Constitution of the United States*, pp. 1–132.
Orth, S. P., and Cushman, R. E., *American National Government*, pp. 52–66, 71–80.
Schuyler, R. L., *The Constitution of the United States*, pp. 85–127.
Stevens, C. E., *Sources of the Constitution of the United States*, pp. 35–58.
Thorpe, F. N., *A Short Constitutional History of the United States*, pp. 18–34.
Warren, Charles, *The Making of the Constitution*, pp. 55–732.

Chapter Ten

THE BATTLE OVER RATIFICATION

I T is fallacious to think that the completed Constitution was received with rejoicing by the people of the United States. On the contrary, it met with bitter and determined opposition. The leading authorities are agreed that the ratification of the Constitution would have been defeated had it been submitted to a popular referendum in which the privilege of voting was not limited by property qualifications. As it was, no direct vote was ever taken on the question of ratifying. The only opportunity offered for a popular expression on the subject was in the election of delegates to attend the state ratifying conventions. Thus about 160,000 men, or about five percent of the total population of the thirteen states, voted indirectly for or against the ratification of the Constitution. As will be shown in the consideration of the state conventions, a goodly portion of the votes, even though cast by men having enough property to meet the qualifications for voters which prevailed generally, were given to delegates pledged to oppose ratification.

ATTITUDE OF THE FRAMERS TOWARDS THEIR WORK

The framers of the Constitution were obviously pessimistic regarding the fate of the document. The fact that a number of delegates had left the Philadelphia convention before its work was completed, because they were dissatisfied with what was being done, was not a hopeful sign. The refusal of three delegates to sign the completed Constitution did not serve to make the outlook brighter. The closing session of the convention was shrouded in gloom. Even Benjamin Franklin's address, appealing for unanimity on the part of the delegates present, was tinged with pessimism. Edmund Randolph, in explaining his refusal to sign, predicted that the new Constitution would not be ratified "and confusion must ensue." Referring to a statement by Alexander Hamilton to the effect that the choice was "anarchy and convulsion on one side" and the possibility of good from the new Constitution on the other side, Randolph declared that the anarchy feared would surely result if the Constitution were presented to the people as the only alternative for anarchy. This view was agreed to by another non-signer, Elbridge Gerry, who expressed a fear that a civil war might result from the existing crisis in the United States. Even the resolution adopted during that last session entrusting to George Washington the journal and other papers of the convention, to be retained by him subject to instructions from the new Congress "if ever formed under the Constitution," reflected the pessimistic attitude of the delegates.

Assuredly, the "Fathers of the Constitution" did not feel that they had accomplished a super-human task. They would have been filled with amazement to hear their work described, as it was many years later by Gladstone, as "the greatest work ever struck off at a given time by the brain and purpose of man." But history proves that they had done their work better than they themselves realized, for the Constitution which they pessimistically submitted to the country was not only ratified but proved workable in practice. Not only that but, during a period of over one hundred and forty years since the Constitution became operative, it has been found possible to adapt it to a country which has undergone vast changes, territorially, socially, and economically. There is no reason why it cannot continue indefinitely to be adapted to the changing needs of the United States through the same means that have thus far proved effective, namely, formal amendment, legislation by Congress, judicial interpretation, executive action, and the influence of custom and tradition.

THE PROCESS OF RATIFICATION

The framers of the Constitution were well aware that they had accomplished a revolutionary action, a peaceful, bloodless revolution it is true. The convention had been called to revise the Articles and, without exception, the delegates had been instructed by the state legislatures, which had chosen them, to carry out the announced purpose of the convention. Yet, early in their proceedings, they had agreed to put aside the Articles and to devote their efforts to the preparation of an entirely new framework of government.

Having prepared a new Constitution, they went further and provided a special procedure for the ratification of the document. The Articles of Confederation unequivocally stated that no "alteration" should be made in them "unless such alteration be agreed to in a Congress of the United States, and be afterwards confirmed by the Legislatures of every State." The report of the Annapolis convention suggested the calling of the convention had proposed that this procedure be followed, for it stated that those selected to go to Philadelphia were "to devise such further provisions as shall appear to them necessary to render the constitution of the federal government adequate to the exigencies of the Union," after which they were "to report such an act for that purpose to the United States in Congress assembled, as, when agreed to by them, and afterwards confirmed by the legislatures of every state, will effectually provide for the same." The official call for the convention, issued by the Confederation Congress on February 21, 1787, had also stated that the revisions to the Articles of Confederation to be proposed by the convention should be submitted to Congress and to "the several legislatures" and should be "agreed to in Congress, and confirmed by the states."

However, in the fifteenth resolution of the Virginia plan, which, as has been pointed out, was early accepted by the convention as the basis for its further deliberations, it was stated that the "amendments . . . to the Confederation" should "after the approbation of Congress . . . be submitted to an assembly or assemblies of Representatives, recommended by the several Legislatures to be expressly chosen by the people, to consider & decide thereon." Thus, it is clear that the framers of the Constitution early agreed that their work, when completed, should be ratified by state conventions.

In view of the fact that Rhode Island was not represented in the convention it was obvious to the delegates that it would be extremely difficult to secure ratification of the Constitution by all of the states. As the work of the convention proceeded, doubt increased concerning the probability of unanimous ratification. The result of this doubt was that, in the seventh and last article of the completed document, it was provided that "The ratification of the Conventions of nine States, shall be sufficient for the Establishment of this Constitution between the States so ratifying the Same." Thus, the framers of the Constitution cast aside the accepted procedure for changing the existing government and provided a method which they felt would have a better chance to succeed. To quote Professor J. W. Burgess, "Had Julius or Napoleon committed these acts they would have been pronounced *coups d'état*."

Before adjourning, the convention adopted two resolutions relating to the ratification of the Constitution. One outlined the procedure whereby the document was to be made effective after its ratification by nine states. The other defined the procedure for securing ratification, as follows, "Resolved, That the preceding constitution be laid before the United States in congress assembled, and that it is the opinion of this convention, that it should afterwards be submitted to a convention of delegates, chosen in each state by the people thereof, under the recommendation of its legislature, for their assent and ratification; and that each convention assenting thereto, and ratifying the same, should give notice thereof to the United States in congress assembled." It should be noted that, nowhere in this resolution, was it stated that the approval of the Confederation Congress should be given to the Constitution before its transmittal to the states.

These resolutions, together with the completed and signed Constitution, were transmitted to Congress, then meeting at New York, by George Washington. Accompanying these documents was a letter which had been prepared by the committee on style but which was signed by Washington as president of the convention. This letter explained that "The friends of our country have long seen and desired" that additional powers should be given to "the general government of the Union" and that "executive and judicial authorities" should be established. But, continued the letter, "the impropriety of delegating such extensive trust to one body of men is evident—hence results the necessity of a different organization" than the Confederation

Congress. The delegates, the letter went on to say, had kept constantly in view "that which appears to us the greatest interest of every true American, the consolidation of our Union, in which is involved our prosperity, felicity, safety, perhaps our national existence." The states represented in the convention had shown a willingness to yield "on points of inferior magnitude" with the result that "the Constitution, which we now present, is the result of a spirit of amity, and of that mutual deference and concession which the peculiarity of our political situation rendered indispensable."

This letter further stated that, while "the full and entire approbation" of each state was hardly to be expected, each should consider that, if its interests alone had been "consulted," other states would have been injured or dissatisfied. The letter closed by saying that the Constitution was "liable to as few exceptions as could reasonably have been expected, we hope and believe; that it may promote the lasting welfare of that country so dear to us all, and secure her freedom and happiness, is our most ardent wish."

Those members of the Constitutional Convention who were also delegates to the Confederation Congress hastened to New York as soon as possible after signing the Constitution so as to defend the document when it was presented to congress. On September 20, 1787, it was received by congress and immediately it became the object of bitter attacks, particularly by Richard Henry Lee of Virginia and Nathan Dane of Massachusetts. It is not surprising that opposition to the Constitution should have been expressed in congress, if for no other reason than that the convention had far exceeded its authority both in casting aside the Articles of Confederation and in providing an extra-legal method of ratification which did not call for approval of the Constitution by congress. Furthermore, if it were agreed to send the Constitution to the states and if it were subsequently ratified by nine states, the Confederation Congress would soon after cease to exist.

Obviously, congress could have nullified all the work of the convention by refusing to transmit the new Constitution to the states. Fortunately it did not pursue this course. After a few days of discussion, congress, on September 28, voted unanimously, eleven states being represented at the time, to transmit the Constitution, with the accompanying resolutions and letter, to the state legislatures "in order to be submitted to a convention of delegates chosen in each State by the people thereof, in conformity to the resolves of the Convention made and provided in that case." In no way did congress indicate whether it approved or disapproved the Constitution.

FEDERALISTS AND ANTI-FEDERALISTS

It took some time after this action before public opinion could be expressed concerning the new framework of government. Such opinions as were expressed at first were largely favorable and it seemed that there would be no formidable opposition to ratification. But it was not long before opposition began to be noticeable. As soon as people in all parts of the country had opportunity to study the document carefully they began to take a stand for or against it. In a short time the country was divided into two parties. Those who favored the Constitution assumed for themselves the name Federalists, and applied to their opponents the name Anti-Federalists.

These two parties were the first real national parties in the history of the United States. During the colonial period there had been parties favoring or opposing the colonial governments. With the development of opposition to British imperial control the people divided into Whigs and Tories or, as they were frequently called, patriots and loyalists. But these groups could hardly be called national parties. During the Confederation period the parties which existed were limited to the individual states. Controversial issues were subject to decision by the state legislatures while even national questions depended on the state legislatures since they chose the delegates to the Confederation Congress. Hence it was in the states that political parties, such as "paper money" parties, were organized for the purpose of controlling elections of the state governmental officials. But the ratification of the Constitution was a national question of interest to the people from New Hampshire to Georgia. Though the matter of ratification was to be decided by individual states, the forces favoring or opposing the document were not divided by state lines.

Generally speaking, the same classes who had agitated for a stronger government prior to the convention rallied to the support of the Constitution. Those who were interested in business, in commerce, in a stable money market, in settling the question of the western lands, and in the redemption of government securities, were to be found, for the most part, in the ranks of the Federalists. Likewise those who wished to have a government that could command respect abroad and which could force compliance with its wishes at home took a stand for ratification. The signers of the Constitution became leaders in the Federalist party and used their best efforts to secure ratification.

But not all of the prominent men of the country were Federalists. As will become apparent when the actions of the individual states are considered, some of the outstanding men of the whole country, such as Patrick Henry, became Anti-Federalists. Other men of prominence in the states, but who were not so well known nationally, also actively opposed ratification. Those men who had formed the paper money parties in the states naturally became Anti-Federalists. The debtor classes had no reason to desire a stronger central government so they too were Anti-Federalists. Also the small farmer class was generally to be found in this party. But it should not be supposed that all who opposed the Constitution were animated only by materialistic considerations. There were those who, like Elbridge Gerry, felt that the document was too democratic. Conversely, men like Richard Henry Lee held that it was not democratic enough. Others were Anti-Federalists chiefly because the Constitution contained no bill of rights. The arguments brought out in the state conventions reveal a variety of reasons for opposition to the Constitution on other than economic grounds.

Within each state, local conditions had much to do with the development of Federalist or Anti-Federalist strength. But, in a general way, it may be said that the chief strength of the Federalists lay in the cities and in the area comparatively near the coast, while the Anti-Federalists were stronger in the "back country." This was well demonstrated by Professor Orin G. Libby in a scholarly analysis of *The Geographical Distribution of the Vote of the Thirteen States on the Federal Constitution, 1787–1788,* published in 1894.

THE DEBATE OVER THE CONSTITUTION IN CONTEMPORARY PUBLICATIONS

As might have been expected at a time when it was customary to write letters to the newspapers expressing opinions on all sorts of questions, the public was regaled, during the latter part of 1787 and, particularly, the first part of 1788, with the printed opinions of various prominent men who, however, signed their letters with pseudonyms. In these published discussions, reference was often made to the political philosophers with whom the Americans of the time were familiar, such as Montesquieu, Hobbes, Milton, Halifax, Blackstone, and Locke.

One of those who took up his pen in opposition to the Constitution was Richard Henry Lee, the Virginian who had introduced the Declaration of Independence resolution in the Second Continental Congress in 1776. In 1787 he wrote *Observations leading to a Fair Examination of the System of Government, proposed by the late Convention. . . . In a number of Letters from the Federal Farmer to the Republican.* In the following year he published *An Additional Number of Letters from the Federal Farmer to the Republican.* Lee's letters were characterized by a noteworthy attitude of fair-mindedness. While criticizing parts of the Constitution he did not hesitate to praise what he regarded as satisfactory portions of the document. It was Lee's main contention that the Constitution was undemocratic and that it would subject the majority to the will of the minority. He claimed that the new instrument of government did not reflect the judgment of the people as a whole. Lee severely criticized the haste of the Federalists to secure ratification. He declared that he was not seeking delay in order to destroy the Constitution but merely to make certain that it would be accepted or rejected on its merits.

Lee denied that existing conditions were such as to demand the immediate ratification of the document as the Federalists were contending. He asserted that conditions were improving steadily, an assertion which substantially agreed with a statement made by Benjamin Franklin in 1787. As a matter of fact that year seems to have been the turning point towards increased prosperity and general improvement in economic affairs. Lee blamed much of the confusion and disorder that had characterized the Confederation period on the War for Independence but, said he, peace was rapidly restoring the ravages wrought by the war. It must be admitted, he declared, "that our federal system is defective, and that some of the state governments are not well administered" but, he continued, "we impute to the defects in our governments many evils and embarrassments which are most clearly the result of the late war."

Continuing, he cleverly argued, "It is natural for men, who wish to hasten the adoption of a measure, to tell us, now is the crisis—now is the critical moment which must be seized or all will be lost; and to shut the door against free enquiry, whenever conscious the thing presented has defects in it, which time and investigation will probably discover."

Lee's letters were doubtless the outstanding contribution to the public debate over the Constitution so far as the Anti-Federalists were concerned. Of course, others of the party also expressed their views publicly; for instance, in Philadelphia a number of letters were published signed by one who called himself "Centinel." But it is apparent that the Federalists were much more blessed with literary talent than were their opponents.

Among those who wrote in support of the Constitution were a group of literary men in Connecticut known as the "Hartford Wits." These included John Trumbull, Timothy Dwight, Joel Barlow, Lemuel Hopkins, David Humphreys, Richard Alsop, Theodore Dwight, Elihu H. Smith, and Mason F. Cogswell. As Vernon Louis Parrington describes them, "Nearly all were Yale men with a pronounced Yale predilection for Calvinism and Federalism, admirable representatives of the oligarchical upper class of the provincial Connecticut society." All of them were ardently opposed to democracy and gladly joined in the fight for the Constitution as a means of combating the forces of democracy.

Francis Hopkinson of Philadelphia was another of the literary men of the period who wrote in support of the Constitution. As a delegate to the Second Continental Congress from New Jersey he had signed the Declaration of Independence eleven years earlier. In relation to the Constitution, he wrote two clever satires which revealed "a good-natured contempt for the democratic underling and all his ways." These were entitled, *The New Roof* and *Objections to the Proposed Plan of a Federal Government for the United States, on Genuine Principles*.

Another advocate of the Constitution was John Dickinson. In defence of the document which he had helped formulate, he wrote nine *Letters of Fabius*. There was, however, nothing original in them; in fact, they contained "not a single illuminating comment." It is not likely that these letters had much influence on contemporary thinking.

Others, as Noah Webster, Peletiah Webster, and James Wilson, likewise contributed arguments in favor of the Constitution. But by far the most important contribution to the Federalist cause was a group of eighty-five letters published in 1787 and 1788 over the signature "Publius." These letters or essays which first appeared in the *Independent Journal*, the *New York Packet*, the *Daily Advertiser*, and other New York newspapers, were gathered together in 1788 and reprinted in a volume under the title, *The Federalist*. Later editions of *The Federalist* have also been published, notably those under the editorship of Henry Cabot Lodge, E. G. Bourne, and Paul Leicester Ford. These three scholars could not agree as to the authorship of all of the letters. Fifty-one have been credited to Alexander Hamilton and five to John Jay, but it is a question whether or not the remaining twenty-nine should be credited to James Madison. There is no doubt but that Madison wrote fourteen. There is ground for thinking that Hamilton and Madison were joint authors of three others while, in the case of the other twelve, there is doubt as to whether Hamilton or Madison was the author.

The letters were addressed "To the People of the State of New York" and were designed to influence public opinion in that state in favor of the ratification of the Constitution. But they were copied by papers outside of that state and doubtless had some influence in promoting the Federalist cause throughout the union. Whether or not *The Federalist* had much influence on contemporary public opinion, there can be no doubt concerning the caliber of the letters themselves. *The Federalist* has been acclaimed as the outstanding treatise on federal government so far produced.

In the first letter Hamilton sought to show that, in considering the Constitution, there was involved "nothing less than the existence of the UNION, the safety and welfare of the parts of which it is composed, the fate of an empire in many respects the most interesting in the world." This letter further set forth the purpose of the following essays and so may be regarded as an introduction to the whole series. Without attempting a detailed analysis of *The Federalist* it may be observed that full discussions were presented of such matters as "Dangers From Foreign Force And Influence," "The Insufficiency Of The Present Confederation," "The General Power Of Taxation," "General View Of The Powers Conferred By The Constitution," "The House Of Representatives," "The Senate," "The Executive Department," and "The Judiciary Department." In fact, on any point involved in the Constitution, one may find in *The Federalist* a lucid exposition of the viewpoint of the Federalists as well as their arguments for the ratification of the document.

EARLY STATE RATIFICATIONS

The honor of being the first state to ratify the Constitution belongs to Delaware. That state, being one of the smallest of the thirteen, was pleased with the concession obtained through the great compromise, as were the other small states, and so it acted speedily and decisively. On November 10, 1787, its legislature passed a resolution calling for the election, on the 26th of that month, of delegates to a state ratifying convention. Those who participated in the election were all freeholders owning fifty acres of land, of which twelve acres were improved "or otherwise worth £40 lawful money." No contest of any consequence developed and the delegates who assembled at Dover on December 3 were overwhelmingly in favor of the Constitution.

After only four days of discussion the document was unanimously ratified on December 7, 1787, thirty delegates being present at the time.

One of the large states, Pennsylvania, soon added its approval, but only after a bitter fight. There the first step to secure ratification was taken even before it was known that action would be taken by congress to transmit the Constitution to the states. The initiative was taken by George Clymer, a delegate to the Constitutional Convention, who, after the signing of the new instrument of government, had taken his place in the Pennsylvania legislature of which he was also a member. Since the legislature was scheduled to adjourn on September 29, Clymer and others feared that congress would not act in time for the Pennsylvania legislature to call a state convention before adjournment. Therefore he moved that a convention be summoned to meet in Philadelphia for the purpose of acting on the Constitution. In vain some of the legislators protested that the action would be irregular for the motion prevailed. After deciding to call a convention, the legislature adjourned until the afternoon of the same day, leaving the method of selecting delegates and the date of the convention unsettled. The opponents of the action then sought to block further action by refusing to attend any more sessions of the legislature, hoping thereby to prevent business from being transacted because of the lack of a quorum.

At this juncture the news arrived that congress had decided to submit the Constitution to the states. This news made "regular" the previous action of the legislature in calling a convention. The Federalist members, determined to complete their action, sent officers after the absent members who, with the help of a Federalist mob, were forcibly taken to the legislative hall. With a quorum thus secured, the legislature set November 6 as the date for electing delegates. The qualifications of those voting for delegates were that they must be freemen, aged twenty-one or over, residents of the state for at least a year, and who, furthermore, were taxpayers. It was claimed that only about thirteen thousand out of approximately seventy thousand eligible voters participated in the election of delegates. Whether this was due to pure indifference, ignorance, or, as the opponents of ratification asserted, to the short time allowed before the election for discussion of the matter, and to a belief that the call for the convention was illegal, is an unsettled question. The main strength of the opposition was manifested among the agrarian classes of the interior. It is interesting to note that the majority of the delegates who opposed ratification were farmers. On the other hand, Philadelphia and vicinity proved to be strong Federalist territory.

After the Pennsylvania convention was assembled the Federalists quickly forced through a ratification resolution. The final vote, taken on December 12, 1787, was forty-six to twenty-three. Following their defeat in the convention, twenty-one Anti-Federalist delegates drew up an address to the people protesting against the whole procedure from the time the Constitutional Convention had been called to the ratification of the Constitution by the state convention. But protests were in vain; the Federalists had achieved their first important victory. Had Pennsylvania failed to ratify the Constitution, the cause of the Federalists would have been practically hopeless.

Following the Pennsylvania action came the ratification of the document by New Jersey. The call for a convention was issued by the New Jersey legislature on November 1, 1787. Delegates were to be elected on the twenty-seventh of that month and the convention was to meet on December 11. Those who voted for delegates were required to be worth fifty pounds in lawful money. Perhaps the Anti-Federalists were not given enough time to organize before the election of delegates took place but at any rate they showed negligible strength. The Federalists made a "clean sweep" of the election and were thus able to secure a unanimous vote of the thirty-eight delegates present in the convention on December 18, 1787 in favor of ratification.

Likewise in Georgia no difficulty was experienced in securing favorable action on the Constitution. The legislature, on October 26, 1787, ordered that, on December 4, three delegates should be elected from each county to meet in convention at Augusta on December 25. Those privileged to vote for delegates were white males who owned property valued at ten pounds "and liable to pay tax" or who were "of any mechanic trade." No contest developed in the selection of delegates and, on January 2, 1788, the twenty-six delegates present in the state convention voted unanimously to "fully and entirely assent to, ratify, and adopt, the said Constitution." It is probable that Georgia, which was in imminent danger of Indian attacks, ratified so speedily because of a desire for a strong central government capable of furnishing protection against the Indians.

One week following the action by Georgia came the ratification by another small state, Connecticut. A state ratifying convention was called by the legislature on October 11, 1787. The election of delegates was to take place on November 12. Voters were required to be at least twenty-one years of age, to possess a freehold yielding forty shillings or seven dollars a year, or to possess personal property worth forty pounds. The larger towns elected delegates favorable to the Constitution while the opposition delegates were mostly chosen by the small inland towns. In support of the Constitution in Connecticut, Oliver Ellsworth prepared and published a series of essays which seem to have been widely circulated and read and which doubtless had considerable influence on public opinion. Be that as it may, the Federalists were overwhelmingly in the majority in the convention which met on January 3, 1788. When the vote was taken on January 9, 1788, one hundred and twenty-eight votes were cast in favor of and only forty against ratification.

THE BATTLE IN MASSACHUSETTS

The first close battle over the ratification of the Constitution took place in Massachusetts. For a time it appeared doubtful that the Federalists could achieve a victory in that state but they eventually won the day by a narrow margin. A resolution was passed by the state legislature on October 24, 1787, providing for the election of delegates "as soon as may be" to meet in a convention at Boston on January 9, 1788. Those who voted for delegates were required to possess a freehold estate yielding an annual income of three pounds or any estate worth sixty pounds. The vote in the eastern part of the state resulted in substantial Federalist majorities but in the middle and western sections the Anti-Federalists proved to be in the majority, according to Professor O. G. Libby. This result revealed a conflict of interests between the commercial and the agricultural classes, between the propertied and the debtor classes, and between the "natural aristocracy" and the "turbulent democracy" of the state.

Had a vote been taken in the convention when it first assembled it is apparent that the ratification of the Constitution would have been defeated. However, during the period of almost a month during which the convention was in session the Federalists were able to win over enough delegates to secure ratification by a small majority. It was later charged that bribery was resorted to as a means of influencing delegates to vote for the Constitution, but careful investigators of the charge have dismissed it as having been unfounded.

A large variety of arguments was presented by the Anti-Federalists to show that the Constitution should not be ratified. A résumé of these arguments will reveal some of the objections which the Anti-Federalists of Massachusetts had to the new framework of government. The Constitution was attacked as "unconstitutional." That is, the Philadelphia convention had been called to revise the Articles of Confederation but the delegates had exceeded their instructions by drawing up a new document. Another objection was that it was obscure and ambiguous instead of being so simple and explicit "that the most illiterate may understand it." It was argued that the expression "We the people of the United States" would annihilate the states and tend to bring about a consolidation of the states. The whole Constitution would operate to destroy the sovereignty of the states.

In regard to the proposed Congress, it was declared that the number of representatives was too small to secure adequate representation. Two years was declared to be too long a term for representatives and would lead to tyranny by the legislature. Annual elections would make the representatives dependent on the people. The six year term for senators would make them too independent and would ultimately lead to life tenure. Furthermore, it was declared that equal representation in the Senate would be unfair to the large states in view of the fact that direct taxes were to be paid in proportion to population. Several members of the Massachusetts convention deplored the lack of religious qualifications for members of Congress, saying that this lack would lead to corruption of morals in the government. It was also argued that members of Congress should be required to possess property for "when men have nothing to lose, they have nothing to fear." This last, however, could hardly be regarded as a typical Anti-Federalist argument. Objection was also raised to the payment of members of Congress out of the national treasury on the ground that they would thus feel no dependence on the people of the states. Fear was expressed that the power of Congress to regulate the time, place, and manner of holding elections to Congress might result in poor election laws and might deprive the people of their choice. Congress might even keep itself in office indefinitely by regulating elections.

The powers granted to Congress by the Constitution were subjected to strong attacks. It was declared that the powers of Congress would involve a union of the purse and the sword. The power of Congress to tax was unlimited and therefore dangerous. The power to enforce the payment of taxes would destroy the sovereignty of the states. The states would be burdened with a "standing army of ravenous collectors." The power of taxation to pay the debts was not confined to existing debts but would lead to new ones, it was correctly prophesied. Likewise, the term "general welfare" would allow expenditures for any purpose desired. The power of taxation given to Congress was equal, it was claimed, to that possessed by the English government before the Revolution, and which had proved so distasteful.

Objections were also raised to the powers to raise armies and navies, to establish a separate national capital, and to erect and control forts and arsenals. Standing armies were dangerous and would lead to national consolidation. In fact, it was claimed, the granting of such great powers to Congress as were enumerated in the Constitution would bring about the consolidation of the thirteen states.

Particular objection was made to the Constitution because it did not contain a bill of rights. Accused persons were not guaranteed an impartial trial nor was there any provision for trial in the vicinity of the alleged offence. There was no provision for indictments by grand juries, nor was there any constitutional limitation on the power of Congress to define criminal procedure other than the requirement of trial by jury. A bill of rights, it was declared, was necessary for the safety of the people.

The Federalists were ready with strong arguments of their own to answer the objections of their opponents. For instance, they declared that the Constitution offered a good government, one that could prevent such anarchy as had "recently existed" in Massachusetts. This government would not become tyrannical since the representatives in Congress would always be controlled by public opinion in their home states.

In answer to the objection that the membership in the House of Representatives was too small, it was pointed out that, as population increased, the number would be enlarged. If the representatives were to be elected annually, the senators, it was said, would outweigh them in importance. The senators, said the Federalists, were to be ambassadors of the states and so should have some permanency of tenure. They should not be brought directly under popular control as that would, it was asserted, obliterate the states and lead to the consolidation which the opponents of the Constitution professed to fear. Political control, it was pointed out, would prevent members of Congress from voting themselves excessive salaries. In regard to the lack of religious qualifications for members of Congress, it was argued that such qualifications would cause injury and privation of civil rights to those otherwise well fitted for office. Dishonest men would subscribe to any doctrine to make themselves eligible. It would be incumbent on the people to see that men were elected to Congress who were worthy without regard to their religion.

The powers granted to Congress were also explained and defended. The want of power, it was pointed out, was "the defect" in the existing Confederation. The power to raise armies would not be abused for, it was asked, "How could an army be raised from the free men of this country to enslave the country itself?" There was no need to fear a military usurpation of power. The limitation of appropriations for military purposes to a two year period would prevent an alliance of the legislature and the army.

In regard to the taxing power, it was declared that the power conferred on the national government in that respect was necessary to preserve the national dignity, to maintain the national safety, and to pay debts. Political control would prevent abuse of the power in view of the fact that all money bills were to originate in the popularly elected House of Representatives. No government could exist without the power to collect taxes. The lack of such power, the Federalists pointed out, was one of the fundamental weaknesses of the Confederation government. Unless the central government should be given the power to levy and collect taxes to pay the debts to foreign countries, those countries would undertake the collection of such debts by force of arms, or at least they would make reprisals on American commerce with ruinous effect on the whole country. Unlimited power of taxation was necessary to provide for such exigencies as war. As for direct taxes, they would be levied, declared the friends of the Constitution, only in times of emergency.

An argument, which was advanced by the Federalists in defence of the power of Congress to regulate commerce, and which was especially effective in Massachusetts, was that such power would bring great prosperity to the New England states. Furthermore, the power would enable Congress to retaliate against foreign nations which imposed restrictions on American trade. It was also contended that the Constitution would result in securing to American ships the carrying of the trade of the United States.

In answer to the charge that the Constitution would destroy the state governments and result in consolidation it was declared that the opposite would be true. The Constitution would guarantee the continued existence of the states whereas, under the Confederation, the state governments were rapidly destroying themselves. The ratification of the new framework of government would not result in the consolidation of the states but merely in a "consolidation of strength." Congress would have no power to change the internal organization of any state.

There could be no usurpation of powers by the central government, declared the Federalists, because of the system of checks provided by the Constitution. Not only were the three branches of government to act as checks on each other but, in addition, there would be checks by the people themselves since each branch of the government, it was claimed, would be derived directly or indirectly from the people. The "spirit of the people" as well as the separate state governments would preserve liberty.

As for a bill of rights, the Federalists argued that such a

bill was unnecessary since the powers granted to Congress were "express" powers and therefore in no need of limitation. The Constitution, it was declared, was not concerned with the rights of individuals and so there was no need of enumerating such rights in the document.

These arguments for and against the Constitution may be regarded as typical of those presented in other state ratifying conventions. Of course there were some variations but, for the most part, these were unimportant. For this reason no attempt will be made to give an analysis of the debates in other states.

In order to secure the ratification of the Constitution by the Massachusetts convention it was necessary for the Federalists to agree to a list of nine proposed amendments. These amendments were not made a condition of ratification but were submitted as recommendations to be acted on after the new government should become operative. This procedure won over Samuel Adams and a few others whose votes were needed to insure ratification. It should be mentioned that all of the states which ratified after Massachusetts followed the example and drew up lists of recommended amendments to the Constitution.

In securing the agreement to ratify the Constitution with recommended amendments, Governor John Hancock played a prominent part. He had been elected governor of the state by the vote of the "Shaysites," the class who had participated in or sympathized with Shays's Rebellion. Naturally, he was not numbered among the Federalists. When the ratifying convention met he was elected as its presiding officer. For a time he did not attend its sessions, pleading that he had the gout. It has been charged that he made this an excuse to stay away until it was pointed out to him that, if Virginia failed to ratify, he would be a logical man for the office of president in the new government. At any rate, he appeared in the convention and used his influence for ratification, which was secured on February 6, 1788 by a vote of one hundred and eighty-seven to one hundred and sixty-eight. A change of ten votes would have defeated ratification. With victory for the Constitution achieved, the Federalists of Boston proceeded to celebrate the event in an appropriate manner as the Philadelphia Federalists had done a little earlier.

Maryland was the seventh state to give its approval to the new Constitution. Even before the Constitutional Convention had completed its work, one of the Maryland delegates, Luther Martin, had withdrawn, and had returned to his home state with the avowed purpose of preventing the ratification of the new instrument of government. In November, 1787, he appeared before the Maryland legislature and delivered a strong attack on the Constitution. But, after James McHenry, another delegate to the Philadelphia convention, had replied, the legislature voted "unanimously" to call a state ratifying convention which, however, was not to meet until April 21, 1788. Eligibility to vote for delegates was, generally speaking, limited to persons having a freehold of fifty acres of land or possessing property in the state valued at thirty pounds "current money." But, of the approximately twenty-five thousand eligible voters in the state, less than one-fourth participated in the election of delegates. For almost a week the convention remained in session listening to the strong denunciations of the Constitution hurled by Martin and a few others. The Federalists said little for they knew that they were in control of the situation. When the vote was finally taken on April 26, 1788, the ratification of the Constitution was approved by a vote of sixty-three to eleven. In connection with the resolution of ratification, a list of twenty-eight recommended amendments was adopted.

South Carolina took no action regarding the Constitution until January, 1788. On the eighteenth of that month, the legislature unanimously issued a call for a convention to meet at Charleston on May 13. The qualifications of those who participated in the election of delegates included ownership of fifty acres of land, or a town lot, or the payment of taxes equal to the tax on fifty acres of land. The delegates elected were

overwhelmingly Federalist so that, after less than two weeks
of discussion, the convention, on May 23, 1788, ratified the
Constitution by a vote of one hundred and forty-nine to seventy-
three. Four resolutions were also adopted in lieu of recommending definite amendments.

The ninth state to ratify was New Hampshire. In that state
the resolution calling a convention was passed by the legislature
on December 14, 1787. The time for the convention to assemble
was fixed at the thirteenth of the following February. A considerable portion of the adult males were eligible to vote for
delegates since the suffrage had been extended by the state
constitution of 1784 to freeholders and taxpayers, including
those who merely paid a poll tax. After the convention assembled it became apparent that the majority of the delegates were
Anti-Federalists, though most of the outstanding men present
were Federalists. A number of the opponents of the Constitution were won over but they still considered themselves bound
by their instructions to oppose ratification. To give these delegates an opportunity to consult with those who had elected
them, the Federalists secured an adjournment until June. By
some this was regarded as a setback for the Constitution but,
as the event proved, it was good strategy. When the convention reassembled, the final debate was quickly disposed of and,
on June 21, 1788, the vote on ratification was taken, resulting fifty-seven to forty-six in favor of the Constitution. Twelve
recommended amendments to the document were adopted by
the convention at the same time.

RATIFICATION BY VIRGINIA

Though the approval by New Hampshire insured the required number of states to put the Constitution into effect, it
would have required a super-optimist to expect success for the
new government without the support of Virginia. On October
25, 1787, the Virginia legislature passed a resolution calling a
state convention which was to assemble on June 2, 1788. Those
eligible to vote for delegates included persons who owned
twenty-five acres of improved land or fifty acres of unimproved
land together with "certain artisans" who lived in Norfolk and

Williamsburg. In numbers the Federalists and Anti-Federalists in the convention appeared to be divided fairly evenly. Both groups had able leaders. Among the proponents of the Constitution were James Madison, John Marshall, and Edmund Randolph, who, after having refused to sign the Constitution at the close of the Philadelphia convention, had decided to support its ratification. George Washington did not attend the ratifying convention but he used his personal influence, through correspondence and otherwise, to secure the approval of the Constitution. On the Anti-Federalist side, outstanding leaders were George Mason, James Monroe, and Patrick Henry.

It will not be possible here to consider in detail the arguments delivered in the Virginia convention for and against the new instrument of government. The arguments were in most respects similar to those used in Massachusetts. Probably the outstanding feature of the whole debate was the oratory of Patrick Henry who fought stubbornly to prevent ratification. One of the strongest contentions of the Anti-Federalists was that the Constitution should contain a bill of rights. There was danger that they would secure the defeat of the document unless amendments were agreed to. Ultimately, it was decided to ratify the Constitution and accompany the action with a recommendation for the adoption of twenty-nine amendments in addition to a bill of rights. The vote, taken on June 25, 1788, revealed eighty-nine in favor of ratification and seventy-nine opposed. A change of six votes would have defeated the ratification resolution.

THE NEW YORK RATIFICATION BATTLE

For the success of the new union it was extremely important to secure the ratification of the Constitution by New York. Otherwise the states forming the new government would have been split into two sections. The governor of the state, George Clinton, was a strong opponent of the proposition to change the central government, and he had great influence with the people. Nevertheless, a resolution to call a state ratifying convention was put through the legislature by a very slight majority in each house. Instead of limiting the right to vote to those who possessed property, the legislature decreed that the principle of manhood suffrage should apply to the election of delegates. The result was that two-thirds of the sixty-four delegates elected were Anti-Federalists while only one-third were Federalists. That ratification was finally secured through the conversion of some of the Anti-Federalists was a remarkable tribute to the persuasive ability of Alexander Hamilton, John Jay, R. R. Livingston, and other Federalist leaders. *The Federalist* essays doubtless had some influence but, after all, it was on the floor of the convention that the friends of the Constitution won their battle for ratification. This they did in spite of the best efforts of Governor Clinton and other Anti-Federalist leaders, including the two delegates to the Philadelphia convention, Lansing and Yates, who, it will be recalled, had left that convention in the middle of its session.

The New York convention assembled at Poughkeepsie on June 17, 1788, and remained in session until July 26, 1788, when a ratification resolution was passed by a vote of thirty to twenty-seven. To secure this result it was necessary for the Federalists to agree to thirty-three recommended amendments and a number of resolutions. They were forced also to agree to a recommendation that another national convention should be called to revise the Constitution. In accordance with this recommendation, the New York legislature, on February 5, 1789, adopted a resolution calling on the newly-elected Congress to call another national convention immediately. It was declared that only confidence that such action would be taken "and an invincible reluctance to separate from our sister states" had secured ratification of the Constitution by New York.

THE DELAYED RATIFICATIONS BY NORTH CAROLINA AND RHODE ISLAND

Though North Carolina started ratification proceedings early, it was not until some months after the Constitution had become operative that its ratifying convention gave approval to the document. The call for a convention was issued by the legislature on December 6, 1787, the election of delegates was held in the following March, and, on July 21, 1788, the convention assembled. Those who voted for the delegates were required to be taxpayers. The paper money and debtor parties were strong in the state and, as usual, they were found arrayed with the Anti-Federalists in opposition to the Constitution. From the beginning of the convention it was clear to the Federalists that ratification would be defeated if brought to a vote. Rather than risk a decision, they secured, in August, 1788, by a vote of one hundred and eighty-four to eighty-four, a *sine die* adjournment.

One of the early accomplishments of the first Congress to meet after the Constitution went into effect was to pass a tariff act imposing duties on foreign imports, and also imports from North Carolina and Rhode Island. In the face of this commercial coercion, the North Carolinians decided to hold another convention and, finally, on November 21, 1789, by a vote of one hundred and ninety-three to seventy-five the Constitution was ratified. In spite of the fact that Congress had already submitted a list of twelve amendments to the states for ratification, the North Carolina convention drew up and adopted a list of twenty-six recommended amendments.

Rhode Island remained out of the new union even longer than did North Carolina. The paper money party controlled that state so effectively that no delegates had been sent to the national convention at Philadelphia. Naturally they had no desire to see their state a party to the new Constitution. Because of this Rhode Island made no move to ratify the new instrument of government until March, 1790. At that time a convention was assembled but the Anti-Federalists who controlled it avoided action by securing an adjournment until May. It was then that Congress resorted to drastic measures as a means of forcing ratification. A bill was passed by the Senate, authorizing the president to suspend all commercial relations with Rhode Island and also to demand that the state pay its share of the national debts. The bill was not acted on by the House of Representatives because the Rhode Island convention reassembled and, on May 29, 1790, ratified the Constitution by a vote of thirty-four to thirty-two. Twenty-one amendments to the Constitution were also recommended by the convention.

The ratification by Rhode Island brought to a close the long

238 AMERICAN CONSTITUTIONAL HISTORY

drawn out battle to provide for the United States a strong
central government. Whether the new Constitution would
prove workable was yet to be proved. That the faith of its
advocates was well founded has, however, been demonstrated
by subsequent history. It is the purpose of the remainder of
this volume to examine that history in order to learn, in a
general way, how the Constitution has worked in practice.

SELECTED REFERENCES

Beard, C. A., *An Economic Interpretation of the Constitution of the
United States*, pp. 217–325.
Beck, J. M., *The Constitution of the United States*, pp. 173–197.
Chandler, J. A. C., *Genesis and Birth of the Federal Constitution*,
pp. 301–330.
Channing, Edward, *History of the United States*, Vol. III, pp. 516–524.
Farrand, Max, *The Fathers of the Constitution*, pp. 143–166.
Fiske, John, *The Critical Period of American History 1783–1789*,
pp. 306–350.
Gay, S. H., *James Madison*, pp. 115–127.
Greene, E. B., *The Foundations of American Nationality*, pp. 603–613.
Johnson, Allen, ed., *Readings in American Constitutional History 1776–
1876*, pp. 126–134.
Landon, J. S., *The Constitutional History and Government of the United
States*, pp. 111–124.
Lodge, H. C., *Alexander Hamilton*, pp. 65–83.
Lodge, H. C., *George Washington*, Vol. II, pp. 35–46.
Magruder, A. B., *John Marshall*, pp. 57–87.
McLaughlin, A. C., *The Confederation and the Constitution 1783–1789*,
pp. 277–317.
Norton, T. J., *The Constitution of the United States, Its Sources and Its
Application*, pp. 185–193.
Parrington, V. L., *The Colonial Mind 1620–1800*, pp. 279–320.
Schlesinger, A. M., *New Viewpoints in American History*, pp. 192–198.
Schuyler, R. L., *The Constitution of the United States*, pp. 128–167.
Thorpe, F. N., *A Short Constitutional History of the United States*,
pp. 82–120.
Warren, Charles, *The Making of the Constitution*, pp. 733–782.

Chapter Eleven

THE CREATION AND GROWTH OF GOVERN-MENTAL AGENCIES UNDER THE CONSTITUTION

THE enthusiasm of the Federalists over ratification of the Constitution by the first nine states found expression in celebrations on July 4, 1788. Not only was the day one for rejoicing over the Declaration of Independence adopted twelve years earlier, but, to the advocates of the new instrument of government, added significance was given to the occasion by the fact that they were assured of success. An account of one of these celebrations carried the following statement which well reveals the exuberance of the Federalists at the time. The "sloop Anarchy," it declared, "was ashore on Union Rock, the old scow Confederation, Imbecility master, had put to sea, and the good ship Federal Constitution had come into port bringing a cargo of Public Credit and Prosperity."

This rejoicing on the part of the friends of the Constitution was perhaps a little premature since several states had not yet ratified and it still remained to be seen whether the "good ship Federal Constitution" would actually bring "a cargo of Public Credit and Prosperity."

PROVISIONS FOR ESTABLISHING THE NEW GOVERNMENT

The framers of the Constitution had not left to chance or to the caprice of the Confederation Congress the determination of the method whereby the new federal government was to be set up after nine states had completed ratification. In the second resolution, adopted at the closing session of the Constitutional Convention and forwarded to congress with the completed Constitution, it had been stated "That it is the opinion of this convention, that as soon as the conventions of nine States shall have

239

ratified this constitution, the United States in congress assembled" should fix a day for the appointment of electors, a day on which the electors should meet to vote for president, "and the time and place for commencing proceedings under this constitution." Members of the new Congress were to be elected and were to meet at a time and place to be set by the Confederation Congress. The new Senate was to choose a temporary president "for the sole purpose of receiving, opening, and counting the votes for president." After the choice of a president had taken place, he and Congress "should without delay proceed to execute this constitution."

Compliance with these directions of the convention constituted the last important act of the Confederation Congress. On July 2, 1788, the president of the congress arose to announce that nine states had ratified the new instrument of government. Thereupon a committee was appointed to report a bill for putting the Constitution into effect among the states which had completed ratification. Twelve days later such a bill was reported and, after a period of debate, was passed on September 13, 1788. This "empowering act" set the first Wednesday in the following January as the date for the choice of presidential electors and members of the new Congress. The electors were to meet on the first Wednesday in February and, on the first Wednesday in March, Congress was to meet at New York.

THE NEW GOVERNMENT ORGANIZED

While the terms of the empowering act were being carried out, the Confederation Congress died a natural death. After October 10, 1788, a quorum of the states was never present. However, occasional meetings were held up to March 2, 1789, but nothing was done except to check the roll of delegates and then adjourn. Between March 2, 1789 and the time when the new Congress began to function, the machinery of the central government was virtually at a standstill.

When March 4, which was the first Wednesday in March, arrived, only thirteen representatives and eight senators were present, not enough to constitute a constitutional quorum in either house. Consequently, those in New York were forced to meet day after day, call the roll, and adjourn until the majority necessary to do business should arrive. On April 1, thirty members of the House of Representatives were found to be present whereupon that body proceeded to organize by choosing Frederick Augustus Conrad Muhlenberg of Pennsylvania as the first speaker. Five days later a quorum was also present in the Senate which then chose a temporary presiding officer so that the task of counting the electoral vote could proceed.

Only ten of the states, it appeared, had participated in the first presidential election. Rhode Island and North Carolina were still out of the union while New York failed to take part due to a deadlock between the two houses of the state legislature over the choice of electors. The potential electoral vote of the remaining ten states was seventy-three but two electors from Maryland and two from Virginia failed to vote on February 4, 1789, the date set by the empowering act. The count before the joint session of Congress revealed that George Washington had been the unanimous choice of the sixty-nine electors whose votes had been cast.

It was the theory of the framers of the Constitution that the electors would choose the best qualified man in the country to be president. For this office a majority vote was required. As each elector voted for two persons it was assumed that the man regarded as next best qualified would receive enough votes to be elected vice president. However, a majority of the votes was not required for election to this office under the original Constitution; the man who received the second highest vote would be elected. This system soon broke down because of the rise of political parties and had to be changed. This, as will be explained later, was accomplished through the twelfth amendment. But, in the first election, the provision worked as intended and John Adams of Massachusetts was elected vice president by virtue of receiving thirty-four out of the sixty-nine ballots cast by the electors. The remaining thirty-five votes were divided among no less than ten different men, which illustrates the difficulty experienced by the electors in deciding who was the second best qualified man in the country. After the system of choosing electors through political parties developed this difficulty disappeared, for then the electors voted for their party's candidates.

Some time was required after the counting of the electoral vote to notify Washington of his election as president. Further time elapsed before he could arrange his affairs and make the trip to New York. After he started, his progress was delayed by the repeated ovations he received from an admiring populace. Frequent banquets, receptions, and parades were held in his honor. Finally, after being rowed from the New Jersey shore to the City of New York in a barge manned by thirteen sea captains, he reached his destination. On April 30, 1789, the first inaugural ceremony was conducted in Federal Hall, a building on the corner of Wall Street and Broadway which had been remodelled to serve as a capitol.

After a parade from the residence which Congress had secured and prepared for his use, the President-elect proceeded to Federal Hall accompanied by committees representing the two houses of Congress. They escorted him to the Senate chamber where Vice President Adams, who had already been installed in office, received him. The party then proceeded to a gallery which opened on Broadway so the assembled people could see the President take the oath of office. The oath was administered by Robert R. Livingston, the chancellor of the state of New York. After administering the oath, Livingston shouted, "Long live George Washington, the President of the United States!" This was answered by the cheering of the crowd and firing of salutes from cannon. Returning to the Senate chamber, the President delivered the first inaugural address, thus establishing a custom which has been followed by all succeeding presidents.

In this address, President Washington declared that he had left his private affairs behind with considerable regret. Belittling his qualifications for the office to which he had been elected, he said that "the magnitude and difficulty of the trust to which the voice of my country called me . . . could not but overwhelm with despondence one who . . . ought to be peculiarly conscious of his own deficiencies." The address contained no specific recommendations though reference was made to the desirability of amending the Constitution so as to remove objections which had been raised to it. The President also informed those assembled that he did not wish any compensation for his services other than the payment of actual expenses. In closing his brief address,

President Washington appealed "to the benign Parent of the Human Race in humble supplication that, since He has been pleased to favor the American people with opportunities for deliberating in perfect tranquillity, and dispositions for deciding with unparalleled unanimity on a form of government for the security of their union and the advancement of their happiness, so His divine blessing may be equally *conspicuous* in the enlarged views, the temperate consultations, and the wise measures on which the success of this Government must depend."

With the President duly installed in his office it was possible for Congress to legislate for the purpose, not only of giving effect to its directly delegated powers, but also of setting up such agencies of government as appeared necessary and proper. During Washington's eight years in office only three hundred and eighteen laws were passed by Congress but most of them were of great importance as they were designed to give practical application to constitutional provisions. During this period when the new instrument of government was being applied, it was in charge of its friends. No less than eleven of the senators and nine of the representatives in the first Congress had been members of the Constitutional Convention. Most of the others elected to that Congress were also Federalists though a few who had opposed it were also elected. With a Federalist Congress and a Federalist president, it is not difficult to see why such a broad view of the Constitution was taken in the years when it was first being put in operation.

Liberally interpreting the clause in the Constitution which stated that the president "may require the Opinion, in writing, of the principal Officer in each of the executive Departments" Congress proceeded, in 1789, to create several such departments. On July 27, an act was passed setting up a Department of Foreign Affairs similar to that which had been established by the Confederation Congress. A little later it was decided that this department should be given charge of certain domestic functions also, and, on September 15, 1789, its name was changed to the Department of State. As the secretary in charge of this department, President Washington appointed Thomas Jefferson who, at the time, was still filling the office of minister to France. Jefferson was the only important appointee of Washington who was not fully in accord with the Federalist ideas of government. For the most part, President Washington appointed only such men to office as were in harmony with his views. In this policy may be discerned the beginning of the spoils system in the national government, the origin of which has been blamed on President Jackson by the uncritical.

Congress also proceeded to create a Treasury Department to handle the federal finances. The financial affairs of the Confederation Congress, in the last years of its existence, had been in charge of a board of treasury consisting of three members. Its duties had been chiefly in the nature of accounting for there had been little money to handle. But, with Congress granted such broad financial powers by the Constitution, it was anticipated that the newly created department would have important work to do. The task of determining its form, powers, and duties took considerable time so that it was not until September 2, 1789 that the law creating the Treasury Department was finally passed. To preside over this department, President Washington turned to his colleague of the war period, Alexander Hamilton.

A third executive department created by the first Congress was the Department of War, by an act passed on August 7, 1789. As secretary of war in charge of this department, the President appointed General Henry Knox who had been in charge of the war department of the Confederation Congress. Knox's duties as Secretary of War included control of the army which consisted of about eight hundred and forty men, mostly on the western frontier, supervision of an arsenal at Springfield, Massachusetts, and also supervision of the public lands and regulation of Indian affairs.

The office of attorney general was also created in order that the president might have a legal adviser. However, it was not until about ninety years later that a department was created for the attorney general. To be the first attorney general, Edmund Randolph was appointed by the President. The office of postmaster general was also created in 1789, and Samuel Osgood was appointed to the office by President Washington.

There still remained the necessity of legislating for the purpose of bringing into existence the third branch of the government, the judiciary. While Congress was not obligated by the

Constitution to create any courts besides a Supreme Court, it was decided to create a complete federal judicial system. So well did Congress perform this task that, to this day, the basis of the federal court system is the same as it was in 1789.

The Judiciary Act, which was passed on September 24, 1789, was drafted by a Senate committee of eight headed by Oliver Ellsworth. It provided for a Supreme Court consisting of a chief justice and five associate justices. In each state, and also in Kentucky and Maine, there was to be established a federal district court presided over by a district judge appointed by the president with the advice and consent of the Senate. Similarly appointed were to be the district attorneys and United States marshals. It was also provided that each district should be visited annually by two of the Supreme Court judges who, with the district judge, should sit as a circuit court to hear appeals from the district court. The procedure and jurisdiction of the courts were defined and it was specifically provided that the federal courts should have appellate power over decisions by state courts in cases involving the national Constitution, treaties, and laws.

To be the first chief justice, President Washington appointed John Jay of New York, while as associate justices he appointed John Rutledge of South Carolina, William Cushing of Massachusetts, John Blair of Virginia, James Wilson of Pennsylvania, and James Iredell of North Carolina. All of these men were strong Federalists and three of them, Rutledge, Wilson, and Blair, had helped draft the Constitution.

Shifting of its personnel and lack of strong leadership kept the Supreme Court from having much influence at first. Jay's service was interrupted in 1794 when he was sent to England on a diplomatic mission. In the next year he resigned in order to run for the office of governor of New York, which he apparently considered more important. His successor,[1] Oliver Ellsworth, was handicapped by ill health as Jay had been. In 1799, Ellsworth was sent to France on a diplomatic errand which practically brought his judicial service to a close. He resigned in 1800 and, in the next year, was succeeded by John

[1] John Rutledge was appointed in 1795 to succeed Jay but he only served one term as his appointment was not confirmed by the Senate.

Marshall who was destined to give to the court the leadership needed to make it a powerful and respected branch of the federal government. Up to the time Marshall was appointed chief justice, only fifty-five decisions had been handed down by the Supreme Court.

Besides creating the first executive departments and a federal judiciary, the first Congress also created a considerable number of subordinate offices, as in the customs service. It continued the postal system of the Confederation period which included, in 1789, seventy-five deputy postmasters. By an act passed in 1792, the postal system was extended and postage rates were established. By 1800 the number of post offices had increased to nine hundred and three.

THE SALARIES OF FEDERAL OFFICIALS

Salaries for various officials, from the president down, were also established by law. In spite of President Washington's expressed wish to receive only what was necessary for his expenses, he was given a salary of $25,000 and an official residence free of charge. In 1873 the annual salary was increased to $50,000. There was appropriated for the presidential office during the fiscal year from July 1, 1931, to June 30, 1932, a total of $472,-380. Of this, $75,000 was for the salary of the president as fixed by a law passed in 1909. An additional $30,000 was for the salaries of three secretaries to the president while another $19,-600 was paid to three executive clerks. The vice president received $15,000 compared to the $5,000 received by the first vice president. Most of the balance was expended for the expenses of the White House, the president's official residence in Washington, and for travel expenses.

The salaries of the secretaries of the State and Treasury Departments were originally fixed at $3,500 a year. The salary awarded to the secretary of war was $3,000. The attorney general and the postmaster general were awarded only $1,500 annually. In 1853 the salaries of the heads of all executive departments were fixed at $8,000 a year. In 1907, the amount was increased to $12,000 and, in 1925, it was further increased to $15,000.

At first the salary awarded to the chief justice was $4,000 a year while the annual amount granted to the associate justices was $3,500 each. The present annual salaries, as fixed by an act of Congress passed in 1927, are: $20,500 for the chief justice, $20,-000 for associate justices, $12,500 for judges of the circuit courts of appeals (created in 1891), and $10,000 for district judges.

Salaries for clerks, as fixed by the first Congress, varied from five hundred to eight hundred dollars a year. In 1923, Congress passed a Classification Act which divided the governmental administrative workers into various grades and fixed the salaries for each. At the top of the scale were placed the professional and scientific workers, divided into seven grades, with annual salaries varying from $1,860 to $7,000. Next came the sub-professional employees, divided into eight grades, with salaries ranging from $900 to $3,000 a year. The administrative and fiscal clerks were classified in fourteen grades with salaries of from $1,140 to $7,500 each year. "Custodial" employees, divided into ten grades, were allowed salaries varying from $600 to $3,000 a year. At the bottom of the scale were placed clerks performing mechanical work. They were divided into five grades with a wage scale of from forty-five cents to ninety cents an hour.

Naturally, the first Congress did not overlook the matter of providing for their own salary. The salary fixed in 1789 was six dollars a day for both senators and representatives. In 1815, the salary was set at $1,500 a year, but this aroused such public indignation that, in 1817, the salary was changed to eight dollars a day. In 1855, the annual salary was made $3,000 a year and, in 1865, it was increased to $5,000. Congress, in 1871, passed what was denounced as the "Salary Grab Act." It not only increased the salary of future members of Congress to $7,500 a year but granted the salary to the existing membership. Again the public disapproval was so strong that, in 1874, the salary was lowered to $5,000. It was not until 1907 that the salary was finally increased to $7,500. In 1925, the annual salary of representatives and senators was fixed at $10,000, with $15,-000 allowed the speaker of the House.

In addition to salary, members of Congress have, from the beginning, been allowed mileage going to or from the capital. At first this mileage was fixed at six dollars for each twenty miles travelled. Since 1865 the travel allowance has been twenty cents a mile. It has been the custom of representatives and senators to collect their mileage regardless of whether or not they have expended the amounts allowed. Furthermore, the members of Congress are allotted $4,000 a year for clerical help. Since they may expend this sum as they see fit, it has been a common practice for congressmen to employ members of their own families. Yet another benefit conferred by members of Congress on themselves is the mail franking privilege allowing them to send their mail free of charge. They also are allowed free stationery.

The economic depression of the period after 1929 caused Congress, in 1932, to order general reductions of eight and one-third percent in the salaries paid government officials. By an act passed on March 16, 1933, the president was empowered to reduce the salaries of all federal officials and employees by as much as fifteen percent.

CONGRESSIONAL EXPANSION

During the period since 1789, Congress has been greatly expanded. The Constitution provided for an initial membership of sixty-five in the House of Representatives and twenty-six in the Senate but these figures were actually less until Rhode Island and North Carolina ratified the document and took their place in the union. The growth in the size of the House began following the census of 1790. The first apportionment act passed that year, allowing one representative for 33,000 people, resulted in increasing the House membership to one hundred and six. Thereafter, due to the rapid increase in population, the number of representatives increased by leaps and bounds. In 1860, with the electoral quotient fixed at 127,381, the number of representatives stood at two hundred and forty-three. After the census of 1910 this number had almost doubled, for it stood at four hundred and thirty-five, though the electoral quotient was then fixed at 211,877.

The House had grown so large as to be unwieldy. It was impossible for it to function effectively as a debating and deliberative group. Yet the prospect was that it would grow even larger. After the 1920 census, Congress avoided the responsibility of dealing with this problem by failing to pass a new reapportionment act. However, a decade later action was taken to prevent the membership from increasing above four hundred and thirty-five. There was considerable opposition to this as it meant that some states would lose a number of representatives while others which had gained population very rapidly would have the size of their congressional delegations increased.

In spite of the opposition, which naturally came from the states that would have their representation decreased, an act was passed by Congress in June, 1929, which directed the president to submit to Congress, after the 1930 census, tables showing the number of representatives each state would be entitled to if the total number remained at four hundred and thirty-five. This apportionment, worked out by the census bureau, was to become effective unless Congress passed a new reapportionment act. However, Congress did not pass such an act so the census bureau apportionment, submitted to Congress by President Hoover in December, 1930, went into effect. Under this new arrangement, sixteen states retained the same number of representatives as before while twenty-one states lost a total of twenty-seven representatives which were, in turn, gained by eleven other states. California led the list with a gain of nine and Michigan was second with a gain of four.

Whether the Senate has reached its maximum size is a question. By the addition of new states to the union the number of senators has been increased automatically to ninety-six. At the present time there are three organized territories, Alaska, Hawaii, and Porto Rico. There is no immediate prospect of their being admitted to the union as states but if such action should be taken the Senate would, of course, gain two members from each. The only other possibility of increasing the size of the Senate would be through the creation of new states out of already existing states. There appears little likelihood of this happening in the near future.

Because of the unwieldy size of both branches of Congress, it has been found convenient to perform through committees the major portion of the task of legislating. The Constitution conferred on the House of Representatives the power to "choose their Speaker and other officers." Acting under this power a complex legislative machine has been created. In this machine the speaker has always been an important part. Through his position as a party leader, and through his authority to maintain order, to recognize members wishing to speak, and to decide disputed points of order, he has wielded great influence. Even more important was the power, long enjoyed by the speakers, to appoint members of the House committees. This power was taken from the speaker in 1911 by a vote of the House. Since that date the committees have been elected by the House itself.

In adopting a committee system in 1789, the House of Representatives was following precedents established by the British House of Commons, the early state legislatures, and the Confederation Congress. At first the practice prevailed of referring all business to special or select committees set up for the purpose. This proved to be entirely too clumsy in practice. In the third Congress which met from 1793–1795 there were about three hundred and fifty select committees. In place of these select committees there was developed a system of standing committees, each to have charge of a certain kind of business. By 1800 there were six such committees; by 1893, the number had increased to fifty; and, by 1923, the number had grown to sixty.

The number of standing committees in the House in 1930 was forty-seven. These vary in size from two in the committee on the disposition of useless executive papers to thirty-five in the appropriations committee. One of the most important of the House committees is the committee on rules which draws up all rules for the House and determines the order of business. The committee on ways and means has charge of all measures for raising revenue. The committee on appropriations is in charge of all bills providing for the expenditure of money by the federal government. Other very important committees are those on rivers and harbors, public lands, enrolled bills, invalid pensions, territories, printing, accounts, claims, military affairs, naval affairs, judiciary, labor, interstate and foreign commerce, immigration and naturalization, agriculture, banking and currency, foreign affairs, education, District of Columbia, education, and World War veterans legislation. To these committees are referred most of the bills introduced during a session of Congress.

The remaining committees perform a comparatively small amount of work; some of them, in fact, do not meet during an entire session of Congress.

In the Senate there is a similar system of standing committees. From the first all Senate committees have been elected by that body itself. By 1921, the number of committees in the Senate had increased to seventy-five. Most of them were unimportant while some were obsolete with no duties to perform. One committee had not met for thirty years. In view of this, the list of committees was reduced to thirty-four. The most important Senate committees are those on appropriations, banking and currency, commerce, District of Columbia, education and labor, finance, foreign relations, immigration, interstate commerce, judiciary, military affairs, naval affairs, and privileges and elections. In recent years the committees on agriculture, pensions, public buildings and grounds, and territories and insular affairs have also been of considerable importance.

While committees of both branches of Congress are elected by the respective branches, the personnel is determined in advance by what is known as the caucus, a meeting of the members of each house belonging to the same party. In the makeup of the committees, the chairman and the majority of the members are selected from the ranks of the party controlling the House of Representatives or the Senate, as the case may be.

All bills, after introduction by a representative or a senator, are referred to the committee having charge of the matters referred to in the bill. The committee may then decide to report the bill back to the House or the Senate with a recommendation that it be passed or it may reject the bill entirely. If the committee wishes, it may revise the bill, rewrite it, or use part of it together with parts of other bills to form a new bill. Often, if the bill is of particular importance or if it deals with a question concerning which there is wide divergence of opinion, the committee may hold public hearings or it may call in experts for advice. It is seldom that a bill is passed after its rejection by a committee but the House or Senate may instruct the committee to report a rejected bill. If a bill is reported back to the House or the Senate it is placed on what is called the "calendar" indicating the day on which it is to be debated and perhaps brought to a vote. The debate takes place in what is called the committee of the whole, which is an old parliamentary device for speeding up business. After the committee of the whole has completed consideration of a bill it is reported to the House or Senate for final action, which may result in passage, rejection, or resubmission to the committee which originally reported it.

This brief account of the committee system of the two branches of Congress gives but a faint idea of the complex organization of the national legislature that has been developed during the period since the Constitution became operative. It would require many pages to describe this organization adequately.

EVOLUTION OF THE ADMINISTRATIVE DEPARTMENTS

Since the creation in 1789 of the first executive departments, Congress, acting under its implied powers, has from time to time provided for new departments to assist the president in the performance of his increasingly complex executive and administrative duties. Meanwhile, the duties assigned to the older departments have also been multiplied. In addition, numerous independent offices have been established to perform special functions. The result of this evolution has been the creation of a vast executive and administrative machine that functions not only in Washington, but throughout the whole of the United States and its possessions and, for that matter, in all parts of the world.

This administrative machine, having been created by Congress, is subject to the control of that body. Any part of it may be changed or even abolished by the national legislature. New duties may be assigned to any branch of the administrative system or duties may be transferred from one to another as has frequently been done. On the other hand, every part of this system is subject to the direction of the president. He, with the advice and consent of the Senate, appoints the chief officers, of whom there are some 15,000. Since he is charged by the Constitution with the duty of executing the laws, he is responsible for the manner in which his appointees perform their tasks. If they fail to act in accordance with his wishes, he may remove them. Thus, it is apparent that the control of the national executive and administrative organization is of a dual character, being divided between Congress and the president.

GROWTH OF THE DEPARTMENT OF STATE

Turning to an examination of the historical evolution of this organization, attention should first be directed to the Department of State, the first executive department to be created in 1789. From the first, this department has been in charge of the foreign relations of the United States. Under its control are the diplomatic and consular services of the United States. Until 1924 these two services were separate but, by the Rogers Act of that year, they were unified. The diplomatic officers are stationed in the capitals of foreign countries where they act as the direct representatives of the president and the secretary of state. Their duties are many and complex for on them depends to a large degree the maintenance of friendly relations with the countries to which they are accredited. The chief diplomatic representatives are designated as ambassadors and ministers. An officer serving temporarily in place of an ambassador or minister is called a *chargé d'affaires*. Attached to each diplomatic mission is a staff of secretaries and *attachés*. At the beginning of 1932, the United States was represented in fifteen of the most important countries by ambassadors, and in forty-two other countries by ministers.

The consular service, also under the direction of the Department of State, has functions quite different from those of the diplomatic service. The consuls are stationed in the more important cities of the world. It is their chief function to protect and promote American trade and business in the countries in which they are stationed. They furnish reports on business conditions and information regarding foreign markets to the home government and, in various ways, they seek to promote American foreign commerce. In addition various duties have been assigned to them in connection with the administration of the United States immigration and naturalization laws, the quarantine laws, the tariff laws, and regulations pertaining to the American merchant marine and its personnel. In 1932 American consuls were stationed in no less than sixty-eight countries or colonial dependencies of such countries. In Great Britain alone there were eighteen consulates, while in China there were fifteen. On the other hand, in Norway and Siam there was only one each.

Among the domestic functions at first assigned to the Department of State were the taking of the census, the administration of the patent and copyright laws, and the administration of the territories of the federal government. These functions have, however, been transferred to other more recently created departments. At present, the duties of the department include the preservation, editing, and publication of the laws and resolutions passed by Congress; the proclamation of constitutional amendments; receiving the electoral votes from the states and transmitting them to Congress; and keeping the seal of the United States and affixing it to proclamations and commissions and other documents as required by law.

As the duties of the Department of State have become more complex, its organization has also been greatly enlarged. Thomas Jefferson, the first secretary of state, carried on the work with the aid of six employees and a few diplomatic representatives, at a total annual expense of $8,000. Now the organization includes about six hundred officials and employees in Washington and about three thousand others scattered throughout the world, requiring, in 1932, an appropriation of $18,506,306. The chief officers in the department in Washington include, in addition to the secretary of state whose regular salary is $15,000 a year, an under secretary at $10,000 a year, and four assistant secretaries at $9,000 a year. In addition there is a legal adviser, a special assistant to the secretary, an executive assistant to the assistant secretary, an economic adviser, an historical adviser, and a chief instructor of the foreign service school maintained to train those about to enter the diplomatic or consular service in subordinate positions. Each of these receives an annual salary of from $6,500 to $9,000. Then there are eighteen divisions, bureaus, and offices with chiefs who receive from $3,300 to $9,000 a year. These are the divisions of foreign service personnel, Far Eastern affairs, Latin American affairs, western European affairs, eastern European affairs, Mexican affairs, passports, current information, foreign administration, treaties, protocols, communications and records, visas, the translating bureau, the bureau of accounts, the office of coördination and review, the foreign service buildings office, and the consular commercial office.

During the period since the office of secretary of state was created, it has been filled by some of the most notable men in the political history of the United States. Six of the early presidents received training in foreign affairs through their occupancy of the office. In fact, for a time it appeared that an appointment as head of the department would mean advancement to the presidency. While Jefferson did not step directly into the presidential office the next three presidents, James Madison, James Monroe, and John Quincy Adams, did so. Martin Van Buren and James Buchanan were the last secretaries of state to later become presidents of the United States. Other outstanding men who have headed the department include John Marshall, Henry Clay, Edward Livingston, Daniel Webster, John C. Calhoun, Lewis Cass, William H. Seward, James G. Blaine, Richard Olney, John Hay, Elihu Root, William J. Bryan, Charles E. Hughes, and Frank B. Kellogg.

DEVELOPMENT OF THE TREASURY DEPARTMENT

Next to the Department of State in prestige and importance is the Treasury Department. Through this department are collected all the revenues of the United States from every source provided by law. It administers the customs service and the income tax laws, and collects the internal revenue taxes. It pays out, on properly executed warrants, all money appropriated by Congress. Under the authority granted by Congress, it borrows money and, under the same authority, it pays the debts of the United States. It also controls the coinage system of the country and supplies all paper money. In addition, it manages the coast guard which performs many functions including the prevention of smuggling; it operates the public health service; and it arranges for and supervises the construction of public buildings. From 1920 to 1930 it was also in charge of the enforcement of the prohibition laws but, during the latter year, Congress, complying with a request made by President Hoover, ordered this function transferred to the Department of Justice.

In size, the Treasury Department is exceeded only by the Post Office Department. Scattered throughout the United States are thousands of officials and employees who constitute a part of the Treasury Department organization. The most important of these are the collectors of the customs and the collectors of internal revenue. Heading the department in Washington is, of course, the secretary of the treasury who receives $15,000 a year. Next in rank is the under secretary who receives $10,000 annually, followed by three assistant secretaries who are each paid $9,000 annually. Next is an executive assistant to the under secretary, and three assistants to the secretary, each receiving an annual salary of from $6,000 to $8,000. There are six divisions each presided over by chiefs whose salaries vary from $5,400 to $8,000 a year. One of these divisions is the secret service, the two chief duties of which are to prevent the counterfeiting of the money and securities of the United States and to protect the president. The other divisions are appointments, supply, loans and currency, accounts and audit, and bookkeeping and warrants.

Other officials include the commissioner of the public debt, the register of the treasury, the commissioner of accounts and deposits, the chief economist, the government actuary, the comptroller of the treasury, and the treasurer of the United States. These receive annual salaries of from $4,600 to $9,000. The commissioner of internal revenue, who receives $10,000 a year, is in charge of the collection of internal revenue taxes and income taxes. The commissioner of customs, who likewise receives $10,000, supervises the far-flung customs service of the United States. A recently created office, also paying $10,000 a year, is that of the farm loan commissioner. Five members of the federal farm board, each receiving $10,000 a year, have also been included in the Treasury Department since the passage of the farm relief act of 1929. The director of the mint, whose salary is $8,000 a year, has oversight of the making of the coins and medals provided for by laws passed by Congress. The director of the bureau of engraving and printing, who receives $9,000 annually, supervises the manufacture of all paper money and government securities.

In charge of the public health service is the surgeon-general who is paid $8,000 a year. This service had its origin in 1798 when the Treasury Department established a marine hospital service to care for sick sailors and so keep them from carrying diseases into the country. This work, in extended form, is now carried on through the quarantine service operating at ninety-six ports of entry. In one year this service excluded over a thousand diseased persons seeking to enter the United States. Through its hygienic laboratory, the public health service scientists are constantly studying the causes, remedies, and prevention of diseases.

The commandant is the title of the Treasury Department official in charge of the United States coast guard. He receives $8,000 annually. Other important treasury officials are the commissioner of industrial alcohol and the commissioner of narcotics, each receiving an annual salary of $9,000.

In 1932, the total amount appropriated by Congress for the Treasury Department was $268,937,417.

THE EXPANSION OF THE WAR DEPARTMENT

During the period of history since 1789 the War Department has experienced a considerable expansion. Its functions are not purely military for it is in charge of such matters as the construction of harbor and river improvements and the building of dams and bridges. The army engineering corps performed the gigantic task of constructing the Panama Canal after others had failed. At present the secretary of war supervises the Panama Canal Zone. Another duty assigned to the War Department is the supervision of the Philippine Islands and Porto Rico.

Though it performs civilian duties, the War Department is, naturally, chiefly concerned with military affairs. Its business is to see that preparations are made for war insofar as it is possible through the appropriations made by Congress, and, in time of war, to devote its energies to the end that victory may be secured.

During most of its existence the department has been presided over by civilians. The secretary of war who is head of the department receives $15,000. Next is an asistant secretary whose annual salary is $10,000 while another assistant secretary, in charge of developing the army air service, receives $9,000 a year.

An administrative assistant draws a salary of $8,000 a year. These officials are all civilians. All the other important officials of the War Department are army officers. First among these is the chief of staff who is paid $10,200 annually. He is in charge of the general staff of the army which was created by an act of Congress passed in 1903. The general staff is made up of five divisions which are military intelligence, personnel, operation and training, supply, and war plans. The chief of staff, the general of the army, the assistant secretary, and the secretary of war were designated by the National Defence Act of 1920 as the "war council" to formulate the policies of the War Department.

The other important officers of the War Department, whose duties may be inferred from their titles, are the adjutant-general, the inspection-general, the judge-advocate-general, the quarter-master-general, the surgeon-general, and the chiefs of engineering, ordnance, signal corps, coast artillery, air corps, chemical warfare service, infantry, cavalry, field artillery, and finance. Each receives an annual salary of $8,000.

The total appropriation for the War Department in 1932 was $460,078,650. This included the cost of maintaining the Panama Canal as well as the amounts appropriated to carry out other non-military functions of the department.

CREATION AND DEVELOPMENT OF THE NAVY DEPARTMENT

Until 1798, the administration of naval affairs was vested in the War Department. In that year, however, the threat of a war with France led to the establishment of the Navy Department. When created it had only three vessels under its jurisdiction, one of which was the famous *Constitution* built a short time previously. The so-called "Naval War with France," fought without a declaration of war during the years 1798–1799, led to a rapid increase in the size of the navy so that by the end of the latter year the United States had thirty-three vessels.

The department grew slowly until it reached its present size. The secretary of the navy, who is a civilian, presides over the department. He, like the other executive department heads, receives $15,000 a year. Other civilian officials are the assistant secretary, and the assistant secretary of aeronautics, each of whom receives $9,000 annually, and a chief clerk who receives a yearly salary of $6,000. The other important members of the department are all naval officers. These include the chief of naval operations, the judge-advocate-general, the president of the naval examining board, the director of naval intelligence, the superintendent of the naval observatory, the hydrographer in charge of the hydrographic office, and the chiefs of the bureaus of yards and docks, navigation, ordnance, construction and repair, engineering, and supplies and accounts. The salaries of these officers range from $6,000 to $10,200 a year. The total appropriation for the Navy Department in 1932 was $360,101,593.

THE DEPARTMENT OF JUSTICE

For many years the attorney-general was a cabinet officer without a department over which to preside. In fact, at first, he was not even a full-time official. He was expected to be available so that his advice on legal matters could be secured by the president and the department heads, but this did not interfere with his private law practice. Gradually his governmental duties increased so much that he had to give up his law practice. From time to time Congress found it necessary to provide officials to assist him in carrying on the legal business of the government. Finally, in 1870, the Department of Justice was created and the attorney-general was designated as its head.

The most important official in the department, next to the attorney-general, is the solicitor-general, whose chief duty is to represent the government in cases before the national Supreme Court. He receives an annual salary of $10,000. There are eight assistant attorney-generals who receive annual stipends of $9,000 each; an administrative assistant to the attorney-general who is paid $7,000 each year; and a chief clerk and general agent whose annual salary is $6,500. The Department of Justice also furnishes solicitors for the Treasury Department and for the Departments of Commerce and Labor. Each of these three is paid $8,500 annually.

The director of the bureau of investigation receives $9,000 a year while the director of the bureau of prisons receives $10,000 annually. Under the jurisdiction of the latter are the three federal prisons at Atlanta, Georgia, Leavenworth, Kansas, and McNeil Island, state of Washington; the federal industrial reformatory for men at Chillicothe, Ohio; the federal industrial institute for women at Alderson, West Virginia; the federal house of detention in the city of New York; and the national training school for boys. The total number of inmates of the federal penitentiaries on May 31, 1931 was 13,473.

In 1930, the function of enforcing the prohibition laws was transferred, by the Williamson Act, to the Department of Justice from the Treasury Department. This added about three thousand employees to the department. The prohibition bureau is presided over by a director who receives an annual salary of $9,000. The country is divided into twelve administrative districts while Porto Rico and Hawaii are additional districts. Some idea of the activity of this bureau may be gained from the facts that, in the fiscal year, 1930–1931, 56,938 prohibition violation cases were tried in the federal courts, resulting in 51,360 convictions and pleas of guilty. Fines totalling $5,606,331 were assessed. During the year a total of 63,177 arrests were made. Prohibition agents seized 8,499 automobiles, 76 boats, 21,541 stills, 14,904 fermenters, 5,319,613 gallons of beer, 1,934,628 gallons of spirits, 291,582 gallons of wines, and a vast quantity of distilling and brewing materials. The budget estimate for prohibition enforcement in 1931–1932 was $11,530,680.

Another important function of the Department of Justice is to supervise the United States district attorneys and marshals. All applications made by federal prisoners for pardons or paroles are considered by the department which then makes recommendations to the president in whom the Constitution vests the sole power to grant pardons and paroles.

In 1931–1932 the amount appropriated by Congress for the Department of Justice totalled $51,229,201.

EXPANSION OF THE POST OFFICE DEPARTMENT

Though the office of postmaster-general was created in 1789 and though the postal system of the Confederation government was continued by action of Congress at the same time, it was not until the beginning of the Jackson administration in 1829 that the office was given cabinet rank, and not until 1874 that the postal organization was recognized by law as constituting a co-ordinate department.

During the period since 1789 the seventy-five post offices then existing have been increased to about fifty thousand. In the fiscal year 1929–1930 mail was carried on the railroads of the country for a total of 564,801,022 miles at a cost of $103,970,436. In addition much mail was carried on ships and by the air mail service inaugurated in 1918.

At first, only letters were carried and even for them such high postage rates were charged as to discourage the use of the postal service. The postal officials were allowed to use their own discretion in the matter of carrying newspapers and periodicals. However, the service has been extended so that not only letters and post cards, but newspapers, magazines, and other literature may be sent through the mails at comparatively low rates. Since 1913 it has been possible to send even bulky packages through the mail as a result of the inauguration of the parcel post system in that year.

Since 1855 it has been possible to protect valuable first class mail through registration. The free mail delivery system inaugurated in 1863 has been extended to cities, even the smaller ones, all over the United States. The cost of this service alone in the year 1929–1930 was $146,531,671. The money order system has been in existence since 1864. It was first established as a convenience for federal soldiers during the Civil War. From a modest beginning in 1896, the rural free delivery system has been expanded until it includes over 45,000 routes with a total mileage of over 500,000. In 1911 a postal savings system was instituted whereby any person may make a deposit of any amount from one dollar to two thousand five hundred dollars and receive two percent interest on the deposit. The total amount of the postal savings, at the close of the fiscal year 1929–1930, was $175,271,686.

So gigantic is the postal system of the United States that it includes about one-half of all the federal civilian employees. Besides the postmaster-general, who presides over it, there are a number of extremely important officials in the department. There are four assistant postmaster-generals, each of whom draws an annual salary of $9,000. One is in charge of the moving of the mail; another assists in the selection of postmasters and other postal employees, supervises the maintenance of post office buildings, and manages the dead letter office; a third controls the postal savings system, money orders, the parcel post system, and administers the financial affairs of the department; and the fourth regulates the rural free delivery service. Other important officials are the chief clerk and superintendent of buildings, the directors of the division of postal savings and the international postal service, the solicitor, the purchasing agent and administrative postmaster-general, the personnel officer, the superintendent of the division of money orders, the general superintendent of the railway mail service, the superintendent of the division of dead letters and dead parcel post, and the chief inspector. These officials receive salaries each year varying from $3,600 to $8,500.

The total amount appropriated for the Post Office Department in the year 1931–1932 was $831,483,777. Of this the department was expected to earn $646,483,777, leaving a deficit of $195,000,000 to be paid out of the treasury. This deficit is not unusual for, ever since the postal system was inaugurated, the cost of the service has exceeded the income. Congress has sought, without success, to discover some means of making the service self-supporting. While the annual deficits are large, it should be kept in mind that the social and economic benefits derived from the postal system are of inestimable value. Experience has demonstrated that an increase in postage rates in the hope of eliminating the deficits defeats its own purpose since the people will not use the mail service as much as when the rates are cheaper.

THE ESTABLISHMENT AND EXPANSION OF THE DEPARTMENT OF THE INTERIOR

In 1849, Congress created the Department of the Interior to take over various domestic duties that had been assigned to the older departments. For example, it was assigned the administration of the copyright laws, since assigned to the Library of Congress; and the management of the census office and the patent office, since transferred to the Department of Commerce.

One of the most important duties assigned to the department was the administration of the public lands. At the time of the department's creation, the policy of the government was to sell the land at a price fixed by law. Under this system speculation was encouraged with consequent harmful effects on the country. One of the chief causes of the panic of 1837 had been the wild orgy of land speculation which preceded it. In 1862, Congress passed the famous Homestead Act by which, under the direction of the Department of the Interior, the major portion of the public domain was parceled out to settlers mostly free of charge. The department also administered the Morrill Act of 1862 whereby public land was granted to the states to encourage them to inaugurate and maintain college courses in military training, agriculture, and the mechanic arts. The colleges and universities of the country which have benefited from the Morrill Act are known as "land grant colleges."

The Department of the Interior also administered the forest and mineral lands. For years the policy of the government was to allow such land to be acquired like any other land. By the "Timber and Stone Act" of 1878, forest land could be purchased at a minimum cost of two and a half dollars an acre. But, in 1891, an act was passed by Congress which permitted the president to withdraw forest lands from entry. While Presidents Cleveland and McKinley acted under this law, it was President Theodore Roosevelt who really inaugurated the forest conservation policy of the United States. He withdrew 150,000,000 acres from disposal to private interests. Following a recommendation by President Roosevelt, Congress, in 1901, created the United States forest service in the Department of the Interior to replace the inadequate bureau of forests. Since that time the forest conservation policy has been administered by this service which, however, has been a division of the Department of Agriculture since 1905.

Until 1910, mineral lands were also disposed of by the Department of the Interior in accordance with the lavish policy established by the national laws. But, in that year, Congress extended the conservation policy to such lands. One law decreed that thereafter all mineral rights under lands granted or sold for agricultural use should be reserved to the government. Furthermore, it was ordered that a large area rich in minerals should be reserved from public sale. Another act created the bureau of mines in the Department of the Interior to administer the mineral conservation policy. This bureau, in 1925, was transferred to the Department of Commerce.

Another important function of the Department of the Interior is the administration of the reclamation policy of the United States. While some attention has been given to the reclamation of marshy or swamp lands, by far the most important work has been done in connection with the reclamation of arid or desert lands. One has only to travel through New Mexico, Arizona, and California, or other western states to see the marvelous results that have been accomplished through the reclamation policy.

The beginning of the reclamation policy was in 1877 when the Desert Act was passed, allowing the purchase of desert land at a price of one dollar and twenty-five cents an acre provided that the purchaser would irrigate the land. In 1894 the Carey Act was passed which granted to the states of the west large tracts of arid lands on condition that they would provide irrigation facilities. This attempt to encourage state reclamation projects did not prove eminently successful so, in 1902, Congress, on the strong recommendation of President Roosevelt, passed the Reclamation Act or what is often called the Newlands Act after its sponsor, Senator F. G. Newlands of Nevada. The act provided that a reclamation fund should be established with the proceeds of public land sales in thirteen western states and territories. The proceeds were to be used, under the direction of the secretary of the interior, to provide irrigation facilities for the purchasers of arid lands. In 1907, the bureau of reclamation was set up in the department to administer the reclamation policy outlined by Congress.

Up to 1930, twenty-eight national reclamation projects had been established in fifteen states in which were located arid lands. Among these are the Salt River project in Arizona, the water for which is supplied by a reservoir created by the Roosevelt Dam. This reservoir serves 255,000 acres of land. Other projects are the Milk River project in Montana, the North Platte project in Nebraska and Wyoming, the Newlands projects in Nevada, the

Yuma project in Arizona and California, the Uncompahgre project in Colorado, the Minidoka project in Idaho, the Lower Yellowstone project in Montana and North Dakota, the Belle Fourche project in South Dakota, the Shoshone project in northwestern Wyoming, the Boise project in Idaho, the Huntley project in Montana, the Klamath project in southern Oregon and northern California, the Umatilla project in northeastern Oregon, the Rio Grande project in Texas and New Mexico, the Strawberry Valley project in Utah, the Okanogan project in Washington, the Sun River project in Montana, the Orland project in the Sacramento Valley in California, the Grand Valley project in western Colorado, the King Hill project in southwestern Idaho, the Riverton project in Wyoming, the Owyhee project in southern Idaho and eastern Oregon, the Vale project in eastern Oregon, the Yakima project in south central Washington, the Carlsbad project in New Mexico, and the Salt Lake Basin project in Utah.

The latest to be started is the Boulder Canyon project authorized by an act of Congress approved on December 21, 1928. The feature here is the great Hoover Dam being constructed in the Black Canyon where the Colorado River flows between the states of Arizona and Nevada. Included in the Boulder Dam project is the All-American Canal to furnish irrigation water for the Coachella and Imperial valleys of southern California. This project, when completed, will rank as the greatest of all engineering feats in the world's history, and it will outrank all other projects in the amount of electrical energy it will produce and in the amount of land it will irrigate.

Up to 1930, the reclamation bureau had constructed fifty-two storage dams creating reservoirs with a storage capacity of 4,763,-394,000,000 gallons of water. To carry the water, 16,557 miles of canals, ditches, and drains had been completed. Water is available to irrigate 1,992,330 acres of land in the irrigation projects and also to supply, under the Warren Act of 1911, land privately developed outside the projects to the extent of 1,480,-040 acres. The cumulative value of the crops produced on land irrigated by government projects, from the time the first water was supplied in 1906 to 1930, was $1,642,267,680. In 1931, the reclamation projects included 40,354 irrigated farms with a total population of 165,956 and, in addition, 213 cities and towns with a total population of 472,723.

When the Department of the Interior was first organized it took over from the War Department the management of Indian affairs. Through the bureau of Indian affairs, the 340,541 Indians of the country are cared for on about one hundred and forty reservations. In 1867 there was created a department of education headed by a commissioner, but, in the next year, it was made a bureau in the Department of the Interior. It has advisory and informative duties for the most part. Other functions of the Department of the Interior include the supervision of the national parks, the administration of the geological survey, the management of federal affairs in the territories of Alaska and Hawaii, the administering of several government hospitals, and the conduct of Howard University, a college for negroes established in the District of Columbia by act of Congress following the Civil War.

The organization of the Department of the Interior includes, besides the secretary of the interior, a first assistant secretary, an assistant secretary, an administrative assistant, two executive assistants, a solicitor, a chief clerk, commissioners and assistant commissioners of the general land office, Indian affairs, education, and reclamation, a director of the geological survey, an administrative geologist, a chief engineer, a director and assistant director of the national park service, and the governors of Alaska, Hawaii, and the Virgin Islands. These officials each receive from $6,500 to $10,000 a year. The total appropriation for the Department of the Interior in the year 1931–1932 was $85,295,-107.

It is obvious that the national government, through this department, is rendering important social and economic services to the people of the United States.

THE DEVELOPMENT OF THE NEWER DEPARTMENTS

Of great benefit to the rural population has been the Department of Agriculture. As early as 1836 Congress assigned to the commissioner of patents the duty of distributing seeds to farmers. During the Civil War, Congress created a Department of Agriculture in charge of a commissioner who, however, did not rank with the cabinet officers. Not until 1889 was the department made coördinate with the other executive departments. Through the Hatch Act of 1887 which authorized the establishment of experimental stations, the department has greatly aided in the improvement of farm products. The Smith-Lever Act of 1914 has made it possible to conduct extension work at strategic points.

The bureau of public roads in the Department of Agriculture administers the large federal appropriations for road building and coöperates with the state road building agencies in the development of a national system of all-weather roads. The bureau of home economics carries on experiments of interest and value to home makers.

Not only does the department render important services to the farmers along economic lines but it also performs important social services for the whole population. The bureau of chemistry enforces the Pure Food and Drug Act passed in 1906 to prevent the manufacture, transportation, and sale of "adulterated, or misbranded, or poisonous, or deleterious" food and drugs. The bureau of animal husbandry enforces the Meat Inspection Act, also passed in 1906, which requires sanitary conditions in meat packing establishments and also requires that all meat pass a rigid inspection.

An enumeration of the chief officials in the Department of Agriculture will reveal some of the other functions of the department. In addition to the secretary in charge of the department, there are an assistant secretary, a solicitor, a librarian, directors of scientific work, regulatory work, extension work, personnel and business administration, information, plant quarantine and control administration, grain futures administration, food and drug administration, experiment stations, coöperative extension work, and chiefs of the bureaus of weather, animal husbandry, dairy industry, plant industry, forest service, chemistry and soils, entomology, biological survey, public roads, agricultural economics, home economics, and agricultural engineering. The annual salaries of these officials vary from $4,600 to $9,000. The amount appropriated for the department during the fiscal year 1931–1932 was $247,283,130.

The growing importance of business and labor led to the establishment, in 1903, of the Department of Commerce and Labor. In 1913, it was deemed advisable to divide the department so as to form the Department of Commerce and the Department of Labor. Included in the Department of Commerce is the bureau of foreign and domestic commerce which has as its special function the promotion of trade. In this department are located the patent office, the census bureau, the bureau of standards, the bureau of fisheries, the bureau of navigation which administers the federal laws regarding navigation and steamboats, the steamboat inspection service, the coast and geodetic survey, the bureau of lighthouses, and the bureau of mines.

Since Herbert Hoover became the secretary of commerce in 1921, the department has become an important factor in the government. The most important officers in the department, other than the secretary, are the assistant secretary, the assistant secretary in charge of aeronautics, the administrative assistant to the secretary, the secretary to the secretary, the chief clerk and superintendent, the chiefs of the divisions of appointments, publications, and purchases and sales, the directors of the bureaus of the census, foreign and domestic commerce, standards, mines, radio, and of the coast and geodetic survey, the commissioners of fisheries, lighthouses, navigation, and patents, and, finally, the supervising inspector-general of the steamboat inspection service. The salaries of these officials are governed by the classification act of 1923. The total amount appropriated for the department in the year 1931–1932 was $54,335,230.

The tenth and last of the executive departments is the Department of Labor created, as has been mentioned, in 1913. The functions which it performs are largely of social significance. Its most important divisions are the immigration bureau, the naturalization bureau, the bureau of labor statistics, the women's bureau, and the children's bureau. The department also maintains an employment service which was established during the World War. The conciliation division has been established to offer its services as a mediator in labor disputes. Many strikes and lockouts have been averted through its activities.

Besides the secretary of labor, the chief officers of the department are the assistant secretary, the second assistant secretary, the chief clerk, the appointment clerk, the disbursing clerk, the supervising director of the United States employment service, the director of conciliation, the director of the women's bureau, the chief of the children's bureau, and the commissioners of general immigration, naturalization, and labor statistics. The annual salaries of these officials vary from $3,200 to $9,000. The 1931–1932 appropriation for the department was $14,994,-200.

THE INDEPENDENT OFFICES

In addition to the ten executive and administrative departments, Congress has from time to time created what are known as the independent offices. These perform not only administrative duties but they also exercise quasi-judicial and quasi-legislative powers. The purpose of Congress in establishing these offices has apparently been to secure for them greater independence and freedom from political interference than if they were placed in the regular departments. In the budget for 1931–1932 provision was made for thirty-three independent establishments.

Considered from the standpoint of the money which it spends, the veterans' administration is the most important of these. It was formed in 1930 through a consolidation of the veterans' bureau, the bureau of pensions, and the national home for disabled volunteer soldiers. Since so much controversy exists over the government's policy towards war veterans, it seems in order to present a brief historical analysis of that policy.

The policy of granting pensions or other rewards to veterans started with the War for Independence. After the Constitution became operative, the function of administering veterans' affairs was entrusted to the War Department in which there eventually developed the bureau of pensions. Up to the beginning of the Civil War in 1861, the federal government had paid to the veterans of the War for Independence, the War of 1812, the Mexican War, and various Indian wars, a total of $90,000,000 in pensions and, in addition, had granted them as bounties a total of 65,000,000 acres of land.

The Civil War, the Spanish American War, and the Indian wars following the Civil War, greatly increased the list of pensioners. The peak was reached in 1902 when 999,446 persons, including 260,003 widows of veterans, were paid $137,504,267. By June 30, 1931, the number of pensioners had decreased to 451,433, of whom 188,288 were widows of veterans, but, due to more liberal allowances, the total amount of the pensions had increased to $234,419,721. Of this amount, $121,993,750 represented Civil War pensions, $102,256,480 represented Spanish American War pensions, while $10,169,491 represented pensions for veterans of other wars.

The soldiers' homes were created following the Civil War and their administration was assigned to the Department of the Interior. These homes, now known as the veterans' administration homes, are eleven in number. In 1931 they cared for 63,879 veterans.

When the World War began in 1917, Congress took steps to prevent the pension system from being extended to the veterans of that war. A system of insurance was provided for, the administration of which was delegated to the bureau of war risk insurance. Those insured, it should be mentioned, had the premiums for this insurance deducted from their meagre pay. After the war, a large proportion of those insured dropped their government insurance. However, during the calendar year 1931, the veterans' administration enjoyed an income of $107,329,206.60 from premiums, interest, and other sources connected with veterans' insurance. This amount should be deducted from the total annual appropriation for the benefit of veterans. A system of compensation was also provided for those disabled in the service by wounds, injuries, or disease. Following the World War, all affairs of the veterans of that conflict were consolidated in the hands of a veterans' bureau created for the purpose. This bureau carried on the work of administering the war risk insurance law and its amendments, as well as a large number of new laws passed since the war. These laws included the adjusted compensation law or, as it is often called, the soldiers' "bonus" law, passed in 1924 over the successive vetoes of Presidents Harding and Coolidge. The purpose of this law was to give to the veterans extra pay for their war service, the payment, however, being delayed for twenty years.

Meanwhile, by legislation passed in 1931, the veterans have been permitted to borrow up to fifty percent of the face value of their adjusted compensation certificates. The duties of the veterans' bureau were further increased by the law passed in 1930 which granted disability allowances to men disabled to the extent of twenty-five percent or more, but who could not connect their disability with their military service. In the years following the World War many disabled veterans were given vocational training which enabled a large portion of them to resume their places as useful members of society. Many have been hospitalized, for the most part in government built and operated hospitals scattered over the United States. The total number hospitalized up to the end of the fiscal year 1930–1931 was 534,431.

On June 30, 1931, a total of 299,288 veterans disabled by their war service were receiving compensation; 93,334 beneficiaries of such veterans who were deceased were also being compensated; 6,364 emergency officers who had been disabled in the war were drawing retirement pay; and 229,568 veterans who could not connect their disabilities with the war were drawing disability allowances. A total of 35,055 were still in hospitals while another group of 19,264 disabled World War veterans were in veterans' administration homes.

The total budget for the veterans' administration for the year 1931–1932 was $947,439,878. This, it must be remembered, included the pensions for veterans of wars prior to 1917 and the cost of maintaining the soldiers' homes, as well as the amounts paid to veterans of the World War. In connection with the latter it included all veterans' insurance disbursements. These disbursements were far exceeded by the payments made by about 644,000 veterans to the insurance division of the veterans' administration.

It is apparent that the amounts spent on veterans in the future will be much less than in the past. On March 16, 1933, Congress passed an act, on the request of President Franklin D. Roosevelt, giving him virtual lawmaking power whereby he may reduce

payments to veterans by an amount estimated as high as $400,-
000,000.

Many more pages would be required for a thorough discussion of the veterans' administration and for the presentation of
arguments for or against the government's policy towards the
veterans of its wars. It is possible to look upon the payments
made as a just reward for hazardous and sacrificial service in
time of national danger or, on the contrary, to regard the
amounts spent on veterans as so much plundered from the
treasury by a class seeking special favors for themselves. If one
is inclined to take the latter view, it should be kept in mind
that the veterans are not the only class who have been or are
being aided by the government. The substantial aid given to the
railroads, to steamship lines, to air lines, to business through
protective tariffs and otherwise, the provision for retirement
pay for the personnel of the regular army and the navy, and
the pension system for civilian employees are but a few instances of how the government's bounty has been and is being
bestowed on others than the veterans. There should be no question about the obligation of the government to aid veterans
who were disabled in the national service during a period of
war.

Another important independent agency of the federal government is the United States shipping board created by act of
Congress in 1916. Its great work was done during the World
War in the development of a merchant marine adequate to
meet the war emergencies. The various commissions that have
charge of communication, transportation, and power development are all very important. These are the interstate commerce
commission, the federal radio commission, and the federal power
commission. The tariff commission, the federal trade commission,
and the civil service commission also perform important functions.
The federal farm board, created in 1929, and the reconstruction finance corporation and the home loan board, created in
1932, have been established to aid the country to recover from
the economic depression. Other special establishments worthy of
special mention are the Smithsonian Institution, the Federal reserve board, the federal board for vocational education, the
bureau of efficiency, and the general accounting office. The total

amount appropriated, in the fiscal year 1931–1932, for the thirty-three independent establishments then existing, was $1,-145,565,043.

OBSERVATIONS ON THE ADMINISTRATIVE SERVICE

From the small beginning of 1789, the administrative service of the United States has grown into a large army, consisting of 616,837 persons on June 30, 1931. Of these, 71,693 were employed in the District of Columbia, the rest outside of the district. Something over 90,000 of the civil service employees in 1931 were women.

Through this vast army of civilian employees the federal government performs a multitude of services for the people. Most of the functions are important but some are of little value and might well be eliminated. The tendency has constantly been in the direction of paternalism, that is, the government has assumed many functions which the people might perform for themselves. More and more, the government has entered into business in competition with private businesses. The ultimate outcome of this trend will be a complete system of state socialism. If the people wish to have a great bureaucracy performing innumerable services, they must be willing to pay the price, not only in the form of increasing taxes but also in the curtailment of their liberty. It is doubtful whether the American people realize the extent to which their liberties have already been curtailed, particularly through the establishment of administrative agencies exercising police powers, as well as judicial and legislative powers, contrary to the principle of separation of powers.

It should be obvious that, through the far-flung administrative organization established by Congress, representing the people, the police powers of the national government have been extended to every nook and corner of the land. The most noticeable manifestation of this police power has been through the activities of the prohibition enforcement agents, but the power is being constantly applied in other ways. Government agents swarm through the land ferreting out violators of the numerous laws for the execution of which they have been made responsible. Secret service agents are seeking out counterfeiters; immigration officials are ready to pounce on persons who are suspected of entering the country illegally or who have remained too long after entering on a permit; postal inspectors are trailing violators of the postal laws; representatives of the narcotics office are on the alert for those trespassing against the anti-narcotics laws; the revenue officers are busy dealing with tax evaders; the coast guard is ever watchful to prevent smuggling; and the meat inspectors are busy condemning unfit meat.

On a larger scale, the radio commission exercises the power to close radio stations which it decides are not in the public interest; the interstate commerce commission restrains railroads from indulging in unfair practices such as granting rebates; and the federal trade commission guards against the violation of the anti-trust laws. And so one might go on to enumerate dozens of other examples of the application of combined federal police and judicial power in everyday life, a power which has been implied through a broad interpretation of the Constitution. Truly, the federal government has departed a long way from the ideal expressed by Thomas Jefferson when he said, "That government is best which governs least."

Even a casual observer can see that there has been considerable duplication and not a little inefficiency in the national administrative service. During the presidency of Herbert Hoover, some progress was made in the direction of reform but his hands were tied by a hostile Congress. However, through an amendment to the treasury-post office appropriation bill, finally passed on March 3, and signed by President Hoover as one of his last acts on March 4, 1933, President Franklin D. Roosevelt was given wide powers to reorganize, merge, or even to abolish government bureaus, offices, and commissions. By impounding the appropriations for the support of some of these administrative agencies, the president will be able to save many millions of dollars annually. The president is to enjoy these extensive powers for two years. Meanwhile, no presidential reorganization order can be negated by Congress except by a two-thirds vote of each house of Congress. This authority placed directly on the shoulders of President Roosevelt the responsibility for eliminating duplication and inefficiency in the federal administrative service.

THE EXPANSION OF THE NATIONAL JUDICIARY

In keeping with the expansion of the legislative and executive branches of the government, the national judiciary has also experienced a considerable growth. This has been necessary because of the great increase in the volume of judicial business brought before the federal courts as a result of the numerous applications of the federal police power.

The first attempt by Congress to increase the size of the federal judiciary was, at least in part, for political reasons and this led to its failure. In 1801, the "lame duck" Federalist Congress passed a judiciary act which relieved the Supreme Court judges of all circuit court duties. Sixteen separate circuit court judges were authorized to "ride the circuits" which were increased to six in number. The Democratic-Republicans, headed by President Thomas Jefferson, came into office shortly after the passage of this act. Taking the view that the new judgeships were unnecessary and that they had been created to give life positions to defeated Federalists, the Jeffersonians, in 1802, secured the passage of an act abolishing the new judgeships though the six circuits were retained. This was the only instance in the national history of the United States where Congress eliminated judgeships without making other provision for the judges. The constitutionality of such elimination was never decided.

No further change in the federal judiciary, other than the extension of the system to new states and territories, was made until 1869. In that year, Congress created nine separate circuit judges for the nine circuits then in existence. The Supreme Court justices were relieved of circuit riding except for one term in each two year period. With the increase in Supreme Court business they ceased circuit riding altogether.

By 1890, the judicial business of the country had become so great that the existing courts were not adequate to dispose of it. During that year, there were 1800 cases on the Supreme Court docket, not more than a fourth of which could be handled. Accordingly, Congress created, in 1891, nine circuit courts of appeals which assumed the appellate jurisdiction of the circuit courts. To lessen the burden of the Supreme Court, the new courts were given final appellate jurisdiction except in certain specified types of cases. The old circuit courts were superfluous after 1891 but they were not abolished until 1911 when their judges were assigned to the circuit courts of appeals. In 1929 the number of the circuit courts of appeals was increased to ten. Three judges preside over each circuit court of appeals. The total number of these judges in 1931 was thirty-nine. While the Supreme Court justices are each assigned to a circuit court of appeals, they are not obligated to sit as members of that court and, as a result, very rarely do so.

From time to time, Congress has created special courts to handle particular kinds of cases. For instance, in 1855 there was established the court of claims to adjust all claims against the United States government. At first the functions of the court were largely advisory but, in 1866, Congress bestowed on it the authority to render final judgments in regard to claims which should be binding on all parties, subject to review by the Supreme Court. The court of claims consists of a chief justice and four associate justices. Each of the five receives an annual salary of $12,500.

In 1909, Congress created a special court of customs appeals, a title which was changed to the United States court of customs and patent appeals in 1929. This court renders final decisions on appeals from the United States customs court (formerly called the board of general appraisers) and from the patent office. Under certain conditions specified in an act passed in 1914, the decisions of the court may be reviewed by the Supreme Court of the United States. The court of customs and patent appeals consists of a presiding judge and four associate justices; the customs court is made up of nine judges.

Exercising judicial functions though it is not a court, is the independent establishment known as the United States Board of Tax Appeals. It was created by the Revenue Act of 1924 to hear appeals in relation to the national tax laws. The board consists of a chairman and fifteen members at the present time. The circuit courts of appeals have appellate jurisdiction over the decisions of this board.

Another part of the federal judiciary is the court system of the District of Columbia. Purely local matters in the district are handled by police courts, justice of the peace courts, the municipal court, and the juvenile court. Above these are courts which deal not only with cases arising in the district but also with cases arising in any part of the United States. The supreme court of the District of Columbia has the same functions as a United States district court, in addition to its functions in the seat of the national capital. This court consists of a chief justice and eight associate justices. Appeals from this district supreme court may be taken to the court of appeals of the District of Columbia which consists of a chief justice and four associate justices. Because they are located at the seat of the national government these District of Columbia courts dispose of many cases which have their origin in all parts of the country.

In the various territories and dependencies of the United States separate judicial systems have also been established. In certain countries, notably China, the United States has created, under treaties made with those countries, what are called consular courts. These are conducted by American consuls and exercise civil and criminal jurisdiction over United States citizens in those countries. Since 1906, the United States has maintained in China an "extra-territoriality" court to review decisions made by consular courts.

Not only have new courts been created by Congress, but the older parts of the national judiciary have been considerably expanded. The number of Supreme Court justices has been altered several times. Beginning with six in 1789, the number of judges was increased to eight in 1837, and to ten in 1863. In 1866, the number was ordered reduced to seven but did not actually decrease to less than eight. In 1869, the size of the court was fixed, as at present, at nine members. During the period since 1789, eleven men have occupied the position of chief justice. They have been John Jay, John Rutledge, Oliver Ellsworth, John Marshall, Roger B. Taney, Salmon P. Chase, Morrison R. Waite, Melville W. Fuller, Edward D. White, William H. Taft, and Charles E. Hughes.

The growth of the district courts has been especially noticeable. It is these courts which handle the bulk of the federal judicial business. From the small beginning of 1789, the number of districts courts has increased to eighty-one, while the number of active district judges had been expanded to one hundred and thirty-nine in 1931. While some states have only one district court and one judge, others have several. In 1931, there were four districts in New York, with their work subdivided among seventeen judges.

Apparently, the only way to stop the federal court system from being further expanded is to cease the tendency to extend the application of the federal police powers.

SELECTED REFERENCES

Bancroft, George, *History of the Constitution*, Vol. II, pp. 351–367.
Bassett, J. S., *The Federalist System 1789–1801*, pp. 3–26.
Beard, C. A., *American Government and Politics* (Fourth edition), pp. 222–241, 284–289, 303–322.
Channing, Edward, *History of the United States*, Vol. IV, pp. 29–59.
Corwin, E. S., *John Marshall and the Constitution*, pp. 1–24.
Hart, A. B., *American History Told by Contemporaries*, Vol. III, pp. 257–272.
Haskin, F. J., *The American Government*, pp. 51–484.
Johnson, Allen, ed., *Readings in American Constitutional History 1776–1876*, pp. 151–157, 178–186, 206–213.
Landon, J. S., *The Constitutional History and Government of the United States*, pp. 125–146.
Lodge, H. C., *George Washington*, Vol. II, pp. 47–75.
McMaster, J. B., *History of the People of the United States*, Vol. I, pp. 525–568.
Ogg, F. A., and Ray, P. O., *Introduction to American Government* (Third edition), pp. 197–233, 279–346, 347–395, 425–440.
Orth, S. P., and Cushman, R. E., *American National Government*, pp. 243–268, 317–386, 387–488, 489–544.
Schuyler, R. L., *The Constitution of the United States*, pp. 168–205.
Stanwood, Edward, *History of the Presidency*, Vol. I, pp. 20–31.
The World Almanac and Book of Facts, 1932, pp. 182–209.
Wilson, Woodrow, *History of the American People*, Vol. III, pp. 98–108, 116–126.
Young, J. T., *The New American Government and Its Work*, pp. 10–41, 45–74, 76–91, 273–295.

EXPANSION OF THE CONSTITUTION
THROUGH AMENDMENT

ONE of the fundamental defects of the Articles of Confederation was its rigidity. It could only be amended by the consent of all of the states and this in practice meant that it could not be amended at all. As has been mentioned, every attempt to change the Articles met with failure. In view of this unsatisfactory experience during the Confederation period, it is easy to understand why the framers of the Constitution placed in that document an article providing for an easier method of amendment. But even the method provided has not resulted in a high degree of flexibility as is demonstrated by the fact that only twenty amendments have been added to the Constitution in a period of over one hundred and forty years.

THE PROCESS OF AMENDING THE CONSTITUTION

The process of amending the Constitution is outlined in Article V of the Constitution. There are four possible methods by which amendments may be added to the document, that is, there are two ways by which amendments may be proposed and two by which they may be ratified. An amendment may be proposed by Congress, a two-thirds vote being required for the purpose. Ratification may be either by three-fourths of the state legislatures or by conventions in three-fourths of the states, "as the one or the other Mode of Ratification may be proposed by the Congress." This accounts for two methods of amendment. Amendments may also be proposed by a convention called for the purpose by Congress on the application of the legislatures of two-thirds of the states. The ratifying methods are the same as for amendments proposed by Congress. This accounts for the other two methods of adding to the Constitution.

In practice, only the first method described has been used,

for all twenty amendments so far added to the Constitution have been proposed by Congress and have been ratified by three-fourths or more of the state legislatures. In 1930, District Judge William Clark of New Jersey ruled that the eighteenth amendment had not been properly ratified because the method of ratification had been by state legislatures instead of by state conventions. It was Judge Clark's contention that an amendment designed to curtail personal liberty to the extent provided for by the prohibition amendment should be submitted to conventions fresh from the people before being considered valid. The Supreme Court quickly overruled this strange decision, holding, in the case of the *United States vs. Sprague* in 1931, that the eighteenth amendment had been properly ratified. The Constitution plainly gives to Congress the right to determine whether ratification shall be by legislatures or conventions.

Several other questions have also arisen in regard to the amending process. May a state which has once ratified an amendment reverse its action and withdraw its ratification? May a state which has rejected an amendment later take action to ratify it? The first question may be answered in the negative. After a state has ratified, its action is considered final regardless of any later action which it may take. This question has never been decided by the Supreme Court but Congress has passed an opinion on it. After the fourteenth amendment had been ratified by three-fourths of the states, three of them reversed their action and attempted to withdraw their ratifications. These were Ohio, New Jersey, and Oregon. The ratifications of the first two were necessary to make the constitutional three-fourths of the states. The secretary of state, whose duty it was to proclaim the amendment, was undecided what to do. He finally decided to proclaim it to be effective provided the ratifications of Ohio and New Jersey were valid. Congress immediately adopted a concurrent resolution enumerating the states which it declared had ratified the fourteenth amendment. Ohio, New Jersey, and Oregon were included in the list. In view of these ratifications, Congress resolved "That said fourteenth article is hereby declared to be a part of the Constitution of the United States, and it shall be duly promulgated as such by the Secretary of State."

The second question may be answered in the affirmative.

Technically, it is not possible for a state to reject an amendment. Ratification may be refused at one time but there is nothing to prevent a state from deciding later to ratify an amendment. Refusal to ratify has the same legal effect as a failure to act at all.

Another question in relation to the process of amendment is whether a state legislature may ratify an amendment subject to approval by the people of the state in a popular referendum. In the case of *Hawke vs. Smith* in 1920, involving the eighteenth amendment, the Supreme Court ruled that this could not be done. The case originated in Ohio where, under a provision of the state constitution, the action of the state legislature in ratifying the prohibition amendment had been submitted to the voters of the state for approval or disapproval.

The question has also arisen as to whether or not Congress may place a time limit on the process of ratifying an amendment. In the case of both the eighteenth amendment and the twentieth amendment it was provided that ratification must be completed within seven years. Those opposed to the eighteenth amendment seized upon this provision as the basis for an attempt to have the amendment ruled invalid. The attempt failed for the Supreme Court in 1921, in the case of *Dillon vs. Gloss*, decided that Congress had properly exercised its legislative power in fixing a time limit for ratification. There has been no decision regarding the length of time an amendment submitted without a time limit shall remain before the states before it is considered dead. The proposed child labor amendment, submitted to the states in 1924, is still "alive" as is demonstrated by its ratification in 1933 by Oregon and other states.

Yet another question regarding the process of amendment has to do with the part, if any, to be played by the president. The Constitution states that "Every Bill" passed by Congress "shall before it become a Law, be presented to the President" for signature or veto. Was it required that this procedure be followed also in the case of proposed constitutional amendments? As early as 1798, in the case of *Hollingsworth vs. Virginia* which arose in connection with the eleventh amendment, the Supreme Court decided that it was not necessary to secure the approval of the president. Proposed amendments are not even submitted to him but one of the executive heads, the secretary of state, has been designated by law to send proposed amendments to the states, to receive ratification returns, and to proclaim the amendments after three-fourths of the states have ratified.

Recently another question has come up in connection with the amending process. Does Congress have the authority to order a national referendum on a proposal to amend the Constitution? During the early part of 1932 there was much talk of a referendum on the repeal of the eighteenth amendment. It is difficult to see how Congress could order such a referendum. In the first place, there is no authority in the national Constitution for a referendum on any question. Certainly there is no provision in Article V which could possibly be construed to permit or authorize a popular vote on a proposed constitutional amendment. Even if Congress should order a referendum, an action which would require the broadest kind of interpretation of its implied powers, the result would be purely advisory.

Not only does Congress clearly lack the authority to hold a national referendum on a proposed constitutional amendment but it lacks the facilities for holding such a referendum. The conduct of elections has always been in the hands of the states. Congress could not force the states to go to the expense of conducting a referendum even though it were held in connection with a regular election.

Of course, when political parties take a stand in their platforms for or against proposed constitutional amendments, it is possible to secure some sort of popular expression on such questions. Yet there are so many issues generally involved in a regular presidential election that there can be no certainty that voters supported a party's candidates because of their stand or because of the platform statement in regard to any particular matter. It is just as apt to be true that the party was supported at the polls by many voters in spite of rather than because of its stand on a certain question.

In the 1932 presidential campaign, the platform of the victorious Democratic party carried a promise to secure an amendment to the Constitution repealing the eighteenth amendment. It would be absurd to claim that all who voted for the Democratic ticket favored this plank. Nevertheless, the Democratic leaders, interpreting the election as a mandate to secure repeal, proceeded to put through Congress an amendment for that purpose.

Because of the difficulty, under the present system, of ascertaining the real will of the people in regard to constitutional amendments it might be well to amend the Constitution so as to permit a real national referendum on such questions.

LIMITATIONS ON THE AMENDING POWER

Only two limitations were placed by the Constitution on the amending power and of these one has long been obsolete. This was the provision in Article V "that no Amendment which may be made prior to the Year One thousand eight hundred and eight shall in any Manner affect the first and fourth Clauses in the Ninth Section of the first Article." These clauses stated that Congress could not prohibit the importation of slaves prior to 1808 nor impose a tax of more than ten dollars a head on slaves brought into the country.

The second limitation on the amending power is the provision "that no State, without its Consent, shall be deprived of its equal Suffrage in the Senate." Since the Constitution went into effect, there has been considerable discussion of the desirability of changing the provision in Article I which states that there shall be two senators from each state. This, it will be recalled, was one of the most important points in the "Great Compromise" of the Constitutional Convention. While it may not seem fair that Nevada and Rhode Island, for example, should be represented in the Senate on an equal basis with California and New York there is nothing to be done about it. It is not likely that the small states will, at any future time, consent to a change in this matter.

The question has been raised as to whether or not there were any implied limitations on the amending power. This question was raised particularly in connection with the eighteenth and nineteenth amendments. In the case of the former it was charged that it violated personal liberty, that it was contrary to the tenth amendment, and that it would deprive persons of their liberty without due process of law. But in the *National Prohibition*

Cases, decided in 1920, the Supreme Court ruled that there were no implied limitations which could be invoked against the amendment.

Similarly, it was claimed that the nineteenth or women's suffrage amendment violated the rights of states to regulate the suffrage but the Supreme Court, in the case of *Leser vs. Garnett* in 1922, ruled that this was not an implied limitation on the amending power. The decision referred to the precedent established in 1870 by the fifteenth amendment designed to secure the voting privilege for negroes.

THE BILL OF RIGHTS

The process of amending the Constitution began with the first Congress in 1789. It will be recalled that all of the state ratifying conventions except the first five had proposed changes in the new framework of government. While the proposals dealt with many different points, a large number of them were designed to protect individual liberty and to prevent the federal government from encroaching on the powers belonging to the states. The Constitution as ratified contained some safeguards of liberty, such as the prohibition of religious tests for national office holders, the definition of treason, the prohibition of titles of nobility, the right of habeas corpus, the right to jury trials, and the prohibition of bills of attainder and ex-post-facto laws, but more guarantees were demanded.

In order to secure ratification of the Constitution, its friends had been forced to promise that they would seek to amend it as quickly as possible after it became operative. In accordance with this promise, James Madison, who had been elected to the first House of Representatives, arose in that body on June 8, 1789, and, in a lengthy speech, proposed that the Constitution be amended so as to remove the chief objections to it. He called attention to the many persons "respectable for their talents and patriotism, and respectable for the jealousy they have for their liberty" who were "much inclined to join their support to the cause of Federalism" if they were assured of the protection of their liberty. "We ought not," continued Madison, "disregard their inclination, but, on principles of amity and moderation, conform to their wishes, and expressly declare the great rights of mankind secured under this constitution." Furthermore, he declared that guarantees of liberty should be added to the Constitution to help overcome the objections of Rhode Island and North Carolina which had not yet ratified the document.

Madison's proposed additions to the Constitution were referred to a select committee which reported back to the House a list of seventeen amendments. Twelve of these met with the approval of the Senate and were sent to the state legislatures for ratification on September 25, 1789. Two of the proposed amendments failed to secure the support of three-fourths of the states but the rest were ratified by all the states except Georgia, Connecticut, and Massachusetts and became effective on November 3, 1791.

These first ten amendments constitute the national bill of rights. The first eight deal with specific individual rights while the ninth and tenth are more general in character. The bill of rights, it should be emphasized, limits the powers of the federal government and not the state governments. This was made clear by the Supreme Court in 1833 in the case of *Barron vs. Baltimore*. The decision in this case held that the due process clause of the fifth amendment could not be invoked against the city of Baltimore which was interfering with a wharf owned by Barron. However, since the fourteenth amendment was added to the Constitution, it has been found possible, through its "due process clause" to invoke the protection of the national safeguards of liberty against the operation of arbitrary state laws.

The first amendment begins with a statement that "Congress shall make no law respecting an establishment of religion, or prohibiting the free exercise thereof." During the colonial period several of the colonies had "established" churches, that is, churches supported by the government through taxation. When state constitutions were first adopted, the idea of state churches had not wholly disappeared. In Virginia, it required a determined fight under the leadership of Thomas Jefferson to secure, in 1784, the famous "Statute for Religious Freedom." At the time the national Constitution was being ratified and put into effect there was a strong feeling that the power of Congress in the matter of religion should be limited and it was for this reason that the religious guarantees were placed in the first amendment.

While Congress is prohibited from establishing a state church, it should be noted that there is nothing to prevent individual states from doing so unless their constitutions contain guarantees similar to those in the national bill of rights. Furthermore, it should be pointed out that the Supreme Court has made it clear that religious freedom does not mean complete freedom of action. A person may not, in the practice of his religion, interfere with the rights of others or commit criminal or immoral acts. This was definitely stated by the Supreme Court in 1878 in the case of *Reynolds vs. United States*. The decision specifically denied the right of a Mormon to practice polygamy. The case came before the federal courts because it originated in Utah which was then a federal territory.

Another provision in the first amendment prohibits Congress from "abridging the freedom of speech, or of the press." This was included probably because of the attempts made by British officials to suppress freedom of speech and of the press in various colonies. These constitutional guarantees do not, of course, permit the utterance or printing of libels. In time of war, freedom of speech and of the press is subject to considerable curtailment as has been demonstrated several times in American history. In 1798, when there was a war with France impending, Congress passed a Sedition Act to prevent criticism of the government. During the Civil War, freedom of speech and of the press was frequently interfered with by the order of the president. Again, during the World War, there was an almost complete suspension of freedom of speech and of the press through the Espionage Act passed in 1917 and its amendment passed in 1918.

But even in times of peace there is not complete liberty in these matters. The most notable example of peace time interference with freedom of speech and of the press was through the Comstock law of 1873 which is still in effect. This act outlaws printed material of an obscene, lewd, or lascivious nature, and specifically prohibits the dissemination through the mails of birth control information. In 1909, the law was amended so as to outlaw, as "indecent," literature that might incite to arson, assassination, or murder. Congress has conferred on the postmaster-general broad police powers in relation to the exclusion from the mails of second class matter which he deems objectionable, such as newspapers or magazines containing material which he deems to be seditious in character.

A favorite method of stifling newspaper criticism of courts has been to punish the editors for contempt of court. In 1932, Congress passed the Norris-La Guardia bill, designed to provide trials by jury for editors who have been adjudged in contempt. This should have the effect of curbing arbitrary interference with freedom of the press by judges.

Most of the states have laws of one kind or another limiting freedom of speech and of the press. These laws have grown out of the post-war fear of communistic agitators but they have been used to suppress others. Minnesota went so far as to pass, in 1925, what was frankly a "gag law." Under this act, a Minneapolis newspaper called the *Saturday Press* was suppressed for criticizing the local law enforcing authorities. Aroused by a decision of the Minnesota supreme court which upheld the law and its application to the *Saturday Press*, the American Newspaper Publishers' Association, through a committee headed by R. J. McCormick, publisher of the Chicago *Tribune*, appealed from the decision to the national Supreme Court, using as a basis for the appeal the fourteenth amendment clause which states, "nor shall any State deprive any person of life, liberty, or property, without due process of law."

By a five to four vote, the Supreme Court, in June, 1931, ruled the Minnesota "gag law" to be unconstitutional. In reading the majority opinion, Chief Justice Hughes, who, in this case as well as in others, has demonstrated his liberality, traced the historical development of the idea of freedom of the press, and then proceeded to say, in part: "Public officers, whose character and conduct remain open to debate and free discussion in the press, find their remedies for false accusations in actions under libel laws providing redress and punishment, and not in proceedings to restrain the publication of newspapers and periodicals. . . .

"Meanwhile, the administration of government has become more complex, the opportunities for malfeasance and corruption have multiplied, crime has grown to most serious proportions, and the danger of its protection by unfaithful officials, and of the impairment of the fundamental security of life and property by criminal alliances and official neglect, emphasize the primary need of a vigilant and courageous press, especially in the great cities. The fact that the liberty of the press may be abused by miscreant purveyors of scandal does not make any less necessary the immunity of the press from previous restraint in dealing with official misconduct. . . . Charges of reprehensible conduct, and in particular of official malfeasance, unquestionably create a public scandal, but the theory of the Constitutional guarantee is that more serious public evil would be caused by the authority to prevent publication."

New problems in relation to freedom of speech have grown out of the remarkable development of radio. By the act of Congress creating the Radio Commission, that body was given broad powers to censor speech over the radio. The commission, through its power to decide whether or not a radio station is serving the "public interest, convenience and necessity," may order a station to discontinue operation. It did this in the case of a radio station operated in Los Angeles by Rev. R. P. Shuler. Appeal was taken from the ruling of the commission to the District of Columbia court of appeals which, in 1932, upheld the order. Mr. Shuler, it was charged, had been too free in his criticisms of various prominent individuals and of certain religious denominations. Early in 1933, the national Supreme Court refused to review the decision of the lower court though it was asked to do so on the ground that freedom of speech was being interfered with by the Radio Commission. Regardless of the merits of Mr. Shuler's plea, it is of immense importance that the Supreme Court should rule soon on the question of freedom of speech over the radio.

The final provision of the first amendment prohibits Congress from passing laws abridging "the right of the people peaceably to assemble, and to petition the Government for a redress of grievances." This was included also because of colonial experience in petitioning the British government. The frequency with which petitions were presented to that government in the period before the War for Independence indicates the importance which the early Americans attached to the right of petition.

In consequence of this provision in the first amendment, numerous petitions are presented to Congress on every conceivable subject. The only serious attempt to limit the right of petition was made by the national House of Representatives in the period 1836–1844, when it refused to receive petitions asking for the abolition or restriction of slavery. The House finally yielded in the matter and since that time no restrictions have been placed by the national government on the right of petition.

It should be emphasized that when people assemble for the purpose of petitioning they must do so peaceably. In 1932, a number of veterans of the World War from all parts of the country assembled at Washington, D. C. to urge Congress to pay the "soldiers' bonus" immediately. Even after the adjournment of Congress many of them remained. Finally, with the sanction of President Hoover, regular army troops were used to expel them by force from the District of Columbia on the ground that their presence was a menace to the public peace and safety.

The second amendment states that "A well regulated Militia, being necessary to the security of a free State, the right of the people to keep and bear Arms, shall not be infringed." This amendment was designed to enable the states to protect themselves from federal usurpation of military power. At the time of its enactment, it was the general opinion that a "well regulated militia" would make a large standing army unnecessary and, consequently, it was felt that a guarantee was needed in the Constitution to make certain that arms would be available for the militia. The Supreme Court has made it clear that the amendment does not uphold the right to carry concealed weapons. On the other hand, the court has also ruled, specifically in the case of *Presser vs. Illinois* in 1886 and in the case of *Miller vs. Texas* in 1894, that the states may not impose unreasonable restrictions on the right of citizens to bear arms suitable for military use.

It is interesting to note that when Madison proposed this amendment it contained a clause stating that "no person religiously scrupulous of bearing arms shall be compelled to render military service in person." This was finally left out of the amendment but, had it been included, it would have automatically solved the problem of "conscientious objectors," persons who refused to perform military services during the World War.

By the third amendment, the people were protected from having troops quartered in their houses against their wishes by order of the government. This amendment states that "No Soldier shall, in time of peace, be quartered in any house, without the consent of the Owner, nor in time of war, but in a manner to be prescribed by Law." The explanation for placing this provision in the bill of rights is to be found in the obnoxious "quartering acts" passed by the British Parliament in 1765 and 1774 to force the colonies to provide quarters for British troops.

The fourth amendment was added to the Constitution chiefly because of the abuses which had grown out of the use of "writs of assistance" by British law enforcing agents during the colonial period. The language of this amendment is clear in its meaning. It declares that "The right of the people to be secure in their persons, houses, papers, and effects, against unreasonable searches and seizures, shall not be violated, and no Warrants shall issue, but upon probable cause, supported by Oath or affirmation, and particularly describing the place to be searched, and the persons or things to be seized."

It is the purpose of this amendment to protect good citizens and, at the same time, to enable the law enforcing officers to search out and seize criminals and the evidence of crime. There are times when searches and seizures may be made without search warrants and yet not be "unreasonable." In various cases, the national Supreme Court has interpreted the fourth amendment in such a way as to permit searches and seizures without warrants under certain circumstances. For instance, officers of the law may stop and search automobiles or other vehicles as well as boats. This was decided in 1925 in the case of *Carroll vs. United States*. The decision stated that, if a warrant were required to search a vehicle of transportation, it would obviously be impossible to conduct a search at all since the vehicle would be removed from the jurisdiction of the law. It should be pointed out that the federal laws authorizing the issuance of search warrants generally prescribe penalties for officers who make arrests and seizures in an unlawful manner.

In the fifth amendment is begun an enumeration of safeguards for persons accused of crime. In the first place, "No person shall be held to answer for a capital, or otherwise infamous crime, unless on a presentment or indictment of a Grand Jury, except in cases arising in the land or naval forces, or in the Militia, when in actual service in time of War or public danger." The purpose of this is to prevent persons from being brought to trial on charges so flimsy as to make a conviction improbable and also to furnish an accused person with the exact charges against him so that he may prepare a defence. In recent years the grand jury system has been severely criticized as slow and cumbersome, but, as is evident, it would take a constitutional amendment to change the system.

The next provision in the amendment states, "nor shall any person be subject for the same offence to be twice put in jeopardy of life or limb." This is the safeguard against what is known as "double jeopardy." The purpose is to prevent any person from being subjected to a long continued persecution under the guise of justice. Accused persons are entitled to have their trial carried through to a verdict which means that the government prosecutor cannot ask a court to dismiss a case for want of evidence and then institute a new trial when and if more evidence is collected. If an accused person is found not guilty in a federal court, the prosecutor cannot appeal from the decision. On the other hand, if a person is convicted he may appeal from the decision to a higher court, or he may ask the court which convicted him to grant him a new trial. In other words, a convicted person may waive the "double jeopardy" safeguard if he chooses to do so. If a jury disagrees or if, for any other reason, there is a mistrial which prevents a verdict from being rendered, a new trial may be held without the accused person being put in double jeopardy. Unless the federal laws applying to the case prohibit it, a person may be tried in both federal and state courts for the same offence if both federal and state laws have been violated. This was stated in 1922 by the Supreme Court in a prohibition case known as *United States vs. Lanza*.

Next, in the fifth amendment, is the statement, "nor shall be compelled in any Criminal Case to be a witness against himself." The purpose of this provision was to safeguard accused persons against brutality and torture in efforts to force from them confessions of guilt. During the colonial period of American history and in Europe during the corresponding period, torture was an accepted method of extorting confessions from accused persons. Excellent illustrations of this may be found in connection with the witchcraft craze of the seventeenth century.

An accused person may not be forced to testify against himself either before a federal grand jury or in a trial before a federal court. However, if the accused takes the stand in his own defence he waives his immunity, for he must answer all questions put to him by the prosecutor as well as by his own attorneys. A confession secured through force or evidence secured through unreasonable searches and seizures without search warrants cannot be used against an accused person in a federal court. It has been ruled that a person cannot refuse to testify if his testimony would have the effect of humiliating him but not of incriminating him to the extent of warranting prosecution.

One of the most important provisions in the fifth amendment is that known as the "due process clause." It is as follows, "nor [shall any person] be deprived of life, liberty, or property, without due process of law." The origin of this provision can be traced back to the English Magna Carta. While it is difficult to define "due process of law" it may be said, in a general way, that it, at first, merely meant in accordance with legal and court procedures which had become recognized in practice as just and proper. But the federal courts have, in recent years, interpreted "due process" to include more than a guarantee of a person's procedural rights; it has become a guarantee against unjust and arbitrary action of any kind on the part of the national government. The due process clause of the fourteenth amendment has also been interpreted similarly in relation to the actions of the state governments.

A good illustration of how the Supreme Court has extended the meaning of the due process clause of the fifth amendment may be seen in its decision in the case of *Adkins vs. Children's Hospital* in 1923. This case arose from the application of a law passed by Congress providing for a minimum wage scale for employed women and children in the District of Columbia. The court ruled that the law constituted an arbitrary deprivation of liberty without due process of law since it limited freedom to make contracts.

The final provision of the fifth amendment states, "nor shall private property be taken for public use, without just compensation." The purpose of this clause is to limit the national government in the exercise of what is known as the "right of eminent domain." It safeguards against arbitrary seizures and confiscations such as frequently occurred in England at the hands of despotic rulers. It does not prevent the United States from acquiring property which it needs but insures the owner a fair price for it. If a fair price cannot be agreed on by the owner and the government, the matter may be taken to a federal court for settlement. In connection with this limitation on the right of eminent domain, it should be noticed that, by the eighth section of the first article of the original Constitution, it is required that the federal government secure the consent of the legislature of the state within which the property is to be purchased "for the Erection of Forts, Magazines, Arsenals, dock-Yards, and other needful Buildings."

By the sixth amendment, it is provided that "In all criminal prosecutions, the accused shall enjoy the right to a speedy and public trial, by an impartial jury of the State and district wherein the crime shall have been committed, which district shall have been previously ascertained by law, and to be informed of the nature and cause of the accusation; to be confronted with the witnesses against him; to have compulsory processes for obtaining witnesses in his favor, and to have the Assistance of Counsel for his defence."

A person in the United States cannot be held in prison indefinitely without trial as was a common practice in France prior to the Revolution of 1789. Nor may there be any "star chamber" or secret trials. They must be speedy, public, and by "an impartial jury." The Supreme Court has decided that the jury must be that known to common law, consisting of twelve persons whose vote in a case must be unanimous in order to return a verdict. Of course, an accused person may waive a jury trial but he has the right to one if he desires it. The requirement that the trial must be held in the state and district where the crime was committed is to prevent Congress from passing anything like the notorious Administration of Justice Act, passed by the British Parliament in 1774, ordering the transfer of certain cases from Massachusetts to England for trial.

The requirement of a grand jury indictment, together with the right to a writ of habeas corpus mentioned in the original Constitution, insure that a person will not be held in prison without cause. The sixth amendment makes certain that the accused will be informed of the terms of the indictment against him by requiring that he shall receive information concerning "the nature and cause of the accusation." Furthermore, it is required that witnesses against him shall appear in court in person where they are subject to cross-examination by the defence. The Supreme Court has recognized two exceptions to this. The written testimony of a dying person may be admitted by the trial court. Also, the court records of the testimony of a witness may be admitted as evidence in a second trial if the witness has died meanwhile.

The accused is privileged to use the agencies of the court to compel his own witnesses to be present at his trial. Furthermore, he is entitled to a defence attorney. If he is financially unable to secure an attorney, the court must provide one for him at the expense of the public.

In the seventh amendment is included another safeguard of property rights. It provides that "In suits at common law, where the value in controversy shall exceed twenty dollars, the right of trial by jury shall be preserved, and no fact tried by a jury shall be otherwise re-examined in any Court of the United States, than according to the rules of the common law." Obviously, if all cases involving amounts as small as twenty dollars were tried by jury the work of the federal courts would be greatly hindered. But, in practice, it is the general custom for the parties in a case involving small amounts to waive a jury trial, leaving the decision to the judge alone.

The eighth amendment states that "Excessive bail shall not be required, nor excessive fines imposed, nor cruel and unusual punishments inflicted." The prohibitions mentioned in this amendment had become a part of the English Constitution during the previous century so it was natural for the Americans, because of their colonial experience with English law, to feel that similar guarantees should be included in their Constitution. In practice, it is left to the courts to decide what constitutes excessive bail, excessive fines, or cruel and unusual punishments.

Both the ninth and tenth amendments were added to the Constitution in response to the demand expressed in the state ratifying conventions that a provision should be included in the document to prevent the federal government from usurping powers not specifically delegated to it. The ninth amendment declares that "The enumeration in the Constitution, of certain rights, shall not be construed to deny or disparage others retained by the people." The tenth amendment concludes the bill of rights by stating that "The powers not delegated to the United States by the Constitution, nor prohibited by it to the States, are reserved to the states respectively, or to the people."

THE ELEVENTH AND TWELFTH AMENDMENTS

After the bill of rights had been added to the Constitution no more amendments were adopted for seven years. The agitation for the eleventh amendment arose out of a Supreme Court decision in 1793 in the case of *Chisholm vs. Georgia*. Chisholm, a citizen of North Carolina, brought suit against the state of Georgia before a federal court under the provision of Article III of the Constitution which stated that the jurisdiction of the federal courts should extend to controversies "between a State and Citizens of another State." Georgia denied that it, as a sovereign state, could be sued by a citizen of another state but the Supreme Court ruled otherwise. Chief Justice Jay, in delivering the opinion of the court, declared that Georgia, by ratifying the Constitution, had consented to be "suable" in accordance with the constitutional provision. He pointed out that Georgia, at that very time, had a suit against two citizens of South Carolina before the court. Nothing in the constitutional provision, reasoned the Chief Justice, could be interpreted to give a state the right to be a plaintiff and refuse to be a defendant in cases involving citizens of other states.

The decision proved to be unpopular and led to a demand for the removal from the Constitution of the provision on which

it was based. Accordingly, on March 5, 1794, Congress submitted to the states an amendment reading, "The Judicial power
of the United States shall not be construed to extend to any
suit in law or equity, commenced or prosecuted against one of the
United States by Citizens of another State, or by Citizens or
Subjects of any Foreign State." After several years, the necessary number of state legislatures had ratified it and, on January
8, 1798, it became effective as the eleventh amendment to the
Constitution. By this amendment, various states have been able
to repudiate their debts leaving their creditors without recourse.

The reason for the addition of the twelfth amendment to the
Constitution is to be found in the presidential election of 1800.
The framers of the Constitution had prided themselves that, in
devising the electoral system for electing the president and vice
president, they had accomplished something that was beyond
criticism. Yet, it was the electoral system which first broke down.
In the first two elections, the system worked as intended, but
thereafter the influence of political parties began to be felt. In
the election of 1796, the electors still showed some independence
as was shown by the fact that John Adams, a Federalist, was
elected President, and Thomas Jefferson, a Democratic Republican, was elected Vice President.

But by 1800, the electors were all chosen as representatives of
political parties. The Democratic-Republicans won the victory
but complications arose because of the constitutional requirement that each elector should cast two votes without designating
which was for the office of president and which was for the office
of vice president. As a result of this procedure, Thomas Jefferson
and Aaron Burr, the Democratic-Republican candidates, received
the same number of votes. The election then devolved on the
House of Representatives which was authorized by the Constitution to vote on the five highest candidates. The vote was to be
by states, with a majority required for election. The Federalists
were still in control of the House which was holding its "lame
duck" session. Some of them plotted to make Burr President instead of Jefferson, though it had obviously been the intention of
the voters to make the latter the chief executive. Finally, on
February 17, 1801, after thirty-six ballots, Jefferson was elected
President by a vote of ten states to four, with two not voting.

It was this prolonged struggle between Burr and Jefferson for the presidency which led to the proposal by Congress, on December 12, 1803, of an amendment to prevent a repetition of the occurrence. Within a few months all the states, except Connecticut, Delaware, Massachusetts, and New Hampshire, had ratified it and, on September 25, 1804, it was proclaimed as the twelfth amendment to the Constitution. The chief change was in requiring the electors to cast separate ballots for president and for vice president. Election to each office was to require a majority of the electoral votes. In case no person received a majority of the electoral votes for president, the House of Representatives, voting by states, was to choose one of the highest three. A majority of the states was required for election. In case of failure by the House to elect a president by March 4th, the vice president-elect was to act as president. If no person received a majority of the electoral vote for vice president, the Senate was to elect one from the two highest. The successful candidate must receive the votes of a majority of the whole number of senators.

No mention was made in this amendment of political parties and no cognizance was taken of the fact that the election of electors had come to be controlled by such parties. Only once since this amendment became effective has it been necessary for the House to elect a president. That was in February, 1825, when John Quincy Adams was elected after none of the four candidates for the presidency had received a majority of the electoral vote. Likewise, the Senate has only been called on once to elect a vice president. That was in 1837 when Richard M. Johnson was chosen over Francis Granger.

THE CIVIL WAR AMENDMENTS

From 1804 until 1865, no amendments were added to the Constitution. Then, in a period of a few years, three were added, which may be designated as the Civil War amendments because they were directly related to the outcome of that war. During the war, the problem of slavery proved very troublesome to the federal government. This problem was only partly solved by the various war measures taken by Congress and President Lincoln. A portion of the slaves were freed as a result of confiscation acts passed by Congress while others became free through the operation of the Emancipation Proclamation of January 1, 1863. But there still remained, in 1865, in the border states and in parts of the south which had been conquered prior to the proclamation, a large number of slaves whose status had to be determined. After considering a proposition to purchase the freedom of such slaves, Congress decided in favor of the more drastic plan of freeing the slaves through a constitutional amendment.

Accordingly, there was submitted to the states, on February 1, 1865, a proposed amendment which stated that "Neither slavery nor involuntary servitude, except as a punishment for crime whereof the party shall have been duly convicted, shall exist within the United States, or any place subject to their jurisdiction." Congress was to have power to enforce the amendment "by appropriate legislation." It is interesting to note that all of the seceded southern states except Texas ratified the amendment and their ratifications were counted. The ten so ratifying had been reconstructed in accordance with the requirements of Presidents Lincoln and Johnson. Congress, during its session of 1865–1866, refused to recognize the validity of the presidential reconstruction measures but, nevertheless, no action was taken to annul the ratification of the anti-slavery amendment by the southern states. However, had only the votes of the states which remained in the union been counted, the amendment would have been ratified as only two border states, Delaware and Kentucky, refused to ratify. The thirteenth amendment was proclaimed to be in effect on December 18, 1865.

The fourteenth amendment was added to the Constitution in the process of carrying through the congressional program for the political reconstruction of the south. When Congress assembled, on December 4, 1865, for its first regular session following the close of the Civil War, it found that ten of the seceded states had been reconstructed in accordance with the presidential plan and had elected senators and representatives to sit in Congress. But the two houses of Congress, acting under their constitutional power to "be the Judge of the Elections, Returns and Qualifications" of their members, refused to admit the southern members-elect. Instead of accepting the presidential plan of reconstruction, Congress set up a joint reconstruction committee of fifteen members to recommend a new program.

One of the acts passed on the recommendation of this committee was the Civil Rights Act, early in 1866. This was vetoed by President Johnson but was repassed over his veto. The president's veto message, however, created doubt as to the constitutionality of the act so it was decided to make it a part of the Constitution. Accordingly, the reconstruction committee drafted an amendment which was approved by Congress in June, 1866. Congress then passed an act informing the southern states that they would be considered reconstructed if they ratified the amendment.

President Johnson advised the southern states to refuse ratification. Ten of them followed this advice but Tennessee ratified and was declared by Congress to be a bona fide member of the union. Following the rejection of the amendment by most of the ex-Confederate states, Congress resorted to more drastic measures. In 1867, over President Johnson's veto, it passed the "military reconstruction act" which imposed drastic conditions on the southern states which must be fulfilled before they would be considered as members of the union. Ratification of the fourteenth amendment was one of the conditions. By June, 1868, all the southern states, except Virginia, Mississippi, and Texas, had fulfilled all the conditions of the military reconstruction act, including the ratification of the fourteenth amendment, and were, accordingly, admitted to the union. Meanwhile, the northern states were engaged in submitting their ratifications so that, on July 23, 1868, it was possible to proclaim the amendment to be effective. Twenty-three northern states ratified it while Delaware, Kentucky, and Maryland refused ratification. One state, California, failed to act on it. As has been pointed out, New Jersey, Ohio, and Oregon attempted unsuccessfully to withdraw their ratifications.

The first section of the amendment includes the important provisions which had been embodied in the Civil Rights Act. These were a provision defining citizenship in such a way as to include the freed slaves and a provision guaranteeing civil rights to citizens. The purpose of these provisions was to give the ex-slaves all the privileges of citizenship, including the privilege of voting. Citizenship was defined as follows, "All persons born or naturalized in the United States, and subject to the jurisdiction thereof, are citizens of the United States and of the State wherein they reside." This definition of citizenship is the only one appearing in the Constitution. Following this definition, is the guarantee of civil rights which reads, "No State shall make or enforce any law which shall abridge the privileges or immunities of citizens of the United States."

To make more certain that this provision would be observed, there was added the due process clause which declares, "nor shall any State deprive any person of life, liberty, or property, without due process of law," and also the clause, "nor deny to any person within its jurisdiction the equal protection of the laws." In practice, it is the due process clause which has proved to be the most important provision in the fourteenth amendment.

The second section of the amendment stated that representatives should be apportioned among the states according to their total population. This provision replaced the one in the original Constitution which stated, in effect, that only three-fifths of the slaves were to be counted in determining the total population of the states.

Also contained in this section was the statement that any state denying the suffrage right to adult male citizens "except for participation in rebellion, or other crime," should lose representation in Congress in proportion to the number of citizens deprived of their right to vote. This provision has not been enforced since the close of the reconstruction period. For that matter, none of the provisions in this amendment which were designed to protect the negroes have proved of much benefit to members of the colored race. The southern states have virtually nullified the first two sections of the fourteenth amendment so far as negroes are concerned.

By the third section of the amendment, the right to hold state or national office was denied to persons who had engaged in rebellion after having previously taken an oath to support the Constitution of the United States. This disability could be removed only by a two-thirds vote of Congress. Most of the ex-Confederates affected by this provision were pardoned by Congress in 1872 but it was not until 1898 that the last of them had their civil disabilities removed.

The fourth section proclaimed the validity of the debts incurred by the federal government during the Civil War and also declared the debts incurred in promoting the rebellion to be illegal and void. Incidentally, it was stated that neither the United States nor any state should assume or pay "any claim for the loss or emancipation of any slave."

The fifth and final section of the fourteenth amendment gave Congress the power to enforce the previous sections "by appropriate legislation."

Fearful that the southern states would seek to deprive the negroes of the privilege of voting, the radical Republicans in control of Congress decided to forestall such action by adding another amendment to the Constitution. Accordingly, on February 27, 1869, an amendment was submitted to the states declaring that "The right of citizens of the United States to vote shall not be denied or abridged by the United States or by any State on account of race, color, or previous condition of servitude." On March 30, 1870, it was proclaimed in effect as thirty states had ratified it. California, Delaware, Kentucky, Maryland, and Oregon refused to ratify it while Tennessee did not act on it. Three of the southern states, Virginia, Mississippi, and Texas, were required to ratify this fifteenth amendment, as well as the fourteenth amendment, before being re-admitted to the union.

In the years since the close of the reconstruction period, the fifteenth amendment has been, for all intents and purposes, nullified in the south. Voting by negroes is so limited as to be a negligible factor in the states in that region. Congress has not attempted, since 1876, to use its power to enforce the amendment through "appropriate legislation."

EXPANSION OF THE CONSTITUTION
THROUGH AMENDMENT
(*Continued*)

AFTER the fifteenth amendment was added to the Constitution, a period of more than forty years was to elapse before the adoption of another amendment. Then, within the space of a score of years, five more amendments were destined to be added to the Constitution while two other amendments were submitted to the states by Congress in the same period.

THE INCOME TAX AMENDMENT

During the Civil War, one of the devices for raising money resorted to by the federal government was the levying of a tax on incomes. In 1886, more than a score of years after the war had closed, and fourteen years after the income tax laws had been repealed, the Supreme Court, in the case of *Springer vs. United States,* declared that such taxes had been constitutional. The decision stated that taxes on incomes were not direct taxes but, rather, were excise taxes and so did not have to be apportioned among the states according to their population. Only poll taxes and taxes on real estate, said the court, were direct taxes.

This decision seemed to settle once and for all the constitutionality of income taxes. For several years the question was dormant until, in 1894, Congress passed a new revenue act which provided for taxes on incomes in excess of $4,000 annually. The constitutionality of the new income tax provision was immediately attacked in the federal courts. Early in 1895, in the case of *Pollock vs. Farmers' Loan and Trust Company,* the Supreme Court ruled that a tax on income from land was a direct tax and so could not be levied by Congress. The court also ruled that a tax on income derived from municipal or state bonds was unconstitutional because it was a tax on state agencies. At the time, only eight judges were sitting and they were evenly divided concerning the constitutionality of taxes on other incomes. Finally, after the ninth judge took his place on the bench, it was decided, by a vote of five to four, that taxes on incomes from salaries, stocks, bonds, and other sources were direct taxes and were therefore unconstitutional.

In their 1896 platforms, both the Democratic and Populist parties severely criticized the Supreme Court for declaring unconstitutional the income tax of 1894. Thereafter, from time to time, suggestions were made to the effect that an income tax law should be passed that would satisfy the Supreme Court. President Theodore Roosevelt made such a suggestion in his annual message in 1907. In the next year, the Democratic party included in their platform a recommendation that an amendment should be added to the Constitution to permit the levying of income taxes.

President-elect Taft did not favor an amendment. He felt that an income tax could be levied that would be upheld by the courts. In the revenue act of 1909, Congress provided for a tax of one percent on the net income of certain corporations in excess of $5,000 a year. This tax was described as a special excise tax imposed in return for the privilege of doing business and so was not a direct income tax. Because of the difficulty in framing an income tax law that would make possible the taxing of all incomes, it was decided to submit to the state legislatures a constitutional amendment. This was done on July 12, 1909 and, on February 25, 1913, the sixteenth amendment was proclaimed a part of the Constitution. This amendment states that "The Congress shall have power to lay and collect taxes on incomes, from whatever source derived, without apportionment among the several States, and without regard to any census or enumeration."

It will be noticed that this amendment does not indicate whether an income tax is a direct tax or not. What it does is to relieve Congress of the necessity of levying such taxes on the states in proportion to their population. In 1916, in the case of *Brushaber vs. Union Pacific Railroad Co.*, the Supreme Court ruled that the amendment did not grant Congress any additional taxing powers but merely removed a restriction on the method of levying a particular kind of tax. In other words, Congress is not empowered by the amendment to tax salaries of state and local governmental officials, city or state income, or income derived from state and municipal bonds. The court further declared that a tax on income derived from property is a direct tax but, because of the amendment, Congress could tax such income without complying with the previous requirement of apportionment. However, income taxes, like any other federal taxes, must be uniform throughout the United States.

Because of the sixteenth amendment, income taxes have become one of the most important sources of federal income. From $71,381,275 in 1913, the income tax receipts rose to $4,286,486,257 in 1918, the peak year. During the fiscal year 1931–1932, in spite of the depression, the federal government derived $1,056,756,697 or over one-third of its tax receipts for the year from taxes on incomes. During the same year, all the various forms of internal revenue taxes yielded $1,557,729,043 while the customs duties amounted to $327,752,291.

DIRECT ELECTION OF SENATORS

In the Constitutional Convention of 1787, various methods of electing members of the Senate were considered. One proposed method was election by the national House of Representatives; another was selection by the national executive; a third was election by the people; while a fourth method proposed was election by the individual state legislatures. This last method was finally incorporated in the Constitution in spite of the effort of James Wilson of Pennsylvania to secure the adoption of a provision for direct election of senators.

From time to time, after the organization of the government under the Constitution, proposals were made to amend the Constitution so as to provide for popular election of members of the national Senate. Such a proposal was made in the House of Representatives in 1826 but it did not come to a vote. In 1834, President Jackson, irked by the action of the Senate in censuring him for his part in the so-called removal of the deposits from the Bank of the United States, proposed popular election of senators as a means of making them more responsive to the people. Andrew Johnson, as a Representative, Senator, and President, between 1851 and 1868, was a persistent advocate of direct election of senators.

In 1866, Congress, acting under its constitutional power to regulate the time and manner of electing members of Congress, passed a law establishing a uniform method of electing senators to be followed by all the state legislatures. The purpose of the law was to prevent deadlocks in senatorial elections. Deadlocks in the California legislature in 1851, 1855, and 1856, had resulted, in each case, in a failure to elect a senator. Similar difficulties had been experienced in other states also. This law, however, did not prove effective in preventing deadlocks which became increasingly annoying. During the period from 1891 to 1905, there were forty-six deadlocked senatorial elections with fourteen of them resulting in no elections at all. There were cases when a whole legislative session was devoted to the election of a senator, to the detriment of state affairs.

The growing dissatisfaction with the election of senators by legislatures found expression in the platform of the Populist party in 1892. This platform contained a plank advocating direct election. The Democratic platforms, in 1900, 1904, and 1908, contained similar planks, as did the Prohibition party platform in 1904 and the Independence party platform in 1908. Furthermore, popular election of senators was advocated by new political leaders of both of the major political parties. These new leaders, imbued with progressive ideas, felt that the people should have a greater voice in their government. They therefore advocated direct election of senators together with other devices designed to "restore the government to the people," such as primary elections, the recall of officials, the initiative and referendum, and woman suffrage.

Though numerous petitions were sent to Congress from all parts of the country, the movement for a constitutional amendment proceeded very slowly, due to the opposition of the Senate. This led to a movement to secure a national convention, by request of two-thirds of the state legislatures, for the purpose of revising the Constitution. By 1909, thirty state legislatures had joined in the request.

Pending a constitutional amendment, various states provided for what was practically direct election of senators by requiring their legislatures to elect as senators men nominated for the office in direct primaries. By 1912, twenty-eight states had made such provision, in one form or another.

The persistent public demand for direct election of senators was destined eventually to break down the stubborn resistance of the Senate. Up to 1889, thirty-nine resolutions for an amendment had been introduced in Congress but without result. But in 1893, 1894, 1898, 1900, and 1902, amendment resolutions were adopted by the House of Representatives. In each case the Senate failed to concur. Not until February 28, 1911, did the Senate go so far as to even vote on an amendment. The proposed amendment then voted on had been submitted by Senator William A. Borah on behalf of the Senate judiciary committee. The vote resulted 54 to 33 in favor of the amendment which was thus defeated because of the lack of a two-thirds majority.

But, in the sixty-second Congress, there was a happier result. An amendment, modelled after that which Senator Borah had proposed in the previous session, was introduced in the House by Representative William H. Rucker, and was passed by the House on April 13, 1911, by a vote of 296 to 16. On June 12, 1911, it was passed, in a different form, by the Senate, the vote being 64 to 24. The House refused to agree to the Senate changes so a deadlock ensued. Not until May 13, 1912 did the House recede from its position and agree to the amendment in the form adopted by the Senate.

Within ten months, thirty-six state legislatures had ratified the amendment and, on May 31, 1913, it was proclaimed by Secretary of State William J. Bryan as the seventeenth amendment to the Constitution. The twelve states which failed to ratify it were Alabama, Delaware, Florida, Georgia, Kentucky, Louisiana, Maryland, Mississippi, Rhode Island, South Carolina, Utah, and Virginia. All but two of these, it will be observed, were states with large negro populations.

The seventeenth amendment provides for the election of

senators from each state by those qualified to vote for members
"of the most numerous branch of the State Legislatures."
There is also provision for the filling of vacancies through
appointments by state governors with the added provision
"That the Legislature of any State may empower the Executive thereof to make temporary appointment until the people fill the vacancies by election as the Legislature may direct."

Since this amendment went into effect, it has been claimed
that the calibre of the senators has been lessened. But this is
merely a matter of opinion. There appears to be no valid ground
on which to base such a claim. It may be that the Senate in
1933 is not superior to that of 1906, for example, but, on the
other hand, it is doubtful if it is inferior. Whether or not the
calibre of the Senate has been changed by direct election, there
can be no doubt but that the seventeenth amendment has proved
beneficial in relieving the state legislatures of the burden of
electing the senators.

THE PROHIBITION AMENDMENT

No amendment added to the Constitution has affected American life so much or aroused so much controversy as the so-
called prohibition amendment. The adoption of this amendment came as the culmination of many years of agitation against
the use of intoxicating liquors. The organized movement against
strong drink in the United States got under way as early as
1826. During the decade of the 1840's, the agitation was carried on by what were called "Washington Societies." Up to that
time the movement had as its object the promotion of temperance and total abstinence. Dissatisfied with the results of their
efforts, the reformers changed their tactics and began to work
for absolute prohibition through action by the state legislatures.
Maine led the way in 1846 with the first state-wide prohibition law in the history of the United States. Ten years later,
thirteen states had taken action to prohibit the sale of intoxicants.
Most of these states later repealed their laws but Maine, New
Hampshire, and Vermont have remained loyal to the prohibition cause.

The modern fight for prohibition had its real beginning in

1869 when the Prohibition party was organized. It has participated in every presidential election since that time. Though it has never polled a large portion of the popular votes, it has served the purpose of keeping the question of prohibition before the people. In 1874, under the leadership of Frances E. Willard, there was organized the Women's Christian Temperance Union. It has been a powerful influence in support of the prohibition movement. The year 1895 saw the formation of the Anti-Saloon League which has proved to be the most potent of all the groups opposed to the liquor industry. It has an elaborate organization with branches in the various states. It has served to coördinate the various forces working for prohibition, such as the religious denominations of the country. In 1916 there was formed what was called the Prohibition National Executive Committee composed of members from each state of the union. It exerted considerable influence in the final fight for national prohibition.

By slow degrees, the prohibition advocates gained ground. In 1893, eight states had prohibition laws while twelve others had partial prohibition under local option laws which permitted local governmental units to decide for themselves whether or not they would have prohibition. In the other states, the saloons were operated under a license system. By 1915, approximately three-fourths of the area of the United States was dry territory. There were only three states which had not adopted either local option or state-wide prohibition.

This remarkable success of the prohibition movement prior to the entrance of the United States into the World War can be explained on several grounds. The old argument that the use of intoxicating liquors was wrong morally had much influence, especially through the churches and Sunday schools. In the public schools, the children were taught that alcohol was physically harmful to people and this, naturally, gained many converts for the prohibition cause. Propaganda designed to show the sinister influence of the liquor interests in local, state, and national politics also had great effect on public opinion. But even more influential were the economic arguments against the use of liquors. It was demonstrated that the use of alcoholic liquors lessened the efficiency of workers and made it more dangerous for them to operate machines or to perform hazardous duties such as were required of railroad workers, for example. Furthermore, it was argued that the vast sums spent for liquors would be diverted to the purchase of other goods if prohibition were made effective.

The arguments cited indicate the type of propaganda used by the prohibitionists to achieve the results they had attained by the time the United States entered the World War. The war itself hastened the adoption of the national prohibition amendment in a very direct way. On August 10, 1917, Congress passed the Lever Act providing for the conservation of food. Among other things it forbade the use of foods, food materials, or feeds in the production of distilled spirits for beverage purposes. The president was authorized by the same act to prohibit the use of food materials in the production of malt or vinous liquors for beverage purposes.

This legislation was followed by the Federal War Time Prohibition Act of November 21, 1918, which became effective on June 30, 1919. This act provided that, until the close of the war "the date of which shall be determined and proclaimed by the President," the sale of distilled spirits or of beer, wine, or other intoxicating malt or vinous liquors for beverage purposes should be unlawful.

Meanwhile a program for adding a prohibition amendment to the federal Constitution was under way. The amendment was introduced in the Senate by Senator Morris Sheppard of Texas. It was adopted on August 1, 1917, and sent to the House for concurrence. There it was amended and passed on December 17, 1917, by a vote of 282 to 128. On the next day the Senate concurred in the House action, and the eighteenth amendment was submitted to the state legislatures for ratification. Within a little more than a year it was ratified by forty-six states. Only Connecticut and Rhode Island refused to ratify it.

On January 29, 1919, the eighteenth amendment was proclaimed a part of the Constitution and, on January 16, 1920, it became effective. The most important part of this amendment states, "After one year from the ratification of this article the manufacture, sale, or transportation of intoxicating liquors within, the importation thereof into, or the exportation thereof from the United States and all territory subject to the jurisdiction thereof for beverage purposes is hereby prohibited." It further states that "The Congress and the several States shall have concurrent power to enforce this article by appropriate legislation."

Before the time arrived for the amendment to become effective Congress passed the National Prohibition Act, or what has been popularly called the Volstead Act, for its enforcement. In its final form, this act was passed by the Senate on October 8, 1919, and by the House two days later. It was vetoed by President Wilson who held that war time prohibition measures were no longer necessary. The veto was promptly overridden by both houses of Congress, the vote in the Senate being 65 to 20 and the vote in the House being 176 to 55. By the Jones Act, approved by President Coolidge on March 2, 1929, Congress made the prohibition enforcement measures more drastic than before. In March, 1933, Congress took a step in the opposite direction, when, on the recommendation of President Franklin D. Roosevelt, it passed an act legalizing beer with an alcoholic content of 3.2 percent.

Since the prohibition amendment became effective it has been subjected to attack on every possible ground but the Supreme Court has upheld it in every particular. Determined efforts have also been made by the opponents of prohibition to arouse public sentiment against it. For this purpose, there was organized, in 1921, the national Association Against the Prohibition Amendment. For the same purpose, there was formed, in 1929, the Women's Organization for National Prohibition Reform. Also in 1929, there was formed a national organization known as The Crusaders to work for the repeal of the prohibition amendment.

The propaganda of these organizations has proved to be very effective. Many people have become convinced that prohibition regulation is not a proper national function but, rather, that it is a matter to be dealt with by the individual states through the exercise of their police powers. Other people have become convinced that prohibition on a national scale cannot be enforced. For over a decade they have seen the prohibition enforcement laws flaunted by persons in places of power and influence as well as by people of less influence. They have seen the development of "bootlegging" on a mammoth scale and, in connection with it, the growth of gangster activity and "racketeering." They know that "speakeasies," dispensing liquors illegally, exist all over the country. As a result of these apparent facts, people, in increasing numbers, have turned against prohibition.

The anti-prohibition sentiment in the country has made itself strongly felt since 1930. On March 14, 1932, a proposal to give the states the right to repeal or abolish the eighteenth amendment was brought to a vote in the House of Representatives but was defeated 227 to 187. Since that time, important developments have taken place.

Both the Republican and Democratic parties included prohibition planks in their 1932 platforms. The former favored submission of an amendment to the states, to be acted on by conventions, allowing the "States to deal with the problem as their citizens may determine, but subject always to the power of the Federal Government to protect those States where prohibition may exist and safeguard our citizens everywhere from the return of the saloon and attendant abuses." The Democratic plank favored outright repeal of the amendment and demanded "that the Congress immediately propose a constitutional amendment to truly representative conventions in the States called to act solely on that proposal."

As a result of the 1932 election, the Democrats won an overwhelming victory. Both houses of Congress, it appeared, would have large "wet" majorities after March 4, 1933. But the repeal forces were not content to await a change of administration before seeking to put through Congress an outright repeal amendment. On December 5, 1932, the opening day of the session, under a suspension of rules, such an amendment was voted on in the House of Representatives but failed by a narrow margin to secure the necessary two-thirds majority. The vote was 272 to 144. In the Senate, a differently worded amendment was brought to a vote on February 16, 1933, and was passed by a vote of 63 to 23. On February 20, 1933, the House concurred in the amendment by a vote of 289 to 121, and it was sent to the states for ratification. This amendment, which may

become a part of the Constitution as the twenty-first amendment, reads as follows:

"Section 1. The Eighteenth article of amendment to the
Constitution of the United States is hereby repealed.

"Section 2. The transportation into any State, Territory
or possession of the United States for delivery or use therein
of intoxicating liquors, in violation of the laws thereof, is
hereby prohibited.

"Section 3. This article shall be inoperative unless it shall
have been ratified as an amendment to the Constitution by
conventions in the several States, as provided in the Constitution, within seven years from the date of the submission
hereof to the States by the Congress."

Naturally, the dry forces, organized as "The Allied Forces
for Prohibition," will make desperate attempts to defeat the
amendment in the state conventions. They will need to hold
only thirteen states in the prohibition column. There are twelve
states which are regarded as almost certain to reject the repeal
amendment so, if the dry forces can hold those states and win
one of the eight states regarded as doubtful, they can prevent the
ratification of the amendment.

On the other hand, the repealists can rely on the support of
the fourteen states that have repealed their state prohibition
enforcement laws as well as Maryland which has never had an
enforcement law. No less than eight states, through popular
referenda in 1932, repealed or approved repeal of their enforcement laws while four voted in favor of the repeal of the
eighteenth amendment. With forty-three state legislatures in
session in 1933, the battle over ratification in conventions called
by legislatures should be well advanced before the end of the
year. However, it would not be surprising if the repeal effort
should require the full seven years allowed for completion or
if it should finally fail.

Since the proposed amendment contains no provision designed
to prevent the return of the great social evil known as the
saloon, there will be nothing, except state laws, to prevent their
reëstablishment. Furthermore, it will be solely the duty of the
states to curb the use by drunken persons of the 26,000,000

automobiles and trucks in the United States if the accident rate is to be held down. The lack of safeguards against these evils affords strong arguments to the opponents of repeal. Nor is there any assurance that bootlegging, racketeering, and gangster activities will disappear with the repeal of the national prohibition amendment. The taxing of liquors by the national, state, and local governments will no doubt result in attempts to evade the taxes. Those states which choose to remain "dry" will have the same difficulties in preventing the illegal manufacture, transportation, and sale of intoxicating liquors as they had under national prohibition and also before the adoption of the eighteenth amendment. In short, there is reason to doubt that the repeal of the national prohibition amendment will produce better conditions in the United States than have existed.

WOMAN SUFFRAGE

Another constitutional amendment which became effective in 1920 was the so-called woman suffrage amendment. This, too, was added to the Constitution after many years of agitation.

The organized movement for woman suffrage in the United States may be said to have been inaugurated by a woman's rights convention held at Seneca Falls, New York, in 1848. The delegates attending this convention drew up a "Declaration of Women's Rights" in which they asserted that "all men and women are created equal." Equality with males was demanded in the matter of the suffrage and also in economic and educational matters.

Though some progress was made in securing educational and economic rights for women, no progress was made for many years in the matter of securing the voting privilege. When the fourteenth amendment was being drafted the woman suffrage leaders sought to have it so worded as to grant the suffrage to women but in this they were unsuccessful. Nevertheless, the women contended that their citizenship gave them the right to vote. A test case was brought before the Supreme Court of the United States which ruled that the privilege of voting was not a necessary attribute of citizenship.

When the fifteenth amendment was being acted on by Congress, that body was flooded with petitions asking that women be placed on at least an equal basis with negroes in the matter of voting, by including the word "sex" in the amendment. Again, the effort proved fruitless.

In May, 1869, under the leadership of Elizabeth Cady Stanton and Susan B. Anthony, there was formed the National Woman Suffrage Association with the avowed purpose of securing an amendment to the national Constitution permitting woman suffrage. In November of the same year, there was organized the American Woman Suffrage Association for the purpose of securing woman suffrage through state action. Lucy Stone and Julia Ward Howe were the chief leaders of this second association. In 1890, the two organizations merged to form the National American Suffrage Association.

The women attained their first success through the action of the state of Wyoming. When it was organized as a territory in 1869, Wyoming granted to women the privilege of voting. In 1890, when it was admitted to the union as a state, Wyoming placed in its constitution a woman suffrage provision. Colorado, after a popular referendum, extended the suffrage privilege to women by a law passed in 1893. Utah and Idaho were the next to sanction woman suffrage. Their action was taken in 1896. Then followed a long period in which no apparent progress was made. But, in 1910, Washington granted suffrage to women; California followed in 1911; Arizona, Kansas, and Oregon, in 1912; Alaska, in 1913; Montana and Nevada, in 1914; New York, in 1917; and Michigan, Oklahoma, and South Dakota, in 1918. In 1916, women were also allowed to vote in Illinois for presidential electors. Twenty other states, by 1915, allowed women to vote in some elections, such as school elections.

Meanwhile, the agitation for a national woman suffrage amendment had been carried on persistently. In 1878, an amendment drafted by Susan B. Anthony was introduced in the Senate by Senator A. A. Sergeant of California. It was referred to a committee which reported it unfavorably. Thereafter, in each succeeding Congress, the same amendment was proposed until it was finally adopted. In 1887, the proposal was brought to a vote in the Senate but was rejected. It was not voted on again by that body until 1914 though it received favorable committee reports eight times. In the House of Representatives the proposed amendment was not voted on until 1915, though it twice received favorable committee reports. It is amusing to read the arguments delivered in Congress against the amendment. Among the reasons advanced against woman suffrage was the allegation that women were not capable of performing military duty, labor in the fields, engineering feats, or jury service. Further, it was argued by one Senator that the granting of the suffrage would compel "the very large class of intelligent, virtuous and refined females, including wives and mothers who have much more important duties to perform, to leave their sacred labors at home, relinquishing for a time their God-given important trust, which has been placed in their hands, to go contrary to their wishes to the polls and vote, to counteract the suffrage of the less worthy class of our female population."

The Prohibition party had endorsed woman suffrage as early as 1872, but no major party declared in favor of it until 1912. In that year, the Progressive party, headed by Theodore Roosevelt, pledged itself "to the task of securing equal suffrage to men and women alike." In 1916, both the Republicans and Democrats had platform planks on the subject. The Republican plank stated that the party "favors the extension of the suffrage to women, but recognizes the right of each state to settle the question for itself." The Democratic plank declared, "We recommend the extension of the franchise to the women of the country by the states, upon the same terms as to the men."

These platform statements by the parties may be explained by the fact that the woman suffrage forces were then conducting a militant fight to bring their long struggle to a successful culmination. On March 19, 1914, they had succeeded in bringing the proposed amendment to a vote in the Senate but it had failed by eleven votes to secure the necessary two-thirds majority. In the House, a vote had been taken on January 12, 1915, which had resulted in 174 votes for and 204 votes against the amendment. In the debates on the proposition, the states rights argument was much in evidence, the members of Congress from the southern states in particular stressing it.

The unwillingness of the major parties to endorse the proposed woman suffrage amendment led to the formation, in 1916, of a Woman's party in the twelve states which allowed women to vote. They devoted their efforts in particular to securing the defeat of congressmen who had opposed the amendment. After Congress began its session in December, 1916, members of this group of women conducted militant demonstrations in Washington, D. C. in order to attract attention to their cause.

After President Wilson summoned Congress for its special war session in April, 1917, the woman suffrage amendment was introduced in both houses. It was not until January 10, 1918, that it came to a vote in the House of Representatives. The result of the vote was 274 to 136. Thus the amendment was adopted by the House by a bare two-thirds majority. In the Senate, the vote on the question was delayed until October 1, 1918. On the previous day, President Wilson appeared before a joint session of Congress and delivered an address in which he strongly urged the adoption of the amendment. The President, who had previously stood for suffrage through state action, had been convinced that woman suffrage was "clearly necessary to the successful prosecution of the war." In his war message, on April 2, 1917, he had declared that the United States was entering the war "to make the world safe for democracy." He had been persuaded that such an aim could not be consistently pursued unless democracy was made a reality in the United States first.

In spite of his support, the Senate rejected the amendment by a vote of 62 to 34. A change of two votes would have resulted in the needed two-thirds majority. This reversal caused the woman suffrage advocates to redouble their efforts. Nevertheless, the amendment was again defeated in the Senate on February 10, 1919, by a vote of 63 to 33, a gain of one vote.

A new Congress, elected in 1918, met in special session in the spring of 1919 on the call of President Wilson. As he was in France at the time, attending the peace conference, he cabled a message to Congress urging the adoption of the woman suffrage amendment. The House of Representatives soon agreed to the proposal by a vote of 304 to 89. On June 5, 1919, the Senate finally capitulated and adopted the amendment by a vote of 66 to 30.

The proposed amendment is worded as originally written by Susan B. Anthony. It states that "The right of citizens of the United States to vote shall not be denied or abridged by the United States or by any State on account of sex." Congress is given the power to enforce this provision "by appropriate legislation."

The National American Woman Suffrage Association, headed by Mrs. Carrie Chapman Catt, and the Woman's party, headed by Miss Alice Paul, had planned in advance a program to secure ratification. Part of the program was to secure the calling of state legislatures for special sessions to ratify the amendment. In five days, ratification by Wisconsin and Michigan was secured. Then followed, in rapid succession, ratification by other states, until March 22, 1920, when thirty-five states had ratified. Pressure was then brought to bear on states which had not ratified in order to secure action by the needed thirty-sixth state. The Republican party platform of 1920 urged Republican legislatures to act while the Democratic platform made a similar appeal to Democratic legislatures. Both President Wilson and the Democratic presidential candidate, James M. Cox, sent personal messages to the Democratic states urging ratification. Finally, on August 16, 1920, ratification by the state of Tennessee was secured and, on August 26th, the nineteenth amendment was proclaimed to be effective. Five days later, the lower house of the Tennessee legislature rescinded its ratification but no attention was paid to the action.

Of the thirty-six ratifications, it is of interest to note that twenty-nine were secured in special sessions of state legislatures. In twelve of the states ratification was secured by unanimous votes of both houses of the legislatures. Twenty-six of the legislatures which ratified were controlled by Republicans and seven by the Democrats while three were divided between the two parties. One state, Florida, failed to act on the amendment while nine states, Delaware, Maryland, Virginia, North Carolina, South Carolina, Georgia, Alabama, Mississippi, and

Louisiana, rejected it. Connecticut and Vermont, both Republican states, ratified the amendment after it had become effective.

As a result of the speedy ratification of the nineteenth amendment, the women were able to participate in the 1920 election in every state except Georgia and Mississippi. In those states, legal requirements for advance registration were in effect and consequently the women there could not qualify as voters in 1920.

Whether woman suffrage has been a success or not is a debatable question. Certainly it has not produced utopian conditions such as some of its advocates assured the country would result if the women were enfranchised. For instance, it was contended that woman suffrage was essential to the success of the prohibition movement, yet, after a little more than a decade of nation-wide voting by women, the movement to repeal national prohibition was well under way while the effort to repeal state prohibition regulations was also being crowned with success. As voters, the women generally have proved to be no more—and no less—idealistic than the men.

As in the case of the men, many women have proved indifferent towards the voting privilege. In the presidential election of 1920, the voting percentage of the country dropped from sixty-five in 1916 to fifty-two. In 1924, the percentage remained the same but in 1928 it rose to about sixty and to slightly over sixty in 1932. While no adequate statistical proof is available it would seem that whereas women at first voted in less numbers than men they are now about on a par with the latter. In short, one sex is about as indifferent as the other in the matter of choosing governmental officials. There is no reason for urging the abolition of woman suffrage for the women certainly have as much right to vote as the men. On the other hand, the record does not indicate any reason for being especially enthusiastic over woman suffrage.

An interesting result of woman suffrage may be observed in the presence of several women in Congress. In the election of 1932 one woman, Mrs. Hattie W. Caraway of Arkansas, was elected to the United States Senate. She is the first woman to be regularly elected to that body. Four women were elected at the same time to the House of Representatives.

THE "LAME DUCK" AMENDMENT

For many years, one of the most unsatisfactory features of the national government was the short session of Congress held following the election of a new Congress. In this short session sat many members who had been defeated for reëlection. These defeated members were popularly called "lame ducks" and the short session, held from the first Monday in December of each even year until March 4 of each odd year, came to be known as the "lame duck" session.

This short session was inaugurated with the first Congress elected after the Constitution became effective. Having once become established it was impossible to change by law the procedure without shortening the term of those representatives and senators in office at the time of the change. A constitutional amendment was needed to make possible the shortening of the terms of the members of Congress.

In the early years of this nation's history there was good reason for postponing the first regular meeting of a newly elected Congress until thirteen months after election and, meanwhile, to have a meeting of the old Congress. The lack of swift transportation facilities made such procedure imperative. But as steamboats, railroads, automobiles, and airplanes speeded up transportation the need for delay in assembling a new Congress was removed. This, coupled with dissatisfaction with the "lame duck" session, led to the demand for a constitutional amendment to make possible the meeting of a new Congress shortly after election.

Accordingly, Senator George W. Norris of Nebraska introduced in 1923 an amendment designed to abolish the "lame duck" sessions. The amendment passed the Senate in 1924 but failed in the House. Senator Norris persisted in his attempt to secure approval of the amendment but without success until 1932. Six times the Senate gave its approval but each time the measure failed in the House of Representatives. But in the 1931–1932 session a victory for the amendment was finally secured. The two houses did not agree on its final wording so it was necessary for a conference committee to arrange a compromise. This was done on February 27, 1932. Three days later the House gave its approval to the amendment while the Senate accepted it on March 2.

Ratification of the "lame duck" amendment was accomplished in record time. By August 12, 1932, fifteen states had ratified, and, on January 22, 1933, Missouri, the thirty-sixth state, added its ratification. Up to February 6, 1933, when the twentieth amendment was officially proclaimed a part of the Constitution, forty-five states had ratified it. Only Florida, Maryland, and Vermont had failed to act on it by that date.

Public attention has been concentrated on the first two sections of the amendment which contain the "lame duck" provisions, while the third and fourth sections have been generally overlooked. The first section fixes noon on January 3 "of the years in which such terms would have ended" had the amendment not been ratified as the time at which the terms of senators and representatives shall end. The terms of the president and vice president of the United States are to end at noon on January 20. By the second section it is provided that Congress shall meet at noon on each third of January "unless they shall by law appoint a different day." If Congress should change this time of meeting it obviously must make some arrangement for counting the electoral vote, unless the Constitution is further amended to do away with the electoral system.

These first two sections of the twentieth amendment, it is provided by a fifth section, are to become effective on October 15th, following the ratification of the amendment. This means October 15, 1933. Therefore the terms of the representatives elected in 1932 will expire on January 3, 1935, while the terms of senators elected at the same time will end on January 3, 1939. The terms of President Franklin D. Roosevelt and Vice President John N. Garner will expire on January 20, 1937.

The attempted assassination of President-elect Roosevelt at Miami, Florida on February 15, 1933, caused many people to ask the question "Who would become president in case the president-elect died before taking office?" The answer is contained in the third section of the twentieth amendment which states, "If, at the time fixed for the beginning of the term of the President, the President-elect shall have died, the Vice-President-elect shall become President." This section also provides for the possibility of a president not being chosen or not being qualified before the time arrives for his term to begin. In such cases the vice president-elect is to act as president "until a President shall have qualified."

This section further provides for the possibility of a presidential term ending without either a new president or vice president having qualified to take office. Such a situation almost occurred in 1877, when a dispute over the electoral votes of four states delayed the selection of a president and vice president until a short time before the term of President U. S. Grant was scheduled to expire.

The new provision for such a contingency gives to Congress the power to settle the difficulty. This portion of the twentieth amendment says, "and the Congress may by law provide for the case wherein neither a President-elect nor a Vice-President-elect shall have qualified, declaring who then shall act as President, or the manner in which one who is to act shall be selected, and such person shall act accordingly until a President or Vice President shall have qualified." This provision would enable congress to fill the office of president if both the president-elect and vice president-elect died before taking office.

By the fourth section of the amendment a further safeguard is provided against the possibility of a presidential term coming to a close without a president or vice president having been elected to take office. This section reads, "The Congress may by law provide for the case of the death of any of the persons from whom the House of Representatives may choose a President whenever the right of choice shall have devolved upon them [under the provisions of the twelfth amendment,] and for the case of the death of any of the persons from whom the Senate may choose a Vice President whenever the right of choice shall have devolved upon them."

It will be noticed that this amendment does not specifically mention the procedure to be followed in case of the death or disqualification of a presidential or vice presidential candidate prior to the meeting of the electors. This omission is easily explained by reference to the twelfth amendment. Theoretically the electors use their own judgment in voting for a president and vice president; in practice, they vote for the candidates of their party. Technically, there is no president-elect or vice president-elect until the electoral vote has been cast. In the popular election held every four years the voters merely choose electors pledged to support their party's candidates. Therefore, if a party's candidate for either the presidency or the vice presidency should die or become disqualified before the electors cast their votes, it would appear that the electors would be free to vote for whom they pleased. In practice, however, the party's national committee would step in and name a new candidate or candidates for whom the electors would then vote. This was done in 1912 when James S. Sherman, the Republican candidate for the vice presidency, died. Mr. Sherman's death occurred a few days before the popular election but the Republican national committee waited until the election had been held and then named his successor. It so happened that this action was a mere formality as the Republicans had gained only eight electoral votes in the popular election. However, the action established a precedent for the future.

OTHER AMENDMENTS PROPOSED BY CONGRESS

During the period since the Constitution went into effect in 1789, hundreds of amendments have been introduced in Congress. Of these, only twenty-six succeeded in securing the approval of Congress. Twenty were added to the Constitution through ratification by the states, four failed of ratification, while two are still before the states.

As has been mentioned, the first Congress proposed twelve amendments to the states, only ten of which were ratified by a sufficient number of states to make them effective. One of the defeated amendments related to the apportionment of members of the House of Representatives. It stated that "After the first enumeration required by the first article of the Constitution, there shall be one Representative for every thirty thousand, until the number shall amount to one hundred, after which the proportion shall be so regulated by Congress, that there shall be not less than one hundred Representatives, nor less than one Representative for every forty thousand persons, until the number of Representatives shall amount to two hundred, after which the proportion shall be so regulated by Congress, that there shall not be less than two hundred Representatives, nor more than one Representative for every fifty thousand persons."

The second of the original amendments which was defeated had to do with the compensation of members of Congress. It stated that "No law, varying the compensation for the services of the Senators and Representatives, shall take effect, until an election of Representatives shall have intervened."

Another amendment, which was adopted by Congress and submitted to the states but which failed of ratification, had to do with titles of nobility. This amendment, placed before the states on May 1, 1810, stated that "If any citizen of the United States shall accept, claim, receive or retain any title of nobility or honor, or shall, without the consent of Congress, accept and retain any present, pension, office or emolument of any kind whatever, from any emperor, king, prince, or foreign power, such person shall cease to be a citizen of the United States, and shall be incapable of holding any office of trust or profit under them, or either of them."

The purpose of this amendment was to supplement the provisions in the second article of the Constitution whereby both the national government and the state governments were forbidden to grant titles of nobility and also whereby persons holding a federal office were forbidden to "accept of any present, Emolument, Office, or Title, of any kind whatever, from any King, Prince, or foreign State" unless they secured the consent of Congress. The amendment failed to secure ratification by the necessary three-fourths of the states. Twelve states ratified it, and four acted unfavorably on it. As there were seventeen states in the union at the time the amendment was proposed, twelve ratifications were not sufficient.

Following the defeat of this amendment, no further attempts were made to amend the Constitution until the eve of the Civil War. After a number of southern states, led by South Carolina, had seceded from the union, an attempt was made to coax them back into the union by giving them assurance that Congress would not interfere with slavery within any state. For this purpose an amendment was passed by Congress and submitted to the states on March 2, 1861. It stated that "No amendment shall be made to the Constitution which will authorize or give to Congress the power to abolish or interfere, within any State, with the domestic institutions thereof, including that of persons held to labor or service by the laws of the said State."

This amendment fell far short of satisfying the southern states while in the north it met with little favor. When it was adopted by Congress it was too late to serve any useful purpose. Only three states, Ohio, Maryland, and Illinois, ratified the amendment.

Not until 1924 was another amendment that failed of speedy ratification submitted to the states by Congress. Then the so-called child labor amendment, which is still (in 1933) before the states, was approved by Congress and sent to the state legislatures for ratification.

The agitation for child labor regulation by the national government arose because of the increasing number of children who were employed in factories. In the period following the Civil War, due to the rapid transformation of the economic life of the United States, the number of children employed in factories and in other gainful occupations increased very greatly. Thus, by 1880, a total of 1,118,356, or 16.8 percent of the children between the ages of ten to fifteen years, were gainfully occupied. By 1910, the number had increased to 1,990,225 or 18.4 percent.

Various states early began to give attention to the matter and, by 1929, all of them had passed some sort of legislation to regulate child labor. However, there has been no uniformity in the laws and in some states they were not made stringent enough to prevent the gainful employment of children. The most drastic laws are in force in Alabama, Arkansas, Delaware, Indiana, Louisiana, Missouri, Pennsylvania, and Wisconsin. These states prohibit the gainful employment of children under fourteen years of age in any occupation at any time. Eleven states and the District of Columbia prohibit such children from working during school hours. Seven states forbid the employment of such children in certain specified industries during the periods when schools are in session. In the remaining states, labor by children under fourteen is prohibited in certain industries without special reference to non-school or school time.

It was for the purpose of securing greater uniformity as well as greater stringency in the regulation of child labor that Congress was urged to legislate in the matter. Finally, a bill was passed by Congress and signed by President Wilson on September 1, 1916, forbidding the shipment, in interstate commerce, of goods produced by the labor of children less than fourteen years of age, or by children from fourteen to sixteen years of age, under certain specified conditions. But hardly had this Keating-Owen Bill, as it was called, become effective than it was declared unconstitutional by the Supreme Court of the United States in 1918 in the case of *Hammer vs. Dagenhart.* The decision was reached by the court by a vote of five to four.

The majority opinion held that the aim of the law was to standardize the age at which children could be employed in the United States. The goods, the shipment of which was prohibited, were in themselves harmless and, furthermore, no evil or harm would result from them after they reached their destination. The law, said the court, was therefore unconstitutional because it transcended the delegated power of Congress over commerce and because it extended the federal authority over a matter which was purely a state matter, namely, the regulation of the hours of labor by children in factories and mines.

The minority opinion of the court, read by Associate Justice Holmes, contended that Congress had unqualified power to regulate commerce and that the power was sufficient to exclude the products of child labor from interstate commerce. He cited several precedents, including the Pure Food and Drug Act of 1906 whereby Congress had applied its power over interstate commerce to destroy an obvious evil. It made no difference, contended the judge, whether "the supposed evil precedes or follows the transportation." It was not for the court to say that regulation of commerce by Congress was "permissible as against strong drink but not as against the product of ruined lives."

The majority decision led to much criticism of the Supreme Court and did much to promote agitation to limit the power of the court in passing on the constitutionality of laws. Nothing came of this agitation then or later. The chief result of the decision was the attempt to pass a new law that would meet the objections of the Supreme Court. On February 25, 1919, a measure which had been introduced by Senator Atlee Pomerene, became effective as a part of the war Revenue Act of 1918. This measure provided for an excise tax of ten per-cent in excess of all other taxes, on the net profits received from the disposal or sale of the products of canneries, manu-facturing plants, mills, mines, or quarries employing children contrary to the standards set up by the act, which standards were similar to those provided for by the act of 1916.

In May, 1922, this second attempt by Congress to regulate child labor was also declared unconstitutional by the Supreme Court in the case of *Bailey vs. Drexel Furniture Co.* The court decided that the purpose of the tax was not merely to raise a revenue and incidentally to restrain and regulate but rather to regulate with a heavy tax as a penalty. Therefore, it was a legitimate use of neither the taxing nor commerce power of Congress. Since the real purpose of the measure was obviously the regulation of child labor within the states it was unconstitu-tional, declared the court, because such regulation was an ex-clusive state function, falling within the powers reserved to the states by the tenth amendment to the Constitution.

These decisions of the national Supreme Court in relation to child labor laws were interesting in that they revealed the lack of appreciation, on the part of the majority of the judges, of the need of social legislation in a modern industrial age. It would have been just as easy for the court to hold the laws constitutional as to declare them unconstitutional. It would have required no more liberal interpretation of the Constitution to uphold the regulation of child labor by act of Congress than has been required in declaring many other laws constitutional. The Supreme Court has reversed itself before so it is con-ceivable that more liberal judges, with a clearer social outlook, will, at some future date, approve a national law for child labor regulation, even though the Constitution is not amended to permit such a law.

However, the advocates of child labor regulation by Congress were not content to wait for a more liberal court. They immediately undertook to get a child labor amendment added to the Constitution, with the result that such an amendment was adopted by the House of Representatives, on April 26, 1924, by a vote of 297 to 69, and by the Senate, on June 2, 1924, by a vote of 61 to 23.

The proposed amendment reads as follows:

"Section 1. The Congress shall have power to limit, regulate, and prohibit the labor of persons under eighteen years of age.

"Section 2. The power of the several states is unimpaired by this article except that the operation of State laws shall be suspended to the extent necessary to give effect to legislation enacted by the Congress."

The opponents of the amendment, including the National Manufacturers' Association, the "Sentinels of the Republic," the Moderation League of Maryland, the Women's Constitutional League of Maryland, the Woman Patriot Publishing Company, and others, immediately concentrated their forces to defeat ratification of the amendment. One of the most absurd charges made against the amendment was that it had been promoted on direct orders from Moscow and that it had been prepared in the "interlocked interests of socialism, pacifism, internationalism and bureaucracy." The amendment, it was further argued by its opponents, would cause great expense; it would result in the breakdown of state power; it would affect the poor but not the rich; it would lead to further measures to regulate, limit, or prohibit the employment or even the leisure of people of any age; it would be a step from liberty to despotism; and it would represent the greatest step towards centralization in the history of the United States.

It was further asserted by those opposed to the amendment that, if it became a part of the Constitution, Congress would prohibit all labor by those under eighteen years of age, that it would even regulate the labor of children in the homes and on the farms, that it would regulate or even close the parochial schools, and that it would interfere with the public school system.

These arguments were answered by the advocates of the amendment who asserted that the citizenship of the country as a whole was affected by the employment of large numbers of children and therefore the ratification of the amendment was a matter of national concern and interest. Furthermore, national regulation of child labor was necessary, declared the friends of the amendment, to protect states having effective regulation from the unfair competition of states not having satisfactory regulation. It was a duty of the national government to see that the children of the country were conserved and rescued from poverty and ignorance. The charges that Congress would abuse the power granted by the amendment were dismissed as "unthinkable."

Among the organizations which have been supporting the child labor amendment are the National Child Labor Committee which was organized in 1904, the National League of Women Voters, the National Education Association, the Consumers' League, the Young Men's and the Young Women's Christian Associations, the American Federation of Labor, the General Federation of Women's Clubs, the American Association of University Women, and the National Women's Trade Union League.

In spite of the support of these powerful groups little headway has been made in securing ratification by the states. There are those who have pronounced the amendment dead but it seems that their verdict has been a little premature. Since the beginning of 1931, five states have ratified it: Colorado, Oregon, Washington, North Dakota and Ohio. The other five states which have ratified (up to March 25, 1933), are Arizona, Arkansas, California, Montana, and Wisconsin. It has also been ratified by one house of the legislature in New Mexico and Nevada. Six states have taken no action at all. In the Iowa legislature, the vote on the amendment was postponed indefinitely. In five of the remaining states the amendment has been rejected by one house of the legislature. The other twenty-four state legislatures have definitely voted against ratification. In the spring of 1933, however, ten additional states were considering ratification resolutions.

Since only thirteen states are necessary to defeat an amendment, it would seem that there is slight chance of this one being ratified. However, it should be mentioned that there is no time limit on the child labor amendment so it may remain before the states indefinitely. The indications are that states which have rejected it will reverse this action and finally ratify the amendment. At any rate, the child labor amendment cannot be pronounced dead. Agitation for it will doubtless continue as long as serious abuses exist in the matter of child labor. Though the number of children between the ages of ten and fifteen who are gainfully employed declined to 667,118 or 4.7 percent in 1930, the advocates of strict regulation will not be satisfied until they have eliminated the abuse entirely.

The sixth unratified amendment to be proposed to the states by Congress is the one designed to repeal the eighteenth amendment. It has already been discussed so it requires no comment here.

ADDITIONAL SUGGESTED AMENDMENTS

Of the numerous other amendments introduced in Congress but not accepted by that body, only a few are of enough importance to require mention. Among the suggested amendments have been some designed to make it easier to amend the Constitution. Thus, in 1913, Senator Robert M. LaFollette of Wisconsin suggested that the method of proposing amendments should be so changed as to permit proposal by a popular referendum in ten states, by the petition of ten state legislatures, or by a majority vote of the two houses of Congress. Ratification would be by a popular referendum in connection with the first regular congressional election following the proposal of the amendment. A majority vote in a majority of the states would be required for ratification, according to the LaFollette plan.

On the other hand, amendments have been suggested in Congress designed to make subsequent amendment of the Constitution more difficult. Such suggestions were made with some frequency after 1920, particularly by those who were disgruntled at the prohibition and woman suffrage amendments. For instance, a resolution introduced in Congress in 1923 by Senator James W. Wadsworth, Jr., provided for the proposal of amendments as described in the original Constitution but sought to make ratification more difficult. Ratification in each state was to be by a state convention or by a direct popular referendum, the choice of the method being left to the state. A state which had ratified was to have the right to reverse its action at any time prior to the ratification by three-fourths of the states. If more than one-fourth of the states rejected an amendment "said rejection shall be final and further consideration thereof by the States shall cease." Ratification of an amendment, according to the proposal, would have to be completed within eight years.

Nothing came of the proposals either to make the amending process easier or more difficult. In recent years little has been said about the amendment of Article V of the Constitution.

Other suggested amendments include one to give women equal rights in all matters, and not merely in the matter of voting as provided for by the nineteenth amendment; one to prohibit the issuance of tax-exempt securities; and one to give Congress "power to make laws, which shall be uniform throughout the United States, on marriage and divorce, the legitimation of children, and the care and custody of children affected by annulment of marriage or by divorce."

Another suggested amendment which has been much discussed but which has not received favorable consideration would substitute direct popular election of the president and vice president for the long obsolete indirect method of electing them through electors. As it is, everyone knows, following the popular election in November of each fourth year, who the next president will be, yet no president or vice president is officially elected until the electors have cast their ballots and Congress has canvassed the result. It would not be surprising if the electoral system were amended out of the Constitution in the near future.

These suggested amendments are but a sample of the numerous proposals that have been made in Congress. Obviously, the amending process has been used very conservatively in the period since 1789. The fact that it has been possible to adapt the Constitution to changing conditions through legislative action, judicial interpretation, executive action, and through custom, has made unnecessary many amendments which might otherwise have been adopted.

SELECTED REFERENCES

(*For Chapters XII and XIII*)

Ames, H. V., "The Amending Provision of the Federal Constitution in Practice," *Proceedings of the American Philosophical Society*, Vol. LXIII (1924), pp. 62–75.

Beard, Charles A., *American Government and Politics* (Fourth edition), pp. 81–94.

Burdick, C. K., *The Law of the American Constitution*, pp. 34–52, 342–434.

Haines, B. M., and Haines, C. G., *The Constitution of the United States*, pp. 186–213.

Johnson, Allen, ed., *Readings in American Constitutional History 1776–1876*, pp. 135–150, 214–224, 500–508, 518–527, 572–578.

Johnson, Allen, and Robinson, W. A., eds., *Readings in Recent American Constitutional History 1876–1926*, pp. 150–161, 186–196, 272–284, 467–476.

MacDonald, William, *A New Constitution for a New America*, pp. 202–217.

Martin, C. E., *An Introduction to the Study of the American Constitution*, pp. 154–205.

McBain, H. L., *The Living Constitution*, pp. 72–113.

Munro, W. B., *The Constitution of the United States*, pp. 135–163.

Norton, T. J., *The Constitution of the United States, Its Sources and Its Application*, pp. 197–262.

Ogg, F. A., and Ray, P. O., *Introduction to American Government* (Third edition), pp. 179–189.

Orth, S. P., and Cushman, R. E., *American National Government*, pp. 82–101, 118–144.

Steven, C. E., *Sources of the Constitution of the United States*, pp. 207–242.

Thorpe, F. N., *A Short Constitutional History of the United States*, pp. 250–290.

Chapter Fourteen

JUDICIAL INTERPRETATION OF THE CONSTITUTION

T HOUGH the framers of the Constitution intended the federal judiciary to be coördinate with the legislative and executive branches of the government, the courts, in fact, played a minor part during the first decade of their existence. Not until after John Marshall became Chief Justice of the Supreme Court in 1801 did that court assume its rightful place in the government. The real importance of the Supreme Court dates from 1803 when, in the case of *Marbury vs. Madison*, Chief Justice Marshall claimed and assumed for the court the right to pass on the constitutionality of acts of Congress.

THE DOCTRINE OF JUDICIAL REVIEW

In declaring this right, Marshall was not originating a new idea. He was simply confirming a principle, basic in the philosophy of constitutional government, namely, that in the interests of free government, the agencies of government must be subject to external control. The doctrine of judicial review as stated by Marshall in *Marbury vs. Madison* held that, under the Constitution, the courts, and finally the Supreme Court, were to decide whether or not the agencies of government were keeping within their constitutional bounds.

The idea of constitutional limitations upon government was inherent in the English system, under the notion that, while the power of Parliament was supreme in relation to legislation, that body was subject to the limitations of "common right and reason" in its acts. This did not involve the right of any court to declare acts of Parliament void as inconsistent with right and reason. The control over Parliament along these lines was to be strictly political, that is, through the force of public opinion. This idea that Parliament was subject to the rule of "common right and reason" was stated by Sir Edward Coke in 1612.

The first appearance in America of this idea of limits upon the power of Parliament was in 1761, when James Otis in the *Writs of Assistance Case* argued that any act of Parliament contrary to English constitutional practice and "against natural equity," could be declared void by the court. In this assault against Parliament's supremacy he went much further than had Coke, who would never have asserted that any other body than Parliament could declare its acts void. As a matter of fact, there was no legal justification for Otis's argument; on the contrary, a previous case had decided against it. However, the argument of Otis was in line with the colonial opposition to England at the time, and had its later influence.

In 1766 the highest court of the colony of Virginia declared the Stamp Act not binding on Virginia, on the ground that it was unconstitutional, and in 1776 a Massachusetts judge charged a jury not to apply certain acts of Parliament, as they were void.

Despite the general existence of legislative supremacy under the state constitutions established in the period of the Revolution, there were several cases in which the state courts, in various forms and on different bases, asserted the right of the courts to hold unconstitutional acts of the legislature not justified by constitutional provisions. Chief among these were the case of *Holmes vs. Walton*, decided in the New Jersey courts in 1780; the case of *Trevett vs. Weeden*, decided in 1786 by the Rhode Island courts; and the case of *Bayard vs. Singleton*, decided just prior to the Constitutional Convention, in 1787, in North Carolina. Of these three, the most influential in the formation of public opinion was that of *Trevett vs. Weeden*, although in this case the declaration of the court that the act of the legislature was void was based upon the alleged impossibility of execution of the law, and not on a question of its constitutional justification. Nevertheless, the case was important as an example of judicial review of an act of the legislature.

In the Constitutional Convention of 1787 the majority of the important members of that body declared either directly or indirectly for a judicial review of legislative acts. The Virginia Plan as introduced in the convention contained a provision for a "council of revision" to pass on acts of the legislature. This body was to be composed of the executive and judiciary officials, and was to pass on all laws, not only on a basis of their expediency, but on a basis of their accordance with or opposition to the provisions of the Constitution. The obvious objection to such an institution was the extent to which it destroyed the principle of the separation of powers in government, a fundamental doctrine of the revolutionary period. At any rate, the plan itself was an indication of the desire of the convention for a limitation of the powers of the legislative branch.

This desire was a natural reaction from the revolutionary emphasis upon popular sovereignty, which had resulted in the primacy of the legislature in the state governments established in that period. The groups chiefly represented in the convention were of the opinion that a government was desirable which should give due protection to property rights. These property rights were in the hands of a comparatively few individuals, and could best be protected from the encroachments of the many by the establishment of some form of check upon majorities such as through judicial review of acts of the legislature. The conservative influence of the courts along these lines had been felt during the period of the Confederation, and they had on that basis been the object of popular opposition by those who were interested chiefly in the securing of social and economic equality.

In addition to the proposed council of revision, the Virginia Plan contained a provision for giving to Congress a veto upon actions of the state legislatures. This proposal met the opposition of those who felt that it would constitute too great an invasion of the independence of the state governments. The fundamental idea involved was that some safeguard must be set up against the violation of the Constitution by the states, and the problem was finally solved in the convention by making the Constitution the "supreme law of the land" enforceable by the courts of the states. This would allow judicial review within the states, on a basis of the conformance or non-conformance of acts of the state legislatures with those provisions of the Constitution which touched the states.

The Constitution, besides being declared the supreme law of the land, contained the provision that the judicial power of the United States should extend to all cases arising under it. No direct provision is made in the Constitution for judicial review or judicial interpretation of the Constitution, but the discussions in the convention indicate that the general understanding was that the judicial power implied judicial review. This was the opinion expressed by leading members of the convention, both in that gathering and in the later advocacy of the Constitution before the country and in the ratifying conventions.

Of particular interest in the light of later events is the opinion of Marshall himself as expressed in the Virginia ratifying convention. In discussing the possibility of the national government invading the sphere of state rights he clearly indicated that in case of this or any other infringement of the Constitution by the national government, the courts would declare the act to be void.

The growth of the idea of judicial review from 1789 until its establishment in the national system by Marshall in 1803 is indicated by its acceptance in the various states up to that time. By 1803, judicial review had been established in a majority of the states in the union, through the instrumentality of judicial practice.

Despite this tendency in the state courts, the early history of the Supreme Court was unimpressive. Few cases were decided, and the tendency of the court to limit its own functions seemed to relegate it to a secondary place in the national structure. In 1792, in the *Case of Hayburn*, several justices of the Supreme Court, sitting as a circuit court, refused to act as a commission on a non-judicial matter. They took the view that their function was limited strictly to the judgment of actual cases at law. In the following year President Washington and his cabinet attempted to secure from the justices of the Supreme Court their opinion on the rights and duties of the United States as a neutral nation, under the laws and treaties of the United States. The court replied that it could not depart from its function of deciding cases at law, and stated that the power of the President to call upon the heads of departments for opinions was limited to the "executive departments."

In that same year the Supreme Court decided in the case of *Chisholm vs. Georgia* that, under the Constitution, a state could be sued in the courts of the United States by citizens of another state. This decision was taken as a serious invasion of the sphere of state rights, in subordinating the states to the jurisdiction of the national courts, and as a result, in 1798, the eleventh amendment was passed, expressly denying to the national courts any jurisdiction over suits against states by citizens of other states or of foreign nations. Thus the first important limitation of state sovereignty by the court was protested by the people, and placed under the ban of the Constitution.

The case of *Calder vs. Bull*, in 1798, afforded the Supreme Court an opportunity to interpret and define the words of the Constitution, and to judge the validity of a state law under it. The state law in question was claimed to be in violation of the provision in the Constitution prohibiting ex-post-facto laws. In judging the case the court decided what the Constitution meant by an ex-post-facto law but, though it had no doubt of its capacity to declare the law in question void if in conflict with the Constitution, it actually did declare the statute constitutional.

THE CASE OF MARBURY VS. MADISON

Finally, in 1803, the case of *Marbury vs. Madison* afforded an opportunity for Marshall to declare the doctrine of the right of the Supreme Court to review acts of the national legislature and to declare them void if in conflict with the terms of the Constitution. Briefly the circumstances of this famous case were as follows: The Federalist party was defeated in the election of 1800, but between the date of the election and the coming of the new officials into office, in March, 1801, the party, through its control of Congress, attempted to entrench itself in the national government by creating new offices in the judiciary which were to be filled with members of the Federalist party. William Marbury was one of the new appointees, but his commission as justice of the peace in the District of Columbia had not been delivered when President Thomas Jefferson, with James Madison as secretary of state, took office on March fourth. The new administration refused to deliver this and other commissions so Marbury filed suit, asking the Supreme Court to grant a writ of mandamus to compel Madison to deliver the commission. The granting of such a writ was authorized by the Judiciary Act passed by Congress in 1789, but Marshall held that the court could not do so, as this act of Congress, in enlarging the powers of the court, exceeded the power granted to Congress by the Constitution, and was therefore void.

The doctrines declared were that the Constitution, as defining the powers of government, was expressive of the will of the people. It was the function of the Supreme Court to interpret the Constitution and, in case of conflict between it as the will of the people, and a law of Congress as an act of government, it was the duty of the court to deny the validity of the law and uphold the Constitution. Thus Marshall stated the basic principle of constitutional government, which is that in such a government the exercise of governmental functions is subject to limitation in the interest of the people.

The importance of the decision, however, lay not in the statement of this principle, but in the assumption by the court of the power of judging whether the constitutional safeguards were being observed. On the basis of this power the court has since determined the development of government under the Constitution along two chief lines, namely, as to the extent and nature of the powers of the national government, and as to the extent and nature of the powers of the state governments. In both of these respects Marshall took a nationalistic attitude, an attitude which favored the power and development of a strong national government, and throughout his career as Chief Justice the court was dominated by his ideas, despite changes in personnel designed to change its composition. The decisions of Marshall laid the legal basis for a strong national government which, however, was to become an actual fact through a course of historical development in which the factors of centralization and localism were to be in conflict. To Marshall in large measure goes the credit for the statesmanlike function of laying the legal basis for later reality.

The nature of the influence exerted by the decision that the Supreme Court could declare void acts of Congress contrary to the Constitution is seen by the fact that the next case in which the court so acted was that of *Dred Scott vs. Sanford,* decided in 1857. By that time the membership of the Supreme Court had changed to such an extent that Marshall's nationalistic ideas no longer controlled it, and the decision in that case was in direct opposition to Marshall's doctrine of expansion of national powers under the "necessary and proper" clause of the Constitution. It should be mentioned also that the prestige of the Supreme Court suffered from this decision, due to the questionable circumstances under which it was given, involving what was termed a gross abuse of trust by that body.

In considering the decisions of the Supreme Court, under Marshall and since his time, it is easily seen that they have dealt not only with the powers of the national government but also with the question of the powers of the state governments. This has been because the Constitution attempts to divide powers between the national and state governments. The difficulty of separating the two aspects of governmental development under the Constitution will be seen in the consideration of the various cases, but such cases will be classified on a basis of whether they deal primarily with the powers of the national government, or with the powers of the state governments.

THE PRINCIPLE OF IMPLIED POWERS

An important power of the national government is that of handling its finances. The government under the Articles of Confederation, as has been pointed out, was characterized by the lack of an adequate power to regulate its own finances, being dependent upon the individual states for contributions to its support. The Constitution was designed to remedy this situation, by giving the national government the power of collecting taxes directly from the people, without the intervention of the states. This power was necessary to the existence of a strong government under the Constitution, as the carrying out of any of its other powers was dependent naturally upon adequate financial support.

In several important cases the Supreme Court has defined the powers of the national government in relation to its financial powers. In 1819 the case of *McCulloch vs. Maryland* was decided by the Supreme Court. This case involved the establishment in Baltimore of a branch of the Bank of the United States. This bank had been chartered in 1816 by Congress to facilitate the administration of the national finances. Among other things, the bank was authorized to establish branches in the states. These, as well as the main bank at Philadelphia, were to be exempt from taxation. The bank met widespread opposition, due to financial difficulties for which it was blamed, and several states attempted to regulate the branch banks in their jurisdictions. The Maryland legislature passed a law taxing heavily banks not chartered by the state legislature which obviously included the branch of the Bank of the United States located at Baltimore. McCulloch, the cashier of this branch, refused to pay the taxes and appealed to the Supreme Court of the United States against the Maryland action.

Two chief points were involved in the case. The first was as to the right of the United States government to establish a bank, in the carrying out of its financial powers. No provision for a bank was contained in the Constitution, and it was argued that therefore no such power existed. In connection with this point Marshall enunciated the famous doctrine of implied powers. This doctrine was based on that clause of the Constitution which grants to Congress all powers "necessary and proper" to carry out its definitely delegated powers. Those who opposed the strengthening of the powers of the national government argued that this clause justified the use by Congress of only such powers as were absolutely indispensable to the carrying out of the definitely delegated powers. Marshall, however, declined to accept such an interpretation, declaring that by the word necessary was meant not vital, but convenient or useful. In other words, the "necessary and proper" clause was an enlargement of the delegated powers of Congress, not a limitation of them. This, in brief, constitutes the doctrine of implied powers, under which Marshall held constitutional the establishment of a bank to handle national finances.

But the other chief point in the case was equally important. Could the State of Maryland tax the branch bank located within its jurisdiction? The power of the state to tax, within its boundaries, was an important one, an attribute of its character as a sovereign state, and one without which its government could not exist long. On the other hand, if the state could tax instrumentalities of the national government, this would imply a superiority of the state over the national government. What was still more important, was the fact which Marshall pointed out, that the power to tax meant the power to tax out of existence, and such a power of the states over instrumentalities of the national government would involve the absolute control of the national government by the states. Therefore, declared the Chief Justice, in cases of conflict between the powers of the states and those of the national government, the national government must be supreme, as it was the expression of the will of the whole people, in contrast to the states which were the expression of the will only of parts of the people.

In 1824 this question was again similarly decided in the case of *Osborn vs. the Bank of the United States,* a case which arose through an attempt of Ohio to tax a branch bank within its jurisdiction. The decisions of the Supreme Court in these cases were met with widespread protests on the part of those who disapproved of the broad interpretation of the "necessary and proper" clause in the interest of the extension of the powers of the national government, and who felt that the denial to the states of the right to tax instrumentalities of the national government within their jurisdictions was an undue invasion of state sovereignty.

On the other hand, while such cases established the broad powers of the national government in the carrying out of its financial measures, and the immunity of national financial instrumentalities from taxation by the states, this latter rule works both ways. In 1871 it was decided in the case of *The Collector vs. Day,* that the federal government has no power to tax instrumentalities of the state governments. The court admitted that there was no express denial in the Constitution of such a power in the hands of the national government, but claimed that it was a necessary implication resulting from our dual form of government under the Constitution. The case arose on a question of whether or not Congress had the power to tax the salaries of judicial officers of a state. Such a power, it was held, would be inconsistent with the existence in the states of an independent judiciary, and would constitute an unjustified invasion of the sphere of state sovereignty.

The extent of the national power to tax was further considered in the case of *Bailey vs. Drexel Furniture Co.*, in 1922. This case involved an attempt on the part of Congress, in 1919, to tax the products of child labor. The tax was not imposed for the purpose of securing revenue, but was an effort on the part of Congress to prevent the use of child labor. Could the taxing power be used thus, to regulate conditions of labor within the states? Such regulation was properly within the sphere of state control. A previous effort to prohibit child labor through the power of Congress to regulate interstate commerce had been declared void by the court in the case of *Hammer vs. Dagenhart*, in 1918. This case will be considered more fully later.

In *Bailey vs. Drexel* the Supreme Court declared that the power of Congress to tax was limited to the purpose of securing revenue, that the extent of the tax was unlimited if it were imposed with such a purpose; but that if it were imposed for the accomplishment of a purpose not properly within the powers of the national government, it was void. To decide otherwise would have meant the taking of control by the national government over powers reserved to the states by the Constitution.

In respect to the general powers of Congress to establish rules for the carrying on of its own business, the case of *Anderson vs. Dunn* further states the doctrine of implied powers. This case, decided by the Supreme Court in 1824, had to do with the right of the House of Representatives to punish persons outside its body for contempt of the House, even to the extent of imprisonment. The decision was that such a power did exist, as being necessary to the delegated power of Congress to make rules for its procedure, and to enable it to do business. In the course of his decision Justice Johnson said, "The idea is utopian that government can exist without leaving the exercise of discretion somewhere. . . . The science of government is the most abstruse of all sciences . . . and practically consists in little more than the exercise of a sound discretion applied to the exigencies of the state as they arise."

Obviously the exercise of discretion in government was to be moderate and within the intent of the Constitution. The important fact, however, is that within such limits the character of the government under the Constitution depends upon the personnel of the government. The government of the United States is thus as much "of men" as "of laws."

A further illustration of the doctrine of implied powers is seen in the case of *American Insurance Co. vs. Canter*. This case, decided in 1828, involved the powers of Congress to acquire and govern new territory. Marshall, in giving the decision in the case, stated that the power to acquire and govern new territory was implied in the constitutional grant to the national government of the power to make war and to make treaties. This was, thus, not the result of any definite grant of the power in the Constitution, but was to be inferred from those powers which were there granted.

In relation to the executive department, the Supreme Court, in the case of *Martin vs. Mott*, extended the doctrine of discretionary powers to the executive. This case was decided in 1827 and involved the right of the president to call out the militia in cases of invasion. It was claimed that no actual or threatened state of invasion existed, and that therefore the act of the president in calling out the militia was unjustified.

In deciding the case the Supreme Court strengthened the independent position of the executive branch of the government, by stating that in such action the president is the sole judge as to whether such an emergency has arisen, and his judgment cannot be reviewed by any other authority in the government. This strengthening of the discretionary powers of the executive, and the refusal of the Supreme Court to attempt any control of his acts was in accord with the doctrine of the separation of powers, and was on a basis of the implied powers of the national government.

INTERPRETATION OF THE COMMERCE CLAUSE OF THE CONSTITUTION

In 1824 another significant case was decided by the Supreme Court. This was the case of *Gibbons vs. Ogden*, which involved the powers of Congress in relation to commerce. The necessity for a government capable of regulating interstate and foreign commerce was an important cause of the move for a new constitution to supplant the Articles of Confederation. The case of *Gibbons vs. Ogden* decided the extent and nature of that power in the hands of Congress, and the relation of this power to the rights of the states.

The circumstances giving rise to the case were as follows: The legislature of the state of New York had granted the exclusive right of steamboat navigation upon New York waters to Robert R. Livingston and Robert Fulton, who could in turn license others in the exercise of this privilege. Ogden had secured such a license. When Gibbons also engaged in the business without such a license, Ogden secured an injunction from the New York courts prohibiting him from so doing. Gibbons, in his own defence, claimed that a license which he had secured from the federal government permitted him to navigate the waters over which New York had asserted its jurisdiction. This case came before the Supreme Court of the United States on appeal from the decision of the New York courts.

In giving his decision, Chief Justice Marshall again stated the necessity for a broad interpretation of the constitutional grants of power to the national government. Commerce, the object of national control, was therefore defined as including not only the buying and selling of commodities, but their transportation. Commerce between the states was defined as intercourse, and as such it included navigation. Therefore the act of Congress under which Gibbons received his license to engage in navigation was within the constitutional powers of that body.

What was to be the relationship between this power of Congress and the attempts of the states to regulate commerce within their boundaries? In deciding this, Marshall invoked the same rule as he had laid down in the case of *McCulloch vs. Maryland*, namely, that in case of conflict between the powers of the national government and those of the states, the national powers were supreme.

This combination of a broad definition of what constituted interstate commerce with the principle of national power over it laid the basis for nationalism of an economic type. It laid the legal framework for a national regulation of interstate economic contacts, which was to result in the elimination of those conflicting and often discriminatory state attempts at regulation which were such a cause of friction during the days of the Articles of Confederation.

Furthermore, Marshall's broad definition of commerce as "intercourse" made it possible at a later date to bring under the control of the national government all the agencies of interstate communication, such as telephone and telegraph lines, ferries between states, even though they transported persons only, and interstate bridges.

The question as to when interstate commerce ceased to be interstate in character and became internal commerce of a state was dealt with in the case of *Brown vs. Maryland*. Congress cannot regulate commerce which is strictly the internal commerce of a state, hence the importance of defining what constitutes such commerce.

In the decision handed down in this case in 1827 Marshall laid down the principle that the sale of the goods imported into a state in interstate commerce was as much interstate as was the importation of those goods. But such goods ceased to be in interstate commerce when they had become mixed with the general mass of property in the state, and this Marshall stated as occurring when the goods were taken from the original package in which they were imported. This is the so-called "original package" doctrine.

According to this doctrine the state could not tax or regulate the sale of imported goods unless they had been taken from the packages in which they were imported. Here again was a decision that, in case of conflict between national and state powers under the Constitution, the powers of the national government are supreme.

As has already been mentioned, the broad interpretation of the taxing power of the national government did not imply any application of this power to matters beyond the national jurisdiction. No more could the power to regulate interstate commerce be applied to the accomplishment of ends not within the power of Congress to accomplish.

By the "police power" is meant the authority to pass laws for the protection of the health, safety, morals, public order and general welfare of the community. This power is not granted to Congress by the Constitution, and is therefore reserved to the states under the tenth amendment. But Congress has under broad interpretation of its definitely granted powers, enacted much legislation the effect of which has been to control those interests of the people otherwise protected by the "police power" of the states.

The greatest amount of this police regulation has been accomplished through the control of Congress over interstate commerce. Through this instrumentality Congress has passed federal safety-appliance acts, employers' liability laws, and antitrust legislation. The courts have held that this is justified by the fact that the aim of Congress in these acts is the safety and efficiency of interstate commerce itself.

Also, the courts have held that the power of Congress over interstate commerce may be used to prevent the use of the agencies of that commerce in the transportation of harmful products or the promoting of undesirable transactions. Along this line has been upheld the prohibition of the agencies of interstate transportation to lottery tickets, impure food or drugs, or animals infected with contagious diseases. This represented a real attack upon national social and economic problems, under the guise of the regulation of commerce.

The question inevitably arose, however, as to how far the national government could go in such a course of regulation. Could any truly national problem of morals, health, or general welfare be dealt with under the definitely delegated powers of the national government, despite the invasion of the legitimate sphere of state action? The case of *Hammer vs. Dagenhart*, decided by the Supreme Court in 1918, defined the limits to which the national authority could extend.

The case arose in connection with the attempt of Congress to deal on a national scale with the problem of child labor. The law in question prohibited the transportation in interstate commerce of goods in the production of which child labor had been used. The Supreme Court declared the law unconstitutional, stating that it was aimed, not at a legitimate regulation of interstate commerce for its own preservation and safety, but at the handling of the problem of child labor itself. This problem, the court stated, could only be dealt with under the police power reserved to the states, and any attempt of the national government to do

so would be in violation of the rights of the states. The products
of child labor could not be barred from interstate commerce
because of any harmfulness of the products themselves, but because of the conditions of their manufacture, and the conditions
of manufacturing within the states were not subject to national
regulation. To sanction regulation of the type involved here
would be in effect to bring the whole problem of labor conditions
under the power of the national government.

The position of the court in this case was the result of a five
to four vote of that body. The decision caused much discussion,
its opponents feeling that it was inconsistent with the previous
sanction of what amounted to police regulations under the commerce clause. In the final analysis the case simply represented a
halt in the tendency of the courts to sanction the increasing development of national powers.

THE SUPREME COURT AND STATE POWERS

Concern thus far has been primarily with the development by
the Supreme Court of its interpretation of the nature and extent
of the powers of the national government. The place of the
states in the federal system has been considered only insofar as
the powers of the national government discussed have involved
limitations upon the powers of the state governments. Consideration will now be given to the direct influence of the Supreme
Court in the determination of the extent and nature of state
powers under the Constitution.

The decisive case in the establishment of the right of the
Supreme Court to pass on the constitutionality of acts of the
state legislatures was that of *Fletcher vs. Peck,* which came before the court in 1810. This case involved a grant of land, made
in 1795 by the state of Georgia. In 1796 the act granting the
land was repealed on ground that bribery had been used to secure its passage. The Supreme Court stated that the original
grant was a contract by the state of Georgia not to reassert its
title to the land, and the fact that the state legislature had
acted corruptly in making the grant was no ground for holding
the legislation invalid.

Since the original grant was a contract, it could not be revoked by a later act of the legislature, for to do so would involve the denial of the sanctity of contracts, expressly guaranteed in the Constitution. This guarantee was a limitation upon the legislative power of the states, and would be enforced by the Supreme Court of the United States. This meant that the state governments would be forced to regard the Constitution as the "supreme law of the land," and that an agency of the national government would apply this supreme law to them.

This case indicates the vital difference between the government under the Articles of Confederation and that under the Constitution. The chief problem of the period just before the adoption of the Constitution had been that of securing some means whereby the states could be forced to live up to their obligations under the Articles of Confederation. Under the Articles no means of accomplishing this could be found, and the provision in the Constitution that the Constitution, laws, and treaties of the United States should be the "supreme law of the land" was an effort to guarantee that under that instrument of government the states should live up to their obligations. That the Supreme Court should enforce the law of the land upon the states was natural, as this would give an outside check upon their actions, but it was opposed as implying the subjection of the states to the agencies of the national government.

In the case of *Dartmouth College vs. Woodward* the Supreme Court decided in 1819 that a charter granted to a private institution, which does not set up a public institution capable of being regulated by the state government, is a contract, and cannot be revoked by the state. Such revocation would be a denial of the sanctity of contracts, guaranteed by the Constitution, and would therefore be declared void by the courts.

In this case the trustees of Dartmouth College had been granted a charter by the English Crown in 1769. The state attempted to change the entire character of the institution, in 1816, by legislative action, but upon the case being carried to the Supreme Court it was decided that the state had no right to do so. The effect of the decision has been to limit the states in the regulation of corporate rights, thus affecting the economic interests of the states in a conservative direction. The decision was of great importance to those who had money to invest, giving them assurance of practical freedom from legislative interference in conducting the business of chartered corporations. The decision has, however, made it possible for corrupt state legislatures to grant charters contrary to the public interest, without the possibility of future legislative regulation of corporations thus set up.

In later years the importance of the Dartmouth College decision was considerably lessened when the state legislatures began inserting in corporation charters provisions for the future changing of the charters. These provisions thus became a part of the contract itself and made it possible for later legislatures to alter charters completely or even to revoke them.

The Supreme Court has ruled that the terms of charters must be strictly interpreted in favor of the public, and that no privileges may be secured by a charter unless they are expressly granted in it. This is the doctrine established in the case of *Charles River Bridge vs. Warren Bridge,* decided by the Supreme Court in 1837. The case involved a franchise granted to the proprietors of the Charles River Bridge, to build a bridge between Cambridge and Boston and receive tolls for seventy years. Somewhat later another franchise was granted to the proprietors of the Warren Bridge, to build a bridge between the same two places. This bridge was to be made free six years after its completion. This would destroy the value of the franchise granted the Charles River Bridge proprietors, and they claimed it was an invasion of the sanctity of contracts.

The Supreme Court ruled, however, that their charter implied no exclusive right to build bridges between these two points, and that such contracts must be interpreted in the interest of the public, not of the holders of the charters.

While these cases in relation to the validity of the acts of state legislatures and the right of the national courts to judge the constitutionality of such acts were being decided, a further question arose. Could the Supreme Court review the decisions of state courts, in case the "supreme law of the land" was involved? Such a right of review was claimed to be in practical denial of the independence of the state courts, making them subservient to the national government, and was thus asserted to be an unjustifiable invasion of state sovereignty. On the other hand there was the necessity, already alluded to, for securing some means of assuring the adherence of the states to the Constitution and the performance of their duties under it. If the decisions of the state courts could not be reviewed to this end, there was no assurance that they would enforce the terms of the Constitution within the limits of their respective states.

Therefore in the case of *Martin vs. Hunter's Lessee,* decided by the Supreme Court in 1816, it was declared that the limitation of the right of the Supreme Court to hear appeals, to cases arising in the federal courts, would be a limitation of the power of that court to judge cases arising under the Constitution, the laws and the treaties of the United States. In order to guard the Constitution from possible violation under the influence of state and local interest, the Supreme Court must have the right to review decisions of the state courts.

This right of the Supreme Court to review decisions of the state courts was declared in the case of *Cohens vs. Virginia,* to include even those cases in which a state was a party. The case, decided by the Supreme Court in 1821, involved the sale by Cohens of lottery tickets, contrary to a law of the state of Virginia. He claimed, in defence of his action, that an act of Congress permitted such sales. Upon his appeal to the Supreme Court, the state of Virginia claimed that the court had no jurisdiction over the case, as a state was the defendant in the case, and such jurisdiction would subject the state to the control of the national government.

In upholding the jurisdiction of the Supreme Court in such cases, Marshall reaffirmed the principle of the supremacy of the Constitution as a check upon state action which had previously been stated in the case of *Martin vs. Hunter's Lessee.* He further upheld the fundamental principle that "the general government, though limited as to its objects, is supreme with respect to those objects."

It was not without opposition, however, that the principle of national enforcement of the Constitution upon the states was declared. The prestige of the Supreme Court suffered a serious blow in connection with the decision in the case of *Worcester vs. Georgia,* given in 1832. The question in this case was the right of the national government alone to regulate and control Indian territory within the states. Marshall upheld this right, and declared void laws of the state of Georgia which extended the jurisdiction of that state over the Indian territory within her borders.

The state of Georgia, however, defied the mandate of the Supreme Court, and President Jackson refused to enforce it, on the grounds of his opposition to the policy of depriving the states of their right to control Indian territory in their limits. This was a setback to the doctrine of the supremacy of the national government in the carrying out of its powers, and a blow to the right of the Supreme Court to review state laws as to their constitutionality. It should be mentioned that President Jackson was within his constitutional rights in refusing to enforce the decision of the Supreme Court. Ordinarily the president would naturally coöperate with the Supreme Court but to compel him to enforce the court's decisions which were contrary to his own judgment would tend to destroy the principle of separation of powers.

Some very important decisions have resulted from the interpretation by the Supreme Court of the fourteenth amendment in relation to state exercises of the police power. As a matter of fact, more cases have been interpreted under the fourteenth amendment than under any other constitutional provision. This amendment was one of that group passed after the Civil War, in the effort to prevent the denial to the negro of his civil and political rights by the southern states. It was doubtless expected by the originators of this amendment that among such rights would be classed all the common civil rights, among which were those safeguarded by the bill of rights in the Constitution. Previously, these rights had been protected by the states, but the framers of this amendment expected to bring these rights under the protection of the national government.

This was contrary to the whole history of American federalism. Dual citizenship, in both state and nation, was implied in the Constitution, which in the final analysis was, in one aspect at least, an attempt to divide sovereignty between state and nation. To establish as a fact the protection by the United States of all those civil rights involved in state citizenship would have been to reduce the states to impotence.

The question of the interpretation of the fourteenth amendment in this respect arose in connection with the grant by the reconstruction government in Louisiana of a monopoly of the slaughterhouse business. This monopoly in the hands of a single concern was secured by corrupt influence, and abridged the right of numerous other concerns to operate in the same business. By these concerns it was claimed that the law granting the monopoly violated the fourteenth amendment which prohibited the deprivation of liberty and property without due process of law, and which guaranteed the equal protection of the laws to all.

The Supreme Court, however, decided, by a bare majority of five to four, that there was a difference between state citizenship and national citizenship, and that the due process of law clause did not limit the states in the exercise of their police power. It was a limit upon the states to prevent the invasion by them of the rights of individuals which flowed from their citizenship in the United States, but these rights did not include the ordinary rights to liberty, property, and the equal protection of the laws.

The minority of the court dissented from such views, pointing out the fact that if the fourteenth amendment only prohibited the states from invading rights of citizens derived from United States citizenship, then it was merely stating an already accepted fact, for the states had never had the power of doing this. Thus the *Slaughterhouse Cases,* as they were called, as decided in 1873, placed no new power in the hands of the Supreme Court to limit state action.

Along the same lines was decided the case of *Munn vs. Illinois,* in 1876. This case involved the right of the state of Illinois to regulate charges for the storage of grain in warehouses. It was urged that the laws passed to this end were in violation of the fourteenth amendment, as the rates provided for were unjust and thus involved the deprivation of property without due process of law. But the court again decided that the amendment provided no check against the state exercise of the police power, and that the police power could justifiably be extended to the regulation of businesses invested with a public interest. As a matter of fact, all businesses are invested with a public interest, and the concern of the courts must be to determine the extent of public interest necessary to justify legislative interference with their freedom of action.

The tendency of the Supreme Court in these early cases was not to be the final one, however. In later cases the court has abandoned its early stand on the question, and has brought under the fourteenth amendment all exercises of the police power of the states. Thus, under its review has come the question in each case considered, as to whether the regulations imposed by the states are justifiable limitations upon the freedom of action of the individual, or whether they are limitations without "due process of law." The Supreme Court has given no definition of "due process of law," except to say that it does not necessarily involve any special legal procedure. The emphasis is therefore more on a just process of law than on any particular rules of procedure.

As a result of this, in judging whether or not a particular state police regulation is to be upheld, the Supreme Court bases its decision fundamentally on whether the invasion of individual rights which it involves is necessary or desirable. Along these lines the court has decided a large number of cases involving the regulation of business, of labor conditions, and the general social and economic conditions of modern industrialism. Obviously, the decision of whether such regulation is necessary or desirable will depend not upon reference to a particular law or statute, but upon a study of the social situation to which the regulation is to be applied.

An example of such a procedure is to be seen in the case of *Lochner vs. New York*, in which the court judged as to whether a law of the state of New York regulating hours of labor in bakery industries was a limitation of the right of the individual to freedom of contract, which could be justified as due process of law. In this case, decided in 1905, the chief consideration of the court was given to the question of whether the conditions of labor in bakery industries justified such a limitation on the freedom of the individual to contract. The court decided that the conditions of labor involved did not make reasonably necessary the regulations proposed, and therefore declared the law unconstitutional. Later cases have emphasized even more the basis for decisions on such matters, as being the personal opinions of the members of the court on matters of abstract justice.

What are the implications of this fact in the evolution of

American constitutional government? As has been pointed out above, the fundamental basis of the Constitution is the belief in the necessity for external restraints upon government, for the purpose of securing the dominance of the public interest. It has also been pointed out that this rule of law was conceived as being promoted by the function of the court in applying the law through the interpretation of the Constitution and the review of governmental actions as to their constitutionality. But it must be seen that in the application of the "due process of law" clause there has been developed a degree of judicial discretion quite apart from the interpretation of the law itself.

Numerous other cases might be cited to illustrate the judicial interpretation of the Constitution but, even if this whole volume were devoted to the subject, only a small proportion of the hundreds of cases could be mentioned. The cases that have been mentioned are typical and indicate some of the more important trends of interpretation. There can be no doubt that decisions of the Supreme Court have aided greatly in the expansion of the Constitution.

SELECTED REFERENCES

Babcock, K. C., *The Rise of American Nationality 1811–1819*, pp. 290–308.

Beard, C. A., *The Supreme Court and the Constitution*, pp. 1–127.

Bizzell, W. B., *Judicial Interpretation of Political Theory*, pp. 1–63.

Burdick, C. K., *The Law of the American Constitution*, pp. 90–142.

Cooley, T. M., et. al., *Constitutional History of the United States as Seen in the Development of American Law*, pp. 29–235.

Corwin, E. S., *The Doctrine of Judicial Review*, pp. 1–78.

Cushman, R. E., *Leading Constitutional Decisions*, pp. 17–20, 33–42, 68–79, 93–105, 155–161, 203–213, 225–234, 241–261.

Elliot, Edward, *Biographical Story of the Constitution*, pp. 125–146.

Haines, C. G., *The American Doctrine of Judicial Supremacy*, pp. 1–353.

Johnson, Allen, ed., *Readings in American Constitutional History 1776–1876*, pp. 140–142, 241–298, 310–316, 436–445.

Johnson, Allen, and Robinson, W. A., eds., *Readings in Recent American Constitutional History 1876–1926*, pp. 1–195, 308–369, 477–506.

Martin, C. E., *An Introduction to the Study of the American Constitution*, pp. 95–126.

McBain, H. L., *The Living Constitution*, pp. 237–271.

McLaughlin, A. C., *The Courts, The Constitution and Parties*, pp. 3–107.

Meigs, W. M., *The Relation of the Judiciary to the Constitution*, pp. 7–240.

Merriam, C. E., *American Political Ideas*, pp. 145–211.

Munro, W. B., *The Constitution of the United States A Brief and General Commentary*, pp. 95–113.

Orth, S. P., and Cushman, R. E., *American National Government*, pp. 545–571.

The Federalist (Everyman's Library Edition), Nos. 78–83, pp. 394–436.

Warren, Charles, *Congress, The Constitution, and The Supreme Court*, pp. 128–302.

Willoughby, W. W., *The American Constitutional System*, pp. 100–110, 122–153.

Wilson, Woodrow, *Constitutional Government in the United States*, pp. 142–172.

Chapter Fifteen

LEGISLATIVE EXPANSION OF THE CONSTITUTION

WHEN the first Congress under the Constitution met early in 1789, it was faced by great responsibilities. It was necessary to pass legislation for the purpose of bringing into existence other agencies of government such as the judiciary and the executive departments. In legislating for these purposes Congress, as has been demonstrated, took a broad view of its powers. But it was necessary for Congress to go further and give practical application to its other powers. One of the chief purposes in drafting a new framework of government had been to secure a central legislative body with adequate powers, particularly in the matters of taxation and commercial regulation. Should those powers be interpreted narrowly, or should a broad application be made of them?

LIBERAL VERSUS STRICT CONSTRUCTION

As the Federalists were in control of Congress during the period when the Constitution was being applied "to the exigencies of the union," the tendency was to take a broad view of the legislative powers. This tendency was strenuously objected to by Thomas Jefferson and his followers who contended that the powers delegated to Congress should be interpreted strictly, and that nothing should be done unless it was specifically authorized by the Constitution. Ever since Congress began to function there have been those two schools of thought, the one favoring liberal or free interpretation and the other advocating strict construction of the Constitution. Even a superficial examination of legislative history since 1789 will reveal that the liberal construction group have most frequently been in control.

Backed by a Supreme Court which has likewise, during much of its history, been inclined to interpret the Constitution liber-

355

ally, Congress has passed a large number of laws dealing with matters not expressly referred to in the list of enumerated powers. Much of such legislation has been made possible by a broad interpretation of the power to tax in order to "provide for the common defence and general welfare of the United States." This is the so-called "elastic clause" of the Constitution. The "necessary and proper" clause has also been frequently used to justify legislation for which no other authority could be found. This is the clause which states that Congress shall have the power "To make all laws which shall be necessary and proper for carrying into execution" the enumerated powers of Congress, "and all other powers vested by this Constitution in the government of the United States, or in any department or officer thereof." From the "necessary and proper" clause has chiefly developed the doctrine of implied powers. However, the tendency, historically, has been to take a broad view of all of the powers and to imply from them the authority to legislate in ways not dreamed of by the framers of the Constitution. For instance, who among the "Fathers of the Constitution" could have foreseen that the power to regulate commerce would, within a hundred and forty years, be applied successively to the regulation of railroads, telephones, telegraphs, pipe lines, airplanes, and radio?

While permitting broad construction of the powers of Congress, the Constitution also provides certain limitations on the national legislature. The fact that the powers are delegated is one limitation. This limitation was strengthened greatly by the tenth amendment to the Constitution. Then there is the limitation which grows out of the dual nature of the government. Congress cannot legislate in such a way as to interfere with the states within their own spheres. For example, Congress cannot tax state agencies or the salaries of state officers. Furthermore, there are definite limitations stated in the Constitution. All duties, imposts, and excises must be uniform throughout the United States; direct taxes must be levied on the states only in proportion to their population; and no duties may be levied on exports. No bills of attainder or ex-post-facto laws may be passed and the "privilege of the writ of habeas corpus shall not be suspended, unless when in cases of rebellion or invasion the public safety may require it." No state may be given preference in the matter of commercial or revenue regulations, "nor shall vessels bound to, or from, one State, be obliged to enter, clear, or pay duties in another." Besides these limitations contained in the original Constitution, the first nine amendments specifically imposed other limitations on Congress in matters pertaining to the rights and liberties of the people.

TARIFF LEGISLATION

One of the first legislative acts passed by the first Congress in 1789 was designed to supply the new government with much-needed revenue. This was a tariff act placed on the statute book on July 4, 1789. It provided for specific duties on more than thirty commodities; for ad valorem duties ranging from seven and a half to fifteen percent on certain enumerated articles; and for a duty of five percent on all articles not enumerated. A few days later, on July 20th, a tonnage act was also passed. It placed a tax of six cents a ton upon vessels built in the United States and owned by Americans; thirty cents a ton on vessels built in the United States but owned by foreigners; and fifty cents a ton on foreign built and foreign owned vessels. A little later a law was passed to provide a customs service for the collection of duties. Thus were the powers of Congress to levy and collect duties and to regulate foreign commerce given their first application.

In the years since 1789, Congress has continued to enact, from time to time, tariff and tonnage acts. Though at first the tariff acts were purely revenue measures, Congress, acting under the broad construction theory, placed on the statute books in 1816 an act that was intended to offer protection to American manufacturers. Ever since, the protective policy has been maintained, though the rates have fluctuated considerably. Since the beginning of the Civil War the tendency has been to impose very high protective rates. The latest legislation on the subject was the Smoot-Hawley tariff act passed in 1930. At all times there have been those who have insisted that tariffs should be imposed for revenue only but even when the advocates of that point of view have been in control of Congress they have not attempted to do away with protection entirely. Some of the leading American industries of the present time have developed largely because of the protection against foreign competition offered by protective tariffs.

FINANCIAL LEGISLATION AS RECOMMENDED BY HAMILTON

Among the most important powers granted to Congress was that which gave it the right to levy and collect taxes, duties, imposts, and excises to pay the debts and to provide for the common defence and general welfare of the United States. It also had the power to borrow money. By the time of the Constitutional Convention, the credit of the United States had been practically exhausted at home and abroad. The Confederation government had been absolutely powerless to pay even the interest on its domestic and foreign debts. Naturally, one of the first concerns of the new Congress under the Constitution was to exercise its financial powers in such a way as to restore the credit of the government.

Accordingly, Alexander Hamilton, the Secretary of the Treasury, was requested to make a report to the legislature on the condition of the finances. The result was his famous series of reports submitted to Congress during the years 1790 and 1791. So important were the results of the policies recommended by Hamilton that Daniel Webster, many years later, was moved to pay him the following tribute: "He smote the rock of national resources and abundant streams of revenue gushed forth; he touched the dead corpse of public credit and it sprang upon its feet."

The first of Hamilton's reports was on the subject of the state and national debts. In regard to the foreign debt he recommended that new government bonds should be sold in the United States to the amount of $12,000,000 and the proceeds used to pay both the principal and interest owed to foreign nations or individuals. Concerning the domestic debts, he urged the issuance of new securities to cover the full value of the amounts owed, although the old national securities had been selling at only a fraction of their face value. Many of them had been bought up by speculators at low prices, and these men would thus stand to make large profits from the action which Hamilton recommended.

Opposition to the injustice thus done the original holders of the securities, who had loaned the government money when its necessities were urgent during the Revolution, was expressed in Congress. It was urged that speculators should be paid the prevailing prices at the time they had purchased the securities, and that the balance should be given the original holders. But this was obviously impossible from a practical point of view, and would have prevented the very effect which Hamilton desired, namely, the securing of the support of the moneyed interests as a guarantee of the continued existence of the government under the Constitution. Another object which was secured through the adoption by Congress of Hamilton's proposition was the creation of a large amount of fluid capital in the shape of the new government securities. This capital could be the basis for expansion in trade and industry. Hamilton believed in the creation of a national debt for this purpose.

In regard to the state debts, Hamilton recommended that they be assumed by the national government, as they had been incurred by the states in a common cause during the Revolution. Hamilton believed that their assumption by the national government would again tend to consolidate the allegiance of the creditor class to the national, instead of the state governments. The Constitution gave no power to the national government to assume the state debts, but they were so assumed, after heated debate, in a practical illustration of the power of Congress, to a limited extent at any rate, to expand the Constitution by interpretation.

Final funding of these obligations by the national government raised the national debt to almost seventy-three million dollars, a huge sum as judged by the finances of the government at that time. In line with Hamilton's desire for a large debt as a basis for the expansion of industry and trade, only two percent of the debt could be paid off each year. This was to be by the creation of a sinking fund.

Only once since the Constitution went into effect has the United States been out of debt. That was in 1835, during President Jackson's administration. The general tendency of Congress has been to follow Hamilton's idea that it is a good thing for the government to be in debt. This idea has not always worked beneficially for it has encouraged Congress at times to be extravagant with the people's money.

EXCISE LEGISLATION

A second report submitted near the end of the year 1790 recommended a tax on distilled liquors. This was for the combined purpose of revenue and the extension of the control of the central government over the areas which would be most affected by the tax. Upon the refusal of groups in western Pennsylvania to pay the tax, which had the flavor of the type of taxation so much objected to when applied by England in pre-revolutionary days, Hamilton, in 1794, advised the calling out of the militia to force obedience to the national government. By this means the "Whiskey Rebellion," as it was termed, was quelled, and the important power of the national government, which it had lacked under the Articles of Confederation, not only to levy taxes but to collect them, by force, if necessary, was sustained. Thus, in this case as in that of the debts, Hamilton's policies strengthened the new government.

In 1802, this first excise law was repealed since Thomas Jefferson and his party, who were then in power, did not believe in that form of taxation. For many years internal revenue taxes were not levied. But the necessity for more revenue during the Civil War caused Congress to again resort to their use. The favorite objects of such taxation have been tobaccos and liquors though in periods of war or other stress numerous other articles have been taxed. The taxes being paid by the American people in 1933 on theater admissions, automobiles, radios, and other commodities, activities, or functions, were partly survivals of war taxes and partly new internal revenue taxes imposed to make up other revenues which had declined due to the depression. These taxes have all been levied in accordance with Hamilton's idea of taxation as expressed in his report on the excise. It has required a broad interpretation of the taxing power to permit these internal excises to be levied.

LEGISLATION REGARDING BANKS

A third report, submitted by Hamilton on the same date as the second, recommended the establishment of a national bank as a necessity in the handling of national finances. It would issue currency, act as an agent for the sale of national bonds, and serve as a depository for government funds. In return for these services it would have the use of the national funds for investment purposes, and enjoy a monopoly in this respect. This latter fact was used as an argument against it, as was the more important claim that it was an unconstitutional exercise of power by Congress. Nevertheless, the First Bank of the United States was chartered in 1791 for a period of twenty years.

This bank was not rechartered but, in 1816, Congress chartered another institution similar to it, likewise for a period of twenty years. Though the Supreme Court twice ruled that this bank had been created through a proper exercise of congressional power, opposition to it continued as long as it existed. In 1832, President Jackson successfully used his veto power to prevent its recharter. He opposed the bank as unconstitutional but he had other more valid reasons for the veto of the recharter bill, the most important of which was clear evidence that the bank was playing politics.

After Jackson had removed the government deposits from the Bank of the United States, state banks were for a time used as fiscal agents of the national government. In 1840, Congress created the Independent Treasury system for the purpose of enabling the government to handle its own money. This system was suspended for a short time by the repeal of the law creating it, but, in 1846, the law was reënacted and the Independent Treasury system remained in existence until 1920. Meanwhile its functions had been assumed by the Federal Reserve system.

The act of Congress in 1913 creating the Federal Reserve system is an excellent illustration of the expansion of the Constitution by legislative action. This system has been of great importance to the economic life of the nation during the years since its creation. In the period of the Civil War, Congress had authorized the creation of a system of national banks authorized to issue paper money under certain prescribed conditions. But, as the years passed, it became apparent that there was a fundamental weakness in the monetary system of the country. There was a lack both of elasticity and mobility in the currency. That is, it could not be quickly expanded or contracted to meet changing conditions nor was it possible to get money quickly to places where it was needed in larger amounts than usual, as in the grain producing section during the harvest season.

It was for the purpose of promoting elasticity and mobility of the currency that the Federal Reserve system was created. The country was organized into twelve districts, with combinations formed of member banks within the districts. It was intended that local financial emergencies should be relieved by a reserve bank of the district which could loan to member banks upon approved collateral. This district reserve bank was to be formed by the member banks themselves. This act was a major attempt to secure nation-wide financial stability.

In 1916, as a means of aiding the farmers of the country to secure easier credit, Congress authorized the creation of federal farm loan banks. A still more recent illustration of how Congress has used its financial powers is the system of home loan banks established under an act of Congress in 1932.

The Reconstruction Finance Corporation, likewise created by act of Congress in 1932, is another excellent example of how the legislative power has been expanded. This corporation was created to make loans to business concerns which, though in good condition otherwise, were in need of refinancing. The R.F.C., as it is called, was also authorized to make loans to local governmental agencies for relief purposes. This corporation was created to combat the deplorable economic conditions growing out of the depression which set in during the fall of 1929. The farm board, created by Congress in 1929, with authority to make loans and to buy up surplus crops as a means of stabilizing agriculture, is another good example of the expansion of the Constitution by Congress.

THE BUDGET ACT OF 1921

Quite illustrative of the present day tendency in regard to the relations of Congress and the president in the national government, is the Budget Act of June, 1921. By this act Congress gave into the hands of the president considerable power to direct its financial policies. Previous to this the allotment of appropriations from the federal treasury had been determined by the committees in the House of Representatives, each committee indicating the requirements of that portion of the federal government with which it was particularly concerned. This old method involved the division of responsibility for the budget as a whole, and a lack of coördination so vicious in its consequences of waste and misuse of funds, that it could only be accounted for by the jealousy of the House for the preservation in its own hands of all its legislative power.

The Budget Act of 1921 placed the responsibility for the allotment of federal expenditures squarely in the hands of the president, subject of course, to the legislative approval of Congress. This was a step towards that coördination and coöperation between the legislature and the executive which Alexander Hamilton desired and attempted to gain in the first administration of President Washington.

The budget for 1932 illustrates not only the variety of objects for which Congress must make appropriations but also indicates the total of governmental expenditures. For the payment of legislative expenses there were appropriated $27,075,335. For the executive office the total appropriated was $472,380. These amounts were increased, by appropriations for the ten departments, for thirty-five independent establishments, and for the District of Columbia, to a total of $3,624,564,012. In addition $411,946,300 were appropriated for payment of principal and $605,000,000 for the payment of interest on the public debt. This made the total appropriations for the year $4,641,510,312.

THE MONEY SYSTEM OF THE UNITED STATES

The Constitution granted to Congress the power to coin money. This power had also been conferred on the Confederation Congress but no steps had been taken to establish a mint. The country had long been forced to rely on foreign coins with the result that there was constant confusion. The coins differed in value, many of them were mutilated, and counterfeiting was common. The lack of an efficient money system made it difficult to carry on business in a satisfactory manner. Realizing this, Secretary Hamilton, early in 1791, made a report to Congress recommending the establishment of a mint. Congress acted on the recommendation and, in 1792, passed an act for the establishment of a mint at Philadelphia and for what is known as the decimal system of coinage. In more recent years additional mints were established at Denver and San Francisco.

From time to time the coinage regulations have been changed by law. The most important act in recent years was the Currency Act of 1900 which placed the United States on the gold standard. This action was taken after a long but unsuccessful fight had been waged for the maintenance of the bimetallic standard. In 1896 the famous "free silver" campaign was carried on with William Jennings Bryan, the Democratic candidate, pledged to keep silver on a parity with gold in the coinage system in spite of the great depreciation in the market value of silver. The Democratic defeat was interpreted by a Republican Congress as an authorization for the establishment of the gold standard, as mentioned above.

Backed by its gold and silver coins, Congress has from time to time authorized the issuance of paper currency known as gold and silver certificates. Other paper money which circulates is in the form of National Bank Notes or Federal Reserve Notes, issued under the authority of the National Bank Act of 1863 and the Federal Reserve Act of 1913. A comparatively small part of the paper money in circulation consists of greenbacks. Originally, greenbacks were purely "fiat" in character, issued by the authority of Congress during the Civil War. They were, in effect, a forced loan from the people, and were issued under the constitutional power to borrow money. A small portion of the greenbacks were called in and canceled after the war but, due to persistent demands for "cheap and easy" money, most of them were left in circulation. They were, however, made redeemable in specie which is maintained in reserve in the national treasury under the provisions of the Currency Act of 1900.

In accordance with its power to punish counterfeiting, Congress has enacted strict laws to deal with those who attempt to counterfeit the coins, paper money, or securities of the United States.

USES OF THE CONGRESSIONAL POWER IN PROMOTING TRANSPORTATION FACILITIES

The legislative power of Congress has been used in a variety of other ways to promote the general welfare of the United States. In the first part of the nineteenth century there was developed great interest in road building. Road building companies were organized in all parts of the United States, then sufficiently populated, for the purpose of building what were called "turnpikes." These companies were financed by sales of stock and the investors received their dividends through the collection of tolls paid for the use of the roads. State governments encouraged these enterprises by subscribing to stock and attempts were even made to secure federal aid through congressional action.

Congress had already made appropriations for the improvement of harbors and rivers so the inland communities felt that it was only fair that appropriations should be made to aid their road projects. Accordingly, Congress entered upon a program of aiding any road project that could get enough political support. But, in 1830, President Jackson succeeded in limiting appropriations for aiding road companies through his veto of what was known as the Maysville Turnpike bill. He took the view that Congress could not properly appropriate money for aiding a project located entirely within the borders of a state. This veto did not stop the spending of money for internal improvements, but thereafter it was necessary that the project aided should be of an interstate character or obviously for the general good. During the period between 1811 and 1838, the federal government itself built what was known as the Cumberland road from Cumberland, Maryland, to Vandalia, Illinois, at a cost of about $4,300,000. It was held that appropriations for this road were justified on the ground that it would promote the general welfare and also the common defence by facilitating military movements.

Due to the necessity for good roads in an age of automobile

transportation, Congress has, in recent years, voted large sums to aid the states in building through or "primary" highways. Coöperation with state road building agencies is promoted by the bureau of public roads in the Department of Agriculture. After the railroad building era got under way, Congress was importuned to give aid in their construction. In 1850 the policy of granting aid in the form of gifts of land was inaugurated. During the Civil War and post-war period, extensive land grants were made to various transcontinental railroads. Altogether almost 160,000,000 acres of land were actually given to the railroads by the national government. Approximately 42,000,-000 additional acres were granted but the government revoked the grants because railroads were not built as promised. Other aid was also given to railroads by direction of Congress. To the present time they have enjoyed subsidies in the form of contracts for carrying the United States mail.

Similarly, by the use of mail carrying contracts, aid has been given to steamship companies engaged in trans-oceanic commerce. During the World War the government itself went into the shipbuilding business in order to secure enough ships to carry troops and supplies to France. The building and operation of these ships was under the direction of the United States Shipping Board and the Emergency Fleet Corporation created under an act of Congress passed in 1916. Since the war it has been the policy of the government, through congressional action, to dispose of these ships to private companies on favorable terms.

The development of commercial aviation has also been directly stimulated by subsidies in the way of mail carrying contracts. The great commercial air lines of the United States could not have been developed without government aid. Congress has been justified in aiding aviation and the other forms of transportation by a liberal interpretation of the Constitution.

THE REGULATION OF INTERSTATE COMMERCE

During the period of American history up to the 1880's, Congress pursued a policy of *laissez-faire* for the most part towards various forms of economic enterprise. Through protective tariffs, subsidies, and other grants-in-aid, it encouraged the development of manufactures, railroads, and business in general. But little attempt was made to interfere with that development through exercise of the constitutional power to regulate interstate commerce.

The wide possibilities in the use of this power were forecast in Chief Justice Marshall's decision in the case of *Gibbons vs. Ogden* in 1824 but they were not realized until some time after this decision prepared the way.

In connection with the development of railway transportation there arose the necessity for the exercise by Congress of its full powers in this respect. The adoption by the railroads of discriminatory rates, rebates, and other unjust practices made regulation necessary, and under the sanction of the courts the states had assumed this responsibility, because of the lack of action by Congress. Confusion resulted when the Supreme Court in 1886 forbade the states to control interstate commerce even indirectly, and the demand for federal regulation was increased.

The result was the Interstate Commerce Act of 1887, which attempted to prevent unjust practices in railroad rate-making, and created an Interstate Commerce Commission with authority to enforce the act. The Supreme Court decided that the commission's powers did not include the fixing of maximum rates, and imposed other restrictions upon its actions, resulting in the Elkins amendments of 1903 and the Hepburn Act of 1906, which facilitated the enforcement of the act and allowed to the Interstate Commerce Commission the fixing of maximum rates. By the Hepburn Act, the commission was also given the power to regulate sleeping car companies, express companies, bridges, ferries, terminal facilities, and pipe lines. Activities of the commission were decided by the courts to be subject to their review only upon a question of the legal powers of the commission, and not upon the practicality of its actions.

Further modifications of the policy of the government on this subject came in 1910 and 1920. The Mann-Elkins Act of the former date established among other things a short-lived commerce court, with special jurisdiction over cases involving Interstate Commerce Commission rulings. By this act the jurisdiction of the commission was extended to cable, telegraph, telephone, and wireless companies. The Transportation Act of 1920 marked an entirely new attitude of Congress on the subject of the regulation of the railroads. Its previous efforts had been limited to the fixing of rates in the prevention of injustice to specific localities. The new emphasis, brought forward by the increasing difficulty of the railroads in maintaining adequate services, was in the direction of fixing rates to guarantee an adequate income for the railroads, to provide for services and replacement. In securing this end, Congress assumed the power to regulate rates, not only in interstate commerce, but upon commerce entirely within a state if incidental to the welfare of interstate commerce. This invasion of the sphere of state rights is indicative of the increasing expansion, in practice, of the powers of Congress in this respect.

The remarkable development of radio broadcasting after 1922 made necessary special legislation for its regulation. After five years of increasing confusion, Congress passed, on February 23, 1927, the Radio Act. It provided for a radio commission of five members to regulate this new but already mammoth industry.

Aviation has also been subjected to federal governmental regulation. This form of commercial transportation is in charge of the Department of Commerce. All private and commercial pilots must be licensed by that department.

REGULATION OF BUSINESS

The power of Congress to regulate commerce is not limited to transportation and communication facilities. The rise, after the Civil War, of what is known as "big business" created a public demand for the regulation of business combinations which warred on their competitors for the purpose of securing monopolies of trade. Congress, entering upon this form of regulation under its power to control interstate commerce, passed the Sherman Anti-Trust Law of 1890. The purpose of this law was to declare illegal all combinations in restraint of trade.

Early interpretation of this act in the courts tended toward the doctrine that all such combinations were prohibited under it, without discrimination as to whether the combination had a good or bad effect. This interpretation was later abandoned by the Supreme Court which adopted what is known as the "rule of reason," namely, that the Sherman Act was intended to prohibit only those combinations in restraint of trade which were harmful to the public interest. The court also adopted the attitude that illegal restraint of trade need not necessarily be directly in interstate commerce. Any combination which "tended" harmfully to restrain interstate commerce was declared to be unlawful.

To facilitate the regulation of combinations in restraint of trade, Congress, in September, 1914, created the Federal Trade Commission, with power to investigate all corporations in interstate trade except common carriers and banks, and with the power to refer cases of wrongdoing to the courts. As an extension of the Sherman Act there was also passed in 1914 the Clayton Anti-Trust Act, making it unlawful for combinations in restraint of trade to be formed through the purchase by one corporation of a controlling interest in another.

NATURALIZATION AND IMMIGRATION

It will not be possible here to give any elaborate analysis of the manner in which Congress has exercised all of its legislative powers. Brief mention must suffice to indicate what has happened. The power to naturalize foreigners was given practical application through a naturalization act passed on March 26, 1790. It required a minimum of two years for the naturalization process. With the exception of a short time during the John Adams administration when the time required for naturalization was extended to fourteen years, the naturalization period has been, for the most part, five years.

Up to 1870 only white persons were eligible for naturalization; since that time persons of African nativity or descent have also been eligible. Orientals are specifically excluded from naturalization. An interesting change in the naturalization laws was made in 1922 when Congress decided that married women should have the privilege of becoming naturalized on their own account and, further, that the citizenship status of married women should no longer depend upon their husbands. Applicants for naturalization, even women, are debarred from citizenship unless they definitely declare their willingness to bear arms in defence of the United States. In a decision in the case of the *United States vs. Schwimmer* in 1929 the Supreme Court upheld the right of a lower court to refuse citizenship to a woman who would not express a willingness to bear arms. In 1931, in the case of the *United States vs. MacIntosh*, a similar decision was rendered. This case was brought to the Supreme Court on the appeal of a Yale University theological professor who had been refused citizenship.

Naturalizations are in charge of the naturalization bureau of the Department of Labor but the actual process of naturalization must be completed in a state court of record or in a federal district court. Many millions of foreigners have gone through the naturalization process and have proved to be loyal citizens of the United States.

Closely related to naturalization is the matter of immigration. Nowhere in the Constitution is Congress granted the power to regulate immigration. Nevertheless the power has been assumed and has been carried, in recent years, to an extreme in sharp contrast to the early policy of allowing anyone to come into the United States who wished. Since 1882, Congress has prohibited the immigration of Chinese coolies. Regulations have also been in effect since that time to bar from entry certain persons physically or socially undesirable. In 1917, over President Wilson's veto, Congress passed an act requiring immigrants to pass a literacy test.

After the World War, a great influx of Europeans began. This hastened the passing of a law in 1921 placing immigrants on a quota basis. The immigration from any country annually could not exceed three percent of the number of persons born in that country who were residents of the United States in 1910. This was not restrictive enough so Congress, in 1924, reduced the quotas to two percent of the foreign residents in 1890. This act of 1924 specifically barred from immigration into the United States Asiatics not eligible to citizenship. This proved very irritating to Japan. The 1924 act also provided that, after three years, the quota plan should be abandoned for a "national origins" plan. This latter plan, which was not actually put into effect until 1929, provided that only 150,000 persons were to be admitted to this country each year. Of these, each country was to be allowed a number in proportion to the number of persons "of that national origin" to the whole population of continental United States in 1920. During the year 1930–1931, the actual immigration totalled 97,139 as compared with 1,218,-480 in 1914. During 1932 more aliens were leaving the United States than were entering. The administration of the immigration laws is in the hands of the immigration bureau of the Department of Labor.

MISCELLANEOUS LEGISLATION

To give practical application to its power "To promote the progress of science and useful arts by securing for limited times to authors and inventors the exclusive rights to their respective writings and discoveries," Congress early enacted copyright and patent laws. The first copyright act was passed on May 31, 1790. It granted to authors exclusive rights to their books, charts, or maps for a period of fourteen years with the right of renewal for another fourteen years. The present copyright law protects a much larger number of productions, including musical compositions, lectures, periodicals, works of art, photographs, illustrations, motion pictures, and motion picture plays. The copyright period was later set at twenty-eight years and was renewable for another twenty-eight years. In 1931, the copyright period was extended to fifty years after the death of the copyright holder. The copyright office of the Library of Congress is in charge of registering copyrights.

The first patent law was passed on April 10, 1790. It granted to inventors a right to their inventions for fourteen years. The present law grants protection for seventeen years. Up to the Jackson administration only about three thousand patents had been issued, yet, it is amusing to note, the official in charge of patents offered his resignation because he felt that everything worthwhile had been patented so that his position was superfluous. He did not dream that, during 1930 alone, 48,322 patents would be issued or that, by 1933, the total number of patents issued would be over 1,800,000. Patents are issued by the patent office which, since 1925, has been in the Department of Commerce.

In acts passed in 1905 and 1920, Congress, acting under its power to regulate commerce between the states, with foreign nations, and with Indian tribes, provided for the protection of trade-marks used in such commerce by registration in the patent office. Previous acts passed by Congress in 1870 and 1876 had been invalidated by the Supreme Court, in the case of *United States vs. De Witt* in 1870 and in the *Trade-mark Cases* in 1879, because protection was granted to all trade-marks whether used in interstate commerce or not.

Congress has also provided for a bureau of standards, which is now in the Department of Commerce, to carry out the power to "fix the standard of weights and measures." This bureau is the authority on all weights and measurements used in scientific experiments or in commerce. It also carries on research work in connection with weights and measurements.

To provide a basis for computing representation and direct taxes, Congress, on March 1, 1790, passed the first census law. The direction of the task of taking the first census in 1790 was assigned to the Department of State. The census is now in charge of a permanent bureau of the census in the Department of Commerce. It has functioned continuously since 1902. Before that a temporary organization had to be set up every ten years. At first the census reports as published contained only statistics regarding population. Now there are published every ten years a whole series of volumes containing much information of value to investigators, particularly in the fields of history, sociology, and economics. Not only do they contain elaborate tables regarding the number, color, nationality, and citizenship status of the people and regarding prisoners, paupers, delinquents, and the physically defective, but also concerning the economic life of the country, such as its mines, agriculture, and manufactures.

By the Constitution, Congress was empowered "To exercise exclusive legislation in all cases whatsoever, over such district (not exceeding ten miles square) as may, by cession of particular States, and the acceptance of Congress, become the seat of the government of the United States." In some of the state ratifying conventions fear was expressed that dire consequences would

follow the creation of a separate district for the federal government. It is amusing to read of the argument presented against
the creation of such a district on the ground that the federal
government might convert it into an invincible fortified stronghold. What should be thought of the argument offered, in all
seriousness, by George Mason in the Virginia ratifying convention, to the effect that it would be dangerous to give Congress
exclusive jurisdiction over such a district because it might become
"the sanctuary of the blackest crimes" and felons might "receive
an asylum there"? In the New York ratifying convention
Melanchthon Smith proposed an amendment to the Constitution
for the purpose of giving the states the right to collect taxes in
and exercise legal jurisdiction over the proposed federal district.

In spite of the fears expressed no change was made in this constitutional provision. Congress, in 1790, proceeded to take the
first steps for the creation of the federal seat of government.
There was considerable jealousy among the states over the location of the district. Both the northern and southern states
wished to secure the capital. Finally, Alexander Hamilton
arranged a political "deal" whereby the southerners who had
been opposing the assumption of state debts agreed to support
that measure in return for votes needed to secure the location
of the national capital in the south. Accordingly, an act was
passed which provided that the capital should be moved from
New York to Philadelphia. There it should remain for ten
years until 1800 when it was to be moved to the District of
Columbia, an area ten miles square, located on the Potomac
River, ceded to the national government by Maryland and Virginia. Congress further made the necessary appropriations to
have the city of Washington laid out and governmental buildings erected. This new capital was taken over by the United
States government during the latter part of the John Adams
administration. It should be mentioned that, in 1846, Congress
returned to Virginia that portion of the district which lay south
of the Potomac River.

Until 1871, the city of Washington was governed by a mayor
appointed by the president of the United States and a two house
council elected by property owning residents. After a brief transition period, Congress, in 1874, abolished local self-government

and provided for the present form of government for the whole district, including the city of Washington. The executive and administrative branch of the government consists of three commissioners, two appointed by the president for three year terms from among the residents of the district and the third appointed by the president from among the officers of the army engineering corps to serve for an indefinite term. The judiciary of the district consists of a court of appeals and a supreme court. These courts deal with cases of national scope as well as with local district cases. Congress itself is the legislative body for the district. Persons resident in the District of Columbia are completely disfranchised unless they can claim legal residence in one of the states and so vote there.

Congress has also carried out its power to exercise its "authority over all places purchased by the consent of the legislature of the State in which the same shall be, for the erection of forts, magazines, arsenals, dockyards, and other needful buildings." The country is dotted with federal buildings and the number is being constantly increased.

The powers granted to Congress in regard to the army, navy, and militia were also of extreme importance. The discussion of these powers and their expansion by Congress will be taken up later in the consideration of "The Constitution in Time of War."

CONGRESS AND SLAVERY

Up to the close of the Civil War, the problem of negro slavery was one of increasing importance. The Constitution gave recognition to the institution of slavery but did not grant to Congress adequate power to deal with it. In a number of the ratifying conventions, particularly in Massachusetts and New York, objection was raised to the provision which stated that three-fifths of the slaves should be counted as population in apportioning representation and direct taxes. Objection was also made to the provision which stated that Congress could not prohibit the importation of slaves prior to 1808. In the Massachusetts convention these objections were answered by a declaration that it was not "in the power of the Constitution" to do anything about slavery in the southern states for each state was sovereign and independent to a degree. It was further argued that ratification of the Constitution would not make the members of the Massachusetts convention "partakers of other men's sins." New states, it was declared, could not claim the right to the "migration or importation" of slaves since that right was "confined to the states now *existing only*." Ratification of the Constitution, it was claimed, would not prevent the eventual abolition of slavery. In fact, it was further asserted, the exercise by Congress of its power to prohibit slave importations beginning with 1808 would cause slavery to die out gradually. How fallacious these arguments were is revealed by subsequent history.

On the other hand, in the southern states, the Constitution was criticized because of its failure to safeguard existing property in the form of slaves. For instance, George Mason in the Virginia ratifying convention raised this objection, declaring further that there was no constitutional provision to prohibit the laying of "a tax on slaves amounting to manumission." This argument, too, was fallacious in view of the fact that Congress was prohibited from imposing a tax of more than ten dollars a head on imported slaves. No authority existed in the Constitution for Congress to tax other slaves directly. James Madison pointed out that there was a safeguard to property in slaves in the provision for the return of fugitive slaves which was contained in the fourth article of the Constitution, as follows, "No person held to service or labor in one State, under the laws thereof, escaping into another, shall, in consequence of any law or regulation therein, be discharged from such service or labor, but shall be delivered up on claim of the party to whom such service or labor may be due."

In 1793, Congress passed the first national fugitive slave law to give force to the provision just quoted. The act was opposed by many in the north because it denied fugitive slaves the right to trial by jury. Numerous petitions were sent to Congress in subsequent years protesting against the alleged kidnapping of free negroes in northern states by persons acting under the protection of the fugitive slave law.

Acting under its power to admit new states, Congress proceeded in the years following the adoption of the Constitution to pass "enabling acts" under which Vermont, Kentucky, Tennessee, Ohio, Indiana, Illinois, Louisiana, Alabama, and Mississippi entered the union, all before 1820. Seven of the original thirteen states had, by their own action, done away with the institution of slavery. All the new states north of the Ohio, in accordance with the Northwest Ordinance of 1787 which had been re-enacted by Congress under the Constitution, prohibited slavery through their constitutions. Vermont also entered the union as a free state, making a total of eleven free states by 1820. All the new southern states permitted slavery so the total number of slave states by 1820 was also eleven. This gave to each group equal representation in the United States Senate.

But in 1820 the issue of slavery became acute in connection with the proposed admission of Missouri as a slave state. Missouri was to be created out of the Louisiana territory, the treaty for the purchase of which had stated that future states created from the territory should be admitted to the union on an equal basis with the existing states. The proposal to permit slavery in Missouri met opposition in Congress and brought up a question as to whether or not the power of Congress to admit states implied the power to regulate the conditions of such admission. The final outcome of the dispute was the Missouri Compromise whereby Maine was admitted as a free state and Missouri as a slave state to preserve the balance in the Senate. However, slavery was prohibited in the rest of the Louisiana purchase north of 36° 30'. This quieted the excitement over slavery for a time.

Nevertheless, anti-slavery sentiment continued to grow in the north and, in a few years, demands were being made for the abolition of slavery or, at least, for the elimination of slavery in the District of Columbia and in the territories. Petitions poured in on Congress to legislate against the institution. The influence of pro-slavery men in the House of Representatives resulted in the adoption by that body in May, 1836, of a rule providing that all such petitions should be laid on the table without any action being taken on them. This came to be known as the "Gag Rule." This action was clearly in violation of the constitutional guarantee of freedom of petition, contained in the first amendment to the Constitution. On this ground it was opposed by J. Q. Adams, the ex-president, then a member of the House of Representatives, who assumed the task of attempting daily to present the ever increasing number of petitions to the House.

Despite this, the House in 1840 adopted what was known as the "Twenty-first Rule," which stated that no petition for the abolition of slavery or in relation to the slave trade could be received or entertained in any way by that body. This had the effect of strengthening the "Gag Rule." The results of these actions were the promotion of anti-slavery feeling in the north, and the increase in the number of the petitions. Finally, in 1844, the House restored the freedom of petition. For this action J. Q. Adams deserves the chief credit.

The war with Mexico, 1846–1848, with the resultant acquisition of territory by the United States, brought the slavery controversy again to an acute stage. During the war, Representative David Wilmot and others persistently but unsuccessfully attempted to secure the adoption by Congress of what came to be known as the "Wilmot Proviso," designed to prevent the extension of slavery to any territory that might be acquired from Mexico. After the territory had actually been acquired, the slavery forces insisted that the line 36° 30′ should be extended to the Pacific coast thus permitting slavery in the new territory.

Due to the rush of population to California following the discovery of gold there, steps were quickly taken to organize a state government. A constitution was drafted prohibiting slavery and Congress was petitioned to admit California to the union with this constitution. This precipitated a crisis which resulted in the famous Compromise of 1850. This, in reality, consisted of a series of acts passed by Congress.

These included the admission of California as a free state, the abolition of the slave trade in the District of Columbia, the setting up of territorial governments in Utah and New Mexico, and the enactment of a new fugitive slave law.

In the north the new fugitive slave law proved particularly displeasing. It provided that a commissioner should hear the evidence in support of the contention that a negro seized as a fugitive was the rightful property of the claimant. No jury hearing was provided for, nor could evidence be given by the accused. If the commissioner hearing the case gave a verdict deciding that the negro was the property of the claimant, he received a fee of ten dollars, but he received only half that amount if he set the negro free. No provision was made for the writ of habeas corpus, but no specific mention was made of its suspension. However, as was pointed out at the time, the writ would in no case protect a negro from the operation of the fugitive slave law.

The denial of a trial to the accused, at the place where taken into custody, was an element of injustice, as was also the arrangement of fees. The act seems to have been characterized throughout by discrimination against the accused negro, and this was a major cause of the tremendous opposition to it aroused in the north, subsequent to its enactment. This accounts for its wholesale violation in the north during the period up to the Civil War.

The Compromise of 1850 was considered, and hoped, to be a final settlement of the question of slavery extension. It was only a short time, however, until the whole problem was reopened. Nebraska wished organization as a territory, but as it was north of the line of 36° 30', and would thus be organized without slavery, the southern slavery advocates would not coöperate to allow its organization. A move was set on foot, however, to make Nebraska a territory, allowing the people there to decide on the question of slavery. This would nullify the provision of the Missouri Compromise which guaranteed that slavery would be excluded from this territory. A bill to that effect was passed by Congress in 1854, with the added provision that two territories were to be created instead of one. Kansas, the southern of the two territories, was expected to be settled by pro-slavery men, and Nebraska, the northern one, by anti-slavery men.

The Kansas-Nebraska Bill, as it was called, definitely repealed the Missouri Compromise. The basis of this repeal was the claim that Congress had no right to legislate on the subject of slavery in the territories. The decision on this subject was to be made by the inhabitants of the territory, on the basis of "popular sovereignty."

In opposition to this was the view that the territories were subject to regulation by Congress, and that this regulation included the right to prevent slavery there. Slaves, it was said, were not property in themselves, but were naturally free, being slaves only by virtue of the laws in the slave states. When they came out from the jurisdiction of those laws they were no longer slaves. The decision in the case of *Dred Scott vs. Sanford,* given by the Supreme Court, in March, 1857, supported the views of the pro-slavery men on the subject of slavery in the territories.

The effect of the fugitive slave law, the Kansas-Nebraska act, and the Dred Scott decision was increased sectional bitterness over the question of slavery. The inability of Congress to settle the question led to the secession of eleven southern states. The Civil War which followed settled once and for all the question which had threatened the complete break-down of the Constitution.

CONGRESS AND THE ACQUISITION OF TERRITORY

Brief mention should be made of the part which Congress has played in the acquisition of territory whereby the original United States has not only been expanded across the North American continent but also to distant parts of the world. Most of the territorial expansion has been brought about through the exercise of the treaty making power by the president acting with the advice and consent of the Senate. It was thus that the vast Louisiana territory was purchased from France in 1803; Florida from Spain in 1819; what is known as the Gadsden purchase from Mexico, for the purpose of extending the southern boundary of the territory of New Mexico, in 1853; Alaska from Russia in 1867; and the Virgin Islands from Denmark in 1917. These treaties, however, all required action by both houses of Congress because appropriations were required for the respective purchases.

In the case of the Mexican cession of 1848 and the acquisition of Porto Rico, Guam, and the Philippine Islands in 1898, only the consent of the Senate was required since those territories were acquired by treaties ending wars. The island of Tutuila in the Samoan group was also definitely acquired in 1899 through a treaty arrangement with Germany and Great Britain, but in this case no war settlement was involved. Similarly, the so-called Oregon country was secured for the United States from Great Britain in 1846 through a treaty negotiated by the president and ratified by the Senate.

This leaves Texas and the Hawaiian Islands to be accounted for. Both of them were annexed to the United States as a direct result of congressional action. After a treaty for the annexation of Texas had failed to secure the two-thirds vote in the Senate necessary for ratification, a joint resolution providing for such annexation was introduced and passed by each house of Congress by a simple majority in 1845.

As a matter of fact, what was provided for was the erection of a new state out of the territory of Texas, to be admitted to the union upon the adoption of a suitable frame of government. The admission of new states to the union is a legitimate power of Congress, and, in this sense, the annexation of Texas by this process may be considered as constitutional.

In 1898, however, Hawaii was annexed by the same procedure, and the case of Texas was given as a precedent. There is a difference between the two cases, however, as Hawaii was not by this action taken into the union, but merely annexed as a territory. Thus it may well be doubted whether Congress was acting under its constitutional powers in annexing Hawaii by a joint resolution of the two houses.

There has never been any question of the right of Congress to dispose of the public lands either by sale or on other conditions such as under the Homestead Act of 1862. But it is another question whether Congress has the power to alienate, politically, territory which has once been acquired by the United States. Such alienation is provided for in an act passed by Congress in January, 1933, over the veto of President Hoover, which is designed to give the Philippine Islands their independence after the elapse of ten years. While Congress has no direct power to dispose of territory thus, the power can certainly be implied from the Constitution just as the power to annex territory by a joint resolution was implied.

THE TREND TOWARD SOCIAL LEGISLATION

With the transformation of the United States from a predominantly agricultural nation to one highly industrialized, it has, perhaps, been inevitable that Congress should have a tendency to pass not only an increasing number of laws dealing with economic affairs but also legislation to deal with social problems. This latter trend was greatly stimulated by the depression following 1929.

Illustrations of the trend are the laws which created the women's bureau and the children's bureau, now in the Department of Labor. The two child labor laws, passed by Congress in 1916 and 1919, but which were declared unconstitutional by the Supreme Court, indicate what Congress might do if the Supreme Court would not stand in the way. Pension laws for veterans of the various wars in which the United States has participated are an old form of social legislation but the insurance, compensation, and rehabilitation laws for those who served in the World War represent an advance in the treatment of veterans. Nor should the pension system established by act of Congress for civilian employees of the government be overlooked in noting the recent trend toward social legislation.

The prohibition legislation of the period following 1920, such as the Volstead Act and the Jones Act, may well be considered as social legislation. The Norris-LaGuardia bill passed by Congress in 1932 affords an excellent illustration of social legislation. This act prohibits the use of the blanket injunction in labor disputes and so removes what has been a grievance of labor since it was first used in the Pullman strike of 1894. The act also prohibits the so-called "yellow dog" contract whereby employers bound their employees not to join a union.

Many other illustrations might be given to demonstrate the increasing tendency of Congress to pass social legislation but two more must suffice. The 1932 legislation creating the Reconstruction Finance Corporation, which has already been mentioned, has been of great importance not only in an economic way but also socially because of the provision for loans to local government agencies for relief work. Before 1929 such legislation would have been denounced as socialistic. An even better example of the distance Congress has gone in passing social legislation is the bill passed in 1932 whereby the Red Cross was authorized to have wheat and cotton owned by the United States Farm Board converted into flour and cloth after which it was to be distributed to the needy.

THE ELECTORAL POWER OF CONGRESS

Under the Constitution, Congress enjoys, in addition to legislative powers, what may be called electoral powers. Under the original Constitution it was provided that, if the electoral college failed to elect a president, the choice should devolve on the House of Representatives, which, voting by states, should select a president from among the five who had received the highest electoral votes. The year 1801 brought the first case in which the election of the president was thrown into the House of Representatives. In this year, the two Democratic-Republican nominees both received the same number of electoral votes. The house then proceeded to settle the question of who should be the next president, by a vote by states, each state having one vote. On the thirty-sixth ballot support of states controlled by the Federalist party was swung to Thomas Jefferson, and he was elected by the vote of ten states out of the sixteen then represented in the Congress.

The twelfth amendment was added to the Constitution to prevent a situation like that of 1800–1801 from again developing. However, in the election of 1824–1825 the House was again called upon to elect a president while in the 1836–1837 election the Senate was forced to elect a vice president.

The disputed presidential election of 1876 affords an excellent illustration of the expansion by Congress of its electoral power. The election of that year resulted in the securing by Samuel J. Tilden, the Democratic candidate, of one hundred and eighty-four electoral votes, or one less than the necessary number for election. Rutherford B. Hayes, the Republican, had one hundred and sixty-five votes. There were a total of twenty votes in dispute, from the states of Florida, Louisiana, South Carolina, and Oregon. By securing one of these votes, Tilden would be elected, but Hayes would need all of them to win.

There was no precedent by which to decide who should settle the question of the disputed votes. The Constitution makes no provision for such a case. Each house of Congress attempted to devise a plan, and it was finally decided that an electoral commission should be appointed, to be composed of five members of each house, and five justices of the Supreme Court. The final result of the choice was that this electoral commission was composed of eight Republicans and seven Democrats.

As would probably be expected in such a case, the decision was in favor of the Republican candidate. In the two cases where there was a division of opinion on the returns in question, those from Florida and Louisiana, the commission decided for the Republican candidate, by an eight to seven vote. In the case of the Oregon and South Carolina returns, the decision was unanimous in favor of Hayes.

The interesting point in connection with the position of the commission is that the basis for their decisions was that they had no right to go back of the returns made by the proper state authorities. The Republican majority claimed that if mistakes had been made, they were made by the state authorities whom Congress had no power to correct.

In January, 1886, Congress further expanded its electoral power by passing the Presidential Succession Act. By an act of 1792 it had been provided that, in case of the removal, death, resignation, or disability of both the president and vice president, the president of the Senate *pro tempore* should succeed to the office, and that in case of his removal, death, resignation, or disability, the speaker of the House should succeed.

The death of President Garfield, after a long period of almost complete disability, brought the question again into prominence. Congress provided in the law of 1886 for the succession to pass, under the same circumstances as provided in the act of 1792, to the various members of the president's cabinet in the following order: secretary of state, secretary of the treasury, secretary of war, the attorney-general, the postmaster-general, the secretary of the navy, and the secretary of the interior. The one succeeding to the office was to act as president until the disability of the regular incumbent was removed, or until an election was held.

In 1887 the Electoral Count Act was passed, in an attempt to establish the principle that in case of disputed electoral counts, such as had occurred in the case of the election of 1876, the decision of the appropriate state authorities in relation to the votes from the states would be final.

This legislation has been defective in that no provision was made for the succession in case of the disqualification or death of a president-elect or vice president-elect before their inauguration. But the twentieth amendment, added to the Constitution in 1933, authorizes Congress to legislate in such a manner as to remedy this deficiency.

OTHER POWERS OF CONGRESS

Congress also possesses what are called judicial powers. Among these are the power of each house to judge the elections, returns, and qualifications of their own members. In practice this has come to mean that each house may exclude anyone elected to it for any reason that it sees fit. In such a case the rejected person has no judicial recourse. The only thing he can do is to seek another election from his state and attempt again to take his seat as a representative or senator, as the case may be.

Each house also possesses the power to compel persons to testify before it or its committees. Refusal to so testify may result in punishment for contempt. This is assuredly a broad interpretation of the Constitution.

Probably the most important judicial power of Congress, however, is the impeachment and trial of civil officers of the United States. In such cases the House of Representatives possesses the sole power of impeachment, that is, the drawing up of charges and conducting the prosecution if the case comes to trial before the Senate which has the sole power to try impeachments. Only twelve persons have been impeached by the House and of these only eight were tried by the Senate while, on March 4, 1933, a ninth trial was scheduled to begin on the opening day of the first session of the seventy-third Congress. The individual who was to be tried by the Senate was District Judge Harold Lauderback of San Francisco, California, who was impeached by the House on February 24, 1933. Of those tried and acquitted two were district court judges, one was a cabinet officer, one was an associate justice of the Supreme Court, while one, Andrew Johnson, was president of the United States. Two of those convicted were district judges while the third was an associate judge of the United States commerce court. The trial of the first man to be impeached, Senator William Blount of Tennessee, was refused by the Senate in 1798 on the ground that he had already been expelled from that body. In 1914, proceedings against a district judge were abandoned after he had been impeached by the House. In 1926, a district judge escaped trial by resigning after his impeachment had been voted by the House.

Another power belonging to Congress may be called "constituent" power, that is, the right to propose amendments to the Constitution. All the amendments so far added have been initiated and submitted to the states by Congress.

DECLINE IN THE PRESTIGE OF CONGRESS

In the procedural character of the House of Representatives is to be found the type of influences which tend to decrease its importance in the national government. Originally intended to represent the people of the nation, the House has to a large extent become absorbed in questions of local interest. Its large and unwieldy membership prevents it from being a real debating body, and has resulted in the development of what has been called "committee government." Committees dictate the policies of the House, which is thus, in reality, divided into a large number of smaller legislative assemblies. The House has no direct communication with the nation; its lack of debate prevents public knowledge of its processes. The result of this has been the tendency of the people to look to the president for information, and to trust to him the custody of the national interests.

The Senate, having a relatively small membership, can indulge in debate, and although often blamed for delaying action in debate, there is no doubt that it thus arouses public opinion and serves a valuable purpose. Due to the longer term, the Senate tends to attract a superior type of personnel, and a de-

gree of continuity of outlook is secured in its membership by
the fact that only one-third of the senators stand for reëlection
every two years.

Despite the fact that the powers of Congress under the Constitution have been greatly expanded, there is little doubt that
the importance of the president is at present tending to increase
at the expense of Congress. This is due to the relative coördination of functions and efficiency in the determination of policy on
the part of the chief executive.

SELECTED REFERENCES

Babcock, C. K., *The Law of the American Constitution*, pp. 143–254,
272–341.

Bassett, J. S., *The Federalist System 1789–1801*, pp. 27–41.

Beard, C. A., *American Government and Politics* (Fourth edition),
pp. 242–283, 363–441.

Dewey, D. R., *Financial History of the United States* (Ninth edition),
pp. 60–117, 143–270, 331–498.

Haines, B. M., and Haines, C. G., *The Constitution of the United States*,
pp. 110–144.

Johnson, Allen, ed., *Readings in American Constitutional History 1776–
1876*, pp. 206–213, 225–228, 237–245, 299–307, 405–453, 538–
546.

Johnson, Allen, and Robinson, W. A., eds., *Readings in Recent American
Constitutional History 1876–1926*, pp. 52–149, 197–207, 229–239,
284–307.

Landon, J. S., *The Constitutional History and Government of the United
States*, pp. 97–225.

Luce, Robert, *Congress an Explanation*, pp. 94–154.

Luce, Robert, *Legislative Principles*, pp. 448–491.

Martin, C. E., *An Introduction to the Study of the American Constitution*,
pp. 49–61.

McBain, H. L., *The Living Constitution*, pp. 202–236.

McCall, S. W., *The Business of Congress*, pp. 1–28, 180–199.

MacDonald, William, ed., *Documentary Source Book of American History
1606–1926*, pp. 233–243, 259–261, 282–288, 302–306, 311–318,
341–343, 374–377, 383–394, 397–405, 488–646, 649–665, 687–
704.

Munro, W. B., *The Constitution of the United States*, pp. 30–65.

Myers, W. S., *American Democracy Today*, pp. 65–97.

Norton, T. J., *The Constitution of the United States, Its Sources and Its
Application*, pp. 8–98.

Ogg, F. A., and Ray, P. O., *Introduction to American Government*
(Third edition), pp. 456–596.

Orth, S. P., and Cushman, Robert Eugene, *American National Government*, pp. 573–702.

Pease, T. C., and Roberts, A. S., eds., *Selected Readings in American History*, pp. 190–203, 287–291, 568–586, 670–679, 683–689, 773–776.

Reinsch, P. S., *American Legislatures and Legislative Methods*, pp. 3–125, 228–330.

Stevens, C. E., *Sources of the Constitution of the United States*, pp. 86–116.

The Federalist (Everyman's Library edition), Nos. 23–26, 52–66, pp. 110–175, 268–342.

Wilson, Woodrow, *Constitutional Government in the United States*, pp. 82–141.

Chapter Sixteen

THE RÔLE OF THE EXECUTIVE UNDER
THE CONSTITUTION

THE office of president as established in the Constitution in 1787 was the result largely of the experience of the American people with the executive in government. This experience began with the colonies, and extended through the period of the Revolution and of the Articles of Confederation. As the Constitutional Convention of 1787 considered the problem of establishing an executive its members drew upon this accumulated experience to guide their deliberations. A brief review of the colonial and early state governments will make clear what the American experience with executives had been.

COLONIAL EXPERIENCE WITH THE EXECUTIVE

The executive functions had been exercised by royal governors in the eight colonies which were royal provinces at the outbreak of the Revolution. The powers and duties of these governors had been defined in their commissions, given them upon entering the office by royal appointment. These commissions had been supplemented by instructions sent from England. In general, the governors had represented the interests of the Crown in the colonies, and had also acted as the executive heads of the local governments. They had enjoyed a power of veto over acts of the colonial legislatures, and, in addition to this, there had been the further requirement that acts passed by these colonial legislatures should be subject to a veto by the Crown.

In the three colonies which remained proprietary up to the Revolution the power held by the proprietor had corresponded practically to that of the king over the royal colonies. The chief difference between the governors of the proprietary colonies and the royal colonies had been that the former represented the proprietor instead of the king. In the corporate colonies, the governors, who had been chosen by the qualified voters of the colony, had played but minor rôles.

There had been a constant struggle between the governors and the legislative bodies, especially in the royal provinces. The effort on the part of the colonies had been to secure popular government through the legislatures, and to use every means possible to thwart the power of the governors over legislation, as involved in the veto. The chief means used for this purpose had been to deny the governor his salary unless he complied with the wishes of the representatives of the people. On the other hand, the royal governors had been under pressure from the Crown to act in its interest.

Under the guise of insisting upon the rights of Englishmen, the colonists had succeeded to a large measure in curbing the control of the governors over the actions of the colonial legislative bodies. But to overcome the royal veto had proved much more difficult. By the time of the Revolution, largely because of the efforts of George III to enforce his prerogative in the colonies, there had been built up a large body of opinion opposed to the institution of monarchy and hereditary succession. A source of this opposition was indicated in the Declaration of Independence where, among other indictments against the king, he was charged with using his power to veto acts of the colonial legislatures to prevent much legislation which was designed to further colonial interests. Thomas Jefferson in the Declaration of Independence merely expressed the feelings of many of the colonists in this respect.

Perhaps the most effective propagandist against the English Crown had been Thomas Paine. In attacking the right of the king to control colonial actions, and in urging independence as the only way out, he had struck at the whole institution of monarchy and hereditary succession. He had termed the king "the Royal Brute of Great Britain," and had declared that, in America, the law and not any man should be king.

This revolutionary opposition to and hatred of the king had been reflected in the new constitutions which had been adopted by the colonies upon their revolt from Great Britain. For the most part, though a theoretical separation of powers had been claimed in these governments, the executives had been granted little power. The chief power, as has been demonstrated, had been concentrated in the hands of the legislative branch of the government. In only three of the states had the executive been given a veto power, and even in those cases the power had been qualified.

THE ARTICLES OF CONFEDERATION AND THE EXECUTIVE POWER

The revolutionary attitude toward the executive was exemplified to an extreme extent in the Articles of Confederation. In that document, as has been made clear, no provision was made for a separate executive and no attempt was made to separate the executive and legislative functions. However, in carrying out its executive functions, the Confederation Congress followed the precedent established by the Second Continental Congress in setting up committees composed of its own members. In some cases, the congress went so far as to appoint men who were not members of that body to perform certain administrative duties. For instance, Robert Morris had been appointed superintendent of finance while John Jay had been selected to serve as secretary for foreign affairs. A result of the lack of any department of the government devoted exclusively to the execution and administration of the laws had been to force congress to consider on its floor every item of both legislative and administrative policy. It had thus been unable to deal thoroughly with either aspect of its function.

THE CONSTITUTIONAL CONVENTION AND THE EXECUTIVE

In the Constitutional Convention the revolutionary fear of the executive was tempered by the experience under the Articles of Confederation. A primary problem of the convention was the instituting of a central government with sufficient coercive power. An executive with power to act upon individuals was thus necessary. In addition to this, efficiency in the carrying out of governmental functions demanded an executive independent of the legislature. But a chief ground of discussion was the extent to which the independence of the executive should be carried and the manner in which his conduct of the office could be controlled if he were not dependent upon the legislature.

Practically all the opinion in the convention agreed upon personal separation of the executive from the legislative branch of the government, that is, upon the idea that the executive should not be a member of Congress. Even the small states which would naturally fear an invasion of their rights by a strong executive intent upon increasing the power of the national government, agreed to this necessity. There was, however, in the convention, a strong opinion, represented most effectively by Roger Sherman, that the election of the executive should be by the legislature, thus subordinating him to that body.

The opposition to election by the legislature was led by James Wilson. Fundamental in his notion of the executive was that he should be dependent upon, and controlled by, the people alone. Thus he should be elected by them, either directly or indirectly, and should be responsible to them. This notion was based upon the idea of the desirability of the separation of powers in government. In an executive dependent upon the legislature, Wilson and those agreeing with him saw instability and executive weakness. The executive would be controlled by the politics of the legislative body, and the system in general would mean legislative supremacy in the government.

In the final result, the executive was largely a compromise of the two views: the one favoring an executive with strong and independent powers, with responsibility only to the people, and with a check upon the legislature in the shape of the veto; the other view favoring separation from the legislature only in respect to personnel. In the end, the veto power granted to the executive was qualified by the provision that it could be modified by a two-thirds vote of each house of Congress; the responsibility of the executive to perform his duties and not to usurp power or misconduct himself was strengthened by the possibility of legislative impeachment; and the idea of a long term to insure independence and stability was compromised by final decision upon a short term with reëligibility.

The attitude of the advocates of the Constitution toward the executive as finally provided for in that document was well stated in the writings of Alexander Hamilton in *The Federalist*. This series of papers, written to secure a favorable public opinion for the Constitution, gave the reasons for support of the executive as established. The popular voice in the choice of the executive was urged as involving a popular control over that office, a weak argument since the electoral college provided for by the Constitution was not designed to secure the popular election of the president. The executive, though powerful, was different from the king of England, in that his veto was strictly limited, and in that he was subject to impeachment and removal upon the misconduct of his office.

A strong executive, it was argued, was a necessity for good government. The elements in his strength were unity, long term in office, sufficient support of a financial sort, and adequate powers. Over against this strength were to be balanced his dependence upon the people for election, and "a due responsibility."

Despite the need for executive dependence upon the popular will, it was not to be claimed, said Hamilton, that this meant dependence upon the legislative department. The two should be independent. Appointments were rightfully to be made by the president rather than by Congress, he further declared, as it was considered that Congress would be more interested in politics than the president would be and would therefore have a tendency to choose officials on a basis of "uniting the suffrages of the party." Hamilton did not foresee the extent to which the president, through his very character as a popular representative, would come to control his party and thus direct the appointment of officers along the very line which was here feared.

EVOLUTION OF THE PRESIDENT'S POWERS

During the years since the Constitution became operative in 1789, the powers of the president have gone through an interesting evolution resulting in a great expansion of the presidential office. The power to execute the laws of the United States and the powers implied from the obligation expressed in his oath to "preserve, protect and defend the Constitution" have been interpreted in a broad way, as has been the provision that "he may require the Opinion, in writing, of the principal Officer in each of the executive Departments, upon any Subject relating to the Duties of their respective Offices." President Washington interpreted this in such a way as to permit him to call the department heads together for oral consultation, thus originating the cabinet as an organ of the government.

Not only is the president an executive officer in the narrow sense but he is forced to perform many administrative duties. The ten executive departments with a multitude of sub-divisions and bureaus, not to mention special officers and commissions, have been created to help execute and administer the laws, but the president remains as the chief director of administration. His is the responsibility for carrying out the laws and he can require his administrative appointees to do his bidding. If he is not satisfied with the manner in which one of his subordinates is conducting his office he may summarily remove him as President Jackson did in the case of his secretary of the treasury in 1833 and as President Wilson did in the case of Secretary of State Lansing early in 1920.

In connection with the execution and administration of laws, the presidents have assumed what is known as ordinance making power, that is, the power to issue instructions and regulations to supplement laws passed by Congress. Examples of such ordinances are the immigration regulations, the instructions to consuls, and the army and navy regulations.

In connection with his administrative duties it has been proposed that the president be given the power to reorganize the various administrative offices. President Hoover had been given such power but, in January, 1933, following his overwhelming defeat for reëlection, the Democratic members of the House of Representatives decided to block his reorganization plans with a view to giving the power to reorganize to his successor, Franklin D. Roosevelt.

By the provision of the Constitution giving them the appointing power, the presidents have vastly increased the importance of their office. The president is empowered to nominate and, with the advice and consent of the Senate, to "appoint Ambassadors, other public Ministers and Consuls, Judges of the supreme Court, and all other Officers of the United States, whose Appointments are not herein otherwise provided for, and which shall be established by Law." Furthermore, he is to commission all the officers of the United States. By custom, and finally by the sanction of the Supreme Court, the presidents have all enjoyed the right to remove office holders, though the Constitution is silent on the matter of removals. Historically, it was in the Jackson administration that the greatest controversy was aroused over power assumed by the president to make removals. It was charged that President Jackson was making a "clean sweep" of the office holders though, as a matter of fact, not more than one-eleventh of them were removed in the first year and a half of Jackson's presidency and not over one-fifth during the eight years he was in office.

Through the exercise of his removing and appointing power it is possible for the president to build up a vast political machine in support of himself and his party. Thus President Hoover built up a machine by which his renomination for the presidency was secured in 1932 with hardly a ripple of opposition. However his machine could not overcome the forces of discontent produced by the economic depression and secure his reëlection. By the use of his political machine a president may go so far as practically to dictate the choice of his successor, as President Jackson did in 1836 when he secured the nomination and election of Martin Van Buren or as President Theodore Roosevelt did in 1908 when he virtually made William Howard Taft the President-elect.

The opposition of the Senate may block presidential appointments, but comparatively few appointments have been rejected by that body. Congress "may by Law vest the appointment of such inferior Officers, as they think proper, in the President alone, in the Courts of Law, or in the Heads of Departments." Insofar as minor officials are appointed by judges they are beyond the executive control but all of the thousands of officials whose appointment has been vested by law in the department heads are, in the final analysis, subject to presidential control because of the president's power over the heads of departments.

While the Senate is not in session, the president may make what are called "recess appointments" which shall expire at the end of the next session of that body unless the appointments are meanwhile confirmed. But there is nothing to prevent the president from giving a recess appointment to an individual even after the Senate has refused to confirm his appointment. President Jackson did this in 1832 in the case of a man named Samuel Gwin. In fact Gwin was nominated by President Jackson no less than four times before the Senate yielded and confirmed his appointment in the spring of 1833.

The president's power of appointment has been somewhat curtailed by the Civil Service Reform Act passed in 1883. By this act the president was authorized to classify such governmental offices as he saw fit. Appointments to these offices were to be made from those who had received the highest grades in competitive examinations conducted under the direction of a civil service commission appointed by the president. At first only about 14,000 offices in the Treasury and Post Office Departments were classified but, by order of successive presidents, the classified service was so enlarged that, by 1930, it included 462,083 offices or about three-fourths of all the civil service of the United States.

Since the Constitution made it possible for the central government to act on individuals and punish them for violations of the federal laws, it was necessary to give to some agency of the government the power to grant reprieves and pardons. Accordingly, the power was granted to the president with the proviso that it should not extend to cases of impeachments. In the exercise of this power, the presidents have relied greatly on the advice of their attorney-generals. The most extended application of the pardoning power occurred during and after the Civil War when Presidents Lincoln and Johnson both issued proclamations of amnesty or pardon to Confederates under certain conditions. As one means of preventing President Johnson from carrying out his reconstruction plans, Congress submitted to the states what became the fourteenth amendment to the Constitution. In this amendment was a provision which prevented the president from pardoning leading Confederates and so conferring on them the right to hold office, if they had once, as federal or state officers, taken an oath "to support the Constitution of the United States" and then had "engaged in insurrection or rebellion against the same, or given aid or comfort to the enemies thereof." Such persons could have their political disabilities removed only by a two-thirds vote of the two houses of Congress.

The power conferred on the president by the Constitution to make treaties with the advice and consent of the Senate has resulted in giving to him the direction of the foreign policy of the United States. From the administration of President Washington to the present time it has been the president who has been forced to take the initiative in the negotiation of treaties. Following the refusal of the Senate to advise President Washington in regard to an Indian treaty, the phrase "with the advice and consent of the Senate" was virtually made to mean merely "with the consent of the Senate." In other words, the Senate takes no formal action in relation to a treaty until it is presented to that body by the president for ratification for which the Constitution requires a two-thirds vote of those present.

In connection with foreign relations, the president possesses the constitutional power to appoint all ambassadors, ministers, and consuls. The practice has been to regard such officers as not only representatives of the United States but also as personal representatives of the president, sympathetic with his viewpoints and in political harmony with him.

By the power conferred on him by the Constitution to "receive Ambassadors and other public Ministers" the president has it within his province to recognize or to refuse to recognize a nation. Thus, in 1793, by receiving Citizen Genet, President Washington gave official recognition to the revolutionary government of France and established a precedent which has been followed by later presidents. Refusal by a president to receive a representative from a newly established government is tantamount to a refusal to recognize that government. For example, Presidents Wilson, Harding, Coolidge, and Hoover, all refused to receive a representative from the Union of Socialist Soviet Republics (Russia) with the result that the United States has had no official relations with the Soviet government.

It is possible for the president to make agreements with foreign countries without the formality of action by the Senate. Such an agreement was reached with Japan in 1907 by President Theodore Roosevelt whereby that country agreed not to issue passports to Japanese laborers seeking to go to the United States. This agreement, at least temporarily, quieted the excitement over Japanese immigration which had developed in California. In 1905, President Roosevelt established a financial protectorate over the Dominican Republic by an executive agreement with that country after the United States Senate had refused to ratify a treaty for the purpose.

The president may conduct foreign affairs in such a way as to bring about hostilities with another country before Congress has declared war. This was true of President Polk whose executive actions helped bring on a clash in 1846 between Mexican and American troops which clash was then used as a ground on which Congress was asked to declare war on Mexico. In other cases, the president may conduct relations with another country in such a way as to leave no alternative for Congress except to declare war.

In connection with foreign relations it is the president chiefly who determines what, if any, protection shall be afforded to American citizens in countries experiencing internal disorders. The several armed interventions in Nicaragua, the last of which was terminated in January, 1933, were by the orders of various presidents. The Nicaragua intervention is also an illustration of how the armed forces of the United States may be involved in actual fighting by executive order without a declaration of war by Congress.

The use of the military and naval forces of the United States to protect American lives and property is not only an illustration of the president's control of foreign relations but it also represents an exercise of his constitutional power as commander-in-chief of the army and navy of the United States. The forces may be used in other ways by the chief executive in time of peace if he sees fit. President Cleveland, for example, ordered federal troops to intervene in the railroad strike of 1894 on the ground that the movement of the United States mail was being interfered with by the strikers. Later, in 1932, President Hoover ordered the federal troops to expel the so-called "Bonus Expeditionary Force" from the national capital. Both actions were subjected to sharp criticism but in each case the president was undoubtedly within his constitutional rights. Whether or not the actions were wise and expedient is another question.

Mention will be made later of the great war powers conferred on President Lincoln during the Civil War. Even broader powers were conferred on President Wilson during the World War. In time of war the president is an extraordinarily powerful individual because of his position as commander-in-chief. No president has actually taken the field in time of war but there is no constitutional provision to prevent him from doing so.

Not the least of the president's powers has been derived from the constitutional provisions that "He shall from time to time give to the Congress Information of the state of the Union, and recommend to their Consideration such Measures as he shall judge necessary and expedient; he may, on extraordinary Occasions, convene both Houses, or either of them, and, in Case of Disagreement between them, with Respect to the Time of Adjournment, he may adjourn them to such Time as he shall think proper."

Through their annual messages delivered at the beginning of the regular sessions of Congress as well as through special messages, the presidents have been able to exert much influence on legislation. The chief executive is in a position to secure information not ordinarily available to congressmen and, therefore, can make definite recommendations to the legislative body. While the annual messages generally deal with a variety of matters, President Cleveland, in 1887, departed from precedent and devoted his whole message to the subject of tariff reform.

Especially in financial matters Congress has had to depend upon the executive branch of the government for information and advice because the Treasury Department alone is in a position at all times to know what the financial status of the country is. Since the passage of the budget act in 1921, the executive has exerted even greater influence on financial legislation.

The presidents have not depended on formal messages alone to influence congressional action. When the majority of the two houses are of the same political party as the president it is possible for him to use his position as the party leader to secure desired legislation. Furthermore, the presidents exert a considerable influence on congressional action through private and unofficial conferences with prominent senators or representatives. President Coolidge's favorite method of arranging such conferences was to invite various members of Congress to the White House for breakfast. Another method by which some presidents, notably Theodore Roosevelt, have sought to influence congressional action, has been by means of appeals for public support made through public speeches or through newspapers. All the presidents from Jefferson to Buchanan had newspapers called "official organs" which served to present their views to the public. The presidents, beginning with Lincoln, have had to depend on the good will of the press in general to secure for themselves favorable publicity. President Franklin D. Roosevelt has not only made effective use of newspapers but he has made even more use of the radio in rallying the people to his support.

Yet another way in which the presidents have influenced legislation has been through their subordinates. Frequently the heads of departments or other executive or administrative officers are consulted by congressional committees or are even asked to prepare drafts for proposed bills.

Finally, and probably most important, the presidents have influenced legislation through the veto. It is very difficult to muster the two-thirds vote required to override a presidential veto and, consequently, comparatively few acts have been repassed after their rejection by the executive. At times an unofficial warning given by the president through some member of Congress or through the press that a bill will be vetoed if passed is sufficient to prevent the passage of such a bill. On the other hand, the members of the legislature are inclined to resent such warnings as unwarranted interferences with the legislative function.

PRESIDENT WASHINGTON'S CONCEPTION OF HIS OFFICE

During the administration of President Washington the process of applying the provisions of the Constitution to the actual exigencies of government was begun. In his administration important precedents as to the conduct of the executive office were established. These involved chiefly the relation between the president and Congress.

It had been expected by President Washington that the Senate, insofar as it was associated with the president in such matters as treaty making and the appointing power, would act as an advisory council, somewhat in the nature of the councils which, in the colonial governments, had acted both as branches of the legislature and as executive bodies in giving advice to the governors. The Senate, however, was of a different mind. It insisted on its character as a legislative body. In attempting to secure the advice and consent of the Senate, President Washington proposed to go before that body, to present his facts, and to receive the Senate's opinions at first hand. But the Senate chose not to act along such lines, insisting that it would debate the president's proposals uninfluenced by his presence.

Similarly, neither house of Congress would allow the heads of the executive departments to speak before it, despite the efforts of Secretary of the Treasury Hamilton to secure this privilege. Hamilton would have preferred the institution of a modification of the English cabinet system, to allow executive guidance of legislative policy. The cabinet itself was not expressly provided for in the words of the Constitution, but was implied, and had been debated at some length in the Constitutional Convention. It will be recalled that a number of the original state constitutions had provisions for advisory executive councils. Various plans had been suggested for a similar council to advise the national chief executive, but most of them involved a practical breaking down of the separation of powers. The omission of any direct reference in the Constitution to such an organization was the cause of no little dissatisfaction among the delegates. There were movements in several of the state ratifying conventions to secure an amendment to the Constitution to provide for the creation of an advisory council, but nothing came of this.

The laws creating the various executive departments, passed during Washington's first administration by Congress, also provided for the appointment of heads of these departments. Upon the basis of the constitutional provision for the securing by the president of the advice of these officers on questions of policy, there developed the institution of the cabinet as a purely extra-legal body.

The law of Congress creating, in 1789, the executive department having charge of foreign affairs, had in it a provision giving the president the power to remove from office the head of that department. This provision was opposed in the legislature, on the grounds that the Senate, being associated with the president in the appointment of such officers, should also be associated in their removal. This question was also debated in connection with the creation of the War and Treasury Departments, but was uniformly decided in favor of an independent power of the president to remove such officers. This question was to be debated from various points of view until 1926, when the Supreme Court finally decided that the power of the president to appoint involved also the power to remove.

In relation to the power of the president over foreign relations there developed a further struggle between him and the legislative department. In 1793, President Washington issued a proclamation of neutrality, stating the position of the country in relation to the war then going on in Europe. Congress was not then in session. Did the power of Congress to declare war imply a power in its hands to maintain neutrality? The advocates of legislative control insisted that it did so. On the other hand, this power was not denied to the president or placed in other hands, by the Constitution, and on these grounds the supporters of executive power claimed it for the president.

In connection with the Jay Treaty of 1795 there was considerable debate as to the extent of the treaty making power. Did the power of the president in this respect, in association with the Senate, extend to objects which were within the proper sphere of the legislature? The Senate claimed that it did not. The House of Representatives demanded the correspondence and papers relating to the negotiation of the treaty, but the president refused to produce them, on the ground that to do so would sanction undue interference on the part of the legislature with the prescribed duties of the chief executive. Any treaty made by him, and approved by the Senate, was asserted to be legal. After further debate the House realized the futility of attempting to supervise this exercise of executive discretion, and voted the measures necessary to put the treaty into effect.

This same question arose again in 1803 in connection with the passage by the House of the necessary measures to carry out the terms of the Louisiana Purchase Treaty. In this case, however, the parties were reversed. The Federalists, who had formerly desired the extension of executive power as an aid to efficient government, now opposed the measures necessary to the carrying out of the treaty negotiated by the executive department. The supporters of President Jefferson, formerly opposed to the extension of executive power, now insisted on the independence of the executive in the exercise of the power to negotiate treaties, and urged the support of this power by appropriate legislation by the House.

In the matter of the suggestion of legislation, President Washington also followed a course designed to enlarge the influence of the executive. His messages to Congress were read to the legislative body in person. This was the case also with President John Adams, but President Jefferson sent his messages to the legislature to be read by someone else, thus observing at least a technical separation from that body. This remained the practice until President Wilson in 1913 reverted again to the practice of Presidents Washington and Adams.

THOMAS JEFFERSON AND THE PRESIDENCY

The election of 1800–1801 put into the office of president Thomas Jefferson, the leader of the opposition to the Federalist party of Hamilton, Washington, and Adams. Jefferson had opposed the Federalists partly on a basis of their advocacy of a strong executive department in the government. This, he claimed, showed them to be in sympathy with monarchy and aristocracy in government. He accused them of wishing to make a monarchy out of the government under the Constitution.

Jefferson, himself, in line with his democratic beliefs, advocated the primacy of the legislative body in the national government, as being more directly derived from, and responsible to, the people. On the other hand, there is evidence to prove that Jefferson did not desire the entire dominance of government by the legislature. Legislative tyranny, said he, is no better than the tyranny of one man, and perhaps worse. The eight years during which he occupied the presidential office were not marked by legislative dominance in the national government. Two examples of President Jefferson's executive leadership in national affairs were the purchase of Louisiana and the Embargo of 1807. Thus it appears that, while he advocated legislative supremacy, President Jefferson, in practice, actually exerted considerable executive leadership.

President Jefferson did not hesitate to engage in a struggle with the third branch of the national government, the judiciary. Within the Supreme Court and the minor federal courts was entrenched the last remnant of the Federalist governmental personnel, otherwise driven from national office by the election of 1800. The system of circuit courts, established by the Federalists as a party measure toward the close of the Adams administration, was destroyed, and President Jefferson attempted to break the influence of Chief Justice Marshall in the Supreme Court by appointing to that body only those judges who agreed with the Jeffersonian interpretation of the Constitution.

The case of *Marbury vs. Madison* was an incident in connection with this war upon the judiciary conducted by Jefferson. The circumstances of this case have already been described. Incidental to the decision in the case, the relation of the courts to the executive was defined by Marshall. The courts, he said, could not control the political acts of the executive done under his discretion or that of his department heads. But if the legislature should prescribe certain duties for the executive to perform he would then be amenable to the control of the courts. Thus, if Marshall had considered constitutional the act of Congress providing for the issuance by the Supreme Court of writs of mandamus, he would not have hesitated to issue such a writ upon an executive department to secure the carrying out by it of duties prescribed by act of Congress.

PRESIDENT JACKSON AS REPRESENTATIVE OF THE PEOPLE

In no respect was the influence of the legislature upon the executive more important up to 1824 than in the matter of the nomination of candidates for the presidency and vice presidency. The Constitution provided the machinery of election, but it did not provide any means of uniting the opinions of the electors upon a candidate of a particular party group. Candidates were usually put in nomination by the state legislatures and, in an attempt to unite the party on a particular candidate, the members of Congress belonging to it met in "caucus" to choose the official candidate of the party. This choice had no legal binding power upon the members of the party.

The caucus was opposed on the ground that it limited the expression of the popular will in the choice of the president. As a matter of fact the Constitution did not provide for a popular choice of the president. In the election of 1824 the caucus nominated William H. Crawford as the candidate of the Republican or Democratic-Republican party, but in the popular election he ran a poor third. The choice of the majority of the electorate was Andrew Jackson, but he failed to secure the majority in the electoral college necessary for his election. The choice was thus made the duty of the House of Representatives, and that body chose John Quincy Adams as president. The congressional caucus as a device for nominating presidential candidates has not been used since 1824. In 1828 the candidates were nominated by state legislatures, newspapers, and mass meetings. During the campaign of 1832 national conventions were first used and, ever since, they have been the means of selecting party candidates for the first office of the land.

The overthrow of the congressional caucus as a method of choosing party candidates for the presidency was a symbol of the rising democratic desire for a popular voice in the choice of the president. The election of Jackson in 1828 was a democratic election, in the sense that, at that time, only one state, South Carolina, chose its presidential electors by vote of the legislature. In the country as a whole the president had become practically dependent upon popular choice for his election.

The natural result of this was a revolution in the character of the presidential office. It had become a representative institution, to be popularly controlled. It was no longer to be considered a stronghold of the aristocratic influence in government. Further, since it was an office representative of the people of the

nation as a whole, it was a fit instrumentality for the securing
of the popular will. President Jackson was thoroughly convinced
that he represented "the people" and this led him to assert in no
uncertain terms his authority in the government. Regarding himself as the representative of the American people as a whole, he
advocated the nationalistic point of view, as in the nullification
controversy with South Carolina in 1832–33.

In his contests with the legislature President Jackson's attitude
on executive power was best exemplified. By previous presidents
the veto had been used a total of nine times. President Jackson
used it twelve times in his two administrations. He claimed the
right of the president to judge as to the desirability or constitutionality of acts of Congress. In respect to their constitutionality,
he asserted that he was not limited by the opinion of the Supreme Court, which, after all, was but one of three independent
agencies in the national government. It was not the duty of the
president to enforce a law which was unconstitutional, and it was
within his right to judge as to the constitutionality of laws coming up for his approval. The president, as well as the judges, had
taken an oath to support the Constitution, and this he must do
according to his own conscience. These views were brought out
in 1832 in his veto of the bill for the recharter of the Second
Bank of the United States.

Among the members of Congress the attitude of President
Jackson on the veto aroused a storm of protest. Henry Clay
insisted that this use of the veto power would mean the break-
down of the principle of the separation of powers in government. It would involve eventually the power of the president
to initiate legislation, and would thus make him the virtual ruler
of the nation. Could the president, asked Senator Clay, know
the national will as well as the two hundred and ninety-four
members of the House and Senate?

Jackson further asserted the right of the president to control the actions of members of his cabinet. When, accordingly,
he ordered the secretary of the treasury to remove the deposits
of national funds from the Bank of the United States his actions
aroused further legislative opposition. The Senate passed, in
1834, a resolution of censure condemning his actions, and to
this he replied that the Constitution had granted no power to

that body to censure acts of the executive. The only way in which the president could be punished by Congress was through impeachment and even then, the president reminded the Senate, the articles of impeachment must be drawn up by the House of Representatives. President Jackson further insisted that he had a right to order the removal of the deposits and to insist that his secretary of the treasury carry out the order because he, the President, was the people's representative and had received a mandate from them through his overwhelming victory in the election of 1832 to proceed with his policy in relation to the bank.

In reply to this Daniel Webster made a speech, in the course of which he denied the character of the presidency as representing the people. He pointed out the fact that the Constitution did not name the president as a representative of the people, and that it provided for no direct election by them. In denying the representative character of the presidency Webster went contrary to the dominant public opinion of the time. Incidentally, Jackson finally won the fight over the resolution of censure for, in January, 1837, the Senate ordered it to be expunged from its journal.

But it was not only in relation to the legislature that President Jackson asserted the independent authority of the executive. As has been pointed out, he asserted the duty of the president to protect the Constitution, on an equal basis with the courts. In so doing he maintained that he was not bound by decisions of the court on constitutional questions. If, in denying the validity of court decisions, he should exceed his authority and misinterpret the Constitution, it would then be a matter for impeachment, which was his risk.

In the case of *Worcester vs. Georgia,* President Jackson, it will be recalled, refused to enforce a decision of the Supreme Court, claiming that he was not required to support decisions of that body which departed from his own opinions on constitutional questions.

A prime factor in securing for President Jackson the independence which he assumed was his control over the party organization. As much as any other one factor, the appointive power of the president insured his dominance in his party and his power among the electorate. The power to appoint to political office naturally became the source of political influence, and caused the concentration of power in the hands of the executive. This was seen by men of the time, who insisted that, combined with the power of the veto and the power to control actions of heads of the executive departments, it meant a practical concentration of influence in the hands of the executive.

President Jackson's attitude on the veto power was later assumed by President Polk, when, in his message of December 5, 1848, he stated the highest duty of the executive to be the protection of the Constitution from legislative infraction. The use of the veto on this ground had been indulged in before Jackson's time, and opposition to the use of the veto had also antedated him. However, members of Congress felt that he was using the veto too frequently and so was abusing his power. But presidents since his time have far exceeded him in the use of this check upon the legislature. For example, President Cleveland vetoed three hundred and fifty-eight bills most of which were private pension bills; Theodore Roosevelt used the veto forty times; while President Wilson vetoed twenty-six bills.

President Jackson's denial of the right of the Supreme Court to bind the president by its decisions was reversed by President Buchanan, in connection with the Dred Scott case. In this case it was decided that the people of a territory had the right to determine whether or not they would have slavery in their territory. This denied the right of Congress to legislate on the subject. President Buchanan stated that he would submit to the dictate of the Supreme Court in this matter.

PRESIDENT LINCOLN'S WAR LEADERSHIP

Under President Lincoln the exigencies of war caused the expansion of executive power to an unprecedented extent. This will be discussed in the later chapter on "The Constitution In Time Of War." The general effect of this large use of his powers by President Lincoln was to establish him as the most powerful executive the nation had yet known. In addition to this use of the war powers, President Lincoln's guidance of public opinion made him the chief figure in the nation. His great efforts in the cause of human equality gave him a world significance as a leader, and elevated the office which he held.

LOSS OF EXECUTIVE PRESTIGE UNDER PRESIDENT JOHNSON

On the other hand, his successor in the presidential office became involved in an unsuccessful struggle with Congress. President Johnson was temperamentally unsuited for the difficult situation in which he found himself. The problems of reconstruction were to be dealt with, the question being as to who should handle them, the president or Congress. Friction over this question was intensified by the attempt of Congress, through the Tenure of Office Act, to deny to the president the right to control his own cabinet. This act denied the right of the president to remove from office officials appointed by himself, without the consent of the Senate. This denied a right which had always been conceded as belonging to the president and, in defence of this right, President Johnson refused obedience to the act. The result of this was his impeachment by the House and subsequent trial by the Senate in 1868.

The result of the trial was the acquittal of the president by the narrow margin of one vote. The question arose, as to what constituted "high crimes and misdemeanours" for the commission of which the president could be convicted upon impeachment. Were they necessarily acts criminal before the law, or merely any acts which in the opinion of the senators disqualified the chief executive from further tenure of office? No precise definition was given by the Constitution so the Senate must decide in each case whether the acts involved constitute sufficient grounds for impeachment. The acquittal of President Johnson was fortunate for the later development of the executive department, for any other outcome of the trial would have meant practical annihilation of the independence of the executive and virtual destruction of the principle of separation of powers.

The case of *Mississippi vs. Johnson* in 1867 was an attempt to secure an injunction to prohibit President Johnson from carrying out the reconstruction acts, on the ground of their unconstitutionality. The Supreme Court refused to issue an injunction, on two grounds: first, that they could not issue a writ of injunction against the president, who might not obey it, and second, that the alleged unconstitutionality of the act was not sufficient reason for the interference by the court with the official duties of the president. This decision in support of the doctrine of the separation of powers in the government, and of executive independence was very timely in view of the hostility of Congress toward President Johnson but it did not prevent him from being impeached.

PRESIDENT HAYES AND THE VETO POWER

Under President Hayes there was some agitation for an extension of the veto power, to allow the President to negative specific provisions of appropriation bills. This was the result of the practice of Congress of tacking onto appropriation bills provisions of a different nature. This meant a considerable pressure upon the president to approve such bills in order to save necessary appropriations. This change was not secured, though it had been advocated previously by President Grant. Consequently, down to the present time, Congress has continued this practice of attaching "riders" to bills that are rather certain to receive the executive approval. Thus, on March 2, 1901, an army appropriation bill was passed with a "rider" known as the Platt amendment which had the effect of making Cuba a protectorate of the United States.

A further attempt in regard to the veto power was to secure a provision requiring a two-thirds vote of *all* members of Congress to override an executive veto, instead of a two-thirds vote of all those present. This also failed of adoption.

PRESIDENT CLEVELAND AND EXECUTIVE INDEPENDENCE

President Cleveland came into office in 1885 pledged to a program of civil service reform. He was the first Democratic president in twenty-four years, and his accession to the presidency afforded the first opportunity the Democratic party had had in that time to share in the federal offices. The Senate was inclined to insist upon the right to pass on suspensions from office. When this right was refused them by President Cleveland, the Senate refused to approve his nominations for office.

In an effort to get at the reasons for suspensions from office the Senate sought, from the department heads, papers relating to the conduct of their offices. These papers were refused. The Senate based its demand upon its asserted right to supervise the actions of departments created by legislative action in which the Senate had participated.

President Cleveland himself claimed that his pledges for civil service reform had been made to the people, and that he was responsible to them alone for their carrying out. To the Senate he refused to submit his official actions for approval or condemnation.

EXECUTIVE LEADERSHIP BY PRESIDENTS THEODORE ROOSEVELT AND WILSON

Along much the same line was the conduct of the executive office by Presidents T. Roosevelt and Wilson. These two presidents represented what may be called the "strong president" school of conduct of the executive office. Their view was that the president should guide public opinion, not that he should merely seek to know what it was. As long as the president could secure popular approval he should lead the country and guide legislative action in accord with his concept of the best public policy.

As far as the extent of the powers of the chief executive was concerned, these two leaders refused to accept the idea that only those duties could be performed by the president, for which a positive grant of power could be found in the Constitution. They held to the view that the president could and should do anything he was not expressly forbidden to do by the Constitution or the laws. This was a broadened concept of the executive power. President Franklin D. Roosevelt has not only adopted this point of view but has gone further than any of his predecessors in asserting executive leadership.

President Taft, on the other hand, took an opposite view. While he emphasized the importance of the veto power as a protection to the Constitution, and urged reform to give the president the control of the budget and to allow members of the cabinet to debate in the legislature, he insisted that the actions of the president must be limited to the positive grants of power in the Constitution or laws of the land, or to powers justly to be implied from such express grants. A mere belief on the part of the executive that the exercise of powers by him would be for the public good he denied would be justification for the use of those powers.

In general, the tendency in present day governmental and political practice is in the direction of placing still more emphasis upon executive leadership. As between the president and Congress, the trend seems to be in the direction of presidential domination. The continuance of this tendency will depend of course upon the quality of the personnel in the executive and legislative departments. It seems, however, in the light of modern emphasis upon administrative management, in the light of the large political influence of the president, and his superior situation and facilities for creating public opinion, that the tendency of recent years is due to continue for some time to come.

From time to time various proposals have been made for changing the presidential system. Among the proposals most seriously considered has been that for giving cabinet members a seat in one or both houses of Congress with the right to discuss measures but not to vote. President Taft, as has been mentioned, favored such a proposal. Another proposal has been not only to give the heads of departments a voice in Congress but to make them full members of that body. Others have proposed to go still further and give bills drawn up by the president and members of his cabinet priority over all other bills introduced in Congress. These last two proposals particularly are designed to make the American system of government more like the cabinet system as in England.

But there is little likelihood of such proposals receiving serious consideration in the United States if for no other reason than that their adoption would tend to destroy one of the fundamental principles inherent in the Constitution, that of separation of powers. As history has shown, strong presidents have been able to exercise a large measure of leadership, not only in their own spheres, but in matters of legislation and so have considerably weakened the principle. But to destroy entirely the "presidential system" and substitute for it the "cabinet system" is unlikely at any future time to win much favor in this country. The American people can hardly be expected to scrap their constitutional system merely because some other countries have successfully used the cabinet system. It would be a simple matter to admit cabinet members to the floor of Congress and give them the right to participate in debate but not to vote and perhaps even to give them the right to introduce bills personally rather than through representatives or senators as at present. These changes could be made by an act of Congress but to go further would require a revision of the Constitution and a complete scrapping of the presidential system.

PROPOSALS TO MAKE THE PRESIDENT A DICTATOR

Following the move begun in Congress in February, 1933, to give President Franklin D. Roosevelt power to reorganize the federal administrative service, proposals were made, through newspapers and otherwise, to make the president a dictator. Some of these proposals were mild, calling for the delegation to the chief executive by Congress of necessary powers to deal with the economic emergency in much the same way as President Wilson was empowered to deal with the war emergency in 1917–1919. Walter Lippmann denies that bestowing such war powers on the president would be equivalent to making him a dictator since the president would still be subject to the control of the people or their representatives. A dictator is one who holds his position by force and who admits no responsibility to the people or anyone else.

By the amendment to the treasury-postoffice appropriation bill signed by President Hoover on March 4, 1933, President Roosevelt was given extensive power in relation to the reorganization of the administrative branch of the federal government. This power is greater than any president has previously enjoyed in time of peace. The new president, in his inaugural address, made it clear that he would not hesitate to ask Congress for any additional powers that might be needed. His ideas on executive leadership and what have been called dictatorial powers may best be indicated by quoting from his address, as follows:

"If I read the temper of our people correctly, we now realize as we have never realized before our interdependence on each other; that we cannot merely take, but we must give as well, that if we are to go forward we must move as a trained and loyal army willing to sacrifice for the good of a common discipline, because without such discipline no progress is made, no leadership becomes effective.

"We are, I know, ready and willing to submit our lives and property to such discipline because it makes possible a leadership which aims at a larger good. This I propose to offer, pledging that the larger purposes will bind upon us all as a sacred obligation with a unity of duty hitherto evoked only in time of armed strife.

"With this pledge taken, I assume unhesitatingly the leadership of this great army of our people dedicated to a disciplined attack upon our common problem.

"Action in this image and to this end is feasible under the form of government which we have inherited from our ancestors. Our constitution is so simple and practical that it is possible always to meet extraordinary needs by changes in emphasis and arrangement without loss of essential form.

"That is why our constitutional system has proved itself the most superbly enduring political mechanism the modern world has produced. It has met every stress of vast expansion of territory, of foreign wars, of bitter internal strife, of world relations.

"It is to be hoped that the normal balance of executive and legislative authority may be wholly adequate to meet the unprecedented task before us. But it may be that an unprecedented demand and need for undelayed action may call for temporary departure from that normal balance of public procedure.

"I am prepared under my constitutional duty to recommend the measures that a stricken nation in the midst of a stricken world may require. These measures, or such other measures as the Congress may build out of its experience and wisdom, I shall seek, within my constitutional authority, to bring to speedy adoption.

"But in the event that the Congress shall fail to take one of these two courses, and in the event that the national emergency is still critical I shall not evade the clear course of duty that will then confront me. I shall ask the Congress for the one remaining instrument to meet the crisis— broad executive power to wage a war against the emergency, as great as the power that would be given to me if we were in fact invaded by a foreign foe.

"For the trust reposed in me I will return the courage and the devotion that befit the time. I can do no less.

"We face the arduous days that lie before us in the warm courage of national unity; with the clear consciousness of seeking old and precious moral values; with the clean satisfaction that comes from the stern performance of duty by old and young alike. We aim at the assurance of a rounded and permanent national life.

"We do not distrust the future of essential democracy. The people of the United States have not failed. In their need they have registered a mandate that they want direct vigorous action. They have asked for discipline and direction under leadership. They have made me the present instrument of their wishes. In the spirit of the gift I take it.

"In this dedication of a nation we humbly ask the blessing of God. May He protect each and every one of us. May He guide me in the days to come."

President Roosevelt had hardly been in office a day before he began giving practical application to his ideas of executive leadership. On March 5, 1933, he proclaimed a national bank holiday and issued a call for a special session of Congress to begin on March 9. On that day he asked for and received from Congress extraordinary power over the banks of the country. He followed with a request for unprecedented power to reduce the salaries of federal office holders as well as the power practically to fix the amounts to be spent on veterans. This request was speedily granted.

Within ten days the new President, by his courageous direct action, had done more to restore the morale of the American people than had been accomplished during the whole period following 1929.

SELECTED REFERENCES

Beard, C. A., *American Government and Politics* (Fourth edition), pp. 163–221.

Black, H. C., *The Relation of the Executive Power to Legislation*, pp. 1–40, 55–148, 181–191.

Chambrun, A. De, *The Executive Power in the United States*, pp. 94–115, 125–222, 258–277.

Cleveland, Grover, *The Independence of the Executive*, pp. 1–82.

Corwin, E. S., *The President's Control of Foreign Relations*, pp. 1–207.

Haines, B. M., and Haines, C. G., *The Constitution of the United States*, pp. 145–157.

Hill, J. P., *The Federal Executive*, pp. 1–237.

Jameson, J. F., ed., *Essays in the Constitutional History of the United States*, pp. 116–185.

Johnson, Allen, ed., *Readings in American Constitutional History 1776–1876*, pp. 1–9, 18–33, 151–187, 197–205, 370–404, 509–517, 547–550, 553–561.

Johnson, Allen, and Robinson, W. A., eds., *Readings in Recent American Constitutional History 1876–1926*, pp. 208–271.

Mason, E. C., *The Veto Power*, pp. 124–140.

Mathews, J. M., and Berdahl, C. A., *Documents and Readings in American Government*, pp. 104–289.

McBain, H. L., *The Living Constitution*, pp. 114–149.

McLaughlin, A. C., *Steps in the Development of American Democracy*, pp. 96–116.

Merriam, C. E., *The Written Constitution and the Unwritten Attitude*, pp. 1–33.

Norton, T. J., *The Constitution of the United States, Its Sources and Its Application*, pp. 99–130.

Ogg, F. A., and Ray, P. O., *Introduction to American Government* (Third edition), pp. 208–302.

Orth, S. P., and Cushman, R. E., *American National Government*, pp. 269–316.

Salmon, L. M., "History of the Appointing Power of the President," American Historical Association, *Papers*, I, No. 5, pp. 9–116.

Stevens, C. E., *Sources of the Constitution of the United States*, pp. 117–177.

Taft, W. H., *Our Chief Magistrate and His Powers*, pp. 1–157.

Thach, C. C., "The Creation of the Presidency, 1775–1789," Johns Hopkins University, *Studies in Historical and Political Science*, Series XL, No. 4, pp. 55–177.

The Federalist (Everyman's Library edition), Nos. 67–77, pp. 342–394.

Wilson, Woodrow, *Constitutional Government in the United States*, pp. 54–81.

Chapter Seventeen

CONSTITUTIONAL EFFECTS OF CUSTOM AND TRADITION

DURING the period since the Constitution was put into operation, it has been vastly expanded, not merely through acts of Congress and judicial interpretation, but also by numerous customs and traditions. These customs and traditions make up the unwritten portion of the Constitution of the United States. In some cases, they have come to have as much constitutional effect as though they were written into the fundamental law of the land. Some of the institutions which have come into existence without any provision for them in the written Constitution or even in the laws passed by Congress are just as important parts of the machinery of government in the United States as those which owe their existence to the Constitution and to the laws of the land. Among such institutions are the political parties and the president's cabinet. Likewise, there are important traditions which effectively limit the activities and policies of the various agencies of the national government. Typical of such traditions are the one which limits a president to two terms and the one which prevents the United States from entering into entangling alliances.

THE EVOLUTION OF POLITICAL PARTIES

One searches the Constitution in vain for a provision which could be interpreted to authorize, directly or indirectly, the formation of political parties. Nowhere in the original Constitution or in its amendments is there the slightest recognition given to parties. Nor was any recognition given to political parties by the laws of Congress until about a decade of the twentieth century had passed. Then Congress acted merely for the purpose of regulating party expenditures in elections. However, prior to that time, there had been some regulation by the individual states.

Should one depend on a perusal of the Constitution and of the laws of the United States, it is obvious that a very incomplete idea of the government would be obtained. One would learn of the three branches of the government and would secure information concerning the remarkable expansion of these branches, but no adequate knowledge would be acquired regarding the procedure whereby the most important governmental officials secure their offices. One would come away from such a perusal with the notion that the president and vice president are chosen by electors who regard them as the best qualified men in the country whereas, in reality, political parties made the electoral system an obsolete device before the Constitution had been in effect for twelve years. One would, furthermore, be convinced that the members of Congress are the true representatives of the people though, in fact, they are representatives of the political parties which promoted their election.

During most of the period since 1789, there have been two major parties in the United States contending for the control of the national government. Since the administration of George Washington, the chief governmental officials have been elected or appointed because of their adherence to one party or another. It is with truth that the government of the United States has been described as a government of political parties.

The first real national parties in the United States were the Federalists and Anti-Federalists. They came into existence during the battle over the ratification of the Constitution. After their defeat in this battle, the Anti-Federalists disappeared. The government, as first organized under the Constitution, was controlled by the Federalists. Gradually, under the leadership of Thomas Jefferson, an opposition party developed. This party, which assumed definite form in 1793, was called the Republican or Democratic-Republican party. It was the ancestor of the present Democratic party. Under Jefferson's leadership, this party stood for two fundamental principles: strict interpretation of the Constitution and the principle that the government exists for the benefit of the people.

As a result of the election of 1800 the Democratic-Republicans gained control of the national government. The Federalists gradually lost strength and, in 1816, they participated for the last time in a presidential election. During the elections of 1820, 1824, and 1828, the Democratic-Republican party alone occupied the national political arena. In 1824, four members of the party divided the popular and electoral vote in such a way as to force the House of Representatives to elect a president. In 1828, the party split into an Adams and a Jackson faction which led to the subsequent formation of new parties. The successful Jackson faction continued to use the name, Democratic-Republican, until 1831, when they began to use the shortened form, Democratic, as their party designation. Ever since, the Democratic party has remained as one of the major parties in the United States.

In 1829, the Adams faction of the Democratic-Republican party assumed the name National Republican. This party supported Henry Clay for the presidency in 1832. In 1834, the National Republicans merged with other groups opposed to President Jackson to form the Whig party. It remained as a major party through the election of 1856.

In 1854, the present Republican party was formed as a result of the opposition to the extension of slavery to the western territories as was permitted by the Kansas-Nebraska Act of that year. In 1856, as a result of its first participation in a presidential election, the Republican party became a major party and has continued to hold that position ever since. In fact, it has been in control of the national government during most of the period since 1860.

Besides the major parties which have become a fixed tradition in the United States, various minor parties have been formed from time to time. Their main function has been to stress issues which have been avoided by the major parties. Occasionally, the minor party agitation of issues has been so effective that the major parties have been compelled to adopt the issues in question. Among the minor parties, of national scope, which have been formed in the United States, mention might be made of the Anti-Masonic party which took part in the presidential election of 1832 and which won the electoral vote of Vermont that year. It was the first minor party to secure electoral votes, a feat which few other minor parties have equaled.

Prior to the Civil War, several minor parties were organized to combat the extension of slavery. The first of these was the Liberty party which took part in the elections of 1840 and 1844. Next came the Free Soil party which was active in 1848, and it was followed, in 1852, by the Free Soil Democrats. The Republican party, of course, was a minor party until after participation in its first national election.

The American or "Know-Nothing" party, which took part in the election of 1856, was opposed to the holding of office by Catholics or foreign-born persons. The Constitutional Union party, which participated in the 1860 election, stood for the preservation of the union, the continued existence of which was threatened by the sectional quarrel over slavery.

Following the Civil War, numerous minor parties sprang up. Some have achieved a degree of permanence while others soon disappeared from the political arena. The oldest of the present minor parties is the Prohibition party which was organized in 1869 and which has participated in every presidential election since that time. In 1892, the Socialist Labor party began participating in presidential elections while the Socialist party has taken part in elections since 1899, when it was organized. Other minor parties of the post-Civil War period included the National Greenback party, standing for a legal tender national currency, which had a presidential candidate in the field in 1876; the Liberal Republican party, which was active in 1872; the Populist or People's party which took part in the election of 1892 and several subsequent elections; the "Silver Republicans" and the "Gold Democrats," who participated in 1896; the Progressive party which took part in the election of 1912 with Theodore Roosevelt as its presidential candidate; and the Independent Progressive party which supported Robert M. La-Follette, Sr. for the presidency in 1924.

Other parties have sprung up from time to time but those mentioned have been the most important. Practically every presidential election finds six or more parties taking part. For example, in 1932, besides the Democratic and Republican parties, there were six minor parties which participated in the presidential election. These were the Socialist, Communist (or Workers), Prohibition, Liberty, the Farm-Labor, and the Socialist Labor parties. It is significant that all of these minor parties polled in 1932 less than a million votes out of a total of almost 40,000,000—less than three percent. In 1912, the Socialist party alone polled about six percent of the total popular vote.

In connection with the activities of the national government at Washington, D.C., there has developed the custom of lobbying. By means of lobbies various organized groups seek to secure legislation which is favorable to them. So important has lobbying become that it has been asserted that the lobbies constitute a third branch of the legislature. William Allen White, in his book *Politics: the Citizen's Business,* has referred to lobbies as a "government outside of government."

Some lobbies are conducted for the purpose of securing legislation for the general good; others are for the purpose of promoting the selfish interests of small groups. The lobbyists are very skillful in bringing pressure to bear on members of Congress. Not only do they exert this pressure through personal interviews but they also are adepts at the art of propaganda by which they seek to create public opinion favorable to their program and so bring indirect pressure on the congressmen.

If the truth were known, one would find that much of the legislation passed by Congress has been influenced by lobbies. Often a measure is favored by one or more groups of lobbyists and opposed by others. In such cases, the noise of the battle outside of the legislative halls may be heard all over the country. For example, in connection with legislation for World War veterans, powerful lobbies are maintained at Washington. Thus, in 1933, there were to be found at Washington lobbyists representing the American Legion, the Disabled American Veterans of the World War, and other veterans' organizations, on the one side; and lobbyists representing the National Economy League, the United States Chamber of Commerce, and allied groups, on the other side.

Similarly, in connection with the prohibition question, powerful lobbies have been maintained for years at the national capital. For a long period, the Anti-Saloon League supported at Washington what was, by common consent, one of the most powerful lobbies in the nation's history. In recent years, the National Association Against the Prohibition Amendment and allied organizations have conducted an obviously effective lobby of their own in opposition to prohibition.

And so one might examine almost any other subject of national legislation with a similar result. In each case there would probably be found a lobby working for or against the legislation. Thus, the farm organizations, such as the American Farm Bureau Federation, have maintained lobbies to work for farm relief. If railroad legislation is desired, a railroad lobby will descend on the national capital; if banking legislation is to be considered, a lobby of bankers will be present to influence the actions of the members of Congress, and so on.

Little has been done to control lobbying but some sort of regulation appears to be necessary. If left uncontrolled, the custom of lobbying will have pernicious effects on the country. Congressmen, after all, are only human and cannot be expected to withstand the terrific pressure brought to bear on them by various lobbies. To quote William Allen White, "This government outside of government which we are building up in America in order that men of like minds may reach one another and form militant minorities may look harmless, but they are charged with dynamite. They are here, these new organs of government; they cannot be ignored nor destroyed, but they must be publicly controlled for the common good."

THE ELECTION OF A PRESIDENT

The constitutional method of electing a president and vice president of the United States is through the electoral system. This method was purposely included in the Constitution so as to remove from the people the choice of these two officials for it was not the intention of the "Fathers of the Constitution" to promote democracy. The method of electing the electors from each state, equal in number to that state's representatives and senators in Congress, was left to the state legislatures.

Though the members of the Constitutional Convention were of the opinion that the electoral system which they had devised was the least susceptible to criticism of all the provisions in the

Constitution, it was the first to break down in practice. This was because of the early rise of political parties. By 1800, presidents and vice presidents were being elected, not because they were the best men in the country but because they were the nominees of a party which had been able to elect a majority of the electors. Instead of being free to choose a president and vice president, the electors have been bound to support the candidates of their party.

In 1821, an elector by the name of William Plumer of New Hampshire refused to be bound by the custom and cast his vote for John Q. Adams though all the other electors voted for James Monroe for the office of president. No elector since that time has dared defy the custom of voting according to the dictates of his party. It is a question what would happen to a delegate who dared to exercise his constitutional freedom of choice by voting for some other persons than those nominated by his party. He would certainly become an outcast from his own party and would perhaps suffer general ostracism because of his defiance of a custom that has come to be as binding as though written into the Constitution itself. As Vice President Thomas R. Marshall declared, the electors have become merely "animated rubber stamps" to record officially the verdict of their party.

Not only has custom deprived the presidential electors of their freedom of choice but it has also brought about what is virtually popular election of the president and vice president, contrary to the intentions of the framers of the Constitution. At first, the tendency was to select the electors through the state legislatures but this method gradually gave way to selection by popular vote. South Carolina clung to the legislative method of selection until the Civil War but, beginning with the election of 1868, it, too, has employed the method of popular election. In 1876, Colorado resorted to the legislative method of electing electors but since that time it has used the popular election method.

With all of the states using the method of electing electors by popular vote, the election of a president and vice president is practically completed in the popular elections held in November of every fourth year. The later meeting of the electors in each state for the purpose of casting their votes and the subsequent ceremony of counting those votes before a joint session of Congress are mere matters of form. These acts have no real significance and might very well be omitted. However, it would require a constitutional amendment to eliminate the obsolete and useless electoral system. Until such an amendment is forthcoming the people of the country must continue to go through the motions of electing electors instead of voting directly for a president and vice president.

In connection with the election of the president and vice president, custom has entered in to fix the method whereby each party nominates its candidates. For a time, the congressional caucus was the customary device for making such nominations. In the caucus, the representatives and senators belonging to the same party met and recommended candidates for the presidency and vice presidency. The congressional caucus method of nominations apparently was used as early as 1796. In 1800 the method was used by both the Democratic-Republicans and the Federalists and the former continued to use it until 1824. Presidents Jefferson, Madison, and Monroe were all the nominees of the congressional caucus.

With the growth of democracy in the country, the caucus method of nomination fell into disfavor. In 1824, William H. Crawford, the caucus nominee for the presidency, ran a poor third. Andrew Jackson and John Q. Adams who had been nominated by state legislatures, newspapers, mass meetings, and so on, far outstripped him. In 1828, the two presidential candidates, Adams and Jackson, were again nominated by the same irregular methods as before. It remained for a new minor party to introduce into national politics a different method of placing a presidential ticket in the field, for, in September, 1831, the Anti-Masonic party held a national convention at Baltimore and nominated William Wirt of that city for the presidency. Incidentally, this Anti-Masonic convention adopted an address to the people setting forth its principles and policies, chief among which were opposition to the Masonic fraternity and to all secret societies in general. This address, for all intents and purposes, may be regarded as the first political party platform in the history of this country. By 1840, the drafting of a platform by the party conventions had become a customary procedure.

In December, 1831, the National Republican party followed the example of the Anti-Masons by holding a convention at Baltimore. They nominated Henry Clay for the presidency and also drew up an address to the people. In May, 1832, the Democrats likewise held a convention at Baltimore. Declaring that the reëlection of President Jackson was being demanded by the people, they felt that it was unnecessary for the convention to nominate him formally. In fact, the work of the first Democratic national convention was confined largely to the nomination of Martin Van Buren for the vice presidency.

The conventions of 1831 and 1832 served to establish a precedent which has been followed ever since. Thus, custom has not only fixed the method of electing presidents and vice presidents but it has also established the national convention system as the method for placing them before the people as the party candidates. In connection with the conventions themselves a number of important customs have developed, in addition to the custom of drawing up a platform, but these need not be discussed here.

THE NO THIRD TERM TRADITION

It will be recalled that there was much diversity of opinion in the Constitutional Convention over the length of time a president should be allowed to serve. The matter was finally settled by fixing the presidential term of office at four years with no limit placed on the number of terms. Nevertheless, custom has entered in to limit presidents very effectually to a maximum of two terms.

The no third term tradition originated with the first president, George Washington. He had accepted the presidency with considerable reluctance and it was with difficulty that he was persuaded to serve a second term. As the time approached for another presidential election, he issued, on September 19, 1796, what has come to be called his "Farewell Address," in which he stated that he had decided "to decline being considered among the number of those, out of whom a choice is to be made." His reasons for so declining were, however, personal. In no way did he hint that he was refusing another term in office because he believed there should be a time limit placed on the holding of the presidency.

His successor, John Adams, served only one term and then was defeated for reëlection. But the third president, Thomas Jefferson, decided to follow Washington's example by declining to serve more than two terms. James Madison and James Monroe, who followed in the presidency, likewise served but two terms each, thus helping to fix the tradition of no third term. After the single term of John Q. Adams, Andrew Jackson came into the presidential office. He favored limiting the president to a single term of four or six years. In his first annual message to Congress and in five subsequent messages he recommended that such limitation should be provided by a constitutional amendment. Nevertheless, he, himself, accepted a second term. But in 1836 he emulated Presidents Washington, Jefferson, Madison, and Monroe by declining to be a candidate for a third term.

Not until General U. S. Grant became the chief executive did another president have the opportunity to accept or decline a third term. President Grant demonstrated that he would be willing to accept a third term but the House of Representatives, through a resolution adopted in 1876, sharply reminded him that there was a no third term tradition. For a president to accept a third term would be "unwise, unpatriotic, and fraught with peril to our free institutions," declared the resolution. Perhaps the fact that the House was controlled by the Democrats while Grant was a Republican had something to do with the resolution but, be that as it may, he was not a candidate for another term. However, four years later, after he had returned from a triumphal tour of the world, an attempt was made to nominate him as the Republican candidate for the presidency. In the party's national convention, Grant actually was in the lead for the nomination until the thirty-sixth ballot when James G. Garfield was nominated as a compromise candidate. This defeat of Grant helped to fix the no third term tradition.

Until the presidency of Theodore Roosevelt, no one, except Grover Cleveland, had an opportunity to break the tradition.

Cleveland served two terms with the administration of Benjamin Harrison intervening. However, as the end of his second term approached, Cleveland gave no indication of a desire for a third term but even had he desired a renomination he could not have secured it as he was out of harmony with the majority of his party.

Theodore Roosevelt became President in 1901, being elevated to the office from the vice presidency by the assassination of President William McKinley. In 1904, he was elected to the presidency in his own right. This raised the question as to whether or not he would be entitled to another term if he desired it as he had served less than a full term after succeeding McKinley. But Roosevelt settled the matter himself by declaring, after the popular election in November, 1904, that "The wise custom which limits the President to two terms regards the substance and not the form, and under no circumstances will I be a candidate for or accept another nomination." In 1907, he declared that he had not changed his mind and would not be a candidate for another term.

But, during the campaign of 1912, he did change his mind, becoming an active candidate for the Republican presidential nomination. He failed to secure this nomination but was subsequently nominated by the Progressive or, as it was popularly called, the "Bull Moose" party. During the ensuing campaign the no third term tradition was cited frequently as a reason why he should not be elected. So much was made of this that a fanatic was inspired to attempt his assassination. After shooting and wounding Roosevelt at Milwaukee, the would-be assassin explained that he had shot him "because he was a menace to the country. He should not have a third term. I shot him as a warning that men must not try to have more than two terms as President."

Roosevelt ran second in the election of 1912, leaving the no third term tradition still in effect. It has been claimed that Woodrow Wilson desired a third term and would have been a candidate in 1920 had his health been good. Third term talk was revived as President Calvin Coolidge approached the end of his administration. He had come into office from the vice presidency in 1923 following the death of President Harding and then had been elected in 1924 to serve a term in his own right. As the discussion of whether or not he should be elected for another term was going on, he settled the matter by issuing to the press a typically terse statement saying, "I do not choose to run." His death early in 1933 insures the continuance of the no third term tradition. Should Franklin D. Roosevelt be re-elected in 1936 or should ex-President Hoover be elected then for a second term, the question may come up four years later but the tradition is safe until 1940 at least.

THE PRESIDENTIAL SUCCESSION

Another custom which has developed in relation to the presidency is that of designating the vice president as "the president" when he is accidentally called upon to perform the duties of the presidental office. The Constitution states that "In case of the removal of the President from office, or of his death, resignation, or inability to discharge the powers and duties of the said office, the same shall devolve on the Vice President." The implication of this statement is that the vice president shall be the acting president.

However, in every case in which the presidential office has been vacated by the death of the incumbent, the vice president has assumed the title of "president" without any objection being made to this procedure. In no case have the duties of the president devolved upon the vice president except through the death of the president. Six presidents have died in office, three of them as the result of assassins' bullets.

William Henry Harrison was the first president to die while in office. His duties were immediately assumed by Vice President John Tyler who established a precedent by referring to himself as "the president." The next president to die was Zachary Taylor who was succeeded by Millard Fillmore. On the assassination of Abraham Lincoln, Vice President Andrew Johnson became the president. After the death of James A. Garfield as the result of a bullet wound inflicted by an assassin, Vice President Chester A. Arthur assumed the title of "the president." Vice President Theodore Roosevelt did likewise following the assassination of President William McKinley. The last accidental president was Calvin Coolidge who assumed the presidential office after the death of Warren G. Harding. These six cases have firmly established the custom of regarding "accidental" presidents as presidents in fact and not merely as acting presidents.

THE PRESIDENT'S CABINET

Nowhere in the Constitution is mention made of the president's cabinet, nor was there any reference to it in the laws passed by Congress until 1907. Yet the cabinet has existed since early in the presidency of George Washington and has grown to be an important part of the national governmental machinery.

As has been pointed out, an unsuccessful attempt had been made in the Constitutional Convention to provide in the new Constitution for an executive advisory council similar to those which existed in several of the states at that time. Following the establishment of the new federal government in 1789, President Washington sought to secure advice from the Senate but met with a cold reception from that body. This forced him to rely on the heads of the executive departments from whom the Constitution authorized him to secure opinions in writing. Seeking a less cumbersome method of securing advice, Washington, in 1792, began holding meetings for the purpose of consulting the department heads. By 1793, these cabinet meetings, as they came to be called, were being held more frequently and had come to be regarded as a fixture of the government. Other presidents followed the example of the first president, thus firmly fixing the custom of holding cabinet meetings.

In Washington's cabinet were included the secretaries of state, war, and the treasury, together with the attorney-general when he was present in the capital. Not until the Jackson administration was the postmaster-general admitted to cabinet meetings. As other departments have been created, their heads have automatically become, by custom, members of the cabinet. With the creation, in 1913, of separate Departments of Commerce and Labor, the membership of the cabinet was increased to ten. During the presidency of Warren G. Harding, 1921–1923, Vice President Calvin Coolidge was invited to attend cabinet meetings. However, when Charles G. Dawes became vice president in 1925 he made it clear that he did not wish the precedent to be followed in his case, thus preventing a new custom from being established.

It should be emphasized that the cabinet is subject entirely to the president's will. The meetings are held as he pleases and the members hold office at his pleasure. He has the power to dismiss any or all of them though their offices can be abolished only by authorization of Congress. President William Howard Taft once remarked that "The Cabinet is a mere creation of the President's will. . . . If the President desired to dispense with it, he could do so." Legally and constitutionally, the president could dispense with the cabinet altogether but it is doubtful if any president would attempt to do so and thus destroy a custom which is almost as old as the Constitution itself. President Jackson for a time suspended cabinet meetings because of discord among its members. But, in 1831, he got rid of all but one of the cabinet through resignations or virtual dismissals and appointed new department heads after which cabinet meetings were resumed. This cabinet upheaval created considerable popular excitement and for months it was a subject for heated public discussion and controversy.

While the cabinet meetings were suspended and, for that matter, throughout his whole administration, President Jackson relied largely on informal advice secured from a group of men sneeringly referred to by enemies of the president as the "Lower Cabinet" or the "Kitchen Cabinet." Some of those from whom he thus received advice informally were members of the regular cabinet for a time. These included Martin Van Buren, John H. Eaton, and William T. Barry. Others, such as Amos Kendall and William B. Lewis, were given subordinate positions in the government at Washington in order that they might be at hand to advise the president. Francis Preston Blair, Sr., editor of the *Washington Globe*, the "official organ" of the administration, was an important member of the "Kitchen Cabinet."

From all the contemporary criticism and the criticisms found in many histories covering the period, one might judge that President Jackson was guilty of great wrongdoing in thus consulting persons informally. As a matter of fact, he had a perfect right to do so as much as he wished. It was just as constitutional for him to have a so-called "Kitchen Cabinet" as for him to meet with the regular cabinet. Later presidents have also had their informal advisers. Thus, President Theodore Roosevelt had a so-called "Tennis Court Cabinet," a group of men with whom he frequently played tennis and with whom he consulted on various matters. Similarly, President Woodrow Wilson leaned heavily on Colonel Edward M. House who had no official connection with the government. There is no reason why the president should not seek advice from anyone whom he chooses to consult.

INFLUENCE OF TRADITION ON FOREIGN RELATIONS

By custom, the president has been left to carry on the foreign relations of the United States without consulting the Senate except when its approval is required for a treaty. As has been explained, the executive's powers in dealing with other countries are very extensive. He may recognize new governments and he may so conduct affairs as to bring the nation to the verge of war.

But in one important respect, tradition limits the president from proceeding as he pleases and that is in the matter of forming alliances with other nations. During the whole period since the Declaration of Independence in 1776, the United States has been involved in only one treaty of alliance. That was the French alliance formed in 1778. This alliance proved of great benefit to the Americans during the last years of the War for Independence but the experience following the war was not so pleasant. In 1793, following the revolution whereby they destroyed their monarchial form of government, the French sent Citizen Genet to this country to seek aid in a war which had broken out between France and Great Britain. President Washington, however, decided that it would be disastrous for the United States to enter the war so, on the advice of the cabinet, he issued a proclamation of neutrality.

This irritated the French greatly, and their anger was intensified by the Jay Treaty negotiated by this country with Great Britain in 1794–1795. To the French, it appeared that this treaty favored the British and ignored French rights under the treaty of alliance of 1778. Matters went from bad to worse until President John Adams broke off all diplomatic relations with France. The "Naval War" with that country broke out in 1798, without a declaration of war, and continued until 1800 when Napoleon came into power in France as First Consul. He negotiated a convention with the United States whereby this nation was released from the treaty of alliance. The unsatisfactory experience which had grown out of this French alliance did much to fix the tradition of no entangling alliances.

Of great influence, also, in developing the no alliance tradition were the words of Presidents Washington and Jefferson. In his "Farewell Address" in 1796, the former said, in part:

"The great rule of conduct for us, in regard to foreign Nations, is, in extending our commercial relations to have with them as little *Political* connection as possible. . . . So far as we have already formed engagements, let them be fulfilled with perfect good faith. . . . Here let us stop. . . .

"Europe has a set of primary interests, which to us have none, or a very remote relation. . . . Hence she must be engaged in frequent controversies, the causes of which are essentially foreign to our concerns. . . . Hence therefore it must be unwise in us to implicate ourselves, by artificial ties in the ordinary vicissitudes of her politics, or the ordinary combinations and collusions of her friendships, or enmities.

"Our detached and distant situation invites and enables us to pursue a different course. . . .

"Why forego the advantages of so peculiar a situation? Why quit our own to stand upon foreign ground? Why, by interweaving our destiny with that of any part of Europe entangle our peace and prosperity in the toils of European ambitions, rivalship, interest, humor, or caprice?

"It is our true policy to steer clear of permanent alliances with any portion of the foreign world, so far, I mean, as we are now at liberty to do it; for let me not be understood as capable of patronizing infidelity to existing engagements. . . .

"Taking care always to keep ourselves, by suitable establishments, on a respectably defensive posture, we may safely trust to temporary alliances for extraordinary emergencies."

This quotation indicates that President Washington was not opposed to all alliances but merely to permanent alliances. His views have been frequently misquoted in recent years, particularly by some of those who have sought to keep the United States out of the League of Nations and even out of the Permanent Court of International Justice on the ground that joining the League or adhering to the Court would be equivalent to entering entangling alliances.

President Jefferson went further than Washington for, in his first inaugural message in 1801, he declared that one of the fundamental principles which would govern his administration was "peace, commerce, and honest friendship with all nations, entangling alliances with none."

All subsequent presidents have followed Jefferson's policy of no entangling alliances; at least, no international agreement has been entered into by this country which has been admitted to be an alliance. Even during the World War, when the conduct of the war was under the general direction of the Supreme Council representing the nations opposed to Germany and when the American Expeditionary Force in France under General John J. Pershing was placed under the supreme command of the French Marshal Foch, the United States would not admit that it was in an alliance. The nations joined in the war against Germany and her allies were always officially referred to as "The Allied and Associated Nations"—the United States being the "Associated" nation while the rest were formally allied. In spite of the technical distinction this country was, for all practical purposes, allied with Great Britain and the other members of the British Empire, France, Italy, and the other avowed allies.

Another traditional influence on the foreign relations of the United States is the Monroe Doctrine. Though this doctrine has not been incorporated in either the Constitution, the laws or the treaties of this country, it has come to have a constitutional effect. The doctrine was first enunciated in 1823 by President James Monroe in his regular message to Congress. It appears that the drafting of the doctrine was chiefly the work of Secretary of State John Q. Adams but, as President Monroe, in the final analysis, was responsible for it, it properly bears his name.

The doctrine was called forth by several circumstances. Most of the Spanish colonies in the western hemisphere had revolted from Spain and their independence had been recognized by the United States. However, the so-called "Holy Alliance," composed of the leading European nations with the exception of Great Britain, was planning to aid Spain in restoring her lost colonies. Then, too, Russia was scheming to make settlements on the coast of what is now the state of California and was otherwise pursuing an aggressive policy in the far northwest.

CUSTOM AND TRADITION 433

Referring to the Russian encroachments, President Monroe stated "that the American continents, by the free and independent condition which they have assumed and maintain, are henceforth not to be considered as subjects for future colonization by any European powers." This statement has proved to be the most important part of the doctrine. Successive presidents have accepted it as their guide and have made their own interpretations of it. It was applied at the close of the American Civil War to force the French out of Mexico after they had conquered that country and set up a puppet government. Again, it was given practical application during President Cleveland's second administration when the Venezuelan boundary dispute was raging. The British, by agreeing to arbitrate the dispute, recognized the validity of the doctrine as did the American Congress by supporting the president in his determination to force arbitration.

Likewise, this part of the doctrine has been the chief basis for the establishment of United States protectorates in the Caribbean Sea area. To prevent intervention or the seizure of territories by European powers because of political disturbances in, or failure to pay obligations by, various small Latin American countries, the United States has itself intervened to restore order and financial stability. It is of interest to note that the non-colonization feature of the Monroe Doctrine has been extended to Asiatic as well as to European powers. Specifically, Japan has been prevented from colonizing or establishing a naval base in any part of the region south of the United States.

The doctrine also contained a pledge of non-interference in European wars, stating, "In the wars of the European powers in matters relating to themselves we have never taken any part, nor does it comport with our policy to do so." Any attempt to extend the European political system to any portion of the western hemisphere, it was further declared, would be considered "as dangerous to our peace and safety." Then followed a pledge that, "With the existing colonies or dependencies of any European power we have not interfered and shall not interfere." The final portion of the Monroe Doctrine was designed to protect the independence of the newly created republics in the Americas. It reads as follows:

"But with the governments who have declared their independence and maintained it, and whose independence we have, on great consideration and on just principles, acknowledged, we could not view any interposition for the purpose of oppressing them, or controlling in any other manner their destiny, by any European power in any other light than as the manifestation of an unfriendly disposition towards the United States."

OTHER TRADITIONS AFFECTING THE PRESIDENT

A number of other important traditions have developed in the course of American history affecting the powers and actions of the president. For instance, the Constitution states that the president shall make appointments "with the advice and consent of the Senate." In practice this has come to mean merely "with the consent of the Senate." However, there has developed a custom known as "Senatorial Courtesy" whereby the president is expected to consult one or preferably both of the senators from a state in which an office about to be filled is located. In case such consultation has not taken place and the approval of the senator or senators been secured, the Senate, acting under the custom of senatorial courtesy, will generally refuse to confirm the president's appointee. The custom is not always followed, particularly when there is no senator from the state belonging to the same party as the president.

There are certain offices, however, which tradition decrees the president shall be free to fill as he pleases. This tradition applies particularly to the department heads who are to constitute the president's cabinet. Only twice since the Civil War has the Senate rejected a president's appointee for a cabinet position. One was President Johnson's appointee to the office of attorney-general in 1868, and by a coincidence, the other was President Coolidge's appointee to the same office in 1925.

It has been the custom for the president, ever since George Washington assumed the office, to make removals as he saw fit, though the matter was not referred to in the Constitution. This custom was tenaciously clung to in spite of attempts on the part of Congress to limit the freedom of the chief executive in the matter. The custom was finally fixed once and for all by a Supreme Court decision in 1926.

Another tradition which limits the chief executive is that he shall not take the field in time of war as the active commander of the armed forces of the United States. The Constitution designates the president as the commander-in-chief of the army and navy but, in practice, he exercises merely a general directive power. Most of his power is delegated by him to the secretaries of the War and Navy Departments who, in turn, rely greatly on the trained officers of the army and the navy. It is an historical fact that no president has undertaken to assume the active command of the armed forces in time of war. None of the war presidents has been qualified to do so. But even if a military man should happen to be in the presidential office during a period of war, he would not be likely to break the established tradition by undertaking active field service. If the tradition were not sufficient to prevent him from doing so, his multitudinous duties as chief executive would serve to keep him at the national capital.

Until 1918, there was a tradition that the president should not leave the country during his term in office. President Wilson broke the tradition when he decided to head the American delegation to the Peace Conference at Versailles, following the armistice which ended the World War fighting. In 1923, President Harding left the country to visit Alaska while, in 1928, President Coolidge went to Havana, Cuba, to address the Pan-American Conference which was in session there.

Yet another custom relating to the president is the delivery of an inaugural address at the beginning of the presidential term. President Washington established the precedent and every president has followed the example. The inaugural address, delivered personally by the incoming president, has come, by custom, to be as integral a part of the inauguration ceremony as the taking of the presidential oath which is prescribed by the Constitution.

The presentation of messages by the president to Congress at the opening of its sessions is also the result of custom. The Constitution merely states that "He shall from time to time give to the Congress information of the state of the Union, and recommend to their consideration such measures as he shall judge necessary and expedient." Custom has decreed that such information and recommendations shall be presented at the beginning of the annual or special sessions of Congress. Of course, the president may also send special messages to Congress at any time after its sessions have begun. The first two presidents delivered their messages orally, in person, but President Jefferson refused to follow the precedent and sent his messages in writing. All succeeding presidents, until 1913, followed his example, thus apparently establishing the custom. However, President Wilson chose to break the long established precedent by delivering his more important messages through a personal address before a joint session of Congress. President Harding followed the example of his predecessor but President Coolidge, in 1924, reverted to the old custom of sending written messages to Congress.

CONGRESSIONAL COMMITTEES

Herbert W. Horwill, an Englishman, who has written the most complete account of the effects of custom and traditions in his interesting book, *The Usages of the American Constitution*, takes the position that congressional committees should not be regarded as one of those usages. However, since these committees represent a definite expansion of the form of the national legislature beyond what is provided for by the Constitution, there seems no logical reason for ignoring them. Since these committees have already been considered in connection with "The Creation and Growth of Governmental Agencies," it is not necessary to consider them at length here. Let it suffice to say that the custom has developed in both houses of Congress of referring all proposed legislation to standing or special committees. These committees have become so important that they practically determine what measures shall or shall not be enacted into legislation. Thus, by custom, the congressional committees have become almost more important than the Congress described in the Constitution, formally divided into a Senate and a House of Representatives. Should one ignore this custom of relying on congressional committees, a very incomplete idea would be obtained of the actual process whereby the national laws are enacted.

THE PARTY CAUCUS

Since the members of the two houses of Congress are, in reality, representatives of political parties, it is inevitable that they should seek to promote the programs of their respective parties. In order to unify the actions of the party members, there has developed the custom of holding what is called the party caucus. Thus, before the organization of a new Congress, the members of each house assemble in the caucus of their own party to determine general policies, to decide on committee memberships, and to select party candidates for the various positions to be filled in the house in question, such as clerkships. An important function of each party caucus in the House of Representatives is to select a candidate for speaker of the House.

During the sessions of Congress, it is customary to hold a party caucus when it seems necessary to secure unified action on some measure. A good illustration of such use of the caucus was afforded by that held by the Democratic members of the House of Representatives in February, 1933 for the purpose of securing united action in favor of the proposed prohibition repeal amendment. While the caucus did not succeed in forcing all the Democratic members to vote for the measure, enough votes were assured to make the vote in the House on February 20th a mere formality. In this case the caucus was felt to be necessary because the House, at the beginning of its session, had rejected a similar proposal.

Generally speaking, a party member is bound to vote in accordance with the decision of the majority of the caucus. Refusal to do so may result in punishment such as deprivation of important committee assignments or loss of influence in connection with the filling of offices. A member may be excused from supporting a caucus measure if he is bound by a definite pledge to his constituents or if the party organization in his home district or state has taken action contrary to that of the caucus. On the other hand, the caucus serves as a device to shield members who wish to vote contrary to the known wishes of many of their constituents. They can excuse their vote by saying that they were bound by the caucus.

The importance of the party caucus varies from time to time

but the tendency in recent years has been in the direction of increasing importance.

Since the World War there has developed an interesting device for promoting legislation of a non-partisan nature for the relief of agriculture. Senators and representatives, without distinction as to parties, met together to decide on ways and means to promote the type of legislation which they desired for the benefit of the agricultural interests. This non-partisan group, which first made its appearance in 1921, has been popularly referred to as the "Farm Bloc." It, or any similar group of senators and representatives promoting any kind of legislation, might appropriately be referred to as the "non-partisan caucus."

OTHER TRADITIONS AFFECTING CONGRESS

A number of other customs of importance have developed in connection with the House of Representatives and the Senate. For example, there is the custom of electing a leader of the majority party as the speaker of the House. The Constitution merely states that "The House of Representatives shall choose their Speaker and other officers," leaving the House absolute freedom of choice in the matter. The House would not have to choose one of its own members to fill the position but could, if it wished, select someone else to act merely as presiding officer. However, custom has made the speaker not only a presiding officer but a partisan leader as well. As the majority party leader he exerts powerful influence on all actions taken by the House.

Another custom requires that representatives shall reside in the district from which they are chosen. There is no such requirement in the Constitution, however. Theoretically, members of the House of Representatives could be chosen from any part of a state to represent a certain district as is the custom in England in the election of members of the House of Commons.

The Constitution gives to the House of Representatives the exclusive power to initiate financial bills. The Senate, however, is given the power to amend such bills. Custom has so expanded the Senate's power to amend as to give that body what is virtually the power to determine what the legislation shall be.

Examples of this are not hard to find. As an illustration, the tariff bill passed by the House of Representatives in 1894 was so changed by the Senate as to be hardly recognizable. Altogether, the Senate added six hundred and thirty-four amendments to the House bill, changing its character almost entirely.

Mention should also be made of the custom which prevails in both houses of Congress of adding "riders" to bills which are rather certain to secure presidential approval. The rider or amendment may have no relation to the bill to which it is attached but is added merely because it is a convenient way to secure the enactment of a measure which would be apt to fail if an attempt were made to enact it separately.

The custom of holding public sessions of the two houses of Congress should also be referred to. Though the sessions of the Continental and Confederation congresses had been closed to the public, the first House of Representatives to meet in 1789 established the precedent of opening its sessions to the public. Not until 1793 did the Senate open its doors to the public. Even after that the Senate often held secret or "executive" sessions to consider treaties or presidential appointments. The proceedings of these executive sessions are not published until many years later. For instance, the proceedings of the executive sessions of the Senate during the presidency of Andrew Jackson were not published until about a half century later. The Senate does not always hold secret sessions when dealing with treaties or appointments, however. A new precedent was set when it held open sessions in 1919 and 1920 to consider the Versailles treaty.

THE COURTS AND THE CONSTITUTIONALITY OF LAWS

The most important power enjoyed by the federal courts is to pass on the constitutionality of laws. Yet there is nothing in the Constitution or the laws conferring on them this power. The power was assumed by the Supreme Court under the leadership of Chief Justice John Marshall in 1803 in the famous case of *Marbury vs. Madison*. Ever since, the federal courts have continued to pass on the constitutionality of laws without any effective opposition being made to the procedure. It should be noticed, however, that the Supreme Court will not give an opinion on a law until a test case is brought before it. This custom of not rendering advisory opinions was established shortly after the Supreme Court was first set up.

There are, nevertheless, occasions when the Supreme Court states opinions which have no direct relation to the case being decided. Thus, in 1857, in the Dred Scott case, the court was merely called upon to decide whether or not the negro, Dred Scott, was a citizen entitled to institute a suit in the courts. The majority decision was in the negative and nothing further was required of the court. In spite of this, the majority decision proceeded to declare that the Missouri Compromise, passed in 1820 and repealed in 1854, had never been constitutional as slaves were property and, as such, could be taken anywhere in the United States. This addition to the basic decision in the case was what is known as an "obiter dictum." The custom of issuing court opinions in the form of obiter dicta has been of considerable influence in American history.

No further discussion of custom in connection with the federal courts is needed here as the matter has been discussed more fully in connection with "Judicial Interpretation of the Constitution."

SELECTED REFERENCES

Adams, R. G., *A History of the Foreign Policy of the United States*, pp. 95–111, 164–179, 356–386.

Beard, C. A., *American Government and Politics* (Fourth edition), pp. 125–188.

Brooks, R. C., *Political Parties and Electoral Problems*, pp. 47–424.

Bruce, H. R., *American Parties and Politics*, pp. 3–307.

Fish, C. R., *American Diplomacy* (Third edition), pp. 94–107, 126–139, 203–219.

Holcombe, A. N., *The Political Parties of To-day*, pp. 14–38.

Horwill, H. W., *The Usages of the American Constitution*, pp. 26–212.

Latané, J. H., *A History of American Foreign Policy*, pp. 1–22, 72–100, 169–196, 686–708.

Munro, W. B., *The Makers of the Unwritten Constitution*, pp. 1–147.

Ogg, F. A., and Ray, P. O., *Introduction to American Government* (Third edition), pp. 208–233, 615–643.

Orth, S. P., and Cushman, R. E., *American National Government*, pp. 165–242, 305–316.

Sait, E. M., *American Parties and Elections*, pp. 141–312, 377–594.

Schlesinger, A. M., *New Viewpoints in American History*, pp. 266–287.
Tiedeman, C. G., *The Unwritten Constitution of the United States*, pp. 46–53.
Wilson, Woodrow, *Constitutional Government in the United States*, pp. 198–222.
Woodburn, J. A., *Political Parties and Party Problems in the United States* (Third edition), pp. 3–370.

Chapter Eighteen

STATE AND FEDERAL RELATIONS

THE Constitution of the United States not only outlines the form and powers of the national government but it also imposes definite limitations on the states. Furthermore, through the tenth amendment, it specifically reserves to the states or to the people "The powers not delegated to the United States by the Constitution, nor prohibited by it to the States." However, there has been a very noticeable tendency on the part of the federal government to encroach on powers reserved to the states. Such encroachment has proceeded with considerable rapidity since the opening of the twentieth century. Through federal subsidies, through the activities of federal administrative agencies, and through judicial interpretation of the due process clause of the fourteenth amendment, the federal government has reduced the states to a subordinate position. The tendency, in fact, has been to break down the dual system of government established by the Constitution and substitute for it a centralized system with the chief authority emanating from Washington, D. C.

It is obvious that the Constitution would not have been ratified and put into operation if this tendency towards centralization at the expense of state sovereignty had been foreseen. As it was, fears were expressed in various of the ratifying conventions that the federal government would usurp powers belonging to the states. It was believed, however, that the tenth amendment would prevent such usurpation. History proves that this belief was not well grounded.

DUAL GOVERNMENT IN THE UNITED STATES

A fundamental weakness of the government under the Articles of Confederation was that it did not have enough power because the states had retained too much power for themselves.

The new Constitution undertook to establish a more satisfactory dual system of government in which the powers would be more equitably distributed between the federal government and the state governments. Thus, certain definite and exclusive powers were delegated to the federal government, such as the power to regulate foreign and interstate commerce, to coin money, to establish a postal system, to punish piracies and felonies committed on the high seas, to declare war, to raise and support armies, and to provide and maintain a navy.

Through the tenth amendment it was made clear that the powers not delegated to the federal government or prohibited to the states should be reserved to the states. Such powers would include the right of each state to regulate the conduct and activities of the people within the boundaries of the state.

In certain matters, the Constitution, at least by implication, grants to the federal and state governments concurrent powers. Both, for instance, may levy and collect taxes and both may borrow money. Here may be discerned one of the features of dual government which is most susceptible to criticism. The system of taxation which had developed in this country forces the people to pay their money directly into both the federal and state treasuries, not to mention the treasuries of the local governments. Similarly, the people are subject in many matters to regulation, control, and even punishment by the federal, state, and local authorities. As an example, consider the matter of meat inspection. First there is federal inspection, then state inspection, and in many cases inspection by local governments. Of course, it is desirable and necessary for the welfare of the people that meat should be inspected and approved before it is offered for sale but why the necessity of two or three different agencies of inspection? Such duplication, often unnecessary and always an expense to the taxpayers, has grown out of the application of the concurrent powers of the federal and state governments.

Certain powers are prohibited by the Constitution to the federal government. Thus it is prohibited from suspending the writ of habeas corpus "unless when in cases of rebellion or invasion the public safety may require it." Neither may the federal government impose duties on articles exported from any states; levy taxes, duties, or imposts which are not uniform throughout the United States; give preference to the commerce of one state over the commerce of another; force vessels from one state "to enter, clear, or pay duties in another"; make appropriations for the army for more than two years; pay out any money from the treasury except "in consequence of appropriations made by law"; nor levy direct taxes except on the states in proportion to their population. In addition to these prohibitions there was the provision that Congress could not prohibit the importation of slaves until 1808, nor tax imported slaves more than ten dollars each. This prohibition has been obsolete since 1808 when the importation of slaves was definitely prohibited by law.

Besides the prohibitions imposed on the federal government by the original Constitution, other prohibitions are contained in the amendments making up the bill of rights. These have been discussed in connection with the "Expansion of the Constitution Through Amendment."

Some powers are prohibited to both the state and federal governments. Neither may pass bills of attainder or ex-post-facto laws, nor may either grant any title of nobility. The thirteenth amendment prohibits the federal government, the states, and individuals from setting up a system of slavery or involuntary servitude. The fifteenth and nineteenth amendments limit both the federal and state governments in the matter of prescribing qualifications for voters.

CONSTITUTIONAL LIMITATIONS ON THE STATES

There are also a number of powers which the Constitution prohibits the states alone from exercising. In the first place, no state may "enter into any treaty, alliance, or confederation." The purpose of this definite prohibition was to centralize the conduct of foreign affairs in the hands of the federal government and so avoid confusion such as existed during the Confederation period. Obviously, if states were allowed to form alliances and confederations, the union would soon be broken up. The only attempt since 1789 to form a confederation came in 1861 when eleven states seceded from the union and formed what they called the Confederate States of America. After four years of Civil War, this attempt to form a confederation contrary to the Constitution was defeated.

It should be pointed out that individual states may, with the consent of Congress, enter into agreements or compacts with other states or foreign powers. This provision, so far as it applies to foreign powers, has proved to be of no importance but a number of compacts between states have been made with the consent of Congress. Over forty such compacts, in fact, have been entered into. An illustration of such an interstate compact was that entered into by a number of western states which paved the way for the Boulder Canyon Project Act of 1928 under which the mammoth Hoover Dam is being constructed.

Next in the Constitution is the provision prohibiting any state from granting letters of marque and reprisal, that is, commissioning privateers to prey on the commerce of another country. If states had been allowed to send out privateers it would have been equivalent to giving them power to declare war since privateering could be carried on only in time of war. Since the time of the American Civil War, privateering has been outlawed by international agreement so the power granted to the federal government exclusively to grant letters of marque and reprisal means nothing.

No state, declares the Constitution, may "emit bills of credit." This was interpreted by the Supreme Court in the case of *Craig vs. Missouri*, decided in 1830, to mean that a state cannot issue bonds or other evidences of indebtedness in small denomination with the intent of circulating them as money. Seven years later, the court ruled, in the case of *Briscoe vs. Bank of Kentucky*, that paper money issued by banks chartered by states should not be considered as bills of credit, the issue of which is prohibited to the states. At present, no state bank bills are in circulation though they are perfectly legal. This is to be explained by the fact that Congress, in 1865, through an amendment to the national banking act passed two years earlier, placed a tax of ten percent on all issues of such paper money. In connection with the consideration of bills of credit, it should be mentioned that no state may "make anything but gold or silver coin a tender in payment of debts." This provision was designed to prevent the enactment of state laws such as existed during the Confederation period, in Rhode Island, for example, whereby creditors, merchants, and others were required to accept the depreciated "fiat" paper money of the state in payment of debts, payment for goods, and so on.

The Constitution specifically declares that no state shall pass any "law impairing the obligation of contracts." The full meaning of this limitation was brought out in the famous Dartmouth College case decided by the Supreme Court in 1819 and in other decisions.

"No State," the Constitution further declares, "shall, without the consent of the Congress, lay any imposts or duties on imports or exports, except what may be absolutely necessary for executing its inspection laws: and the net produce of all duties and imposts, laid by any State on imports or exports, shall be for the use of the Treasury of the United States; and all such laws shall be subject to the revision and control of the Congress." Nor may any state impose tonnage duties without the consent of Congress. These prohibitions on the states insure to the federal government the exclusive power to regulate and control foreign and interstate commerce and, incidentally, to monopolize the revenues secured from import duties and tonnage taxes which it alone has unlimited power to impose.

The states are also definitely prohibited from keeping "troops, or ships of war in time of peace." This has been interpreted to mean that the states cannot maintain standing armies or permanent navies. It does not prohibit the states from training their militia. Nor may a state "engage in war, unless actually invaded, or in such imminent danger as will not admit of delay." These provisions were intended to prevent the states from waging war on their own account. The declaration of war as well as the conduct of a war are in the hands of the federal government exclusively. There is nothing in the Constitution, however, to prevent a state from giving aid to the federal government in time of war. In this connection, it is of interest to note that the state of California was still, in 1933, seeking to collect from the federal government a sum of several million dollars for expenses incurred during the Civil War.

Brief mention should also be made of the important limitations placed on the states by the fourteenth amendment. These limitations, as stated in the first section of that amendment are: "No State shall make or enforce any law which shall abridge the privileges or immunities of citizens of the United States; nor shall any State deprive any person of life, liberty, or property, without due process of law; nor deny to any person within its jurisdiction the equal protection of the laws."

In addition to the direct prohibitions imposed on the states by the Constitution, there are important indirect or implied limitations as well. One of these limitations is that a state may not interfere in any way with the exercise of the functions of the federal government or with the administration of the national laws. Attempts have been made by the states to interfere but the Supreme Court has emphatically denied their right to do so. Some states, as will be pointed out later in this discussion, have gone so far as to nullify or attempt to nullify federal laws.

A state may not exercise its police or judicial power on government property unless the consent of the federal authorities is first obtained. Thus, early in 1933, a session of one of the superior courts of Los Angeles County was held at Sawtelle, California, in the soldiers' home, to try a case involving a veteran confined in the hospital there. This was done with the consent of the Veterans' Administration officials, secured in advance.

Likewise, a state may not exercise its right of eminent domain in respect to federal property, including buildings, land, forts, navy yards, and so on. For instance, a state could not build a road through a federal military reservation or any other land owned by the federal government without the consent of the proper federal officials, given voluntarily.

The famous Supreme Court decision in the case of *McCulloch vs. Maryland* in 1819, made it clear that states could not tax any agency of the federal government. Later Supreme Court decisions have made it clear that exemption from state taxes extends to federal property, salaries paid by the federal government to its officials and employees whether in the civil or the armed service, and to federal bonds.

INTERSTATE RELATIONS

Included in Article IV of the original Constitution are a number of provisions designed to secure friendly relations between the states by imposing on them certain definite obligations. Obviously, these provisions were designed to prevent some of the bad feeling which existed between the states during the Confederation period.

Thus, in the first section of this article it is stated: "Full faith and credit shall be given in each State to the public acts, records, and judicial proceedings of every other State. And the Congress may by general laws prescribe the manner in which such acts, records and proceedings shall be proved, and the effect thereof." The importance of this provision is very apparent. It means, for example, that legal papers, such as deeds, mortgages, wills, and contracts, properly executed in one state, shall not be questioned in any other state.

A marriage legally performed in accordance with the laws of one state cannot be ruled invalid by another state. For instance, a California couple, unwilling to comply with the state law requiring a three day legal notification period before a marriage license will be issued, may and do cross the state line into Arizona where there is no such requirement, have a marriage ceremony performed, and return to California where they must be legally recognized as man and wife.

Similarly, divorces granted by the courts of one state must be recognized in all other states. However, it must be established that the court granting the divorce had proper jurisdiction in the case. For instance, if a person who is a resident of New York, where a divorce may be secured only on the ground of adultery, desires an easier method of securing a divorce, he or she may go to Nevada, remain for six weeks in order to establish residence and so give the Nevada courts jurisdiction, and obtain a divorce on any one of eight grounds. While such divorces are generally recognized in other states they may be questioned or even be declared invalid if it is shown that the residence established in another state was not bona fide but was merely for the purpose of evading the laws of the state in which the party was a resident before securing the divorce.

One of the most noticeable characteristics of the people of the United States is their mobility. An examination of the census reports indicate that this has always been a national trait for they reveal that in every state, at every census period, were many people from other states. This mobility has been made possible by the provision in Article IV of the Constitution which states that "The citizens of each State shall be entitled to all privileges and immunities of citizens in the several States." This has made it possible for people to move freely from one state to another without interference. On coming into one state from another they have not been burdened with special discriminatory restrictions. Instead, they have been able to come and go with the same freedom as citizens of the state entered. Thus, a person from California may travel to New York and back with complete freedom. He may enter into contracts or transact any other legal business in any of the states through which he passes on the same basis as citizens of that state. However, if he wishes to become a citizen of another state he must comply with its legal qualifications before becoming eligible to vote or hold office.

Next appears the extradition provision of the Constitution which states that "a person charged in any State with treason, felony, or other crime, who shall flee from justice, and be found in another State, shall on demand of the executive authority of the State from which he fled, be delivered up, to be removed to the State having jurisdiction of the crime." While this provision appears to require the delivery of the fugitive from justice to the state from which he has fled, there is no way of forcing a state governor to grant an extradition request from the governor of another state. In 1861, the Supreme Court ruled that extradition could not be enforced through the federal courts.

The third section of Article IV of the Constitution states that "No person held to service or labor in one State, under the laws thereof, escaping into another, shall, in consequence of any law or regulation therein, be discharged from such service or labor, but shall be delivered up on claim of the party to whom such service or labor may be due." It was on this provision that the Fugitive Slave Acts of 1793 and 1850 were based. Since the thirteenth amendment was added to the Constitution this section has been obsolete insofar as it pertained to slaves.

CONSTITUTIONAL GUARANTEES TO THE STATES

In the third and fourth sections of Article IV are also contained a number of important guarantees to the states. First, following the statement that Congress may admit new states to the union, is the guarantee that "no new State shall be formed or erected within the jurisdiction of any other State; nor any State be formed by the junction of two or more States, or parts of States, without the consent of the legislatures of the States concerned as well as of the Congress."

Another provision declares that "The United States shall guarantee to every State in this Union a republican form of government." Congress has it within its power to see that a state, at the time of its admission to the union, has made provision for a republican form of government. After a state has once become a member of the union it is also, according to the Supreme Court, the function of Congress to determine whether changes in the government of a state constitute a departure from the "republican form." This has been ruled to be a political question with which the Supreme Court will not deal.

Likewise, through the Constitution, the United States guarantees to protect each state against invasion by an enemy. This does not mean that the federal government must prevent such invasion for that may be impossible as was demonstrated during the War of 1812 when New York and Louisiana, for example, were invaded by British troops. In practice the provision means that the federal government will use its military and naval forces in attempts to prevent the invasion of any state and will also use its forces to drive out the invaders should they succeed in entering a state.

The Constitution also guarantees that the United States government will protect each state "against domestic violence" if the state legislature, or the state executive "when the legislature cannot be convened," requests such protection. If violence within a state threatens federal property or the exercise of a federal function, the president may order federal troops to deal with the disorder without a request from a state government or even in spite of the expressed wish of the state governor that such action should not be taken. Thus, President Cleveland did much to break the Pullman strike of 1894 by ordering federal troops to Chicago to guard trains carrying United States mail. The troops were used in spite of objections of the governor of Illinois.

Among the other guarantees to the states may be mentioned that which insures the equality of all the states in the United States Senate; that which gives to the states a part in the process of amending the Constitution, and, finally, that which is contained in the eleventh amendment, granting to each state immunity from suits in the federal courts by citizens of another state or of a foreign country.

CONTROL OF STATE REPRESENTATION IN CONGRESS

Ostensibly each state has the right to send any properly qualified citizens that it pleases to represent it in the federal House of Representatives and in the Senate. In practice, however, this right is limited by the constitutional powers granted to the House and to the Senate to "be the judge of the elections, returns and qualifications of its own members," and to expel members by a two-thirds vote. On occasion, this power has been used by the House or the Senate to deprive states of their freedom of choice and even to deprive them temporarily of their full representation in Congress. Thus, for example, Frank L. Smith of Illinois and William S. Vare of Pennsylvania, who were elected to the United States Senate in 1926, were excluded from that body on the ground that money had been improperly used to secure their election. This procedure was attacked without result as a violation of state rights.

INFLUENCE OF FEDERAL SUBSIDIES ON THE STATES

One of the most effective methods whereby the federal government has been able to influence and even to control state action has been through the use of subsidies. The practice of granting subsidies to the states antedates the Constitution for it was in 1785 that the Confederation Congress passed its famous land ordinance which set aside one section in each township for the support of schools. Through the Morrill Act of 1862, Congress granted to each state a portion of the public domain, the proceeds of which were to be used to support institutions of higher learning which offered instruction in the mechanical arts, in agriculture, and in military science and tactics. After the bureau of education in the Department of the Interior was created, it was charged with the administration of the act and its amendments and the secretary of the interior was authorized to deny to any state its share unless it complied with the conditions imposed by Congress.

Through the Department of Agriculture and the subsidies which it administers, the federal government in large measure regulates agricultural education and experimentation in the states. Should any state fail to comply with the federal regulations it would find its subsidies withheld.

In 1914, Congress passed the Smith-Lever Act which appropriated money out of the national treasury for the promotion of extension work by the state agricultural colleges and the Department of Agriculture. To secure its share of the money, a state must provide a sum equal to its portion of the federal appropriation and must also comply with the conditions imposed by the law.

This was followed in 1917 by the Smith-Hughes Vocational Education Act which was intended to benefit the urban rather than the rural sections. It granted money to the states for the purpose of aiding them in providing instruction in home economics, in the trades, and in industrial subjects. The act was to be administered by the Federal Board for Vocational Education.

The federal policy of aiding the states in road building was revived in 1916 through the Federal Highway Act. In 1930, a total of $979,592,093 was spent on roads in the United States, of which $155,343,529 came from the federal treasury.

In 1921, Congress passed the Sheppard-Towner Act which granted money to the states to be used in promoting the welfare of mothers and their infants during the period of child birth. The children's bureau of the Department of Labor was charged with the administration of this law.

During the Hoover administration, due largely to the depression which set in during 1929, the federal policy of granting subsidies to the states was greatly extended. The most outstanding example of the extension of the policy may be seen in the establishment in 1932 of the Reconstruction Finance Corporation. The act creating this corporation provided $300,-000,000 to be loaned to the states for relief purposes. This is only one illustration of the tendency on the part of the states to look to the federal government for help in dealing with social and economic problems, the handling of which, it would appear, fall within the category of the powers reserved to the states. In the face of nation-wide distress, however, there has been a growing inclination to ignore academic considerations which have to do with such matters as reserved powers and state rights.

Unquestionably, the subsidies granted by the federal government to the states have proved of great benefit to the people of the states and the nation as a whole. But, in accepting the subsidies, the states have surrendered much of their control over their internal affairs. Gradually, the distinction between the federal and state government has tended to become obliterated. The continuation of the tendency will result in more or less complete centralization of power in the hands of the federal government.

While struggling with the devastating forces of economic depression it cannot be expected that much will be done to halt the tendency; in fact, the effect of the depression, as has been indicated, has been to promote the trend. But as soon as conditions will permit, it might be well for the people to take stock and decide what the future policy shall be. Whether the states should be left to exercise their reserved powers without being interfered with, influenced, or controlled by the federal government is a question that should be answered in the near future.

BEGINNING OF THE "STATE RIGHTS FETISH"

In the early period of the history of the United States, much more stress was placed on state rights than has been the case in recent years. It should not be supposed that the advocacy of state rights has been limited to any one section of the country or to any one group of people. States in all parts of the country and political parties of very diverse views have been devoted to what Professor A. M. Schlesinger calls "The State Rights Fetish." In fact, the advocacy of state rights has, in many cases, been merely a matter of expediency. States or political parties have been prone to raise the cry of state rights when it would serve their purpose to do so. At other times, the same states and parties have been found taking a strong nationalistic stand.

"The State Rights Fetish" really began before the Constitutional Convention, as Professor Schlesinger points out in his stimulating *New Viewpoints in American History*, as follows:

> "The origin of the great controversy is to be found in the Federal Constitutional Convention. In a less direct sense, the state rights question is not to be regarded as an American problem at all, but rather as the inevitable fruit of any attempt to reconcile centralized federative control with local self-government. In this sense, the Revolutionary War may be regarded as a victory for state rights, or colonial self-government, carried to the point of secession; and the Articles of Confederation were a codification of that victory in the guise of a formal constitution under which the separate states became freer of their own central government than they as colonies had desired to be of the British home government. The chief task that confronted the leaders of the Federal Constitutional Convention was, in its essence, the same that the British government had failed to solve a dozen years before: the problem of harmonizing central unified control with state sovereignty."

As has been previously mentioned, objections were made to the Constitution in the state ratifying conventions on the ground that it would bring about the "consolidation" of the states. But this and other objections were overcome and the new instrument of government was ratified and put into effect. But, the new federal government had hardly begun to function before the state rights advocates were making themselves noticeable. Their activity at that time was largely devoted to opposition to the Hamiltonian policy of broad construction of the Constitution. In other words, the first state rights advocates under the Constitution were strict constructionists. They objected to such things as the First Bank of the United States and the assumption of the state revolutionary debts on the ground that the Constitution did not directly authorize them.

The first important formulation of the state rights doctrine, outside of the halls of Congress, appeared in 1798 and 1799 in the form of the famous Kentucky and Virginia resolutions. The former were drafted by Thomas Jefferson and were adopted by the Kentucky legislature while the latter were drawn up by James Madison and were adopted by the Virginia legislature. The purpose of the resolutions was to rally public opinion against the Federalists who had passed through Congress the obnoxious Alien and Sedition Acts.

In the Kentucky resolutions, adopted on November 19, 1798, it was resolved:

"That the several states composing the United States of America are not united on the principle of unlimited submission to their general government; but that, by compact, under the style and title of a Constitution for the United States, and of amendments thereto, they constituted a general government for special purposes, delegated to that government certain definite powers, reserving, each state to itself, the residuary mass of rights to their own self-government; and that whenever the general government assumes undelegated powers, its acts are unauthoritative, void, and of no force."

Each state, it was asserted, *has an equal right to judge for itself, as well of infractions as of the mode and measure of redress.*" In the Kentucky resolutions, adopted on November 22, 1799, it was declared that the individual states not only had "the unquestionable right to judge of the infraction" but, further, *"That a nullification, by those sovereignties, of all unauthorized acts done under color of that instrument* [the Constitution], *is the rightful remedy."*

After Thomas Jefferson had been elected President and the Democratic-Republican party had come into power, an interesting change took place. This party became the broad constructionists while the Federalists became the strict constructionists. The Louisiana Purchase and the Embargo of 1807 could only be justified by taking a broad view of the Constitution. The Federalists opposed both actions as not warranted by the Constitution, though shortly before members of that party had been instrumental in securing congressional action which certainly was not directly authorized by the basic law of the land.

Strong objection was expressed in New England, particularly, to the War of 1812. The climax of the opposition came in the holding of the Hartford Convention in 1814. All five of the New England states were represented in this convention. Just what was discussed in this gathering has never been revealed but it is probable that secession was considered. However, the only action recommended publicly was the addition of seven amendments to the Constitution. The close of the war brought the New England state rights agitation to an abrupt halt.

NULLIFICATION IN SOUTH CAROLINA

Following the War of 1812, the charter of the Second Bank of the United States caused another flare-up of the state rights doctrine. Maryland and Ohio, in particular, asserted their right to tax branches of the bank but, as has been mentioned, the Supreme Court denied their right to do so.

During the early part of the Jackson administration, Georgia effectively nullified a Supreme Court decision favoring the Indians over whom the state had extended its authority.

But the most dramatic expression of state sovereignty came from South Carolina which actually attempted to nullify a federal law. In 1816, John C. Calhoun and other representatives from that state had been among the most active in securing the passage by Congress of what was the first real protective tariff in this nation's history. However, a decade later, Calhoun and others had come to the conclusion that a protective tariff was injurious to the interests of their state, so they decided that it was unconstitutional. In 1827, the South Carolina legislature adopted an "Exposition" (which, it was learned several years later, had been written by Calhoun) declaring that a state had a right to nullify a law which it regarded as unconstitutional.

Because of dissatisfaction with the tariffs of 1828 and 1832, a convention was held in South Carolina and, on November 24,

1832, a nullification ordinance was adopted. Among other things, this ordinance stated:

"We, therefore, the people of the State of South Carolina in Convention assembled, do declare and ordain, and it is hereby declared and ordained, that the several acts and parts of acts of the Congress of the United States, purporting to be laws for the imposing of duties and imposts on the importation of foreign commodities, and now having actual operation and effect within the United States, . . . are unauthorized by the Constitution of the United States, and violate the true meaning and intent thereof, and are null, void, and no law, nor binding upon this State, its officers or citizens; and all promises, contracts, and obligations, made or entered into, or to be made or entered into, with purpose to secure the duties imposed by the said acts, and all judicial proceedings which shall be hereafter had in affirmance thereof, are and shall be held utterly null and void."

This nullification ordinance met with vigorous action on the part of President Jackson. On December 10, 1832, he issued a proclamation to the people of South Carolina urging them not to support the nullification policy of their leaders. Later he sent a special message to Congress asking for authority to use force in dealing with the situation. Congress responded by passing, on March 2, 1833, what was known as the "Force Bill" but which was denounced by the nullifiers as the "Bloody Bill."

Nullification was scheduled to become effective on February 1, 1833, but, before that date, the nullifiers decided to postpone action until Congress should have the opportunity to revise the tariff. Before adjourning, Congress, on March 2, 1833, passed what came to be known as the compromise tariff providing for a gradual reduction of the tariff over a ten year period until it reached a maximum of twenty percent. The nullifiers, influenced by this compromise and by the fact that other states had shown no willingness to support their action, held another convention and rescinded the nullification ordinance. At the same time, as a gesture of defiance, the convention proceeded to nullify the Force Bill.

SECESSION AND COERCION

The passing of the South Carolina nullification crisis did not silence the advocates of state rights. From 1833 until the Civil War, the slavery interests were the chief exponents of state rights but there were instances in which the anti-slavery sections asserted the doctrine of state sovereignty. These occurred at the time of the annexation of Texas and also during the Mexican War, when various northern states took strong stands against the actions of the federal government. After the passage of the Fugitive Slave Act in 1850, a number of northern states passed what were generally known as Personal Liberty Laws for the purpose of obstructing the operation of the act. The supreme court of the state of Wisconsin went so far as to approve the use of the writ of habeas corpus to free an alleged fugitive slave held in custody by a United States marshal. This action, which amounted to nullification of the federal law, was vigorously denounced by the United States Supreme Court in 1859 in the case of *Ableman vs. Booth*. The decision of the Wisconsin court was reversed on the ground that a state court had no authority to interfere with the administration of a federal law.

While the South Carolina nullification ordinance of 1832 had threatened secession if the federal government attempted to coerce the state, it so happened that no actual attempt at secession was made until over a quarter of a century later. As the years passed, the controversy over slavery became more and more acute and the sectional breach between the northern and southern states gradually widened. The anti-slavery interests sought, in particular, to do away with the slave trade in the District of Columbia and to prevent the extension of slavery to the western territories. On the other hand, the slavery interests insisted that they had a right to deal with the question of slavery as they pleased; that it was a state matter and not a question for the federal government to deal with.

Following the Mexican War which added a vast territory to the United States the feeling between the sections grew so bitter that secession was actually considered by a number of southern states. The crisis was temporarily avoided by the Compromise of 1850 but a decade later the threatened secession took place. Angered by the election of Abraham Lincoln, the Republican candidate for the presidency, on a platform calling for the non-extension of slavery, South Carolina called a convention which, on November 7, 1860, adopted an ordinance of secession. It repealed the action of the state convention which, on May 23, 1788, had ratified the Constitution and declared "that the union now subsisting between South Carolina and other States, under the name of the 'United States of America,' is hereby dissolved."

By the time President Lincoln was inaugurated on March 4, 1861, six states had followed the example of South Carolina and the Confederate States of America had been organized under a provisional constitution which carefully safeguarded state rights. The firing on Fort Sumter, at Charleston, South Carolina, by Confederate troops on April 12, 1861, precipitated a Civil War which was destined to last for four years. Three days after the Fort Sumter incident, President Lincoln issued a call for seventy-five thousand militia to suppress the combination of states obstructing the federal laws as this combination was "too powerful to be suppressed by the ordinary course of judicial proceedings, or by the powers vested in the marshals by law."

The President's proclamation went on to say, "I appeal to all loyal citizens to favor, facilitate, and aid this effort to maintain the honor, the integrity, and the existence of our National Union, and the perpetuity of popular government; and to redress wrongs already long enough endured." Thus the President made the preservation of the union the avowed object of the war so far as the federal government was concerned.

This led to the secession of four more states so that, by June 8, 1861, there were eleven seceded states in all: South Carolina, Mississippi, Florida, Alabama, Georgia, Louisiana, Texas, Virginia, Arkansas, North Carolina, and Tennessee.

It is not necessary here to discuss the Civil War. Suffice it to say that the spring of 1865 saw the final defeat of the Confederates and the destruction of the Confederate States of America. After several years all of the seceded states were restored to the union but only after they had complied with the conditions imposed by Congress. The final success of the federal government dealt a death blow to the notion that state rights could be carried to the extreme even of secession from the union. It was hardly necessary for the federal Supreme Court to declare, as it did in 1869, in the case of *Texas vs. White*, that secession was a constitutional impossibility.

THE STATE RIGHTS DOCTRINE SINCE THE CIVIL WAR

Since the close of the Civil War, the expressions of state rights have been mild compared to the period before that war. The tendency, as has been pointed out, has been to minimize state sovereignty while the federal government has steadily become more important. While it is true that the southern states have virtually nullified the fourteenth and fifteenth amendments, at least to the extent of depriving most negroes of the voting privilege, they have accomplished this result chiefly through indirect methods without openly and defiantly proclaiming their intention to nullify.

During the recent period, some use of the state rights doctrine was made in the fight to prevent a national woman suffrage amendment. Both the Democratic and Republican parties avoided taking a stand on the question as long as possible, but in 1916 both declared in favor of woman suffrage through state action. Had it not been for the World War, it is doubtful whether the nineteenth amendment would have been added to the Constitution.

Up to date, the state rights doctrine has been effective in preventing the ratification of the proposed child labor amendment. During the period since national prohibition became effective, much has been heard about the right of states to deal with the liquor question as they may wish. It was interesting to note that, after Congress submitted the prohibition repeal amendment to the states in February, 1933, some of the supporters of the amendment sought to secure congressional action to set up ratifying conventions in the states. In other words, while advocating the amendment in the interest of state rights, they were willing to take from the states what is clearly a reserved power to call their own ratifying conventions. This merely illustrates that advocacy of state rights is largely a matter of expediency rather than of conviction.

If those who profess to be devoted to the doctrine of state

rights are sincere, they will not stop with their attempt to secure the repeal of the prohibition amendment. They will seek to have the federal government withdraw from the states and leave them to exercise their reserved powers as they see fit. What the future of the state rights doctrine will actually be, only time can tell.

SELECTED REFERENCES

Babcock, K. C., *The Rise of American Nationality*, pp. 150–167.
Beard, C. A., *American Government and Politics* (Fourth edition), pp. 442–450.
Beck, J. M., *The Vanishing Rights of the States*, pp. 13–84.
Burgess, J. W., *The Civil War and the Constitution*, Vol. I, pp. 74–137.
Channing, Edward, *History of the United States*, Vol. IV, pp. 211–246; Vol. V, pp. 404–432; Vol. VI, pp. 256–280.
Frankfurter, F., and Landis, J. M., "The Compact Clause of the Constitution—a Study in Interstate Adjustments," *Yale Law Journal*, Vol. XXXIV (May, 1925), pp. 685–758.
Garver, F. H., "The Distribution of Governmental Powers," *The Historical Outlook*, Vol. XVIII (March, 1927), pp. 122–124.
Holcombe, A. N., "The States as Agents of the Nation," *Southwestern Political Science Quarterly*, Vol. I, (March, 1921), pp. 307–327.
Ogg, F. A., and Ray, P. O., *Introduction to American Government* (Third edition), pp. 136–155.
Orth, S. P., and Cushman, R. E., *American National Government*, pp. 703–718.
Schlesinger, A. M., *New Viewpoints in American History*, pp. 220–244.
Tiedeman, C. G., *The Unwritten Constitution of the United States*, pp. 110–128.
Willoughby, W. W., *The American Constitutional System*, pp. 61–189, 263–290.
Wilson, Woodrow, *Constitutional Government in the United States*, pp. 173–197.

Chapter Nineteen

THE CONSTITUTION IN TIME OF WAR

THAT the Constitution was not designed solely to govern the concerns of this nation in time of peace is indicated by the provisions of the document itself. In accord with the idea that even war, upon which depends the very existence of the state, must be conducted in such a way as to preserve the fundamental character of the government and to preserve popular liberties, the Constitution provides for the conduct of war, and for the necessities of a military establishment. Such provisions are necessary if the government under the Constitution is to protect itself against such threats to its existence as internal disorder or foreign aggression.

THE WAR POWERS OF CONGRESS

In the hands of Congress the Constitution places most of the definitely delegated powers in relation to war. Congress is given the power to declare war, and to raise and support armies. Appropriations for the latter purpose are limited to a period of two years. This is in order to prevent the creation of a permanent armed force with a financial independence which would relieve it from responsibility to the people. Congress may also "provide and maintain a navy," and provide for the calling out of the militia of the states to "execute the laws of the Union, suppress insurrections, and repel invasions."

In relation to the militia organization, intended to be trained by the states, Congress is authorized to provide regulations for its organization, arming and disciplining, and for its control while in the service of the United States.

Indirectly related to its powers in the conduct of war are the powers of Congress to levy and collect taxes to "provide for the common Defence," and the power to determine the punishment of treason, defined in the Constitution as levying war against, or adhering to the enemies of, the United States. It must be said, further, that, for the carrying out of these delegated powers, Congress may enact all laws "necessary and proper."

WAR POWERS OF THE PRESIDENT

In contrast to the somewhat numerous powers granted to Congress in the carrying out of war, the sole mention of the president in this respect is to make him the commander-in-chief of the army and navy of the United States, and of the militia when called into the national service. This involves the control of the actual conduct of war. In addition, the control of the president over foreign relations vests in him, in connection with the Senate, the power to make peace, this power not being vested in Congress as a whole. The executive function of the president furthermore makes him the agent for carrying out the powers of Congress in relation to war.

The enumeration of the provisions of the Constitution in relation to war would seem to vest in Congress the chief powers along this line. It may safely be said, however, that actual practice under the Constitution has been decidedly in the direction of the domination by the executive in this respect. In no case has the power of the president been subject to greater expansion than in this. Further, the actual exercise of the war powers by the national government has inevitably involved the limitation of private rights, the exact relation of which to the power of making war has been a major point of controversy during war times. Thus the actual enumeration of the war powers presents a very inadequate picture, when considered in the light of interpretation and practice. A survey of the history of the exercise of the war powers will indicate the interpretations of the Constitution in the face of the actual problems of war times.

DECLARATIONS OF WAR

To Congress is given the power of declaring war. As a matter of fact, however, the actual declaration of war may be unnecessary for the initiation of warlike measures, and in cases where warlike measures are not begun until after the declaration of war, action of Congress along this line is likely to be merely the culmination of a course of foreign policy carried out under the direct control of the president.

The power of the president to defend the United States against foreign aggression without a formal declaration of war by Congress is seen in the case of the war with the Tripolitan pirates, during President Jefferson's administration. In this case Tripoli declared war against the United States due to the failure of this country to pay tribute. President Jefferson, recognizing the need for defensive measures to protect American shipping in the Mediterranean Sea, sent there a naval squadron which engaged the Tripolitan fleet. This was done without a declaration of war by Congress.

In the case of the Civil War, previous to any declaration of war by Congress, President Lincoln ordered a blockade of the southern ports, called for volunteers for the national army, beyond the number authorized by law, and ordered the suspension of the writ of habeas corpus. These acts were supported in a special session of Congress meeting in July, 1861, and the Supreme Court in its decision in the *Prize Cases* upheld the validity of acts of war taken on the initiative of the president, previous to a declaration of war by the Congress.

The nature of war as an incident in foreign relations, together with the control of the president in this sphere, indicate the inevitability of the determination by the president as to whether or not war shall take place. Granting the power of Congress formally to declare war, it is obvious that the power of the president to guide the course of foreign relations gives him the power, within the limits of political accountability, to prevent or to bring on war.

Examples of this in history are not difficult to find. The War of 1812 might easily have begun earlier than it did except for President Jefferson's determination to avoid it if possible, through his control over foreign relations. The war with Mexico, begun in 1846, was the direct result of the manipulation by President Polk of American relations with that power, culminating in armed conflict previous to any declaration of war by Congress. Although, in Congress, this was asserted to be an unconstitutional assumption of power by the president, that body formally recognized the state of war with Mexico. This was in direct contrast to the previous opposition by Congress to such a war.

In the presidential election of 1916 an important factor in the reëlection of President Wilson was the campaign slogan, "He kept us out of war." This was a recognition of the obvious fact that as went the course of foreign relations under executive guidance, so would be determined the question of entry into or avoidance of war. Despite this campaign emphasis upon the executive leadership in keeping the nation out of war, slightly over a month after he came into office for the second time, President Wilson sent his war message to Congress, and that body voted a declaration of war.

This indicates the nature of the direct influence of the executive over a declaration of war by Congress. A declaration of war is a simple legislative act, and may be subject to the same forms of direct presidential control as any other act of Congress. Apart from the political influence of the president upon legislation by Congress, he may also influence it by making recommendations in messages to that body, and by the use of the veto. So largely is Congress dominated in the exercise of its power to declare war by the control of foreign relations by the president, that by the time a declaration of war is imminent, the question of presidential approval of such action is never in doubt. For all practical purposes, a declaration of war, involving the statement of national policy on the question, is the message of the president recommending that Congress adopt a declaration of war.

In the case of the War of 1812, for example, Congress was thoroughly in favor of a war with England, but would not act until President Madison sent his message recommending a declaration of war.

Further examples could be cited to indicate the extent to which the power of Congress to declare war has, in actual practice, come under the entire domination of the executive. In this case the separation of powers between legislature and executive has clearly broken down, to the ultimate advantage of the executive, who has become the policy-determining agent.

THE RAISING OF TROOPS

A further power of Congress, in relation to war, is that of raising and supporting armies, in which it is limited, in making appropriations of money, to a term of not over two years. To a large extent control over the raising of armies has passed into the hands of the president, either through delegation to him by Congress of this power, or through an extra-legal assumption by the president of this function.

In the larger number of cases Congress has delegated to the president powers along this line. This procedure was followed before and during the War of 1812, when general acts of Congress delegated to the president, within certain limits, the power of determining the number of troops to be raised. During the Civil War, however, President Lincoln at first assumed the power of raising troops, without any legal sanction by Congress. His call for volunteers during the early days of the war, previous to the meeting of Congress, was in answer to the necessities of the situation, and not the result of the delegation of this power by Congress.

When Congress did meet in 1861, it authorized President Lincoln to raise troops to a certain number. A law of 1862 gave him the power to enlist volunteers as replacements for regular troops, to any number he desired. A congressional act of 1863, amended in 1864, allowed the president to conscript troops without limitation as to number.

In connection with the Spanish-American War and the World War, Congress authorized the executive to raise troops to an unlimited number to carry on the war. The National Defense Act of 1916 was in a way preparatory to the World War. Among other things, it gave the president the power to draft the units of the national guard into the service of the United States. By the Selective Service Act of May, 1917, the president was given the additional power of drafting as many men into the armed forces as he saw fit, and this power was extended by Congress in 1918. Thus to all intents and purposes the power of raising armies has become an attribute of the executive. Congress has, in practice, lost control over military policy in this respect by executive assumption of the power, and by delegations of control.

The Constitution does not prescribe the method of raising armed forces. Two possibilities exist. Armies may be raised either by voluntary enlistment, or by compulsory draft. The use of conscription in the World War introduced no new idea in this respect. The draft had been used during the Revolutionary War by the colonies. James Monroe, the secretary of war during the War of 1812, had suggested its use by Congress, but it was then opposed as unconstitutional.

During the Civil War, conscription was introduced by President Lincoln in connection with an act of July, 1862, for the calling out of the militia. The power of the president to establish regulations in respect to the calling out of the militia under this act was made by him the basis for the institution of the draft. A later act of Congress, in March, 1863, specifically provided for the draft as the method of raising troops, but the institution of conscription by the executive under the act of 1862 was attacked as an undue extension of executive power. It amounted practically to an exercise of legislative power by the president.

The draft, as used in the Civil War, was inefficient, due to lack of popular coöperation and to an inadequate system of administration which allowed evasions of the regulations. In some localities, as in the city of New York, the attempt to apply the draft led to mob violence of serious proportions.

Despite this popular opposition, the courts declared the conscriptive method of raising troops to be constitutional. Such decisions were rendered in state and lower federal courts; no Civil War conscription case was taken before the Supreme Court.

Upon the entry of the United States into the World War, a compulsory draft law, technically called the Selective Service Act, was passed on May 18, 1917. It provided for universal conscription within certain age limits and subject to certain regulations. Such a method of raising troops had been adopted almost universally by the nations already engaged in the war. Nevertheless, the constitutionality of the law was attacked in the courts in several cases which were dealt with simultaneously by the Supreme Court under the title of the *Selective Draft Law Cases*. The unanimous decision of the Supreme Court was that the law was constitutional, as being a "necessary and proper" exercise by Congress of its power to raise troops.

Further, it was held, such power had been exercised by the states previous to the establishment of the Constitution. By that document, Congress had taken over all powers in this respect previously exercised by the states, so it followed that it had the right to exercise this power. Conscription was held not to involve involuntary servitude as prohibited under the thirteenth amendment, but only such service as every citizen could rightfully be forced to perform in the public interest.

The draft, as thus instituted during the World War, was vastly more efficient than it had been during the Civil War. This was as much due to its popular support as anything, and there is little doubt that in case of a future war conscription will remain the basic method of raising troops, though it is not specifically provided for in the Constitution.

WAR FINANCES

As has been mentioned, Congress has not only the power to raise armies but also the power to support them financially, though no appropriation for this purpose may be made for a period longer than two years. In conferring on Congress a general power of taxation, the Constitution mentions provision "for the common Defence" as one purpose of national finances. This purpose is sufficiently broad to include the support of all varieties of war activities. War taxation, however, is subject to the same limitations as apply in time of peace, such as that all duties, imposts, and excises are to be uniform throughout the United States.

During the Civil War, Congress made full use of its constitutional powers in filling the war chest. Three main methods of raising money were used: borrowing, taxation, and the issuance of paper money. Almost every session of Congress during the war saw some change in the national revenue producing system. Tariff rates were successively increased until, in 1864, the average rate was forty-seven percent. During the war a total of $305,-360,451 was raised through the collections of duties on imports. A wide variety of internal revenue taxes were imposed on luxuries and necessities as well. Liquors, tobaccos, meats, and a large number of other things were taxed. In addition, inheritance and income taxes were levied for the first time in American history. The rate in 1861 was three percent on all incomes in excess of $800; by 1865, the rate had been increased to five percent on incomes between $600 and $5,000, and to ten percent on annual incomes over $5,000. These incomes taxes, it will be recalled, were imposed in spite of the fact that there was no constitutional provision authorizing them. A total of $356,846,136 was secured during the Civil War from internal revenue and income taxes.

By far the largest part of the money needed for the federal expenses during that war was secured through borrowing. Through the sale of bonds, a total of $2,621,916,786 was raised. What was in reality a forced loan from the people was the issuance of legal tender notes or "greenbacks," as they were called. By the end of the war, a total of $431,000,000 in greenbacks had been issued. The Civil War thus saw the national government resort to the issuance of "fiat" money for the first and only time since the revolutionary period.

The money producing methods authorized by Congress during the World War were far more effective than those used during the Civil War. Early in the war it was decided to raise about one-third of the cost of the war through taxation and the other two-thirds through borrowing. Vast amounts were borrowed for short periods through the use of treasury certificates of indebtedness. During the years 1917–1919, the total borrowed in this manner was almost $30,000,000,000. This was repaid during the same period chiefly by other borrowing, by the sale of bonds, and by receipts from taxation.

Five great drives were authorized and staged for the sale of war bonds during the same period. The first four issues of bonds were called "Liberty bonds" while the fifth was the "Victory bond" issue. The issues were all oversubscribed by the American people. Altogether the government asked for $18,500,000,000 but $24,068,231,300 were subscribed. Some of the subscriptions were reduced by the government but a total of $21,474,330,000 in bonds was issued to 66,500,000 subscribers.

Another form of borrowing money was through what were called war savings certificates, and thrift stamps. The certificates were designed to hold twenty war savings stamps which could be purchased at a minimum price of $4.12 each but which, at the end of five years, would be worth $5.00. Thrift stamps were also sold at twenty-five cents each. The issuance of war savings certificates and thrift stamps was for the purpose of reaching those who could not afford to buy bonds. Even the children were thus enabled to "help win the war." The amount received from the sale of war savings certificates and thrift stamps totalled over $1,115,000,000.

In addition to these methods of borrowing, the government put into operation the most stupendous system of taxation this country has ever experienced. The sixteenth amendment, which had been added to the Constitution in 1913, made possible an extensive use of income taxes against which no constitutional objections could be raised. But every other possible form of taxation was also resorted to. About four-fifths of all the money raised through taxation was designed to come from income, war profits, and excess profits taxes. Other forms of taxation provided for by the war revenue acts of 1917 and 1918 included estate taxes; taxes on transportation, insurance, beverages, cigars and tobacco, admissions and dues; excise taxes, stamp taxes, and other special taxes. By the Revenue Act of 1918, the tax rate on the first $4,000 of net income was six percent. The rate was increased by a graduated system as the incomes became larger. Extra taxes or surtaxes were also imposed on incomes, beginning with one percent on incomes from $5,000 to $6,000. On some large incomes in excess of $1,000,000 a year, the total tax rate, including the regular tax and the surtax, reached seventy-seven percent. Through the various forms of taxation, including customs duties, a total of about $9,330,000,000 was paid into the United States treasury from the time war was declared on April 6, 1917 to June 30, 1919.

The tax receipts, added to the amounts borrowed through the sale of bonds, war savings certificates, and thrift stamps, totaled about $31,922,000,000. The regular and extraordinary war expenses of the government during the same period were approximately $32,427,000,000. The amazing feat of raising and disbursing these vast sums of money was performed through the exercise of constitutional powers, direct or implied.

THE PRESIDENT AS COMMANDER-IN-CHIEF

In relation to the powers of the president, directly derived from constitutional grants, it must be recognized, in the first place, that a primary function of the president is to execute the laws as enacted by Congress. From such execution of the laws there may be secured to the president large powers of a discretionary nature in relation to the conduct of war. On the other hand, there is at least one important direct grant of power to the executive in the Constitution in relation to war, namely, that he is made the commander-in-chief of the armed forces of the United States. This is a recognition of the necessity for unity of control over the army and navy in time of war in order to provide for the possibility of a well-organized and coördinated military program.

In connection with the conduct of the two greatest wars in which the United States has been involved, namely, the Civil War and the World War, there have been evolved two fundamentally differing approaches to the problem of executive powers in time of war. In the case of President Lincoln there was a violent disagreement between the president and Congress over which should control the conduct of war. President Lincoln claimed the primacy of the executive in this matter, basing his claim on his character as commander-in-chief of the armed forces. As commander-in-chief he inferred that he had the authority to deal with the exigencies of the war. Naturally, if the powers of the president in relation to war were to be determined only by his own inferences from the necessities of the situation, complete executive control over the conduct of war would probably result. To a large measure this is what took place under President Lincoln, who during the Civil War exercised an almost dictatorial power in the national government.

The World War produced also a large expansion in the power of the executive in the national government, but in an entirely different way. In this case there was not the contest between President Wilson and Congress over the exercise of the war powers that had taken place between President Lincoln and his Congress. This was due to several different factors, but its result was that during the World War, Congress enacted legislation, notably the Overman Act of May 20, 1918, giving into the hands of the president the control over practically all agencies for the carrying on of the war. Thus, the power executed by President Wilson was not the result of a disagreement over the rightful location of the war powers, but of a wholehearted desire on the part of Congress for a successful termination of the war, whether through the concentration of power in the hands of the executive or by any other means.

This contrast between President Lincoln and President Wilson, in their attitudes towards and exercises of the executive power in time of war, may best be seen through a review of some of their most important actions during war times.

INTERFERENCE WITH CONSTITUTIONAL RIGHTS
DURING THE CIVIL WAR

The suspension by President Lincoln, in 1861, of the writ of habeas corpus has previously been mentioned as an example of his exercise of war powers prior to a declaration of war by Congress. The writ of habeas corpus, designed to prevent false imprisonment by guaranteeing an inquiry into the causes of imprisonment, is safeguarded by a constitutional provision which prohibits its suspension except in case of necessity during a rebellion or invasion. There is no mention made in the Constitution, however, as to what agency in the government shall possess the power of suspending the writ.

This being the case, when President Lincoln judged a situation to have arisen which demanded the suspension of the writ, he assumed the power to order its suspension. Congress was not then in session, so that even if it had the power it could not have acted on the necessity for a suspension. When the national legislature met, President Lincoln submitted his act to that body for approval. His argument was that in the presence of an emergency and in the absence of a provision in the Constitution deciding whether Congress or the president should have the power of suspending the writ, the president was justified in so doing. This right of the president was to be inferred from his military powers, and from his duty to uphold the Constitution by any means possible.

The chief argument against the right of President Lincoln

to suspend the writ of habeas corpus was contained in Chief Justice Taney's decision in the case of *Ex parte Merryman* in 1861, in which he argued that, in view of the silence of the Constitution as to who should have the power of suspending the writ, Congress should do so. This view was supported by the prevailing opinion up to the time of the Civil War, and by such legal decisions and discussions in Congress as had previously taken place.

In response to the President's request for ratification of his action, Congress passed the Habeas Corpus Act of 1863. This act did nothing to settle the question as to whether Congress or the president had the right to suspend the writ.

President Lincoln's policy in regard to the suspension of the writ of habeas corpus was typical of his attitude on the extent of his powers in time of war. He believed in his power to suspend the writ and, on this basis, he acted, leaving the matter of legislative approval or disapproval to be considered later.

Closely connected with the suspension of the writ of habeas corpus under Lincoln was the recourse to arbitrary arrest and trial by irregular processes. Together with the suspension of the writ of habeas corpus, these measures were taken by order of the president in an effort to check the activities of those disloyal to the government in the existing emergency.

The fourth amendment to the Constitution provides safeguards against "unreasonable searches and seizure." Searches and seizures may not be made except by the authority of warrants issued "upon probable cause, supported by oath or affirmation," and describing the person or things to be seized. It is obvious that the right to a writ of habeas corpus would be necessary to secure an examination of the basis of an arrest, so that the real safeguard against arbitrary arrest lay in the writ. Its suspension early in the war thus paved the way for numerous cases of arrest of those suspected of disloyal activities. Of this group there were many, especially in the states bordering on the south. The most effective means for their suppression was their arrest, sometimes on suspicion of disloyalty and sometimes on evidence of disloyal practices such as supplying information to the enemy, obstructing the draft, or encouraging desertion from the army.

These arrests were sometimes made by the local authorities,

and sometimes by federal officials. The position of President Lincoln on the subject was that the suspension of the guarantees of the fourth amendment was necessary during time of war, and that it was within his power, as commander-in-chief of the armed forces, to order such suspension.

The object in making the arrests was not the institution of court proceedings against those held in custody. The larger number of those arrested was arrested arbitrarily, held an indeterminate length of time, and released in a manner quite as arbitrary as they had been arrested.

In some cases, however, there were instituted trials of citizens, in areas not in the war zone, by courts-martial or military commissions. A notable instance of this occurred in Ohio in 1863 when C. L. Vallandigham was arrested by military officers, court martialed, and sentenced to imprisonment. The president commuted the sentence to banishment to the south. Vallandigham made his way from the south to Canada from which he conducted his campaign as the anti-war Democratic candidate for governor of Ohio. He lost the election, however, and was forced to remain in exile. This method of handling Vallandigham and others was contrary to the fifth amendment to the Constitution which guarantees the right of judicial proceedings for those accused of illegal acts. By its terms it is provided that no one "shall be held to answer for a capital, or otherwise infamous crime, unless on a presentment or indictment of a Grand Jury," except in cases involving the members of armed forces of the United States when engaged in actual conflict.

The attitude of President Lincoln on this constitutional guarantee was similar to his position on the right of freedom from arbitrary arrest, namely, that the war emergency justified its suspension. Congress, far from passing legislation in support of the action of the president, provided, by the Habeas Corpus Act of March 3, 1863, that, in case no grand jury indictment was returned within twenty days against those arrested and imprisoned, they were to be liberated. This provision of the act was not enforced.

The position of Congress on the matter of the validity of constitutional guarantees in time of war was upheld by the Supreme Court in the case of *Ex parte Milligan*, decided after the war, in 1866. The case involved the right of a citizen, in territory outside the actual area of warlike operations, to a trial by the regular civil courts, instead of by a military commission. Milligan, an anti-war Democrat of Indiana, had been arrested, tried by a military tribunal, and sentenced to imprisonment, in 1864. The decision in the case covered the general field of the right of the government to suspend constitutional guarantees. By a five to four vote, the Supreme Court decided that war does not destroy civil rights in territory not the scene of actual military operations. The necessities of war must be subject to the limitations of the Constitution. As this decision was made after the Civil War had ended, it was of no service to those who had been deprived of their constitutional rights during the war. It was, at best, a moral victory for those who had opposed the arbitrary acts of the government during the war.

PRESIDENT LINCOLN AND SLAVERY

A further striking illustration of President Lincoln's tendency, during the Civil War, to assume powers which he might or might not be legally entitled to, was in his actions on the emancipation of the slaves. His position, before his election to the presidency, had been that there should be no interference with the institution of slavery in the states where it already existed, but that there should be no spread of the institution to the western territories. In accordance with this position, there was no attempt, other than to confiscate slaves as property, to interfere with slavery during the early days of the Civil War. This attitude, however, could not be maintained in the face of the growing desire in the north for the abolition of slavery.

In accordance with the prevailing opinion in the north, Congress enacted several laws which involved indirect applications in relation to slavery in the south. Acts for the confiscation of enemy property, passed on August 6, 1861 and July 17, 1862, were to be applied to any property used against the United States in the war. Further, captured slaves or slaves who sought refuge within the federal lines were to be freed.

President Lincoln's own preference in relation to the freeing of the slaves was that it should be by some form of coöperation between the states and the national government, involving compensation to slave owners for the loss of their property. It was, however, obvious that no such plan could be put into operation.

The result was that President Lincoln, recognizing the demand in the north for emancipation, and seeing the impossibility of the execution of the plan he favored, decided for emancipation by presidential proclamation, and after issuing a preparatory proclamation some three months earlier, issued, on January 1, 1863, his famous Emancipation Proclamation.

The basis upon which the president claimed the power of thus freeing the slaves by proclamation was primarily his position as commander-in-chief of the armed forces of the nation. This action he justified as a war measure, based upon the military necessity of hindering the southern states in carrying on the war. Such an action as freeing the slaves within the states, he had previously considered unconstitutional, as an undue interference with the internal affairs of the states, but in time of war it could be justified by the necessity of preserving the Constitution against those who would attack it. Thus the chief point in view was the preservation of the Constitution.

The Emancipation Proclamation decreed freedom for the slaves in the regions then in rebellion against the United States. The slaves were to be freed as soon as the federal troops conquered the regions referred to in the proclamation. Slaves in other places, including the border states and such parts of the south as had already been conquered by the federal troops, were in no way affected by President Lincoln's action. President Lincoln has been given more credit in connection with the slaves than he is entitled to. A goodly portion of the slaves did not receive their freedom until the thirteenth amendment was added to the Constitution in 1865.

POLITICAL RECONSTRUCTION OF THE SOUTH

After the Civil War, there developed a struggle between Congress and the executive, over the control and direction of the policy of reconstruction of the seceded southern states. President Lincoln assumed the power to reconstruct the south, inferring the power from his position as commander-in-chief. President Johnson attempted to carry on Lincoln's policy but was blocked by the actions of Congress which claimed that reconstruction was a legislative problem. Since the Constitution makes no provision for the secession of states, it naturally contains no provision whereby states which have seceded may be restored to the union. The Tenure of Office Act, President Johnson's disregard of it, and his subsequent impeachment and trial have been discussed in relation to the executive. The policy of congressional reconstruction was included in several acts passed in 1867, which were the basis of its policy, and which, with the Tenure of Office Act, insured primacy of Congress over the executive in this function.

Briefly, these acts provided for the setting up of military government in the southern states; the adoption of a constitution in each state, to be drawn up by a convention elected by the votes of all qualified citizens, whether white or colored; and the adoption of the fourteenth amendment by the legislature created by this constitution. Appropriate machinery for the execution of this plan was provided. The purpose was to enfranchise the negroes, and to attempt to prevent their subsequent disfranchisement by the whites. This was to be accomplished by dictating the type of state governments to be set up.

These acts of Congress were vetoed by President Johnson, but passed over his veto. The grounds of his disapproval of them were that military rule in the south was for the purpose of coercing the people there into the adoption of forms of government which they did not approve. This was a type of military despotism which was unjustified, as the war had been ended. Control by the national government over the direct details of the adoption of state constitutions he declared unjustified and an invasion of the rights of the states.

PRESIDENTIAL POWERS DURING THE WORLD WAR

The World War, as has already been suggested, saw a largely different development of executive power. President Wilson doubtless exercised more power as a "war President" than President Lincoln had during the Civil War. But his powers were the result chiefly of legislation by Congress which granted him large discretionary powers in connection with the administration of national affairs. In case he doubted whether he could rightfully exercise powers required by specific situations, he proceeded to secure congressional action granting him the powers necessary. Congress took the view, natural in the light of the difficulties of war, that a concentration of control would secure the most efficient and best coördinated program for the winning of the war. As a result, examples of the extension of executive power in the hands of President Wilson as a result of grants by Congress of control over the conduct of war activities are not difficult to discover.

MOBILIZATION OF WAR RESOURCES DURING THE WORLD WAR

An early example of this kind is in connection with the Selective Service Act of May, 1917, which gave the executive the right to determine the rules for the administration of the draft. As a result, the President issued as many as thirteen proclamations, as well as other regulations, for the organization and administration of the national system of conscription. This was a virtual exercise by the President of legislative power, delegated to him by Congress.

The magnitude of operations during the World War was such as to bring to bear on the problem of securing victory practically all the activities of the American people. It was a time when, particularly, the economic strength of the nation had necessarily to be mobilized and the economic effort controlled, so as to avoid waste and duplication of effort, and to secure a program of activities guided toward the one end of winning the war. This control of the national economic life was sought in a program of congressional legislation which brought under national control the conduct of finance, industry, foreign trade, labor, communication and transportation, food production and sales, and the production and consumption of fuel, to mention the most important ones.

To a large extent the legislation passed by Congress delegated to the President the power to decide upon questions of economic policy. It was not a matter of Congress deciding upon a policy and delegating to the President the mere execution of the law, although this was also involved. The discretionary power of the President was great, putting in his hands, to use or guide in its use by others, a degree of governmental control over the economic life of the nation unprecedented in its history.

As good an illustration as any of the powers thus granted the President by Congress was the control which the war made necessary over the agencies for producing and distributing food and fuel products, and to secure economy in their consumption. This aspect of governmental control, as much as any other, was felt by the people at large, whose efforts in coöperation with the government were an important part of the war activity.

The necessity for control of food and fuel in order to supply the allies and prevent excessive costs to domestic consumers was recognized by Congress in the enactment of the Food and Fuel Control Act, on August 10, 1917. Besides a number of provisions definitely penalizing such actions by the public as the hoarding of food or fuel products, or the establishing of monopolies in them, the act gave to the President broad powers to carry out the general aims of the act.

These powers included the institution of a system of licensing of business activities connected with food and fuel, in order to control their activities. The President was authorized to requisition food or fuel for public use on just compensation; to buy and sell such commodities; to regulate conditions of trade in these commodities in order to prevent price fluctuation or manipulation; to fix prices for commodities; and to prevent the use of food products in a manner not calculated to secure a sufficient supply of food for the public, notably in their use in the making of liquors. Above all, he was authorized to make all regulations and to issue all orders necessary to carry out the provisions of the act.

The extent to which the President was thus to become the regulator of the everyday life of citizens of the nation was unprecedented in American history. It was, of course, impossible that he should directly administer the national policy of food and fuel control, but the act gave him entire freedom to set up the necessary administrative machinery and to control its actions. In accord with this President Wilson set up the United States Food Administration by an executive order issued on the very day that Congress passed the Food and Fuel Control Act. Herbert Hoover was designated as the head of the Food Administration. On August 23, 1917, the Fuel Administration was set up with Harry A. Garfield as it head. These administrative agencies were typical of those set up under other war legislation by the President, and under which his powers of control were carried out.

In addition to the President's control over food and fuel through such administrative agencies, his powers granted by the act of 1917 were also exercised directly. The use of the licensing system for business concerns handling food and fuel products was instituted as a means of subjecting them to regulation and control. The licensing system was established through a series of proclamations by the President under the power given him by Congress to institute all regulations necessary to carry out the general aim of the Food and Fuel Control Act. There was a general use of executive orders in relation both to food and fuel. By such orders, the President not only set up administrative agencies, but took direct control of the formulation of policy, despite the delegation of large measures of this power by him to those working under him and subject to his approval.

In a similar manner, there were set up the War Trade Board, headed by Vance McCormick; the Shipping Board, headed by Edward N. Hurley; and the Railroad Administration with William G. McAdoo as the director-general.

The mention of the increases of power in the hands of the President as a result of action by the legislature brings out a basic tendency along this line, but it is not to be assumed that the President failed to exercise independently of Congress those powers specifically granted him by the Constitution. Notable among the cases in connection with which President Wilson extended his control over the economic life of the nation by virtue of his position as chief executive and commander-in-chief of the armed forces, was his creation, without definite legislation by Congress, of various independent administrative agencies.

But even in these cases there was indirect congressional authority through the National Defence Act of 1916. This act provided for a Council of National Defence consisting of six cabinet members with an advisory committee of seven members. This organization was set up in February, 1917, and, by the time the United States entered the war in April, it was ready to function. On the recommendation of the Council of National Defence, the President set up numerous committees which performed important war functions without definite legislative sanction. For example, there was established in this way on April 9, 1917, the General Munitions Board which later became the War Industries Board headed by Bernard M. Baruch. The Railroads' War Board which preceded the Railroad Administration further illustrates how the executive power was employed in the creation of war agencies.

WORLD WAR REORGANIZATION OF GOVERNMENTAL AGENCIES

In addition to his power of instituting new administrative agencies to carry out the functions delegated to him by Congress, the President was given a further control over administration by the Overman Act of May 20, 1918. By this act Congress recognized the need for coördination of existing executive departments and administrative agencies. The President was given power to coördinate or consolidate these bureaus in such a way as to eliminate duplication of efforts in relation to the conduct of the war. He was not given the power to abolish any executive departments under the law, but could recommend such abolition to Congress. The control of the President in this direction was not a general control, as it extended only to the purposes of the war. The act provided that the power granted to the President should last six months after the end of the war.

CONTROL OF PUBLIC OPINION

The control exercised by President Wilson over the course of governmental policy in relation to the World War was not merely the result of the desires of Congress. It also had the backing of public opinion throughout the nation as a whole. This is not to say that there existed no opinion hostile to the government's war policies. As a matter of fact an extremely significant activity of the government during the World War was its efforts to control public opinion. In the same way in which control by the government was extended to practically the entire economic life of the nation was an effort made by the government to control the development of public opinion. The very fact that the waging of war had become a matter involving the everyday life of the individual made the active coöperation of all a matter of vital interest in the winning of the war.

The influence of the government in the matter of public opinion was exerted in two directions. These were, first, toward positive control of public opinion through agencies for the creation of a public opinion of a certain type, and, second, toward negative control of public opinion, or the effort to prevent the creation of a public opinion along lines unfavorable to the successful prosecution of the war. In other words, the government spread propaganda of a type calculated to secure united coöperation of the people for the winning of the war, while, at the same time, it took strong measures to prohibit the spread of propaganda aimed in the opposite direction.

The most important agency for the creation of a public opinion favoring the successful prosecution of the war was the Committee on Public Information, headed by George Creel, which was created by the executive order of President Wilson, on April 14, 1917. This organization was the first of its kind in American history. There was no precedent for it in any previous war, and it, with the other agencies for controlling public opinion brought into use during the World War, may be taken as symbols and expressions of the modern tendency for war to involve the whole population of a nation, and to wipe out many of the former distinctions between combatant and non-combatant classes.

The activities of the Committee on Public Information may be divided into two groups, those involving foreign, and those including domestic activities, but only the domestic activities will be considered here. These bore upon the control of public opinion in America. They included a division of news which was interested primarily in securing the coöperation of the press in order to prevent the printing of war news that should be kept secret. The division of news also served as a clearing house for all news in relation to the war, except actual dispatches from the front. Except for such dispatches, the division became the chief source of war news, thus controlling to a large extent the creation of public opinion by the press.

In addition to this the committee organized the "Four Minute Men," a group of speakers, who discussed brief topics along lines suggested by material prepared and sent out from Washington. The committee supervised the preparation of a large amount of published material which was distributed widely. It also created public opinion through the use of motion pictures, posters, commercial advertising, and other agencies.

While the activities of the Committee on Public Information were typical of efforts along this line, they were not the only ones pursued. Such organizations as the food administration, the Liberty Loan organizations, the Red Cross, and the welfare organizations such as the Young Men's Christian Association and the Knights of Columbus, conducted their own campaigns of publicity, all designed to create such attitudes on the questions of the war, as would in the estimation of the government, best secure eventual victory.

The extra-constitutional character of these activities is not only illustrated by the creation of the Committee on Public Information by executive order in 1917, but by the fact that for a considerable length of time its activities were not even supported financially by Congress. The net cost of its operations was about four million dollars, which came largely from the one hundred million dollar emergency war fund granted the President for war use, as well as from income from the activities of the committee itself.

Viewed thus, the Committee on Public Information is to be seen as a tremendous extension of executive control in war time, a control exerted by the President over the very minds and thoughts of the people. The nature of this control depended solely upon the desires of the President and his immediate associates. Yet this control was accepted by the nation as a whole, which not only consented to it, but aided it by a spirit of strong opposition to any who refused to adopt the opinions which it sought to foster.

Although America was declared to have entered the World War to foster world-wide democracy, it is plain that the conduct of the war itself involved considerable inroads on the liberty usually associated with a democratic form of government. This was justified on the same grounds as were President Lincoln's interferences with constitutional rights during the Civil War. From his point of view, temporary departures from the Constitution could be justified for the purpose of its preservation from absolute destruction. In the same way, if during the World War democracy was to be saved as a principle, its libertarian connotations had necessarily to be suspended temporarily. How this was done was graphically described by Alfred E. Smith, the Democratic party presidential candidate in 1928, in a speech delivered on February 7, 1933, in which he advocated that wartime measures should be applied to the current depression. Ex-Governor Smith said, in part, "And what does a democracy do in a war? It becomes a tyrant, a despot, a real monarch. In the World War we took our Constitution, wrapped it up and laid it on the shelf and left it there until it was all over."

The most important efforts of the government to prevent the creation of a public opinion along lines which seemed to it unfavorable to the successful conduct of the war were undertaken under the Espionage Act of 1917 and its amending act of the following year. The essential effects of these laws were to make criminal the uttering of any statements criticizing war policies of the government, whether such statements were true or false, whether they had any known criminal results or not, and regardless of their motivation. By many, these laws were held to be unconstitutional, as violating the provision in the first amendment guaranteeing freedom of speech and of the press. The significant fact is, however, that these acts were passed with popular approval, were largely upheld in the courts as constitutional, and could be strictly enforced due to the almost unanimous public coöperation with the government. This seems a justification of Alexander Hamilton's statement that no provision safeguarding freedom of speech should be contained in the Constitution, as freedom of speech would not depend upon law, but upon the prevailing public opinion, for its definition and its existence.

Although such temporary denials of fundamental rights during time of war may be justified on a basis of immediate necessity, the ultimate public benefit demands that suspension of constitutional rights be confined to the period of war. The immediate effect of the limitation upon freedom of speech under the Espionage Act and its amendment may or may not have been good. It is at least debatable whether the gain in social solidarity was not overbalanced by the loss in desirable criticism of governmental policy during the war. But there should be no doubt whatever as to the ultimate bad effect of the lasting, and not temporary, effect of these repressions of free speech upon American national life since the war. The popular war-time approval of repression of free speech has undeniably carried over into the post-war period. It is this tendency for a definite carry-over into post-war psychology which makes war-time departures from the Constitution of peace time so grave, and which should cause hesitation in taking such steps. However, in America, self-confidence, and not hesitancy, has been the usual characteristic of popular majorities which, for better or for worse, have usually exhibited a tendency to rush blithely in where angels fear to tread. Democracy is to be judged, not by its name, but by its works.

PEACE TIME PREPARATIONS FOR WAR

It is well to keep in mind that the national government has not only the powers necessary to carry on war but, by the same token, the powers to prepare for war. Until the period of the World War, little was done in times of peace to prepare for war. The fears, which were expressed in various state ratifying conventions, in 1787–1788, concerning the "union of the purse and the sword" by constitutional provisions, have persisted throughout American history. Consequently, the United States entered all of its wars with little preparation.

Even as late as the beginning of the world conflict in Europe in 1914, the typical American attitude was apparently that expressed by William J. Bryan when he declared that, in case the United States became involved in war, "a million men would spring to arms over night." As the war progressed and the likelihood of the United States becoming involved increased, tardy attention was given to military and naval preparations. In June, 1916, the National Defence Act was passed, providing for an increase in the size of the regular army and the national guard and for the development of a reserve officers' system through summer training camps for qualified civilians. Also in 1916, a Naval Appropriation Act was passed which authorized the building of ten dreadnaughts and six battle cruisers over a period of three years. However, this preparedness program had hardly got under way when the United States entered the war.

The war proved the fallacy of Bryan's prediction concerning the million men springing to arms. The men were available but the arms were not. Furthermore, the men were not trained in the intricacies of modern warfare. The result was that about a year passed before this country could become a potent factor in the war.

After the war, Congress and a large portion of the public were determined that never again should the United States be forced to enter a war unprepared.

The navy had made great strides during the war and, after the conflict was over, it attained approximate equality with the British navy. The extreme advocates of preparedness were determined that the United States navy should be the largest in the world. In Great Britain and Japan were those with similar desires for their own navies. The result was a post-war navy building competition which threatened ruin to all concerned. A halt was called by an agreement reached at the famous Washington Conference in 1922 whereby it was agreed that the leading naval powers should limit the number of their "capital" ships by what is known as the 5–5–3 ratio. This ratio placed the United States and Great Britain on a par, while Japan was allowed three-fifths as many "capital" ships. Through the London Conference of 1930, these three powers agreed to limit other types of naval vessels as well. The ratio for capital ships allowed the United States, Great Britain, and Japan, respectively, was changed to $10:10:3\frac{5}{8}$, while new ratios were established for other vessels, as follows: aircraft carriers, $10:10:6$; cruisers with larger than six-inch guns, $10:8\frac{1}{10}:6$; cruisers with six-inch guns, $10:13\frac{4}{10}:7$; destroyers, $10:10:7$; and submarines $10:10:10$. These ratios, representing in each case a stated maximum tonnage, are to be in effect until 1936.

The object of these limitations was to prevent disastrous

armament races and, at the same time, it was the object of the United States to maintain a navy on a par with that of Great Britain and superior to that of any other power. The ratios decided on apparently fixed the desired equality or superiority. In practice, however, the United States has not built up to the maximum treaty limitations, nor has this country maintained its full quota of vessels in commission.

According to the report of the secretary of the navy, the United States had, in 1932, eleven battleships in commission, one in "reduced commission," and three in the process of being modernized. Great Britain had fifteen and Japan ten battleships in full commission. At the same time, the United States had in commission only eight heavy cruisers, compared to twelve for Japan and seventeen for Great Britain; and ten light cruisers compared to twenty for Japan and twenty-five for Great Britain. To quote another portion of the report, "Of 101 destroyers, the United States has seventy-two in full commission, ten in reduced commission and nineteen in rotating reserve. Of 121 British destroyers, seventy-four are in full commission and forty-seven in reserve commission. Eighty Japanese destroyers are fully manned. Of fifty-four United States submarines, forty-two are in full commission, eleven are in rotating reserve, and one in reduced commission. Of fifty-two British submarines, forty-four are in full commission and eight in reserve commission. Sixty-two Japanese submarines are fully manned."

From this report, it is apparent that the United States is pursuing a comparatively mild program of naval preparedness. If this country should build up to the limits set by the London treaty it could not fairly be criticized for such action. It certainly was in the power of this nation, following the World War, to develop the most powerful navy in the world. The willingness to submit to limitations suggests that the United States naval preparedness program has been characterized by a high degree of reasonableness.

The military preparedness program following the World War was outlined in the National Defence Act of 1920. This act embodied the lessons learned from participation in the great conflict during the years 1917–1918. Under this act, the army of the United States was to be composed of three main branches: the regular army, the national guard, and the organized reserve.

In 1932, the regular army included 12,180 officers and 119,888 enlisted men whereas the Defence Act provided for a maximum of 280,000 officers and men. The national guard consisted of 174,137 enlisted men and 13,250 officers, instead of 210,000 men with a proportionate number of officers. Instead of 120,000 reserve officers on the active list there were only 83,808 of whom only 22,388 received active duty training during the fiscal year 1931–1932. During the previous year 117,423 young men received training in the Reserve Officers' Training Corps in various schools, colleges, and universities scattered throughout the country. During the same year, 39,061 young men received military training in fifty-three Citizens' Military Training Camps. It is the purpose of the R.O.T.C. and the C.M.T.C., as they are commonly designated, to prepare men for commissions as reserve officers. Should the United States become involved in a war, it is contemplated that the reserve force should constitute the largest branch of the army. The reserve officers are assigned to skeleton organizations which would be speedily brought to war strength through the application of a selective draft.

The internal organization of the army is too complicated to be described here. Within the limits set by Congress, the armed forces of the United States have been kept in a high state of preparedness for war. Whether the statutory limits on preparedness are too high or too low is a question concerning which there is and has been much controversy. However, compared with other countries, the United States has tended, since the World War, to carry on a very modest program of military preparedness. This country has amply demonstrated its willingness to limit its war preparations if other countries will do likewise. Meanwhile it would seem to be good judgment to maintain a reasonable degree of preparedness. The problem of the American people is to see that its government steers a middle course between the extreme pacifists on the one side who would have the United States disarm regardless of the world situation and the extreme militarists on the other side who would have this country prepare against any possible combination of foes.

SELECTED REFERENCES

Atkisson, H. L. B., "Constitutional Sources of the Laws of War," *Senate Documents*, 65th Congress, 1st Session (1917), Doc. No. 86, pp. 5–36.

Berdahl, C. A., *War Powers of the Executive in the United States*, pp. 11–270.

Burdick, C. K., *The Law of the American Constitution, Its Origin and Development*, pp. 62–63, 77–80, 84–85, 255–271, 355–373.

Burgess, J. W., *The Civil War and the Constitution 1859–1865*, Vol. I, pp. 74–137, 226–242; Vol. II, pp. 72–88, 114–118, 214–233.

Chafee, Zechariah, *Freedom of Speech*, pp. 1–160, 395–397.

Chambrun, A. de, *The Executive Power in the United States*, pp. 116–124, 237–257.

Corwin, E. S., "Freedom of Speech and Press under the First Amendment: A Resume," *Yale Law Review*, Vol. XXX (November, 1920), pp. 48–55.

Corwin, E. S., *The President's Control of Foreign Relations*, pp. 126–167.

Cushman, R. E., *Leading Constitutional Decisions*, pp. 114–129.

Hughes, C. E., "War Powers Under the Constitution," *Senate Documents*, 65th Congress, 1st Session (1917), Doc. No. 105, pp. 3–14.

Mathews, J. M., *The American Constitutional System*, pp. 280–289.

Paxson, F. L., *Recent History of the United States 1865–1927*, pp. 462–553.

Powell, T. R., "Constitutional Law 1919–1920. III." *Michigan Law Review*, Vol. XIX, pp. 288–300.

Randall, J. G., *Constitutional Problems under Lincoln*, pp. 1–530.

Schlesinger, A. M., *Political and Social History of the United States 1829–1925*, pp. 210–260.

Willoughby, W. F., *Government Organization in War Time and After*, pp. 3–358.

Appendix A

ARTICLES OF CONFEDERATION—
1781–1789

TO ALL OF WHOM THESE PRESENTS SHALL COME, WE THE UNDERSIGNED DELEGATES OF THE STATES AFFIXED TO OUR NAMES, SEND GREETING.
Whereas the Delegates of the United States of America in Congress assembled did on the fifteenth day of November in the Year of our Lord One Thousand Seven Hundred and Seventy-seven, and in the Second Year of the Independence of America agree to certain articles of Confederation and perpetual Union between the States of Newhampshire, Massachusetts-bay, Rhodeisland and Providence Plantations, Connecticut, New York, New Jersey, Pennsylvania, Delaware, Maryland, Virginia, North-Carolina, South-Carolina and Georgia in the Words following, viz.

Articles of Confederation and perpetual Union between the States of Newhampshire, Massachusetts-bay, Rhodeisland and Providence Plantations, Connecticut, New-York, New-Jersey, Pennsylvania, Delaware, Maryland, Virginia, North-Carolina, South-Carolina and Georgia.

Article I. The stile of this confederacy shall be "The United States of America."

Article II. Each State retains its sovereignty, freedom and independence, and every power, jurisdiction and right, which is not by this confederation expressly delegated to the United States, in Congress assembled.

Article III. The said States hereby severally enter into a firm league of friendship with each other, for their common defence, the security of their liberties, and their mutual and general welfare, binding themselves to assist each other, against all force offered to, or attacks made upon them, or any of them, on account of religion, sovereignty, trade, or any other pretence whatever.

Article IV. The better to secure and perpetuate mutual friendship and intercourse among the people of the different States in this Union, the free inhabitants of each of these States, paupers, vagabonds and fugitives from justice excepted, shall be entitled to all privileges and immunities of free citizens in the several States; and the people of each State shall have free ingress and regress to and from any other State, and shall enjoy therein all the privileges of trade and commerce, subject to the same duties, impositions and restrictions as the inhabitants thereof respectively, provided that such restrictions shall not extend so far as to prevent the removal of property imported into any State, to any other State of which the owner is an inhabitant; provided also that no imposition, duties or restriction shall be laid by any State, on the property of the United States, or either of them.

If any person guilty of, or charged with treason, felony, or other high misdemeanor in any State, shall flee from justice, and be found in any of the United States, he shall upon demand of the Governor or Executive power, of the State from which he fled, be delivered up and removed to the State having jurisdiction of his offence.

Full faith and credit shall be given in each of these States to the records, acts and judicial proceedings of the courts and magistrates of every other State.

Article V. For the more convenient management of the general interest of the United States, delegates shall be annually appointed in such manner as the legislature of each State shall direct, to meet in Congress on the first Monday in November, in every year, with a power reserved to each State, to recall its delegates, or any of them, at any time within the year, and to send others in their stead, for the remainder of the year.

No State shall be represented in Congress by less than two, nor by more than seven members; and no person shall be capable of being a delegate for more than three years in any term of six years; nor shall any person, being a delegate, be capable of holding any office under the United States, for which he, or another for his benefit receives any salary, fees or emolument of any kind.

Each State shall maintain its own delegates in a meeting of the States, and while they act as members of the committee of the States.

In determining questions in the United States, in Congress assembled, each State shall have one vote.

Freedom of speech and debate in Congress shall not be impeached or questioned in any court, or place out of Congress, and the members of Congress shall be protected in their persons from arrests and imprisonments, during the time of their going to and from, and attendance on Congress, except for treason, felony, or breach of the peace.

Article VI. No State without the consent of the United States in Congress assembled, shall send any embassy to, or receive any embassy from, or enter into any conference, agreement, alliance or treaty with any king, prince or state; nor shall any person holding any office of profit or trust under the United States, or any of them, accept of any present, emolument, office or title of any kind whatever from any king, prince or foreign state; nor shall the United States in Congress assembled, or any of them, grant any title of nobility.

No two or more States shall enter into any treaty, confederation or alliance whatever between them, without the consent of the United States in Congress assembled, specifying accurately the purposes for which the same is to be entered into, and how long it shall continue.

No State shall lay any imposts or duties, which may interfere with any stipulations in treaties, entered into by the United States in Congress assembled, with any king, prince or state, in pursuance of any treaties already proposed by Congress, to the courts of France and Spain.

No vessels of war shall be kept up in time of peace by any State, except such number only, as shall be deemed necessary by the United States in

ARTICLES OF CONFEDERATION—1781–1789 493

Congress assembled, for the defence of such State, or its trade; nor shall any body of forces be kept up by any State, in time of peace, except such number only, as in the judgment of the United States, in Congress assembled, shall be deemed requisite to garrison the forts necessary for the defence of such State; but every State shall always keep up a well regulated and disciplined militia, sufficiently armed and accoutred, and shall provide and constantly have ready for use, in public stores, a due number of field pieces and tents, and a proper quantity of arms, ammunition and camp equipage.

No State shall engage in any war without the consent of the United States in Congress assembled, unless such State be actually invaded by enemies, or shall have received certain advice of a resolution being formed by some nation of Indians to invade such State, and the danger is so imminent as not to admit of a delay, till the United States in Congress assembled can be consulted: nor shall any State grant commissions to any ships or vessels of war, nor letters of marque or reprisal, except it be after a declaration of war by the United States in Congress assembled, and then only against the kingdom or state and the subjects thereof, against which war has been so declared, and under such regulations as shall be established by the United States in Congress assembled, unless such State be infested by pirates, in which case vessels of war may be fitted out for that occasion, and kept so long as the danger shall continue, or until the United States in Congress assembled shall determine otherwise.

Article VII. When land-forces are raised by any State for the common defence, all officers of or under the ranks of colonel, shall be appointed by the Legislature of each State respectively by whom such forces shall be raised, or in such manner as such State shall direct, and all vacancies shall be filled up by the State which first made the appointment.

Article VIII. All charges of war, and all other expenses that shall be incurred for the common defence or general welfare, and allowed by the United States in Congress assembled, shall be defrayed out of a common treasury, which shall be supplied by the several States, in proportion to the value of all land within each State, granted to or surveyed for any person, as such land and the buildings and improvements thereon shall be estimated according to such mode as the United States in Congress assembled, shall from time to time direct and appoint.

The taxes for paying that proportion shall be laid and levied by the authority and direction of the Legislatures of the several States within the time agreed upon by the United States in Congress assembled.

Article IX. The United States in Congress assembled, shall have the sole and exclusive right and power of determining on peace and war, except in the cases mentioned in the sixth article—of sending and receiving ambassadors—entering into treaties and alliances, provided that no treaty of commerce shall be made whereby the legislative power of the respective States shall be restrained from imposing such imposts and duties on foreigners, as their own people are subjected to, or from prohibiting the exportation or importation of any species of goods or commodities whatsoever—of establishing rules for deciding in all cases, what captures on land or water shall be legal, and in what manner prizes taken by land or naval forces in the service of the United States shall be divided or appropriated —of granting letters of marque and reprisal in times of peace—appointing courts for the trial of piracies and felonies committed on the high seas and establishing courts for receiving and determining finally appeals in all cases of captures, provided that no member of Congress shall be appointed a judge of any of the said courts.

The United States in Congress assembled shall also be the last resort on appeal in all disputes and differences now subsisting or that hereafter may arise between two or more States concerning boundary, jurisdiction or any other cause whatever; which authority shall always be exercised in the manner following. Whenever the legislative or executive authority or lawful agent of any State in controversy with another shall present a petition to Congress, stating the matter in question and praying for a hearing, notice thereof shall be given by order of Congress to the legislative or executive authority of the other State in controversy, and a day assigned for the appearance of the parties by their lawful agents, who shall then be directed to appoint by joint consent, commissioners or judges to constitute a court for hearing and determining the matter in question: but if they cannot agree, Congress shall name three persons out of each of the United States, and from the list of such persons each party shall alternately strike out one, the petitioners beginning, until the number shall be reduced to thirteen; and from that number not less than seven, nor more than nine names as Congress shall direct, shall in the presence of Congress be drawn out by lot, and the persons whose names shall be so drawn or any five of them, shall be commissioners or judges, to hear and finally determine the controversy, so always as a major part of the judges who shall hear the cause shall agree in the determination: and if either party shall neglect to attend at the day appointed, without showing reasons, which Congress shall judge sufficient, or being present shall refuse to strike, the Congress shall proceed to nominate three persons out of each State, and the Secretary of Congress shall strike in behalf of such party absent or refusing; and the judgment and sentence of the court to be appointed, in the manner before prescribed, shall be final and conclusive; and if any of the parties shall refuse to submit to the authority of such court, or to appear or defend their claim or cause, the court shall nevertheless proceed to pronounce sentence, or judgment, which shall in like manner be final and decisive, the judgment or sentence and other proceedings being in either case transmitted to Congress, and lodged among the acts of Congress for the security of the parties concerned: provided that every commissioner, before he sits in judgment, shall take an oath to be administered by one of the judges of the supreme or superior court of the State where the cause shall be tried, "well and truly to hear and determine the matter in question, according to the best of his judgment, without favour, affection or hope of reward": provided also that no State shall be deprived of territory for the benefit of the United States.

All controversies concerning the private right of soil claimed under different grants of two or more States, whose jurisdiction as they may respect such lands, and the States which passed such grants are adjusted, the said grants or either of them being at the same time claimed to have originated antecedent to such settlement of jurisdiction, shall on the petition of either party to the Congress of the United States, be finally determined as near as may be in the same manner as is before prescribed for deciding disputes respecting territorial jurisdiction between different States.

The United States in Congress assembled shall also have the sole and exclusive right and power of regulating the alloy and value of coin struck by their own authority, or by that of the respective States—fixing the standard of weights and measures throughout the United States—regulating the trade and managing all affairs with the Indians, not members of any of the States, provided that the legislative right of any State within its own limits be not infringed or violated—establishing and regulating post-offices from one State to another, throughout all the United States, and exacting such postage on the papers passing thro' the same as may be requisite to defray the expenses of the said office—appointing all officers of the land forces, in the service of the United States, excepting regimental officers—appointing all the officers of the naval forces, and commissioning all officers whatever in the service of the United States—making rules for the government and regulation of the said land and naval forces, and directing their operations.

The United States in Congress assembled shall have authority to appoint a committee, to sit in the recess of Congress, to be denominated "a Committee of the States," and to consist of one delegate from each State; and to appoint such other committees and civil officers as may be necessary for managing the general affairs of the United States under their direction—to appoint one of their number to preside, provided that no person be allowed to serve in the office of president more than one year in any term of three years; to ascertain the necessary sums of money to be raised for the service of the United States, and to appropriate and apply the same for defraying the public expenses—to borrow money, or emit bills on the credit of the United States, transmitting every half year to the respective States an account of the sums of money so borrowed or emitted,—to build and equip a navy—to agree upon the number of land forces, and to make requisitions from each State for its quota, in proportion to the number of white inhabitants in such State; which requisition shall be binding, and thereupon the Legislature of each State shall appoint the regimental officers, raise the men and cloath, arm and equip them in a soldier like manner, at the expense of the United States; and the officers and men so cloathed, armed and equipped shall march to the place appointed, and within the time agreed on by the United States in Congress assembled: but if the United States in Congress assembled shall, on consideration of circumstances judge proper that any State should not raise men, or should raise a smaller number than its quota, and that any other State should raise a greater number of men than the quota thereof, such extra number shall be raised, officered, cloathed, armed and equipped in the same manner as the quota of such State, unless the legislature of such State shall judge that such extra number cannot be safely spared out of the same, in which case they shall raise officer, cloath, arm and equip as many of such extra number as they judge can be safely spared. And the officers and men so cloathed, armed and equipped, shall march to the place appointed, and within the time agreed on by the United States in Congress assembled.

The United States in Congress assembled shall never engage in a war, nor grant letters of marque and reprisal in time of peace, nor enter into any treaties or alliances, nor coin money, nor regulate the value thereof, nor ascertain the sums and expenses necessary for the defence and welfare of the United States, or any of them, nor emit bills, nor borrow money on the credit of the United States, nor appropriate money, nor agree upon the number of vessels of war, to be built or purchased, or the number of land or sea forces to be raised, nor appoint a commander in chief of the army or navy, unless nine States assent to the same: nor shall a question on any other point, except for adjourning from day to day be determined, unless by the votes of a majority of the United States in Congress assembled.

The Congress of the United States shall have power to adjourn to any time within the year, and to any place within the United States, so that no period of adjournment be for a longer duration than the space of six months, and shall publish the journal of their proceedings monthly, except such parts thereof relating to treaties, alliances or military operations, as in their judgment require secresy; and the yeas and nays of the delegates of each State on any question shall be entered on the journal, when it is desired by any delegate; and the delegates of a State, or any of them, at his or their request shall be furnished with a transcript of the said journal, except such parts as are above excepted, to lay before the Legislatures of the several States.

Article X. The committee of the States, or any nine of them, shall be authorized to execute, in the recess of Congress, such of the powers of Congress as the United States in Congress assembled, by the consent of nine States, shall from time to time think expedient to vest them with; provided that no power be delegated to the said committee, for the exercise of which, by the articles of confederation, the voice of nine States in the Congress of the United States assembled is requisite.

Article XI. Canada acceding to this confederation, and joining in the measures of the United States, shall be admitted into, and entitled to all the advantages of this Union: but no other colony shall be admitted into the same, unless such admission be agreed to by nine States.

Article XII. All bills of credit emitted, monies borrowed and debts contracted by, or under the authority of Congress, before the assembling of the United States, in pursuance of the present confederation, shall be deemed and considered as a charge against the United States, for payment and satisfaction whereof the said United States, and the public faith are hereby solemnly pledged.

Article XIII. Every State shall abide by the determinations of the United States in Congress assembled, on all questions which by this confederation are submitted to them. And the articles of this confederation shall be inviolably observed by every State, and the Union shall be perpetual; nor shall any alteration at any time hereafter be made in any of them; unless such alteration be agreed to in a Congress of the United States, and be afterwards confirmed by the Legislatures of every State.

And whereas it has pleased the Great Governor of the World to incline the hearts of the Legislatures we respectively represent in Congress, to approve of, and to authorize us to ratify the said articles of confederation and perpetual union. Know ye that we the undersigned delegates, by virtue of the power and authority to us given for that purpose, do by these presents in the name and in behalf of our respective constituents, fully and entirely ratify and confirm each and every of the said articles of confederation and perpetual union, and all and singular the matters and things therein contained: and we do further solemnly plight and engage the faith of our respective constituents, that they shall abide by the determinations of the United States in Congress assembled, on all questions, which by the said confederation are submitted to them. And that the articles thereof shall be inviolably observed by the States we respectively represent, and that the Union shall be perpetual.

In witness whereof we have hereunto set our hands in Congress. Done at Philadelphia in the State of Pennsylvania the ninth day of July in the year of our Lord one thousand seven hundred and seventy-eight, and in the third year of the independence of America.

On the part & behalf of the State of New Hampshire.

JOSIAH BARTLETT,   JOHN WENTWORTH, JUNR.,
                           August 8th, 1778.

On the part and behalf of the State of Massachusetts Bay.

JOHN HANCOCK,   FRANCIS DANA,
SAMUEL ADAMS,   JAMES LOVELL,
ELBRIDGE GERRY,   SAMUEL HOLTEN.

On the part and behalf of the State of Rhode Island and Providence Plantations.

WILLIAM ELLERY,   JOHN COLLINS.
HENRY MARCHANT,

On the part and behalf of the State of Connecticut.

ROGER SHERMAN,   TITUS HOSMER,
SAMUEL HUNTINGTON,   ANDREW ADAMS.
OLIVER WOLCOTT,

On the part and behalf of the State of New York.

JAS. DUANE,   WM. DUER,
FRA. LEWIS,   GOUV. MORRIS.

On the part and in behalf of the State of New Jersey, Novr. 26 1778.

JNO. WITHERSPOON,   NATH. SCUDDER.

On the part and behalf of the State of Pennsylvania.

ROBT. MORRIS,   WILLIAM CLINGAN,
DANIEL ROBERDEAU,   JOSEPH REED,
JONA. BAYARD SMITH,   22d July, 1778.

    On the part & behalf of the State of Delaware.

THO. M'KEAN,   NICHOLAS VAN DYKE.

    Feby. 12, 1779.

JOHN DICKINSON, May 5th, 1779.

    On the part and behalf of the State of Maryland.

JOHN HANSON,   DANIEL CARROLL,
    March 1, 1781.   Mar. 1, 1781.

    On the part and behalf of the State of Virginia.

RICHARD HENRY LEE,   JNO. HARVIE,
JOHN BANISTER,   FRANCIS LIGHTFOOT LEE.
THOMAS ADAMS,

    On the part and behalf of the State of No. Carolina.

JOHN PENN, July 21, 1778.   JNO. WILLIAMS.
CORNS. HARNETT,

    On the part & behalf of the State of South Carolina.

HENRY LAURENS,   RICHD. HUTSON,
WILLIAM HENRY DRAYTON,   THOS. HEYWARD, JUNR.
JNO. MATHEWS,

    On the part & behalf of the State of Georgia.

JNO. WALTON,   EDWD. LANGWORTHY.
    24th July, 1778.
EDWD. TELFAIR,

CONSTITUTION OF THE UNITED STATES—
1789–

WE THE PEOPLE of the United States, in Order to form a more perfect Union, establish Justice, insure domestic Tranquillity, provide for the common defence, promote the general Welfare, and secure the Blessings of Liberty to ourselves and our Posterity, do ordain and establish this CONSTITUTION for the United States of America.

ARTICLE I.

Section 1. All legislative Powers herein granted shall be vested in a Congress of the United States, which shall consist of a Senate and a House of Representatives.

Section 2. The House of Representatives shall be composed of Members chosen every second Year by the People of the several States, and the Electors in each State shall have the Qualifications requisite for Electors of the most numerous Branch of the State Legislature.

No person shall be a Representative who shall not have attained to the Age of twenty-five Years, and been seven Years a Citizen of the United States, and who shall not, when elected, be an Inhabitant of that State in which he shall be chosen.

Representatives and direct Taxes shall be apportioned among the several States which may be included within this Union, according to their respective Numbers, which shall be determined by adding to the whole Number of Free persons, including those bound to Service for a Term of Years, and excluding Indians not taxed, three fifths of all other Persons. The actual Enumeration shall be made within three Years after the first Meeting of the Congress of the United States, and within every subsequent Term of ten Years, in such Manner as they shall by Law direct. The Number of Representatives shall not exceed one for every thirty Thousand, but each State shall have at Least one Representative; and until such enumeration shall be made, the State of New Hampshire shall be entitled to chuse three, Massachusetts eight, Rhode Island and Providence Plantations one, Connecticut five, New York six, New Jersey four, Pennsylvania eight, Delaware one, Maryland six, Virginia ten, North Carolina five, South Carolina five, and Georgia three.

When vacancies happen in the Representation from any State, the Executive Authority thereof shall issue Writs of Election to fill such Vacancies.

The House of Representatives shall chuse their Speaker and other Officers; and shall have the sole Power of Impeachment.

Section 3. The Senate of the United States shall be composed of two Senators from each State, chosen by the Legislature thereof, for six Years; [1] and each Senator shall have one Vote.

Immediately after they shall be assembled in Consequence of the first Election, they shall be divided as equally as may be into three Classes. The seats of the Senators of the first Class shall be vacated at the Expiration of the second Year, of the second Class at the Expiration of the fourth Year, and of the third Class at the Expiration of the sixth Year, so that one-third may be chosen every second Year; and if Vacancies happen by Resignation, or otherwise, during the Recess of the Legislature of any State, the Executive thereof may make temporary Appointments until the next Meeting of the Legislature, which shall then fill such Vacancies.[2]

No Person shall be a Senator who shall not have attained to the Age of thirty Years, and been nine Years a Citizen of the United States, and who shall not, when elected, be an Inhabitant of that State for which he shall be chosen.

The Vice President of the United States shall be President of the Senate, but shall have no Vote, unless they be equally divided.

The Senate shall chuse their other Officers, and also a President pro tempore, in the Absence of the Vice President, or when he shall exercise the Office of President of the United States.

The Senate shall have the sole Power to try all Impeachments. When sitting for that Purpose, they shall be on Oath or Affirmation. When the President of the United States is tried, the Chief Justice shall preside: and no Person shall be convicted without the Concurrence of two thirds of the Members present.

Judgment in Cases of Impeachment shall not extend further than to removal from Office, and disqualification to hold and enjoy any Office of honor, Trust or Profit under the United States: but the Party convicted shall nevertheless be liable and subject to Indictment, Trial, Judgment and Punishment, according to Law.

Section 4. The Times, Places and manner of holding Elections for Senators and Representatives, shall be prescribed in each State by the Legislature thereof; but the Congress may at any time by Law make or alter such Regulations, except as to the Places of chusing Senators.

The Congress shall assemble at least once in every Year, and such Meeting shall be on the first Monday in December, unless they shall by Law appoint a different Day.

Section 5. Each House shall be the Judge of the Elections, Returns and Qualifications of its own Members, and a Majority of each shall

---

[1] Changed by the seventeenth amendment.
[2] Changed by the seventeenth amendment.

constitute a Quorum to do Business; but a smaller Number may adjourn from day to day, and may be authorized to compel the Attendance of absent Members, in such Manner, and under such Penalties as each House may provide.

Each House may determine the Rules of its Proceedings, punish its Members for disorderly Behaviour, and, with the Concurrence of two thirds, expel a Member.

Each House shall keep a Journal of its Proceedings, and from time to time publish the same, excepting such Parts as may in their Judgment require Secrecy; and the Yeas and Nays of the Members of either House on any question shall, at the Desire of one fifth of those present, be entered on the Journal.

Neither House, during the Session of Congress, shall, without the Consent of the other, adjourn for more than three days, nor to any other Place than that in which the two Houses shall be sitting.

Section 6. The Senators and Representatives shall receive a Compensation for their services, to be ascertained by Law, and paid out of the Treasury of the United States. They shall in all Cases, except Treason, Felony and Breach of the Peace, be privileged from Arrest during their Attendance at the Session of their respective Houses, and in going to and returning from the same; and for any Speech or Debate in either House, they shall not be questioned in any other Place.

No Senator or Representative shall, during the Time for which he was elected, be appointed to any civil Office under the Authority of the United States, which shall have been created, or the Emoluments whereof shall have been increased during such time; and no Person holding any Office under the United States, shall be a Member of either House during his Continuance in Office.

Section 7. All bills for raising Revenue shall originate in the House of Representatives; but the Senate may propose or concur with Amendments as on other Bills.

Every Bill which shall have passed the House of Representatives and the Senate, shall, before it become a Law, be presented to the President of the United States; if he approve he shall sign it, but if not he shall return it, with his Objections to that House in which it shall have originated, who shall enter the Objections at large on their Journal, and proceed to reconsider it. If after such Reconsideration two thirds of that House shall agree to pass the Bill, it shall be sent, together with the Objections, to the other House, by which it shall likewise be reconsidered, and if approved by two thirds of that House, it shall become a Law. But in all such Cases the Votes of both Houses shall be determined by Yeas and Nays, and the Names of the Persons voting for and against the Bill shall be entered on the Journal of each House respectively. If any Bill shall not be returned by the President within ten Days (Sundays excepted) after it shall have been presented to him, the Same shall be a Law, in like Manner as if he had signed it, unless the Congress by their

Adjournment prevent its Return, in which Case it shall not be a Law.

Every Order, Resolution, or Vote to which the Concurrence of the Senate and House of Representatives may be necessary (except on a question of Adjournment) shall be presented to the President of the United States; and before the Same shall take Effect, shall be approved by him, or being disapproved by him, shall be repassed by two thirds of the Senate and House of Representatives, according to the Rules and Limitations prescribed in the Case of a Bill.

Section 8. The Congress shall have Power to lay and collect Taxes, Duties, Imposts and Excises, to pay the Debts and provide for the common Defence and general Welfare of the United States; but all Duties, imposts and Excises shall be uniform throughout the United States;

To borrow Money on the credit of the United States;

To regulate Commerce with foreign Nations, and among the several States, and with the Indian Tribes;

To establish an uniform Rule of Naturalization, and uniform Laws on the subject of Bankruptcies throughout the United States;

To coin Money, regulate the Value thereof, and of foreign Coin, and fix the Standard of Weights and Measures;

To provide for the Punishment of counterfeiting the Securities and current Coin of the United States;

To establish Post Offices and post Roads;

To promote the Progress of Science and useful Arts, by securing for limited Times to Authors and Inventors the exclusive Right to their respective Writings and Discoveries;

To constitute Tribunals inferior to the supreme Court;

To define and punish Piracies and Felonies committed on the high Seas, and Offences against the Law of Nations;

To declare War, grant Letters of Marque and Reprisal, and make Rules concerning Captures on Land and Water;

To raise and support Armies, but no Appropriation of Money to that Use shall be for a longer Term than two Years;

To provide and maintain a Navy;

To make Rules for the Government and Regulation of the land and naval Forces;

To provide for calling forth the Militia to execute the Laws of the Union, suppress Insurrections and repel Invasions;

To provide for organizing, arming, and disciplining the Militia, and for governing such Part of them as may be employed in the Service of the United States, reserving to the States respectively, the Appointment of the Officers, and the Authority of training the Militia according to the discipline prescribed by Congress;

To exercise exclusive Legislation in all Cases whatsoever, over such District (not exceeding ten Miles square) as may, by Cession of particular States, and the Acceptance of Congress, become the Seat of the Government of the United States, and to exercise like Authority over all Places purchased by the Consent of the Legislature of the State in which the

Same shall be, for the Erection of Forts, Magazines, Arsenals, dock-Yards, and other needful Buildings;—And

To make all Laws which shall be necessary and proper for carrying into Execution the foregoing Powers, and all other Powers vested by this Constitution in the Government of the United States, or in any Department or Officer thereof.

Section 9. The Migration or Importation of such Persons as any of the States now existing shall think proper to admit, shall not be prohibited by the Congress prior to the Year one thousand eight hundred and eight, but a Tax or duty may be imposed on such Importation, not exceeding ten dollars for each Person.

The Privilege of the Writ of Habeas Corpus shall not be suspended, unless when in Cases of Rebellion or Invasion the public Safety may require it.

No Bill of Attainder or ex post facto Law shall be passed.

No Capitation, or other direct, tax shall be laid, unless in Proportion to the Census or Enumeration herein before directed to be taken.

No Tax or Duty shall be laid on Articles exported from any State.

No Preference shall be given by any Regulation of Commerce or Revenue to the Ports of one State over those of another: nor shall Vessels bound to, or from, one State, be obliged to enter, clear, or pay Duties in another.

No Money shall be drawn from the Treasury, but in Consequence of Appropriations made by Law; and a regular Statement and Account of the Receipts and Expenditures of all public Money shall be published from time to time.

No Title of Nobility shall be granted by the United States: And no Person holding any Office of Profit or Trust under them, shall, without the Consent of the Congress, accept of any present, Emolument, Office, or Title, of any kind whatever, from any King, Prince, or foreign State.

Section 10. No State shall enter into any Treaty, Alliance, or Confederation; grant Letters of Marque and Reprisal; coin Money; emit Bills of Credit; make any Thing but gold and silver Coin a Tender in Payment of Debts; pass any Bill of Attainder, ex post facto Law, or Law impairing the Obligation of Contracts, or grant any Title of Nobility.

No State shall, without the Consent of the Congress, lay any Imposts or Duties on Imports or Exports, except what may be absolutely necessary for executing it's inspection Laws: and the net Produce of all Duties and Imposts, laid by any State on Imports or Exports, shall be for the Use of the Treasury of the United States; and all such Laws shall be subject to the Revision and Controul of the Congress.

No State shall, without the Consent of Congress, lay any Duty of Tonnage, keep Troops, or Ships of War in time of Peace, enter into any Agreement or Compact with another State, or with a foreign Power, or engage in War, unless actually invaded, or in such imminent Danger as will not admit of delay.

ARTICLE II.

Section 1. The executive Power shall be vested in a President of the United States of America. He shall hold his Office during the Term of four Years, and, together with the Vice President, chosen for the same Term, be elected, as follows

Each State shall appoint, in such Manner as the Legislature thereof may direct, a Number of Electors, equal to the whole Number of Senators and Representatives to which the State may be entitled in the Congress: but no Senator or Representative, or Person holding an Office of Trust or Profit under the United States, shall be appointed an Elector.

The electors shall meet in their respective States, and vote by ballot for two persons, of whom one at least shall not be an inhabitant of the same State with themselves. And they shall make a list of all the persons voted for, and of the number of votes for each; which list they shall sign and certify, and transmit sealed to the seat of the Government of the United States, directed to the President of the Senate. The President of the Senate shall, in the presence of the Senate and House of Representatives, open all the certificates, and the votes shall then be counted. The person having the greatest number of votes shall be the President, if such number be a majority of the whole number of electors appointed; and if there be more than one who have such majority, and have an equal number of votes, then the House of Representatives shall immediately chuse by ballot one of them for President; and if no person have a majority, then from the five highest on the list the said House shall in like manner chuse the President. But in chusing the President, the votes shall be taken by States, the representation from each State having one vote; a quorum for this purpose shall consist of a member or members from two-thirds of the States, and a majority of all the States shall be necessary to a choice. In every case, after the choice of the President, the person having the greatest number of votes of the electors shall be the Vice President. But if there should remain two or more who have equal votes, the Senate shall chuse from them by ballot the Vice-President.[1]

The Congress may determine the Time of chusing the Electors, and the Day on which they shall give their Votes; which Day shall be the same throughout the United States.

No person except a natural born Citizen, or a Citizen of the United States, at the time of the Adoption of this Constitution, shall be eligible to the Office of President; neither shall any Person be eligible to that office who shall not have attained to the Age of thirty five Years, and been fourteen Years a Resident within the United States.

In Case of the Removal of the President from Office, or of his Death, Resignation or Inability to discharge the Powers and Duties of the said Office, the Same shall devolve on the Vice President, and the Congress

---

[1] Changed by the twelfth amendment.

may by Law provide for the Case of Removal, Death, Resignation or Inability, both of the President and Vice President, declaring what Officer shall then act as President, and such Officer shall act accordingly, until the Disability be removed, or a President shall be elected.

The President shall, at stated Times, receive for his Services, a Compensation, which shall neither be encreased nor diminished during the Period for which he shall have been elected, and he shall not receive within that Period any other Emolument from the United States, or any of them.

Before he enter on the Execution of his Office, he shall take the following Oath or Affirmation:—"I do solemnly swear (or affirm) that I will faithfully execute the Office of President of the United States, and will to the best of my Ability, preserve, protect and defend the Constitution of the United States."

Section 2. The President shall be Commander in Chief of the Army and Navy of the United States, and of the Militia of the several States, when called into the actual Service of the United States; he may require the Opinion, in writing, of the principal Officer in each of the executive Departments, upon any Subject relating to the Duties of their respective Offices, and he shall have Power to grant Reprieves and Pardons for Offences against the United States, except in Cases of Impeachment.

He shall have Power, by and with the Advice and Consent of the Senate, to make Treaties, provided two thirds of the Senators present concur; and he shall nominate, and by and with the Advice and Consent of the Senate, shall appoint Ambassadors, other public Ministers and Consuls, Judges of the supreme Court, and all other Officers of the United States, whose Appointments are not herein otherwise provided for, and which shall be established by Law: but the Congress may by Law vest the Appointment of such inferior Officers, as they think proper, in the President alone, in the Courts of Law, or in the Heads of Departments.

The President shall have Power to fill up all Vacancies that may happen during the recess of the Senate, by granting Commissions which shall expire at the End of their next Session.

Section 3. He shall from time to time give to the Congress Information of the state of the Union, and recommend to their Consideration such Measures as he shall judge necessary and expedient; he may, on extraordinary Occasions, convene both Houses, or either of them, and, in Case of Disagreement between them, with Respect to the Time of Adjournment, he may adjourn them to such Time as he shall think proper; he shall receive Ambassadors and other public Ministers; he shall take Care that the Laws be faithfully executed, and shall Commission all the Officers of the United States.

Section 4. The President, Vice President and all civil Officers of the United States, shall be removed from Office on Impeachment for, and Conviction of, Treason, Bribery, or other high Crimes and Misdemeanors.

ARTICLE III.

Section 1. The judicial Power of the United States, shall be vested in one supreme Court, and in such inferior Courts as the Congress may from time to time ordain and establish. The Judges, both of the supreme and inferior Courts, shall hold their Offices during good Behaviour, and shall, at stated Times, receive for their Services, a Compensation, which shall not be diminished during their Continuance in Office.

Section 2. The judicial Power shall extend to all Cases, in Law and Equity, arising under this Constitution, the Laws of the United States, and Treaties made, or which shall be made, under their Authority;—to all Cases affecting Ambassadors, other public Ministers and Consuls;—to all Cases of admiralty and maritime Jurisdiction;—to Controversies to which the United States shall be a Party;—to Controversies between two or more States;—between a State and Citizens of another State;—between Citizens of different States,—between Citizens of the same State claiming Lands under Grants of different States, and between a State,[1] or the Citizens thereof, and foreign States, Citizens or Subjects.

In all Cases affecting Ambassadors, other public Ministers and Consuls, and those in which a State shall be Party, the supreme Court shall have original Jurisdiction. In all the other Cases before mentioned, the supreme Court shall have appellate Jurisdiction, both as to Law and Fact, with such Exceptions, and under such Regulations as the Congress shall make.

The Trial of all Crimes, except in Cases of Impeachment, shall be by Jury; and such Trial shall be held in the State where the said Crimes shall have been committed; but when not committed within any State, the Trial shall be at such Place or Places as the Congress may by Law have directed.

Section 3. Treason against the United States, shall consist only in levying War against them, or in adhering to their Enemies, giving them Aid and Comfort. No Person shall be convicted of Treason unless on the Testimony of two Witnesses to the same overt Act, or on Confession in open Court.

The Congress shall have Power to declare the Punishment of Treason, but no Attainder of Treason shall work Corruption of Blood, or Forfeiture except during the Life of the Person attainted.

ARTICLE IV.

Section 1. Full Faith and Credit shall be given in each State to the public Acts, Records, and judicial Proceedings of every other State. And the Congress may by general Laws prescribe the Manner in which such Acts, Records and Proceedings shall be proved, and the Effect thereof.

Section 2. The Citizens of each State shall be entitled to all Privileges and immunities of Citizens in the several States.

[1] This paragraph was changed by amendment eleven.

A person charged in any State with Treason, Felony, or other Crime, who shall flee from Justice, and be found in another State, shall on Demand of the executive Authority of the State from which he fled, be delivered up to be removed to the State having Jurisdiction of the Crime.

No Person held to Service or Labour in one State, under the Laws thereof, escaping into another, shall, in Consequence of any Law or Regulation therein, be discharged from such Service or Labour, but shall be delivered up on Claim of the Party to whom such Service or Labour may be due.

Section 3. New States may be admitted by the Congress into this Union; but no new State shall be formed or erected within the Jurisdiction of any other State; nor any State be formed by the Junction of two or more States, or Parts of States, without the Consent of the Legislatures of the States concerned as well as of the Congress.

The Congress shall have Power to dispose of and make all needful Rules and Regulations respecting the Territory or other Property belonging to the United States; and nothing in this Constitution shall be so construed as to Prejudice any Claims of the United States, or of any particular State.

Section 4. The United States shall guarantee to every State in this Union a Republican Form of Government, and shall protect each of them against Invasion; and on Application of the Legislature, or of the Executive (when the Legislature cannot be convened) against domestic Violence.

ARTICLE V.

The Congress, whenever two thirds of both Houses shall deem it necessary, shall propose Amendments to this Constitution, or, on the Application of the Legislatures of two thirds of the several States, shall call a Convention for proposing Amendments, which, in either Case, shall be valid to all Intents and Purposes, as Part of this Constitution, when ratified by the Legislatures of three fourths of the several States, or by Conventions in three fourths thereof, as the one or the other Mode of Ratification may be proposed by the Congress; Provided that no Amendment which may be made prior to the Year One thousand eight hundred and eight shall in any Manner affect the first and fourth Clauses in the Ninth Section of the first Article; and that no State, without its Consent, shall be deprived of its equal Suffrage in the Senate.

ARTICLE VI.

All Debts contracted and Engagements entered into, before the Adoption of this Constitution, shall be as valid against the United States under this Constitution, as under the Confederation.

This Constitution, and the Laws of the United States which shall be made in Pursuance thereof; and all Treaties made, or which shall .be made, under the Authority of the United States, shall be the supreme Law of the Land; and the Judges in every State shall be bound thereby, any Thing in the Constitution or Laws of any State to the Contrary notwithstanding.

The Senators and Representatives before mentioned, and the Members of the several State Legislatures, and all executive and judicial Officers, both of the United States and of the several States, shall be bound by Oath or Affirmation, to support this Constitution; but no religious Test shall ever be required as a Qualification to any Office or public Trust under the United States.

ARTICLE VII.

The ratification of the Conventions of nine States, shall be sufficient for the Establishment of this Constitution between the States so ratifying the Same.

DONE in Convention by the Unanimous Consent of the States present the Seventeenth Day of September in the Year of our Lord one thousand seven hundred and Eighty seven, and of the Independance of the United States of America the Twelfth. In witness whereof We have hereunto subscribed our Names,

Gº: WASHINGTON—
Presidt., and Deputy from Virginia.

New Hampshire.

JOHN LANGDON,	NICHOLAS GILMAN.

Massachusetts.

NATHANIEL GORHAM,	RUFUS KING.

Connecticut.

WM. SAML. JOHNSON,	ROGER SHERMAN.

New York.

ALEXANDER HAMILTON.

New Jersey.

WIL: LIVINGSTON,	WM. PATERSON,
DAVID BREARLEY,	JONA. DAYTON.

Pennsylvania.

B. FRANKLIN,	THOS. FITZSIMONS,
THOMAS MIFFLIN,	JARED INGERSOLL,
ROBT. MORRIS,	JAMES WILSON,
GEO. CLYMER,	GOUV. MORRIS.

Delaware.

GEO. READ,	RICHARD BASSETT,
GUNNING BEDFORD, JUN.,	JACO : BROOM.
JOHN DICKINSON,	

Maryland.

JAMES MCHENRY,	DAN. CARROLL.
DAN. JENIFER, of St. Thomas,	

Virginia.

JOHN BLAIR,	JAMES MADISON, JR.

North Carolina.

WM. BLOUNT,
RICH'D DOBBS SPEIGHT,

HUGH WILLIAMSON.

South Carolina.

J. RUTLEDGE,
CHARLES COTESWORTH PINCK-
NEY,

CHARLES PINCKNEY,
PIERCE BUTLER.

Georgia.

WILLIAM FEW,
Attest:

ABR. BALDWIN.
WILLIAM JACKSON, Secretary.

ARTICLES IN ADDITION TO, AND AMENDMENT OF, THE CONSTITUTION OF THE UNITED STATES OF AMERICA, PROPOSED BY CONGRESS, AND RATIFIED BY THE LEGISLATURES OF THE SEVERAL STATES PURSUANT TO THE FIFTH ARTICLE OF THE ORIGINAL CONSTITUTION.

ARTICLE I.

(The first ten Articles declared in force November 3, 1791)

Congress shall make no law respecting an establishment of religion, or prohibiting the free exercise thereof; or abridging the freedom of speech, or of the press; or the right of the people peaceably to assemble, and to petition the Government for a redress of grievances.

ARTICLE II.

A well regulated Militia, being necessary to the security of a free State, the right of the people to keep and bear Arms, shall not be infringed.

ARTICLE III.

No Soldier shall, in time of peace, be quartered in any house, without the consent of the Owner, nor in time of war, but in a manner to be prescribed by law.

ARTICLE IV.

The right of the people to be secure in their persons, houses, papers, and effects, against unreasonable searches and seizures, shall not be violated, and no Warrants shall issue, but upon probable cause, supported by Oath or affirmation, and particularly describing the place to be searched, and the persons or things to be seized.

ARTICLE V.

No person shall be held to answer for a capital, or otherwise infamous crime, unless on a presentment or indictment of a Grand Jury, except in cases arising in the land or naval forces, or in the Militia, when in actual service in time of War or public danger; nor shall any person be subject for the same offence to be twice put in jeopardy of life or limb; nor shall be compelled in any Criminal Case to be a witness against himself, nor be deprived of life, liberty, or property, without due process of law; nor shall private property be taken for public use, without just compensation.

ARTICLE VI.

In all criminal prosecutions, the accused shall enjoy the right to a speedy and public trial, by an impartial jury of the State and district wherein the crime shall have been committed, which district shall have been previously ascertained by law, and to be informed of the nature and cause of the accusation; to be confronted with the witnesses against him; to have compulsory process for obtaining witnesses in his favor, and to have the Assistance of Counsel for his defence.

ARTICLE VII.

In suits at common law, where the value in controversy shall exceed twenty dollars, the right of trial by jury shall be preserved, and no fact tried by a jury shall be otherwise re-examined in any Court of the United States, than according to the rules of the common law.

ARTICLE VIII.

Excessive bail shall not be required, nor excessive fines imposed, nor cruel and unusual punishments inflicted.

ARTICLE IX.

The enumeration in the Constitution, of certain rights, shall not be construed to deny or disparage others retained by the people.

ARTICLE X.

The powers not delegated to the United States by the Constitution, nor prohibited by it to the States, are reserved to the States respectively, or to the people.

ARTICLE XI.

(January 8, 1798)

The Judicial power of the United States shall not be construed to extend to any suit in law or equity, commenced or prosecuted against one of the United States by Citizens of another State, or by Citizens or Subjects of any Foreign State.

ARTICLE XII.

(September 25, 1804)

The Electors shall meet in their respective States, and vote by ballot for President and Vice-President, one of whom, at least, shall not be an inhabitant of the same State with themselves; they shall name in their ballots the person voted for as President, and in distinct ballots the person voted for as Vice-President, and they shall make distinct lists of all persons voted for as President, and of all persons voted for as Vice-President, and of the number of votes for each, which lists they shall sign and certify, and transmit sealed to the seat of the Government of the United States, directed to the President of the Senate;—The President of the Senate shall, in the presence of the Senate and House of Representatives, open all the certificates and the votes shall then be counted;—The person having the greatest number of votes for President, shall be the President, if such number be a majority of the whole number of Electors appointed; and if no person have such majority, then from the persons having the highest numbers not exceeding three on the list of those voted for as President, the House of Representatives shall choose immediately, by ballot, the President. But in choosing the President, the votes shall be taken by states, the representation from each state having one vote; a quorum for this purpose shall consist of a member or members from two thirds of the states, and a majority of all the states shall be necessary to a choice. And if the House of Representatives shall not choose a President whenever the right of choice shall devolve upon them, before the fourth day of March next following, then the Vice-President shall act as President, as in the case of the death or other constitutional disability of the President. The person having the greatest number of votes as Vice-president, shall be the Vice-President, if such number be a majority of the whole number of Electors appointed, and if no person have a majority, then from the two highest numbers on the list, the Senate shall choose the Vice-President; a quorum for the purpose shall consist of two-thirds of the whole number of Senators, and a majority of whole number shall be necessary to a choice. But no person constitutionally ineligible to the office of President shall be eligible to that of Vice-President of the United States.

ARTICLE XIII.

(December 18, 1865)

Section 1. Neither slavery nor involuntary servitude, except as a punishment for crime whereof the party shall have been duly convicted, shall exist within the United States, or any place subject to their jurisdiction.
Section 2. Congress shall have power to enforce this article by appropriate legislation.

ARTICLE XIV.

(July 23, 1868)

Section 1. All persons born or naturalized in the United States, and subject to the jurisdiction thereof, are citizens of the United States and of the State wherein they reside. No State shall make or enforce any law which shall abridge the privileges or immunities of citizens of the United States; nor shall any State deprive any person of life, liberty, or property, without due process of law; nor deny to any person within its jurisdiction the equal protection of the laws.

Section 2. Representatives shall be apportioned among the several States according to their respective numbers, counting the whole number of persons in each State, excluding Indians not taxed. But when the right to vote at any election for the choice of electors for President and Vice-President of the United States, Representatives in Congress, the Executive and Judicial officers of a State, or the members of the Legislature thereof, is denied to any of the male inhabitants of such State, being twenty-one years of age, and citizens of the United States, or in any way abridged, except for participation in rebellion, or other crime, the the basis of representation therein shall be reduced in the proportion which the number of such male citizens shall bear to the whole number of male citizens twenty-one years of age in such State.

Section 3. No person shall be a Senator or Representative in Congress, or elector of President and Vice-President, or hold any office, civil, or military, under the United States, or under any State, who, having previously taken an oath, as a member of Congress, or as an officer of the United States, or as a member of any State Legislature, or as an executive or judicial officer of any State, to support the Constitution of the United States, shall have engaged in insurrection or rebellion against the same, or given aid or comfort to the enemies thereof. But Congress may by a vote of two-thirds of each House, remove such disability.

Section 4. The validity of the public debt of the United States, authorized by law, including debts incurred for payment of pensions and bounties for services in suppressing insurrection or rebellion, shall not be questioned. But neither the United States nor any State shall assume or pay any debt or obligation incurred in aid of insurrection or rebellion against the United States, or any claim for the loss or emancipation of any slave; but all such debts, obligations and claims shall be held illegal and void.

Section 5. The Congress shall have power to enforce, by appropriate legislation, the provisions of this article.

ARTICLE XV.

(*March 30, 1870*)

Section 1. The right of citizens of the United States to vote shall not be denied or abridged by the United States or by any State on account of race, color, or previous condition of servitude.

Section 2. The Congress shall have power to enforce this article by appropriate legislation.

ARTICLE XVI.

(*February 25, 1913*)

The Congress shall have power to lay and collect taxes on incomes, from whatever source derived, without apportionment among the several States, and without regard to any census or enumeration.

INDEX

Ableman vs. Booth (1859), 458.

Adams, John, on causes of American Revolution, 82-3; defends British soldiers, 103-4; at First Continental Congress, 111; estimates American attitude on Revolution, 115; drafts treaty with France, 129; and Massachusetts Constitution of 1779, 149; Minister to Great Britain, 172, 173, 190; elected Vice President, 241-2; elected President, 296; foreign relations under, 430-1.

Adams, John Quincy, Secretary of State, 255, 432; elected President, 297, 404; upholds freedom of petition, 376-7.

Adams, Samuel, radical leader, 109; at First Continental Congress, 111; on committee to draft Articles of Confederation, 131; absent from Constitutional Convention, 190.

Adkins vs. Children's Hospital (1923), 292.

Administration of Justice Act, 106, 294.

Administrative agencies, national, 243-4, 252-74; reorganization of during war time, 480, 481. *See also* Executive Institutions, Departments.

Admission of new states, under Virginia Plan, 193; under New Jersey Plan, 196; under Constitution, 450.

Advisory opinions of Supreme Court, 335.

Albany Conference of 1684, and colonial union, 66.

Albany Congress of 1754, 75-7; called by English Board of Trade, 75; colonies represented, 75; Peters' Plan of Union, 76; Franklin Plan of Union, 76-7.

Alexandria Convention, 179.

Amendments, proposed for Articles of Confederation, 170-1, 173-4; under Virginia plan, 193; Constitutional provision for, 211; process of making, 279-83, 329-30, 451; limitations on power of making, 283-4; bill of rights proposed, 284-5.

Amendments ratified: first, 285-9, 376-7, 484-5; second, 289-90; third, 290; fourth, 290, 473; fifth, 285, 290-3, 474; sixth, 293-4; seventh, 294; eighth, 294-5; ninth, 295; tenth, 295, 356, 442-3; eleventh, 295-6, 336, 451; twelfth, 296-7, 321; thirteenth, 297-8, 442, 446-7, 460, 477; fifteenth, 301, 460; sixteenth, 302-4, 470; seventeenth, 304-7; eighteenth, 280, 281, 282, 307-13; nine-

teenth, 313-8, 460; twentieth, 281, 319-22, 384; text of amendments ratified, 509-14.

Amendments not ratified: approved by Congress, 322-9, 460; proposed to Congress, 329-30, 456.

American Commonwealth, The, J. B. Bryce, 207.

American Insurance Co. vs. Canter (1828), 342.

Anderson vs. Dunn (1824), 341.

Andros, Sir Edmund, 23, 31.

Annapolis Convention, issues call for revision of Articles of Confederation, 180, 183.

Anthony, Susan B., and woman suffrage, 317.

Anti-Federalists, oppose ratification of Constitution, 219-38; win under Jefferson, 402; in national government, 417-8.

Anti-Saloon League, and prohibition, 308.

Appointive power, of president, 393-5, 406-7, 409-10, 434.

Armed forces, raising and supporting of, 466-8.

Arms, right to bear, under second amendment, 289.

Articles of Confederation, 130-2, 157-81; background of, 130-1; committee drafts, 131; approved by states, 132; general character of, 157-8; form of government under, 158-60, 390; powers of Congress under, 160-2; conduct of government under, 162-81; text of, 491-8.

Austrian Succession, war of, 70-2.

Bacon, Nathaniel, 14.

Bailey vs. Drexel Furniture Co. (1922), 326, 341.

Banks, national, Supreme Court on, 338-40; Andrew Jackson on, 361, 405-6.

Barbary pirates, American relations with, 176-7.

Barron vs. Baltimore (1833), 285.

Bayard vs. Singleton (1787), 333.

Berkeley, Sir William, 13-4.

Bienville, Celeron de, expedition of, 73-4.

Bill of Rights, 2.

Board of Trade, English, calls Albany Congress, 75; functions of, 88; recommends Proclamation of 1763, 94.

"Boston Massacre" of 1770, 103-4.

Boston Port Act, 105, 110.

"Boston Tea Party," 104-5; causes Coercive Acts, 105.
Bradford, William, Governor of Plymouth Colony, 16, 18.
Briscoe vs. Bank of Kentucky (1837), 445.
"Broad construction," 355-6.
Brown vs. Maryland (1827), 344.
Brushaber vs. Union Pacific Railroad Co. (1916), 303-4.
Buchanan, James, Secretary of State, 255; on relation of president to courts, 407.
Budget Act of 1921, 362-3.

Cabinet system, origin of, 393, 400-1; proposals for reform of, 411-2; influence of custom and tradition on, 428-30, 434.
Calder vs. Bull (1798), 336.
Calhoun, John C., and nullification, 456.
Calvert, Cecilius, and Maryland Colony, 34-6.
"Cambridge Agreement, The," 21.
Caraway, Mrs. Hattie W., elected senator, 318.
Carroll vs. U. S. (1925), 290.
Carver, John, and Plymouth Colony, 17, 18.
Case of Hayburn (1792), 335.
"Caucus" system, of nominations, 403-4, 423; for legislative control, 437-8.
Census, provided for in Constitution, 208; legislation by Congress on, 372.
Champlain, Samuel de, establishes Quebec, 64.
Charles River Bridge Co. vs. Warren Bridge (1837), 348.
Child labor, legislation on, 324-5, 381; Supreme Court decisions on, 325-7, 341, 345-6; proposed amendment on, 327-9, 460.
Chisholm vs. Georgia (1793), 295, 335-6.
Citizenship, defined in fourteenth amendment, 299-300.
Civil Rights, and fourteenth amendment, 298-300.
Civil Service Reform Act, 395.
Clay, Henry, on veto power, 405.
Clayton Anti-Trust Act, 369.
Cleveland, Grover, conduct of presidential office by, 409-10; and third term tradition, 425-6; and Pullman strike, 451.
Coercive Acts, 105-7.
Cohens vs. Virginia (1821), 349.
Coke, Sir Edward, 332-3.
Colbert, Jean Baptiste, promotes French colonization in America, 64-5.
Collector vs. Day, The (1871), 340.
Colonization in America, English, early delay in, 4-5; motives for, 5-6; attempts at by individuals, 6. *See also* individual colonies by name.
Commerce, national regulation of, under New Jersey Plan, 194-5; debated in Constitutional Convention, 202-3; provided for in Constitution, 209; in Supreme Court decisions, 342-6; by Congress, 357-8, 366-9.
Committee of Detail, 201-2.

Committee on Public Information, 482-3.
Committee on Style, 204-5.
"Committee system" in Congress, 249-52, 385-6, 436.
Committees of Correspondence, 109.
Compact theory, in Connecticut Colony, 28.
Compromise of 1850, 377-8, 458.
Concord, Battle of, 117.
Concurrent powers, state and federal, 443.
Confederate States of America, 444-5, 459.
Congress, *Continental:* First, 109-15; Second, 117-32.
    Confederation: structure, 158-60; powers of, 160-2, 442-3; calls Constitutional Convention, 183; puts Constitution into effect, 239-40.
    National: provided for in Constitution, 207-9; first election of, 240; sets up governmental agencies under Constitution, 243-8, 252-78; expansion and organization of, 248-52; sessions of, under twentieth amendment, 319-20; approved amendments not ratified, 322-9; amendments submitted to, not approved, 329-30; implied powers of, 338-42, 355-6; limitations on powers of, 356-7, 443-4; tariff legislation by, 357-8; financial legislation by, 358-65; internal improvements by, 365-6; transportation subsidies by, 366; regulation of commerce by, 366-9; regulation of naturalization and immigration by, 369-71; miscellaneous legislation by, 371-4; and slavery, 374-9; acquisition of territory by, 379-80; trend toward social legislation by, 381-2; electoral power of, 382-4, 451; judicial powers of, 384-5; "constituent" power of, 385; decline in prestige of, 385; influence of president over, 398-9; President Washington and, 399-402; and nomination of president, 403-4, 423; President Jackson and, 405-6; effect of lobbies on, 420-1; effect of custom and tradition on, 436-9; concurrent powers of, 443; and interstate relations, 445; war powers of, 462-3; exercise of war powers by, 463-81, 484-8. *See also* House of Representatives, Legislative Institutions, Senate.
Connecticut, settled in 1635, 28; governed under Fundamental Orders of Connecticut, 29-30; New Haven Colony joined to, 30; under charter of 1661, 31; in New England Confederation, 62-4; at New York Conference of 1690, 67; at Albany Congress of 1754, 75; at Stamp Act Congress, 99; on independence question, 125; ratifies Articles of Confederation, 132; adopts state constitution, 137; interstate relations during "critical period," 178; ratifies U. S. Constitution, 227.
Conscription, 466-8.
Conservation of natural resources, 263-4.
Constitution, *State:* 134-56; Second Continental Congress advises adoption of, 134-5; New Hampshire, 135-6; South

Carolina, 136-7; Rhode Island, 137; Connecticut, 137; Virginia, 138-9; New Jersey, 139-40; Delaware, 140-1; Pennsylvania, 141-3; Maryland, 143-5; North Carolina, 145-6; Georgia, 146-7; New York, 147-9; Massachusetts, 149-53; general features of, 153-6.

National: framing of, 183-206; analysis of, 206-13; ratification of, 214-38; development of governmental agencies under, 240-78; amendment of, 279-330; judicial interpretation of, 280-1, 283-95, 302-4, 325-7, 332-53, 355-6, 367, 370, 372, 379, 403, 406, 408, 439-40, 445-7, 450, 456, 458, 460, 464, 467-8, 472-5; legislative expansion of, 355-86; role of executive under, 388-414; influence of custom and tradition on, 416-40; state and federal relations under, 442-61; in time of war, 462-88; text of, 499-514.

Continental Association, formed by First Continental Congress, 113; nature of, 113-4; backed by public opinion, 114.

Continental Congress, *First:* 109-15; background of, 109-10; colonies represented, 110-1; prominent delegates, 111; Suffolk resolves adopted, 112; "Declaration of Rights" adopted, 112-3; Continental Association formed, 113-4; sets date for Second Continental Congress, 114; effects of, 114-5.

Second: 117-32; meets May 10, 1775, 117; assumes governmental functions, 117-8; organization of, 118; military measures, 118-20; financial activities, 120-1; Declaration of Independence adopted, 121-9; French treaties, 129-30; Articles of Confederation adopted, 130-2.

Contracts, sanctity of, in Supreme Court decisions, 346-9, 446.

Convention, Constitutional, 183-213; suggested by Annapolis Convention, 180; called by Congress of Confederation, 183; economic interests represented at, 183-4, 190-1; organization of, 184; personnel of, 185-91; Virginia plan, 191-3, 197-8; Pinckney plan, 193-4; New Jersey plan, 194-6, 198-9; Hamilton plan, 196-7, 199; debates in, 197-205; "Great Compromise," 199-201; Committee of Detail, 201-2; compromise on representation in lower house, 202; "Commerce Compromise," 202-3; "Executive Compromise," 203-4, 390-1; judicial branch discussed, 204; committee on style, 204-5; adoption of final draft, 205-6; analysis of completed Constitution, 206-13.

Convention system, 403-4, 423-4.

Coolidge, Calvin, and third term tradition, 426-7.

Corporate colonial government, in Virginia, 7-8, 9, 10, 55; in Massachusetts Bay, 20-3, 24-5, 56-7; in Rhode Island, 26-8; in Connecticut, 31; in New York, 38-9, 55; in Delaware, 49, 55; proposals to abolish, 87.

Cotton, John, 21.

Council for New England, grants land to Pilgrims and Puritans, 16, 20; grants land to Mason and Gorges, 31-2.

Council of National Defence, 480-1.

Court of Common Pleas, 3.

Court of Exchequer, 3.

Court of King's Bench, 3.

Courts, *see* Judicial Institutions, Supreme Court.

Coxe, Daniel, Plan of Union, 70.

Craig vs. Missouri (1830), 445.

Creel, George, heads Committee on Public Information, 482.

Cultural Americanism, and American Revolution, 85-6.

Custom and tradition, effect on Constitution, 416-40.

Customs Board, English, 88.

Dartmouth College vs. Woodward (1819), 347-8, 446.

Debts, state and national, 358-60.

Declaration of Independence, 121-9; background of, 121-4; Lee Resolution for, 124-6; formal Declaration adopted, 126; public opinion on, 127; analysis of, 127-9; recognition of by Great Britain, 163; on Royal veto, 389.

"Declaration of Rights," of First Continental Congress, 112-3, 128.

Declaration of war, control of president over, 463-5.

Declaratory Act, 100, 101.

Delaware, settled by Swedish under charter, 49; proprietary government in, 49; at Stamp Act Congress, 99; on independence question, 125, 126; ratifies Articles of Confederation, 132; adopts state constitution, 140-1; interstate relations during "critical period," 180; ratifies Constitution, 224-5; refuses to ratify thirteenth, fourteenth and fifteenth amendments, 298-9, 301.

Democratic party, origin of, 417-8.

Departments, executive, State, 243-4, 253-5; Treasury, 244, 255-7; War, 244, 257-8; Navy, 258-9; Justice, 259-60; Post Office, 260-2; Interior, 262-6, 452; Agriculture, 266-8, 452; Commerce, 268, 428; Labor, 268-9, 428, 453. *See also* Administrative Agencies, Executive Institutions.

Dickinson, John, at Stamp Act Congress, 99; writes "Letters of a Pennsylvania Farmer," 102; at First Continental Congress, 111; on independence question, 125, 126; on Committee to draft Articles of Confederation, 131; at Annapolis Convention, 180; at Constitutional Convention, 188-9, 198, 206; supports ratification of Constitution, 223.

Dillon vs. Gloss (1921), 281.

District of Columbia, control of Congress over, 372-4.

"Dominion of New England," 23-4, 41.

Dongan, Thomas, Governor of New York, 65; secures alliance with the Iroquois,

65-6; and Albany Congress of 1684, 66.
Dred Scott vs. Sanford (1857), 337-8, 379, 407, 440.
Due process of law, under fifth amendment, 292-3; under fourteenth amendment, 292, 300, 350-3.
"Duke's Laws," in colonial New York, 40-1.
Duquesne, Marquis, 74.

Economic influences, in colonization of America, 5-6; in American Revolution, 83-4, 89-98, 101-5; in move for Constitution, 168-81; in Constitutional Convention, 183-4, 190-1; on ratification of Constitution, 220; and eighteenth amendment, 308-9; and lobbies in Congress, 421.
Education, national subsidies to states for, 451-2.
Electoral Count Act, 384.
Emancipation Proclamation, 476.
Eminent domain, limits on state right of, 447.
English precedents for American Constitution, 1-4, 250, 292, 332-3.
Espionage Act, 286, 484-5.
Evolutionary character of American Constitution, 1.
Executive institutions, under English Constitution, 2.
    Colonial: Virginia, 9-10, 11-4; Plymouth, 18; Massachusetts Bay, 20-1, 22-4; Rhode Island, 26, 27; under New Haven Confederation, 30; New Hampshire, 32; Maryland, 36, 37-8; New York, 39, 40-2; New Jersey, 43, 44-5; Pennsylvania, 47, 48; North Carolina, 51, 52; South Carolina, 52, 53; Georgia, 54; general colonial, 57-9, 388-90; in Franklin's Plan of Colonial Union, 76-7.
    State: New Hampshire, 135-6; South Carolina, 136-7; Rhode Island, 137; Connecticut, 137; Virginia, 139; New Jersey, 140; Delaware, 140-1; Pennsylvania, 142; Maryland, 144; North Carolina, 145-6; Georgia, 147; New York, 148; Massachusetts, 151; general character of in state constitutions, 153-4.
    National: under Articles of Confederation, 159-60, 390; under Northwest Ordinance of 1787, 166-7; in Virginia Plan, 192-3; in New Jersey Plan, 195; in Hamilton Plan, 196-7; debated in Constitutional Convention, 203-4, 390-1; provided for in Constitution, 209-10; discussed in The Federalist, 224, 392; set up by Congress under Constitution, 243-5, 246-8, 252-78; under twelfth amendment, 296-7; under twentieth amendment, 319-22; and development of president's powers, 392-9; under Washington, 399-402; under Jefferson, 402-3; under Jackson, 403-7; under Lincoln, 407-8; under Johnson, 408-9; under Hayes, 409; under Cleveland, 409-10; under T. Roosevelt, 410; under Wilson, 410;

under Taft, 410-1; under F. D. Roosevelt, 410, 412-4; suggested changes in, 411-2; influence of custom and tradition on, 421-30, 434-6; in time of war, 463-7, 471-5. See also Administrative Agencies, President.
Ex parte Merryman (1861), 472-3.
Ex parte Milligan (1866), 475.
Ex post facto laws, prohibited by Constitution, 336, 444.
Extradition, and interstate relations, 449-50.

Family Compact, 71.
Farrand, Max, on Pinckney plan, 194.
Federalist, The, 223-4, 392.
Federalist Party, favors ratification of Constitution, 219-38; opposes Louisiana Purchase, 402; in national government, 417-8.
Federal Reserve System, 361-2.
Federal Trade Commission, 369.
Fiat money, in Massachusetts Colony, 93; in states during "critical period," 171; use by national government, 469.
Financial powers, British colonial legislation under, 93, 94; of Second Continental Congress, 120-1; under Congress of the Confederation, 160, 169-71; national, under Virginia Plan, 193; national, under New Jersey Plan, 194-5; debated in Constitutional Convention, 201; provided for in Constitution, 209; Treasury Department administers, 244, 255-7; expenditures under, 246-8, 254, 257-62, 264-6, 268-73, 276; Committee of House on, 250; and income tax, 304; and Supreme Court decisions, 338-41; legislation under by Congress, 357-65; Hamilton's program under, 358-61, 363-4; of executive branch, 362-3, 398; President Jackson and, 405-6; of Senate in legislation, 438-9; states under Constitution, 445-6; in war time, 462, 468-70.
Fletcher vs. Peck (1810), 346-7.
Food and Fuel Control Act, 479-80.
Force Bill, 457.
Foreign relations, under Second Continental Congress, 129-30; under Congress of the Confederation, 160, 172-7; under Department of State, 243-4, 253-5; power of president over, 396-8, 400-2, 430-4, 464-5; influence of tradition on, 430-4.
France, colonizes in North America, 64-5; in rivalry with England in America, 64-79; treaties of Second Continental Congress with, 129-30, 162; relations with, under Articles of Confederation, 172; relations with, under Constitution, 430-2.
Franchise, see Voting qualifications.
Franklin, Benjamin, seeks royal government for Pennsylvania, 48; plan of colonial union, 76-7; at Second Continental Congress, 117; made Postmaster General, 120; favors independence, 126;

negotiates treaty with France, 129-30; proposes confederation of colonies, 130-1; presides over Pennsylvania state convention, 141; negotiates Treaty of Paris, 162; at Constitutional Convention, 186, 200-1, 205-6, 214; on conditions in America, 1787, 222.

Freedom of the press, in colonial New York, 42; in Virginia Constitution of 1776, 138; in Pennsylvania Constitution, 143; in Maryland Constitution, 145; in North Carolina Constitution, 146; in Massachusetts Constitution, 152; in first amendment, 286-8; in time of war, 481-5.

Freedom of speech, in Virginia colony, 13; in Pennsylvania Constitution, 143; in Massachusetts Constitution, 152; in first amendment, 286-8; in time of war, 481-5.

French and Indian War, 72-9; causes of, 72-5; Albany Congress of 1754, 75-7; French successes, 77; English successes, 78; Treaty of Paris concludes, 78; results on colonies, 78-9; result on English debt, 95.

Fugitive slave law, of 1793, 375, 449-50; of 1850, 377-8, 449-50, 458.

Fundamental Articles of New Haven, 30.

Fundamental Orders of Connecticut, 29-30.

Fur trade, influence on Anglo-French rivalry, 65, 73.

"Gag Rule," of House of Representatives, 376-7.

Galloway, Joseph, leads moderates at First Continental Congress, 112.

Georgia, *Colonial period:* motive for colonization, 53-4; proprietary government in, 54-5; royal government in, 55; not represented at First Continental Congress, 110; ratifies Articles of Confederation, 132; adopts state constitution, 146-7; finances during "critical period," 171; ratifies U. S. Constitution, 226-7.
    National period: Chisholm vs. Georgia, 335; *Worcester vs. Georgia,* 350-1, 456.

Gibbons vs. Ogden (1824), 342-4, 367.

Gorges, Fernando, and Maine, 32.

Grant, Ulysses S., and third term tradition, 425.

Great Britain, relations with, under Articles of Confederation, 172-4.

Grenville Acts, 96-8; Sugar Act, 96-7, 100-1; Stamp Act, 97-100; Quartering Act, 98, 100; American reactions to, 98-100.

Guarantees to states, under Constitution, 450-1.

Habeas Corpus, writ of, in England, 3; in Northwest Ordinance of 1787, 168; under Constitution, 294, 443; and Fugitive Slave Law of 1850, 378, 458; suspension of during Civil War, 464, 472-3.

Habeas Corpus Act, 473.

Hamilton, Alexander, at Annapolis Con-

vention, 180; at Constitutional Convention, 188, 196-7, 204-5; favors ratification of Constitution, 215, 223-4, 236, 392; Secretary of Treasury, 244; legislative program of, 358-61, 363-4, 454-5; on protection of individual rights, 484.

Hammer vs. Dagenhart (1918), 325, 341, 345-6.

Hancock, John, at Second Continental Congress, 117; absent from Constitutional Convention, 190; on ratification of the Constitution, 232.

Hanson, John, 159.

Hartford Convention, 456.

"Hartford Wits," 222.

Hawke vs. Smith (1920), 281.

Hayes, Rutherford B., conduct of presidential office by, 409.

Health service, public, 256-7.

Henry, Patrick, formulates "Virginia Resolves," 98-9; at First Continental Congress, 111; declines to attend Constitutional Convention, 190; opposes ratification of Constitution, 220, 235.

Hepburn Act, 367.

Hollingsworth vs. Virginia (1798), 281.

Holmes vs. Walton (1780), 333.

Hooker, Thomas, founds Connecticut Colony, 28.

Hoover, Herbert, President, 249, 255; Secretary of Commerce, 268; and reform of administrative agencies, 274, 393; vetoes Philippine independence bill, 380; renominated in 1932, 394; and subsidies to states, 453; heads Food Administration during World War, 480.

Hopkinson, Francis, supports ratification of Constitution, 223.

Horwill, Herbert W., 436.

House of Burgesses of Virginia, 11-5; first meets in 1619, 11; bicameral in form, 1676, 12; and taxation, 13-4; Parliament submitted to, 1652, 13; passes "Virginia Resolves," 98-9; adopts "Virginia Resolves" of 1769, 103; issues call for First Continental Congress, 110.

House of Representatives, described in Constitution, 207-9; discussed in *The Federalist,* 224; expansion and organization of, 248-52; and right of petition, 289; and election of president, 297, 382, 404; implied powers of, 341-2; adopts "Gag Rule," 376-7; "committee government" in, 385; and treaty-making power, 401-2. See also Congress, Legislative Institutions.

Hutchinson, Mrs. Anne, founds Portsmouth, 25-6.

Immigration, regulation of by Congress, 370-1.

Impeachment, *Under state constitutions:* New Hampshire, 136; Virginia, 139; Delaware, 140; Pennsylvania, 141-2; North Carolina, 145; New York, 148; Massachusetts, 150-1.

National period: in Virginia plan, 193; in New Jersey plan, 195; under Constitution, 210; power of Congress, 384-5; attempt to impeach President Johnson, 408, 477.

Implied powers, in clause of Constitution, 209; growth of administrative functions under, 252-74; in Supreme Court decisions, 338-42; exercised by Congress, 355-86.

Inaugural address, of president, 435.

Independent offices, 269-74.

Independent Treasury system, 361.

Individual rights, under English Constitution, 3; under Virginia Charter of 1606, 7-8; in Rhode Island Colony, 27; in New York Colony, 42; in New Jersey Colony, 44.

In state constitutions: Connecticut, 137; Virginia, 138; Delaware, 141; Pennsylvania, 142-3; Maryland, 144-5; North Carolina, 146; Georgia, 147; New York, 149; Massachusetts, 152-3; New Hampshire, 154.

National period: in Northwest Ordinance of 1787, 168; in Bill of Rights, 213, 284-95, 357, 444; and fourteenth amendment, 287, 292, 298-301, 350-3; proposed amendment for, 330; limitations on powers of Congress for, 356-7; during war times, 472-5, 483-5.

Internal improvements by Congress, 365-6.

Interstate Commerce Act, 1887, 367.

Interstate relations, under Articles of Confederation, 158, 160, 178-81; in New Jersey plan, 196; under Constitution, 210-1, 448-50; under eleventh amendment, 295-6.

"Intolerable Acts," 105-7.

Jackson, Andrew, and direct election of senators, 305; and Supreme Court, 350; and Bank of the United States, 361; vetoes Maysville Turnpike bill, 365; asserts right of removal, 393, 394; chooses his successor, 394; and appointments, 395; conduct of presidential office by, 403-7; and third term tradition, 425; and cabinet system, 429-30; and nullification, 457.

Jay, John, at First Continental Congress, 111; Secretary for Foreign Affairs, 172, 176, 190, 390; negotiates treaty with Great Britain, 174; supports ratification of Constitution, 236; Chief Justice of Supreme Court, 245, 277.

Jefferson, Thomas, at Second Continental Congress, 117; drafts Declaration of Independence, 126, 128, 389; drafts Virginia Declaration of Independence, 138; drafts Ordinance of 1784, 165; Minister to France, 172, 190; characterizes personnel of Constitutional Convention, 189; Secretary of State, 243-4, 255; on expansion of governmental functions, 274; and religious freedom in Virginia, 285; elected Vice President,

296; elected President, 296; and Federal judiciary, 336; opposes broad construction, 355, 455; opposes excise law, 360; conduct of presidential office by, 402-3, 455-6; leads anti-Federalist party, 417-8; and third term tradition, 425; foreign relations under, 431-2; and messages to Congress, 436; and state rights idea, 455-6; and war powers of president, 464.

Jeopardy, double, under fifth amendment, 291.

Johnson, Andrew, quarrel with Congress, 299, 477; on direct election of senators, 305; and pardoning power, 395-6; conduct of presidential office by, 408-9.

Judicial institutions, under English Constitution, 3.

Colonial: Virginia, 13; Massachusetts, 24; Rhode Island, 26; New Haven federation, 30; Maryland, 35, 36; Pennsylvania, 46; North and South Carolina, 54; Georgia, 54; general colonial, 59-60, 87, 102.

State: New Hampshire, 136; South Carolina, 137; Rhode Island, 137; Connecticut, 137; Virginia, 139; New Jersey, 140; Delaware, 141; Pennsylvania, 142; Maryland, 144; North Carolina, 146; Georgia, 147; New York, 148-9; Massachusetts, 151-2.

National: under Articles of Confederation, 160; in Virginia plan, 193; in New Jersey plan, 195; in Hamilton plan, 197; debated in Constitutional Convention, 204; provided for in Constitution, 209, 210-1; discussed in *The Federalist,* 224; created by Congress, 244-6; expansion of, 275-8; struggle of Jefferson with, 403; custom and tradition and, 439-40. *See also* Supreme Court.

Judicial review, in Constitutional Convention, 204, 333-4; in Constitution, 213; development of doctrine of, 332-5; in Supreme Court decisions, 336-7, 346-50; custom and tradition of, 439-40.

Judiciary Act of 1789, 245, 336-7.

Jurisdiction of courts, *see* Judicial institutions.

Kansas-Nebraska Bill, 378-9.

Kentucky, refuses to ratify thirteenth, fourteenth and fifteenth amendments, 298, 299, 301.

Kentucky and Virginia Resolutions, 455-1.

King George's War, 70-2; causes, 70-1; in America, 72; results, 72.

King William's War, 66-8; causes for, 66-7; in America, 67-8; and New York Conference of 1690, 67-8.

Knox, Henry, Secretary of War, 244.

"Lame duck" session of Congress, 319-20.

Land Ordinance of 1785, 163-5.

League of Augsburg, and King William's War, 66-7.

Lee, Richard Henry, and Stamp Act, 98; at First Continental Congress, 111; ad-

vocates independence, 124-5; proposes confederation, 130; absent from Constitutional Convention, 190; opposes ratification of Constitution, 218, 220-2.
Legislative institutions, under English Constitution, 2-3.
Colonial: Virginia, 11-2, 13, 14; Massachusetts Bay, 20-1, 22, 24, 58; Rhode Island, 26, 58; Connecticut, 29, 58; New Haven Confederation, 30; New Hampshire, 32; Maryland, 35, 36; New York, 40, 41-2; New Jersey, 43, 44; Pennsylvania, 46-8; North Carolina, 51; South Carolina, 52; general colonial, 58-9, 389; in Franklin's plan of colonial union, 76.
State: New Hampshire, 135-6; South Carolina, 136; Rhode Island, 137; Connecticut, 137; Virginia, 138-9; New Jersey, 139-40; Delaware, 140; Pennsylvania, 141; Maryland, 143-4; North Carolina, 145; Georgia, 147; New York, 147-8; Massachusetts, 150-1; general characteristics of, in state constitutions, 153.
National: under Articles of Confederation, 158-62; under Northwest Ordinance of 1787, 166-7; in Virginia plan, 192; in New Jersey plan, 196; in Hamilton plan, 196; debated in Constitutional Convention, 197-202; provided in Constitution, 207-9; Jefferson and supremacy of, 402-3. *See also* Congress, House of Representatives, Senate.
Leisler, Jacob, leads rebellion in colonial New York, 41.
Leser vs. Garnett (1922), 284.
Lexington, Battle of, 116-7.
Libby, Orin G., on ratification of Constitution, 220-1.
Limitation of armaments, 486-8.
Lincoln, Abraham, and slavery, 297; and pardoning power, 395; and war powers of president, 398, 459, 464, 466-7, 471-7, 484; general conduct of office by, 407-8; and state rights issue, 458-9.
Lobbies, effect of on legislation, 420-1.
Lochner vs. New York (1905), 352-3.
Locke, John, drafts "The Fundamental Constitutions of Carolina," 51-2; natural rights philosophy of, 103; ideas of, in Declaration of Independence, 128; influence on state constitutions, 153; referred to in debate on ratification of Constitution, 221.
London Company, created by Charter of 1606, 7-8.
Lords of Trade, 88.
Louisburg, taken by English, 1745, 72; restored to France, 72.

Madison, James, at Annapolis Convention, 180; at Constitutional Convention, 185-6, 191, 204, 206; supports ratification of Constitution, 223, 235; Secretary of State, 255, 336; proposes Bill of Rights, 284-5, 289; and third term tradition, 425; and state rights idea, 455; and war powers of president, 465.
Magna Carta, 2.
Mann-Elkins Act, 367-8.
Manor system, in colonial Maryland, 35.
Manufacturing Acts, 92-3, 94.
Marbury vs. Madison (1803), 332, 336-7, 403, 439.
Marriage and divorce laws, and interstate relations, 448-9.
Marshall, John, not present at Constitutional Convention, 190; supports ratification of Constitution, 235; becomes Chief Justice, 245-6, 277; interpretation of Constitution by, 332, 335-40, 342-4, 347-50, 403.
Martin vs. Hunter's Lessee (1816), 349.
Martin vs. Mott (1827), 342.
Maryland, *Colonial period:* granted to Cecilius Calvert, 34-5; settled, 35-6; proprietary colonial government in, 35-8; religious toleration in, 37; royal colony, 38; proprietary rights in, restored, 38; at Albany Conference of 1684, 66; at New York Conference of 1690, 67; at Albany Congress of 1754, 75; at Stamp Act Congress, 99; on independence question, 122, 125; ratifies Articles of Confederation, 132, 163-4; adopts state constitution, 143-5.
National period: interstate relations during "critical period," 179-80; ratifies Constitution, 233; refuses to ratify fourteenth and fifteenth amendments, 299; and Bank of the United States, 338-40.
Mason, George, draws up "Virginia Resolves of 1769," 103; on seat of federal government, 373.
Mason, Captain John, and New Hampshire, 32.
Massachusetts, *Colonial period:* 16-25; Plymouth Colony in, 16-9; Massachusetts Bay Colony, 19-25; at Albany Congress of 1754, 75; fiat money in, 93; at Stamp Act Congress, 99; on independence question, 125; ratifies Articles of Confederation, 132; adopts state constitution, 149-53.
National period: Shays's Rebellion in, 171; interstate relations during "critical period," 178-80; ratifies Constitution, 227-33.
Massachusetts Bay Colony, 19-25; absorbs Plymouth Colony, 19; established by Puritans, 19-21; Charter of 1629, 20, 21; settlement, 1630, 21; theocratic government in, 21-3; representative government in, 22-4; colonial self-government in, 23-5; in "Dominion of New England," 24; in Massachusetts Colony, 24; absorbs Maine and New Hampshire, 32-3; in New England Confederation, 62-4; at Albany Conference of 1684, 66; at New York Conference of 1690, 67.
Massachusetts Government Act, 105-6.
"Mayflower Compact," 18.

INDEX

McCulloch vs. Maryland (1819), 338-40, 343, 447.

McLaughlin, A. C., on Pinckney plan, 194.

Mercantilism, in British colonial policy, 89-107.

Message to Congress, presidential, 398, 402, 435-6.

Miller vs. Texas (1894), 289.

Minnesota, passes "gag law," 287.

Mississippi vs. Johnson (1867), 408.

Missouri Compromise, 376; repealed, 378, 440.

Molasses Act of 1733, 91-2, 94.

Monetary system of the United States, 363-5.

Monroe Doctrine, and force of tradition in foreign relations, 432-4.

Monroe, James, opposes ratification of Constitution, 235; Secretary of State, 255, 467; and third term tradition, 425; and Monroe Doctrine, 432-4.

Montesquieu, influence on state constitutions, 153; referred to in debate on ratification, 221.

Morrill Act, 452.

Morris, Gouverneur, at Constitutional Convention, 187, 204, 205.

Morris, Robert, opposes independence, 126; and finances of the Confederation, 169, 390; at Constitutional Convention, 187.

Mount Vernon Convention, *see* Alexandria Convention.

Munn vs. Illinois (1876), 351.

National Defence Act of 1916, 466, 480-1, 485-6; of 1920, 487-8.

National Prohibition Cases (1920), 283-4.

Natural resources, conservation of, 263-4.

Naturalization, regulation of by Congress, 369-70.

Navigation Acts, effects on Virginia Colony, 14, 90-2, 94.

"New colonial policy," 94-107; King George II and, 94; Proclamation of 1763, 94-5; English domestic debt and, 95-6; Grenville Acts, 96-8; American reaction to Grenville Acts, 98-100; Townshend Acts, 101-4; American reaction to Townshend Acts, 102-4; result of "Boston Tea Party" on, 104-5; "Coercive Acts," 105-7.

New England Confederation, 62-4; members of, 62; causes of, 62-3; results of, 63-4.

New England Restraining Act, 116.

New Hampshire, settled 1623, 32; absorbed by Massachusetts Bay Colony, 32; becomes a Royal colony, 1679, and 1692, 32-3; in Dominion of New England, 32; proprietary colony, 32; at Albany Congress of 1754, 75; on independence question, 122, 125; ratifies Articles of Confederation, 132; adopts state constitution, 135-6; interstate relations during "critical period," 178-80; ratifies Constitution, 234.

New Haven Colony, 30; in New England Confederation, 62-4.

New Haven Confederation, 30.

New Jersey, *Colonial period:* proprietary government in, 43-4; Royal government in, 44-5; at Stamp Act Congress, 99; on independence question, 122, 125; ratifies Articles of Confederation, 132; adopts state constitution, 139-40; finances during "critical period," 171.

National period: interstate relations during "critical period," 178, 180; delegation at Constitutional Convention, 188; plan at Constitutional Convention, 194-6, 198-9, 201; ratifies Constitution, 226.

New Netherlands, settled by the Dutch, 38-40; "patroon system" in, 39; government of, by Dutch, 39-40; seized by Duke of York, 40, 63.

New Viewpoints in American History, A. M. Schlesinger, 454.

New York, Dutch settle, under charter, 38-9; seized by Duke of York, 40; representative government, colonial, 40-2; royal colony, 41-2; in Dominion of New England, 41; freedom of speech, colonial period, 42; at Albany Conference of 1684, 66; at New York Conference of 1690, 67; at Albany Congress of 1754, 75; at Stamp Act Congress, 99; on independence question, 122, 125, 126; ratifies Articles of Confederation, 132; adopts state constitution, 147-9; opposes tariff amendment under Confederation, 171; finances during critical period, 171; trade controversies during "critical period," 178-80; ratifies Constitution, 235-6.

New York Conference of 1690, caused by King William's War, 67-8; plans for defence at, 67-8.

New York Weekly Journal, 42.

Nobility, titles of, 323, 444.

Nomination, of president, 403-4, 423-4.

Norris-La Guardia Bill, 381.

North, Lord, and Townshend Acts, 103; recommends Coercive Acts, 105; proposes conciliation of Americans, 115-6.

North Carolina, proprietary government over, 50-2; royal government over, 53; separation from South Carolina colony, 53; declares opposition to independence, 122; ratifies Articles of Confederation, 132; adopts state constitution, 145-46; finances during "critical period," 171; interstate relations during "critical period," 180; ratifies Constitution, 236-7.

Northwest Ordinance of 1787, 166-8.

Nullification, by South Carolina, 405, 456-8; of fourteenth and fifteenth amendments, 460.

Oath of office, in Pennsylvania Colony, 48; in Georgia Colony, 54; in Constitution, 211.

"Obiter dictum," 440.

INDEX

Office-holding qualifications, in Connecticut Colony, 29; in state constitutions, 154-5; under Northwest Ordinance of 1787, 167; provided in Constitution, 207.

Oglethorpe, General George, and colonization of Georgia, 53-4.

Ohio Company, and Virginia Colony, 74-5.

Ohio Company of Associates, 165.

"Old Colonial Policy," 86-94; and colonial self-government, 87-9; mercantilist theory of, 89; trade regulation in, 90-2; regulation of manufacturing in, 92-3; financial legislation in, 93; failure to enforce, 93-4.

"Olive branch" petition, 122.

Ordinance of 1784, 165-6, 167.

Osborn vs. the Bank of the U. S. (1824), 340.

Otis, James, 333.

Overman Act, 471, 481.

Paine, Thomas, publishes *Common Sense,* 123-4; opposes monarchy, 389.

Pardoning power of president, 395-6.

Parliament, origin of, 2; powers and privileges of, 2-3; supremacy of, 332-3.

Parties, political, and choice of president, 297, 321-2, 394, 403-5, 421-4; and president's influence on legislation, 398-9; and president's power of appointment, 406-7; rise and growth of, 416-20.

Patents, regulation of by Congress, 371-2.

Paterson, William, presents New Jersey plan, 194-6, 198-9; on grand committee, 200.

"Patroon system," in colonial New York, 39.

Penn, William, and New Jersey Colony, 44; and Pennsylvania Colony, 45-8; proposes Penn Plan of Union, 68-9.

Pennsylvania, *Colonial period:* 45-9; royal grant to William Penn, 45-6; proprietary government in, 46-9; settlement of, 46-7; religious toleration in, 47; Royal government in, 47; at Albany Congress of 1754, 75; at Stamp Act Congress, 99; on independence question, 125, 126; ratifies Articles of Confederation, 132; adopts state constitution, 141-3.

National period: finances during "critical period," 171; interstate relations during "critical period," 178, 180; ratifies Constitution, 225-6.

Personal liberty laws, 458.

Peters, Richard, plan of union, 76.

Petition of Right, 2.

Petition, right of, in first amendment, 288-9; in Congress, 376-7.

Pilgrims, settle in Leyden, 16-7; motives for migrating to America, 17; secure grant of land from Virginia Company, 17; settle at Plymouth, 18; form "Mayflower Compact," 18; secure patent from Council for New England, 19; absorbed in Massachusetts Bay Colony, 19.

Pinckney, Charles, plan at Constitutional Convention, 193-4.

Pinckney, C. C., at Constitutional Convention, 189.

Plymouth Colony, 16-9; founded by Pilgrims, 17-8; "Mayflower Compact" for government of, 18; patent for, from Council for New England, 19; absorbed by Massachusetts Bay Colony, 19; in New England Confederation, 62-4; at New York Conference of 1690, 67.

Plymouth Company, created by charter of 1606, 7.

Police power, and national administration, 273-4; and national judiciary, 275, 278; in Supreme Court decisions, 344-6, 350-3.

Politics: the Citizen's Business, William Allen White, 420.

Polk, James K., and president's control of foreign relations, 397; and war powers of president, 464-5.

Pollock vs. Farmers' Loan and Trust Co. (1895), 302-3.

Popular sovereignty, in Connecticut Colony, 28; revolutionary period, 127; in Constitution, 212.

Preamble of Constitution, 207.

Preparedness for war, 485-8.

President, provided for in Constitution, 210; Washington first holds office of, 241-3; relation to executive departments, 252-3; election of, under twelfth amendment, 296-7; succession to office of, 320-2, 383-4, 427-8; proposed amendment on election of, 330; implied powers of, 342; and Congress, 362-3, 382-4, 391, 403-4; increasing prestige of, 386; development of powers of, 392-9, 412-36; various concepts of office of, 399-414; proposals for change in office of, 411-2; proposed "dictatorship of," 412-4; custom and tradition and office of, 421-36; war powers of, 463; actual importance of in war time, 463-7, 471-85.

Presidential Succession Act, 383.

Presser vs. Illinois (1886), 289.

Privy Council of England, and colonial government, 87-8; veto over colonial legislation, 88.

Prize Cases (1863), 464.

Proclamation of 1763, 94-5.

Prohibition, enforcement of, 260; and eighteenth amendment, 307-13, 460; laws as social legislation, 381; lobbies on, 420-1.

Property, protection of, under fifth amendment, 293; under seventh amendment, 294; under fourteenth amendment, 300; and judicial review, 334.

Proprietary colonial government, in New Hampshire, 31-2, 56; in Maryland, 34-8, 56; in New York, 40-1; in New Jersey, 43-4, 56; in Pennsylvania, 45-9, 56; in Delaware, 49-50; in North Carolina, 50-2; in South Carolina, 52, 56; in Georgia, 53-5; proposal for abolition of, 87; the executive in, 388-9.

Public lands, 263.

Public opinion, control of during war time, 481-5.
Puritans, motives for migration to America, 19-20; Charter of March, 1629, secured by, 21; settle Massachusetts Bay Colony, 21; institute theocratic government, 21-3; religious persecution by, 23.

Quartering Acts, 98, 100, 106, 290.
Quebec Act, 106.
Queen Anne's War, causes for, 69; concluded, 70.

Racial factors and American Revolution, 84.
Radio Act, 368.
Randolph, Edmund, at Annapolis Convention, 180; at Constitutional Convention, 186, 191, 201, 206, 214-5; supports ratification of Constitution, 235; becomes Attorney-General, 244.
Randolph, Peyton, President of First Continental Congress, 111.
Ratification, of Massachusetts Constitution of 1779, 149-50.
    Of Constitution of 1787: under Virginia Plan, 193; provided by Convention, 211-2, 216-8; party divisions on, 219-21; writings on, 221-4; by Delaware, 224-5; by Pennsylvania, 225-6; by New Jersey, 226; by Georgia, 226-7; by Connecticut, 227; by Massachusetts, 227-33; chief arguments for and against, 227-33; by Maryland, 233; by South Carolina, 233-4; by New Hampshire, 234; by Virginia, 234-5; by New York, 235-6; by North Carolina, 236-7; by Rhode Island, 237-8.
Reapportionment, provided for in Constitution, 208; enacted by Congress, 248-9; amendment on, approved by Congress, 322-3.
Reclamation policy, 264-6.
Reconstruction Finance Corporation, 362, 381, 453.
Reconstruction period, amendments to Constitution during, 297-301; executive powers during, 408-9, 476-7.
Religious freedom, in England, 16, 19-20, 21, 34, 45.
    Colonial: Massachusetts Bay, 21-2, 25-6; Virginia, 14; Rhode Island, 25-7; Connecticut, 28, 29; Maryland, 34, 36-7; New York, 41; New Jersey, 43, 44; Pennsylvania, 45, 47; North Carolina, 50; South Carolina, 52; Georgia, 54; and American Revolution, 84.
    In state constitutions: Virginia, 138; Maryland, 145; North Carolina, 146; New York, 149; Massachusetts, 152.
    National: in Northwest Ordinance of 1787, 168; in first amendment, 285-6.
Removal, right of president, 393, 394, 434.
Representative government, Colonial: Virginia, 11-2, 13; Plymouth, 18-9; Massachusetts Bay, 20, 22-3, 24; Rhode Island, 26, 27; Connecticut, 29-31; Maryland,

35, 36; New York, 39-40, 41; New Jersey, 43; Pennsylvania, 47-8; North Carolina, 51; South Carolina, 52; Georgia, 55; general colonial, 58; in Franklin's plan of colonial union, 76; American view on representation, 99-100.
    Under state constitutions: New Hampshire, 135; South Carolina, 136; Virginia, 138-9; New Jersey, 139-40; Delaware, 140; Pennsylvania, 141; Maryland, 143; North Carolina, 145; Massachusetts, 150.
    National: under Articles of Confederation, 158; under Northwest Ordinance of 1787, 166-7, 168; in Virginia Plan, 192; debated in Constitutional Convention, 198-201, 202; provided in Constitution, 207-8, 212; and expansion of Congress, 248-52; under fourteenth amendment, 300; proposed amendment on, 322-3; effect of custom on, 438.
Republican party, origin of, 417-8.
Resources, economic, mobilization of during war, 478-81.
Revolution, American, Causes: views on, 81-2; John Adams on, 82-3; American economic independence and, 83-4; religious dissent and, 84; racial factors and, 84; social factors and, 84-5; cultural Americanism and, 85-6; English colonial government and, 86; "old colonial policy" and, 86-94; "new colonial policy" and, 94-107; First Continental Congress and, 109-15.
    Conduct of: by Second Continental Congress, 117-132.
Reynolds vs. U. S. (1878), 286.
Rhode Island, Colonial period: religious toleration in, 25, 26; Charter of 1633, 27; at Albany Congress of 1754, 75; at Stamp Act Congress, 99; ratifies Articles of Confederation, 132; adopts state constitution, 137.
    National period: opposes tariff amendment under Confederation, 170; finances in, during "critical period," 171; interstate relations during "critical period," 180; ratifies Constitution, 237-8.
"Riders," attached to bills in Congress, 439.
Roosevelt, Franklin D., given virtual legislative powers, 271-2; given power to reorganize administrative agencies, 274, 412; recommends modification of liquor laws, 310; term of, under twentieth amendment, 320; attempted assassination of, 320; asserts executive leadership, 410, 412-4.
Roosevelt, Theodore, inaugurates conservation policy, 263; and income tax, 303; chooses his successor, 394; and president's control over foreign relations, 397; general concept of presidential office, 410; and third term tradition, 426; and "Tennis Court Cabinet," 430.
Royal colonial government, in Virginia, 12-4, 56; in Massachusetts Bay, 23-5,

56-7; Rhode Island, 27; New Hampshire, 32-3, 56; Maryland, 38; New York, 41-2, 56; New Jersey, 44-5, 56; Pennsylvania, 47; South Carolina, 52-3, 56; North Carolina, 53, 56; Georgia, 55, 56; tendency toward bringing colonies under, 87; the executive in, 388-9.

Salaries, of federal officials, 246-8, 323.
  In executive departments: State, 254; Treasury, 256-7; War, 257-8; Navy, 258-9; Justice, 259-60; Post Office, 262; Interior, 266; Commerce, 268; Labor, 269.
Sandys, Sir Edwyn, and Virginia Charter of 1609, 9; and representative government in Virginia, 11; and land grant to Pilgrims, 17.
Saturday Press, 287.
Schlesinger, A. M., on "State Rights Fetish," 454.
Scioto Company, 165.
Searches and seizures, under fourth amendment, 290.
Secession, 444-5; threatened by South Carolina, 1832, 458; and slavery controversy, 458-9; and result of Civil War, 459-60.
Sedition Act, 286.
Selective Draft Law Cases (1918), 467-8.
Selective Service Act, 466-8, 478.
Self-government, colonial, in Virginia, 7, 10, 11-2, 13-4; Plymouth, 18-9; Massachusetts Bay, 20-5; Rhode Island, 26, 27; Connecticut, 29-31; Maryland, 35, 36; New York, 39-40, 41; New Jersey, 43, 44; Pennsylvania, 48; opposed to English imperialism, 82, 87-9; English mercantilism and, 89-107.
Senate, described in Constitution, 207-9; discussed in *The Federalist,* 224; expansion and organization of, 248-52; and election of vice president, 297; discussed in Constitutional Convention, 304; election of, 304-7; compared to House of Representatives, 384-5; and presidential appointments, 394-5, 409-10, 434; relation to executive, 400-2; "executive" sessions of, 439; equality of states in, 451.
Separation of powers, in colonial governments, 60; in Maryland state constitution, 144; in Massachusetts constitution, 153; in state constitutions, 153, 389-90; under Articles of Confederation, 159-60, 168; and judicial review, 334-5, 350, 406; and executive, 350, 390-1, 405-6, 407, 408, 409, 411-2.
Seven Years' War, 72-9. *See also* French and Indian War.
Shays's Rebellion, 171, 232.
Sheppard-Towner Act, 452-3.
Sherman, Roger, at First Continental Congress, 111; on committee to draft Articles of Confederation, 131.
Sherman Anti-Trust Law, 368-70.

Slaughterhouse Cases (1873), 351.
Slavery, introduced into Virginia, 4; prohibited in Georgia Colony, 54, 55; prohibited in Northwest Territory, 166-7; debated in Constitutional Convention, 203; in the Constitution, 203; and thirteenth amendment, 297-8; proposed amendment on, 323-4; in ratifying conventions, 374-5; Congress and, 375-9, 444; and admission of new states, 376-9; in territories, 377-9; and state rights idea, 457-60; abolition of, by Lincoln, 475-6.
Smith-Hughes Act, 452.
Smith-Lever Act, 452.
Social factors, and American Revolution, 84-5.
Sons of Liberty, 109.
South Carolina, colonial period, 50-3; proprietary government over, 52; Royal government over, 52-3; separation from North Carolina Colony, 53; at Stamp Act Congress, 99; on independence question, 126; ratifies Articles of Confederation, 132; adopts state constitution, 136-7; finances during "critical period," 171; ratifies Constitution, 233-4; nullification by, 405, 456-8; threatens secession, 1832, 458; secedes, 458-9.
Sovereignty, state, 442-61.
Spain, relations with, under Articles of Confederation, 174-6.
Speaker of the House, 249-50, 438.
Spoils system, under Washington, 244; under Jackson, 393-4; 406-7; under Hoover, 394.
Springer vs. U. S. (1886), 302.
Stamp Act, 97-100, 102, 109; passed by Parliament, 1765, 97; American reaction to, 99-100; Stamp Act Congress, 99-100; repealed by Parliament, 100.
Stamp Act Congress, 99-100, 109.
State rights idea, origin of, 454, in ratifying conventions, 454, and broad versus strict construction, 454-5; Kentucky and Virginia Resolutions, 455; shift in party views on, 455-6; and nullification in South Carolina, 456-8; and slavery, 457-60; since Civil War, 460-1.
States, admission under Virginia plan, 193; admission under New Jersey plan, 196; relations of, to Federal government, 442-7, 450-61; relations between, under Constitution, 444-5, 448-50.
"Strict construction," 355.
Subsidies, by national government, 366; to states, 451-3.
Succession, presidential, 320-2, 383-4, 427-8.
Suffolk resolves, adopted by First Continental Congress, 112.
Suffrage, *see* Voting qualifications.
Sugar Act, 96-8, 100-1.
Supremacy, national, under Virginia plan, 193, 334; under New Jersey plan, 195-6; under Hamilton plan, 197; in Constitu-

tion, 211, 334-5, 444-7; in Supreme
Court decisions, 337-353.
Supreme Court, provided for in Constitution, 210-1; structure of, set up by Congress, 245; early importance of, 245-6,
332; expansion of business of, 275;
personnel of, 277; interpretations of
Constitution by, 280-1, 283-95, 302-4,
325-7, 332-53, 355-6, 367, 370, 372, 379,
403, 406, 408, 439-40, 445-7, 450, 456,
458, 460, 464, 467-8, 472-5; Jefferson's
struggle with, 403. For cases, see topics
involved.
Swedes, settle in Delaware, 49.
Symnes Company, 165.

Taft, William Howard, and income tax
amendment, 303; Theodore Roosevelt
and election of, 394; general concept of
presidency, 410-1; on cabinet system,
429.
Tariff, legislation on by Congress, 357-8.
Taxation, colonial views on, 13-4, 99-100,
102, 103; under Articles of Confederation, 161; in Virginia plan, 193; in New
Jersey plan, 194-5; debated in Constitutional Convention, 201, 203; provided
for in Constitution, 209, 443-4; discussed in The Federalist, 224; income
tax, 302-4; limits on state power of, 338-
40, 446-7; and Supreme Court decisions,
338-41, 344; Congressional legislation
on, 357-60; in war time, 462, 468-70. See
also Financial powers.
Tenure of Office Act, 408, 477.
Territories, Northwest, 163-8; slavery in,
377-9; acquisition of by Congress, 379-
80.
Texas vs. White (1869), 460.
Theocratic government, in Massachusetts
Bay Colony, 21-3, 24; in New Haven
Colony, 30.
Tory party, views on American Revolution,
81, 219; proportion of Americans in,
115.
Townshend Acts, 101-4.
Trade-mark Cases (1879), 372.
Transportation Act, 368.
Treasury Board, English, 88.
Treaties, Ryswick, 68, 69; Utrecht, 70, 72;
Aix-la-Chapelle, 72; Paris, 1763, 78;
Paris, 1783, 162-3; San Lorenzo, 176;
power of president to make, 396; control
of Congress over making of, 400-2; Jay,
1795, 401; Louisiana Purchase, 402. See
also Foreign relations.
Trevett vs. Weeden (1786), 333.
"Twenty-first Rule," 377.

Union, Colonial: 62-80; New England
Confederation, 62-4; Albany Conference
of 1684, 66; New York Conference of
1690, 67-8; Penn plan of union, 1697,
68-9; Coxe plan of union, 70; Albany
Congress of 1754, 75; Peters' plan of
union, 76; Franklin plan of union, 76-7;

influences toward, in 1763, 79-80; the
Continental Congresses, 109-32.
　National: Articles of Confederation,
157-81; nature of, under Constitution,
442-61.
"United Colonies of New-England, The,"
63.
Usages of the American Constitution, The,
H. W. Horwill, 436.
U. S. vs. De Witt (1870), 372.
U. S. vs. Lanza (1922), 291.
U. S. vs. MacIntosh (1931), 370.
U. S. vs. Schwimmer (1929), 370.
U. S. vs. Sprague (1931), 280.

Van Buren, Martin, Secretary of State,
255; Jackson and election as president,
394.
Vermont, under Articles of Confederation,
178-9.
Veto power, use by governors in colonies,
24, 57, 388-9; in Franklin's plan of colonial union, 77; of Crown over colonial
legislatures, 87, 88, 389; of Privy Council over colonial legislatures, 88; in
South Carolina Constitution, 137; of
New York Council of Revision, 148; in
Massachusetts Constitution, 151; under
Northwest Ordinance of 1787, 167; of
national legislature over state legislatures, 192; under Virginia plan, 192-3;
provided for in Constitution, 210, 391;
influence on legislation, 399; use by
President Jackson, 405, 407; President
Cleveland and, 407; President T. Roosevelt and, 407; President Wilson and,
407; use of by President Hayes, 409.
Virginia, Colonial period: attempts at settlement of, 6-7; Charter of 1606, 7-8;
self-government in, 7-9, 11-2, 13-5; settlement of, 8-9; Charter of 1609, 9-10;
Charter of 1612, 11; tobacco culture in,
10; slavery introduced into, 11; House
of Burgesses, 11-5; as a royal colony,
12-5; as a proprietary colony, 14; Bacon's Rebellion in, 14; settlers from,
move to Carolinas, 51; at Albany Conference of 1684, 66; expansion in Ohio
Valley, 74-5; economic life of, 83; heads
independence movement, 124; ratifies
Articles of Confederation, 132; adopts
state constitution, 138-9.
　National period: interstate relations
during "critical period," 179-80; delegation at Constitutional Convention, 185-6;
plan for Constitution, 191-3, 197-8, 201,
202; ratifies Constitution, 234-5; freedom of religion in, 285.
Virginia Resolutions, 455.
"Virginia Resolves," on Stamp Act, 98-9.
"Virginia Resolves of 1769," on Townshend Acts, 103.
Volstead Act, 310.
Voting qualifications, Colonial: Massachusetts Bay, 21-3, 24; Rhode Island,
27; Connecticut, 30; New Haven Confederation, 30; New Haven, 30; Con-

necticut Charter of 1662, 31; Maryland, 36, 37; New York, 41; New Jersey, 43; Pennsylvania, 47.

In state constitutions: Virginia, 138; general character of, 155.

National: under Northwest Ordinance of 1787, 167; provided for in Constitution, 207; for delegates to state ratifying conventions, 224-7, 233-7; under fifteenth amendment, 301, 444; under nineteenth amendment, 313-8.

War, Quakers in Pennsylvania colony oppose, 48; measures of Second Continental Congress, 118-21; powers under Articles of Confederation, 160-1; powers of Congress, 209, 462-3; powers of president, 210, 397-8, 435, 463-7, 471-85; executive departments for, 244, 257-9; prohibition of powers for, to states, 446; Civil War, and state rights idea, 459-60; declarations of, 463-5; World War, 465-72, 478-88; raising of troops for, 466-8; finances, 468-70; individual rights during, 472-5, 481-5; control of economic life during, 478-81; administrative agencies during, 481; control of public opinion during, 481-5; preparation for, in time of peace, 485-8.
War of the Austrian Succession, *see* King George's War.
War of the Grand Alliance, 67. *See also* King William's War.
War of the Spanish Succession, *see* Queen Anne's War.
Wars for Supremacy, influence toward colonial union, 64; causes for, 64-66; King William's War, 66-8; Queen Anne's War, 69-70; King George's War, 70-2; French and Indian War, 72-9.
Washington, George, in French and Indian War, 74-5; and "Virginia Resolves of 1769," 103; at First Continental Congress, 111; Commander-in-Chief of Continental Army, 118-9; President of Constitutional Convention, 184, 185, 206, 215; transmits Constitution to Congress, 217; becomes first President, 241-3; asks advisory opinion from Supreme Court, 335; originates cabinet system, 393, 428; and president's control of foreign policy, 396, 430-2; conduct of presidential office by, 399-402; and no-third-term tradition, 424-5; "Farewell Address," 424-5, 431; initiates inaugural addresses, 435.
Washington Globe, 429.
Webster, Daniel, on the presidency, 406.
Whig party in England, view on American Revolution, 81, 219.
"Whiskey Rebellion," 360.
White, William Allen, on lobbies, 420-1.
Williams, Roger, 25-6; founds Providence, 25; Patent of 1643 secured by, 26; compared to Thomas Hooker, 28.
"Wilmot Proviso," 377.
Wilson, James, on independence question, 126; at Constitutional Convention, 186-7, 201, 204, 205, 304, 391; supports ratification of Constitution, 223.
Wilson, Woodrow, on woman suffrage, 316, 317; asserts right of removal, 393; and war powers of president, 398, 471-2, 477-85; general concept of presidential office, 410; and messages to Congress, 436.
Winthrop, John, 21, 22, 92.
Woman suffrage, move for, 313-6; and nineteenth amendment, 316-8; results of, 318.
Woolen Act of 1699, 92.
Worcester vs. Georgia (1832), 349-50, 406.
Writs of Assistance, 101, 290.
Writs of Assistance Case (1761), 333.

"Yellow dog" contract, 381.

Zenger, John Peter, and freedom of the press, 42.